of the core values—tribal traditions and ties to the ancestral lands."

—Stewart Udall, secretary of the interior 1961–69
and author of *The Quiet Crisis*

"In an era when so many seek inspiration, Professor Wilkinson has answered the call. He paints a vivid picture of the people whose bravery and courage and dynamic leadership have enabled them to survive challenges and experiences most Americans will never know—the loss of their homelands, their cultures, their languages, their religions, their ways of life, and even their children. These are the native people of this land, our nation's First Americans."

—Senator Daniel K. Inouye

Also by Charles Wilkinson

American Indians, Time, and the Law:
   Native Societies in a Modern Constitutional Democracy

The American West:
   A Narrative Bibliography and a Study in Regionalism

The Eagle Bird:
   Mapping a New West

Crossing the Next Meridian:
   Land, Water, and the Future of the West

Fire on the Plateau:
   Conflict and Endurance in the American Southwest

Messages from Frank's Landing:
   A Story of Salmon, Treaties, and the Indian Way

BLOOD
STRUGGLE

The Rise
of Modern Indian Nations

Charles Wilkinson

W. W. NORTON & COMPANY
New York • London

For information about permission to reproduce selections from this book, write to
Permissions, W. W. Norton & Company, Inc., 500 Fifth Avenue, New York, NY 10110

Manufacturing by R.R. Donnelley, Haddon
Book design by Charlotte Staub
Production manager: Julia Druskin

Library of Congress Cataloging-in-Publication Data

Wilkinson, Charles F., 1941–
Blood struggle : the rise of modern Indian nations / Charles Wilkinson.— 1st ed.
p. cm.
Summary: "The story of the extraordinary gains by Indian tribes over the
second half of the twentieth century"—Provided by publisher.
Includes bibliographical references and index.
ISBN 0-393-05149-8 (hardcover)
1. Indians of North America—Politics and government. 2. Indians of North America
—Government relations. 3. Indians of North America—Social conditions. 4. Self-
determination, National—United States. 5. United States—Race relations. 6. United
States—Social policy. 7. United States—Politics and government. I. Title.
E98.T77W546 2005
323.1197'073'09045—dc22

2004025221

ISBN-13: 978-0-393-32850-9 pbk.
ISBN-10: 0-393-32850-3 pbk.

W. W. Norton & Company, Inc., 500 Fifth Avenue, New York, N.Y. 10110
www.wwnorton.com

W. W. Norton & Company Ltd., Castle House, 75/76 Wells Street, London W1T 3QT

3 4 5 6 7 8 9 0

I dedicate this book,
with my lasting admiration,
  to the Indian tribal leaders
  of the historic post–World War II era,
  who have made their reservations
  into homelands

CONTENTS

INTRODUCTION

In the summer of 1973 I made one of many trips to Menominee County, in Wisconsin. At the time I was an attorney with the Native American Rights Fund, a nonprofit law firm in Boulder, Colorado. My friend Ada Deer picked me up at the Green Bay airport and suggested, since we had no meeting until the next morning, that we ride out to her mother's place. That part of Wisconsin had been mostly cleared for farming, but Menominee County, other than two small towns, remained wooded. A few years before, Congress had recognized the full-bodied Wolf River as one of six great American streams protected by the original Wild and Scenic Rivers Act. The deep forests held wild rice marshes, a healthy deer herd, and many bears. I saw my first wolf there.

After Ada and I passed into Menominee County, we drove through the little Indian settlement of Keshena and soon turned onto a dirt road where, after a couple of miles, the thick woods opened up. We had arrived at Ada's family cabin, set in a small meadow in a bend of the Wolf River, with the birch and white pine forest spreading out beyond.

The cabin was now located in Menominee County because in 1954 Congress had "terminated" the former Menominee Reservation. Termination had been an outright disaster for the Menominee, bringing social and economic ills, forcing many to depart their ancestral woods for the cities, and pushing them to the brink of selling off their magnificent homeland. By the late 1960s the tribe had resolved to reverse termination, a task political observers deemed impossible. Nevertheless, by the time of my trip the Menominee Restoration Act had surmounted nearly all the legislative hurdles. Congress would surely pass it in the next few months.

The chief factor in Menominee restoration, other than the raw injustice of termination, was Ada Deer herself, the tribal leader. She was to achieve much—as one of her tribe's first college graduates and the holder of a master's from Columbia, a distinguished lecturer at the University of Wisconsin's School of Social Work, the Democratic nominee for Congress, and assistant secretary of the interior for Indian affairs in the Clinton administration—but Ada's grandest accomplishment would always be the Menominee Restoration Act, which saved a people and, as much as any one event, signaled that American Indian tribes had revived and would take their rightful seats as sovereign governments in modern America. Menominee restoration had many faces—tribal members, supporters from other tribes, Wisconsin politicians, Washington, D.C., officials and staffers, experts in many fields, lawyers (of which I was one), people from the media, and many more—but it all came back to Ada. Fiery, charismatic, inclusive, strategic, and possessed of energy without end, Ada shaped the plans, brought in the needed people, and marshaled tasks through to conclusion. Presented with a crisis, she turned it first into a cause, then into a movement.

No doubt some of this came from her mother. Ma Deer, as everybody called her, grew up in Philadelphia, became a nurse, and headed off to Appalachia, the Rosebud Sioux Reservation, and finally the woods of Menominee, eager to improve the lot of the Indians. There the young white woman fell in love with Joe Deer, a full-blooded Menominee, married him, and raised five children. Ma Deer did most of the work herself, for Joe drank too much and had trouble fulfilling fatherly roles.

My visit to the family cabin could not have been much better. Although I had not been to her home before, I knew Ma Deer well from various restoration meetings and social occasions. That evening we had a good venison and wild rice dinner. Spirits were high, now that passage of the restoration bill was so close. It detracted from the day hardly a whit when Ma Deer, who fly-specked every event and issue at Menominee, had quite a few words with me, as I knew she would. At issue was my opinion—an opinion held by any lawyer, however much an Indian advocate, after the Supreme Court's *Lone Wolf v. Hitchcock* decision in 1903—that Congress had the power to abrogate Indian treaties. "Break an Indian treaty! What a ridiculous proposition! How can you come out here and tell people things like that? What possesses you to do that?"

"But, Ma Deer—"

The cabin, glorious though its surroundings may have been, was rudimentary, a one-room log structure lacking electricity and indoor plumbing. I tried to imagine Ada's childhood. Obviously, it would be good to be raised in beauty, out in nature, and in a home with warmth and robust conversation. She loved her two brothers and two sisters. But it also must have been hard—hard in the winters, hauling water from the river and clearing the road out to the highway, hard at the schools that were themselves rudimentary and still teaching Indian children that Columbus had discovered America, hard to live in deep poverty, hard to come to grips with the absence of four other siblings lost at birth.

A day later, on my plane ride back to Colorado, I found myself contemplating the immense distance between that cabin and stately Capitol Hill, where the United States Congress soon would make Menominee restoration federal law. How unlikely that such a journey could be made. As the months and years went by, such successes continued to mount as modern tribes changed and improved the complex governmental, cultural, and economic system under which Indians lived. Those advances too flowed from the work of people raised in modest dwellings and saddled with the most difficult social and economic conditions.

Two years after my visit, I went into academia, but much of my writing and research continued to involve Indian law, history, and society. I worked with tribes and the Native American Rights Fund and other Indian organizations on various projects. In many instances, I had the good fortune of witnessing firsthand the history Indian people made.

Over the course of more than thirty years I became preoccupied with a number of questions. What exactly have tribes accomplished? Where have tribal leaders made progress and where have they come up short? Why have tribes been so active in the post–World War II era after generations of being so ineffectual in their dealings with the majority society? And (when I thought not just of Ada but also of many other Indian leaders) how could they have risen from such humble origins to create significant changes in a modern industrialized nation? Finally, where does the Indian sovereignty movement fit in American history? In time I decided to put those ruminations to pen and paper.

THE MIDDLE of the twentieth century, when Ada was a young girl, marked the all-time low for tribal existence on this continent. American Indians faced four overbearing and seemingly intractable problems. First, they were mired in the worst economic and social conditions of any group in America. Their desperate economic plight far outstripped any national depression. Income was low, and unemployment rampant; it was a rare tribe with a jobless rate below 40 percent, and some reached 90. Infant mortality was five times the national average, and life expectancy twenty-five years less than for other Americans. Many a Native family depended on government rations to survive.

Second, Indians suffered a relentless political oppression at mid-century. The Bureau of Indian Affairs controlled the reservations with an iron grip. The law, going all the way back to classic opinions by Chief Justice John Marshall, recognized tribes as governments with the right of self-determination, but at mid-century Marshall's words rang hollow.

Third, and deeply hurtful, the BIA and the churches ran a concerted campaign to suppress tribal religions and traditions and "Christianize" Native Americans. Indian language, dress, and ceremonies all were labeled backward and uncivilized. The BIA and mission schools prohibited the old languages and enforced strict

Western dress codes. Church attendance was often mandatory. Traditional dances, songs, and rituals violated BIA regulations, enforceable in administrative courts. The totality of it—the daily challenge to self-identity, to self-worth—was emotionally and spiritually debilitating. Would our country have tolerated even the smallest measure of this broad-scale persecution if it had been levied against Catholics, Jews, Seventh-day Adventists, or the Amish?

Then, on August 1, 1953, Congress tightened the screws by activating the most extreme Indian program in history. House Concurrent Resolution 108 officially announced the termination policy, a "final solution" that would lead to a sell-off of tribal lands, the withdrawal of all federal support, and the rapid assimilation of Indian people into the majority society. Advocates for termination asserted that many tribes were self-sufficient (and thus ready for termination) and that the others would be ready within a short period of time.

This theory had no basis in the reality of Indian country. Far from being self-sufficient, poverty-stricken Indian people hung on mainly because of meager federal support and the sustenance they could gain from the land. For Indian tribes, virtually nothing could be more threatening to these place-based peoples than the expropriation of their land. The early 1950s—especially since termination now cast its shadow—was a time of hopelessness, confusion, and fear in Indian country. Never had the age-old specter of the "Vanishing Indian" come so close to reality.

Indian leaders responded and by the mid-1960s had set daunting goals: Reverse the termination policy; break the BIA's paternalistic hold and reestablish tribes as sovereign governments within reservation territory; enforce treaty rights to land, water, and hunting and fishing; and at once achieve economic progress and preserve ancient traditions in a technological age. This modern tribal sovereignty movement amounted to a last stand for Native people. As Vine Deloria, Jr., put it, "If we lose this one, there won't be another."

Against all odds, over the course of two generations, Indian leaders achieved their objectives to a stunning degree. Conditions improved, often dramatically, on every reservation. Native people raised the standard of living, made advances in health, housing, and education, revitalized traditional practices, solidified treaty hunting and fishing rights, and expanded the tribal land base. Now tribal governments, not federal or state officials, make the great majority of decisions on the reservations.

To be sure, many problems remain. Economic conditions for most tribes, while significantly improved, continue to lag behind national indicators. Indian people and health specialists have made inroads on the blight of alcoholism, but much work still lies ahead. Diabetes strikes at heartbreaking levels. Yet the dominant fact is the revival. Even on the Pine Ridge Sioux Reservation of South Dakota, in the upper Great Plains, where Indian poverty has been the hardest to crack, the Oglala people have broken the grip of the BIA, the land is secure, the language lives on, and each year Sun Dance has ever more adherents. Indian people have accomplished what would have been unthinkable in the dark days of the 1950s: They have created viable, permanent self-governed homelands.

The Indian revival of the second half of the twentieth century deserves to be recognized as a major episode in American history. The modern tribal sovereignty movement can fairly be mentioned in the same breath with the abolitionists and suffragists of old and the contemporary civil rights, women's, and environmental movements. For all their progress, each of those efforts suffered serious setbacks, and in the case of the modern ones, they continue to face rock-hard obstacles. So too with the tribes, but the relative degree of progress for Native people is comparable to each of the other groups.

This movement presents a fascinating saga, in part because of compelling personalities and the barriers they surmounted, in part because the successes run counter to widely held assumptions. The fact of the progress, much less its extent and nature, is not commonly understood. Further, this is not a story of what federal officials have done for Indians. The vision and actions of Native Americans themselves created the deep change. Tribal leaders, Ada Deer and many others, learned how to use the political and legal system to create a framework within which progress could be made. Then they put those laws and policies to work by painstakingly building creative and effective institutions and programs at home, on the reservations. The modern Indian movement has put on grand display America's truest nobility—its commitment to give dispossessed peoples the chance to thrive—but it took the passionate and informed determination of Indian people to activate that impulse.

Another surprise, at a time when the popular conception links Indians to casino lights, is that the progress in Indian country is not due to gaming. To be sure, gaming has brought significant—in a few cases enormous—financial returns to some tribes. Yet the modern Indian movement had already accomplished much of its program by the time gaming came on the scene in the 1990s. Gaming is an organic part of the system that Indian leaders envisioned a quarter of a century earlier and then fought to make a reality; tribal gaming is possible because it is one of the many sovereign activities that tribes, as independent governments, can undertake on their own terms, not those of the states. Gaming has played an important role, but the scope of the modern tribal sovereignty movement goes far beyond it.

This book, while it will present a far-ranging reform movement in a complex area of national policy, will not focus primarily on the work of federal legislatures, courts, and administrative agencies. Properly understood, modern American Indian history has been made by Indian leaders who seized the initiative, brought forth their grievances and proposed solutions, and, more often than not, accomplished the kind of progress they dared seek. These pages, then, will look first and foremost to Indian country and tell the stories of the personalities, crises, and opportunities that led to the profound changes Indian people have wrought.

AS I EXPLAIN in the acknowledgments that follow the text, numerous people have helped me. Foremost are the many Indian people who have passed on precious information. It was not easy for them. They have ample reason to be reluctant, suspicious of outsiders. My guess is that they knew they had created an important story and concluded that I wanted to tell their story true. I hope I have because for me, Indian tribal sovereignty is one of the noblest ideals that has ever touched my mind—every bit as much so as the ideals of freedom or justice, to which tribal sovereignty is closely related. But claims to sovereignty never come easy, especially for small, ethnic governments within a much larger and more powerful sovereign entity. Tribal leaders knew at the outset that it would be a struggle—a blood struggle—to make their sovereignty a reality in this modern industrial nation. That is where we begin.

Part One

ABYSS

1.

Indian Country: August 1953

By the summer of 1953 America had hit its full stride. The post–World War II boom generated a bursting, chest-pounding optimism that filled the streets and factories with a kind of prosperity no country had ever seen. Working people could now aspire to one of the new television sets, a shiny car from Detroit, and a split-level house. Even the blacks had begun to pull themselves up out of segregation, as Jackie Robinson broke baseball's color barrier and the epic school discrimination case *Brown v. Board of Education* had reached the Supreme Court.

American Indians, however, had been left far behind in the dust on the road to success, farther behind than any identifiable group in the nation. Now it would get worse. Congress was poised to launch the ominous policy of termination, which would liquidate their homelands and cut off lifelines of federal support. Life on three reservations—Red Lake, Pine Ridge, and Quinault—told the story.

ROGER JOURDAIN, born on the Red Lake Chippewa Reservation in northwestern Minnesota in 1912, grew up in his grandmother's home speaking his tribal language. After attending the mission school at Red Lake and being sent off to the Bureau of Indian Affairs' boarding school in Wisconsin, he made it through eighth grade in the reservation's public high school. As a young man, sturdily built with a thick shock of black hair, he worked as a lumberjack in BIA logging camps out in the tribal pine stands, the last forests before the terrain makes its transition into the Great Plains. Then Roger found construction work and became a valued employee, working heavy equipment—bulldozers, scrapers, and power shovels—for the BIA roads department and private contractors.

In 1958, Jourdain rose to the chairmanship of his tribe; he served for three full decades. In time, finding that Indian people all across the country endured a suffocating desperation, he and a small cadre of tribal leaders became catalysts in forging a movement to preserve and revitalize tribal homelands and cultures. But in the summer of 1953 hope was in short supply.

Jourdain found good work on the poverty-stricken reservation, but few tribal members did. Although close to half the potential labor force had seasonal employment—logging in the woods or fishing commercially in Red Lake—fewer than 100 people, of 2,500 tribal members on the reservation, held year-round jobs. Family income stagnated at $1,250, compared with a statewide average of $3,200.

Living conditions at Red Lake were grim. Some Chippewa people had log cabins, but most lived in tar paper shacks, usually a single room, sometimes divided into two rooms by blankets hung from the ceilings. The only buildings served by electricity belonged to the BIA, the school, and the missions. The same was true for indoor plumbing; the Indians were left with outhouses. "Yeah," Jourdain says wryly, speaking of both his youth and the 1950s, "we had running water. Every morning I had to get up and run down to the stream with a bucket."

The land offered a saving grace. Although Red Lake people have always been bitter about the 1863 treaty that greatly reduced their historic homeland, the reservation remains expansive: 800,000 acres, about 1.5 percent of Minnesota. Hourglass-shaped Red Lake—the largest lake in the state, one of the largest in the country, so broad you can barely see the woods on the far shore— dominates the landscape. The reservation also holds more than 200 smaller lakes. Dry land mostly consists of deep woods, made up of pine, birch, and many hardwood species. These forests have

RED LAKE BAND OF CHIPPEWA RESERVATION

been steadily logged since the nineteenth century but remain largely pristine. The Mahnomen River watershed on the north side of Red Lake is as wild as any place in the lower forty-eight states. The land is a treasure to the Red Lake people, and when they talk about it, they commonly allude to the freedom it brings them.

The woods and the lakes brought material, as well as spiritual, benefits to the Chippewa. The backcountry assured abundant deer, bear, moose, and rabbit for the dinner table. In the summer, families set up sugar camps to draw maple syrup and harvest blueberries. Red Lake itself produced a sweet strain of walleye for subsistence and commerce. The reservation's many other lakes provided whitefish and goldeye for smoking, and the people harvested wild rice in the traditional fashion from flat-bottomed boats. Most families kept home gardens, planted in potatoes, corn, lettuce, and other vegetables. Nonetheless, in the 1950s the subsistence living, along with the scattered paychecks and small welfare payments, could not meet all their needs; once a month the big white government truck rumbled in, bearing rations—flour, sugar, beans, canned goods, oleomargarine, cheese, and powdered milk.

In the years just after World War II the Red Lake Band of Chippewa faced another set of problems, at least as deep and insidious as the grinding poverty, all stemming from the fact that a once-independent people now was forced to endure a hard-edged, outside control, a subjugation. They might find freedom in the woods, but not in the schools, churches, or halls of government.

Even as he approached ninety years of age, Roger Jourdain raged against the pervasive influence of the BIA and the churches in those earlier days. "The BIA and the missions ran the reservation, what was left of it. The missions and the BIA were together. Nobody ever challenged them until I came along in the late fifties." All the schools—BIA, mission, and state—ignored tribal traditions and promoted assimilation. "Some parts of Catholic school were all right, but they could never get rid of that missionary enthusiasm. They were very subtle. You didn't know they were doing it. 'We're going to make you Indian girls and boys, you little pagans, into good religious people.' All the schools, they had no respect for our culture."

Jourdain had especially choice words for what he called the old BIA. "They were a bunch of bums. Tramps. The BIA didn't have any quality standards. The superintendents would get assigned because their gramma knew a congressman. Then they come in and ran the place without any respect for Red Lake self-determination or sovereignty. We have every right, as much as anybody else, to run our own affairs. You should be able to do what you want to do in your own community, your own yard."

Larry Stillday, a little boy in the early 1950s, grew up in Ponemah, the most traditional village on the Red Lake Reservation. The people there still bury their dead in the earth under spirit houses, wooden structures the size of a grave with pitched roofs and sides just a foot or two high. Slender and graceful, Stillday talked in his soothing voice about the reservation of his childhood. "We had no sense of entitlement. We had the loss of land. We had the loss of religion to the missionaries. The religion was taken. The absence of children was quite noticeable. Our children were being ripped away, to government boarding schools, to non-Indian foster homes off the reservation. Losing children is like losing the land.

"You talk about losing land, and you talk about acreage, but that is not the whole part. There is the sacredness. During the Korean conflict there were bombings [when the military conducted practice maneuvers]. As a child I'd be swimming in the lake. Jets would come over and drop bombs back in the woods. Boom. Boom. They never had permission to do that. Another intrusion was through logging after the war. It was another form of attack."

As a young man Stillday left the reservation for Minneapolis, and he lived for a while in Europe, staying away for thirty-five years. Now he is a counselor for the tribe in Ponemah. "It was a confusing time, a time of hopelessness. We were aware of all these things, assimilation, acculturation. Kids today have the choice to come back. They know they have an entitlement. They know who they are. They know they're entitled. We didn't have that choice."

OUT ON the Great Plains, 450 miles southwest of Red Lake, Lakota people faced even harsher conditions at the Pine Ridge Reservation in South Dakota, at 2.5 million acres the nation's third-largest Indian reservation. This homeland of the Oglala branch of the Lakota, one of the seven tribes of the Sioux Confederation, offered little in the way of economic opportunity. The Lakota's only possibilities for paying work were cattle grazing, which some families pursued, or a job with the Bureau of Indian Affairs. Statistics are sparse, but unemployment surely ran between 80 and 90 percent.

Sioux country once offered much more. Buffalo were everywhere. At the western edge of Sioux country, the Black Hills, the spiritual center of Lakota life, the Lakota's "Mother's heart and pulse," rose from the plains to an elevation of seven thousand feet. In addition to their cultural significance, the Black Hills held deer

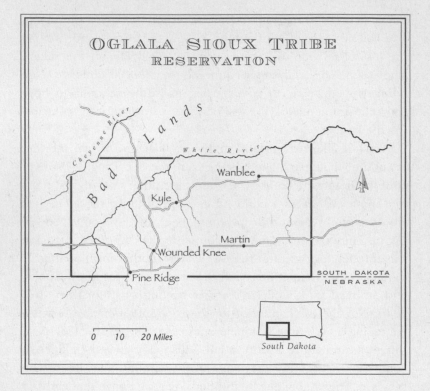

and elk, commercially valuable timber, and gold and silver. The Great Sioux Reservation, created by treaty in 1868, reserved to the tribes of the Sioux Nation a sweeping expanse of land in Dakota Territory, reaching from the Wyoming line to the Missouri River, fully half of what is now South Dakota and part of North Dakota as well. But in a single generation the westward expansion took out the buffalo. The discovery of the Black Hills' mineral riches in 1874 led to the abrogation of the 1868 treaty and the breakup of the Great Sioux Reservation: Congress threw the Black Hills open to mining, designated millions of acres of rangeland for home-steading by non-Indians, and set up six separate Sioux reserva-tions on the remaining lands, with Pine Ridge the largest in both acres and people.

By the 1950s the Lakota, a hunting people with their best hunt-ing land in the Black Hills taken, had endured nearly a century of dependency on the federal government. In the town of Pine

Ridge—small, but the largest on the reservation—Highway 18 laid down a line of demarcation. The west side was the white side, with the BIA office building, the jail, the BIA boarding school, and housing for federal employees. To the east lay a shantytown, home to Indian people, a place devoid of the plumbing and electricity that served the community across the highway. Many old men in Pine Ridge wore their hair in long braids, Lakota style, but the outlying villages—Porcupine, Wanblee, Yellow Bear, Kyle, Allen, and others—were even more resolutely traditional. Out in the backcountry, families sheltered in tipis, tents, and log cabins lived much as the Lakota had for centuries.

One observer aptly described the BIA at the Pine Ridge Reservation in the 1950s as " 'The Company' in a company town." The bureau dominated the economy as employer, purchaser, and consumer. It handed down the laws and ran the police and courts. It controlled the tribe's only economic asset, the fair-to-middling rangelands; far from promoting Lakota interests, the bureau leased vast expanses of grazing land to large non-Indian cattle companies at rates well below market value. Further, bureau policies cut the Lakota ranchers off from market participation. Mario Gonzalez, Lakota and Indian law attorney, explains that "there was one BIA subagent per district, and they were called boss farmers. They controlled everything. You couldn't even sell your cows if you wanted to; you'd need permission." Anthropology Professor Marla Powers described those times: "Back then, in the fifties, the money from leasing went straight to the BIA. Then the Indian people had to go to the government to get vouchers to pay for things. They had to justify what they were spending money on back then. They essentially had to get permission to spend their own money."

BIA and church schools vigorously sought to "Christianize" the Sioux students. Teachers prohibited children from speaking their Lakota language (though it was used exclusively in most of their homes) and cut off their braids. Everything Lakota was pagan and savage. Gerald Clifford, a traditional Sun Dancer as an adult but raised Catholic, remembered that "when we heard drums down below the school the nuns told us it was 'devil worship.' " The pressure to adopt Christianity was felt in the state schools as well: Every Monday the Kyle Day School required the students to attend religious instruction; the only choices were Catholic and Episcopalian.

The tentacles of outside control were perhaps most profoundly felt with respect to Sun Dance, the most important traditional Sioux ceremony. Unlike the Yuwipi or the Sweat Lodge, both more personal in nature, Sun Dance is a grand religious and social occasion embodying all that it means to be Sioux—the ways and stories, the tragedies and the triumphs, the past, present, and future. One experienced Sun Dancer explained that the ceremony represents each of the traditional practices and beliefs, tracing all the way back to the White Buffalo Calf Woman, who taught the Sioux their culture; performing the dance forges a link to the past, to ancestors who because of their own suffering are a source of strength and hope to overcome the challenges of today and tomorrow. Sun Dance has become ever more precious to the Sioux because while the buffalo are nearly gone and the Black Hills confiscated, Sun Dance continues to be a defining symbol of Sioux culture.

Historically the Sioux performed Sun Dance once a year, in June or July, close to the common buffalo hunt. All the tribes gathered to pray, fulfill promises made to Wakan Tanka, offer thanks, socialize, and celebrate life. The people came from all over. One early account estimated the attendance at tens of thousands and described the camp circle around the dance to be at least three-quarters of a mile in diameter.

The ceremony itself, held over four days (preparations lasted weeks or even months), took place inside a large circular arbor, which workers formed by setting two concentric rows of ash posts ten to twenty feet apart. For shade, they laid pine boughs and brush on top of saplings that served as beams. Spectators sat in the arbor, surrounding the dancers. The entrance to the arbor opened to the east.

The dancers performed Sun Dance around a large center pole, the tallest tree a chosen scout could find. Participants consumed neither food nor drink. Piercing was central to the ceremony. Each dancer was prepared by having loose skin on his chest and shoulders pierced in several places; wooden skewers attached by lassos of rawhide were then inserted through the incisions and attached to the center pole. The participant danced with increasing vigor, pulling away from the pole, stretching his skin out, and trying to break it. "Every time a break was made in his skin," as Sarah Olden described the traditional dance, "the relatives of the dancer had to give something to the poor. When all the skin was torn through, the women gathered around him and sang, 'Li! Li! Li! Li! Li! Li! Li!' " to express their admiration for the dancer's endurance and bravery.

In 1881 the Bureau of Indian Affairs, in its drive to assimilate the Sioux, and with the ardent support of the churches, outlawed Sun Dance. Attendance at the ceremony became a crime, punishable in the BIA administrative courts. The outraged Sioux resisted and held a large traditional dance—a single gathering of all the Sioux tribes—in 1883, but after that, as the bureau forcibly broke up gatherings, the public dances ceased. The ban on Sun Dance was punctuated, and the consequences of disobeying federal edicts prohibiting Indian religious ceremonies were underscored, in 1890 by the massacre at Wounded Knee Creek on the Pine Ridge Reservation, where the U.S. military slaughtered more than two hundred men, women, and children. Their wrong had been following the Ghost Dance, a pan-Indian religion holding out hope that the old, free days would return.

Although standard accounts once reported that Sun Dance disappeared after the 1883 ceremony, we now know that the Sioux kept it alive. At Pine Ridge the Lakota continued to hold scattered, underground dances in remote areas of the reservation. By the early 1950s open Sun Dances were being held at Pine Ridge and the other Sioux reservations, but under tightly controlled circumstances: Piercing was not allowed until the late 1950s, and then only upon certification from the BIA in Washington. Though it ultimately failed, the whole long suppression was emotionally and spiritually debilitating, and it left scars. Clamping down on

Sun Dance was like prohibiting devout Christians and their ministers from uttering Jesus' name, using the symbol of the cross, reading the Bible, and congregating on Sundays.

Fortunately, the heavy hands of the Lakota's governmental and religious overseers could not reach everywhere. To a newcomer passing through, the Pine Ridge reservation may seem nothing more than a barren wasteland. There is truth in that, but there are other truths too. To the Sioux, the reservation was the setting for the tribe's long history, the tragic and the uplifting and the ordinary, the place where all the ancestors had been buried in ceremony, the locale for all of Grandfather's stories. The land was a broad, ever-present charter—writ in sky and flowing grass, in low hills and cottonwood hollows and piney ridges—of freedom from the difficulties of daily life. Even the Badlands of the northern part of the reservation, a rough, choppy, eroded-out terrain of gullies and buttes, carried Lakota memories and were home to scattered families on plots far from any road.

So in the years after World War II the Sioux received from the land a little income from ranching, some food from gardening and hunting, and a strong sense of satisfaction and tradition. They did much of their traveling by horseback or horse and wagon. Hunting and trapping were part subsistence and part ceremony, for the Lakota way was to honor the deer and antelope and small game they took—beaver, ducks, rabbits, wild turkeys, and squirrels. The people went out to gather native plants, such as timpsila (a wild turnip), chokecherries, and buffalo berries, for the taste and cultural meaning. The experience of a Lakota elder spoke the heart of many of her fellow Lakota: "I went to St. Louis. Everything there was so fast and busy. I couldn't wait to come back to Pine Ridge. I needed my wide open spaces here, where it's quiet and peaceful, and where I can think."

Yet the Lakota received many firm reminders that the land could give only so much freedom. The priests pressured them to attend church, and most complied, usually out of politeness. The children had to leave their traditions and attend white schools, often boarding schools far from home. And once a month it would come time to go into town for the rations and pick up the trucked-in dry beans, cornmeal, bacon, canned tomatoes, and oleo.

THE LITTLE SETTLEMENT of Taholah lies on the Pacific coast along the south bank of the Quinault River as it empties into the ocean. More rock than sand, this jagged coastline on the Olympic Peninsula receives driving, battering storms for more than half the year. Lodged in a landscape at once harsh and spectacular, furious and giving, Taholah is home to most members of the Quinault Indian Nation.

In the years immediately after World War II the Quinault faced fearsome social problems. The reservation had no schools, and few of its young went off to college; apparently no one in the tribe had obtained a four-year degree. Alcoholism afflicted most families. Diabetes and heart problems hit the Quinault at rates many times those of the general population, and infant mortality brought regular sadness. So did continuing rashes of suicides. "I remember it vividly," said Phillip Martin, a longtime tribal council member. "In the early fifties, five boys in one family all committed suicide. They were all young, between eighteen and thirty-five." Yet the reservation had no health facility, no doctor, dentist, or nurse.

On the other hand, poverty held a looser grip at Quinault than on most other reservations. To be sure, there was need. No one had indoor plumbing, the cedar plank homes regularly housed extended families of a dozen or more, and family income amounted to less than two-thirds of Washington's statewide average. Nearly half the tribal members, most of them seeking better economic opportunities, lived away from the reservation. Yet standard indicators failed to tell the full story. Pearl Capoeman-Baller, the tailored, soft-spoken president of the Quinault Nation, remembered her youth in Taholah: "We knew, of course, that we were poor. But nobody felt poor. Everybody had the same. We shared. There was no difference in social or economic status."

The wealth of the land played a central role in this. The 200,000-acre reservation provides 26 miles of coastline. The

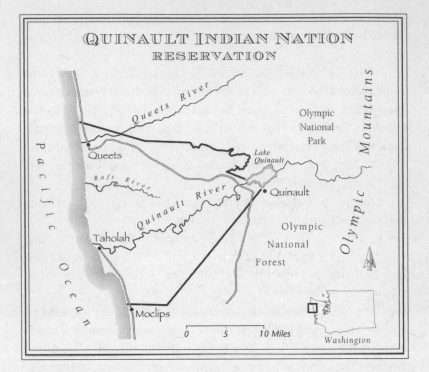

upper, higher end reaches to Lake Quinault, adjacent to Olympic National Park in the Olympic Range. Doused with 70 to 140 inches of rain annually, the reservation, except for the coastal strip and some open prairies, consists of lush rain forest, mainly western redcedar—giant trees rising to canopies two to three hundred feet high—along with hemlock, Sitka spruce, and Douglas fir. The forest floor is a rich, nearly impenetrable tangle of ferns, vine maple, and other vegetation—and fallen behemoths that in time become seedbeds for new growth. The moisture, the vegetation, and the spongy soil make perfect watershed conditions for the Quinault, one of the big rivers that surge down out of the Olympics.

The reservation produced a modest economic base consisting of some 200 jobs, almost all in logging and fishing, to a local adult population of 1,500. Beyond that, the ocean and river were virtual cornucopias. Five species of salmon, notably the Quinault blueback, a succulent delicacy found nowhere else, ran in the Quinault. The runs of the early 1950s, depleted by logging but still healthy, provided some commercial returns. A bounty of salmon from subsistence nets spread throughout Taholah, the other reservation town of Queets, and the backwoods reservation homes as families shared their catches. Abundant razor clams and elk also provided staples on the dinner tables.

The Quinault were a cedar people as well as a salmon people. Traditionally they used all parts of the big trees: planks for housing; woven bark and roots for clothing, baskets, and utensils; and leaves for medicines and ceremonies. The redcedars also made possible a hallmark of Quinault society, the elegant canoes that craftsmen carved from downed logs. By the 1950s some of the light, swift river canoes remained in use, but with the decline in whaling and the construction of inland routes to transport freight, the Quinault no longer employed the larger, stouter ocean canoes that once supported a thriving Native commerce along the northwest coast up into British Columbia.

The Quinault, then, retained some of their traditional society's basic sources of strength. The Sioux might have lost the buffalo, but the Quinault still had their salmon. In addition, although the Bureau of Indian Affairs had pressed Christianizing hard— especially by sending Quinault children off to the federal boarding schools, with their religious and assimilationist orientation, since the 1870s—the missionaries had encroached on Quinault tribal land to a lesser degree. Taholah had two churches (some people went to both), the Natives' own Shaker church, which was well attended, and the Pentecostal church, which also had adherents but did not aggressively proselytize. Nonetheless, whatever tender advantages the tribe may have had, by the early 1950s immense forces that threatened to destroy the salmon runs, the forests, and tribal self-governance—the Quinault way of life—had been set in motion.

In 1887, Congress passed the General Allotment Act, which authorized the BIA to "allot" Indian reservations—that is, to break up tribal ownership by first transferring some tribal lands to individual tribal members and then opening all or a significant part of the remaining reservation land to acquisition by non-Indians. The idea was to turn Indians into farmers—and, implicitly, to allow non-Indians to obtain tribal lands for agriculture, mining, and logging. Allotment brought woe to every tribe it touched, but whatever its merits, it certainly made no sense at Quinault. This was timberland, not farmland. Still, the government dispensed allotments to tribal members, just as if they were agricultural land, the only difference being that the Quinault received 80-acre parcels instead of the 160-acre size in agricultural areas.

Allotment ruined the Quinault forest. The optimum way to manage forestland is to control as large an area as possible and set up a forestry plan that will allow for a sustainable timber harvest. But at Quinault, with most of the land transformed from a single block owned by the tribe into a grid with more than two thousand eighty-acre parcels in individual ownership, the incentives changed dramatically. Allottees could obtain large, one-time payments by clear-cutting their parcels, which held some of the most valuable commercial timber on earth. The system encouraged the stripping of the ancient groves, with all their wildlife and cultural values: Almost no one actually lived on the dense, heavily forested allotments; many allottees had homes off the reservation and had less personal interest in preserving the forests; and non-Indians obtained Quinault allotments upon inheritance or purchase and saw them purely as cash registers for short-term gain.

This put the BIA in a box. The agency is legally a trustee for tribal land and for individual trust land, such as allotments. At Quinault, the bureau now faced steady pressure for rapid clear-cutting from many of the allottees, Indian and non-Indian, as well as from the timber companies eager to get at these rich forests.

The timber harvesting debacle that began in the 1920s, accelerated in the 1950s, and continued well into the 1970s, however, went far beyond the bounds of any acceptable trusteeship or forestry program. The bureau gave little oversight to the non-Indian companies that logged the Quinault forest. Poor road construction triggered excessive erosion. Tractors dragging out the trees tore up the ground in areas where high-lead logging (removing logs by elevated cables) could have been used. Unsupervised

An expanse of slash from clear-cuts on the Quinault forest during the 1970s. Among many other problems, the slash leaves little ground for young trees to regenerate and, in any event, makes access for hand planting nearly impossible. Mount Olympus rises in the background. Photograph courtesy of Larry Workman, Quinault Indian Nation.

logging companies bulldozed gravel out of stream channels to get building material for their roads.

Further, the loggers left huge amounts of slash, the debris—broken trees, stumps, branches, and other wood fiber—that accompanies timber harvesting. Slash, especially in big-tree forests such as the Quinault, stifles growth of young trees, creates a fire hazard, and blocks salmon from reaching spawning beds. All these effects plagued the Quinault forest, where standards for slash removal (and all other aspects of good forestry) were far lower than in the nearby Olympic National Forest, state forestlands, or private timber company forests. David Martin worked for the tribal forestry program in the 1980s, after the tribe took over reservation timber management, and served as vice-chair of the tribal council. He described a scene that still holds true on many landscapes in the tribe's forest: "When I came back after forestry school, looking at it from a forester's perspective, the devastation was horrendous. How can you articulate it without being there, being hit with it? You could never see ground for acres and acres. There were huge piles of slash—hemlock, spruce, cedar. You could walk on top of it for miles, practically, in some areas."

The clear-cuts and the boneyards of slash redefined the Quinault reservation. Fires broke out in the slash heaps. The salmon
runs declined as the result of soil erosion and stream blockages.
Regeneration, essential for sustainable forestry, crept at anemic
levels or, in some locations, not at all. Numerous reports documented the damage. The U.S. Bureau of Sports Fisheries and
Wildlife emphasized a need for better protection of fishery
resources. The Army Corps of Engineers cited the impacts on fish
passage caused by fallen logs left in the streams. An internal BIA
report pithily warned that "the Bureau of Indian Affairs should face
up to the problem and take necessary action to prevent the logging
companies from raping the land and reaping the easy dollar."

Nor did the BIA obtain a fair financial return for the allottees.
The situation was well documented in hearings chaired by Senator Richard Neuberger of Oregon. The committee report listed
several disturbing practices, including the use of outmoded timber prices; underestimating the value of western redcedar, the
dominant species; the use of long-term, high-volume sales, which
effectively eliminated competitive bidding; and failure to meet
minimum standards for scaling (where logs, after being loaded on
a logging truck, are graded for volume and quality to determine
value). One witness testified that "it is a known fact that you could
cross the road there from the Indian reservation on to Olympic
National Forest land and still the National Forest Service obtains
higher prices for their timber than the Indian does, which only
requires crossing the road." As Senator Neuberger put it, "I think
it is a very sorry situation because it seems to me that our Government has not been a vigilant custodian of the property of these
Indians. . . . [E]verywhere along the line where a mistake has
been made it has been made adversely for the Indians so far as the
price of their timber is concerned."

In addition to controlling land use, the Bureau of Indian Affairs
kept down the tribe's ability to govern itself. The repression at Quinault, as elsewhere, was omnipresent, but one incident stands out.

In 1953, Congress complemented the termination policy by
enacting a statute that cut straight to the heart of the sovereignty
of those tribes not immediately slated for outright termination.

Public Law 280, as it is called, part of the then-current program of rapid assimilation, allowed states to assume criminal and civil court jurisdiction over Indian reservations. Now, for the first time, tribal members would have to appear in state courts, before white judges and juries, for offenses committed on the reservation. It would also obviate the need for tribal courts. "Jurisdiction" may sound like a gray, technical term, but to the Quinault, jurisdiction—a commonly used word on the reservation, like sovereignty—meant self-determination, control over their own people and affairs. Washington state officials moved aggressively to take jurisdiction on several reservations. Washington law, however, provided that the state would not take jurisdiction over any reservation unless the tribe passed a resolution in favor of state authority.

The Quinault Nation's constitution designates the general council, comprised of all adult tribal members, as the ultimate decision-making body. The issue of state jurisdiction under Public Law 280 came to the general council in 1958. Tribal member Francis Rosander recalled that "it was a pretty hectic time. There was a problem with lawlessness. The BIA had pulled its policemen out of the village. Some pretty undesirable people came here." Nonetheless, tribal leaders saw Public Law 280 for what it was—a direct attack on tribal sovereignty—and refused to surrender jurisdiction to the state. Phillip Martin attended the emotional general council meetings: "The people were just against Public Law 280. Our sovereignty is sacred to us." Three separate times the general council voted down Public Law 280.

Two days after the last general council meeting, BIA officials called a rump session with the business committee of the tribe, a body that held power to act only at the behest of the general council. The meeting was held in Hoquiam, forty miles south of the reservation, where the nearest bureau office was located. That day, under pressure from the bureau and flying directly in the face of the general council's clear directives, the business committee signed a resolution requesting state jurisdiction under Public Law 280. Shortly thereafter, Governor Albert Rosselini signed a proclamation extending state law to the Quinault reservation.

The Quinault sued to challenge Public Law 280's reach onto the reservation. State court judge Warner Poyhonen found that the business committee could not act for the tribe and struck down both the committee's resolution and Governor Rosselini's proclamation. In an unusually forceful judicial reprimand, Judge Poyhonen rebuked the Bureau of Indian Affairs for its role in the incident:

> I have strong reason to believe that certain employees of the government of the United States actively persuaded, induced, encouraged, and caused said resolution to be signed by the members of the business committee. There is reason to believe that the resolution was in fact prepared by certain employees of the United States government. It is significant that the meeting at which the resolution was signed was held not on the reservation (which was the customary meeting place) but in a room in the U.S. Post Office Building in Hoquiam at which certain Federal employees were present and participated in the discussions.

Another, even more ominous matter darkened the skies over the Quinault and the other northwestern tribes. Most had negotiated treaties with the United States guaranteeing them the right to fish under their own laws both on the reservations and at their traditional sites off the reservations. With the post–World War II population boom bringing in new non-Indian fishing boats and with increased industrialization wreaking damage to the rivers, more fishers competed for fewer fish. The non-Indian fishers and their allies in the state fish and game agencies made Indian fishermen the scapegoats. State game officials began arresting tribal fishermen for violating state license requirements and other laws even though the treaties guaranteed tribal fishers independence from state restrictions. At Quinault, non-Indian fishermen provoked ugly confrontations at off-reservation sites. At least one Quinault fisherman was shot at. Everywhere there was fear of losing the fishing rights, so critical to the Quinault economically, culturally, and spiritually. Although Public Law 280 expressly provided that it did not grant state jurisdiction over fishing or hunting, a main reason that the Quinault voted down Public Law 280 was the belief that one way or another, the state would use it as a lever to get at tribal salmon. Yes, dark times, and getting darker.

THE KINDS of troubles at Red Lake, Pine Ridge, and Quinault plagued all the nation's Indian reservations.

The Bureau of Indian Affairs exercised a nearly unfathomable degree of authority. The local superintendents, selected by the BIA without consulting the tribes, controlled the tribal budgets and manipulated tribal chairmen by disbursing or withholding dollars. Tribal ordinances were subject to BIA approval. The agency used its approval power over the hiring of tribal attorneys to shut out "troublemakers"—that is, lawyers who would actively assert tribal positions.

In addition to governor, the BIA was banker, educator, doctor, and land manager. It controlled most reservation jobs. It ran the schools and the hospitals. It administered tribal and individual bank accounts and leased, and sometimes sold, Indian land. Earl Old Person, who became a leading spokesperson for Native people years afterward, gained a seat in 1954 on the tribal council of the Blackfeet Tribe in northern Montana. Old Person is still haunted by the relentless paternalism: "When I got on the council, we were following what we were told. The BIA was really the people we worked with. If they told us something, we just went along. We didn't know better. And we felt that we couldn't do better. . . . There were these supervised leases of our oil and gas. The BIA would call in all the oil companies and bid on the oil for that tract of land. And whatever the bid was, they got the land. No one had input, tribal leaders or landowners."

In the postwar years the Bureau of Indian Affairs and the churches drove home the message, reinforced by the "America First" pride of the day, that Indianness was a thing of the past and that assimilation into the larger society was both inevitable and good. Indian clothing and languages were remnants of a lost day. Indians should abandon the reservations and move to the cities that offered a modern American way of life. All the old ceremonies, not just Sun Dance, were archaic and pagan. As Alvin

Josephy wrote, "Agents of the Bureau of Indian Affairs looked away from, or even encouraged, missionaries who continued to break up Indian ceremonies or interfere with and punish individual Indians and their families when they tried to revive languages, arts, and other aspects of their traditional cultures."

The campaign made its mark. On the Oregon coast the drums went still; no powwow had been held since World War II broke out. Earl Old Person described the direct impact on individual Indian people: "During this time people didn't want to be associated as Indian. They were afraid. People who talked the Indian language didn't want to talk the Indian language. They were afraid. I think they were still afraid from boarding schools. People would go to school and be beat up for talking the Indian language. And that was still with them. People didn't want to show their Indian way of life."

Desperate social conditions blanketed Indian country. Life expectancy for Native Americans was just 42 years, two decades less than for the general population. Infant mortality claimed 62 Indian babies per 1,000 live births, more than twice the national rate of 26. The educational system failed to connect with Indians at every level. Children stayed away from school at rates far above the national average; at Navajo, the largest reservation, 60 percent of the children remained unenrolled. Less than 5 percent of Indian people held high school degrees. Of course, far fewer entered higher education; many tribes had no university graduates at all, and nationally just a few dozen Indians received college diplomas each year. The number of Indian lawyers could be counted on one person's fingers, and so could the doctors.

Poverty engulfed Indian people. Median income for Indian families was $870, while non-Indian families received $3,750. The unemployment rate among Indians hovered around 50 percent; even in the worst days of the Great Depression, national unemployment never rose above 25 percent. Such standard economic indicators may not precisely reflect actual conditions of reservation Indians, for they do not include goods obtained by barter and by subsistence hunting and fishing, but the naked eye could easily see the deep problems—the shacks; the outhouses; the lack of electrical lines. "There were some tough times," recalled Marlon Sherman of Pine Ridge. "Dad had to leave the rez sometimes for work back in the fifties. We were very poor, but Dad was a good provider, a good hunter, and he helped other people a lot. I think we were probably relatively well-off comparatively. . . . We went to the trading post in Kyle once a month when the welfare check came in. . . . It's funny, but I never knew how I looked until I got to town. When I got to town, I *saw* the patches on my knees, my raggedy clothes. . . ."

In the early 1950s the total Indian population stood at approximately 350,000. About 15 percent lived away from the reservations, and they generally experienced a better economic situation, but not by much. Incomes for off-reservation Indians averaged about 10 percent higher than for reservation residents, although that figure rose to about 25 percent during the decade as various assimilationist programs encouraged reservation Indians, especially those with higher skill levels, to move away from home to cities.

Success in the cities for Indian people during this time was notably uneven. Some made it in blue-collar jobs—the Mohawk high-beam ironworkers on the nation's skyscrapers and bridges became legendary—or even in the professions, but for most, city life was a hand-to-mouth existence. For nearly all, the spiritual loss was palpable: "Adjusting to urban life proved difficult for Indian Americans, who still retained traditional values and viewed life from a native ethos." Urban Indians suffered a nearly universal sense of alienation and dislocation, and alcohol abuse was widespread. In most urban areas in the West, neighborhoods euphemistically called Indian enclaves—"slums" is a more accurate term—grew up. On the outskirts of Great Falls, Montana, Hill 57 was one of too many places where landless Indian people lived in rough shacks or their cars. They lacked medical care and endured miserable, unsanitary conditions without sewage facilities, electricity, or potable water.

As far back as the nineteenth century, common folklore held out the image of "rich Indians" and the idea that all Indians regularly received large government checks. In the twenty-first century there are some wealthy Indians, though their numbers are proportionately small and they are mostly limited to members of a few successful gaming tribes, but no such phenomenon existed before recent times.

In the early 1950s virtually no tribes possessed memberships with income levels as high as the general citizenry of the states where they were located. The average family income of $2,160 at Quinault, for example, was among the highest of all tribes but just two-thirds the income of Washington families. The Klamath Tribe, which seems to have had the highest tribal income at the time, may have slightly exceeded non-Indian income levels in Oregon because of annual per capita payments of $800 per person from the logging of tribal lands. The Blackfeet of Montana, Warm Springs of Oregon, Wind River of Wyoming, and a handful of other tribes all dispensed to their members reasonably significant per capita payments from timber or mineral extraction, but income levels remained well below those in non-Indian communities.

The tribes of eastern Oklahoma—the Choctaw, Chickasaw, Cherokee, Creek, and Seminole, sometimes called the Five Civilized Tribes—presented a special case. These tribes originally lived in the Southeast, but from the beginning days of the Republic, Georgia, Alabama, Mississippi, and other southern states coveted the tribes' large reservations and resented their prosperous economies and elaborate governments. In the 1830s, with the ardent support of the states, President Andrew Jackson succeeded in persuading Congress to remove the tribes to Oklahoma in the series of forced marches called the Trail of Tears. The five tribes, which owned most of eastern Oklahoma by treaties signed in connection with their removal, reestablished their governments— among other things, they organized extensive tribal school systems—only to have most of their reservations expropriated and opened for homesteading and oil exploration by the Curtis Act of 1896, which paved the way for Oklahoma statehood. The remaining lands consisted of scattered individual allotments.

With the reservations broken up, the BIA pressed hard for full assimilation of the Five Civilized Tribes. Life in Oklahoma City, Tulsa, and other cities eventually worked well for some tribal members who joined the ranks of business and civic leaders. Thus, by 1950, of a total population of 64,000, about 550 had obtained college degrees—a small percentage perhaps, but the graduates from those five tribes constituted half of all Indian college graduates in the country. Most members of the five tribes, however, remained on their family allotments in the hills and valleys of eastern Oklahoma, living in poverty-stricken conditions similar to those of Indian people in other parts of the country.

Another tribe in eastern Oklahoma, the Osage, had a distinctive history that also brought success, but only to a few. When oil was discovered in the early 1900s on Osage land, some Osage received staggering sums, rising as high as $8,000 per year in the 1920s, but the flow of money was poisoned by all manner of schemes to defraud financially naïve Osage people and, in the end, by a grisly string of murders. The boom had faded by mid-century, and family income dropped to $2,415. Further, the Osage oil money was distributed unevenly according to a "head rights formula," so that as observed in a Department of Commerce report, "every oil-rich Osage has a score of contemporaries without oil, who continue to farm their lands in Oklahoma as did their grandfathers."

WHILE IT MIGHT be tempting to lay blame on the Bureau of Indian Affairs for the rock bottom that Native people hit after World War II, the difficulties lay much deeper. Administrative agencies take their cues, and their budgets, from Congress, which in turn reflects national sentiment. The American people, to the limited extent they thought about Indians at all, felt vaguely sympathetic and wondered why Indians didn't just get on with the job of becoming "real" Americans, but mostly they were indifferent. Although the status quo had abjectly failed from any point of view, an apathetic Congress appropriated modest amounts of money to perpetuate the existing system of encouraging assimilation and keeping the reservations intact as safety nets for those who continued to live there. The BIA, without sufficient funds or tradition to attract outstanding people, just carried out Congress's and the nation's will, or lack of it. The tribes' despair, and resulting inertia, completed the stagnation.

Everywhere, then, though there were many variations, the essential story was the same. Indian people could find little hope, only the torment of a dilemma. The reservations were dead-end streets economically. Yet were the cities an answer? They might provide, after long and agonizing readjustment, some material gain. But those things held dear—the land and the culture and the bracing freedom and satisfaction they offered—could be found only back home in Indian country.

2.

The Deadening Years

Images of Indian country in the middle of the twentieth century display a certain kind of reality, societies overwhelmed by governmental paternalism, cultural suppression, and poverty at a moment in history. Those snapshots, however, depict only one dimension. They fail to capture time.

The Indian experience encompasses not just the present but layers upon layers of past people and events. To Indians, the past is especially vivid because they are place-based peoples. Unlike most Americans, they know exactly where their parents and grandparents—and all the many generations before—lived. The oral tradition, where stories are told and retold with exactitude, makes the past even more indelible. The coming of the white people and the treaties with them are not distant, hazy memories but sharp occurrences, just yesterday. So for Native people in the 1950s the troubles and burdens of the past were every bit as tangible as those of the moment. While every tribe has its own specific history, the story of the Nez Perce illustrates the contours of the Indian experience across America.

THE VAST and dramatic aboriginal domain of the Nez Perce Tribe, where the people had lived for 10,000 years or more, covered most of central Idaho: to the crest of the Bitterroot Range in the east, nearly to the headwaters of the Salmon River in the south, and to the Palouse River in the north. To the west, Nez

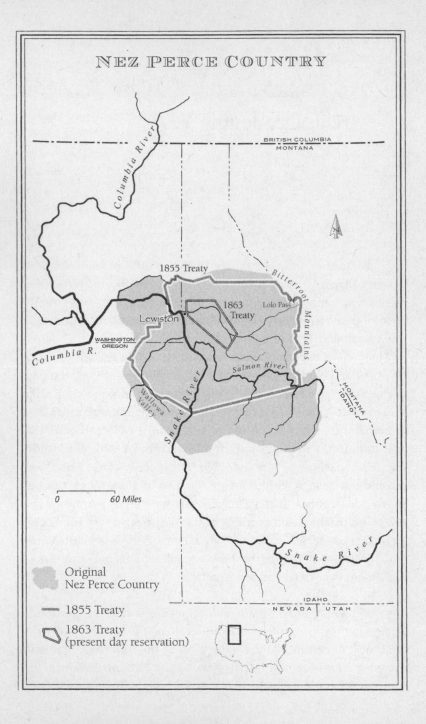

NEZ PERCE COUNTRY

Original
Nez Perce Country

1855 Treaty

1863 Treaty
(present day reservation)

Perce country reached beyond the modern state line to parts of southeast Washington and northeast Oregon, including the Wallowa Valley. The area, mountain ranges and plains cut by river canyons, amounted to thirteen million acres, about one-fourth the size of the state of Idaho.

When the runs came, the Nez Perce lived off the salmon, using the bountiful rivers and tributaries at home and traveling to traditional fishing spots as far west as the fabulous grounds at Celilo Falls on the Columbia. Early Anglo travelers, including the Lewis and Clark Expedition, commonly raved in their journals about the plenitude of salmon, and so did the Nez Perce, as explained by Leroy Seth: "In the springtime the elders would say that the fish runs are like a big parade. It seems like everything comes to life at that time and watches the parade, especially the birds. The plants come to life and that is the cue for us to know when to go catch those fish before they pass by." The Nez Perce people made good use of the forests and grassy meadows, harvesting huckleberries, wild carrots, and the sweet, onionlike root of the camas lily. They also took deer, elk, and, in the broad valleys on the far side of Lolo Pass, buffalo. In the early 1700s the tribe obtained the horse, which made travel easier and quicker.

The horse also solidified the military power of the Nez Perce by increasing their ability both to chase and to escape. The geography facilitated the tribe's control over its homeland; the big Palouse, Clearwater, and Salmon River country, especially the forestland rising toward the eastern sky, afforded the Nez Perce a sturdy measure of insulation from other tribes. Even today this region, along with the canyon country in the American Southwest, makes up one of the largest expanses of remote backcountry in the lower forty-eight states.

When the white people came to the continent, they radically altered Nez Perce existence before ever setting foot on the tribe's soil. As Elizabeth Fenn explains in *Pox Americana*, her study of epidemics in America, the arrival of Europeans "brought an abrupt end to thousands of years of isolation from the infectious diseases of Europe, Africa, and Asia. No one—not a single individual—had acquired immunity to *Variola* [smallpox] or any other Old World pathogen. . . . It was as though a spark had landed in a forest . . . with thousands of years of dried timber. The results were explosive; the consequences, unspeakable." In 1781 and 1782 missionaries or fur traders induced a virulent smallpox epidemic in the Upper Missouri country that killed off three-quarters of the Arikara. Steadily, the disease spread to the Blackfeet and other tribes of the Upper Missouri. All these tribes lived across the Continental Divide from the Nez Perce, but the Nez Perce often traveled east to trade with them. When Nez Perce traders returned home from those journeys, they brought with them a plague against which Native people had no resistance. A generation later the tribe was again devastated by smallpox; this epidemic probably spread from European ships landing far to the west at the mouth of the Columbia River.

European diseases continued to spark gruesome sieges into Nez Perce country during most of the nineteenth century, with cataclysmic results. Although warfare with whites played a role, the germs were far and away the dominant cause in chopping the Nez Perce population from an estimated 6,000 in 1805 (after the first two waves of smallpox had already hit) to 1,500 in 1885.

Because of their isolation, the Nez Perce probably fared somewhat better than most tribes. The silent killers came in many forms. Smallpox. Measles. Scarlet fever. Influenza. Bubonic plague. Diphtheria. Typhus. Cholera. Tuberculosis. Gonorrhea. Ninety separate epidemics, each sweeping over broad reaches of the country, ravaged tribes between the early sixteenth century and the beginning of the twentieth. In addition to actual deaths, the diseases lowered population through decreased rates of fertility and fecundity. Tribal traditions also contributed. The use of sweat baths and a dip in cold river water to treat the ill, a practice of the Nez Perce and many other tribes, only worsened the suffering from smallpox and measles. No tribe escaped the epidemics, and some were extinguished.

The many written accounts leave no doubt about the horrors that tribes passed down by the oral tradition. At Cherokee, a trader witnessed the smallpox epidemic of 1738: "Seeing themselves disfigured . . . some shot themselves, others cut their throats . . .

many threw themselves with sullen madness into the fire." James Mooney described the 1849 Kiowa cholera epidemic: "The Kiowa remember it as the most terrible experience in their history, far exceeding in fatality the smallpox of nine years before. . . . It . . . was particularly dreaded on account of its dreadful suddenness, men who had been in perfect health in the morning being dead a few hours later." The artist George Catlin witnessed the loss of an entire Mandan village to smallpox in 1837:

> The first symptom of the disease was a rapid swelling of the body, and so very virulent had it become, that very many died in two or three hours after their attack, and that in many cases without the appearance of the disease upon the skin. Utter dismay seemed to possess all classes and all ages, and they gave themselves up in despair, as entirely lost. There was but one continual crying and howling and praying to the Great Spirit for his protection during the nights and days; and there being but few living, and those in too appalling despair, nobody thought of burying the dead, whose bodies, whole families together, were left in horrid and loathsome piles in their own wigwams, with a few buffalo robes, etc. thrown over them, there to decay and be devoured by their own dogs. . . .

The impact on Indian people was almost unimaginable. Estimates of pre-Columbian Native populations within the mainland United States have been the subject of considerable debate. Scholars now universally reject as too low Alfred Kroeber's estimate in 1937 of 900,000 and generally regard Henry Dobyns's 1982 figure of 18 million as too high. The commonly accepted range seems to be a Native population of 5 to 7 million before the diseases hit. In 1900 the Indian population reached its all-time low of approximately 250,000, a reduction of 95 percent or more, most of it resulting from the epidemics.

THE WESTWARD EXPANSION ground away at traditional Native societies in many other ways. The insidious effects of alcohol, a drug nearly unknown on the continent, quickly caught the attention of the tribes and the settlers alike. From early colonial days, trade with Indians had been a major issue, and liquor a prime element of Indian trade. The issue had many facets. Some traders defrauded Indians by doing business with intoxicated Natives and by exacting too much for sales of rum and other spirits. Indian people reacted poorly to the new drink, causing disruption and violence within the tribes. This led to resentment against the whites, sometimes manifested in raids and skirmishes. The colonies all adopted their own Indian trading regulations, and most included a prohibition against liquor sales. In 1802, as part of sweeping Indian commerce legislation, Congress outlawed liquor in the Indian trade, a stricture widely ignored by white traders on the frontier.

The Nez Perce first encountered liquor during the 1820s and 1830s, when fur traders held a summer rendezvous each year in various Rocky Mountain locations. These large, colorful congregations allowed the mountain men to obtain furs in exchange for such goods as knives, clothing, coffee, sugar—and alcohol. Unlike most traders, the western fur trappers apparently showed considerable restraint owing not to the faraway federal law that had little impact on them but to their own desire to maintain stable relations with Native trading partners. The mountain men generally got on well with Indian people. Kit Carson, Jim Bridger, Broken Hand Fitzpatrick, and others spoke several Indian languages. They learned the best trails and adopted aspects of the Indian lifestyle, clothing themselves in animal hides and constructing tipis. While they used liquor only sparingly as a trade item, it was very much a part of the ribald socializing that, along with the business conducted, distinguished the rendezvous.

From the comparatively benign beginnings of these yearly gatherings, the Nez Perce's problems with liquor mushroomed. The white population steadily encroached on Nez Perce territory, and by the 1860s, despite entreaties by several tribal leaders urging whites not to sell to the Nez Perce, "liquor became a desperate problem for the Indians." All across Indian country drinking reached plague proportions for peoples who, as historian Angie Debo explained, had no coping strategies for it: "This first taste of alcohol was more significant than anyone could have foreseen.

The European had developed some immunity to its effects or restraint in its consumption through millenniums of use. To the Indian it was wholly ruinous. As tribe after tribe encountered it, it became a large factor in their history."

IF THE MOUNTAIN MEN saw a good deal to admire, indeed emulate, in Native culture, the missionaries going out into Indian country saw only savages in need of change. But change, read conversion, could happen only if their traditional ways were stamped out.

After Europeans reached the New World, clerics in England, Spain, and Portugal soon entered into a far-ranging debate over the nature of the Natives and their rights. It was a given that Indians were, variously, "savages," "heathens," and "infidels." Could such people rightly own land? Could they have governments? Were they human in a full sense? Legal historian Rennard Strickland, an Osage-Cherokee, told me, "You have to understand. These people denied our humanity. Our *humanity*. And it continued well into the twentieth century."

The colonies, reflecting a partnership between church and state on the Indian issue, declared the goal of Christianizing and assimilating Natives. Missionaries converted significant numbers among some tribes, especially in New England. On the whole, however, the coastal settlements had only limited success in the early years, both because the Indians held tenaciously to their traditional ways and because the missionary spirit paled in intensity with the efforts to come.

The movement to "civilize" Natives, fueled by nationhood and an upsurge in Protestant missionary zeal, gained considerable steam in the late 1700s. Washington and especially Jefferson gave prominence to "civilization" in national Indian policy. "Civilize" quickly became a near synonym for "Christianize." Thomas McKenney, superintendent for Indian trade from 1816 through 1822, spearheaded an effort extraordinary by modern lights or, for that matter, by the values of a young nation that had rebelled largely to escape a state religion. In order to save Indians, McKenney advocated a recipe, accepted by Congress in 1819, of paying government subsidies directly to missionaries for educating Indians. He exhorted that "we have the power not only to enhance their happiness in this world, but in the next also; and by our councils, and guidance, save souls that otherwise must perish!" Treaties of the era also called for education funds, which were distributed to churches, but in the 1830s, with the Oregon Trail now open and the nation preoccupied with the West, activist missionaries saw opportunities to convert even more souls, all the way to the Pacific.

The Nez Perce received their first missionary in 1836, when Henry Spaulding, a Presbyterian, arrived at the lower Clearwater River, 20 miles from today's Lewiston, Idaho. Henry and Eliza Spaulding had no background in frontier living and needed help from the Indians, who were glad to give it. Word of Christianity had already spread among the tribes of the Columbia River watershed. In particular, there was much curiosity among the Natives about "the book" that Garry, chief of the Spokane Tribe, had obtained from missionaries farther north. So a number of Nez Perce cut logs and constructed a substantial cabin consisting of small quarters for the Spauldings' residence and a much larger room to serve as church and school. The openness and hospitality of the Nez Perce reflected a susceptibility to the missionaries shared by many other Indian tribes. As tribal member Allen Slickpoo explained in a history sponsored by the Nez Perce Tribe, "The missionaries at first were welcomed with open arms. We were already a very religious people and wanted to learn about the white man's way as well."

Spaulding achieved early success, logging many baptisms and conversions. His training in medicine enhanced his value to the Nez Perce, but within a few years, resentment began to build. Spaulding was determined to eradicate Nez Perce ways. He favored the "progressives"—the converts—and discriminated against the "pagans" by withholding goods. He discouraged the men from hunting, seeking to turn them to agriculture, and objected to traditional clothing and dances. In concert with the local Indian agent, he pushed through a rigid code of conduct, enforceable by lashings, and Spaulding, possessed of a tumultuous temper, personally administered the whippings. After Spaulding left Nez Perce in 1847, his successors, while more diplomatic, pursued the same Christianizing policies.

These early incursions into Native society laid the foundation for tribal divisions and losses of self-identity that were to impact the Nez Perce forever. "The external stress brought on by missionary and government attempts to modify radically Nez Perce social organization," wrote anthropologist Deward Walker, "frequently has exacerbated internal strains to the point of open rupture of relationships between leaders and aspirants for leadership." Allen Slickpoo quoted a fellow Nez Perce: "Later we realized this softening up process of the American Indian, by the introduction of missionaries who played an important role in breaking down our way of life, demoralizing and weakening our cultural values, and ending our power and freedom so that we would be dependent on the whites."

BY THE EARLY 1850s the Nez Perce population had been reduced by more than half to approximately 3,000. The decline in numbers plainly affected the tribe's military capability, and both liquor and the missionaries' work had cleaved fissures in the society, but somehow, as the years to come were to show, the Nez Perce spirit, its sense of nationhood and place, remained strong. At mid-century, however, the United States came at the Nez Perce from yet another angle, by using treaty negotiations to reduce tribal landholdings and open up real estate for settlement by non-Indians.

In 1853, President Franklin Pierce appointed Isaac Stevens governor and superintendent of Indian affairs of the new Washington Territory, which at the time took in northern Idaho. By 1854 Stevens, able and ambitious, had decided to begin drawing up treaties with the territory's tribes to make way for the westward expansion. Stevens's aggressive, bullying tactics got him in trouble from the start. The December 1854 treaty with a group of southern Puget Sound tribes—Stevens designated both the tribes that would be grouped together and the "chiefs" who would represent them—went bad immediately. He forced such a small reservation on the Nisqually that Chief Leschi and his followers would have none of it, leading to a bloody war of outrage.

The Nisqually treaty, the first of thirteen that Stevens negotiated from Puget Sound to western Montana, and the combat that followed chastened him somewhat and, more important, sent stories of the arrogant young American rippling among the tribes of the Northwest. After the Puget Sound treaties, Stevens worked his way south to the Columbia River, calling a treaty council with the Nez Perce and other tribes in May 1855 on Mill Creek in the Walla Walla Valley.

The Walla Walla treaty council, fascinating in many respects, had a grandeur about it. An estimated 5,000 Indian people attended. The Nez Perce rode in: "a thousand warriors mounted on fine horses and riding at a gallop, two abreast, naked to the breech-clout, their faces covered with white, red, and yellow paint in fanciful designs, and decked with plumes and feathers and trinkets fluttering in the sunshine." The personalities and relationships were complex. On the United States' side, Isaac Stevens used strong-arm tactics, but his fellow negotiator, Joel Palmer, who far better understood the Indians' reactions and point of view, repeatedly had to step in, back up, and move down a better track. For the Indians' part, the tribes had divisions among themselves, leading finally to the creation of three reservations, one for the Nez Perce, one for the Umatilla, Cayuse, and Walla Walla, and one for the Yakama and several smaller Columbia River tribes and bands.

But when you read the minutes of Indian treaty negotiations, certainly including these minutes, you find something else, something more profound. It is a point laid out in detail by Alvin Josephy in his great book *The Nez Perce Indians and the Opening of the Northwest*. Josephy teaches us that the stereotype of the Indian leaders at the treaty talks as passive and intellectually overmatched is wrong.

The Nez Perce negotiators and the other tribal leaders at the Walla Walla council had a complete understanding of the situation. The white people wanted their land and had the population and weaponry to take it. The tribes, on the other hand, possessed

considerable leverage; in time they would lose a military campaign, but along the way they could exact heavy costs in money
and human life to fight a war on the fragile, distant edge of American territory.

The calculus was about power, and the tribes could make the
calculations as well as the white people. The tribal negotiators
were sophisticated and used every technique and device available
to them. They strung the proceedings out (the talks began on May
28 and went to June 11), giving them time to caucus, think, and
make what changes they could. They made their arguments precisely and ably. As anthropologist Herbert Spinden put it, Nez
Perce oratory was characterized "by calm reasoning where facts
were to be considered, and by impassioned appeal when the decision depended on sentiment. There was considerable use of ges-
ticulation and a great display of dignity. Statements were concise
and concrete."

Both sides agreed that the land at issue was Indian land. To be
sure, traditionally Indian people did not think in terms of landownership, but they did comprehend national territory. As Owhi,
a Yakama, said at the negotiations, the Creator "made our bodies
from the earth. . . . What shall I do? Shall I give the lands that are
a part of my body and leave myself poor and destitute?" The prevailing view among the tribal leaders, however, seemed to be an
amalgam of tradition and the practical fact that the tribes would
be forced to relinquish some land—and, by the white man's rules,
would be entitled to compensation. Young Chief said this at the
Walla Walla council (the minutes used the term "God" but the
speaker probably used the Yakama term for Creator): "I wonder if
this ground has anything to say: I wonder if the ground is listening to what is said. . . . I hear what this earth says, the earth says,
God has placed me here. . . . God on placing them on the earth . . .
[said], take good care of the earth and do each other no harm. God
said, You Indians who take care of a certain portion of the country should not trade it off unless you get a fair price."

Isaac Stevens knew, as a matter of American real property law,
that the Nez Perce, like all American Indian tribes, had an ownership interest in their land. In its 1846 treaty with Great Britain,

the United States gained clear title to the Pacific Northwest as against all foreign nations. But the United States still had a shared title with the tribes that, under Chief Justice John Marshall's seminal decision in *Johnson v. McIntosh* in 1823, were "rightful occupants of the soil, with a legal as well as just claim to retain possession of it, and to use it according to their own discretion."

· This Indian right of occupancy meant that tribes had a legal right to live on their aboriginal land, to hunt and fish on it, and to use the minerals, trees, and other vegetation. The right of occupancy, while it did not require compensation if taken by the federal government, also included a legal right of possession as against the states and settlers, who would be trespassers upon the tribal title. Under federal law, the United States could obtain title in one of two ways, by conquest—that is, war—or by purchase, the treaty-making process that federal policy preferred and that Stevens had put in motion.

Ground rules in the Walla Walla Valley in 1855, then, were well drawn. The United States had more power, but the tribes had some power. The United States was there to obtain Indian land, not to give land to the tribes, which already had their land, by possession and by federal law. They came to the negotiations as sovereign nations. Given the military superiority of the United States, it was not a negotiation among equals—few negotiations are—but it was definitely a negotiation.

The Nez Perce Treaty of 1855 remains controversial within the tribe to this day. Lawyer, a tribal leader and a Christian, acted as principal negotiator for the Nez Perce, and charges persist that he was too eager to please, that he was manipulated by Stevens and the missionaries. Late in the negotiations, Looking Glass, the Nez Perce war chief, arrived amid great commotion. He had been off hunting buffalo and doing battle with the Blackfeet, across the Continental Divide, and he raced back upon hearing of the council. "My people, what have you done? While I was gone, you have sold my country." He proceeded to designate the reservation he thought was right. He went to Stevens's map and with his finger drew a line precisely around the whole Nez Perce traditional territory. But the die had been cast; it was too late in the council proceedings. The Nez Perce chiefs, including Looking Glass, signed the treaty that Lawyer had agreed to with Stevens.

The Nez Perce retained a reservation of 8 million acres, but ceded away about 5.5 million acres. The size of this cession has continued to cause resentment among the Nez Perce. Yet from one perspective, Lawyer and his fellow negotiators had done well. Typically, other tribes ceded away roughly 80 or 90 percent of their aboriginal land at treaty time. The Nez Perce kept 60 percent of their land, a vast and, however value might be defined, valuable tract.

Further—this grew critical in the modern "salmon wars"—the tribal negotiators refused to relinquish all their rights in the ceded area. If a tribe does not explicitly preserve rights in a ceded area, it normally loses all rights in that land. So the Nez Perce, like other tribes that treated with Stevens, insisted upon keeping specified off-reservation rights for fishing, hunting, gathering, and other purposes. Stevens and Palmer assured them several times during the proceedings that those rights would be protected. The 1855 treaty guaranteed to the Nez Perce Tribe, in addition to exclusive rights on the reservation, "the right of taking fish at all usual and accustomed places in common with citizens of the Territory; and of erecting temporary buildings for curing, together with the privilege of hunting, gathering roots and berries, and pasturing their horses and cattle upon open and unclaimed land."

It is important to mark down the enduring role of the 1855 treaty. Although its promises of a permanent 8-million-acre homeland soon were shattered, its other central structural provisions— the recognition of Nez Perce sovereignty, the federal-tribal trust relationship, and the guarantee of expansive off-reservation fishing, hunting, and gathering rights—all remain fully in place today. And so, in one of a thousand ironies that characterize the federal-tribal relationship, a certain legal stability, of which our legal system can be quite proud, protected some tribal rights while, concurrently, the Nez Perce people experienced almost incomprehensible agony and loss as momentous events continued to sweep across their country.

.   .   .

THE 1855 TREATY came under fire immediately. Miners turned up traces of gold on the Nez Perce Reservation within a year after the treaty. Then, in 1860, refugees from the rich but increasingly crowded California fields hit major strikes in the Clearwater watershed. As a governor of Idaho later put it, the Nez Perce "reservation was overrun by the enterprising miners; treaty stipulations were disregarded and trampled underfoot; towns were established thereon, and all means that cupidity could invent or disloyalty achieve were resorted to shake their confidence in the government." The tribe should have been secure under the treaty; the Nez Perce now possessed complete ownership of its treaty land, protected in a sacred trust by the United States. Nevertheless, whether it was the Cherokee in the 1820s, the California Indians in the forties and fifties, the Sioux in the seventies, or any number of other tribes, gold always obliterated Indian landholdings, and the Nez Perce were no exception.

The inevitable land reduction treaty came in 1863 at Lapwai. Lawyer again took the lead in representing the tribe. His role here, as eight years before, remains clouded in controversy. He may well have been doing the best he could in the face of what amounted to a full-scale invasion by American settlers. But we do know that the leaders of several Nez Perce bands that refused to show up or that walked away from the treaty negotiations never had the slightest intention of seeing their valleys transferred away by surrogate signatories. The minutes of the 1863 negotiations give no indication that Lawyer purported to speak for the other bands when he signed the treaty. Yet the federal commissioners pretended that all the bands had consented. As Alvin Josephy's careful research shows, "In the end, a bold lie was broadcast in the assertion that the entire tribe had agreed to the treaty. That statement was conveyed to Washington without qualification."

In all, the 1863 treaty ceded away more than 90 percent of the magnificent 8-million-acre Nez Perce Reservation created in 1855, leaving only 750,000 acres east of Lewiston. The treaty expressly left in place the other provisions of the 1855 treaty, including the off-reservation fishing, hunting, and gathering rights. Nonetheless, the document blew apart the Nez Perce land base without the consent of many of its chiefs. Josephy and leading historian Angie Debo both use the same word for it, "fraudulent," but fraud seldom slowed the march of expansion. Under the Supreme Court decision in *Lone Wolf v. Hitchcock*, a treaty negotiated by the executive branch and confirmed by the Senate becomes the supreme law of the land, fraud or no.

One chief who refused to attend the 1863 negotiations was Joseph, leader of the band that lived across the Snake River in the high, sublime Wallowa Valley, within Oregon. His son, also named Joseph (his Nez Perce name, Hin-mah-too-yah-lat-kekht, meant, so appropriately, Thunder Traveling to Loftier Heights), studiously followed the events. The younger Joseph lost his father in 1871: "I buried him in that beautiful valley of the winding rivers. I love that land more than all the rest of the world."

By then, because of the words agreed to by others in 1863, it was the land not of the Nez Perce but of the farmers, ranchers, and miners of the United States. To Joseph, the treaty was no treaty at all. His father had refused to sign it. The Wallowa Valley was still Nez Perce country, a place of peace, a place beyond the reach of the United States, beyond the churches and their schools: "They will teach us to quarrel about God, as the Catholics and Protestants do on the Nez Perces reservation, and at other places. We do not want to learn that. We may quarrel with men sometimes about things on this earth, but we never quarrel about God. We do not want to learn that."

Pressure built steadily on Joseph and his people during the 1870s. Oregon Governor Lafayette Grover and other state officials pushed for removal of the Nez Perce from the Wallowa Valley. Joseph, eloquent, sensible, and smart, tried to reason with Indian agent John Monteith, General Oliver Howard, and federal authorities, but they insisted on enforcing the 1863 treaty. Finally, confronting the inevitability of military might, Joseph relented. He would remove to the Lapwai Reservation. The Nez Perce left the Wallowa Valley in mid-May 1877, and as the sad procession neared the reservation, combat with local settlers broke out. Young Nez Perce warriors in Joseph's party were exacting revenge for past killings and violence.

Thus began Joseph's epic 1,300-mile march, assisted by Looking Glass the younger and other able lieutenants, studded with bravery and military genius, across the divide, down to newly proclaimed Yellowstone National Park, and up through central Montana nearly to the Canadian line. There, on a snowy, windswept plain near the Bear Paw Mountains on October 5, 1877, the depleted and exhausted band of 418 Nez Perce, three-quarters of them women and children, surrendered after a final battle that took the lives of Looking Glass and 24 others. Joseph's closing words to the gathered U.S. military officers have lived over the years: "Hear me, my chiefs, I am tired; my heart is sick and sad. From where the sun now stands, I will fight no more forever."

Federal troops took Joseph and the remaining survivors by train to Fort Leavenworth and then to the Indian country of Oklahoma. After suffering eight years of imprisonment, they were returned to the Northwest. Some went to Lapwai, but Joseph and 150 others were sent to the Colville Reservation in Washington, not to Nez Perce and certainly not to the Wallowa Valley.

Modern-day Nez Perce tribal members look down into Joseph Canyon in the Wallowa Valley of northeastern Oregon. Photograph courtesy of Phil Schermeister.

JUST TWO years after their captors allowed some of the Wallowa group to return to Idaho, Congress launched a policy that every bit as much as the Indian wars, every bit as much as the initial treaties and the "renegotiated" treaties, changed the lives of the Nez Perce and other Indian people across the country.

The idea behind the General Allotment Act of 1887 was deceptively simple and seemingly innocuous: To make Indians into farmers by carving lands out of the tribal reservation and providing every tribal member with an individual allotment, a plot of land, usually 160 acres. On a few forested reservations, such as Quinault, 80 acres made an allotment. Not so incidentally, on many reservations—Pine Ridge is an example—much of the tribal land not allotted would be declared "surplus" and opened for settlement by non-Indians.

Allotment remade Indian country once again. When Congress enacted the statute in 1887, Indian landholdings nationally totaled 140 million acres, about 8 percent of all land in what is now the lower forty-eight states. By 1934, when Congress abandoned the allotment policy, tribal landholdings had plummeted to 52 million acres, a loss of nearly 90 million acres, an area the size of Idaho and Washington combined. Teddy Roosevelt called allotment "a mighty pulverizing engine, to break up the tribal mass."

Allotment arose from mixed motives. A child of the nineteenth century's broad-shouldered westward expansion, allotment derived much of its force from the boomers who wanted Indian land. A proponent argued that Indian ownership could not prevent the nation's drive west, which was as "irresistible as that of Sherman's to the sea." A House subcommittee minority report called the allotment policy "greed," asserting that "the real aim of this bill is to get at the Indian lands and open them up to settlement. The provisions for the apparent benefit of the Indian are but the pretext to get at his lands and occupy them."

At the same time, beneficent attitudes, however paternalistic they may have been, also played a role in the adoption of allotment. This was the era of the Friends of the Indian, a group of self-professed Indian advocates, with a significant Christian influence, that met annually in the rarefied atmosphere of a resort on Lake

NEZ PERCE TIME

1950s	Nez Perce lands reduced to 76,000 acres
1948	Nez Perce adopt Indian Reorganization Act
1927	Nez Perce adopt constitution requiring BIA approval for tribal ordinances
1911	98 percent of Nez Perce allotted and leased to non-Indians
1893	Nez Perce receive $3 per acre for 500,000 acres of surplus land opened for homesteading
1889	Alice Fletcher arrives to implement allotment
1885	Nez Perce population estimated at 1,437
1880s	Nez Perce devastated by smallpox epidemic
1877	Chief Joseph leaves the Wallowa Valley, beginning five-month, 1,300-mile march
1863	Lapwai Treaty: Nez Perce territory reduced to 750,000
1860	Gold discovered in Idaho at Orofino Creek
1855	Walla Walla Treaty: Nez Perce guaranteed 8 million acres
1850s	Nez Perce population estimated at 3,000
1836	Henry Spaulding, Nez Perce's first missionary, arrives
1820s	Nez Perce introduced to alcohol
1805	Nez Perce population estimated at 6,000
1780s	Nez Perce devastated by smallpox epidemic
1700s	Nez Perce acquire horses, solidifying control over 13-million-acre domain
10,000 bp	Native Americans settle central Idaho

UNITED STATES TIME

1953	Congress announces termination policy
1941–1945	World War II
1934	Indian Reorganization Act: Congress ends allotment policy
	Native American lands reduced to 52 million acres
1924	Citizenship granted to Native Americans
1901	President Theodore Roosevelt describes allotment as "a mighty pulverizing engine to break up the tribal mass"
1900	Native American population estimated at 250,000
1900s	Native American children educated at BIA boarding schools
1887	General Allotment Act. Native American lands encompass 140 million acres
1885	Fewer than 1,000 buffalo alive
1881	Helen Hunt Jackson's A Century of Dishonor published
1879	BIA boarding school adopts "kill the Indian, and save the man"
1869	Transcontinental railroad completed
1862	Homestead Act
1861–1865	Civil War
1854–1856	Isaac Stevens negotiates treaties in the Pacific Northwest
1848	Gold discovered in California at Sutter's Mill
1836	Trail of Tears: Native Americans removed from Southeast
1832	Worcester v. Georgia (Marshall recognizes tribal sovereignty)
1823	Johnson v. McIntosh (Marshall recognizes tribal land rights)
1819	Congress provides subsidies to missionaries
1815–1890	Indian wars
1804–1806	Lewis and Clark Expedition
1803	Louisiana Purchase
1801	John Marshall becomes chief justice of U.S. Supreme Court
1775–1783	Revolutionary War
1492	Columbus reaches North America
	Native American population estimated at 5 to 7 million

Mohonk in upstate New York. They drew inspiration from Helen Hunt Jackson's *A Century of Dishonor,* published in 1881, and *Ramona,* which came out three years later. Jackson's books may have been overdrawn and surely did not amount to high literature, but she struck a chord and generated national sympathy for the Indians' cause. Her work drew comparisons with *Uncle Tom's Cabin,* and the Lake Mohonk reformers regularly pointed out the similarity to the struggle of blacks. "The time has now come," wrote Lydia Maria Child, "when, without intermitting our vigilant watch over the rights of black men, it is our duty to arouse the nation to a sense of its guilt concerning the red man."

The Friends of the Indian saw allotment as a chance for Natives to share in the fruits of American society. The Jeffersonian ideal still burned brightly, and agrarianism held great, if idealized, appeal. Reformers also thought they could improve on the traditional communal tribal ways. The idea of providing a plot of real estate to each tribal member, though it would diminish or eliminate the tribal land estate, fit nicely with the individualistic tone of American society and the assimilationist views held by the evangelical Christians then active in Indian policy. Idealism aside, the Indian reformers also believed that allotment would be the best tribes could get. The alternative was a wholesale expropriation of Indian lands.

A strange idea, really, to turn Indians who had never farmed into farmers. How many of us could rise to the command "You shall now become a farmer"—or, for that matter, teacher, plumber, doctor, or salesperson? Yet most of the policy making community proceeded on that basis, whether out of straight-faced subterfuge, sincerely held belief, or inattentiveness. Henry L. Dawes, for example, a respected congressman from Massachusetts who shepherded the General Allotment Act (it is often called the Dawes Act) through Congress, was by every account well-meaning and genuinely committed to minority rights. In addition to his sympathy for Indians, he strongly opposed slavery. One of the very few to analyze allotment carefully and forecast its effects—and oppose it—was Colorado Senator Henry Teller: "If I stand alone in the Senate, I want to put upon the record my prophecy in this matter, that when thirty or forty years shall have passed and these Indians shall have parted with their title, they will curse the hand that was raised professedly in their defense to secure this kind of legislation and if the people who are clamoring for it understood Indian character, and Indian laws, and Indian morals, and Indian religion, they would not be here clamoring for this at all."

ALLOTMENT, which was imposed on about three-fourths of the nation's tribes, came to the Nez Perce Reservation in 1889 in the form of Alice C. Fletcher, appointed by the commissioner of Indian affairs as special allotting agent for the Nez Perce. Fletcher, a noted anthropologist, saw herself as a strong supporter of the Indians and was a mainstay of the Lake Mohonk conferences. An ardent believer in allotment, she had carried out the allotting of the Omaha reservation in Nebraska.

The process of allotment at Nez Perce is recorded in *With the Nez Perces,* a remarkable collection of letters by E. Jane Gay, who served as a cook in Fletcher's retinue. Gay's intimate, firsthand accounts give a sense of how the government carried out the policy that made such dramatic changes in Indian societies. Here is Gay's report, viewed through Fletcher's eyes, of Fletcher's first meeting at the agency building with the Nez Perce as she began the process of obtaining the "agreement" of the tribe for the allotment, and opening for homesteading, of their remaining ancestral lands:

> . . . There is tangible silence within; dark forms are ranged against the walls, some on wooden benches, others standing, and some prone upon the floor. The attitude of all is simply that of waiting—waiting to know what is wanted of them.
>
> You catch no inspiration from their faces as you are introduced by the agent in charge, but you make a little speech as graciously as you are able. There is no halfway meeting of your overtures; only the silence which can be felt.
>
> You read the Severalty Act and explain its provisions. You think you make it plain but the rows of old red sandstone sphinxes make no sign. Their eyes are fixed in stony dumbness. They never heard of the "Dawes' Bill"; they cannot take it in. . . .

. . . [A]s Allotting Agent, you stand before them, and, with reddened cheeks and stammering tongue you try to impress them
with the advantages of the proposed arrangement. You had pre-
arranged your arguments and expected to convince this docile
people as easily as you had convinced yourself, but somehow
you weaken. Your arguments give way before the logic of voice-
less helplessness. . . .

Your arteries throb so loudly in the silence that you can think
of nothing to say. . . . Your cravat is tight and you loosen it.
There is a stricture about the cardiac region. You unbutton your
coat and look along the line of dark faces. They do not light up
as they meet your gaze and it is your own eyes that first seek
the ground. But at last an old man rises, with a dignity which
renders invisible his poor garments and his low estate and
makes you do him reverence.

"How is it," he says, "that we have not been consulted about
this matter? Who made this law? We do not understand what
you say. This is our land by long possession and by treaty. We
are content to be as we are." And a groan of assent runs along
the dark line of Sphinxes as the old man draws his blanket about
him, as if forevermore to shut out the subject.

The action rouses you and you gather your forces, while the
next man in less quiet tones asks if you are not "afraid to come
among them on such an errand"! "Our people are scattered,"
says another. "We must come together and decide whether we
will have this law."

You tell them that there is nothing for them to decide; they
have no choice. The law must be obeyed, but you will wait until
they can understand better all about it. And then, with rare discretion, the ad interim Agent adjourns the council.

As the people disperse amid low mutterings in cheerless
tones, you clearly realize that you have not caught your Indian.

But Fletcher was nothing if not determined and resourceful,
and over the ensuing four years she did indeed catch her Indian.
Valley by valley, village by village, family by family, she met with
groups of Nez Perce, who in time became imbued with the
inevitability of Fletcher's, and her government's, plans for them.

The BIA originally held the individual 160-acre allotments of tribal members in trust, meaning that they could not be sold or taxed. The statute, however, made provision for ending the trust status and issuing a fee patent (a deed). Thus the trust was not permanent but would last only 25 years—unless the BIA extended the trust period or, more likely, shortened it upon a finding that an allottee was "competent." Findings of competency tended to coincide with the availability of a farmer or sharp-dealing speculator interested in obtaining Indian land at a bargain basement price. Many other Indians lost their land through mortgage foreclosures or tax defaults. One Nez Perce woman recalled that "I don't know what happened, but about 1920 they just shoved us away from the agency. We didn't have anything to say about it. They gave us the fee patents. We didn't have any choice. About all of us lost the land because of taxes."

A fee patent. No, that is an abstraction. Land. No, something more even than that. Something so sacred that the Nez Perce have regularly reacted in the fashion of Smoholla, whose Dreamer faith moved many Sahaptin-speaking people around the time that Joseph and his followers were being forced on their long trail east. "You ask me to plow the ground," Smoholla began. "Shall I take a knife and tear my mother's bosom? Then when I die, she will not take me to her bosom to rest."

A fee patent. Land. A mother's breast. Not something that can be lost by something called a sale. Not something that can be lost by something called a notice that comes in the mail, written in a foreign language, about something new, called taxes. But it can be.

For those able to hold on to their allotments, few cared to forsake their traditional fishing and hunting ways for a life of farming. In 1898 the BIA agent at Nez Perce reported that only 10 percent of the land was being cultivated and that white people with BIA leases did most of the farming. By 1911, after the agency relaxed its leasing policy, 98 percent of the 136,000 acres of allotted land had been leased to non-Indians.

When Alice Fletcher told the gathered Nez Perce that they had "no choice" and that "the law must be obeyed," she spoke accurately. Once the government decided to make individual allotments on a particular reservation, the only question at issue was where each allotment would be located. If a prospective allottee refused to cooperate, Fletcher, as special allotment agent, could simply designate a parcel.

The surplus land agreements at Nez Perce and the other allotted reservations were even more cynical than the individual allotments. In theory, since Indians would now become farmers, all land except the individual allotments would be "surplus to their needs." In reality, white people simply wanted Indian land. The General Allotment Act required that the surplus land arrangements, unlike the individual allotments, must be the product of consensual agreements with the tribes.

The government obtained signatures, but little real consent, on the surplus land agreements at Nez Perce and elsewhere. Federal Indian agents dictated the terms of the agreements and pressured Indian leaders to sign. The inequality between the United States and the tribes was far greater than it had been during treaty time. Now the tribes had lost their military capability, had been forced off most of their ancestral lands, and subsisted in large part on agency rations. In the case of the Nez Perce, a group of Christian "progressives" signed on behalf of the tribe an 1893 agreement designating two-thirds of the existing reservation, 500,000 acres, as surplus and throwing it open for homesteading. The tribe received three dollars an acre, money that was distributed to tribal members and quickly spent. Those dramatic land rushes in the movies, where a gunshot sounds and hordes of horse-drawn wagons burst forth on the land, depict white settlers charging toward the surplus lands of Oklahoma tribes, where oil patches as well as farm fields awaited. Save for the oil, the rush for Nez Perce land was the same.

None of this stilled the chorus of official enthusiasm for allotment. Five years after the surplus lands agreement, the local Nez Perce BIA agent, like so many others relentlessly optimistic in the belief that Indians could and should be turned into yeoman farmers, advanced his view that allotment was a good thing for the Nez Perce: "It gives the Indian a chance to be a man among men."

But not much of a chance. Allotment ravaged the Nez Perce

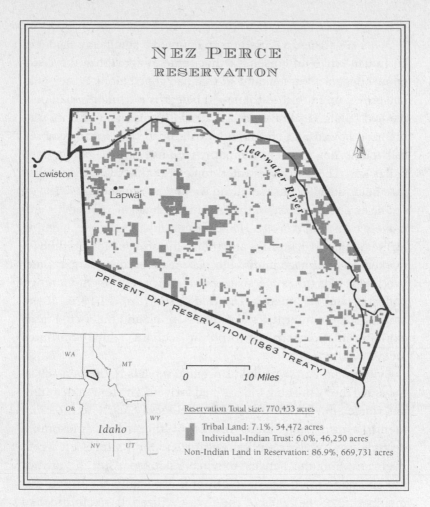

NEZ PERCE
RESERVATION

Lewiston

Lapwai

Clearwater River

PRESENT DAY RESERVATION (1863 TREATY)

WA

MT

OR

WY

Idaho

NV   UT

0   10 Miles

Reservation Total size. 770,433 acres

Tribal Land: 7.1%, 54,472 acres
Individual-Indian Trust: 6.0%, 46,250 acres
Non-Indian Land in Reservation: 86.9%, 669,731 acres

reservation. Anthropologist Deward Walker described allotment as "perhaps the single most important change forced on the Nez Perces by agents of the government," and the assessment rang true for Indian country generally. Of the 750,000 acres in Nez Perce ownership in 1893, just 49,252 acres are held as individual trust allotments and 36,409 acres are owned by the tribe today. The rest—664,000 acres, or 88 percent of all land within the 1863 reservation's boundaries—has been transferred to non-Indians. The tribe has lost more than 99 percent of the land that it owned when it entered the negotiations with Isaac Stevens.

. . .

IN 1894, James Earle Fraser sculpted a small clay model of an Indian brave on horseback that came to symbolize the deadening effect of allotment and all that had gone before. Fraser, who had grown up in the West, knew the depths to which Indian people had fallen. His brave, utterly despondent, sits on his mount, his head bowed and his shoulders slumped. His spear symbolically points down, and in sympathy with its rider, the pony's head hangs low. The sculptor wanted to convey the "idea of a weaker race being steadily pushed to the wall by a stronger."

Fraser, also the artist for the Indian-head nickel, refined his tentatively named *Indian on a Horse* for more than a decade, creating eighteen-inch-high bronzes and then a life-size version. In time he worked up the image in durable plaster on an even larger scale, two and a half times life size, mounted it on an eight-foot-high pedestal, and renamed it *The End of the Trail*. In 1915, at the Panama-Pacific International Exposition in San Francisco, Fraser exhibited his masterpiece to public acclaim, which continues today.

By the time Fraser made his original models in the mid-1890s, the era of the "Vanishing Indian" had arrived. The notion that Indians would simply die out had long held sway; early in the nineteenth century politicians orated of the tribes' "inexorable destiny," and William Cullen Bryant and Sir Walter Scott wrote poems evoking the Natives' inevitable demise. After the turn of the century the effects of allotment, especially the brutal dismembering of the lands of the Five Civilized Tribes in order to pave the way for both oil exploration and Oklahoma statehood, made the "Vanishing Indian" a household phrase. Artists titled popular paintings *The Twilight of the Indian*, *The Last of His Race*, and *The Sunset of a Race*. Edward Curtis named one of his most famous photographs *The Vanishing Race*. An early motion picture was *The Last of His Line*, and Zane Grey's novel *The Vanishing American* appeared as a film in 1926. Joseph Dixon's illustrated book *The Vanishing Race*, published in 1913, was overblown, but its hard-hitting message of impending extinction reached a broad and accepting audience.

With allotment's constriction of the reservations and compul-
sory assimilation fully installed as federal policy, the suffocating
of Indian societies proceeded full tilt. By the 1890s Indian reservations, with their vigilant government and church keepers, had
become places akin to refugee and internment camps. Indian
agents laid down the law. The missionaries, more government
funding in hand, expanded their activities. Churches controlled
the appointment of Indian agents; Nez Perce, for example,
although the Catholics had set up operations, remained a "Presbyterian reservation."

Education became a crucible for assimilation. A military as well
as religious mind-set set the tone. Captain Richard Henry Pratt,
who founded the experimental Carlisle Indian Industrial School
in Pennsylvania in 1879, styled himself as sympathetic to the
Indians' plight but was plain about his methods: "[A]ll the Indian
there is in the race should be dead. Kill the Indian and save the
man." According to Thomas Jefferson Morgan, commissioner of
Indian affairs in the early 1890s, "to fight them is cruel, to feed
them is wasteful, while to educate them is humane, economic,
and Christian." The off-reservation boarding schools opened in
the 1880s, leading to closure of many BIA reservation schools, and
by 1900 the Bureau of Indian Affairs was running twenty-five off-
reservation schools with 7,430 students in all. BIA officials and
school administrators used coercive recruitment tactics, ranging
from zealous persuasion to withholding rations and annuities
from families that kept their children at home. Authorities
assigned the children proper Christian names and forbade them
from wearing traditional clothing and hairstyles and speaking
their native languages. The teachers meted out stiff discipline,
including flogging. Allen Slickpoo explains the jolting experience
for Nez Perce children at Chemawa, near Salem, Oregon, and at
other boarding schools in the Northwest:

> The boarding schools were highly regimented. Many of these
> schools used military discipline and force was the word of the
> day. Many of our students came from homes speaking the Nez
> Perce language and had to learn English in the boarding schools.

This was very difficult since the general feeling was that English had to be beat into the students. Harsh disciplinary measures were taken to enforce the learning of English. Many of us recall the punishments given for failure to learn an English word or words. The students, both boys and girls, were required to wear military-style uniforms. The boys were taught to drill. This style of education was practiced up into the 1940s.

Assimilation became a crazy quilt. Some of it took, but much did not; changing the worldviews of entire peoples does not come easily. Many in the subjugated citizenry will refuse to budge or, if willing to change, find the going difficult or impossible. As one author observed, "Enforced social change, indirectly because of the loss of the buffalo and the hunting lands and directly by policies of the administrator, led to the partial loss of some traditions, the redefinition of traditional prereservation patterns, and the incorporation of some patterns of life of the dominant society, which altogether added up to the establishment of a new way of life indigenous to neither culture—a reservation culture, a colonial 'third culture.' "

Just as federal education practices reverberated throughout tribes, so too did the forced transition to a cash economy. The concept of sharing, integral to Indian societies, did not jibe well with the individualistic, materialistic attitude that drove the nation's economic system. As one Navajo stated, "When a relative needed help you helped them out. When you needed something else you could rely on a relative to help out, it all worked out in the long run. With money it doesn't work anymore, now the relative with money is expected to help out, what is needed for most everything is money and the poor relatives never have any." BIA officials in the early twentieth century regularly complained about practices that prevail even today: giveaways and sharing. An agent at the Yankton Sioux Reservation disdainfully reported that "the Indians' hospitality, so far as means will permit, is boundless. He will divide his last morsel with his neighbor, however thriftless and improvident he may be."

When Indian people did get jobs, this new form of power

opened up still more fault lines within the tribes. Tribal members who had no jobs gravitated toward those who had, thus lowering the status of elders and traditional political leaders. Entry into the cash economy also affected gender roles. Male dominance increased for those with access to economic opportunities, but the hard fact remained that few men could get good work. With their traditional skills less valued, their self-esteem plummeted. One Nez Perce woman lamented, "The money economy has caused a lot of problems for the Indian people because, prior to the money economy, there was a lot of trading done. Men got the meat and fish women needed. They were self-sustained families. When we moved to the money economy, it made it hard because, for men, there were few jobs."

IN 1906 the BIA agent at Nez Perce applied the conventional wisdom about Indians to the tribe under his charge. "It will be," he predicted, "only a few generations before the tribe is extinct." By the 1920s, however, in a pattern seen on many other reservations, glimmers of a tribal revival, however faint, had begun to appear. Despairing over their people's circumstances, Nez Perce tribal leaders, with the help of the local BIA superintendent, drew up what they called the five-year plan. The plan had some elements of a constitution, setting out the need for action (one recital referred to "living in idleness and acquiring the vices of the supposedly superior race"); creating a general council composed of all tribal members that would be the basic decision making body; and establishing a "business committee" that would formally represent the tribe in dealings with the outside world. It also set out objectives in farming, education, health, economic matters, and law and order. The brief document, however, lodged few powers in either the general council or the business committee. In 1927 the tribe adopted a formal constitution, but the hand of the BIA was all too evident. The business committee had few powers and almost no financial resources. Moreover, all its actions had to be approved by the Bureau of Indian Affairs.

In 1948, after years of debate, the Nez Perce Tribe sent out an even stronger reminder of its determination to exercise self-determination. The tribe adopted a new constitution that pro-claimed broader tribal governmental powers and dispensed with the term "business committee," a formulation promoted by the BIA and hardly suggestive of the decision-making body of a sov-ereign government. Although the 1948 constitution did require BIA ratification for constitutional amendments, no longer would bureau approval be required for tribal ordinances.

THE CONSTITUTIONAL WORK at Nez Perce made a state-ment about tribal sovereignty—and about the tribe's refusal to disappear—that reflected heartfelt emotions across Indian coun-try, but in 1948 a new tribal constitution could be only that, a state-ment, a yearning. Whatever words might be put to paper, the bureau remained the real government on the reservations. It wielded the power. The chains of land loss, repression, and poverty that had held the Nez Perce down for so many generations kept all Indian people down.

By 1953, with tribes deep in the abyss into which they had descended after allotment, a new breed of congressional reform-ers had settled on an approach toward Indian affairs. Like allot-ment, it might hold appeal to those who saw themselves as friends of the Indians. Reservations impeded development, sapped the federal budget, and blighted a shining country. Anachronisms, pure and simple. Wouldn't the country benefit by doing away with them? And wouldn't the Indians themselves want to be freed of the Bureau of Indian Affairs?

The next policy hatched in Washington came on quickly and smacked of finality.

3.

Termination

On August 1, 1953, Congress laced its new Indian initiative with an urgency rare for our national legislature. House Concurrent Resolution 108, which formally announced the policy of termination, directed that the end of reservations and federal services and protections be completed "as rapidly as possible." In the short term, five large tribes (the Flathead, Klamath, Menominee, Pottowatomie, and Turtle Mountain Chippewa) and all tribes in four states (California, Florida, New York, and Texas) should be terminated "at the earliest possible time." To expand the program even further, HCR 108 ordered the Interior Department to identify, within five months, additional tribes so they could be terminated "at the earliest practicable date." Two weeks after passage of HCR 108, Congress enacted Public Law 280. This is the statute the Bureau of Indian Affairs attempted to impose on the Quinault, extending state jurisdiction to many nonterminated reservations and authorizing other states unilaterally to take jurisdiction over whatever reservations they wished. In the months and years to come, many other termination-style programs would be adopted.

Termination meant total assimilation, for some tribes now, for the others soon. Apprehension turned into fear and panic as word of HCR 108 spread across Indian country. Even today, half a century later, for Indian people the word "termination" represents the third rail, shorthand for all that is extreme and confiscatory in federal Indian policy.

Although sometimes ascribed to a Republican administration and Congress and to the go-go, America First spirit of the early post–World War II years, termination stems from deep impulses long lodged in American views toward Indians. The United States negotiated treaties, after all, in order to reduce Indian landholdings and political power. Allotment was designed to hasten Indian assimilation, which Congress also promoted through the far-ranging and coercive BIA and church activities. Termination offered full and final relief from the centuries-old weariness with the refusal of Indians to abandon their political and cultural identity. The most specific origins of termination, however, are found in a brief flash of federal policy that aggressively promoted tribal rights but soon activated a backlash that became the extreme assimilationist policies of the 1950s and 1960s.

NATIONALLY, the 1920s saw a spurt of interest in, and concern over, Indian affairs. John Collier, a dynamic and reform-minded social worker familiar with tribes of the Southwest, energetically criticized the BIA in the newspapers and magazines. The idealistic Collier passionately believed in the worth of Indian cultures. Tribes, he asserted, could still create a "Red Atlantis," and the bureau was holding them back. In response to the sympathy aroused by Collier and others, the Institute for Government Research (popularly known as the Brookings Institution) established the Meriam Commission, which held extensive hearings into federal policies toward Indians and released its report in 1928.

The Meriam Report is still considered the most influential formal study in the field of federal Indian affairs. The report, while never overwrought, decried the condition of Indians and the inadequacy of existing federal programs. It laid bare the health, education, and social problems, announcing that "an overwhelming majority of the Indians are poor, even extremely poor, and they are not adjusted to the economic and social system of the dominant white civilization." Its recommendations, which became a guide for Indian policy in the 1930s, underscored a need to revamp BIA programs through increased funding and efficiency. The report did not, however, question the main premise for

Indian policy ever since allotment. The commission regularly referred to "the Indian problem" and made it clear that "the clock cannot be turned backward" and that full assimilation was inevitable: "The national government can expedite the transition and hasten the day when there will no longer be a distinctive Indian problem and when the necessary governmental services arc rendered alike to whites and Indians by the same organization without discrimination."

John Collier's high-visibility advocacy during the 1920s and early 1930s made him an attractive candidate for commissioner of Indian affairs in the Franklin Roosevelt administration, and he avidly pursued the post. When his main competitor, Harold Ickes of Chicago, raised his sights and secured appointment as secretary of the interior, Collier became Ickes's choice for commissioner. The Department of the Interior quickly developed a formidable and generally close-knit Indian reform team. Ickes was one of the few interior secretaries with a strong interest in Indian affairs before coming to the office. The new solicitor, top legal official in the department, was Nathan Margold, a leading New York attorney who had collaborated with Collier on Indian causes. Margold then brought in the brilliant Felix Cohen to serve as assistant solicitor for Indian affairs.

The Meriam Report had given credibility to reform through its central finding that the current approach to Indian policy had failed. Collier's agenda, however, went far beyond the report's actual recommendations or, for that matter, beyond any proposals seriously being put forth. Collier opposed forced assimilation. He advocated abandonment of allotment, a subject barely touched upon in the Meriam Report. He wanted to lodge significant power in tribal governments, and he believed with all his heart and soul in the value of Native cultures: "They had what the world has lost. They have it now. What the world has lost, the world must have again, lest it die."

Radical though his views may have been, the frenetic Collier achieved many of his goals. His successes owed nothing to his personality, for he was irascible, humorless, and often tactless. Rather it was his persistence, the quality of the people around him, and the good fortune of working for a president who could have from Congress almost anything he asked. This applied even if, as in the case here, Roosevelt lent only tepid support.

The Collier years produced the Indian Reorganization Act of 1934, the first comprehensive congressional action since allotment, nearly half a century earlier. The IRA legislated major land reform: It prohibited any further allotments, directed that all allotments still in trust remain so until Congress directed otherwise, allowed tribes to regain many surplus lands that had not been homesteaded, and authorized the interior secretary to proclaim new reservations and expand existing ones. The act also invited tribes to adopt constitutions as instruments of self-government.

During the 1930s Washington changed Indian policy in many ways. Congress strongly boosted funding for Indian education, health, and economic development. To protect Sun Dance and other Indian ceremonies long under ban, Collier ordered that "no interference with Indian religious life or ceremonial expression will hereafter be tolerated." A number of research projects provided justifications for the new policies. D. S. Otis, for example, documented the wreckage of allotment.

The FDR administration made perhaps its finest contribution to Indian affairs in Felix S. Cohen's *Handbook of Federal Indian Law*. Cohen, at twenty-four already an admired scholar in jurisprudence, international law, and legal ethics, had no formal training in Indian law before joining the Roosevelt administration as assistant solicitor. Concerned by the lack of scholarship in the field of Indian law, he trained his imposing intellect on organizing a diffuse body of knowledge, largely forgotten by the time he wrote. This cataloging held great importance to people whose lives were largely controlled by thousands of highly specialized statutes, treaties, court cases, and administrative laws. The result, one of the greatest treatises in all of the law, articulated the special federal trust relationship toward Indians, the nature of Indian treaties, the individual rights of Indian people, and the doctrine of tribal sovereignty. *Cohen's Handbook* became the standard source for judges and lawyers.

Cohen's treatment of tribal sovereignty was especially influential, highlighting as it did one of John Marshall's leading opinions, *Worcester v. Georgia*, in 1832. In that decision the chief justice explained at length that Indians had developed governmental systems millennia before Columbus and that from the beginning European nations and the United States had fully recognized the tribes' sovereignty. Europeans and the Americans had chosen the treaty device precisely because those nations acknowledged tribes to be governments. After the treaties, Marshall held in *Worcester v. Georgia*, Indian tribes governed themselves free of state laws and continued to be "considered as distinct, independent political communities, retaining their natural rights, as the undisputed possessors of the soil, from time immemorial, with the single exception of" laws enacted by Congress. Reviving Chief Justice Marshall's century-old vision of tribal sovereignty, Cohen declared in his *Handbook*: "Perhaps the most basic principle of all Indian law, supported by a host of decisions hereinafter analyzed, is the principle that *those powers which are lawfully vested in an Indian tribe are not, in general, delegated powers granted by express acts of Congress, but rather inherent powers of a limited sovereignty which has never been extinguished.* Each Indian tribe begins its relationship with the Federal Government as a sovereign power, recognized as such in treaty and legislation." [Emphasis in original.]

Cohen's words, which reinforced accounts passed down orally since treaty time, quickly became known in Indian country and, after the termination era, formed the legal basis for the essential points that Indian leaders asserted: Tribes have the right of self-government, and the United States has a special trust obligation to protect the interests of Indian tribes and people. Cohen, the lawyer-philosopher whose pen could be both sledgehammer and artist's brush, also depicted the ethical dimensions of the Indian experience: "It is a pity that so many Americans today think of the Indian as a romantic or comic figure in American history without contemporary significance. In fact, the Indian plays much the same role in our American society that the Jews played in Germany. Like the miner's canary, the Indian marks the shifts from

fresh air to poison gas in our political atmosphere; and our treatment of Indians, even more than our treatment of other minori-
ties, reflects the rise and fall in our democratic faith."

Despite its contributions, Collier's administration and the
Indian Reorganization Act left a mixed legacy. The land reform
measures are unalloyed benefits to Indian people. The IRA's
emphasis on tribal self-government, and the movement away
from forced assimilation, struck the right chords from an Indian
standpoint. Education and health services improved. Cohen's
treatise and sheaths of legal opinions were monumental.

But Collier's regime suffered from a top-down, paternalistic
approach. In spite of his many contacts on the reservations, especially in the Southwest, he brought few Indians into the administration. Although he held ten well-attended "congresses" in Indian
country after the reorganization bill had been introduced and
obtained support from some tribes at that point, he expended little effort to obtain Indian views while the bill was being drafted.
After the IRA became law, each tribe had to decide by popular vote
whether to organize under the act's self-governance provisions.
Collier, convinced that he knew what was "best" for Indians,
stumped on the reservations and pressured tribes to come under
the act. More than half of the tribes did. Others, like the Nez Perce,
adopted constitutions under their own inherent sovereignty
rather than use the IRA process. The IRA constitutions generally
have worked well for most tribes that voted them in, but in several cases, bitterness set in and continues today. Especially at
Hopi and in Sioux country, the Anglo-styled constitutions have
been resisted by traditionalists, thus bringing still another outside
source of divisiveness and factionalism. For all its good ideas and
intentions, the Collier era remained at its core, like the ones
before it, a policy born and bred in the East and handed to the
tribes.

Whatever shortcomings Collier had from the Indian perspective, his problems with congressional leaders ran even deeper. As
early as 1939 the Senate Committee on Indian Affairs, reacting in
part to long-standing accusations that Collier and his ideas were
"Communist," issued a report harshly criticizing the Indian Reor-

ganization Act. The document attacked the act for denying Indian property rights, subjecting tribes to a primitive communalism, and increasing the authority of federal bureaucrats.

In 1943 the Senate Indian Affairs Investigating Subcommittee signaled a strong sentiment against tribal governments and the reservations and in favor of ending federal responsibilities to Indians. Senate Report 310, though it never used the phrase, advocated a full-blown termination program, throwing Indian lands open to taxation and sale, liquidating the Bureau of Indian Affairs, closing all bureau schools, and abandoning Indian health care facilities.

The House Committee on Indian Affairs soon held hearings to consider the recommendations of Senate Report 310. The tenor of the time became all the more evident because the House members represented the more moderate congressional views on Indian matters. Exchanges at the hearings were often arch ("In other words," one congressman inquired of Collier, "you are telling this investigating committee what it shall do?") and committee members made no secret of their belief that eliminating Indian services would save federal budget dollars. Even in the House the working assumptions had shifted away from Collier's protribal recipe. Representative Karl Mundt of South Dakota, who sympathized with the Indians' plight, observed that "the purpose of the Indian Bureau should be to dissolve itself at the first possible opportunity" and requested Collier to "give us concrete suggestions as to what the Congress can do to absolve the Government from its responsibility under treaties and statutes, to entitle the Indian to live as the white men are living."

The Collier principles did serve to fuel a new generation of tribal leaders bent on self-determination two decades later, but his influence on policy began to peter out in the early 1940s and ended with a dull thud in 1945, when he left office, partly the victim of his own bullheadedness and dismissiveness. But it was not just Collier's personality and poor relations with Congress. The times had changed. World War II had ended, and the country, awash in its new global prominence, quickly moved into a sustained economic boom. Anything seemed possible so long as it involved capitalism, expansion, and modernism.

. . .

AFTER THE WAR the Senate Post Office and Civil Service
Committee took the unusual step of subpoenaing acting BIA Commissioner William Zimmerman to testify. On February 8, 1947, in
a hostile hearing, the committee ordered him to supply a listing
of tribes from which federal support could be withdrawn. Zimmerman hastily prepared a list—he submitted it just two days
later—breaking tribes down into three groups: those "predominantly acculturated and ready for immediate withdrawal"; those
"semi-acculturated" and ready within ten years; and those "predominantly Indian" that would need more than ten years of
bureau support. While this list resembled one submitted by Collier three years earlier, it attracted greater notice and marked the
beginning of Congress's active pursuit of termination.

Dozens of Indian land sale and "emancipation" bills followed,
though no legislation passed immediately. Also in 1947, however,
Congress initiated a major study of government efficiency, to be
chaired by former President Herbert Hoover. The 1948 Hoover
Commission included recommendations in Indian policy that
gave yet more speed to termination. "The basis for historic Indian
culture has been swept away. Traditional tribal organization was
smashed a generation ago. . . . Assimilation must be the dominant
goal of public policy."

President Truman found the perfect enforcer to spearhead a
new, and presumably decisive, era in federal Indian policy. Dillon
S. Myer, appointed to lead the BIA in 1950, had no Indian experience but was respected for his efficiency and honesty. He also
possessed a key credential: As director of the War Relocation
Authority he had worked himself out of a job by dismantling the
Japanese internment camps after World War II. (Although phasing out the camps was by any account a laudable goal, Myer had
taken criticism during his WRA years for isolating perceived agi-
tators and requiring loyalty oaths from many internees before
their release.) During his tenure as BIA head, the controversial
commissioner drew the full range of reactions, from Congressman
Toby Morris, who characterized him as "a man of unimpeachable
integrity" and "a very able administrator," to Harold Ickes, who,

after initially recommending him for the post, called Myer a "blundering and dictatorial tin-Hitler." For his part, Myer left no doubt about his unwavering dedication to the rapid and full withdrawal of federal support to American Indians.

Myer's activist administration pushed an assimilationist, pro-withdrawal policy on many fronts. The commissioner embraced the Hoover Commission's goal of "complete assimilation" and put it forth in speeches, congressional testimony, and private meetings. In discussions with tribes, he emphasized that withdrawal (the phrase "termination" had not yet come into use) was both inevitable and imminent. He demoted and reassigned superintendents who disagreed with his views.

Myer implemented his extreme views through departmental policies. He initiated the voluntary relocation program in 1951 in order to encourage "surplus" reservation residents to move to urban areas; relocation soon blossomed into a principal strategy of the termination era. In the boarding schools, Myer established a placement program so that Indian students could benefit from living in non-Indian, Christian homes. To keep tribal governments down, Myer seized on the bureau's power of approval of attorney contracts to force out assertive lawyers; one of his prime targets was Felix Cohen, by then in private practice. Myer also denigrated the abilities of tribal governments and touted the benefits of state jurisdiction in Indian country.

When the Eisenhower administration came in, Myer duly submitted his resignation but apparently expected to be kept on. He had good reason, since he and the new Republican majority were of a similar mind and in any event, Myer had bipartisan support on Capitol Hill. To Myer's credit, in the words of one of his predecessors, he had led "a general 'tightening up' in administration." But his reappointment was not to be, as Republican leaders saw him as a potentially dangerous lightning rod. So Myer left office on March 20, 1953, not as a leader of an exciting and revolutionary era that was about to dawn but rather as an important transitional figure who helped articulate the mission and strategy and put the administrative apparatus in place, ready for the kind of sweeping change that rarely occurs in public policy.

Absolutely crucial to the new era was an underlying reality: Nearly everyone supported some kind of new agenda, and "withdrawal" embodied the more specific notions held by most people in positions of authority. Certainly something had to be done. Poverty in Indian country shocked anyone who saw it. Reservation Indians simply had not joined America; they lacked an enterprising economic spirit, and education levels and health conditions remained abysmal. The Bureau of Indian Affairs, charged to oversee these "wards," epitomized bureaucracy run utterly amok—a nightmare of red tape, ineptitude, manipulation, and oppressiveness.

The idea of "freeing the Indian" hit the mark dead on. So much so, in fact, that a principled and well-meaning senator, representative, or administrator—or, for that matter, well-informed citizen—could find such a policy self-evident.

The only holdouts were a good many Indian people instinctively leery of rapid change imposed from the outside. "Freedom" did sound good, but these matters were hard for anyone to understand. They needed study. Maybe "freedom" through assimilation would entail a loss of land, hunting and fishing rights, health and education benefits—and culture and family too. But at bottom lay a problem. Although some tribal leadership on national issues was beginning to emerge, with few exceptions Indian tribes lacked the equipment to make their case in Congress. They lacked a voice. And you'd better have a voice when a crisis exists, when Congress is ready to move, and when you have serious doubts about the chosen course.

AFTER CONGRESS ADOPTED House Concurrent Resolution 108 in the summer of 1953, members introduced termination bills in rapid-fire fashion, and the air grew thick with inevitability. Assistant Interior Secretary Orme Lewis, an able lawyer from Phoenix, took the lead, marshaling evidence and putting together cases for terminating specific tribes. Both Secretary of the Interior Douglas McKay and BIA Commissioner Glenn Emmons were committed terminationists. On Capitol Hill, Senator Arthur V. Watkins of Utah virtually ran Indian affairs. Most members left it to him. Those who did pay attention generally supported Watkins's objectives. A bit of scattered and sporadic opposition had little impact because Watkins, as chair of the Indian sub-committee, controlled the legislative machinery and knew how to operate it.

Watkins, the son of Mormon pioneers, was born in 1886 and grew up on the small family farm, where he worked. At the age of ten, he took a second job at seventy-five cents a day. After just two years of high school, he went off first to Brigham Young University and then to Columbia Law School. As a young assistant county attorney in Salt Lake City he nearly died from a hemorrhaging duodenal ulcer, which led him to leave the law and manage a ranch near Lehi, Utah. Eventually he became a water developer. In 1946 he won his seat in the U.S. Senate with a low-budget campaign, proud of his independence: "So I went to Washington as a Senator indebted to no contributors, entirely a free agent."

The silver-haired Watkins makes a fascinating study. He quickly became a respected insider in the Senate. Isolationist and antilabor, he normally sided with the conservative wing of his party, but he always followed his convictions. In 1954, in the most celebrated episode of his career, he broke with his Republican colleagues and chaired the Senate Select Committee that censured Senator Joseph McCarthy of Wisconsin. Reflecting the widespread praise that Watkins eventually received, the *New York Times* wrote that he "acquitted himself with firmness and dignity. While the Wisconsin Republican called him 'cowardly' and 'stupid' and said his committee was an 'unwitting handmaiden of the Communist Party,' Mr. Watkins presided with icy reserve, pressing home the case that eventually led to Senator McCarthy's downfall."

This steely determination marked Watkins's pursuit of termination. He had an unbending faith in the rightness of his cause and did not hesitate to use pressure, including the withholding of tribal funds, to force agreement to termination. Perhaps because he believed tribal assent superfluous and doubted the validity of Indian treaties, Senator Watkins resorted to strong-arm tactics in the drive toward termination. He gave witnesses misleading assurances and erroneous information concerning the intent of

Senator Arthur V. Watkins (1947). Photograph courtesy of L. Tom Perry Special Collections, Harold B. Lee Library, Brigham Young University, Provo, Utah.

Congress. He asked leading questions of BIA witnesses to create an optimistic picture of Indian competency for termination and was critical and incredulous when tribal members or senators spoke against it.

The devoutly religious Watkins saw his program for Indian people as the right one. He apparently had few, if any, personal relationships with Native people so that he viewed Indian policy entirely through the lens of his own life as a self-made man and as a beneficiary of the American way. To him, Indians lacked an incentive to work. "They want all the benefits of the things we have," he said, "highways, schools, hospitals, everything that civilization furnishes, but they don't want to help pay their share of it." The federal guardianship had held them back: "They would have learned from carrying responsibility. They would have learned if they had been placed in a position where they would actually have had to go to work and to take care of their own affairs." Although he used hardball tactics along the way, Arthur V. Watkins righteously—and immodestly, considering the comparison to Abraham Lincoln—announced that termination would take its place in American history: "Following in the footsteps of the Emancipation Proclamation ninety-four years ago, I see the following words emblazoned in letters of fire above the heads of the Indians—'THESE PEOPLE SHALL BE FREE!' "

So it may be that Arthur Watkins had good intentions. Believing Indians would benefit from termination, he thought they had only to appreciate all that America had to offer. They could make it if they would just take charge of their lives, if they would just get with the plan, if they would just be more like *him*. Unfortunately, his premises went unexamined. He rushed forward, bullheaded, never pausing to ask even so simple a question as "Is it really a good thing to have Indians sell off their land and to hand them the money?" In time his theory proved as dead wrong as his methods.

Watkins moved quickly to organize committee hearings, debate, and passage of tribal termination bills. He worked closely with the chairman of the House subcommittee, Representative E. Y. Berry, a probusiness Republican of South Dakota. To speed consideration of the bills, the two agreed, in a rarely used procedure, to hold joint Senate-House subcommittee hearings. They scheduled a marathon series of sessions, lasting twenty days and involving dozens of tribes, beginning on February 15, 1954, and continuing into April.

The first hearing involved six Southern Paiute and Shoshone tribes and bands in Watkins's home state of Utah. The circumstances and testimony presaged many difficulties that were to plague the process and substance of termination: questions of tribal readiness for abrupt immersion in mainstream society, informed tribal consent, industry interest in obtaining tribal resources quickly and cheaply, and, ultimately, the wisdom and common sense of the termination program.

At the outset the witness list at the Southern Paiute hearing suffered from a notable absence; the tribes, small and impoverished, could not afford to attend the hearing. Representative Berry asked BIA Commissioner Glenn Emmons if he had contacted the tribes to obtain their consent. Emmons replied, "For discussion purposes. The consent was, of course, not obtained." Paiute education and income levels lagged far behind those in surrounding communities, raising serious questions about their readiness for termination—and their ability to comprehend the lengthy and technical bill. The committee received a letter of support from a Charles H. Harrington, who had met with the Kanosh Paiute Band and found them "more enthusiastic than ever" about termination. It turned out, as the local BIA superintendent explained to the committee, that Harrington had something to gain from the bill's passage. "He represents some oil company, and he desired to negotiate a lease, without going through the usual procedure, without following regulations. . . ." When Joe Garry of the National Congress of American Indians appeared to testify and raise concerns about the termination policy, Berry cross-examined him harshly.

Ernest Wilkinson (no relation to the author), a Washington, D.C., attorney, also appeared to raise a technical issue about the bill's effect on future claims litigation. One line of inquiry, however, caused him to question the underlying logic and wisdom of termination. Representative James Donovan of New York, defending the proposed legislation, asked: "Is this an act that enfranchises and puts these 350 Indians on the same basis as the other inhabitants of the State of Utah that are not Indians?" The witness's answer was succinct: "Not in my judgment. They are enfranchised already. This takes away some privileges that other citizens do not enjoy. But so far as I can see, as applied to these six groups, it doesn't give them any benefits whatever."

The affected Indians, in other words, already held full United States citizenship with the right to vote, hold office, receive state benefits, and so forth. Although Watkins repeatedly said termination would "give" them their land, the tribes already owned it. While in trust, it was nontaxable, like the lands of other governments, federal, state, and local. After termination it would be taxable—and up for sale, perhaps improvidently, just as during allotment. And termination would remove federal health and education programs for Indians.

Congress unanimously passed the Southern Paiute Termination Act five months later.

THIS INITIAL ROUND of hearings also included the two largest tribes up for termination, the Menominee of Wisconsin and the Klamath of Oregon. These closely watched bills offered insight into how the legislative process for termination worked. The way Watkins conducted the hearings also explains why Vine Deloria, Jr., reported that "absolute terror spread through Indian country as the power of the committee was arbitrarily used against the helpless Indian communities."

The Menominee forest blanketed more than 90 percent of the tribe's 233,000-acre reservation. It held eleven kinds of hardwood and eight species of softwood, making it one of the most diverse woodlands in the Northern Hemisphere. Loggers recognized its commercial value as early as the mid-1800s, and in 1908 Wisconsin Senator Robert La Follette, eager to conserve the forest, obtained progressive legislation requiring that the timberlands be managed on a sustained yield basis. He also got funding to construct a tribal lumber mill, state of the art at the time, in Neopit.

For generations the mill served the tribe well. By the time of the termination bill the Menominee, almost unique among tribes, were able to pay for most of the social programs normally funded through the BIA. The Menominee's economic situation, however, was brittle. The tribe had virtually no income other than the timber operation. The mill, nearly a half century old, was now outmoded. Although the Department of the Interior presented the joint committee with a report estimating annual income for most Menominee families at $2,300, the department's regular statistical analysis, completed two years earlier, had estimated family income at just $1,200. Statewide, the figure was $3,300 dollars. With only five college graduates, the tribe had few people trained for management positions.

There had been difficulties with federal timber management. The tribe, asserting that the BIA had mismanaged the resource, sued in the court of claims and prevailed, obtaining a settlement of $8.5 million in 1951. The Menominee were entitled to this money—they had won it in a federal court case—and their congressman, Melvin Laird, introduced a bill in the House to distribute the funds to the tribal members, $1,500 each. The House routinely passed the bill, but Watkins, holding the claims award hostage for termination, buried it in his subcommittee and combined it with the termination bill.

Before the hearings in June 1953, Watkins went up to the reservation to obtain the Menominee's consent. At a general council meeting, Watkins, in the words of historian Verne Ray, "told the tribal members that they were going to be terminated whether they liked it or not, that they would be allowed no more than three years to prepare a plan for termination, and that unless they agreed to termination, their own tribal funds [from the federal claims case] would not be released. . . ." One tribal member asked the senator directly, "[D]o you feel that [termination] for the Menominee Tribe is inevitable?" Watkins responded, "Yes, I do. . . . We have a general policy for the whole United States [referring to House Concurrent Resolution 108] and we can't go on forever as we have. The Congress of the United States is committed to the policy of getting the Indians on their own feet."

Senator Watkins, his brief visit over, left the Menominee alone to consider the matter. After a short discussion those in attendance voted 169–5 (out of a tribal population of 3,059), in support of termination. Watkins had what he wanted. However, less than a month later, the Menominee held another meeting and voted 197–0 against termination, "even though," as the resolution advised the tribal voters, "it means that you will not receive a per capita payment from tribal funds." As became even clearer at the joint subcommittee hearing and later, there was no actual consent by the Menominee—only capitulation in the face of inevitability.

Watkins dominated the three-day congressional hearings on the Menominee bill, forcefully cross-examining and leading witnesses toward his points. He offered soliloquies on his themes of the overbearing BIA guardianship, the freedom that termination offered, and the need to apply pressure so that the Mcnominee would be more industrious: "But here we have a group of people who have innate ability just the same as other people, when they get stimulated with a little ambition and a little necessity. You know, necessity is said to be the mother of invcntion. It is the spur to drive all of us to do things we don't think we can do."

As for coordination with the state, supposedly a prerequisite for termination, Watkins had moved ahead without state consultation. At the Menominee hearing, Harry Harder, Wisconsin tax commissioner, appeared on behalf of the governor. Harder inquired of Watkins, "Now it is my feeling that the Congress has pretty well decided that there is going to be termination . . . of the Menominee Reservation." Senator Watkins responded directly: "If you are basing that on House Concurrent Resolution 108, passed unanimously by both the House and the Senate, then I think your assumption is correct." Harder responded, "So the State of Wisconsin, which wasn't considered at all, in any of this legislation is on the sideline. . . ." Harder and Wisconsin Congressman Laird raised several concerns about the basic wisdom of the complex legislation, but to no avail. Another unusual aspect of the joint subcommittee hearings, especially considering the intricacy and revolutionary nature of termination, was that not a single academic expert was called.

Watkins was especially firm with tribal witnesses. The Menominee could see that the chairman was unbending: "We became convinced that there was *no* alternative to accepting termination. Therefore, all we pleaded for was adequate time to plan this sudden and revolutionary change in our lives!" Several tribal witnesses requested only a delay in implementation. The profound clash in worldviews between the senatorial patriarch and the reservation Indians, and the stark contradiction between "readiness" for termination and Senator Watkins's actual perception of tribal conditions, were manifest in this exchange between Senator

Watkins and Antoine Waupochick, chairman of the Menominee
Advisory Council:

> MR. WAUPOCHICK. Thank you very much. May I have a second
> of additional time to present for the record a few pictures I
> have?

> SENATOR WATKINS. Oh, yes. We are always glad to have pictures.
> They are easier to study than the printed word.

> MR. WAUPOCHICK. They concern pictures of various homes on
> the reservation. Those pictures were taken throughout the
> reservation, and I might say that 55 percent of our people live
> in homes of that nature there.

> SENATOR WATKINS. Now are these supposed to show good homes,
> or bad homes?

> MR. WAUPOCHICK. Both. The condition of the homes.

> SENATOR WATKINS. I didn't see anybody living in a teepee or a
> wigwam.

> MR. WAUPOCHICK. No. But where you visited, you saw the old
> lady that couldn't talk English.

> SENATOR WATKINS. Oh, yes.

> MR. WAUPOCHICK. And you know what she said? She wanted to
> know where that white-haired man was from. And I told her.
> I said, "He is from Washington." She told me, "What is he
> up to?"

> SENATOR WATKINS. I thought she would ask that.

> MR. WAUPOCHICK. And I conversed with her there, and I said,
> "That is a very fine gentleman. He is coming over here to see
> how we live on the reservation." "Well," she said, "I hope that
> he doesn't take this land away from me."

> SENATOR WATKINS. Did you tell her I was trying to give it to her?

> MR. WAUPOCHICK. No.

> SENATOR WATKINS. I was afraid you did not.

> MR. WAUPOCHICK. She was very much concerned because the
> name Washington at any time is a respected item to a group
> of Indians. Anybody coming to Washington from our reserva-
> tion, carries a great honor to come and visit the Great White
> Father, as they say.

SENATOR WATKINS. I hope they did not think I was the Great White Chief himself.

MR. WAUPOCHICK. She wanted to know what you had in mind in coming over. She was quite concerned. She did not even want to have her picture taken with us.

SENATOR WATKINS. I do not blame her. It was a very interesting experience. I appreciated your help in introducing me to those people and giving me the opportunity to see how they lived, how they felt about it. That was one of the most interesting experiences of the whole trip.

MR. WAUPOCHICK. We wish you could have stayed longer.

SENATOR WATKINS. *I had the same experience in visiting Europe, the refugee camps down in the Near East.* A study of people is always an interesting study; it is one of the most interesting in the world to me.

MR. WAUPOCHICK. Thank you very much, Senator. [Emphasis supplied.]

Three months later Congress passed the Menominee Termination Act.

THE KLAMATH TRIBE of Oregon, like the Menominee, owned an expansive, heavily forested homeland. The original reservation, established by treaty in 1864, comprised 1.9 million acres but was steadily eroded by a major surveying error, a congressional grant for a wagon road that ended up in the hands of a timber company, an addition to Crater Lake National Park, and allotment, when many parcels were released from trust and sold. By the time of termination the reservation had been reduced by nearly half.

Nonetheless, at about 1 million acres (865,000 owned by the tribe, the rest by tribal members holding allotments), the Klamath Reservation remained one of the largest in the country. Located in southern Oregon, north of Klamath Falls, it lay in the eastern "dry side" of the state. It is open, big sky country, rich in volcanic activity and flanked by the high Cascade Range to the west. At some vantage points, the arresting snowcapped upswelling of Cal-

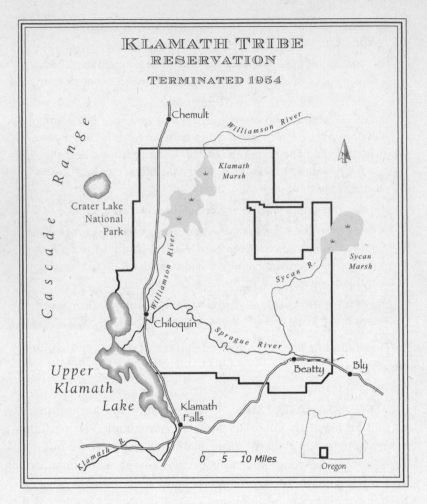

ifornia's Mount Shasta, more than 14,000 feet high, rises in the distance.

Three good-sized, spring-fed tributaries of the Klamath River—the Sycan, Sprague, and Williamson—gave tribal members of the 1950s mullet and some salmon (dams soon blocked off the salmon runs). Marshes, notably the large and dramatic Klamath Marsh, offered beaver and otter trapping. Wetlands also produced the wocus, a pond lily whose seeds the Klamath ground into an excellent flour, and camas and other roots grew in the flats and meadows. Game, especially antelope and deer from the populous

interstate herd that migrated up from California, made up a critical part of the diet. Hunting was a major activity, with families
consuming up to fifteen deer annually. Prime forest, mostly ponderosa and sugar pine, covered 80 percent of the land. This
domain took an hour to traverse from north to south on the state
highway, much longer from east to west on secondary and logging
roads.

Testimony from the Interior Department at the Klamath hearings indicated that family income probably averaged about $4,000,
comparable to the Oregon average. This came mostly from annual
payments of $800 per person produced by timber harvesting on
the magnificent ponderosa pine forest the tribe owned by its
treaty. Such payments, while hardly extravagant, could support a
family. As a result, tribal members had little incentive to work,
and few did. Only five tribal members of 2,100 had graduated from
college, and Klamath were beset by bad consumer choices, unsat-
isfactory living conditions, and serious health and alcohol problems. Like other groups of poor people with low education levels,
the Klamath found that cash payments were not the answer. As
Theodore Stern put it in the standard history of the Klamath, this
situation put its members in "a very special economic niche, and
one which carried grave disadvantages, not only as a preparation
for a career in the outside world, but even for articulation within
the reservation communities."

The Klamath differed from the Menominee in that a significant
tribal faction, led by Wade Crawford, vocally supported liquidation
of the reservation. As early as the 1920s, Crawford had put forth
termination-style proposals for the Klamath. His followers consisted mostly of off-reservation tribal members living in Klamath
Falls and he continued to work on his project, with varying
degrees of tribal support. In the years leading up to termination,
tribal members against liquidation dominated the tribal council,
but the situation was fluid, with various inconsistent votes taken,
making it difficult to assess tribal sentiment. Perhaps the overriding point is that such complex legislation confused the Klamath, a conclusion reached in a 1956 Stanford Research Institute
report and in a report of the American Indian Policy Review Com-

mission. Crawford was not chosen as an official tribal delegate to the joint committee hearings in Congress, but he did attend and testify in favor of the "new policy to give the Indians their freedom, to give them the right to handle their own business, and their own affairs, tribally and individually."

In most termination hearings, Bureau of Indian Affairs witnesses supported the protermination views of Senator Watkins and the administration, but testimony on the Klamath bill proved a notable exception. E. Morgan Pryse, the BIA area director from Portland, who had begun his work in the bureau at the Klamath Reservation in 1920, held firm to his conviction, which turned out to be accurate, that termination would put Klamath landownership at risk:

> REPRESENTATIVE BERRY. I would just like to ask this question. What percentage of this land, in your judgment, would be sold by the individual Indians when they obtain title?

> MR. PRYSE. Well, experience has shown that as fast as the Indian obtains a fee simple title, he generally sells it. There has been sold around 88 million acres of Indian land, probably the best land, by the Indians, since the Allotment Act of 1887.

> SENATOR WATKINS. You mean in this one reservation?

> MR. PRYSE. No; I am talking about the whole United States. There has been quite a lot of forest land pass out of Indian ownership on the Klamath Reservation.

> SENATOR WATKINS. That was quite a long time ago when that was done.

> MR. PRYSE. That is right.

> SENATOR WATKINS. We hope they have made progress in ability to make decisions since that time.

> MR. PRYSE. Most of them would like to retain trust status as to their land, because they feel that once a patent is granted, it is just a question of time until it passes out of Indian ownership.

> REPRESENTATIVE BERRY. What is your opinion on this? Do you think within a reasonably short time they will have disposed of their properties?

MR. PRYSE. If a bill was passed transferring fee simple title to them?

REPRESENTATIVE BERRY. Yes.

MR. PRYSE. Well, I am afraid it would. I am afraid it would pass out of Indian ownership, a great portion of it, in a matter of a few years. That is just my personal opinion. I am not speaking for anyone else, or the Department, but since you asked me for my own personal opinion, that would be my opinion.

SENATOR WATKINS. Is that because the Indian has not the ability to determine whether he ought to sell or not?

MR. PRYSE. Well, probably because they haven't had the experience of making a living and providing for taxes and also withstanding the pressure of people to buy their property.

Some of the most revealing moments during the joint hearings came during the testimony of Boyd Jackson and his polite but pointed exchange with Senator Watkins. Jackson, the official tribal delegate and dead set against termination, knew that some form of legislation was predestined. His best chance lay in shaping the bill and buying enough time to develop alternatives that might minimize the damage. At the same time, as the lawyer Ernest Wilkinson had during the Utah hearings, Jackson felt obligated to address the ultimate flaws in termination, a policy that he saw as allotment writ even larger:

MR. JACKSON. It seems to me that the present move is in a sense a repetition of something that happened years ago and something that has been discussed here during the present time.

In 1917, the Secretary of the Interior and the Commissioner of Indian Affairs set up a policy whereby they felt that the time had come when the individual members of tribes should be dealt with individually as to their tribal properties. The result of that was that fee patents were issued, sort of on the right and left basis. And it also affected us, the Klamath Indians.

In a relatively short time, as to lands, which in those times were relatively low, we woke up and found that we had received fee patents to some hundred thousand or more acres

of land. And those lands represented our best river bottom
and marshlands.

These lands went out of our ownership. Just why and how
the Secretary decided to change his views, I don't know. But
these patents were closed down; that is, the issuing of the
patents at the rate at which they were being issued. And, as a
result of that, we now have something over 136,000 acres of
land, which was discussed here. . . .

SENATOR WATKINS. The thing that is bothering me, Boyd, is this:
You have enough judgment and intelligence you think to
come here and say "no" to us. In effect, you are saying "No,
we don't want this." Haven't you got enough courage to say
"No" to the fellow who comes along and wants to buy your
land?

MR. JACKSON. The loss of a hundred thousand acres of land
shows that we lacked guts at that time when such a thing was
thrown open to us.

SENATOR WATKINS. How long has that been?

MR. JACKSON. 1917.

SENATOR WATKINS. That is a long time, and you have made great
progress since then.

MR. JACKSON. And since that time it has been said that it would
never do to pass anything the size of Klamath over to the Indians because they would lose it overnight. That has been said
not too long ago. And quite a bit of that is quite true.

Jackson, a small rancher from the reservation town of Chiloquin, plainspoken yet firm, understood termination as well as
anyone. He knew that his tribe had problems. He knew that it
owned more than 1.5 percent of Oregon and that the reservation
held some of the best pine stands in the West. He knew too that
this involved more than dollars. His people dated back at least
10,000 years. All the ancestors were buried there, in their homeland. He knew the history, he knew what allotment had wrought,
and Jackson, a careful person, knew something else: Everyone
agreed that something should be done, but no one, including Senator Watkins, had really thought termination through. There hadn't
been enough time.

Congress passed the Klamath Termination Act five months
later.

THE 1954 joint hearings produced six termination acts, all
passed in the same year. Seven more termination statutes followed, until the policy was shelved in the late 1960s and formally
renounced in the 1970s. Congress terminated more than a hundred tribes, including many small, impoverished bands and
rancherias in California and Oregon. Termination affected at least
1.3 million acres and 11,000 people, diminishing Indian trust land
by 2.5 percent and cutting off federal services for 3 percent of all
federally recognized Indians.

The hastily adopted statutes failed to answer basic issues, leaving them to the Department of the Interior to resolve before the
laws took effect. What will happen to the land? Will it be sold and
the proceeds distributed to the members? Or will it be retained by
the tribe? If retained, will it be held by a tribally owned private
corporation or administered by a bank? If funds are distributed to
individuals, should private guardians be appointed for "incompetent" Indians? How will health, education, and social needs services be met?

For smaller tribes, the BIA completed the plans within a year
or two; the agency simply appraised the land and sold it to the
highest bidder. The three tribes with the largest landholdings—the
Menominee, the Klamath, and the mixed-blood Ute (like the terminated Southern Paiute, from Watkins's home state)—all had
detailed administrative plans. The Menominee plan, for example,
was 30 pages long (minuscule type, three columns to a page) in
the *Federal Register*. The Interior Department finalized those three
plans in 1961, seven years after passage of the individual acts.

Every terminated tribe floundered. Members of the smaller
tribes and the mixed-blood Ute got a few hundred dollars apiece for
their sold-off land and migrated to the cities or lived in shantytowns
near their former reservations. They made no measurable improvements. Most found themselves poorer, bereft of health care, and suffering a painful psychological loss of community, homeland, and
self-identity. Lynn Schonchin of Klamath lamented:

What it did to the tribe, that was even more horrible. To see
our tribe, we broke apart, we moved away, family units broke
down, some folks went through the loss of identity, they didn't
feel comfortable with who they were. I can remember going to
Indian rodeos . . . and being told at a couple of them that us Kla-
maths couldn't participate in an all-Indian rodeo because we
were terminated. I mean, even the [other] tribes looked at us as,
"You're not Indian any more." And that's basically what the Termination Act said, "They will no longer be Indians." How do you
deal with that?

The Menominee managed to avoid an immediate sell-off of
their land. But the administrative plan—the mechanism for delivering the promised "freedom"—set up an elaborate, positively
weird private corporation to hold the land. Menominee Enterprises Inc. was organized under state law with all shares of stock
theoretically held by tribal members but voted by a voting trust
that was in turn controlled by the First Wisconsin Trust in Milwaukee. The tribe had expended all its available funds preparing
for termination. As a result the new corporation could not reno-
vate the outmoded timber mill or pay the now-applicable property
taxes. In a move bitterly opposed by the great majority of tribal
members, the voting trust sold 9,600 acres of tribal heartland—
deep woods and lakes—for recreational second homes to pay the
taxes owed by the financially untenable corporation. By the late
1960s the voting trust was poised to make still more land sales. It
was like selling the furniture to pay the mortgage.

Termination also bruised Menominee life. Menominee County
suffered the highest unemployment in Wisconsin. Per capita
income was the lowest and per capita welfare payments the highest. After Congress terminated federal services to the Menominee,
the hospital closed, leaving not a single doctor or dentist in the
county. Moreover, the Department of Health, Education and Welfare found widespread discrimination against Menominee children in the local schools.

THE KLAMATH TRIBE may have suffered the most of all. In
spite of Senator Watkins's rhetoric of "giving" the Indians their

land, termination—as with most of the other tribes—cost the Klamath their million-acre forest-and-river homeland. The BIA and the tribes explored many options during the seven years of developing the termination plan. Finally, the bureau gave each tribal member the choice of "remaining" in the tribe or "withdrawing" from the tribe and being paid a proportionate share of the value of the land. But it was a Hobson's choice, for "remaining" meant only that land not sold would be transferred from a federal administrative trustee to a private institutional trustee, the United States National Bank in Portland. Seventy-eight percent voted to withdraw and received $43,000 apiece for the sale of 600,000 acres. Rather than glut the market by placing such a large amount of timberland up for sale, in the end the administrative plan called for a purchase by the United States and the creation of the Winema National Forest.

The distribution of funds set off an orgy of fraud and exploitation as it became open season on the withdrawn members; local car dealers and appliance stores moved their operations to the edge of the former reservation. A small minority of remaining members invested their distributions well, but most, lacking business experience, quickly lost their funds. The standard study concluded that the withdrawn members "have received few lasting benefits from termination."

The bank trust for the Klamath remaining members never worked. The bankers were not much less bureaucratic than the BIA. After ten years, when given the chance to vote, the remaining Klamath abolished the failed bank trust. This land too was purchased by the United States and added to the Winema National Forest.

The remaining members—474 people, 22 percent of the tribe— received more money and, after the experiences of their fellow tribal members, used it somewhat more wisely. By the 1980s they had received a total of $286,000 per person. Nonetheless, they may also have received "few lasting benefits." The remaining tribal members spent most of the distribution on day-to-day maintenance until the funds were exhausted. A comprehensive survey completed in 1989 found that only 1 percent of all Klamath had attained college degrees. More than 30 percent of them made less than $5,000, and only 5 percent more than $35,000 annually. Many health and social problems continued.

Termination exacted numerous economic costs that Congress never considered in its high-speed rush to liquidate the Klamath Reservation. Termination stripped the Klamath of their right, by virtue of the treaty, to be free of state taxation. In addition, tribal members lost traditional federal health and education services. Before termination, the Klamath, who depended so heavily on hunting, fishing, and trapping, had exclusive treaty rights to use their vast and richly endowed reservation to gather food. After the land became part of the Winema National Forest, non-Indians—now allowed to hunt and fish on the former reservation—took most of the animals. Forest Service clear-cutting and fire suppression practices degraded wildlife habitat, further reducing the deer and antelope herds. Traditionally, tribal members had the right, under assignments from the tribal council, to build homes on the reservation, usually on the sites they selected. Termination ended that valuable tribal prerogative.

Termination contained another loss, hidden and especially poignant. The statutes closed the tribal rolls as of the date of passage—August 13, 1954, in the case of the Klamath. Indian tribes have ever-expanding and ever-contracting memberships as members are born and pass on. But termination mandated a rigid date after which newly born children could not be enrolled—and could not share in the financial distributions. This completely shut out "after borns." Many Klamath families faced arbitrary divisions and termination-imposed contentiousness as some brothers and sisters were born before August 13, 1954, and some after.

THE GOVERNMENT devised many assimilationist programs for tribes not yet slated for termination. In Public Law 280, while it did not fully terminate reservations, Congress cut deeply into tribal sovereignty by allowing states unilaterally to take jurisdiction over criminal and civil cases on Indian reservations. The BIA advocated state assumption of jurisdiction, as it did so blatantly at Quinault, over the wishes of the tribe. In 1968, Congress curtailed the future ability of states to assume Public Law 280 jurisdiction, but by then numerous tribes had come under state court jurisdiction and seen their tribal courts atrophy.

So-called relocation was another major assimilation initiative of the 1950s. The BIA actively encouraged Indians to leave the reservations for the cities. "In the early fifties," Albert DuBray of Rosebud Sioux recalled, "there was a lot of pressure placed on the people. [Relocation] was always considered a voluntary program, but there was a lot of promotion of the program in the early stages." While the poorly funded effort set up transition offices in Denver, Minneapolis, Chicago, Oklahoma City, Oakland, and several other cities to help with housing and employment, relocation had a definite sink-or-swim tenor to it. In all, more than 100,000 Indians moved as part of the formal relocation program, and a similar number left the reservations in response to bureau persuasion or on their own initiative.

Urban life proved wrenching for nearly all the relocatees. Most lacked the education and skills for anything but menial labor. The alarm clock symbolized the many pressures of job, traffic, and concrete so foreign to rural, slow-paced reservation life. Large numbers of new arrivals went straight to slum neighborhoods or skid rows. Many returned home: 75 percent according to some studies, 30 percent by BIA figures. (In time some Indian people learned how to work the system: In the early 1970s, when the relocation program was on its last legs, Mary Cornelius of the Turtle Mountain Chippewa Tribe, who had relatives in Minneapolis, was fond of saying, "I think next week I'll go to the Twin Cities on relocation—again.") Relocation fell into disfavor because of the coercion and ineffectiveness, but one bright light began to shine years later. Although relocation provided few benefits to the people it directly served, many of their children, having grown up in the cities, helped build the Indian professional middle class, which played a central role in revitalizing Indian life in the latter part of the twentieth century.

Nor was Felix Cohen's 1942 *Handbook on Federal Indian Law* safe from the terminationists' zeal. The treatise had become a valued source for tribal leaders and their attorneys. Justice Felix

Frankfurter called it "an acknowledged guide for the Supreme Court in Indian litigation." But in 1958 the Department of the Interior, fearing the force of Cohen's—and John Marshall's—words, issued a revised edition. The new volume, built around the constant theme of denigrating tribal rights, put forth the reasoning for the revision: "Much of the earlier Federal law and many Indian treaties now have only historical significance. As national development and progress continue and as new patterns of policy evolve, legal answers to questions of Federal Indian law will be found predominantly in the latest statutory law and judicial determination of justifiable issues. Those are stressed in this revision for the purpose not only of seeking balance . . . but also for the purpose of foreclosing, if possible, further uncritical use of the earlier edition. . . ." Nothing in recent court opinions had suggested that treaties had lost their force; later cases in fact supported them. True, the termination-era statutes were on the books, and the courts were bound to follow them when they applied. Even so, the original Cohen treatise remained good law in nearly all its aspects. The revised edition of 1958 stands as a monument not to law but to the overreaching of the termination years.

IN RETROSPECT, an intriguing irony emerges from the turbulence of termination. Senator Watkins repeatedly exhorted Indians to get up on their own two feet, to walk on their own. Termination proved the wrong recipe for that. Still, the *fear* of termination had the effect of mobilizing American Indians, though not in a fashion Senator Watkins would have intended. For as the shock waves of termination rolled through Indian country, Indian people realized that something had to be done and that they could count upon nobody save themselves. That realization became a major impetus for the gathering of the modern tribal sovereignty movement.

Part Two  LAST STAND

4. The Making of a Movement

Major political, social, and economic movements demand a multitude of pragmatic tasks. Supporters must develop strategies, create organizations, obtain resources, and do legwork. These jobs run the gamut: drafting legislation and managing litigation, delivering speeches and organizing letter-writing campaigns, fund-raising and lobbying, knocking on doors and stuffing envelopes. Depending on the nature of the movement, the work may also entail the actual operation of a project: running a homeless shelter, installing and carrying out a diversity program in a university or corporation, or cleaning up a river.

Also required, beyond organization and implementation, is a compelling philosophical framework to bind the movement, to inspire and uplift its adherents. A movement needs a set of ideals to which people will make a blood commitment.

As of the 1950s, Indian country, its members poor, scattered, and small in number, seemed an unlikely candidate for any kind of action at all. Also, more subtle but no less significant, many forces aligned against the articulation of a clear, unified, and living philosophy. Each tribe prided itself on its own distinct traditions. Indian cultures relied heavily on the oral tradition, so that writings were scarce and dissemination difficult. Most important, had the philosophy actually survived? Suppose that in its pure form two and a half centuries ago, the Indian worldview housed a complex and valuable set of ideas about gods, nature, ceremony,

family, and sharing that ought to be preserved, that might serve
as a rallying cry for Natives and a healthy segment of the American populace. Suppose also that tribes universally shared these
general philosophical notions, if not all the specifics of tradition
and culture. Suppose, further, that the long-exercised sovereignty
of aboriginal peoples, promised by treaty, is a luminous ideal that
ought to flourish in all nations, certainly in the world's leading
democracy. Even if all of that were true, how could those philosophies and beliefs have any remaining vitality after the centuries
of assimilation and loss? In particular, how could the Indian way
have survived the long, deadening years from allotment in the
1880s through termination? Indianness, it would seem, had
become a relic, or soon would. How could a movement rise up
from those ashes?

HANK ADAMS, Assiniboine and Sioux from the Fort Peck
reservation in Montana and a major intellectual force in the modern Indian revival, believes the answer to how the Indian way survived lies partly in "sustaining Indian figures": "By their respective
historic roles or personal abilities and accomplishments, they
maintained the Indian character in good stead—with a universal-
ity of appeal and respect—among sufficient numbers of the larger
American society that the worst of America's plans and 'final solutions' could not be fully realized" during the difficult times
between the mid-nineteenth and mid-twentieth centuries. These
sustaining Indian figures, all of whom also gave tremendous inspiration to Native people, include the welcoming image of Poca-
hontas; Sacajawea, the guide and interpreter; the warrior Crazy
Horse; Charles Curtis, who ascended to the vice presidency in
1929; the athlete Jim Thorpe; the comedian and philosopher Will
Rogers, Sr.; Ira Hayes, the heroic and tragic World War II veteran;
Maria Tallchief, ballerina; and Jay Silverheels, the Lone Ranger's
Tonto. Indian painters, potters, basket makers, silver workers,
sculptors, and carvers of totems and masks also qualify as sustainers. All the while many thousands of common people in
Indian country carried on the old ways day to day, telling coyote
stories, stacking cordwood, taking the salmon, cooking the stews,

conducting the kiva ceremonies, singing the songs, and dancing the dances. Particulars might have changed—there might be blue jeans, a pickup truck, or a nylon gill net—but they were still the old ways.

The sustainers also included three philosophers. They uplifted Indian people and engaged non-Indians with the power of their ideas. Their work, by paying due intellectual honor to the Indian way, tribal sovereignty, and the homelands, contributed mightily to keeping the central ideas alive during the deadening time.

Charles Eastman, born in 1858, lost his mother soon after birth and was raised by his grandmother in the traditional Santee Sioux way. In 1862, as his father fought in the Sioux battles in Minnesota, the rest of his family fled the Missouri River country north to Canada. At age 15 he received a jolt. His father, long believed hanged for his role in the Minnesota conflict, in fact had been imprisoned. Upon release he sought out the boy. Now a confirmed Christian, the senior Eastman sent Charles, still monolingual in Dakota, to the Santee federal boarding school in Nebraska.

The boy took immediately to this new form of education. After graduating from Santee, he went on to Dartmouth. Smart, dashing, and blessed with the classic Sioux visage, Eastman gained immediate acceptance in white society. With his Dartmouth diploma in hand, he entered medical school at Boston University, where he earned his M.D.

Eastman, in addition to his duties as a physician, became an accomplished author. Much of his early work praised Christianity and the Anglo world, but in time his upbringing took hold, in combination with a life-changing professional experience. In 1890, now a doctor in the Indian Health Service, he was assigned to Pine Ridge. Soon after his arrival the reservation was thrown into upheaval by what the BIA termed "the ghost dance uprising." When news of deaths and shootings reached Eastman, he sought permission to go to the site and treat the survivors, but his superior turned him down. In time he learned that Wounded Knee had been a massacre, not an uprising.

Charles Eastman lived and understood both traditional Indian life and the most cultured side of the larger society in a way that few people ever had. You hear references to Indians being between two worlds, uncomfortable in each society, and some are. Eastman, however, like many Indians to follow, was in both worlds, comfortable and accepted in each.

A prolific writer (he produced seven books and many articles) and active in Indian causes, Eastman became increasingly disillusioned with Christianity and America's treatment of Indians. His grandest contribution was *The Soul of the Indian*, published in 1911, a thin volume that draws upon his boyhood in a Sioux family and depicts the Indian way of thinking "as it was before he knew the white man." Eastman saw beauty and value in the way Indian people saw the world and in their ideals. He was no accomplished wordsmith, but his writing had the kind of vitality and integrity that his contemporary John Muir displayed in his accounts of the wild Sierra Nevada. Both men put down their words in a spare and plain fashion but with exuberance, love, and utter authenticity.

The Soul of the Indian, while brief in pages, is intellectually elaborate and challenging. Eastman blended ceremonies, legends, and stories into his exploration of religion, nature, and sharing and loyalty to family and friends. He explained the place of material goods; social structure, including the high station of women and elders; the theory and etiquette of warfare, crime and punishment; and death, which he called "the border-land of spirits." Always the cornerstone was spirituality, for these societies were theocracies, but with a tenor so different from Christianity:

> The worship of the "Great Mystery" was silent, solitary, free from all self-seeking. It was silent, because all speech is of necessity feeble and imperfect; therefore the souls of my ancestors ascended to God in wordless adoration. It was solitary, because they believed that He is nearer to us in solitude, and there were no priests authorized to come between a man and his Maker. . . . Our faith might not be formulated in creeds, nor forced upon any who were unwilling to receive it; hence there was no preaching, proselytizing, nor persecution, neither were there any scoffers or atheists.

The Indian was a member of the natural world, and this brought relationships and obligations:

> . . . We believed that the spirit pervades all creation and that every creature possesses a soul in some degree, though not necessarily a soul conscious of itself. The tree, the waterfall, the grizzly bear, each is an embodied Force, and as such an object of reverence.
>
> The Indian loved to come into sympathy and spiritual communion with his brothers of the animal kingdom, whose inarticulate souls had for him something of the sinless purity that we attribute to the innocent and irresponsible child. . . . His respect for the immortal part of the animal, his brother, often leads him so far as to lay out the body of his game in state and decorate the head with symbolic paint or feathers. Then he stands before it in the prayer attitude, holding up the filled pipe, in token that he has freed with honor the spirit of his brother, whose body his need compelled him to take to sustain his own life.

Just as Eastman's view of the Indian mind included the humility of silence and a duty to nature, so too it encompassed the morality of simplicity:

> The native American has been generally despised by his white conquerors for his poverty and simplicity. They forget, perhaps, that his religion forbade the accumulation of wealth and the enjoyment of luxury. To him, as to other single-minded men in every age and race, from Diogenes to the brothers of Saint Francis, from the Montanists to the Shakers, the love of possessions has appeared a snare, and the burdens of a complex society a source of needless peril and temptation. Furthermore, it was the rule of his life to share the fruits of his skill and success with his less fortunate brothers. Thus he kept his spirit free from the clog of pride, cupidity, or envy, and carried out, as he believed, the divine decree—a matter profoundly important to him.

Charles Eastman's own sense of loss, and its relationship to Christianity, for which he held a guarded respect, runs through

The Soul of the Indian. He wanted to go back and live the essence of the life he revered but knew he could not, and wondered whether anyone ever would: "As a child, I understood how to give; I have forgotten that grace since I became civilized. I lived the natural life, whereas I now live the artificial. Any pretty pebble was valuable to me then; every growing tree an object of reverence. Now I worship with the white man before a painted landscape whose value is estimated in dollars! Thus the Indian is reconstructed, as the natural rocks are ground to powder, and made into artificial blocks which may be built into the walls of modern society."

Another guiding light was Black Elk, now the best known of all traditional Indian philosophers, the Lakota holy man whose narrative has been brought to us in John Neihardt's *Black Elk Speaks.* The book, presented as Black Elk's words, derives from a series of interviews that Neihardt held with the medicine man in 1931 at his home near Manderson on the Pine Ridge Reservation. Black Elk was nearly seventy at the time (he lived until 1950). As Neihardt explained it, Black Elk embarked on these long and exhausting sessions out of his obligation to "save his Great Vision for men."

Black Elk Speaks recounts Black Elk's inspirational yet tragic life from his birth in 1863 through the Wounded Knee massacre in 1890. He bore witness to a grand panorama of human experience that not only covered major historical episodes of the American West and the United States broadly but also encompassed a wide array of universal societal impulses. This included Lakota life before any assimilation; the creation of the Great Sioux Reservation in the Great Sioux Treaty; the Battle of the Little Bighorn; the suppression of Sioux life by their federal overseers; the elimination of the buffalo from the Great Plains; the white soldiers' luring, and killing, of Crazy Horse; the arrival of the Ghost Dance with all its hope for a return of the old days; and the massacre at Wounded Knee Creek.

Throughout, the book is rich with the details, sometimes humorously told, of Lakota life. Black Elk told of conversations with fish about his bait (" 'You who are down in the water with wings of red, I offer this to you; so come hither' "); the reaction to the 13-year-old Black Elk's scalping of a soldier at the Little Bighorn ("My mother gave a big tremolo just for me when she saw my first scalp"); the naming of every month (May is the Moon When the Ponies Shed, June the Moon of Making Fat); the sweat lodge ("So we brought the sacred pipe back home and I went into the sweat lodge after offering the pipe to the Six Powers"); and the Lakota's love of the land, the horse, and the buffalo that were about to disappear ("Then we got our horses from the brush on the other side of the ridge and came around to the mouth of the draw where the bison would pass as they drifted with the wind").

But at its heart *Black Elk Speaks* is about religion. The book's bloodstream is the medicine man's intricate vision, received when he was nine, that guided Black Elk's life. The vision, and Lakota spirituality, among many other things, looked to the hoop and a flowering tree:

> You have noticed that everything an Indian does is in a circle, and that is because the Power of the World always works in circles, and everything tries to be round. In the old days when we were a strong and happy people, all our power came to us from the sacred hoop of the nation, and so long as the hoop was unbroken, the people flourished. The flowering tree was the living center of the hoop, and the circle of the four quarters nourished it. The east gave peace and light, the south gave warmth, the west gave rain, and the north with its cold and mighty wind gave strength and endurance. . . . The life of a man is a circle from childhood to childhood, and so it is in everything where power moves. Our teepees were round like the nests of birds, and these were always set in a circle, the nation's hoop, a nest of many nests, where the Great Spirit meant for us to hatch our children.

Black Elk Speaks takes us on a winding journey of joy and loss, hope and despair, often mixed together. In his vision the holy man saw a starving man, a bison, a sacred herb, and the nation's hoop: "I know now what this meant, that the bison were the gift of a good spirit and were our strength, but we should lose them, and from the same good spirit we must find another strength." The reservation and its foreign-built houses became part of Lakota life: "After the heyoka ceremony, I came to live here where I am now between Wounded Knee Creek and Grass Creek. Others came too, and we made these little gray houses of logs that you see, and they are square. It is a bad way to live, for there can be no power in a square. . . . Well, it is as it is. We are prisoners of war while we are waiting here. But there is another world."

The last great hope for Black Elk blew in on the gusts of the Ghost Dance, with its promise of a revival and its ghost shirts that would repel the white man's bullets. "As I made these shirts, I thought how in my vision everything was like old times and the tree was flowering, but when I came back the tree was dead. And I thought that if this world would do as the vision teaches, the tree could bloom here too." Black Elk had been nearby but not within the encampment at Wounded Knee Creek on December 29, 1890. Even so, he could have become a casualty, but he evaded the bullets and escaped his pursuers, only to witness the carnage of a people and their ideals at Wounded Knee:

> I did not know then how much was ended. When I look back now from this high hill of my old age, I can still see the butchered women and children lying heaped and scattered all along the crooked gulch as plain as when I saw them with eyes still young. And I can see that something else died there in the bloody mud, and was buried in the blizzard. A people's dream died there. It was a beautiful dream.
>
> And I, to whom so great a vision was given in my youth,—you see me now a pitiful old man who has done nothing, for the nation's hoop is broken and scattered. There is no center any longer, and the sacred tree is dead.

Scholars and Lakota have raised questions about the strict accuracy of Neihardt's translation of the interviews in *Black Elk Speaks*, which Black Elk delivered in Lakota. In later editions, Neihardt changed the by-line from "as told to" Neihardt to "as told through." Also, Neihardt's book, first published in 1932, like a later one by Joseph Epps Brown, presents only Black Elk's Sioux beliefs and his life up to the Wounded Knee massacre. The medicine man, however, later spent many years as a catechist, or lay teacher, for the Catholic Church. For some, this diminishes Black Elk's standing. However, in the complex milieu of Christian-Indian relationships, a common response, probably the predominant one, has been for Indians to participate in both Christian and Native religions. Further, for those who ascribe to both, many hold to the traditional religion and participate in the Christian faith out of politeness, fondness for the minister, or even the need for a meal at church bazaars. In Black Elk's case, he saw similarities between the two religions and may well have viewed them as two different ways of worshiping one God. Important too was the social work element of his work as a catechist, helping people out in a myriad of ways. Black Elk's granddaughter Charlotte Black Elk adds another consideration: She believes that one motivation for her grandfather was that his position as a catechist entitled him to a car, which allowed him to spread the Lakota faith, as well as fulfill his duties to the Catholics, in remote areas of the sprawling reservation. In other words, in this sense Black Elk, like so many other Indian people during the deadening years, adapted as best he could under confusing and difficult circumstances.

In any event, none can deny the influence of *Black Elk Speaks*. Vine Deloria, Jr., himself a Sioux and a leading activist and scholar during the modern era, explains the influence of the medicine man's words two generations after their first publication:

> The most important aspect of the book . . . is not its effect on the non-Indian populace who wished to learn something of the beliefs of the Plains Indians but upon the contemporary generation of young Indians who have been aggressively searching for roots of their own in the structure of universal reality. To them the book has become a North American bible of all tribes. They look to it for spiritual guidance, for sociological identity, for political insight, and for affirmation of the continuing substance of Indian tribal life, now being badly eroded by the same electronic media which are dissolving other American communities.

The third animating Indian voice that articulated and sustained
the Native worldview belonged to D'Arcy McNickle, a member of
the Confederated Salish and Kootenai Tribes of the Flathead
Reservation in Montana. Born in 1904 to an Irish father and Canadian Cree mother, McNickle grew up on the Flathead reservation
(though he had no Salish or Kootenai blood, the tribe took him in
as a member). When he was eleven years old, he was sent off to
Chemawa boarding school in Oregon, which prohibited children
from wearing their hair long or speaking their Native languages.
He never forgot the Chemawa experience, the force and extent of
government assimilation.

McNickle became a man of the world, perhaps the only American Indian of his generation of whom that could be said. He spent
three and a half years at the University of Montana and then sailed
to Oxford University and on to the University of Grenoble. From
1927 through 1936 he lived mostly in New York City, writing, taking courses at Columbia University and the New School for Social
Research, and making ends meet from editing jobs. In 1935 and
1936 he held a staff position with the Federal Writers Project.

McNickle's first published work, *The Surrounded*, appeared in
1936 to praise in the *Saturday Review of Literature* and elsewhere.
He set the novel at the Flathead reservation, the tribal society that
always kept a hold on his heart. So did the reservation's startling
beauty: the Mission Range, "a magnificent barricade against the
eastern sky, the highest jagged crests floating in morning mist
8,000 feet above the valley," and Flathead Lake, "a mirror to the
sky for forty miles." The landscape was so grand and fertile that
whites swarmed in at the first opportunity, during allotment.
McNickle told that story in *The Surrounded*, partly autobiographi-
cal, through a young Indian man trapped in the conflict of cultures, caught in both the insensitivity of the whites and the
fatalistic disengagement of the Indians. McNickle forced no con-
clusions on his reader; he offered facts, a story, and a deep and
personal knowledge of the dilemmas of Indian-white relations.

Just as *The Surrounded* came out, McNickle joined the BIA, then
in John Collier's heyday. The scholarly, tweedy McNickle became
part of Collier's inner circle, loyal to him and his ideals through-

out his life. He continued on with the bureau past Collier's depar-
ture but finally left in 1952, during Dillon Myer's terminationist
administration. McNickle's sixteen years with the BIA brought
him into the policy arena, and the byplay between his writing and
his real-world experience plainly strengthened both.

McNickle left an impressive body of work as novelist, historian,
and anthropologist, in which he examined Indian culture, Indian
history, and, above all, the tangled Indian-white relationship. His
legacy has three aspects. First, from the point of view of an Indian
and a scholar, he explained federal tribal history and the worth of
Native culture. *They Came Here First* (1949), *Indians and Other
Americans* (1959), and *Indian Tribes of the United States* (1962) are
comprehensive and boldly informational ethnohistories, written
at a time when serious and balanced treatment of Indians reached
its nadir. Second, for three decades D'Arcy McNickle was the
strongest and most eloquent Native public advocate for Indian
nationalism. His assertions came in an era when all sense of tribal
sovereignty was being abandoned, when the bureau named tribal
governments "business committees." Department of the Interior
lawyers tried to erase Felix Cohen's words, and Congress distributed court judgments for confiscation of tribal lands not to tribes
but to individual tribal members on a per capita basis. In 1959
McNickle carefully researched and announced the elements of
Indian nationalism, so much at risk and so little known: "sovereignty," "government by consent," "securing Indian people in the
possession of their lands," and tribal "rights, as 'domestic dependent nations,' to govern their internal affairs."

Third, McNickle well knew of bigotry against Indians but he
also saw a much deeper problem. Rather than just racism, Indians
had to overcome insensitivity, ignorance, and closed-mindedness.
He told a story of this ultimate barrier, an inability of two races to
understand each other and communicate meaningfully across the
gulf of history and culture, in his textured preface to *They Came
Here First*:

Trouble had come to one of the Hopi Indian villages. The people had been refusing to dip their sheep. They had even refused

to count their sheep. These were matters which expert range managers considered important. Worse than that, since this was wartime, these Hopi Indians had refused to register for Selective Service, and neither would they sign a paper saying that they had religious scruples against taking up arms. . . .

The government official had to ask why these things were. Perhaps it was a misunderstanding. He was there to make things right. The speaker for the village had come from the fields in work clothes, but he honored the official by slipping a pair of store trousers over his earth-stained dungarees. The afternoon wore to evening while he talked of the things that troubled the villagers. As he talked the troubles which were in his mind settled upon the mind of the government official. And he, who had come to explain away doubt and misunderstanding, found perplexity instead.

The Hopi spokesman was never cantankerous; his voice was not even sharp, but his questions had a terrible urgency.

He said: "When the Hopi people came from the underworld, they found people living in this land before them. These people had been living here a long time, and they knew many things about the world and the right way to live. Our Hopi people went to them and said, 'We would like to live here with you.' They replied, 'All right. You can stay here. We have certain rules here, ways of living and you will have to follow these rules. Then there will be no trouble.' That's how it was. The Hopis did as they were told and they never had trouble. After a while the white men came. They did not ask if they could live with us. They just moved in. They did not ask what our rules were; instead they wrote rules for us to follow. 'Now you just obey these, and you won't get into trouble,' they said. How do you explain that?"

He did not wait for a response. There were too many questions yet to ask. . . .

When the government official came away in the dark, moonless summer night, he thought of all the answers which an intelligent, civilized official must give in defense of his creed and his position. He even wrote them down on paper when he got to a lighted room. . . .

I was present at that conversation on the mesa. I tried to frame answers to the questions. As it turned out, there were hundreds of questions; one led into another and gave the mind no rest.

How did it happen that these Hopi Indians, after four hundred years of sharing their ancient land with invaders from another world, were not crushed? How was it that they could stand off, unhurried, and ask the white man to explain himself?

This was not the vanquished and the vanishing American. Here was a living voice, and a competent voice, asking the white man to justify his works. This was not what one read in the books.

To explain it, I discovered, one had to start way back and explain the Indians. Where did they come from? and when? and how? What was it like when they first came into the land? Where did they make their homes?

Perhaps, if one really tried, one could visualize something of what it was like. One ought to try. It was important.

Wind from an Enemy Sky, McNickle's last book and published posthumously, comprised his life's work in the sense that he had begun it before starting *The Surrounded*, then reworked it many times. Set once again on the Flathead reservation, it involves a proposed dam that the Indians resist in a fatal clash. Two key whites, the dam builder Pell and the Indian agent Rafferty, are well-meaning, not malevolent. Pell, ever the technician, plunges ahead with his project while Rafferty is immobilized by his inability to sort out the cultural differences. Though unable to act in time, Rafferty finds some insight in his musings: "The problem is communication, he said with inward words. . . . These people find it difficult to believe that a white man, any white man, will give them respect, as it is difficult for me to understand why they push me away and keep me from coming into their confidence. The answer, obviously, is that we do not speak to each other—and language is only a part of it. Perhaps it is intention, or purpose, the map of the mind we follow."

D'Arcy McNickle's "enemy sky" with its cold and bitter winds, then, does not symbolize white society per se. Rather, it stands for the wild turbulence of separate storms colliding. Calming that enemy sky could not be the work of whites alone. Indeed, they had little incentive. The tribes had much more to lose. So, if the skies were to brighten, it would be left to Indian people themselves. And D'Arcy McNickle, now in his role as social activist rather than writer, helped lead the way in the borning days of new kinds of initiatives from Indian country.

SINCE COLONIAL TIMES Indian policy has always been federalized. Yet until the 1940s, in spite of such major national initiatives as allotment and the Indian Reorganization Act, Indians had never been able to organize on a national basis. The Friends of the Indians in the late nineteenth century had an entirely white membership. The Association on American Indian Affairs, housed in New York since 1922, had been a good advocate, but as of the 1940s was a nearly all-white organization (it now has many Indian members and staff). Sporadic early-twentieth-century efforts by Indians, such as the Society of the American Indian and the Teepee Order of America (Charles Eastman was active in both), had brief and unproductive tenures. American Indians, a group whose destiny depended on federal policy, had no capability to influence it.

The idea of creating an organization—truly Indian and truly national—to speak for the tribes had been gestating since the early 1940s. John Collier believed in the idea, and D'Arcy McNickle also embraced it. McNickle and fellow BIA employees Ruth Muskrat Bronson (Cherokee), Archie Phinney (Nez Perce), Charles Heacock (Rosebud Sioux), and others formed plans for a national convention.

On November 15, 1944, the inaugural National Congress of American Indians' convention assembled in Denver's Cosmopolitan Hotel. For those hoping for a spirited, defiant gathering, the opening prayer sounded an auspicious note. McNickle described it this way: "Basil Two Bears was asked to give an invocation in Sioux, which he did. But he ended his prayer with what must have been an old Sioux warwhoop, telling us to get in there and give the Bureau hell. Well, it happened that the National Reclamation

Association was meeting in the other half of the ballroom, with only sliding doors between the two meetings, not much to obstruct the sound. The Reclamation Association meeting came pouring out into the hall to find out who had been stabbed."

Turning to less exciting matters, 80 delegates from 50 tribes adopted a constitution, elected officers, and set out a platform based on sovereignty and civil rights. The ambitious enterprise faced initial roadblocks and many potholes in the years to come, just as any organization of independent governments will. Cries went up that the new congress was dominated by the bureau and its membership was both too professional and too Oklahoma. Though its numbers would grow, the fledgling NCAI represented a small minority of tribes. In its early years it operated on a shoestring.

Even so, Indian people took notice. The concept was right: McNickle had insisted that NCAI be Indian only and membership based on tribes, not individuals. And so it was. The times required this kind of organization. The tribes might or might not need this particular National Congress of American Indians, but they did need a national congress. In the years to come, NCAI's fortunes would ebb and flow, but without question the original delegates were wise to launch the venture.

Then along came an unexpected boost, the return of Indian veterans at the end of World War II. Twenty-five thousand young Indians, fully one-third of the eligible Indian population, three times the rate for the general public, had served. They gained a reputation for bravery that, while not measurable, seems well deserved beyond the "Indian warrior" stereotype. Their service filled their tribespeople with pride, an emotion that has endured.

On coming home, the veterans brought with them new attitudes. They had gone into the outside world and succeeded. They had been treated as equals—and expected that to continue. To be sure, they faced disappointments. Reservation jobs were scarce, and old-style BIA domination and manipulation all too familiar. Opportunities in the cities were often lacking. Nonetheless, as Vine Deloria, Jr., wrote in 1970, returning veterans made up a fresh and resourceful leadership corps. "Some spent a few days with the old folks and then left again for the big cities. Over the years they have emerged as leaders of the urban Indian movement. Many of their children are the nationalists of today who are adamant about keeping the reservations they have visited only on vacations. Other veterans stayed on the reservations and entered tribal politics." Whether they settled in Indian country or in the cities, these veterans raised expectations and bred a much-needed impatience and assertiveness. In the words of Helen Peterson, later executive director of NCAI, "World War Two revived the Indians' capacity to act on their own behalf."

The veterans sparked the first episodes of Indian activism. Several western states still denied Indians the right to vote. Outraged veterans in New Mexico and Arizona challenged the state laws. Felix Cohen was called in on both cases, and NCAI lent its support. Frank Harrison, an Apache, prevailed in the Arizona Supreme Court in 1948. Reversing an older decision, the court found that a state constitutional provision denying suffrage to "persons under guardianship" referred to individuals declared by a court to be incompetent for mental or other reasons. Although Indians are "regarded and treated by the United States as requiring special consideration and protection," the special federal relationship with Indians, sometimes referred to as a guardianship, did not prevent Indian suffrage. In the New Mexico case the court also upheld the right of Indians to vote and directly referred to the military service of Miguel Trujillo, a Pueblo Indian and former marine, and his coplaintiffs: "We all know these New Mexico Indians have responded to the needs of the country in time of war. Why should they be deprived of their rights to vote now because they are favored by the federal government in exempting their lands from taxation?"

Joe Garry personified the changes in Indian advocacy. The grandson of Chief Garry, a veteran of the European and Korean conflicts, and the chairman of the Coeur d'Alene Tribe, the handsome and charismatic Garry became president of NCAI in December 1953. He succeeded Napoleon B. Johnson, a Cherokee and Oklahoma judge who had been NCAI's only president to that date. For executive director, Garry selected Helen Peterson, Lakota.

NCAI had not been moribund—it had taken stands on important issues, including Indian suffrage—but neither had it firmly established itself. Ruth Muskrat Bronson's hard work barely held the organization together. Now termination loomed.

Lacking money and office space, Garry and Peterson had little more than Garry's Buick and near-boundless energy. Crisscrossing the country, meeting with tribes on the reservations and supporters in the cities, they struggled to put together a strategy and a network. "Hang on to your lands. Kick and scratch if you have to, but hang on to your lands," Garry was fond of saying to Indian audiences. "Don't sit back and let things happen to you."

Senator Watkins's termination hearings, which opened in early February 1954, came upon them quickly. Garry appeared at the first hearing, involving the Southern Paiute of Utah. If anything, his brief testimony aided the terminationists. Stating that NCAI did not "oppose or favor" the bill, he read a passage from a tepid NCAI resolution. Under questioning, he was no match for Representatives Berry and Donovan, who led him into admissions that the tribes had been properly consulted, that he had no alternative proposals, and that NCAI had no objections other than its "concern" over whether tribes fully understood the legislation. Helen Peterson emphasized the uphill battle NCAI faced. "We had little understanding of what termination really meant, except that it struck terror into the hearts of people. . . . In the NCAI office we did all we could to support, encourage, and back up those people who dared to question termination, but it was pretty much a losing battle. The NCAI was in a tough spot. We were deeply committed to respecting the sovereignty of a tribe. Did the NCAI want to oppose termination even when the people involved wanted it? We never really came to a final answer on that question."

Nonetheless, while NCAI, like Indian tribes generally, could not stop Watkins's steamroller, especially in the early days, Peterson and Garry learned from adversity. They called an emergency conference in Washington, D.C. Garry's announcement of the conference sounded the alert: "[T]he supreme test for our strength and our will to survive, as Indians, is now before us." Held just two weeks after the termination hearings began, the gathering attracted representatives from 43 tribes who threw down the gauntlet, adopting a Declaration of Indian Rights that denounced termination as a "one-sided approach to free the government of responsibilities and obligations guaranteed in treaties and agreements with them."

When the emergency conference ended, more than 100 participants stayed in town for hearings on the Flathead termination bill. Their presence required Senator Watkins to adjourn the hearing and move to a larger room and underscored the rising opposition in Indian country. D'Arcy McNickle came out against the termination of his tribe and its reservation. NCAI also worked against the bill. Most important, the Flathead mobilized support within their congressional delegation, in local communities, and among statewide interest groups.

In the end the Flathead prevailed. So did several other tribes slated for termination. Moreover, while too many tribes fell to the radical policy, it bears emphasis that many escaped and that eventually termination was scrapped entirely. A young but energetic Indian movement was beginning to gather steam.

THE MODERN tribal sovereignty movement has had no single great inspirational leader, no Martin Luther King, Jr., no César Chávez. After all, in spite of a considerable commonality among the tribes, Indian country contains more than 500 separate and independent peoples. Each has its own history, traditions, institutions, and officials. Yet if one person may be singled out, it is Vine Deloria, Jr.

Deloria, a member of the Standing Rock Sioux Tribe, grew up in an intellectual family. His father, the incisive Episcopalian minister Vine Deloria, Sr., was the first Indian named to a national position in the church. Even so, he felt more comfortable as an Indian than as a Christian preacher. The Sioux anthropologist Ella Deloria was Vine's aunt.

Something of a late bloomer, Vine Deloria, Jr., describes himself as having been a "benign delinquent," setting off a thunderous fireworks display over the gym during a high school graduation and jacking up cars outside church, placing chunks of wood under the axles, and laughing at the whir of the spinning wheels when the parishioners attempted to depart. Though later the influence of his father and aunt took hold, the young Deloria cared little for his studies; more than once, rather than endure a tedious (and inattentive) teacher, he leaped out the window during lectures in favor of rabbit hunting. Exasperated, his father arranged for the boy's admission to the Kent School and shipped him off to Connecticut, where he completed his secondary schooling in 1951.

After a stint in the marines, Deloria earned a bachelor's degree from Iowa State. Then, working as a welder, he attended the Lutheran School of Theology in Moline, Illinois. By 1963, now in his thirties and holding a master's in sacred theology, he had yet to find his calling.

Through all this "white" education, Deloria never strayed far from his Indian roots. He followed national developments, and the state of Indian advocacy appalled him. Supposedly NCAI represented the tribes, but membership had dropped precipitously after the departures of Joe Garry and Helen Peterson. Worse, the organization's passivity hampered Indians in a time of growing opportunities. In 1959 the United States Supreme Court handed down the first favorable modern opinion, *Williams v. Lee*, a ringing endorsement of tribal sovereignty, yet when Deloria called the NCAI office, no one had heard of the case. At the same time, by the early 1960s the civil rights movement had become a force. "What you could see," Deloria recalled, "was that the tribes just had to be more aggressive. The government was so terrified by civil rights that if we just threatened to act, we could prevail."

In the fall of 1964 Deloria ran for executive director of NCAI and won. His three years in that post revived the organization and made it into an effective advocate for tribal rights. Nearly bankrupt when Deloria arrived, NCAI quickly became solvent. Membership shot from 19 tribes to 156. NCAI became a presence on Capitol Hill, resisting the continuing threats of termination and proposing new policy directions based on tribal self-determination.

For all his organization building and activism at NCAI, Deloria also began to realize the intellectual bent instilled in him by his father and aunt since childhood. "This is when I started writing. I wanted to give good briefings before Congress. I got to love old documents and learning how to root around in them." When he left NCAI, Deloria had not yet published. In two years he wrote two minor articles, and then, in 1969, *Custer Died for Your Sins* burst upon the world.

Custer embodied its author's personality: sarcastic, witty, iconoclastic, and lightning quick, always poking, sparring, and jabbing. Laced with historical references and vignettes of contemporary conditions and personalities, *Custer* spared hardly anyone. Deloria skewered the usual suspects—the bureau, missionaries, and dominant societal values—but he also went after Democrats, liberals, and Indian tribes, including his own—all, in sum, who fell short or dissembled. *Custer,* widely read and influential, hit the right tone. Never whiny or self-pitying, Deloria framed history, identified problems, and dug into theory and real-world considerations. He also offered better approaches: greater recognition of tribal sovereignty (he called for a "cultural leave-us-alone law") and more stable leadership and management in Indian country. The book simply rang true.

Custer Died for Your Sins altered the political landscape in two ways. For whites, it humanized Indians. Deloria lucidly explained the distinctive cultures and needs of Native peoples. In a text uproariously funny at times, he showed Indian humor in its full flower. No stone-faced Natives here. Deloria's Indians are resourceful people, survivors who endured wave upon wave of tragedy yet somehow never lost either their lightheartedness or the grit to preserve their ways of life.

For Indians, *Custer* inspired empowerment and pride. It offered hope in a time when hope seemed the province of all in America save Natives. It allowed Indians to dream their own real dreams. There had never been anything like it.

Deloria wrote of the "moccasin telegraph," and his book provided proof. Stories are legion of Indian people excitedly reading passages from dog-eared copies to relatives and friends. Folk singer and guitarist Floyd Red Crow Westerman cut a toe-tapping album titled *Custer Died for Your Sins*, sung to traditional tribal melodies; verses were based on the book—for instance, the title

Vine Deloria, Jr. (2000). Photograph courtesy of Fulcrum Press.

song and "Here Come the Anthros." *Custer's* subtitle, *An Indian Manifesto,* aptly described the book. Most of the words involved history, personalities, law, social conditions, and humor, but Indian people knew that at its core *Custer* was an anthem of optimism for the future of a proud, worthy people: "We will survive because we are a people unified by our humanity; not a pressure group unified for conquest. And from our greater strength we shall wear down the white man and finally outlast him. But above all, and this is our strongest affirmation, we SHALL ENDURE as a people."

Vine Deloria, Jr., found common cause with others of his generation who shared his blend of nuts-and-bolts politics and intellectualism. Clyde Warrior, a Ponca from Oklahoma, had been brought up by his traditional grandparents. He spoke his tribal language and learned the techniques that would make him an accomplished fancy dancer. As a teenager, however, he had taken a different tack. The tall, handsome youth posed in traditional regalia for a tourist postcard and, dressed in buckskins, worked at Disneyland, paddling a canoe. By the early 1960s, when he was in his twenties, his dress might be eclectic—a cowboy hat, a Hawaiian shirt, and buckskin all were possibilities—but his commitment to Indian traditions and tribal self-determination registered whitehot. In an election for president of the National Indian Youth Council, his opponent gave a traditional campaign speech while Warrior's announced position consisted of just two sentences: "This is all I have to offer. The sewage of Europe does not flow through these veins."

Warrior won the election, but that kind of talk made many Indians uncomfortable. Their schooling had taught them that Anglo culture was good, that Indian ways were bad. No matter, Warrior never toned down his rhetoric. A compelling public orator and steeped in history and Indian rights, he pressed forward, relentlessly challenging assumptions, breaking the mold, making converts.

Hank Adams, though born Assiniboine and Sioux, grew up on the Quinault reservation. When he was only 14 years old, he was in attendance as the tribe's members sharply opposed state jurisdiction under Public Law 280 in the 1950s. Subsequently the Bureau of Indian Affairs ran roughshod over the tribe's expressed will and wrote up an illegitimate petition to the governor of Washington. The injustice enraged Adams, burning into him a lifelong commitment. Two years of college at the University of Washington bored him stiff, and in 1963 he dived into Indian affairs. Possessed of a photographic memory, the willingness to expend serial all-nighters reading anything bearing on Indian rights, and a Machiavellian instinct for political strategy, Adams became the quintessential activist. That he sometimes appeared to be stark raving mad seemed only to enhance his stature.

Mel Thom, while less outrageous than his fellow activists, nonetheless had strong personal qualities. Persuasive and immediately likable with his broad, sunshine smile, Thom graduated from Brigham Young University and soon became tribal chairman of the Walker River Tribe of Nevada. A consensus builder, Thom labored to bring Indian organizations together in a common reform effort. His efforts on process, however, never let him stray from his conviction that the Indian cause had to aim at deep change: "We had decided that what we needed was a movement. Not an organization, but a movement. Organizations rearrange history. Movements make history."

Deloria, Warrior, Adams, and Thom never formally worked together in the same group or building. While Deloria served at NCAI, the other three focused their energies on the National Indian Youth Council. Warrior and Thom had participated in the National Indian Chicago Conference in 1961. The gathering produced a spirited and important document, the Declaration of Indian Purpose, that set out grievances and a statement of beliefs, written primarily by D'Arcy McNickle. It stated, "We, the Indian people must be governed by high principles and laws in a democratic manner, with a right to choose our own way of life." The young people wanted more. Later that summer Warrior, Thom, the Navajo Herbert Blatchford, and others founded the National Indian Youth Council. Adams joined up with NIYC as an organizer in 1963. NIYC, while it lacked the tribal leadership of NCAI, had a sharper edge.

The four fed off one another, by telephone, sessions at conferences, and long letters about philosophy and strategy. Deloria worked out of Washington, D.C., Warrior spent most of his time in Oklahoma, and Thom lived in Nevada. Meanwhile, Adams was out in the Northwest, driving the salmon fishing disputes. Their time together proved enormously productive, but it lasted just five years. Clyde Warrior put on weight and drank too much bourbon; the alcohol flowed freely in those exuberant early days of the movement. In 1968 he died of liver failure at age 29. Hundreds of people attended his traditional Ponca funeral, conducted at the home of the grandparents who had raised him. The others soldiered on, and the movement Warrior had helped bring to life flourished, but even after the passage of a quarter of a century, people still shake their heads at what more might have been.

. . .

*DURING THE 1960S a new breed of young, college-educated Indians developed an agenda based on history, culture, and law. Termination must be halted. Land must be returned. Traditional Indian ceremonies and religions must be respected. The federal government must fulfill its duty as trustee by protecting and promoting Indian interests. Treaty hunting, fishing, and water rights must be honored. Federal programs must be administered and controlled by Indians. Sovereign Indian tribes—not the BIA, the churches, or the states—must govern the reservations. In each case, as the activists made clear in public forums and numerous protests and demonstrations, the operative word was "must."

The work of the new Indian intellectuals, whose numbers grew steadily, was critical to progress for Indian people. Yet much more would be needed, for success would have to be achieved in many hundreds of reservations, legislatures, courts, and administrative offices. In addition to their own direct accomplishments, the young intellectuals' combination of uplifting ideals, a bold agenda, and action-oriented methods helped galvanize a building restlessness on the reservations and inspired tribal leaders to take more assertive stances. For the only change that could finally matter would be change out on the land.

5.

Leadership on the Reservations

Out in Indian country, tribal leaders had talents of many kinds in the 1950s but not much talent for dealing with the larger society. Tribal action was mostly defensive and mostly ineffective. Congress terminated tribes and their treaties, public works projects grabbed tribal lands, and the states steadily gained jurisdiction over reservations.

Still, ineffective or not, Indian people did resist. The losses created symbols of injustice and taught lessons. The word spread. Bitter defeats on specific local issues, like the fear generated by the national policies of Arthur Watkins, educated Indian people and pulled them together. Gradually, by the 1960s, tribal leaders had grown more skillful in their defensive actions and more determined to move beyond the reactive to the active.

THE END of World War II unleashed America's domestic energies. The unprecedented surge of economic development cranked out a multitude of private initiatives (industrial factories, new consumer products, and residential subdivisions) and public works projects (dams, power plants, and highways) that installed the infrastructure for the private enterprise. Indian tribes from coast to coast found their lands in the crosshairs of federal agencies looking for sites to locate their large-scale projects.

The Seneca Nation's Allegany Reservation lies in a hilly, wooded area of southwestern New York, just above the Pennsylvania line. Five centuries of European settlement long ago eliminated many eastern tribes altogether or forced their members to disperse into towns and cities, but the six nations of the Iroquois Confederacy—the Seneca, Cayuga, Mohawk, Oneida, Onondaga, and Tuscarora—all held on and managed to retain some land. Their reservations are smaller than those of many western tribes, which felt the pressure of national expansion much later.

Cornplanter, a legendary eighteenth-century Seneca chief, knew that his people would be overwhelmed unless they were guaranteed land. Seeking assurances, he traveled to Philadelphia in 1790 to meet with President George Washington, who provided Cornplanter with a letter saying that Seneca lands would remain intact. Four years later the Seneca–United States treaty promised that the United States would "never claim [Seneca lands] nor disturb the Seneka Nation, nor any of the Six Nations . . . in the free use and enjoyment thereof."

The treaty and Washington's letter did not deter the Army Corps of Engineers, the muscular dam-building agency used to having its way on the nation's rivers. The notion of constructing Kinzua Dam on the Allegheny River traced to the early 1900s when Pittsburgh, downriver from the Seneca, began to press for flood protection. The dam, which was to inundate much of the Seneca reservation and change tribal life forever, initially foundered, primarily because the justice and interior departments objected to breaking the Seneca treaty.

By the early 1950s Kinzua Dam had come to the fore again, as part of the postwar development boom. Project proponents now emphasized the cash register of hydropower in addition to flood control. The Eisenhower administration generally had little truck with Indian objections, and of no small moment, the president's aide for public works, Major General John Bragdon, had served with the Army Corps of Engineers in Pittsburgh. The entreaties of the president's son, Major John Eisenhower, who proclaimed it "particularly essential that our word be kept with the Indians," were drowned in the megapolitics of dam-and-reservoir construction. The corps had other viable alternatives but never gave them an airing; as one prominent local attorney quipped, "Flooding the

Conewango Valley would provide more water for Pittsburgh, but it would flood out white folks! They vote." Justice and interior promptly reversed their positions, removing key obstacles to the project. In early 1957 the corps had in hand a preliminary court order paving the way for surveying and construction.

The proposed dam would exact devastating costs on the Seneca. The corps designed it to back up water over a stretch of 35 river miles upstream. The reservoir would flood 10,000 acres of tribal land, about one-third of the reservation. Moreover, the flooded part was the best part, the rich bottomland and low-lying forests down by the river. All the prime berry and fruit gathering places, the finest deer and bear habitat, the best farmland, none of it would ever be seen again. The 160 Seneca families living below the high-water mark, over 600 people, would be uprooted, denied their free-flowing river, the heart of their homeland. The site of the Coldspring Longhouse would be lost. Thousands of Seneca graves, Cornplanter's among them, would be exhumed and moved to higher ground in advance of the flooding.

In retrospect, the Seneca never had a chance. The magnitude of the forces aligned against them, however, give luster to the nobility of their decadelong crusade against Kinzua Dam. Working without any staff or experience in mobilizing public opinion, Chief Cornelius Seneca, in full traditional dress, took his nation's case public through speeches and a national television appearance. After 1959, when the tribe turned to younger leadership, George Heron, a World War II veteran, continued the aggressive opposition.

With virtually no tribal funds, the Seneca raised money to fight the dam by granting highway and pipeline rights-of-way across parts of the reservation and marshaled support from many quarters. The Six Nations Confederacy, National Congress of American Indians, the gathered Indians at the 1961 Chicago Conference, and individual tribes spoke up for Seneca treaty rights. Churches, the American Civil Liberties Union, various politicians, and many other organizations joined in opposition to Kinzua Dam. Journalists pitched in. Especially notable was Alvin Josephy, editor of *American Heritage* magazine and award-winning author. Moved

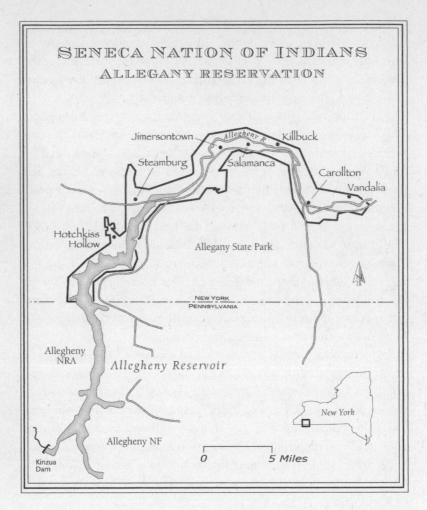

SENECA NATION OF INDIANS
ALLEGANY RESERVATION

Jimersontown   Allegheny R.   Killbuck

Steamburg   Salamanca

Carollton
Vandalia

Hotchkiss
Hollow

Allegany State Park

NEW YORK
PENNSYLVANIA

Allegheny
NRA   *Allegheny Reservoir*

New York

Allegheny NF

Kinzua
Dam   0   5 Miles

deeply by the Indian cause, Josephy wrote passionate articles and books on many Native subjects, including Chief Joseph and the Nez Perce. For the wrongs at Seneca, he titled his piece "Corn-planter, Can You Swim?"

As it turns out, we have no clear answer to the dilemma posed by Josephy's question. Inevitably the corps prevailed. Kinzua Dam plugged the river, and the agency's work inundated much of the Seneca's homeland, including Cornplanter's burial site. Today a monument to him stands on ground high above the reservoir. The memorial purports to be the chief's new resting place, but no one can be sure of that. The corps may or may not have done its job accurately because the army, fearing adverse publicity, kept secret the complicated task of moving the remains of some three thousand Seneca ancestors from their soon-to-be-flooded graves.

The tribe's court challenges, based on the treaty promise "never [to] claim nor disturb" Seneca land, failed. Timing was against it. Just a few years later, when the law toughened and became much more protective of Indian treaty rights, the Seneca probably would have succeeded. Today Kinzua Dam stands in bittersweet irony as a monument to both injustice and a cause that stiffened the resolve of Indian people across the nation to defend their lands and treaties.

IN THE WEST, scores of tribes faced the juggernaut of post-war expansion, public works projects, and powerful, mission-oriented federal agencies. The water and energy buildup of the region proceeded on three main fronts. In the upper Great Plains, the Army Corps of Engineers and Bureau of Reclamation built massive dam-and-reservoir projects for power and irrigation on the Missouri River and its tributaries. In the Pacific Northwest the rush of dam building after the war tamed the Columbia and Snake rivers and most of the steep, coastal rivers. In the Southwest the Big Buildup fueled the massive expansion of urban centers from Denver to Phoenix to Las Vegas to the Southern California cities. Dams, reservoirs, coal mines, power plants, transmission lines, and roads on the lands and rivers of the interior Colorado Plateau—all moved forward inexorably, within two generations transforming towns into cities, cities into metropolises, metropolises into megalopolises. The population of the eleven western states raced from 17 million in 1945 to 64 million at the end of the century.

The dynamic in the West followed the pattern at Seneca. The solidly connected Army Corps of Engineers and Reclamation Bureau effectively lobbied Congress for approval of their projects. Indian land, water, and minerals offered the path of least resistance. The tribes lacked the money, ballot box influence, and political know-how to mount effective opposition. Reclamation and the corps, steamrollers both, saw no need to search for alternative sites or to reconfigure their pork-barrel projects, which regularly failed to meet cost-benefit standards. Treaty promises and trust obligations never entered the equation.

THE PICK-SLOAN AGREEMENT, negotiated between Colonel Lewis Pick of the corps and William Sloan of reclamation in 1944, divided up the construction opportunities in the Upper Missouri Basin between the two agencies. Congress promptly approved the arrangement, which called for 112 dams in the Dakotas, Montana, and Wyoming. The Missouri had always been both lifeline and corridor for the plains tribes, and their reservations were located along the rivers. The big, main stem Pick-Sloan dams tore into eleven Indian reservations in the Missouri Basin; five Sioux reservations lost more than 200,000 acres. Among the upriver tribes, the Fort Berthold reservation lost the most, 155,000 acres. The dams flooded fertile, sheltered bottomlands and their villages, farms, and valuable wildlife habitat. Families and whole towns were forced to relocate on drier and windier sites on the higher, treeless plains.

The agencies stonewalled the tribes from beginning to end. They refused to alter the project plans and, arm in arm with members of Congress who controlled the appropriations process, discussed compensation for the damage only in crabbed terms. Federal negotiators flatly rejected tribal requests for the return of some ancestral lands. Also dismissed were proposals for reduced electrical rates for tribal members and hunting, fishing, and grazing rights along reservoir shorelines. Payments averaged under $100 per acre and included no relocation or reconstruction expenses.

The dealings doubly frustrated the tribes because they had strong leadership and put so much energy into the negotiations with the agencies. Franklin Ducheneaux, Sr., chairman of the Cheyenne River Sioux Tribe, widely recognized as a tough but flexible and creative negotiator, tirelessly reworked the tribe's proposals, but General G. J. Nold made only cosmetic changes in the corps's offer. Ducheneaux finally called off the negotiations, such

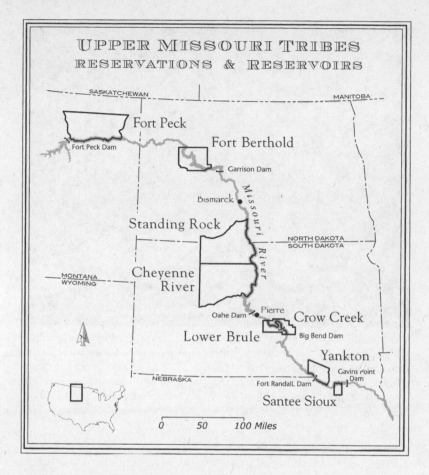

as they were. The corps held all the cards—and was backed up by
E. Y. Berry, the terminationist congressman from South Dakota.
As one observer commented, "the tribe just couldn't deal with the
Corps of Engineers at all."

The Missouri River development hit the Mandan, Hidatsa, and
Arikara Tribes of the Fort Berthold Reservation hardest of all. Garrison Dam in North Dakota took not only homes, farms, and hunting grounds but also inundated a bridge across the Missouri; this
turned a three-mile trip between families into a drive of more than
a hundred miles around the shoreline of the new reservoir. Tribal
chairmen Martin Cross and George Gillette fought the dam but,
like the Sioux, made little progress against the assembled fire-

The Mandan, Hidatsa, and Arikara Tribes of the Fort Berthold Reservation could find no way to stop the inundation of tribal land along the Missouri River for the Garrison Dam and Reservoir Project. Here, in 1950, Interior Secretary J. A. Krug signs a document transferring 155,000 acres (about 240 square miles) from the tribe to the United States. Fort Berthold tribal Chairman George Gillette, hand to face, stands at the left. Photograph courtesy of AP/Wide World Photos.

power. The formal signing ceremony in the secretary of the interior's office in Washington made as sorrowful a public occasion as one will see. "You know that famous photograph of our tribal council back in D.C. at the signing for Garrison Dam?" asked Susan Johnson, a Fort Berthold tribal member. "Sometimes people say that shows how passive our people were. But that's not so. Our tribal chairman, who was wiping away his tears in such incredible anguish in that picture, had done everything he possibly could to stop that dam. So had the other council members. They weren't passive at all. But they were powerless."

THE RUSHING RIVERS of the Pacific Northwest, with their steep, downhill courses, offered some of the best hydroelectric sites in the world. The torrents could be blocked and stored behind dams, then sent blasting down through pipes to spin giant turbines, thus producing electricity. Eager to harness this "cheap" electrical power, regional development interests and federal agencies embarked on one of history's most ambitious dam-building programs. By the 1960s the Columbia, by far the West's largest river, had been dammed from top to bottom and transformed from a wild river into a series of slack-water back-to-back reservoirs; from Portland, Oregon, to the Canadian line, a stretch of nearly 600 miles, only 50 miles of free-flowing water remained. In the Puget Sound area, municipalities and companies built hydro facilities on dozens of rivers. Dams impounded coastal rivers from the Olympic Peninsula down to the Klamath River in Northern California. The Bonneville Power Administration's proud, and accurate, assertion in 1976 about the rapidity and effectiveness of hydro development on the Columbia held true for the Northwest as a region: "In little more than one generation, Man has harnessed the tremendous water power of the Columbia. . . ."

The projects took some reservation land, but the tribes of the Northwest were salmon people; their far greater loss came from the precipitous decline in the runs. Most of the tribes, like the Nez Perce in their 1855 treaty, held off-reservation fishing rights on the rivers they had ceded to the United States. These rights so blanketed the Northwest that virtually every dam threatened tribal treaty rights. By the 1970s, owing primarily to the dams, salmon runs were in free fall.

The salmon tribes possessed no more political equipment than other tribes to prevent the dam building, which came on so fast and hard. Their protests unheard, tribal leaders were left with the pale compensation of cash for the salmon that pervaded their diets, their commerce, and their songs and dances . . . their lives. Hydro dams, some impassable and all injurious to fish, flooded the waterfalls, but the projects could not erase the iconic images of Indian fishermen on their platforms with their hoop nets reaching out over the sturdy currents or the remembrance of grieving blanketed elders looking out on the placid lakes that had replaced their rivers. Photographs of those scenes went out to a receptive public and to the country's Indian leaders, who became even more steeled.

IN AMERICA'S dry Southwest, where postwar development was equally frenetic, dozens of tribes paid the price for hinterland water and power projects designed to benefit the booming cities. The dams went in, as elsewhere, with no concern for impacts on tribal lands. One federally subsidized water project after another lavished reliable water supplies on irrigators, hydro suppliers, and cities—but not on tribes, which by treaties and other federal laws possessed extensive water rights. In 1973 the National Water Commission concluded that "in the history of the United States Government's treatment of Indian tribes, its failure to protect Indian water rights for use on the Reservations it set aside for them is one of the sorrier chapters."

Coal, oil, and gas played a key role in the postwar buildup of the Southwest and in the upper Great Plains. The Crow, Northern Cheyenne, Mescalero and Jicarilla Apache, Northern and Southern Ute, Navajo, and Hopi reservations, among others, all held major mineral deposits. Everywhere the pattern was the same. Mineral companies went directly to the Department of the Interior to negotiate contracts. The BIA, often accompanied by tribal lawyers, then presented the contracts to the tribes for their approval as favorable deals. The tribal councils rubber-stamped them, but they were hardly good deals. Invariably, the tribes received below-market-value returns and damaging environmental impacts on the land, water, and air.

The situation at Hopi gained wide attention and was especially poignant. A 1966 coal lease to the Peabody Coal Company of the fabulous deposit beneath Black Mesa underpriced tribal coal and water and financially disadvantaged the tribe in many other ways. The Kikmongwi, traditional Hopi who represented most of the tribe, recoiled at the idea of locating the sprawling open-pit mining operation, the largest in the country, on the tribe's sacred mesa in remote northern Arizona. Rumors swirled that John Boyden, the non-Indian tribal attorney who controlled the "progressive" tribal council, represented Peabody Coal in secret. Hopi traditional leaders protested in every way they knew, writing letters and petitions to presidents, Department of the Interior officials, and international bodies. Thomas Banyacya, a quiet but riveting speaker and translator for the Kikmongwi, spoke out across the country and in foreign nations: "You pass all kinds of laws without asking us. You will make us landless, homeless people. This land is the only land we have. This is the land of the Great Spirit. European people can go back to their lands. Native people have no place to go." Compelling though the Hopi's pleas may have been, ultimately they could not penetrate the nation's decision-making apparatus. The Big Buildup of the Southwest proceeded apace at Black Mesa.

AMID ALL the losses during the 1950s and in early 1960s, some glimmers of progress began to appear. In Sioux country the tribes took on a patently impossible challenge. The stirring result not only marked the Sioux's first clear victory in their dealings with a non-Indian government since the Great Sioux Treaty and the battle at the Little Bighorn, nearly a century before, but also held up to all tribes a vivid portrait of what could be.

South Dakota had long considered taking jurisdiction over the state's reservations. In 1950, Dillon S. Myer, with termination on his mind, stirred the pot: "The ultimate answer is the assumption of full jurisdiction by the state." A perfect mechanism arrived in 1953, when Congress passed Public Law 280, allowing states to assume jurisdiction unilaterally in Indian country, the statute the BIA used in its devious attempt to transfer jurisdiction at Quinault to the state of Washington. Although South Dakota officials assumed that a state takeover was inevitable, they moved slowly. By 1960 local non-Indian citizens had stepped up their lobbying for decisive action under Public Law 280. The issue went to the state legislature, where a bill taking jurisdiction in Indian country sailed through in 1963. Governor Archie Gubbrud received strong opposition from the Sioux tribes (Cato Valandra, Rosebud tribal chair, called it "the Wounded Knee of 1963") but, with vocal non-Indian support, promptly signed the measure. The same old story seemed to be playing out in the Dakotas.

The Sioux refused to let it lie. Within two weeks they met in Pierre and formed the United Sioux Tribes of South Dakota, with William Whirlwind Horse as president. Time was short; to put the jurisdictional takeover on hold, they had only two months to collect the 14,000 petition signatures needed to place a referendum on the ballot; if passed by the electorate, the measure would overturn the state law. Indian people and their friends did it. Going door to door on and off the reservations, they gathered more than 20,000 signatures. South Dakota's elected representatives had overwhelmingly invoked Public Law 280. Now the state's people would vote on the referendum on November 3, 1964.

Sioux leaders had no experience in state elections, but they proceeded to organize a thoroughly modern campaign. They retained a Sioux Falls advertising firm to handle the public relations work. Polling showed that neither historical injustices nor a concern for tribal culture especially resonated with the public. Instead, the tribes would focus on voters' sense of fairness—the state law was wrong because the Sioux had never consented to it. As the campaign moved into high gear, the churches, at the urging of the tribes, gave their enthusiastic support. Cato Valandra, William Whirlwind Horse, Franklin Ducheneaux, Sr., and other tribal leaders worked the reservations and the cities. As election day drew close, the strategy shifted: To counteract active non-Indian groups opposing the referendum, the tribal spokespeople did much less work outside the reservations, deferring to a hardworking non-Indian organization, named the Keep Faith Committee, created to support the Sioux position. The Public Law 280 referendum became the most closely watched election issue in the state.

On election day the tribes ran a full-bore get-out-the-vote effort. In the past Sioux voter turnout had been minuscule, but on November 3, 1964, an estimated 90 percent of Sioux people voted. Nonetheless, it amounted to a small percentage of the total; South Dakota's non-Indians would have to carry the day. Communities near the reservations, where anti-Indian sentiment ran the strongest, overwhelmingly rejected the referendum, but the Sioux campaign was stunningly successful in Sioux Falls, Pierre, Rapid City, and Aberdeen. The referendum passed in a landslide with 79 percent of the vote—201,389 to 58,289.

Sioux country exploded into dance—the way that great victories had always been celebrated. At Rosebud, where Cato Valandra and others had worked so hard, the tables brimmed with food, and war dance music poured from the loudspeakers. When the Victory Dance began, Tom Boneshirt led the colorful grand entry. The tribal newspaper headline captured the spirit of the moment, unlike any the Sioux had experienced in a great long time: WE SHALL SURVIVE!

INDIAN AFFAIRS had taken on a new attitude by the mid-1960s. Deloria, Warrior, Thom, Adams, and other college-educated younger people brought intellectual vigor, a comprehensive political agenda, and activist strategies. Out on the reservations, a cadre of determined tribal chairmen gained valuable experience through painful setbacks as well as modest successes.

Roger Jourdain of the Red Lake Chippewa and Wendell Chino of the Mescalero Apache were among the most aggressive, flamboyant, and effective. Blunt and irascible, Jourdain took office in 1959 and relentlessly pounded the BIA, promoting Red Lake sovereignty. He scornfully chided a federal official for the meager programs of the 1960s: "You are not giving us anything. You are merely returning a finger of sand for all that you have taken. But you act like you are doing us a kindness." He trained his energies first on housing and health care. In the early 1960s he obtained federal funds for one of the first tribally run housing projects. "We can build them better than HUD or those tramps at the bureau. And we did." He began paving the way for one of the finest health facilities in northern Minnesota. To symbolize sovereignty, Jourdain hatched plans to issue tribal license plates (the Minnesota Supreme Court later ruled that the Red Lake plates must be honored just like the plates of another state) and to require passports for non-Indians to enter the reservation.

Roger Jourdain, ever the firebrand, stands in front of a map of Chippewa land cessions and reminds a group of his tribe's loss of land. Referring to the 1863 Treaty of Red Lake, he scoffs, "Lincoln—the Great Emancipator? He emancipated the slaves and emancipated ten million acres of our land at the same time." Photograph courtesy of the Charles Brill family, reprinted with permission from Red Lake Nation—Portraits of Ojibway Life.

The Apache Wendell Chino, an ordained minister with a booming voice, trumpeted that "Indian people should make decisions about Indian land" and promoted and practiced what he called red capitalism. He wrested control of the land away from the BIA, creating tribally operated timber and cattle companies and establishing the Inn of the Mountain Gods, one of the first tribal resorts. Not above taking a dig at other tribes, Chino was fond of proclaiming, "Navajos . . . make rugs, and the Pueblos make pottery. The Mescaleros make money."

Cato Valandra of the Rosebud Sioux had helped spearhead the South Dakota referendum. Now he set up an innovative housing program and improved reservation roads. Joe Garry, tribal chairman at Coeur d'Alene, had logged a full decade dealing with issues through the National Congress of American Indians and in state government as a member of the Idaho legislature. Robert Jim and Eagle Seelatsee of the Yakama Nation and a growing number of other tribal leaders in the Northwest staunchly defended treaty fishing rights. Other influential tribal leaders of the 1960s included Franklin Ducheneaux, Sr., of Cheyenne River, Osley B. Sinook of Eastern Cherokee, Clarence Wesley of San Carlos Apache, Pete Homer of the Colorado River Tribes, Alan Alex of the Pyramid Lake Paiute, Joe DeLaCruz of Quinault, Norbert Hill of the Wisconsin Oneida, and Ronnie Lupe of White Mountain Apache.

They all had particular concerns at home but were bound together by a passion for tribal rights. Vine Deloria, who worked closely with the tribal leaders during his tenure at NCAI from 1964 through 1967, summed it up: "Look, in many ways these guys were a pitiful group. Their tribes were all poor, and they had termination to worry about. But they knew their stuff. They knew tribal sovereignty. They even knew Felix Cohen's *Handbook*. Somebody would tell them tribes were just social groups or fraternal organizations or whatever, and they'd say, 'The hell we are. Just look at Cohen, page 122. That's your government's publication. We're independent sovereign governments!' "

IN 1964, the same year as the South Dakota Public Law 280 referendum, tribal leaders joined together nationally to achieve a momentous result. President Lyndon Johnson's War on Poverty legislation was moving through Congress to create the Office of Economic Opportunity. Initially, the bill allowed OEO funds to be used to benefit Indians, but the grants could be made only to state and federal agencies, not directly to tribal governments.

In May 1964, Indian leaders came to Washington, D.C., for the "Capital Conference," the American Indian Capital Conference on Poverty. Although tribal offices were still small and administered few grants, the assembled Indians, knowing that tribes would have little say, and get little money, if programs went through the states and the BIA, decided to lobby for direct OEO funding of tribes. Vice President Hubert Humphrey and Secretary of the Interior Stewart Udall attended the conference, and during the

four-day gathering Indians and their supporters fanned out over
Capitol Hill to meet with legislators. When the OEO legislation
passed a few months later, the tribes had won their point: OEO
grants could go directly to tribes.

The work of the Capital Conference contributed just three
words to the OEO statute, specifying "a tribal government" as an
eligible grantee. Nonetheless, for Indian country the action was
nothing short of earthshaking. As Philip S. Deloria explains, the
War on Poverty grants empowered tribes by building tribal capac-
ities, creating independence from the BIA, and knitting tribes
together with other tribes and the country as a whole:

> The 1960s was above all else an Office of Economic Oppor-
> tunity decade. . . . [T]he Great Society programs were the first
> major instance in which Indian tribal governments had money
> and were not beholden for it to the Bureau of Indian Affairs.
> This created an enormous change in the balance of power on
> reservations and in Washington.
>
> Tribes could, to some degree, set their own priorities. They
> could hire, supervise, and fire people on their own. They had
> telephones and copying machines to spread information
> throughout Indian country and the money to hold conferences
> to organize for the common good. They could go to Washington
> whenever they wanted to and not only when the superintend-
> ent or the central office of the BIA told them they could. These
> things altered the nature of the Bureau of Indian Affairs and the
> relationship between tribes and the federal government. They
> changed the face of Indian affairs in a way that will never com-
> pletely be reversed.

This integration of tribal governments into the War on Poverty
in 1964 also stood as a milestone in the long course of federal and
tribal relations. For the first time in American history, Indian people had conceived of a provision to be inserted in national legislation and then lobbied it through Congress into law. The tribes
had wrought no miracles, nor even turned the corner, but a person with a good eye could see that brighter days might well lie
ahead.

6.

Red Power

The Indian movement had a complicated relationship with the civil rights movement. Indian leaders generally remained apart from the strategizing and events of civil rights advocates. They believed that the drive for civil rights, so closely identified with blacks, would inevitably move Native Americans to the fringes. Besides, the issues were different. Tribes strove to protect their sovereignty and land bases, matters outside the scope of civil rights. To Vine Deloria, civil rights too easily equated with sameness: "In the minds of most people in 1963, legal equality and cultural conformity were identical." To appreciate the distinction between the civil rights and tribal movements, one needed only to consider the nature of the wrongs inflicted on each group: Blacks were determined to eliminate segregation and allow integration; Indians sought to reverse forced assimilation.

Indians, then, stayed away from the 1963 March on Washington, when Martin Luther King, Jr., delivered his famous address from the Lincoln Memorial. After civil rights leaders urged Indians to participate in the Poor People's March of 1968, Deloria and Hank Adams discussed it at length but decided not to attend. Some Indians did march but pointedly camped off by themselves rather than stay at Resurrection City, the main tent grounds.

Still, Indians shared considerable ground with the civil rights movement, and the Indian movement reaped many benefits from its larger counterpart. Civil rights put wind beneath the wings of the Indian movement by forcing the nation to confront the virus of racism and the humanity of minority peoples. While the protection of sovereign homelands would always be the greatest "civil right" of Indian people, they also had many traditional civil rights concerns: religious freedom, equality in public schools and employment, and voting rights, as evidenced in the lawsuits brought by the World War II veterans. They also wanted to overturn laws prohibiting mixed marriages and enforce rights in the criminal justice system, such as appointed counsel in court cases and humane treatment in the prisons. In addition, the activist tactics of the civil rights movement, under the right circumstances, could be useful.

On the matter of tactics, Indian leaders had a different style. Tribal council members, then, as now, tended to be conservative— after all, a prime tribal objective was to preserve age-old practices— and they knew all too well the dangers of dealing with the majority society; some tribal leaders, especially the older ones, wanted nothing to do with activist strategies. Perhaps the most common response was to employ peaceful activism situationally, and over the years Indian people have made many a point by marches, sit-ins, and other demonstrations. A few groups, most notably the urban-dominated American Indian Movement in its brief but historic heyday, adopted the kind of militant, and potentially deadly, tactics used by the Black Panthers and Student Nonviolent Coordinating Committee. But one thing is sure, however one adds it up, the ends and means of the civil rights struggle became shaping forces in Indian America, just as they did in America as a whole.

AT 40,000 members, the Lumbee Tribe of North Carolina is one of the country's largest. The Lumbee live in Robeson County, in and around the town of Pembroke. The fast and full Lumbee River runs through the middle of Lumbee territory, and that wet country produces thick woods and numerous swamps, some of them large and open enough to be called lakes. This mostly impenetrable terrain left the Lumbee so isolated that eighteenth-

and nineteenth-century Indian policy passed them by. This saved the Lumbee, unlike other southeastern tribes, from being moved West, but it also left them with no treaty—and no federally protected land base, tribal jurisdiction, or federal services.

North Carolina had jurisdiction over the Lumbee but offered the Natives few benefits. The state constitution designated them "persons of color," denying them voting rights. In the segregated South, Robeson County—triracial, with roughly equal numbers of whites, blacks, and Indians—had separate schools and other facilities for each. Through it all the Lumbee tenaciously clung to their land, owned privately by tribal members. That was the situation in 1958, when the Lumbee produced one of the first successful acts of resistance by Indian people in modern times.

The local Ku Klux Klan was not amused when a Lumbee woman moved into a white neighborhood and began dating a white man. It contacted the Klan's Grand Wizard, James "Catfish" Cole, who agreed to come to Robeson County for a KKK rally and speak on the topic "Why I Am for Segregation." The event would be held in a farm field on a Saturday evening in January. In a prelude, Klan members burned crosses in the front yards of two Indian families.

When Grand Wizard Cole arrived at dusk, he found fewer Klan members than advertised—no more than a hundred. Worse yet from his standpoint, Lumbee and Indians from as far away as Sioux country had shown up in droves—hundreds, probably more than a thousand. Some Klansmen wore their white robes and pointed caps; many packed pistols or shotguns, but so did many of the Indians. A few headlights shone from cars ringing the field, but otherwise the only light came from a single generator-fed light bulb, hung above the speaker's platform in the middle of the meadow. Cole's guards surrounded the platform.

Indians, scuffling with the Grand Wizard's protectors, had pressed in on the speaking area. The Indians were yelling, "Where's Cole?" The local sheriff told Cole, "I can't control this crowd with the few men I've got. I'm not telling you not to hold the meeting, but you see how it is. You've leased the land and have a right to be here. But you see how it is." Cole paused, then, with trepidation, began to walk through the freezing night air toward the makeshift platform.

A shot from an Indian rifle rang out, shattering the light bulb, and the field erupted into pandemonium. The dark of the night was broken only by the flashbulbs of photographers from the Associated Press, United Press, local papers, and *Life* magazine. Shots and screams split the night air, coupled with the hissing from punctured Klan auto tires. Apparently Cole scampered into a nearby swamp to take cover.

No one was killed or seriously hurt. A Robeson County judge sentenced Cole to 18–24 months, and a local Klan member to 6–12 months, for inciting a riot. No Indians were charged. *Life* magazine gave the nation a glimpse into the Indian cause—and encouragement to Indian people—by running a story with a photograph of Simeon Oxendine, a Lumbee Indian and World War II veteran, in celebration at the end of the melee, wrapped in a Ku Klux Klan flag.

The victory lifted the Lumbee, giving them one of the high points in tribal history. One scholar tells of his first Lumbee interview, in 1966. The tribal member carried the eight-year-old *Life* magazine photograph in her wallet. In 2002, Kelvin Sampson, head coach of the University of Oklahoma basketball team, became the first American Indian to take a team to the Final Four of the NCAA tournament. Sampson proudly recalled that his father, a coach of the local Indian school, had been one of the Lumbee in that field in Robeson County 44 years earlier.

INDIAN ACTIVISM gradually increased during the 1960s. Mohawk boycotted public schools because New York refused them the right to vote in school board elections. Cherokee protested against Oklahoma's enforcement of its hunting laws. Indians in the Northwest and Upper Great Lakes asserted treaty rights by staging "fish-ins." Navajo and Hopi demonstrated against coal mining and power plants. Alaska Natives picketed oil and gas development on their traditional lands. Native Hawaiians sat in against hotel construction that threatened to block access to beaches. There were many others. But not until November 20, 1969, on San Francisco Bay's Alcatraz Island, did Native concerns truly penetrate the national consciousness.

The San Francisco Bay Area had become home to one of the largest urban Indian populations. Relocation, the federal assimilation program designed to move reservation Indians to the cities, had targeted the area, and the BIA now ran relocation offices in San Francisco, Oakland, and San Jose. Local Indian centers became social magnets, bringing together Native Americans from different tribes and creating communities where, in the words of a transplanted Oklahoma Indian, "Native people often came to sip coffee, make plans and build indestructible dreams." The California colleges—UC–Berkeley, San Francisco State, and UC–Santa Cruz—all had Indian study programs, adding opportunities for Native faculty and students. Indian people fed off the Bay Area's electric atmosphere, where civil rights sentiments ran strong, the Free Speech Movement flourished, and anti–Vietnam War activism was at its peak. And San Francisco in the 1960s was . . . well, San Francisco in the 1960s.

The government shut down Alcatraz's prison facility in 1963. A year later, a group of Indians, mostly Sioux, boated out to the island and claimed the land—to be used for an Indian university— under the authority of the 1868 Treaty of Fort Laramie with the Sioux and other tribes. News coverage of this modest few hours of occupation soon faded, but the idea of obtaining Alcatraz had been planted in the Indian mind. In 1969 the matter came to a head as the San Francisco Board of Supervisors took up planning for the island's future. Indians had their own plans, crafted on campuses because of strong student interest. In October, Natives made a second takeover attempt, again short-lived. But the determination had grown deep, wide, and fierce.

Thus, on November 20, 1969, some eighty Indians, young and old alike, set out in broad daylight aboard a ragtag collection of vessels for the island of Alcatraz. A genial caretaker welcomed them and showed them around. Then, having named their organization Indians of All Tribes, they claimed the land. Large signs promptly went up. YOU ARE NOW ON INDIAN LAND; PEACE AND FREEDOM. WEL-

COME. HOME OF THE FREE INDIAN LAND; WARNING. KEEP OFF INDIAN
PROPERTY.

Richard Oakes, a Mohawk, good with words and movie star
handsome, became the Alcatraz spokesman for Indians of All
Tribes. Adam Nordwall, Red Lake Chippewa and a small busi-
nessman in San Francisco, mostly stayed on the mainland to
organize a myriad of support tasks: providing food and supplies,
finding boats, complementing Oakes in the media dealings, and
processing the steady stream of donations. The occupiers put
together an Alcatraz Proclamation, at once tongue in cheek and
dead serious. It vested title in Native Americans and offered to
make payment of $24, a precedent set on "a similar island about
300 years ago." It also declared Alcatraz suitable for a reservation,
for the island had "no fresh running water," "no oil or mineral
rights" but is "rocky and unproductive" and "the population has
always been held as prisoners." Indians of All Tribes proclaimed
that the island would be home to five centers of Indian and ecological studies. Oakes, in particular, was able to put forth both the
mood, as well as the agenda, of Alcatraz:

> Alcatraz was symbolic to a lot of people, and it meant some-
> thing real to a lot of people. There are many old prophecies that
> speak of the younger people rising up and finding a way for the
> People to live. The Hopi, the spiritual leaders of the Indian peo-
> ple, have a prophecy that is at least 1,200 years old. It says that
> the People would be pushed off their land from the East to the
> West, and when they reached the Westernmost tip of America,
> they would begin to take back the land that was stolen from
> them. . . .
> Alcatraz was a place where thousands of people had been
> imprisoned, some of them Indians. We sensed the spirits of the
> prisoners. At times it was spooky, but mostly the spirit of mercy
> was in the air. The spirits were free. They mingled with the spir-
> its of the Indians that came on the island and hoped for a better
> future.

Federal officials reacted cautiously during the nineteen-month
occupation. The media response had been immediate and over-

whelmingly positive: Nordwall and others gave chosen reporters confidential briefings in advance, and glowing stories hit the newsstands and television screens in a matter of hours. At first the Coast Guard set up a blockade, mostly unsuccessful, to interdict supply boats but lifted it three days later. The government's decision not to evict the occupants forcibly proved a wise course. The Indians had public sentiment on their side and could do little harm on their rocky outpost. Support for a conservative federal approach grew even stronger six months into the Alcatraz occupation with the horrifying incident at Kent State University in Ohio, where demonstrating students were shot and killed. Off and on, various federal negotiators met with representatives of Indians of All Tribes, but made no headway.

The Indians settled in with an infectious idealism. Thanksgiving Day on Alcatraz, just seven days into the occupation, became a celebration of all celebrations. Rathskeller's Restaurant, on Ghirardelli Square, donated untold numbers of turkeys and trimmings. The color of traditional Native dancing and the singing and drumming of the old songs filled up eyes, ears, and souls. Visitors, Indian and non-Indian alike, swarmed in for the festivities. Spectator boats circled the island, with well-wishers hailing as unique a holiday as they ever would witness.

Many more visitors came through in the months to come. There were celebrities: Buffy Sainte-Marie, Anthony Quinn, Jane Fonda, Candice Bergen, Jonathan Winters, and Merv Griffin, who produced a special on Alcatraz for national television. Native American leaders, present and future, included Vine Deloria and Hank Adams; Wilma Mankiller, later to become principal chief of the Cherokee Nation; Browning Pipestem, Otoe tribal member and a leading Oklahoma lawyer; and John Echohawk, who would soon lead the Native American Rights Fund. Clothes, food, and supplies flowed in from scout troops, churches, and labor unions. Classes came out from Bay Area elementary and secondary schools, as well as colleges and universities.

Yet within two months the occupation began to sour. The settlement was rife with alcohol and marijuana. Too many of the residents were thugs or misfits. Fights and vandalism became commonplace. Unsanitary conditions abounded. The occupiers had no means to deal with illnesses such as heart attacks or with serious accidents; Richard Oakes's little daughter, Yvonne, fell three stories down a stairwell and eventually died.

The residents of Alcatraz had lost their ability to govern, to maintain a civilized society. With so many different tribes represented, and with some Indian people from traditional reservation upbringings and others just discovering their Indianness, the residents of Alcatraz lacked a common bond. Further, it became clear that many people on the island had come not to attain the "freedom" that the Alcatraz Proclamation envisioned but simply to escape any form of authority. The seven-member council fell into disfavor. The "security force," lightheartedly named the Bureau of Caucasian Affairs in the early days, took to administering beatings. Squabbles over money and supplies mushroomed. Oakes, rightly or wrongly the target of much animosity, was voted off the island. Morale suffered from the growing realization that Indians were not going to obtain title to the land. Government attorneys knew that neither Indians of All Tribes nor any other Native group had a legal claim to Alcatraz, whether under the 1868 Fort Laramie Treaty or any other law; the government might hold its fire, but it would not relinquish the island. Accentuating the social ills and evanescence of mission was the bleak reality that Alcatraz stood in San Francisco, not San Diego, Bay; winter on the Rock was miserably cold, foggy, and windy.

People began moving off, going back to work, school, or the city streets. In the spring of 1970 federal negotiators made a serious offer: Title to the island would remain in the United States, but Alcatraz would be made a well-funded federal park, dedicated mostly to Indian culture and designed largely by an Indian committee. The Indians roundly rejected the proposal. The idea sounded like a theme park, and in any event, the fractious group had lost the ability to reach consensus on anything so controversial as a final agreement with the government. The Alcatraz occupation gradually petered out. In June 1971, more than a year and a half after the celebrated landing, federal agents removed the last fifteen occupiers—six men, four women, and five children—who agreed to leave peacefully.

Of the two faces of the Alcatraz occupation, the initial halcyon time, rather than the dreary aftermath, has proved to be the enduring image. America was deeply moved by the bold, assertive announcement that these peoples, so long consigned to the past tense, had a modern life and relevance. The event changed the lives of uncountable Indian people. Richard Oakes recalled: "There was one old man who came on the island. He must have been eighty or ninety years old. When he stepped up onto the dock, he was overjoyed. He stood there for a minute and then said, 'At last, I am free.' " Frances Wise, living in Texas at the time, exemplified the impact far beyond San Francisco Bay: "It affected how I think of myself. If someone asks me who I am, I say, well, I have a name, but Waco/Caddo—that's who I *am*. I have a good feeling about who I am now." In her autobiography, looking back more than twenty years, Principal Chief Wilma Mankiller reflected the feelings of a great many Indian people:

> Although Alcatraz ultimately would not remain a sovereign Indian nation, the incredible publicity generated by the occupation served all of us well by dramatizing the injustices that the modern Native Americans have endured at the hands of white America. The Alcatraz experience nurtured a sense among us that anything was possible—even, perhaps, justice for native people.
>
> . . . The occupation of Alcatraz excited me like nothing ever had before. It helped to center me and caused me to focus on my own rich and valuable Cherokee heritage.

ANOTHER DEVELOPMENT, with origins preceding Alcatraz, would carry its spirit forward. In 1968, Dennis Banks, Clyde Bellecourt, and other Chippewa, living in the Twin Cities at the time, created the American Indian Movement. AIM began as a counterforce to the ills of relocation, the despair, disorientation, drunkenness, and violence that plagued the gritty Indian ghetto of Minneapolis. AIM's early social work focused on health care,

housing, and education, including a survival school, but its innovative "street patrol" soon moved onto more dangerous ground.
Banks and Bellecourt, both of whom had done prison time, knew
that Minnesota's jails held a disturbingly high number of Indian
inmates, many more than the state's 1 percent Indian population
suggested. Almost all the convictions involved alcohol-related
conduct. To head off trouble, AIM sent out its members, dressed
in red jackets and equipped with two-way radios, tape recorders,
and cameras, to scout the Indian bars. They took intoxicated Indians home. Sometimes they picked up police radio calls and sped
to the scene so they could advise detainees of their rights and
monitor arrests for police abuses. The street patrol made the
police edgy, but Indian arrests dropped dramatically.

AIM quickly caught the imagination of Indian people, especially in the cities, and within two years gained a national following. Two key figures joined in 1970. John Trudell, a Santee Sioux
with the build and tenacity of a lightweight boxer, had helped give
life to the Alcatraz occupation by broadcasting his daily *Radio Free
Alcatraz* radio show to an estimated 100,000 listeners from stations
in Berkeley, Los Angeles, and New York. Trudell brought to AIM
valuable organizing, public relations, and speaking skills.

The other new leader, Russell Means, became AIM's most identifiable figure. Oglala from Pine Ridge, he was born on the Yankton Sioux Reservation in 1940 but grew up in Vallejo and other Bay
Area towns. He lived on the rough side of society and experienced
more than his share of alcohol, drugs, and minor crimes. Yet
Means never lost touch with Sioux country, returning in the
summers and being educated in traditional ways by his grandfather. After stints in various colleges and jobs, including construction, data processing, and dance instruction, he moved to
Cleveland, where he worked for an Office of Economic Opportunity program and became active in the Cleveland American
Indian Center. In early 1970, Dennis Banks called Means and
urged him to join Banks and Clyde Bellecourt at an AIM demonstration in Detroit. Means and AIM made an instant match. The
tall, strikingly handsome Means, wearing Lakota-style braids, a
ribbon shirt, and a bone choker and firing off urgent, combative

messages, projected a captivating—and, to some, fearsome—presence.

AIM instigated numerous protest actions. On July 4, 1971, Indians staged a "countercelebration" at Mount Rushmore. On Thanksgiving, Means and Trudell led a demonstration at Plymouth Rock that included painting the rock red. AIM orchestrated short-lived takeovers of Fort Snelling in Minneapolis and the Fort Sill Indian School in Oklahoma. The occupation of an abandoned Coast Guard base by the local AIM chapter in Milwaukee, however, took hold: The Indians used the property for a community school and programs for the elderly and alcoholism treatment.

In 1972 wrath against the evils of white society intensified after a rash of murders. A southern Arizona police officer shot and killed a Papago (now Tohono O'odham) man, Philip Celay. The coroner ruled it justifiable homicide, but a Tucson paper called it "kitchen justice at its worst." In Gordon, Nebraska, a border town south of the Pine Ridge reservation, two white men beat Raymond Yellow Thunder to death. AIM led a caravan of hundreds of Indians to Gordon and participated in negotiations with local, state, and federal officials. This time the protests made headway: Raymond Yellow Thunder's killers were indicted, and the town agreed to establish a human rights commission. Then Indians received a devastating blow with news of the death of Richard Oakes, the hero of Alcatraz. The pattern was all too familiar: Oakes and a white YMCA caretaker named Michael Morgan had an argument; Morgan, who had fired a shot over Oakes's head in an earlier confrontation, claimed the Indian threatened him with a knife (though none was ever found) and then shot Oakes dead; Morgan, claiming self-defense, went free. The word spread, and Indian country was seething.

That summer, at the Rosebud Sioux Sun Dance, Robert Burnette of Rosebud, Vernon Bellecourt of AIM, and others discussed a march on Washington, an Indian version of the 1963 civil rights march. Then a group of about 50 Indian leaders, mostly from activist groups, including AIM and the National Indian Youth Council, met in Denver on September 30, 1972, to lay plans for what they called the Trail of Broken Treaties. Caravans would

The Restless Indian *by Tony Begay, Navajo (1970). Courtesy of Museum of Northern Arizona.*

come in from all parts of the country. They would arrive in Washington during the last week of October, just before the 1972 presidential election, and conduct peaceful demonstrations and Indian spiritual ceremonies. The crusade would be drug- and alcohol-free. "The Caravan must be," Robert Burnette exhorted, "our finest hour."

Three caravans pushed off in early October from Seattle, San

Francisco, and Los Angeles. Each was to wend a zigzag way through reservations, picking up additional troops, and the three would converge in Minneapolis for a strategy session, then continue on to Washington together. The caravans had a comely wing-and-a-prayer quality to them. Russell Means, leader of the Seattle group, started out with just three cars plus a green van sporting large plywood sheets, hung on each side of the van and painted in red letters: TRAIL OF BROKEN TREATIES, UNITED STATES. Their numbers steadily grew, and so, as Means recalled, did problems with their rickety vehicles: "We used walkie-talkies to stay in touch with several Indian auto mechanics who brought up the rear. Whenever a car broke down—which was constantly—we got it off the road and found rides for its passengers while the mechanics fixed it. We traveled slowly and stayed together." They slept on church, schoolhouse, and gymnasium floors.

The Minneapolis meeting produced an important document. The participants broke into work groups, which came up with suggestions on different issues that Indian people confronted. Hank Adams, accompanied only by his own outright genius, then closeted himself in a motel room and drafted a comprehensive proposal since called the Twenty Points.

Adams's central premise, gleaned from a thoroughgoing understanding of both Indian country and the federal apparatus, held that the future for tribes lay not with reform of the BIA but in the sovereignty and land bases of Indian tribes. The Twenty Points therefore emphasized a return to bilateral treaty relations, restoration of 100 million acres of land, full tribal control of the reservations, religious and cultural freedom, and abolition of the BIA. Like all visionary proposals, the document, while roundly accepted by the Indian people in attendance, went farther than the present system could accommodate. But it was a serious declaration and deserved to be treated as such; the Twenty Points put forth, in brave and vivid terms, the earnest dreams of modern Indian country.

The caravan, now composed of several hundred Indians, left Minneapolis and, bright with prospect, neared Washington. To be sure, AIM dominated the Trail of Broken Treaties, and the group's militant tactics arched many eyebrows—a public reaction that the BIA, which knew the caravan was coming, helped foster. Nonetheless, the caravan had mostly lived up to its high, "finest hour" standards, and press coverage of the colorful entourage had been good. The group had strong spokesmen and a provocative manifesto in the Twenty Points. The Trail of Broken Treaties had not engaged the public to the extent Alcatraz had, but a fair comparison seemed in order.

Once the procession reached the nation's capital early in the morning of November 3, however, everything fell apart. Misunderstandings piled up on one another. The advance work had been sloppy, and hundreds of caravaners had no place to stay. A church offered its basement, but it was too small—and infested with rats. An armory had few toilets and no showers. Exasperated, the marchers went to the auditorium at the BIA building to figure out what to do. BIA officials refused to help; Harrison Loesch, the assistant interior secretary with authority over the bureau, had sent out directions back in October not to provide "any assistance or funding, either directly or indirectly," to trail participants. Such rigid instructions hamstrung those employees who wanted to make sensible accommodations. At 5:00 P.M., departmental officials ordered the Indians to leave the auditorium, but this was not a group in the mood to follow orders.

Some 400 Indians proceeded to take over the building, chaining or barricading all the entrances with desks and chairs. Communication between the occupiers and federal officials (who were just days away from a presidential election) ranged from nonexistent to horrible. Deadlines to evacuate, set by court order and administrative fiat, came and went. Police surrounded the building.

Inside, the occupiers, unleashing all their frustration and rage, tore the place apart. They destroyed furniture, broke windows, graffitied walls, and even smashed classic Indian pottery and slashed Native paintings. They raided the agency's file cabinets, burned or otherwise destroyed files, and smuggled an estimated twelve tons of papers out of the building to points never disclosed. Those files may somehow have represented all the evils of the federal government over many generations, but they also held information essential to the lives of Indian people: records of property ownership, trust accounts, probates of estates, water rights, all the many dealings that the BIA has with Indian people.

Hank Adams had not been in the building during the rampage. Now the occupiers chose him to lead a negotiating team. Clenched-jawed federal negotiators offered little. In the end they did agree to recommend that there be no prosecutions for the occupation, to provide some financial assistance so that trail participants could return home, and to study the Twenty Points and respond formally to them. With that, the weary and hungry occupiers began filing out of the Washington office of the Bureau of Indian Affairs. Adams, anguished at this failed attempt to push an aggressive policy agenda in a nonviolent manner, made his way back to the Pacific Northwest. Indian people had attained no victory, not even a scent of it.

THE TRAIL of Broken Treaties had ended in a confused morass, but the American Indian Movement had no intentions of relenting. Russell Means, Dennis Banks, and the rest of the AIM leadership, now highly disciplined and not responsible for the botched housing arrangements in Washington, grew even more resolute. While AIM received most of its Indian support from the cities and had little backing on the tribal councils, its constituency on the reservations was growing. In January 1973, two months after the BIA takeover in Washington, Indian activism reignited. A white man had knifed to death a Sioux, Wesley Bad Heart Bull, outside a bar in Buffalo Gap, a dirt-road South Dakota ranch town just west of the Pine Ridge reservation. Prosecutors charged the defendant with second-degree manslaughter, not murder, and released him on $500 bail. Although Bad Heart Bull had a long record and was apparently the aggressor, charges of racism rang out, and Dennis Banks led a 200-person caravan to Custer, the county seat. The county attorney declined to revise the charges, and a riot broke out. Police responded with nightsticks and tear gas. The Chamber of Commerce offices went up in flames.

The Bad Heart Bull incident in some ways represented a reprise of the murder of Raymond Yellow Thunder a year earlier (though the previous incident was much more clearly racially motivated), but the temperature in 1973 burned hotter. AIM's anger level had skyrocketed. Law enforcement agencies, including the FBI, had many more eyes trained on AIM. And the Pine Ridge Sioux reservation roiled with unrest over wrongs present and past. The tension soon built into the apex moment of Indian militant activism.

In 1972 the Oglala Sioux elected Dick Wilson as tribal chairman in a closely contested race with Gerald One Feather. The stocky, burr-cut Wilson, whose support came mainly from the town of Pine Ridge, immediately drew criticism from traditionals in the outlying areas and from Russell Means, who had just moved from the Twin Cities back to Pine Ridge. Wilson doled out jobs to friends and family, provocatively declaring that "there's nothing in tribal law against nepotism." The Sioux had just won a large court award for the taking of the Black Hills; the traditional tribal members were determined to refuse the payment and hold out for a return of the land, but Wilson favored accepting the money. He also came down on the opposite side from the traditionals on another land issue. During World War II the government had taken over a 133,000-acre parcel in the Badlands region of the reservation for a gunnery range. Now the government wanted permanent title to the land, which had valuable uranium deposits, and Wilson was negotiating with federal officials, not for return of the land but for a cash payment.

The complaints against Wilson went beyond hiring practices and his stands on policy issues. Wilson assembled a tribal security force, widely called goons, to keep law and order. This translated into close and tough surveillance—and, apparently, beatings—of Wilson's political opponents, especially AIM supporters and suspected supporters. In February 1973 a tribal civil rights group, with many AIM sympathizers, initiated an effort to impeach Wilson, a move he narrowly survived at a proceeding in front of the tribal council.

Two hundred Sioux or more, many of them traditionals, believing Wilson and the BIA had fixed the impeachment proceeding, gathered at the Calico Community Hall six miles north of the village of Pine Ridge. By this time the reservation was aswarm with military and law enforcement personnel—FBI agents, 75 members of the elite Special Operations group, state police, BIA police, and Wilson's "goons"—determined to protect the federal buildings in Pine Ridge from an expected AIM takeover attempt. Government soldiers mounted machine guns on the roof of the BIA building. Many of the troops staked out the Calico meeting. Inside the packed hall, people deliberated late into the night. What to do next? Ellen Moves Camp urged that AIM be called in: "We decided that we did need the American Indian Movement in here because our men were scared, they hung to the back. It was mostly the women that went forward and spoke out." The group sent out word to Means and Banks.

Three days later the meeting resumed at Calico, with Means and Banks now in attendance. Indian people once again filled the community hall. The talk went on. Finally, holy man Frank Fools Crow spoke his mind: "Go ahead and do it, go to Wounded Knee. You can't get in the BIA office and the tribal office, so take your brothers from the American Indian Movement and go to Wounded Knee and make your stand there." Everyone there knew this was right. Every Sioux knew the horror visited upon the Lakota there in 1890. The nation knew too: Dee Brown's *Bury My Heart at Wounded Knee*, published three years before, had become a best seller. A caravan of 54 vehicles headed out into the winter night, driving south straight through Pine Ridge—to the surprise of the expectant military gathering, anticipating a confrontation there. The long line of vehicles proceeded east on U.S. 18, then turned left toward deep history, toward Wounded Knee.

The occupiers took control of the little flatlands hamlet, occupying the Sacred Heart Catholic Church, several houses, and the trading post, which they promptly relieved of its considerable stock of hunting rifles, shotguns, and pistols. Within hours, opposing forces set up roadblocks around the village. The combined federal-state-tribal contingent brought in a frightful amount of firepower: Its equipment included 17 armored personnel carriers, .50-caliber machine guns, M-16 rifles with 133,000 rounds of ammunition, M-79 tear gas grenade launchers, and infrared lights. Intermittently, Phantom jets flew overhead. The Indians, mostly

Bury My Heart at Wounded Knee, *styled as "an Indian history" of nineteenth-century tragedies, helped raise the consciousness of the general population toward Indian concerns. On the Pine Ridge reservation, where history blankets everyday life, the Oglala Sioux needed no reminding of the 1890 massacre. Photo courtesy of Ray Ramirez, Native American Rights Fund.*

Sioux, had a couple of automatic rifles, the weapons from the trading post, a scattering of rifles, pistols, and knives, and the makings of Molotov cocktails. The two armies—the modern, fully equipped corps on the outside, the scruffy guerrillas on the inside—would have made a comic scene except that everyone knew the situation was hair-trigger serious.

The standoff lasted 71 days. The Sioux issued a series of demands, including Senate Foreign Relations Committee hearings on Indian treaties (which Chairman William Fulbright suggested he might hold). James Abourezk and George McGovern, the United States senators from South Dakota, came out to inspect the site. Negotiations continued on a regular basis with White House and high Department of the Interior officials. President Richard Nixon spent time on the matter. Across the country and in Europe as well, the media gave the bristling confrontation extensive coverage—often front page, cover story, and top of the broadcast—that far outstripped Alcatraz or the Washington debacle.

The wonder is that the confrontation did not produce more casualties. On several days the government forces fired thousands of rounds into the stronghold. The Indians, with less capability, nonetheless gave nearly as much. Buddy Lamont, Lakota, and Frank Clearwater, Apache, died. Lloyd Grimm, a marshal, took a gunshot in the chest but survived. Others received less serious injuries.

The Indians gained one of their goals: to raise public consciousness. Opponents grudgingly acknowledged AIM's work; an *Arizona Republic* editorial, for example, darkly opined. "As Wounded Knee unfolds in sharper detail, the whole episode is simply too well-organized, too well financed, too slick to have been the impromptu work of AIM. If and when the federal government gets its courage back, it might look into bigger questions of who is really behind the Wounded Knee incident." A Harris poll reported that 93 percent of all Americans had heard of the takeover; 51 percent sympathized with the Indians, 21 percent with the government. To be sure, many people felt jaded or revulsed toward AIM, but there was admiration too. The involvement of Frank Fools Crow and other traditionalists, along with ordinary Lakota people, lent gravity to the problems of reservation Indians.

For its part, the government held the cards and, despite inevitable spates of confusion, played them with savvy. The United States had time on its side. While Indians sometimes broke the perimeter and smuggled in supplies on close-call runs, the government choked off most attempts to bring in food and munitions. It had plans in place to storm the encampment but kept them, and the attendant violence, in reserve. At the same time, the United States had a sword poised above the occupiers' heads, and the Indians knew it. Federal officials negotiated and waited, negotiated and waited some more. Then, with Hank Adams brought in to negotiate on behalf of the Indians for whatever might be salvaged, the two sides reached a settlement. On May 8, 1973, federal personnel withdrew from their bunkers, and the Indians left the Wounded Knee village.

The federal government controlled the aftermath. It had promised to send White House representatives to the reservation to dis-

cuss the 1868 treaty, the Twenty Points, the grievances against
Dick Wilson, and other issues. It did so, but perfunctorily. Matters
of sovereignty and treaties, the White House representatives
patiently—and evasively—explained, were for the Congress, not
them.

The Department of Justice then proceeded to break AIM's back.
From the beginning federal negotiators had made it clear that,
unlike the BIA building takeover, amnesty was off the table. In an
all-out campaign, prosecutors began filing charges even before the
occupation ended and eventually arrested hundreds of AIM members. They filed multiple counts in each case, brought multiple
cases against many defendants, and went for high bail.

AIM put together a formidable defense to the prosecutions.
The Wounded Knee Legal Defense/Offense Committee, which
received loads of contributions but was chronically short of funds
to fight the wave of prosecutions, coordinated and provided much
of the legal representation. The National Lawyers Guild recruited
attorneys. William Kunstler, the activist lawyer who had represented the Chicago Seven, participated. Some of the trials, notably
the Means-Banks prosecution in St. Paul, became media circuses.
The defendants regularly charged government misconduct,
including FBI perjury, improper surveillance, and threatening
witnesses (the Means and Banks St. Paul charges were dismissed
on the basis of misconduct). Judges threw out some charges,
juries found for the defendants in others, and the government
never brought some to trial. In the end, the government's overall
conviction rate was less than 10 percent.

Still, the government won the war against AIM, and though
waged in stately federal courtrooms, war it was. One of the federal
prosecutors left no doubt about the impact, win or lose, of the
wave of criminal trials: "I think to some extent the prosecutions
accomplished as much by getting dismissed or an acquittal as they
would have had there been a conviction. Because I think Russell
Means and Dennis Banks realized even if you get off, sitting nine
months in a courtroom isn't what they want to do, and that's what
potentially would happen if they did this again." There were other
factors. AIM had its own internal dissension and disloyalty (AIM

member Carter Camp shot Clyde Bellecourt, and AIM's director
of security, Douglas Durham, turned out to be an FBI informant).
By the mid-1970s the era of violent resistance had faded in the face
of public weariness and changing times. Yet the prosecution campaign remained the dominant force that led Rex Weyler to con-
clude that "virtually every AIM leader in the country would be
either in jail, dead, or driven underground within the two years
following the occupation of Wounded Knee."

FOR A TIME the AIM warriors became the face of Indian
America. Russell Means, in particular, cut such an imposing figure, erect and elegant in Sioux regalia, with the look of the eagle
in his eye, as he belted out a riveting speech about modern America's moral and legal duties to honor treaties with Indian tribes.
And look what his face replaced: a faded tintype of a nineteenth-
century chief, the despondent brave with his spear pointed down
at *The End of the Trail*, and the drunken Indian. For many Americans, until Means there was no image at all.

Yet the setting was awkward. While sincere in their traditionalism, the AIM leaders lived most of their lives in the cities, not in
Indian country. In a movement directed toward legal recognition
of tribal governments, they were not elected tribal officials and,
though Means nearly unseated Dick Wilson in 1974, rarely would
be. Then there was the matter of hard results. Indian activism
brought the treaties and tribal sovereignty into public view for the
first time in the century, but to what end? How exactly would
the high-visibility demonstrations and takeovers, and the many
quieter ones, make the treaties enforceable?

Vine Deloria, who never failed to acknowledge AIM's contributions, who always gave Russell Means his due, knew that it would
take more than AIM. He and many others looked toward the
Pacific Northwest, where tribal people were trying to combine
activism and court enforcement. "We had to obtain legal protection for the treaties and the sovereignty," Deloria emphasized.
"That's why the treaty fishing cases were so important. That was
the way to make the breakthrough."

7.

The Salmon People

The harvesting of wildlife, and the meals, trading, and ceremonies that follow, have always been at the core of Indian life. By the 1950s and 1960s the reduction of tribal lands, the BIA's pressure to abandon traditional practices, and rising numbers of non-Indian hunters and fishers had all cramped age-old tribal ways. Enforcement of state wildlife laws had become increasingly zealous, forcing Indians underground. Yet tribal practices never died out. As Sue Masten, tribal chair of the Yurok Tribe on the Northern California coast and president of the National Congress of American Indians at the turn of the twenty-first century, announced: "We are salmon people. We couldn't let anyone take that from us." Fishing and hunting, like the land, like the religions and the languages, help define the health and future promise of Native societies.

Indian treaty rights arouse opposition because state wildlife laws—license fees, seasons, bag limits, and other restrictions—do not apply to treaty fishers or hunters. Instead, the tribes' own laws control. Resistance stems from many sources, including generalized state's rights sentiments, competition with non-Indian commercial and sports interests, administrative turf guarding, and outright racism. The Supreme Court has knocked down one well-worn homily: that states "own" wildlife. Rather than ownership, wildlife management is analyzed in terms of which government has jurisdiction—that is, regulatory authority. Congress has often deferred to state wildlife regulations, but Congress, whose statutes and treaties are the supreme law of the land and thus override state law, can trump state wildlife laws for various purposes, such as protection of endangered species and recognition of Indian treaty rights.

The most serious argument for state regulation of Indian fishing and hunting is conservation. For more than a century, but especially after World War II, many animal species have declined, some to extinction. Generally, state fish and game agencies have had responsibility for conservation. The professional employees, mostly biologists, rightly view this as a high calling, a sacred duty.

At the same time, when Indians began to assert their rights aggressively in the 1960s, the politics of state legislatures and their fish and game agencies were seldom so idealistic. They looked to their natural constituencies, the sports and commercial users who paid the license fees that supported the agencies. The Indians, seen as outsiders, made easy scapegoats. When the numbers of salmon or lake trout or elk declined, the user groups and the states pointed their fingers at the tribes. State wardens then cracked down on Indian fishing or hunting in the name of conservation. Later, when these issues went to court, judges found that Indians had not caused the species declines or wasted fish or game. Invariably, large-scale harvests by non-Indians and habitat degradation resulting from development caused the shortages.

Regardless of fault, treaty fishing and hunting became an enormously emotional issue. Tribal people believed to their depths that their ancestors had negotiated with the United States of America and obtained federal protection of their cherished activities and that those promises should be honored. To many in the general public, however, non-Indian commercial and sports fishing were important to the economy and the American way of life. Conservation was obviously a good thing, and people believed that the states were responsible for it.

Further, Indian treaty rights raised fundamental moral issues: Why should one racial group have special privileges? Americans, after all, had fought a war of independence in good part to free themselves of prerogatives based on heredity and to establish a new form of egalitarianism. The skepticism over special rights is compounded when American society, which prides itself on modernism, is presented with special rights lodged in antiquity.

These emotions flashed more over fishing than hunting because fishers find themselves in closer proximity with one another, because fishing is more often done in public view, and because fish are much more commercially valuable than wild game; salmon is a staple in grocery stores, but venison is not. In turn, the states tended to quarrel relatively little over on-reservation fishing. The off-reservation treaty fishing generated far and away the greater heat. Indians were beyond their own lands, out in the larger society—plainly, so it seemed to state officials, under state authority.

Most tribal powers are territorially based within reservations, but Indians can sometimes claim off-reservation rights. A tribe may in a treaty relinquish ownership to most of its aboriginal land (while retaining the reservation) but explicitly reserve in the treaty some rights—usually for fishing, hunting, and gathering— in the area where the tribe surrendered landownership. The Nez Perce of Idaho had insisted upon such off-reservation rights in its 1855 treaty, which reserved to the tribe, in addition to the right to fish on the reservation, "the right of taking fish at all usual and accustomed places in common with citizens of the Territory." The Nez Perce treaty was one of the Isaac Stevens treaties that guaranteed off-reservation rights in much of the Pacific Northwest. In the Great Lakes area large Chippewa treaty reservations were broken up, but with the understanding that the fishing rights would continue on the ceded land and lakes.

While off-reservation treaty rights battles have arisen in the northern Rockies, the Southwest, and the Southeast, the most prominent conflicts have taken place in the Great Lakes area and the Pacific Northwest. Chippewa tribes claimed treaty rights over vast reaches of Lakes Huron, Michigan, and Superior; the Chippewa and other tribes also asserted rights in inland Wisconsin and Minnesota lakes. In epic events, tribes from Northern California up through Oregon and Washington and inland to Idaho brought litigation that directly challenged the basic economic, social, and legal structures and attitudes that northwesterners had adopted for one of the region's icons, the Pacific salmon. Perhaps more than any other issue, fishing rights disputes epitomize the tribes' struggle to revive traditional cultures, treaty rights, and sovereignty.

THE CHIPPEWA (also Anishinabe or Ojibwa), with many bands, were one of the largest and most powerful tribes in aboriginal times. They lived around the Great Lakes, but their domain also took in the pine forests of Michigan, Wisconsin, and Minnesota and reached as far west as parts of North Dakota and Montana. The people depended on fishing, hunting, and ricing. Lakes Superior, Huron, and Michigan held prodigious numbers of lake trout, sturgeon, and whitefish, which the Chippewa harvested with nets, weirs, and spears.

With the end of the War of 1812 and completion of the Erie Canal in 1825, the nation expanded toward what was then the Northwest. Needing land for settlement and new states, the United States negotiated many treaties with Chippewa bands. The initial treaties, which set aside expansive reservations, proved inadequate from the Americans' standpoint as settlers arrived in greater numbers. Beginning in the 1850s, the United States renegotiated the treaties, with the federal side holding much more power than a generation earlier, when the original treaties were signed. The terms varied, and some of the documents were silent, but the historical record shows that the Chippewa understood that relinquishing most of their remaining lands would not mean giving up their fishing and hunting rights at their traditional places.

Whatever legal rights the Chippewa still retained, a larger question loomed: Could the fish themselves survive in harvestable numbers? Tribal fishers had always taken large amounts of lake trout, whitefish, and other species, but nineteenth-century technology brought a new scale to Great Lakes fishing. Pound net fishers used leaders—nets up to 1,400 feet long, hung from the surface and anchored on the lake bottom in water as deep as 90 feet—to guide fish first into a tunnel and then into a pen, where they were harvested. Another method, gillnetting, employed nets sus-

GREAT LAKES CHIPPEWA TRIBES
RESERVATIONS

ONTARIO
USA
Nett Lake
Grand Portage
Vermilion Lake
Red Cliff
Fond Du Lac
Mille Lacs
St. Croix
Lac Court Oreilles
Ontonagon
Bad River
Keweenaw
Lac Vieux Desert
Lac du Flambeau
Mole Lake
Sokaogon
Sault Ste. Marie
Bay Mills
Grand Traverse
Isabella
MI
MINNESOTA
WISCONSIN
MICHIGAN
ONTARIO
Great Lakes
Lake Superior
Lake Michigan
Lake Huron
Lake Erie

0   50   100 Miles

pended vertically in the water with a mesh size that allowed fish to swim in past their heads but entangled them (often in the gills) when the fish tried to withdraw. Indian fishers had long used small gill nets operated from birch canoes, but the new arrivals developed much longer nets, operated from six-foot-tall net spools mounted on large vessels.

The introduction of steam-driven boats in the late nineteenth century capped what Margaret Bogue has called, in her superb environmental history of the Great Lakes fishery, "the technology of massive harvests." The new craft allowed companies to cover much greater distances and to use giant power spools to retrieve nets. In Lake Huron's Georgian Bay alone, the gill net fleet in 1894 ran 2,121 miles of nets. So too was hook-and-line fishing revolutionized; hook gangs, used mainly for lake trout, were comprised of heavy cords several miles long, commonly set with as many as 2,500 to 3,000 hooks. These and other techniques brought more than 100 million pounds of fish to market annually but also resulted in huge losses because of waste. In 1885, for instance, an estimated 400 to 500 tons of Lake Erie whitefish rotted in gill nets. Habitat destruction, mostly from excessive logging and water pollution, also contributed to the free fall of the fishery.

As early as 1881, the *Chicago Times* asked: "What of the great lakes? . . . And where are the fish?" By the 1920s commercial production had gone into steep decline.

Then came the sea lampreys. It is believed that these eels migrated from the Atlantic Ocean up the Hudson River into Lake Ontario. After completion of the Welland Canal, they moved into the other Great Lakes, infesting Erie in the 1920s and Huron, Michigan, and Superior in the 1930s. The lampreys devastated what was left of the lake trout and whitefish. These parasites, with toothed, suction-type mouths, latched onto the sides of fish, which could not shake the invaders, and sucked out the life fluids. By the 1950s the once-teeming fisheries of the Great Lakes, in the words of biologists Michael Hansen and James Peck, "collapsed catastrophically."

The changes in the lakes and the land laid many burdens on the Chippewa. They had sold fish to fur traders and early settlers, but that became much more difficult. In addition to the drop in the Great Lakes fishery, the new technology drove most individual fishers out of the market since only companies could afford the high-cost equipment. Further, by the 1890s A. Booth and Company had taken over virtually all wholesaling, and its monopolistic practices drove down the prices to fishermen, including Indians. State fishing agencies, rejecting the idea of any treaty rights, required Indian fishers to buy state commercial licenses. The combination of land loss and limited opportunities in commercial fishing and logging, the result of widespread deforestation, caused many Chippewa to move away from their traditional areas. By the 1930s one-quarter of them lived in the cities.

The pattern differed in the inland lakes of Wisconsin and Minnesota, where the prized fish were muskellunge and walleye.

Commercial fishing was far less intensive for these species so coveted by sports fishers. While the fisheries never bottomed out, Indians faced increasingly stiff competition from recreationists and lakefront homeowners. Confrontational non-Indians chased Indians off their traditional fishing spots, and the states arrested and prosecuted Indians who fished outside state laws. The state supreme courts upheld the convictions.

Regardless, the Chippewa never stopped fishing.

IN THE MID-1960s, Buck Chosa and Fred Dakota, both members of the Keweenaw Bay Band of Chippewa at the distant southern shore of Lake Superior, were searching for ways to rejuvenate their tribe. The Chippewa bands, from Michigan across to North Dakota, still felt a common bond. It was a time of ferment. The idealism and frustration that had led to AIM had started to brew in Minneapolis and other cities, and Chippewa in their twenties and thirties led the way. There was also ferment out on the reservations, especially at Red Lake, where the land base remained mostly intact.

The two men—Chosa, 48 years old, generally conservative, and an army veteran with a Bronze Star, and Dakota, a generation younger, feeling common cause with the city activists—made an interesting counterpoint: different, but both rebels in the name of tribal nationalism. They traveled over to Red Lake and met Roger Jourdain and others. Sovereignty was all the talk. Fired up, they returned to Keweenaw Bay determined to take on the fishing rights issue. Both men fished (Chosa sold his catches as far away as the Straits of Mackinac, 200 miles to the east), and state enforcement severely limited their operations. They knew too that establishing the fishing rights would further tribal sovereignty and, as they put it, generally "give the tribe room to move."

Buck Chosa had still another reason, a personal one. His father, Jim, had been the lead defendant in *People v. Chosa* in 1930, when Jim and other tribal members had been charged with violating state laws. Article 11 of the band's 1854 treaty provided for off-reservation fishing rights on traditional lands. The Michigan

Supreme Court, reflecting the prevailing view of the "Vanishing Indian," found that "when one becomes a citizen of the United States, he casts off both the rights and obligations of his former nationality and takes on those which pertain to other citizens of the country." Any other result, the court concluded, would be "foreign to our system of government." *People v. Chosa* had ruled that except for on-reservation fishing, the treaty was a nullity.

Chosa and Dakota met with tribal leaders at Keweenaw Bay about challenging the *Chosa* opinion. The tribal chairman, Bill Jondreau, and the others were enthused because they all believed that the opinion was wrong, that the tribal treaty negotiators had preserved the fishing rights. They had heard of protests and court cases over Indian fishing for salmon out on the Pacific coast.

Jondreau wanted to take the lead. He made certain that the issue would be joined by calling state officials and telling them exactly where, and when, he would be fishing for lake trout. Without a state license.

On June 1, 1965, state officials arrested Jondreau for illegal possession of four lake trout taken from Keweenaw Bay. Jondreau, insisting on standing by the treaty, refused to plead guilty and was convicted in the Baraga County trial court. The court of appeals affirmed, and Jondreau then appealed to the Supreme Court of Michigan. His case was a long shot at best. In order to rule his way, the court would have to overrule one of its own opinions, *People v. Chosa*. Bill Jondreau, Buck Chosa, Fred Dakota, and the other Chippewa waited.

THE EFFORTS of the Northwest tribes to enforce their treaty rights rose to such prominence owing to one factor—the fish they sought. For how many things in the world, natural or artificial, can match the Pacific salmon? The creamy succulence of a pink fillet, pan-fried, poached, or slow-cooked over an open alder fire in the traditional Northwest Indian fashion. The solid whack on an anchovy-baited hook far offshore. The twisting, water-spraying aerobatics of a river steelhead on a fly line. The mind-expanding wonder we feel in imagining the 10,000-mile life journey of the

Idaho chinook, their birth in mountain streams near the Continental Divide, their journey to the Gulf of Alaska, their return to spawn in the very place they began. The image, indelible once received, of the silver streaks charging up a waterfall. The profits and jobs from boating, canning, shipping, and serving the big fish. The millions of sports fisher user days, and the way their license fees, equipment, travels, and celebrations spread throughout the economy. The role of the salmon for twelve millennia or more in the lives of hundreds of separate peoples from California up through Canada and Alaska, peoples who both used and revered the fish. The very definition of the broad, green Pacific Northwest, Timothy Egan concluded in *The Good Rain,* "is simply this: wherever the salmon can get to." In a similar vein, James Lichatowich wrote, "When I look at a salmon, I don't just see a silver fish, I see the Northwest."

Any group, it follows, seeking to adjust fundamentally the way that Pacific salmon were harvested and allocated would face a long, twisty, and rocky route.

The Great Lakes pattern of treaties, overfishing, habitat destruction, post–World War II population growth, and state crackdowns on Indian fishing also prevailed in the Northwest. State fisheries agencies in Washington, Oregon, Idaho, and California, urged on by well-organized non-Indian sports and commercial fishing interests and backed by governors and other political leaders, were resolute in bringing off-reservation treaty fishing to an end. To best those forces, the tribes would need to operate at all levels. Down on the rivers, Indian fishers would have to find the fortitude to continue fishing in the face of arrests and prosecutions. The tribes, most of them destitute, would have to retain excellent lawyers. A grass roots campaign should educate the citizenry to the Indians' plight and then mobilize public opinion. Ideally, in time and if everything broke right, because of the trust duty to Indians and because solemn promises of the nation were at stake, the tribes might realign the balance of power with the states by enlisting the support of the United States of America, both its courts and its Department of Justice. The two main arenas would be the Columbia River and Puget Sound.

· · ·

THE COLUMBIA—Frances Victor called it the River of the West—is far and away the Northwest's largest river. Fifteen times the flow of the Colorado, it breaks through the Cascade Range to create the Columbia River Gorge, one of the world's finest fishing grounds. There, along the fifty-mile stretch where the river narrows and crashes down numerous falls, Indian fishers erected their wooden platforms reaching out over the current and nimbly worked their long-handled dip nets. Fishers in the mid-Columbia stretch, and at other main stem and tributary sites, took enormous quantities of salmon—an estimated 42 million pounds per year, many times the amount taken today from the depleted runs. The Columbia River tribes built their societies on the fish.

While the tribes, over 10,000 years or more, learned to limit their take to assure plentiful runs, the arrivals from Europe recognized no limits. The Columbia's first cannery, allowing companies to preserve the fish and market worldwide, opened in 1867. With their prodigious appetites, the canneries opened the floodgates to fishers with long gill nets, large V-shaped fish traps, and fish wheels (Ferris wheel–size contraptions turned by the current). This free-for-all decimated the runs. President Theodore Roosevelt moaned in 1908 that "the salmon fisheries of the Columbia River are now but a fraction of what they were twenty-five years ago," and Dr. Livingston Stone of the U. S. Bureau of Fisheries declared: "[T]he helpless salmon's life is gripped between these two forces—the murderous greed of the fishermen and the white man's advancing civilization—and what hope is there for the salmon in the end?"

That was before the dams. Bonneville, the first impoundment on the main stem Columbia, near Portland, Oregon, started producing electricity in 1938. While fish ladders allowed some fish passage across Bonneville, salmon populations plummeted even further because of the cumulative effects of dam construction. Grand Coulee Dam came next. Completed inland near the Canadian border in 1941, it rose 343 feet, far too high for fish ladders, and shut off more than 1,100 river miles of salmon habitat. The runs that Grand Coulee drove into extinction included the leg-

endary Royal Chinook, the hardy Canadian-born fish with individuals commonly weighing 70 pounds apiece, some reaching 125
pounds.

Bonneville and Grand Coulee, however, marked only the beginning of the drive for supposedly "cheap" hydropower and irrigation water. Within a generation, the once-wild main stem
Columbia was made over by fourteen dam-and-reservoir projects,
all essentially consecutive in that the pool behind each dam
reached upstream to the next dam. Ten more dams control the
Snake, the Columbia's largest tributary. More than 400 others
plugged smaller tributaries. In total, the dams have closed off half
of all Columbia Basin spawning habitat and brought runs in the
remainder of the watershed to ruins. Today's runs, mostly comprised of hatchery fish rather than wild salmon, are estimated at
about one-fifth the size of the runs before Europeans arrived.

CELILO FALLS, deep in the Columbia River Gorge, made the
best fishing place of all. The rocky terrain, resisting the river's
force, narrowed the current and concentrated the fish. In addition
to the main fall, side currents and eddies made for efficient dip
net harvesting. Hundreds of rock shelves and boulders, each
assigned to a family, provided footing for Indian fishers or served
as the bases for platforms that reached out over the water. By the
1940s Celilo had become even more essential. Downriver, the pool
behind Bonneville Dam had buried dozens of prime fishing spots
under 40 feet of water. Those fishers moved up to Celilo Falls.
Some 2,000 fishers from the Umatilla and Warm Springs tribes of
Oregon, the Yakama of Washington, and the Nez Perce of Idaho
depended on Celilo's bounty.

The builders of post–World War II America, however, saw Celilo
Falls in terms of electricity, not salmon. The tribal councils
objected to the proposed The Dalles Dam, just as they did to Bonneville and Grand Coulee, but to no avail. Oregon and Washington
fisheries agencies also opposed The Dalles Dam, but as a gauge of
the anger and misconceptions of the era, state officials gave the
Army Corps of Engineers ammunition by conceding that flooding
Celilo and eliminating Indian fishing (just 1 or 2 percent of the

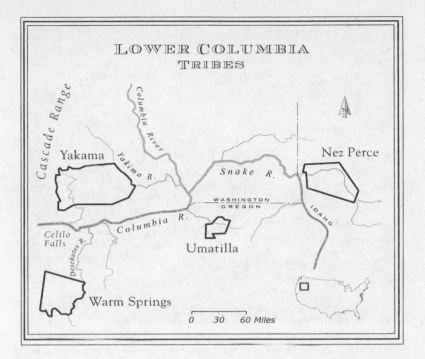

LOWER COLUMBIA TRIBES

Cascade Range

Columbia River

Yakama

Yakima R.

Snake R.

Nez Perce

WASHINGTON
OREGON

IDAHO

Celilo
Falls

Deschutes R.

Columbia R.

Umatilla

Warm Springs

0   30   60 Miles

Columbia River harvest) would be a "direct and outstanding contribution to conservation."

By 1957 the river had backed up behind the concrete impoundment and flooded Celilo Falls. Tommy Thompson, nearly 90 and
the traditional leader and regulator of the tribal fishing, cried
when he saw the rising water that would destroy a magnificent
place and strafe the self-identity of the humans who so revered
and depended upon the place. "There goes my life," Thompson
sobbed. "My people will never be the same."

After the flooding of Celilo, Indian fishing on the Columbia fell
into a lull. The fishers were dispirited. They had lost both the
place and the means to fish; the dipnetting could no longer continue because the eddies, shoots, and falls all had been inundated
by reservoirs. Dipnetting from boats on the still, deep reservoirs
proved futile.

Indian fishing on the Columbia took a slight upturn in the early
1960s. Forsaking dip nets except on undammed tributaries, tribal
fishers turned to an old technology in a new form. Indian fishers

Indian fishermen at Celilo Falls, near the town of The Dalles, Oregon, shortly before the falls were inundated behind the reservoir created by The Dalles Dam. The salmon did not actually "jump" these high falls. Rather, they waited near the base of the falls (when they were most susceptible to hoop netting) until the current had gathered a sufficient amount of force, then leaped partway up the falls and "swam" frantically up the current until they reached the slower river water above. This often required repeated attempts. Photograph courtesy of historicphotoarchive.com.

had long used gill nets made from roots or slender willows, but the modern monofilament gill nets were lighter, much longer, equally strong, and even more effective since the mesh could expand and tighten to secure the fish more completely. A sadness remained, for the fishers could no longer revel in the sounds and smells and force of the wild river. The efficiency of gillnetting, however, offered even greater commercial potential. The fishers returned, now working the pools behind the dams with their boats, gill nets, and buoys.

The Columbia grew increasingly combative. The states, with the fisheries depleted and with many new commercial and sports fishers moving to the Northwest, launched a winched-up crusade

The flooding of Celilo Falls and numerous other fishing areas on the main stem Columbia and Snake rivers made hoop net fishing at those traditional sites impossible. Modern Indian fishers still use the hoop nets on a few of the tributaries. This Warm Springs tribal member is fishing from a wooden platform at the Sherars Bridge tribal fishing grounds on the Deschutes River in central Oregon. Photograph courtesy of Michael L. Sherrill.

against treaty fishing. The agencies adopted new regulations, including a ban on gillnetting above Bonneville Dam, a ploy that infuriated Indians because only Indian netters fished above Bonneville, while non-Indian gillnetters worked the river below Bonneville. State wardens dramatically stepped up the number of arrests.

Tensions also rose because now tribal leaders and fishers of the 1960s resisted with a new aggressiveness and resourcefulness. As

Lillian Tahkeal of the Yakama Nation explained, state officials "thought they were getting the Indians off the river. . . . They thought with Celilo gone, the Indians were gone. It didn't work out that way." The vigorous tribal actions on the Columbia paralleled efforts to the north on Puget Sound, and together they received much notice in Indian country. Thus the salmon people gave courage to many, not the least of whom was Bill Jondreau of the Keweenaw Bay Band of Chippewa, who was soon to dare challenge the established law of Michigan.

The tough, no-nonsense tribal council of the Yakama Nation took the lead on the Columbia. Outraged by the proliferating arrests, Chairman Robert Jim and Vice-Chairman Eagle Seelatsee directed the tribal attorney, Jim Hovis, to protect the treaty fishers. They also bitterly complained to the BIA. In response, the Department of the Interior assigned attorney George Dysart to work on Columbia River Indian fishing issues. This proved to be a significant move, for over the next quarter of a century Dysart was smack in the middle of the treaty rights disputes.

Dysart, a cautious, scholarly man with a traditional legal background, seemed in many ways an unlikely candidate for the emotional Indian and state conflict. Yet convinced that the states were violating the federal laws he had sworn to uphold, he dived into the business of protecting Indian treaties. Dysart worked closely with Hovis, a bulldog of a lawyer whose personality matched that of his Yakama tribal clients. Between them, Dysart and Hovis defended Indian fishers during the 1960s in dozens of prosecutions in county courts on both the Washington and Oregon sides of the Columbia. Most of the juries refused to convict, and eventually the states scaled back their prosecutions. In an era when termination remained in vogue and the BIA still reined in private attorneys by using its power to approve their contracts, Dysart and Hovis were delivering a kind of accomplished and determined lawyering that Indian people had rarely received.

The legal dispute on the Columbia took a major turn when it moved into the federal courts in 1968. David Sohappy, who had grown up in the traditional Yakama way and had served in the army, lived down on the river and made his living from fishing. After an arrest and three nights in a Washington jail, the latest episode in combat that had flared for years, Sohappy and several of his relatives sued the Washington and Oregon fish commissions.

The Yakama Nation refused to support the Sohappy plaintiffs, even though they were tribal members. David Sohappy believed that the treaty protected him not just from state enforcement but from tribal laws as well. The Yakama Nation, like the Nez Perce and Umatilla, had adopted its own regulations for treaty fishing on the Columbia and had no patience with tribal members who disobeyed its conservation requirements. Robert Jim, Eagle Seelatsee, and other Yakama tribal council members, however, could see the potential importance of the *Sohappy* case. They requested Hovis and Dysart to find a way to bring in the United States on behalf of the tribes. Sid Lezak, United States Attorney for Oregon, agreed. Getting the Department of Justice back in Washington, D.C., to authorize the suit was difficult, but Dysart and Lezak relentlessly and successfully made their case; Owen Panner, Warm Springs tribal attorney at the time and later a federal judge, called the federal approval "a miracle."

The government then filed <u>United States v. Oregon</u> in <u>federal court to protect the treaty rights</u>. The Yakama, Umatilla, Warm Springs, and Nez Perce all intervened in the litigation so that the tribes and their own lawyers could participate. Judge Robert Belloni consolidated the cases, bringing the Sohappy plaintiffs, the United States, the four affected tribes, and the two states under one roof.

On July 8, 1969, Judge Belloni handed down a landmark decision. He ruled that the treaties were valid, that state regulation did not normally apply to treaty fishers, and that the state actions were "discriminatory" and not justified by any demands of "conservation." All those points had been upheld directly or indirectly in various federal cases (though some state opinions disagreed), but Judge Belloni broke new ground in addressing an overriding issue: whether tribes had a right to some share of the total fishery. In ruling that tribes are entitled to a "fair share" of the harvestable runs, his opinion raised the specter that tribal rights might force some commercial boats and nets off the water, or reduce the take of sports fishers, in order to meet the needs of the tribes.

The fair share ruling triggered an angry response from non-Indian fishers. The dignified, white-haired Belloni later recalled that "fishermen of all kinds, the sports and commercial fishermen, reacted a lot stronger than I ever thought they would." Nor did the 1969 ruling—handed down before *Custer Died for Your Sins* and Alcatraz, at a time when Indian people still had not effectively articulated their side—make intuitive sense to most people in the general public. Panner, now a federal judge on the same court where Belloni sat, emphasized that "the case took a toll on Belloni. I know how much he worried about it. He lost a lot of friends, commercial fishermen down on the coast. He took a lot of abuse. That decision couldn't have happened without a federal judge who could put up with that kind of static and not have to worry about being reelected."

Judge Belloni's decision could not be the final word. He crafted his fair share test as a broad formulation, hoping that the parties on the Columbia River could then negotiate a detailed settlement within that general framework, as, in 1977, they did. Up in Puget Sound, however, the temperature of Indian fishing rights had risen many degrees higher than in Oregon. State officials, including the attorney general, were in no mood to compromise. Neither were the tribes. Questions now hung over the rivers of the Northwest: What does "fair share" mean? Less than 1 percent in order to match the Indian population? Ten percent? One-third? As much as one-half? The answers came in the adjudication of the fishing rights of the tribes of Puget Sound, one of the most momentous lawsuits in the history of the Pacific Northwest.

THE LONG and violent salmon wars in the Puget Sound region of Washington, simmering for generations, boiled over in the early 1960s. With fewer fish and many more non-Indian fishers, Washington state fish agencies fixed blame squarely on the Indians. Never mind the well-documented environmental damage caused by dams and other development; never mind that

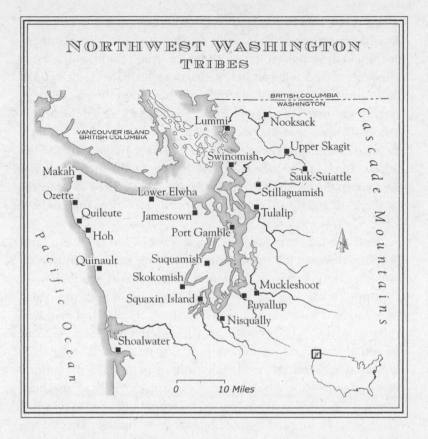

NORTHWEST WASHINGTON TRIBES

BRITISH COLUMBIA
WASHINGTON

VANCOUVER ISLAND
BRITISH COLUMBIA

Cascade Mountains

Pacific Ocean

Lummi
Nooksack
Upper Skagit
Swinomish
Sauk-Suiattle
Makah
Ozette
Lower Elwha
Stillaguamish
Quileute
Jamestown
Tulalip
Hoh
Port Gamble
Quinault
Suquamish
Skokomish
Muckleshoot
Squaxin Island
Puyallup
Nisqually
Shoalwater

0   10 Miles

treaty fishers took just 6 percent of the overall harvest. State officers mounted major raids on the Puyallup, Nisqually, and Green
rivers and on Makah fishers in Neah Bay. From there the state
enforcement effort expanded to all 23 tribes in northwest Washington, where thousands of Indians exercised treaty fishing
rights.

The Muckleshoot Tribe, like most in the Puget Sound area, had
seen its lands carved down to a reservation so small that off-reservation fishing was an absolute necessity for these salmon people.
Reservation visitors commented on how every home seemed to
have fish spears and drying salmon hanging on interior household
walls. In addition to regular salmon meals, Muckleshoot sold fish
to buyers from Aberdeen to Seattle as a main source of income.

The tribal fisheries manager, Cecil Moses, headed the Muck-leshoot resistance to the state's crackdown. A big, burly man, Moses had the toughest job, working the green chain, at the Weyerhaeuser mill. A follower of the Shaker religion, he dedicated his life to protecting the fishing rights of his people from the non-Indians who, in his words, "just take, take, take." He set the Muckleshoot fishing seasons, strategized with other tribal leaders, organized fish-ins, and endured many arrests and seizures of his canoes. Much later, when the salmon wars finally ended, Moses, like most of the resisters from other tribes, was treated as a returning war hero and served on the tribal council for more than twenty years.

The fishing at Muckleshoot, as it always had been, was a family affair. The men did most of the harvesting, working from rock formations with spears and dip nets. Out on the rivers they used aluminum boats and the traditional twenty-foot-long red cedar canoes carved with shovel noses to prevent tipping and operated with ornate maple or yellow cedar paddles and fir pushpoles. The women did the cleaning and the precision task of drying the delicate fillets on alder racks. The children were tasked with various chores. Gerald Moses, Cecil's son, looks back jovially at his childhood days as a "pack horse," when he would lug gunnysacks full of fifteen- to twenty-five pound chinook from the riverbank up the steep sides of the Green River canyon to the women waiting above.

The constant surveillance and threat of arrest took some of the joy and profit out of it. Increasingly, fishers from the Muckleshoot and other tribes had to work the rivers at night: "dark-time fishing." More time went into fighting the state than caring for the equipment and catching the fish. Then, too, the high-visibility conflict created splits within the Indian community. Some tribal leaders, hearing the relentless drumbeat that the off-reservation fishers were "poachers" and "renegades," became openly critical of the resisters.

Many of the confrontations sparked physical violence. Officers forcibly dragged Indian fishermen up rocky banks and landed blows with fists, nightsticks, and long-handled flashlights. Indians usually gave dead weight when arrested, but both sides had their hotbloods. Some of the fishermen fought back, and angry Indian spectators sometimes showered the officers with rocks and chunks of driftwood. With demonstrations rising in support of black civil rights, the states received increased federal funding to quell civil disobedience. In 1964, Billy Frank, Jr., of the Nisqually Tribe, who was to suffer some 50 arrests and gear confiscations going back to 1945, realized the state of Washington was going all out when state officers in riot gear operating a high-speed aluminum boat rammed and capsized his cedar canoe: "These guys had a budget. This was a war."

While the stalwart presence of Indian fishers on the rivers was a sine qua non, the tribes could not prevail without political and legal strategies. From the Washington tribes, Ramona Bennett of Puyallup, Janet McCloud of Tulalip, and Guy McMinds of Quinault took the lead along with the omnipresent Hank Adams. Unlike the Sioux in their campaign to eliminate Public Law 280 from South Dakota, the Northwest fishing tribes did not retain a public relations firm but had a full equivalent, and then some, in Adams's incendiary mind.

The work of these four and others, all in their twenties and early thirties, stands as testament to how, when the time and place are right, the verve and creativity of youth can change the world. They devised a sophisticated, multifaceted strategy. They established good relationships with reporters and church groups; the American Friends Service Committee, an organization of the Quakers, became the first non-Indian organization to support the treaty efforts. A large 1963 demonstration at the state capitol in Olympia attracted wide attention. Many other protests and press conferences followed. Crowds of supporters, anticipating the occasions when squadrons of law enforcement officials would move in for arrests, would be waiting to cheer on the fishers and jeer the intruders. The Indian leaders recruited celebrities, including Marlon Brando, Jane Fonda, and Dick Gregory, who contributed to the combative but upbeat atmosphere. The Indians especially liked Gregory, the black comedian. Once, at a press conference following his release from custody for demonstrating on behalf of Indian fishing, he was asked if he had been offered tribal membership. Gregory replied, "No thanks, I've got enough problems."

The young organizers persuaded Charles Kuralt of CBS to cover the story and instigated three documentaries, most notably Carol Burns's *As Long as the Rivers Run*. They also urged the Friends to put together an independent scholarly account of the fishing dispute. The result was *Uncommon Controversy*, an objective, well-documented—and highly readable—1970 report that went into multiple printings. Taking the long view, a group of Indians persuaded the eminent University of Washington law professor Ralph W. Johnson to begin teaching Indian law. Though lacking experience in the field, Johnson agreed and eventually became both a nationally recognized authority on Indian law and, like so many others who became exposed to the cause, an advocate for Indian treaty rights. "This was," Johnson concluded in his straightforward way, "an injustice. It was entirely wrong. The state was being repressive, racist."

The litigation aspect of the equation was pressing, complicated, and delicate. Ramona Bennett, Guy McMinds, Janet McCloud, and Hank Adams had no legal education (there were only a dozen or so Indian lawyers in the country at the time), but they were imbued with the importance of law to Indian people. When McMinds was a boy, his grandfather had handed him a copy of Felix Cohen's *Handbook of Federal Indian Law* and told him, "Here. Take this book and read it. It will be your future."

They knew about, and understood, the federal court opinions. Early in the twentieth century a fish wheel operator in the Columbia, trying to eliminate competition from Yakama dip net fishers, fenced off a traditional fishing site, blocking access by the Yakama. A federal Department of Justice attorney sued on behalf of the Indians. In a leading Indian law opinion, the Supreme Court held in the 1905 *United States v. Winans* case that—regardless of any contrary state laws—federal treaties continued in force and that the Indian fishers had a right to fish at the site even though a non-Indian, Winans, owned the land. Justice Joseph McKenna, who wrote the opinion, underscored the gravity and dignity of the Indian position by stating that the right to fish was "not much less necessary to the existence of the Indians than the atmosphere they breathed." The cases since then had split; the federal decisions usually upheld the Indian position, while the Washington state court decisions supported state regulation of Indian fishing. The treaties, though, were federal law, and under the Constitution federal laws and federal court decisions interpreting them override any conflicting state laws. The tribes seemed to have a solid legal position.

There remained the matter of lawyers. A few tribes could scrape together funds to hire an attorney, but most could not. The War on Poverty provided the saving grace. By the mid-1960s the Office of Economic Opportunity had opened legal services offices for poor people with several located on reservations. In northwest Washington, Seattle Legal Services not only agreed to take on Indian treaty litigation but dedicated an impressive amount of attorney time. Janet McCloud and Hank Adams urged the Seattle Legal Services attorneys to bring in the Native American Rights Fund, the national Indian law firm in Boulder, Colorado, which was funded mainly by the Ford Foundation but also received OEO support. The SLS attorneys agreed that NARF could bring needed expertise and resources. It proved to be a critical move. David Getches from NARF became a mainstay for the tribes.

News of George Dysart's efforts on behalf of individual Indians on the Columbia quickly made its way up to Puget Sound. By the time the United States filed on behalf of the Columbia River tribes in 1969, it was fully apparent how critical federal support would be. The federal lawyers would bring litigation experience and, in the case of Dysart, deep expertise in Indian law. Litigation on the treaties would require extensive—and expensive—expert testimony, which the federal government would support. Moreover, no one had any doubt about the credibility it would add to the tribes' case if the trial began with a Department of Justice attorney rising to his feet in a high-ceilinged federal courtroom to pronounce, "Your Honor, on behalf of the United States of America, I represent the plaintiff Indian tribes in this action."

Resolving the question of whether the United States would bring litigation to halt the state enforcement required a good deal of jockeying for position. Stan Pitkin, the United States Attorney for western Washington, made it clear in 1969 that he supported filing a lawsuit by the United States as trustee on behalf of the tribes. He left the details of the complaint—as well as the challenging process of obtaining authority from the Department of Justice in Washington, D.C.—to George Dysart. Dysart had to move carefully in order to meet all the formal and informal constraints of the federal system, doubly so because the case clearly had the potential to disrupt established economic interests. The federal lawyer liked, as an impatient Getches put it, "to keep his powder dry." But Dysart's step-by-step approach worked. In September 1970 the justice department launched *United States v. Washington* in Federal District Court in Tacoma. Most of the Washington tribes intervened.

The very first event, the assignment of the case to Judge George H. Boldt, was hardly auspicious for the Indian side. Boldt, an Eisenhower appointee, had earned a reputation as a hard-nosed judge who handed out stiff sentences in criminal cases. He ran a tight ship in the courtroom. In the trial of Vietnam protesters called the Seattle Seven, the defendants repeatedly disrupted the courtroom to the point that continuing the trial would be futile. Frustrated, Judge Boldt finally declared a mistrial, but he was not finished. He proceeded to sentence the Seattle Seven to six months in jail for contempt of court—and refused to lift the sentences for the Christmas holidays. Those and other stories left the Indians and their lawyers rolling their eyes.

THE TRIAL began in Tacoma on August 27, 1973. When the diminutive man entered the packed courtroom in his robe and ever-present bow tie and seated himself behind the bench, no one could know Judge Boldt's predispositions, if any, toward the case. The many Indian people in attendance, who had long believed that the federal judiciary would deliver them justice, watched anxiously. Strange that it would come down to this judge in this regal-looking wood-paneled room. The treaties, the sovereignty, the hopes, all to be decided by this judge in this room. Thirty years later the Nisqually fisherman Billy Frank, Jr., recalled the day well: "We had a whole lot of bad experiences with the state courts. The judges were finding us guilty and throwing us in jail. When we did get a good decision, the state supreme court would reverse it. Then Judge Boldt took our case. We knew he was a conservative judge. In some of the early hearings he made some statements we took as sympathetic. When he was put on the Pay Board [by President Nixon], our case went to another judge, who was really disappointing. Then, when Judge Boldt came back from the Pay Board, it was a big step. It gave us hope. Still, we had a lot of doubts. We looked around, it was standing room only, and it was all rednecks, sports fishermen. These guys got there first and took all the seats. They wanted to show their power. I remember thinking, 'I hope this place isn't rigged.' "

As he stood in the back of the courtroom that day, Billy Frank knew that the cause to which he had dedicated his adult life was nearing a climax. Would this trial be a charade—"rigged"? Or would his fervently held vision of justice be served? This was his tribe's last stand, and the moment of truth was at hand.

Part Three
FOUNDATIONS for SELF-DETERMINATION

8.

Turning Points

Billy Frank had plenty of company, in body and spirit, as he watched the Northwest fishing rights trial unfold in the Tacoma courtroom. By the late 1960s and early 1970s, Native people across the country were seeing hope for the fulfillment of the treaties, for self-determination broadly writ. They longed for the right to make their own decisions and their own mistakes.

American Indians had made clear advances from the dire circumstances of the early 1950s. Many individual tribes fought various schemes to take land, treaty rights, and jurisdiction—and sometimes won, as in the Sioux's 1963 overturn of South Dakota's Public Law 280 jurisdiction. Public demonstrations had raised the nation's consciousness toward Native concerns. Indian leaders embedded tribes in the War on Poverty legislation, and numerous OEO-funded projects had gone to work on the reservations. The fishing rights cases were making their way through the courts.

Still, the tribes had yet to establish a movement with hard results and staying power. The BIA still controlled the reservations. Tribal powers and treaty rights remained very much in doubt. Poverty retained its grip. And termination stood as official government policy.

Although an exact historical moment could never be determined for such a thing, the modern Indian movement had crystallized by the mid-1970s. The termination election at the Colville Reservation, the Menominee Restoration Act, congressional pas-

sage of self-determination legislation, and the Boldt decision in
the Northwest fishing cases were both symbolic and deeply sub-
stantive—not isolated triumphs on individual issues but systemic
advances that benefited tribes broadly. Together they represented
new winds in Indian country and reached all three branches of the
federal government. Together they announced that at last Indian
tribes could shape their own futures.

TERMINATION gradually waned after its powerhouse beginnings. When the Democrats took over the Senate in 1955, Arthur
Watkins lost his subcommittee chairmanship and his ability to
ramrod Indian bills through Congress. Acknowledging the contentiousness over the policy, Secretary of the Interior Fred Seaton
declared in a 1958 radio address that termination without tribal
consent would be "unthinkable." Nonetheless, termination supporters still lurked on Capitol Hill and in the Department of the
Interior. The complex Klamath and Menominee terminations
became final in 1961. Termination proposals continued to come
forward in the 1960s, and several senators expressed strong protermination sentiments at the 1966 confirmation hearings for
Robert Bennett's appointment as BIA commissioner. Kinzua Dam
had already flooded Seneca homelands; now Senator Henry
"Scoop" Jackson of Washington and others proposed to terminate
the Seneca Nation in 1967. But the most visible sign that termination still had life in the late 1960s was Senator Jackson's resolute
campaign to liquidate the 1.1-million-acre Colville Reservation in
his home state.

"Scoop" Jackson cut a formidable figure. First elected to the
House in 1940 and then to the Senate in 1952, the tough, method-
ical Jackson quickly entered the Senate "club." A hawk on military
issues (Nixon wanted to appoint him secretary of defense), Jackson generally took liberal stands on domestic matters. As chairman of the powerful Interior Committee, Jackson was a primary
architect of the National Environmental Policy Act of 1969.

On Indian affairs, Jackson took a hard line. He had chaired the
House Indian Committee in his early congressional years and
consistently supported termination. In particular, he steadfastly

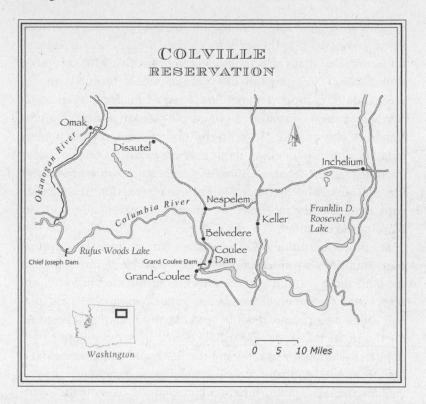

COLVILLE
RESERVATION

Omak
Okanogan River
Disautel
Inchelium
Columbia River
Nespelem
Franklin D.
Roosevelt
Keller
Lake
Belvedere
Rufus Woods Lake
Coulee
Chief Joseph Dam   Grand Coulee Dam   Dam
Grand-Coulee

Washington

0   5   10 Miles

advocated terminating the Colville Reservation, Washington's
largest. In 1956, Congress passed Public Law 772, which restored
land to the Colville Reservation but also gave the tribe five years
to submit a plan for termination. By the time he took over as chairman of the Senate Interior Committee in 1963, Jackson controlled
the fortunes of the Colville.

Internally, members of the Confederated Tribes of the Colville
Reservation found themselves caught in crosscurrents. Tribal society had been fractured by allotment, which allowed non-Indians
to move onto the reservation. A lot of tribal members had moved
away, and many of those who stayed felt less connected to the
tribe and the land. In a confused time, termination seemed a possible solution to the resentment against the paternalism of the
BIA, the label of "government ward," and the image of "blanket
Indian." Alluring too was the prospect of a good return. The

sprawling reservation, bordered on the south by the Columbia River, possessed fine timber stands. The Stanford Research Institute estimated that tribal members might receive $30,000 apiece from a selloff. To many Colville tribal members, termination and the freedom its supporters held out seemed modern and productive while the reservation seemed old-fashioned and cumbersome. As one argued, "To keep the Indians tied to these forests today is almost like telling them that they have to use the horse and buggy in the jet age. There have been some kinds of security for the Indians in the ownership of the reservation in the years gone by, but today most of the Indians are anxious to take their place in the competitive world."

Still, for a decade the Colville tribal council resisted termination. Traditionals wanted no part of it. Colville cited their love of the land and community. "I do not want termination or to sell my reservation," one member wrote the Senate committee. "I am one-half Colville and one-half white but I like my Indian part best." As for the financial issues, the tribal council believed a better path than termination lay in reducing the BIA's role and coaxing out a higher return through improved timber management.

Then, in 1964, protermination candidates took over the council, and the new governing body soon announced its support of Senator Jackson's pending termination bill. The council withdrew the tribe's membership from the National Congress of American Indians and the Affiliated Tribes of Northwest Indians because they opposed termination. The bill went to Senate hearings in 1965. Colville termination looked to be a sure thing.

Jackson, his legislative and administrative allies, and the protermination forces at Colville had not counted on Lucy Covington. The granddaughter of Chief Moses, the last recognized Colville chief, she was raised on the family ranch in a weathered shack amid the reservation's low, rounded hills. Her family ran cattle, and Lucy grew up on a horse. "We all rode. My mother rode. We broke horses." Much of her raising came from Mary Moses, Chief Moses's wife, who died in 1937 at the age of 118. Mary told young Lucy stories nearly every day, some of them about how the soldiers tracked Indian people down before the reservation. "She

Lucy Covington on her family ranch in the late 1960s. Photograph courtesy of Encyclopaedia Britannica, Inc.

wanted me to know somehow how much suffering had happened before we got a home base." Covington carried these lessons with her always: "If an Indian doesn't have land, he has nothing."

She clearly saw the danger at hand. Despite the demands of her ranch, she launched an all-out campaign against the termination bill. Covington enlisted Paschal Sherman, one of the few Indian lawyers, and mobilized able young tribal members, including Mel Tonasket, who later became tribal chair and president of NCAI. Selling off cattle to pay for the airline tickets, she made whirlwind trips back to Washington, D.C., trying to block Jackson's efforts.

Intense and well spoken, believable down to the marrow, she carried her message to every office that would listen. The legislation would be ruinous to the tribe economically and socially. It would strip away an Indian person's very identity. "Termination," Covington implored over and over, "is like giving your eagle feather away."

Then the action shifted from the nation's capital to the reservation. Knowing that the council's support of the bill gave Jackson the cover he needed, Covington organized an antitermination slate for the 1968 tribal election. She and her running mates campaigned across broad Colville country and also made use of the maturing network of Indian leaders nationally. To expose the damage that termination had wreaked on other tribes, Covington invited to the reservation Jim White, the Menominee leader and orator, and Elnathan Davis, who was attempting to reverse the Klamath termination. At a large community meeting they told of a deepening poverty among their tribespeople, how the one-time payments flitted away, how children born after the closure date received no payments at all, how much the loss of the land hurt. The rally also included national leaders Vine Deloria, Jr., Chuck Trimble, and Hank Adams.

Covington's slate swept the 1968 Colville tribal election, and the vote, resounding throughout Indian country and on Capitol Hill, dealt a deathblow to termination. It bespoke an ability of tribes to act decisively, both locally and nationally, for tribalism and the land in the face of enormous pressure from on high. Indian people themselves turned the last termination bill to dust.

MEANWHILE, the tribes that had actually been terminated had to endure what the Colville, Flathead, and a few other candidates for liquidation managed to stave off. There were no success stories among the terminated tribes. With their reservations liquidated, members fled to the cities or remained near their former homeland, the sense of community shattered and their economic status diminished even more.

The Menominee of Wisconsin avoided an outright sale of their land—at least at first. After termination took effect in 1961, the byzantine statute and administrative plan transferred tribal lands to Menominee Enterprises, Inc., a private corporation chartered under Wisconsin law. MEI was no "tribal" company. A voting trust, not individual Menominee, held and voted the corporation's shares. Individuals held only certificates, not actual shares. The voting trust had seven members, four of them Menominee—but five votes were required for valid action. The only power residing in individual Menominee was to vote for the voting trustees, but even that was attenuated: The certificates of minors and "incompetents" were voted by still another trust controlled by the First Wisconsin Trust Company with offices in Milwaukee. This bank held 40 percent of all certificates and (since many individual certificate holders did not vote) regularly cast, as a bloc, 80 percent and more of all votes in the elections of trustees.

Congress had replaced one master with another: first the Bureau of Indian Affairs; now, under the "freedom" of termination, the voting trust and the First Wisconsin Trust Company.

MEI brought with it a cascade of other troubles. Before termination, tribal land (like all government land, federal, state, local, and tribal) could not be taxed. But now MEI, as a private corporation, owed county property taxes, and the state collected sales and income taxes within the former reservation. MEI never had a chance. With forested land its only asset, the corporation staggered ahead with an outmoded 1908 mill, a heavy tax load, and a timber market in sharp decline over the seven years since Congress passed the termination act. The corporation's dearth of cash reserves would have stymied any timber business: After the tribe was inexplicably required to pay $12 million as the federal administrative costs of termination, MEI was left with $1.7 million in liquid assets, which dropped to $300,000 in 1964.

The Menominee people faced all manner of new problems. With the tribal hospital and clinic gone, Menominee County had no doctors, dentists, or health facilities. A tuberculosis epidemic struck 25 percent of all members. Menominee County, created at the time of termination, became the only county in the state without its own public schools. Indian children in the Shawano County schools faced high rates of failure, suspension, expulsion, and—as a federal investigation concluded—racial discrimination. Until termination, Menominee people could build their homes on tribal land for free with tribal permits. MEI, as a for-profit entity, required a purchase of residential land at market value. With tribal jobs eliminated and MEI cutting back, the unemployment rate nearly doubled.

The Menominee people had lost control of their 250,000-acre homeland, a glorious landscape of deep forests, wild rivers, and backcountry lakes. They could no longer determine who would run it, and how. Inexorable economic forces drove them further down month by month.

In the late 1960s MEI proposed a development scheme that galvanized the smoldering rage and sense of wrong among the Menominee. In an effort to stave off bankruptcy, the corporation embarked on a land sale program, called Legend Lake, that would dam streams to make new lakes and impound outlet waters to enlarge existing ones. Lakeside lots would then be sold—mostly, no doubt, to non-Indians. From a corporate standpoint, this may have made good sense; Legend Lake, by offering up prime recreational property, might at least give MEI the chance to right itself financially. From a tribal standpoint, the project promised disaster. It would sacrifice precious heartland and damage the environment. By attracting thousands of new residents, Legend Lake sales would eliminate what little political influence the Menominee still had over their former reservation.

A citizens' group founded in 1970, Determination of Rights and Unity for Menominee Shareholders, or DRUMS, set its sights on stopping the Legend Lake sales, establishing Menominee control over MEI, and, eventually, even reversing termination. In addition to a large and committed grass roots network, DRUMS drew together exceptional leadership. Ada Deer brought inspiration, organizational ability, and conceptual clarity. Jim White, a mesmerizing speaker and DRUMS' first president, often acted as spokesman. Sylvia Wilber, mother of thirteen, Shirley Daly, who had returned from Chicago to Menominee County, and Georgianna Ignace all had strong managerial skills. In the mid-1970s the Menominee Tribe was to see its share of divisiveness. But for

a stretch of some five years, when the unity had to be there, the sense of common mission superseded all else.

DRUMS seemed to spring to life full grown. Within months the Menominee organized a series of well-planned and smoothly executed demonstrations. To disrupt the Legend Lake land development, DRUMS picketed Legend Lake's Menominee County sales office and promotional events in Milwaukee, Green Bay, and Appleton. More than 200 protesters turned out for a major demonstration in Milwaukee at the First Wisconsin Trust building.

In October 1971, DRUMS carried out an eye-opening 220-mile march from Keshena, in Menominee County, to the state capitol in Madison. The march to Madison, like the other DRUMS protests, remained nonviolent but sharp-edged. Jim White, who needed no public address system, told crowds along the way how he saw it: "We read it, the stealing from the Indians and all, and think it happened 100 years ago. The hell it did. It's happening right today." After the 12-day march, Governor Patrick Lucey and an assembled crowd of 600 greeted the marchers on the capitol steps. Lucey met with Menominee leaders to discuss DRUMS' requests. Within a month, Lucey visited Menominee County, and he remained a staunch supporter of the Menominee movement.

The annual election of MEI voting trustees loomed shortly after the march to Madison. DRUMS had put up a four-person slate in opposition to the MEI-sponsored candidates. Their platform included an end to Legend Lake sales, democratization of MEI, and the eventual abolition of the various trusts. The campaign required long, tedious days of gathering proxies and urging Menominee to set aside the wet-blanket hopelessness engendered by years of the bank's domination of the elections. "We felt we had to go all the way," Sylvia Wilber said, "even if it meant going down fighting. The morale of our people as the result of the Madison march was high, and no one wanted to risk this feeling." Amazingly, the DRUMS ticket won by an impressive margin. Ada Deer became the new chair of the voting trust. The new trust named Sylvia Wilber chair of the MEI board of directors and Shirley Daly a member of the board.

As if 1971 had not been sufficiently frenetic for DRUMS, the year also produced a first draft of the Menominee restoration bill. By then the Native American Rights Fund had identified the Menominee effort as a priority, and I had become one of the tribe's attorneys. I shall always treasure those days: The cause was uplifting, the personalities were memorable, and the passion for the land and sovereignty was palpable. I did the bill drafting, an easy task since Ada Deer and the other Menominee leaders well knew what they wanted: reversal of termination and complete restoration. In their minds, only repeal of the termination act, return of the land to trust status, and full recognition of the tribe and its sovereign authority could right the wrongs against their people and their land. The initial draft went to meetings in Keshena and Neopit and to gatherings of tribal members living in Milwaukee, Madison, Green Bay, and Chicago.

By early 1972 the tribe had already obtained an astounding

level of support. Every political leader in Wisconsin, including Governor Lucey, Senators Gaylord Nelson and William Proxmire, and the Menominee's congressman, David Obey, gave whole-hearted approval. Many other senators and representatives were also on board. To be sure, some difficult terrain lay ahead. Senator Jackson listened but remained lukewarm. Passage of the Menominee legislation, after all, would go beyond halting termination, which already had taken place at Colville, to the outright reversal of a policy Jackson had supported for two decades.

The House presented an even greater obstacle: longtime Interior Committee chairman Wayne Aspinall of Colorado, a strong termination supporter. Aspinall, one of the last of the old-guard committee chairmen, kept his hands on every last detail of committee work. And the Menominee restoration bill had to go through his committee.

On the tribe's first visit to Washington, which I attended, Ada Deer asked for a meeting with Aspinall. Instead, we were met by his aide Lewis Sigler. Before moving over to Aspinall's staff, Sigler had been recruited to the BIA by Dillon Myer to work up termination proposals. Sigler explained that the chairman was unavailable to speak with the tribal representatives. On the merits of the restoration proposal, he said—with a straight face—that the Menominee, if they prepared their case carefully, might expect committee hearings within twenty years or so. Sigler also advised the tribal delegation to drop the term "restoration," since it might offend committee members who had supported termination for the Menominee and other tribes. No doubt Sigler had in mind Chairman Aspinall, who could be seen through his open office door, casually reading his mail. Not a good sign.

Yet Menominee restoration had been touched by magic. Gary Orfield, Harvard political scientist and noted civil rights expert, observed, "I have spent a lot of time around Capitol Hill. One of the most remarkable lobbying campaigns I have ever seen was the campaign for Menominee restoration. Nobody was safe from Ada Deer and her supporters. Members of Congress just gave up." Deer's finely tuned sense for the ways of Congress and her shrewd use of experts led her to build a solid record on many fronts:

Ada Deer (1980s). Photograph courtesy of Ray Ramirez, Native American Rights Fund.

history, demographics, business, law, health, education, and eco-nomics. Armed also with her trademark optimism and persist-ence, which, in Orfield's formulation, just made people "give up," Deer made her case by going to, over, or around, as the case need be, the key players on the Hill, in the White House, and in the Department of the Interior, wherever she could make headway.

Nor did fortune fail to smile. In 1972 Henry Jackson decided to run for president. Needing to appeal to a national constituency (one increasingly sympathetic to Indians), he gave his full support to Menominee restoration. A few months after spurning Deer and her colleagues, Wayne Aspinall was upset in the Colorado Demo-

cratic primary and would no longer be committee chair when
Congressmen Lloyd Meeds and Manuel Lujan convened House
field hearings in Keshena in the spring of 1973. Lewis Sigler's 20-
year wait for hearings had become 16 months.

Though it took a prodigious amount of work, the Menominee
Restoration Act moved through Congress with rare speed. President Nixon signed it into law in December of the same year the
bill was introduced. The statute mandated a one-year period for
the tribe and the administration to negotiate a method for
"unscrambling the MEI eggs" and vesting the land in the tribe once
again. That done, in April 1975, Secretary of the Interior Rogers C.
B. Morton completed the restoration in his large ceremonial office
in Washington. At an emotional ceremony thick with tears, hugs,
and justice, Secretary Morton signed the final set of documents
that dissolved MEI and transferred all Menominee lands back to
the tribe, to be held in trust by the United States of America and
governed by the sovereign Menominee Tribe of Wisconsin.

SELF-DETERMINATION, which replaced termination as official United States Indian policy in the 1970s, came about in a different fashion from other steps forward in modern times. Indian
people did not play as direct a role in formulating the policy as
was the case, for instance, with Menominee restoration. Nonetheless, the self-determination doctrine promoted by Presidents
Johnson and Nixon reflected long-standing needs and sentiments
in Indian country.

Ever since the establishment of the reservation system, Native
Americans held dear the impulse to govern their homelands free
of BIA control. Charles Eastman had argued early in the twentieth century that the BIA should be the "servant . . . of the Indians." Robert Yellowtail, from the Crow Tribe of Montana, had
evoked self-determination in testimony before the Senate Committee on Indian Affairs in 1919:

> Mr. Chairman, it is peculiar and strange to me [that] . . . you
> have not upon your statute books nor in your archives of law,
> so far as I know, one law that permits us to think free, act free,

expand free, and to decide free without first having to go and ask a total stranger that you call the Secretary of the Interior; in all humbleness and humiliation, "How about this, Mr. Secretary, can I have permission to do this"? and "Can I have permission to do that"? etc. . . .

Mr. Chairman, your President [Woodrow Wilson] but yesterday assured the people of this great country, and also the people of the whole world, that the right of self-determination shall not be denied to any people, no matter where they live, nor how small or weak they may be, nor what their previous conditions of servitude may have been. . . . I and the rest of my people sincerely hope and pray that the President, in his great scheme of enforcing upon all the nations of the earth the adoption of this great principle of the brotherhood of man and nations, and that the inherent right of each one is that of the right of self-determination, I hope, Mr. Chairman, that he will not forget that within the boundaries of his own nation are the American Indians, who have no rights whatsoever—not even the right to think for themselves.

After World War II, as he embarked on his lonely mission of articulating what Indian policy ought to be, D'Arcy McNickle put forth a philosophy based on "government by consent" and the tribes' "rights, as 'domestic dependent nations,' to govern their internal affairs." And though his prose lacked the grace of Eastman, Yellowtail, or McNickle, Roger Jourdain touched many chords across Indian country by calling for the eviction from the Red Lake Chippewa reservation of the "bums and tramps" who inhabited the Bureau of Indian Affairs.

When I first began to work with Indian people, I was surprised by their emphasis on the BIA. Causes such as treaty rights, land return, and school discrimination resonated much more with me. In time I began to appreciate the reality and symbolism that the federal agency represented. For more than a century, day after day, month after month, for the entire lives of thousands upon thousands of Native people, the BIA had been their keeper, their master. It mattered little that some good souls in the agency worked to protect tribal rights and traditional practices. The oppression, the confiscation of land, the plots to eviscerate a worldview—all been carried out under the auspices of the BIA. Things could not be made right until the brute within was removed.

The term "self-determination" came into general use only in the 1970s, but Indian people had begun practicing it after the Office of Economic Opportunity programs started in 1964. The War on Poverty's boldness opened a broad and bright landscape. Funding flowed not from the hidebound BIA but from the OEO, a brand-new enterprise that prided itself on flexibility and creativity. Further, the direct-funding provision that tribal leaders had formulated at the Capital Conference and lobbied into the OEO legislation now clicked in: The tribes, not the agency, received the grants and spent the funds according to their own priorities. As one wag put it, OEO support—especially compared with the top-heavy, paternalistic BIA-run programs—amounted to "raw cash."

The key OEO institution was the community action program, or CAP, bestowed with the unusually energetic congressional mission statement of "a program which mobilizes and utilizes resources . . . in an attack on poverty." Tribal councils authorized CAPs, which eventually reached 80 percent of the reservation population. Tribal CAPs dedicated the largest amount of funding to Head Start for preschoolers and home improvement. Other areas of emphasis included educational development, legal services, health centers, and economic development.

Needs and programs varied by tribe. The eight northern pueblos in New Mexico, for example, developed an effort to train a hundred silversmiths and started up a plant that turned out adobe bricks for house building. As for the relatively few OEO restrictions, such as the agency's prohibition against construction, enterprising Indian leaders often found a way around them. As Philip Deloria wryly recounted, Roger Jourdain of Red Lake "secured money for a training program for carpenters, plumbers, and electricians, with half a million dollars budgeted for 'training materials.' Remarkably, the 'homework' looked a lot like houses, and both the Red Lake people and the Red Lake sawmill benefited immeasurably."

One premier success of the OEO Indian effort came from Navajo country. Located in Arizona just northeast of Black Mesa in arid, red rock country, the community of Rough Rock exemplifies how hard it is for the Navajo Nation to bring communications, social services, and economic development to an area larger than seven states and nearly the size of Maine: Many of the 200,000 reservation residents live in remote places, places plentifully endowed with sere southwestern beauty but also barriered off from those benefits of the outside world that Navajo people might want to obtain. The Rough Rock Demonstration School rose from the community's will to give its children education that both respected and integrated Navajo culture and prepared young people for dealings with the majority society.

In 1965, Allan Yazzie and other Navajo sent a proposal to the OEO that quickly evolved into a new school at Rough Rock. The building already stood and had originally been intended as a BIA-run facility, but Yazzie, other Navajo, and Robert Roessel, an Anglo education professor at Arizona State University, managed to head off a turf struggle with the agency. The school would be run by Navajo, not the BIA, and it became the first wholly Indian-controlled school since the federal government took over the schools of the Five Civilized Tribes of Oklahoma in the late nineteenth century. Bilingual specialist Wayne Holm stressed how radical the project was: "Whatever OEO did for good or for bad, for the first time, OEO put Navajos in administrative roles. There were just a *handful* of Indians, and particularly Navajos, that had been in administrative roles. [The Rough Rock Demonstration School] must have been shocking to people at the time. [The founders, and local community members] were probably the only people in America that really believed in the fact that Indians could administer their own school programs." Skeptics in the BIA forecast that "Rough Rock won't last for 6 months."

They were wrong. Roessel served as Rough Rock's first director, then turned the position over to Dillon Platero, a Navajo. Anglos taught some classes, but beyond doubt Rough Rock was a true community project. An all-Navajo board of directors governed the school's budgeting, accounting, and planning. Navajo culture and language pervaded the curriculum. Non-Indian staff members received in-service training to familiarize them with Navajo society. The school brought community members, including medicine men, into the classroom. Ever mindful of being a resource for the community, Rough Rock included not just adult classroom education but also projects such as a greenhouse, a poultry farm, a furniture factory, and an ambitious art and crafts project that hired Navajo instructors to teach rug weaving, basketry, silversmithing, sash belt weaving, and other creative endeavors.

Rough Rock's seeds blew out across the country's largest reservation and far beyond. It developed curriculum material and research for use by other institutions. Schools took notice of Rough Rock's bilingual and bicultural curriculum and ways of achieving a high level of community involvement. Other tribes soon set up their own Indian-controlled schools. Rough Rock's success led directly to the creation of the Navajo Community College (now Diné College), the first modern tribal college, a movement that in time expanded to more than thirty higher education institutions. The school (now called the Rough Rock Community School) has attracted many visitors, spawned numerous academic articles, and influenced education as far away as Hawaii and Japan.

The OEO projects injected Indian country with a confidence and determination not seen since the creation of the reservation system. The specific projects brought many benefits, but the generalized gifts of leadership and tribal control proved equally enduring. Not everything worked. The tribes hit many potholes on this road. Rough Rock, for example, had to overcome a stretch in the 1980s when the school suffered from federal budget cuts, high absenteeism, and internal divisions. Nonetheless, a thousand or more Indian people, never before given the chance to assume major responsibilities, took the reins of OEO projects and then moved into leadership positions in the tribal councils, national and regional Indian organizations, and federal and state offices. At long last American Indians had the chance to manage—or mismanage—significant programs. It became almost a mantra with this new leadership class that they finally had the power to make their own mistakes, "the right to be wrong and the right to be right." "We had never been given the chance to fail."

THE OEO community action projects, while they showed the way and mattered on their own, could never be more than part of the solution. Many other Indian programs and responsibilities resided in the BIA, other Department of the Interior agencies, and numerous federal offices beyond Interior. The White House obviously had a powerful voice. Under the Constitution, Congress holds primary authority over Indian affairs. It was time for an overarching philosophy to replace termination and articulate the new role of Indian tribal governments in the American federal system.

The late 1960s and 1970s presented an auspicious political setting for progressive action. The administrations of Johnson, Nixon, and Carter all had generally positive predispositions toward Indian affairs. The Nixon years were especially interesting and productive. The president's staff included a number of liberals, like Daniel Patrick Moynihan and Sallyanne Payton, as counterweights to encourage debate. This "loyal opposition" played an important role in Indian matters, as White House advisers Brad Patterson, Len Garment, and Bobbie Greene Kilberg all advocated for Native Americans. The three pushed hard, for instance, for Menominee restoration, and Patterson and Garment expended large blocks of time in negotiations with Indians during the Alcatraz, BIA, and Wounded Knee occupations.

Congressional leadership saw Indian policy in a new light. In the House, Lloyd Meeds of Washington took over as chair of the Indian subcommittee in 1973 and, with Wayne Aspinall gone, served four years as a stalwart for tribes until running into political opposition from his constituents over fishing rights. Morris Udall, determined to support the Indian cause, became Interior Committee chair in 1975. On the Senate side, James Abourezk of South Dakota was one of the best congressional friends Indians have ever had. Several other senators, notably Mark Hatfield of Oregon, Barry Goldwater and Paul Fannin of Arizona, Frank Church of Idaho, and Lee Metcalf of Montana, took a strong interest, especially when tribes from their own states were involved.

A new way of doing business was reflected in the congressional committee staffs, which exert influence over so many legislative decisions. The year 1971 marked the arrival of Forrest Gerard, a member of the Blackfeet Tribe, to the staff of the Senate Interior Committee. Frank Ducheneaux, an attorney from Cheyenne River Sioux and son of the tribal chair of the same name, joined the House Interior Committee staff in 1973. A few other Indian people, notably Helen Scheirbeck, a Lumbee who had worked on the Indian Civil Rights Act for Senator Sam Ervin, had served as staffers on Capitol Hill. Gerard and Ducheneaux, however, became the first to hold posts on the key Interior Committees where most Indian bills went.

Gerard and Ducheneaux, able professionals both, had the confidence of their members, Senator Jackson in Gerard's case, Meeds and Udall in Ducheneaux's. Previously colleagues in the BIA, the two men worked together, setting priorities and comparing notes. They walked the thin line between their Indian advocacy and their duties to their superiors. Often this took the form of pointed but necessary advice to tribes on how to recast their proposals to meet legal standards and political realities. Gerard had the additional task of gradually softening Jackson's stands on Indian matters. They played central roles in the explosion of Indian legislation beginning in the early 1970s.

IF TRIBAL EXPERIENCE with the OEO and a newly receptive Congress helped lay the foundation for self-determination, the Johnson and Nixon administrations also played pivotal roles in articulating and popularizing the new approach. Good governmental programs often spring from personal creativity and advocacy by agency employees in the field, and Bill King, a maverick superintendent from the Salt River Pima-Maricopa Reservation, had a lot to do with tribal empowerment. On his own, he bent the system to allow the tribe to run most of its BIA programs. In the mid-1960s, Secretary of the Interior Stewart Udall recruited his fellow Arizonan to Washington, where King, with Udall's backing, heralded the idea of adopting the OEO approach for all government Indian programs. In 1968, Johnson delivered a special message to Congress in which he called for "self-determination" as the "new goal for Indian programs." The objective would be a "policy of maximum choice for American Indians."

Partly because the Johnson message was a bit premature (it came before Alcatraz) and partly because his successor's presentation was far more detailed, Richard Nixon's 1970 special message to Congress has become accepted as the landmark enunciation of the self-determination policy. Many well-intentioned people in and out of the White House, including Alvin Josephy, the spirited journalist who took on Kinzua Dam, worked on the message, but there was little consultation with the tribes in spite of the considerable amount of self-determination already being exercised by tribal governments. The federal government had not yet learned how to deal directly with Indian country. Nonetheless, although suspicion initially abounded among Indians, Nixon's 1970 message quickly came to be recognized for what it was, a truly historic and pathbreaking moment in federal Indian affairs.

The message called for a fundamental realignment in the federal and tribal relationship. Nixon flatly proclaimed termination "wrong": It was "morally and legally unacceptable" and produced "bad practical results." As for the tribes' relationship with the BIA, Congress should "empower a tribe . . . to take over the control [of federal programs] . . . whenever the tribal council . . . voted to do so." In addition to articulating broad ideas, the message put forth a laundry list of laws that should be enacted. Nixon urged Congress to reject termination by a new concurrent resolution, adopt sweeping self-determination legislation, return Blue Lake to the Taos Pueblo, support Indian-controlled schools, enact economic development legislation, increase funding for Indian health, and create an independent Indian trust counsel authority to represent Indian interests in the Departments of the Interior and Justice.

While much in Nixon's text was not new, the widely noticed message, with its remarkable force and specificity, opened the throttle on the momentum already building in Indian country. Congress would in time enact virtually all of Nixon's ambitious legislative agenda. Beyond that, as Indians became accustomed to working in the federal legislative arena, tribes would get hundreds of laws on scores of subjects passed.

The centerpiece of the Nixon message became statutory law in 1975, when Congress enacted the Indian Self-Determination and Education Assistance Act. In it, Congress directed the BIA and the Indian Health Service to contract with tribes for the planning and administration of programs. Now, instead of the federal agencies' building a tribal community center, setting up a day care program, running a health clinic, or writing an economic development plan, a tribe could contract with the agency, receive the funding directly, and do the job itself.

The initial self-determination statute brought reform but hardly instant revolution. In the early years the BIA, jealous of its century-old prerogatives, stonewalled requests from tribes to operate their own programs. Funding often proved inadequate. Despite these headwinds, tribal administrators never let up, submitting applications and reapplications to take over BIA programs and regularly enlisting congressional offices to increase the pressure. The new system of self-determination settled in during the 1980s. Statutes expanded tribal rights to contract for government services. Ten years after the self-determination law, Bill Pensoneau, tribal planner for the Ponca of Oklahoma, put it accurately: "In the 1960s, self-determination was a distant dream. We're a lot closer to it now." Tribal control steadily increased in the years that followed.

The meaning of the congressional and presidential announcement of a new policy went far beyond the mechanics of transferring programs to tribal governments. Self-determination proved to be a launching platform for tribal advancement generally. The OEO started it. Now the broader self-determination policy helped expand tribal infrastructures and leadership opportunities. Morale in Indian country brightened as the heavy hand of the BIA lifted, bit by bit. Courts, in ruling on the nature of tribal governmental powers, looked to the concept of self-determination for guidance. In whatever circle—on the reservations, in town, or in the halls of government—the perception of tribes shifted measurably. It is

quite a different calling card to be bound for self-determination
rather than consigned to termination.

FOR TRIBES to break free of the chains that bound them,
they also needed favorable interpretations of the treaties and myriad other laws that played such a major role in the lives of Indian
people. Foremost were the treaty resource rights and sovereignty
that came to a head in *United States v. Washington* when Judge
George Boldt called court to order in Tacoma in August 1973, with
Billy Frank, Jr., the Nisqually fisherman, standing in the back of
the courtroom and worrying to himself that after all the effort, the
proceeding might be "rigged."

But Frank also had good reason to be optimi tic. Court opinions
showed a clear trend toward an expansive reading of treaty fishing rights. Back in Michigan, Bill Jondreau, Buck Chosa, and Fred
Dakota prevailed in their long journey through the court system
to protect Chippewa treaty rights. In 1971 the Michigan Supreme
Court had taken the rare step of overruling one of its own opinions, the 1930 *Chosa* decision. Now the court squarely held that
the state's prosecution of Jondreau for fishing for lake trout outside the state season violated the 1854 treaty with the Keweenaw
Bay Band.

In Idaho, Indian fishermen scored an important court victory.
The Fort Bridger Treaty of 1868 recognized the right of the
Shoshone and Bannock "to hunt on the unoccupied lands of the
United States." State officials took the word "hunt" literally and
arrested Indian salmon fishermen on the ground that only hunting was protected by the treaty. Tribal members knew otherwise;
their ancestors at treaty time had insisted on the right to fish,
which was at the heart of their way of life. In 1972, in *State v.
Tinno,* the Idaho Supreme Court agreed. Neither tribal language,
Shoshone or Bannock, contained separate words for hunting and
fishing. Instead, *tygi* in Shoshone and *hoawai* in Bannock both
meant "to gather wild food." *State v. Tinno* thus issued one more
reminder that treaties are bilateral agreements between two governments and that ever since the great decisions of Chief Justice
John Marshall in the 1830s, American courts have read treaties as

the Indian people would have understood them. The U.S. Supreme Court also handed down treaty decisions in 1968, 1971, and 1973 that, while not decisive, encouraged the Pacific Northwest tribes.

Public opinion and court rulings helped create a rising tide in favor of the Northwest tribes as the trial date in Judge Boldt's courtroom approached. The efforts of church leaders, print and television journalists, filmmakers, scholars, and, most of all, the earnest, defiant Indian people out on the rivers and in the demonstrations combined to depict a genuinely arresting and idealistic movement. The participants felt it as well. In 1972, Harry Sachse, a young lawyer in the Justice Department, had been assigned the oral argument before the Supreme Court in an important treaty fishing case involving the Puyallup and Nisqually tribes. Stationed in Washington, D.C., and working purely from the paper file, he initially felt only a distant connection with the bloodstream of the events 3,000 miles away. That changed for him, as it did for many others, when he met the people and got out on the water:

> The Solicitor General's office does not ordinarily send their lawyers out to see what they are going to be arguing about or meet the people. It is a very intellectual institution. So that summer, on some of my vacation time, I went out to meet the Puyallup Tribe and see the river. I waited at the Chief Leshi Cemetery, which was about all the land the Tribe had, and met with the Council in a war surplus building that they used for meetings. Ramona Bennett, young and beautiful, was Chairperson of the Tribe. . . . It was a simple room, a tribe with hardly anything except a treaty, tradition of fishing and a fighting spirit. . . .
>
> After meeting with the Council, the Tribe set it up for me to spend the next day with Billy Frank. . . . We walked up and down the Puyallup River and I saw salmon swimming up the river making ripples like submarines for the first time in my life. We then went to Frank's Landing and putted around the Nisqually River and the Bay in Billy's boat, looking at the fishing sites and seeing seals. It was a wonderful experience for me, and a typical part of the Frank's Landing method of seeing that

people who are important to their cause—me, because I was
about to argue their cause in the Supreme Court—understood
the cause from the heart as well as the head.

The lengthy, sprawling trial in *United States v. Washington*—
Judge Boldt considered arguments from eleven lawyers, heard
nearly 50 witnesses, received 350 exhibits, and analyzed testimony in a 4,600-page trial transcript—turned ultimately on historical evidence, for Boldt's job was to say what the cryptic treaty
language meant in defining Indian off-reservation rights as: "the
right of taking fish, at usual and accustomed grounds and stations
. . . in common with all citizens of the Territory." Did the state
have any role in regulating Indian fishing? Did the "right of taking
fish" mean that the tribes had the sovereign authority to do their
own regulating? Did "in common with" allocate a share of the fishery to the tribes? How large a share?

In re-creating these ancient negotiations, Judge Boldt was
required to give the benefit of the doubt to the tribes. The
Supreme Court said long ago that any ambiguities in treaty language must be resolved in favor of the Indians. The United States
had written the treaty in its own language and, being militarily
superior, could impose its terms. The law has always, as a matter
of fairness, construed contracts between unequal parties (such as
consumer agreements with banks and insurance companies) in
favor of the weaker parties. The rule of reading Indian treaties in
favor of the tribes also derives from the United States' trust obligation to act in the best interests of the tribes.

This trial about the past hinged on the testimony of Dr. Barbara
Lane, an anthropologist from the University of British Columbia.
Lane, authoritative and precise, speaking in her clipped Canadian
accent, described the treaty negotiations and the backdrop of
Native life in great detail. Judge Boldt gave her the highest judicial
compliment, calling her findings "exceptionally well researched
and reported." Comparing Lane's testimony with that of Dr. Caroll
Riley, the state's expert, Judge Boldt concluded that "in summary,
the court finds that where their testimony differs in any significant
detail, the testimony of Dr. Lane is more credible and satisfactory

than that of Dr. Riley and is accepted as such except as otherwise specified." Years later Judge Boldt validated in simple terms the iron determination of the Indian treaty negotiators: "Historically, the Indians would never sign a treaty unless they'd retained their prerogatives to fish in their usual and accustomed places."

Barbara Lane had company on the witness stand. Toward the end of the trial, Indian elders testified and told, sometimes in their own languages, their stories of the salmon people and the treaties. Some lawyers in the case believe that the words of the elders "won the case." Judge Boldt was rapt, never taking his eyes from Lena Hillaire, Lena Smith, Forrest "Dutch" Kinley, and Esther Ross as they recounted their stories of the rivers, land, ceremonies, and salmon. They related too what their grandfathers had told them about treaty time, confirming and deepening Dr. Lane's academic testimony. Lena Smith said that "once when my grandfather was picked up for fishing and put in jail, we went to the jailhouse, and they were talking about the treaty. Isaac Stevens said to our chiefs that if there was a river or a creek where the Indians fished before, they could fish there after the treaty." Dutch Kinley testified in a similar vein: "We gave up our land without any restrictions. But when it came to hunting and fishing, we wanted exclusive rights in certain areas. We felt that we were giving the citizens a right to fish in common with us." An attorney for a non-Indian commercial fishing association then tested Kinley on cross-examination:

Q: Mr. Kinley, you just said a moment ago that you believe the Indians have exclusive fishing rights to certain locations. I want to point out the obvious: that you certainly were not present at the treaty negotiations, nor have you talked to anyone who was at them, have you?

A: No. My father died at 103 years old, and I think it's been the tradition of our people—you have history books; our people, the duty of our old people was to inform us about our family and about our rights. I think that this is a tradition that has been as accurate as your history books.

Judge Boldt handed down his historic opinion in *United States v. Washington* on February 12, 1974—he intentionally chose Lincoln's birthday—finding for the tribes on every major point. He had immersed himself in the case, explaining later that he had spent "days and days on end reading all the great decisions on Indians and fishing rights. Over and over again, all the great minds who dealt with the problems of Indians put in their opinions that we were taking away from the Indians their rightful heritage." The 203-page decision, replete with historical analysis, worked from the premise that the best understanding of the term "in common with" at treaty time was that the tribal and federal parties meant to divide the resource equally. In this, Judge Boldt boldly moved beyond Judge Belloni's trailblazing "fair share" allocation to the tribes by announcing a "50-50" allocation: The treaties meant to allow tribes an opportunity to harvest one-half of the salmon passing their off-reservation fishing places.

Further, Judge Boldt squarely recognized the sovereign right of tribes as governments to regulate the salmon harvest by tribal members. As a predicate, he debunked the specter that the tribes overharvested or wasted salmon: "With a single possible exception testified to by a highly interested witness and not otherwise substantiated, notwithstanding three years of exhaustive trial preparation, neither Game nor Fisheries [the Washington state agencies] has discovered and produced any credible evidence showing any instance, remote or recent, when a definitely identified member of any plaintiff tribe exercised his off reservation treaty rights by any conduct or means detrimental to the perpetuation of any species of anadromous fish."

The Boldt decision, as *United States v. Washington* became known, set off an explosive reaction from fishing organizations and state agencies. A group called the Steelheaders vociferously led the charge for the sports fishers, but commercial fishers faced the greatest impact; most of the increased Indian allocation (tribal fishers took only about 6 percent before the decision) came from the non-Indian commercial take. There is no underestimating the effects on the non-Indian commercial fishers. Many had to abandon their craft and relocate. Their families and communities suffered. A state and federal "buy-back" program to retire commercial boats helped ease the transition, but the new allocation regime did not settle in until well into the 1980s. In the meantime, it was the Indians who now confronted the fish-ins. "Massive illegal fishing continued for years following the decision," wrote Fay Cohen, author of a leading study on the Boldt decision and its aftermath. In 1977 alone the non-Indian fishers illegally took an estimated 183,000 salmon.

The protesters both ridiculed and defied Judge Boldt. Bumper stickers blared: "Can Judge Boldt, Not Salmon"; "Let's Give 50 Percent of the Indians to Judge Boldt." Federal marshals had to cut down a gill net used to hang the judge in effigy in front of the federal courthouse. More disturbing, state officials were slow to prosecute violators of Boldt's decree; when they did, state judges— covertly undermining the supreme law of the land—usually dismissed the charges.

Eventually the Boldt decision gained acceptance by even its staunchest opponents. The federal court of appeals affirmed it in 1975, and the Supreme Court declined to hear it a year later. State officials, led by Attorney General (later U.S. Senator) Slade Gorton, still refused to give in. Taking a circuitous procedural route, in 1979 they managed to reach the Supreme Court, which, this time issuing a full written opinion, affirmed Judge Boldt's ruling in virtually all respects. In a statement that has few parallels in American jurisprudence, the Court quoted from an earlier court of appeals opinion and underscored the sweep of the Boldt decision, the extreme nature of Washington's response to it, and the epic nature of the issues at bar: "The State's extraordinary machinations in resisting the [1974] decree have forced the district court to take over a large share of the management of the State's fishery in order to enforce its decrees. Except for some desegregation cases, the district court has faced the most concerted official and private efforts to frustrate a decree of a federal court witnessed in this century."

Normally, cases are remembered for their Supreme Court opinions, but the Northwest fishing case, *United States v. Washington*, remains forever known as the Boldt decision. Written and carefully documented by a respected judge after protracted proceedings, the decision carries a rare credibility. Minority rights,

judicial courage, morality, generations of Native persistence, and
the truth of history converged in the federal courthouse in Tacoma
in 1974 to create the kind of elevated justice to which our system
can sometimes rise.

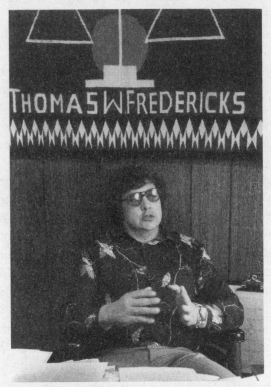

*Tom Fredericks, Mandan, served as executive director
of the Native American Rights Fund from 1975 to
1977 and has represented tribal clients in private
practice for more than twenty years. During the
Carter administration, he was the first Indian to be
appointed associate solicitor for Indian affairs. Under
pressure from Congress, the Department of the Interior established a high-level working group on Indian
fishing rights in the late 1970s. Fredericks, a member
of the group, was instrumental in convincing the
group to abandon a proposal for the United States to
urge the Supreme Court to revisit—and possibly overturn—the Boldt decision. Photograph courtesy of Ray
Ramirez, Native American Rights Fund.*

. . .

BY THE MID-1970s, therefore, tribal action on many different fronts had fundamentally reshaped the circumstances that held sway just a generation before. Congress jettisoned termination, advanced a new policy of self-determination, and began to give relief to terminated tribes. Administrations heard out tribal views and regularly responded favorably to them. Judges, pulled into a highly specialized area of law counterintuitive to most Americans (including the judges themselves), took the trouble to plumb the historical roots and true meanings of treaties and other laws that at first blush seemed to contradict American notions of equality. The cause of Native people resonated with the American public.

This favorable atmosphere would be tested severely and often. As tribes gained political, legal, and economic power, they would face determined opposition, just as the salmon people had. But now the tribes had established the continuing validity of their treaties and their standing as governments. They also had earned the right to be heard and knew how to make the most of it.

9.

Reclaiming Heartlands

Juan de Jesus Romero served as the cacique, the highest spiritual leader, of the Taos Pueblo in New Mexico until his death in 1978 at the age of 101. His life's passion was the return of Blue Lake to his people. He prayed for Blue Lake every morning and evening, gave the people hope, and beseeched them to keep the cause alive. "If our land is not returned to us," he once said, "if it is turned over to the government for its use, then it is the end of Indian life. Our people will scatter as the people of other nations have scattered. It is our religion that holds us together."

The cacique rarely spoke in public, and when he did, it was through an interpreter. Similarly, most of the tribe's elected council members were fluent only in Tiwa. Since a return of Blue Lake would require congressional action, the council appointed Paul Bernal to serve as the pueblo's representative to the outside world. A World War II navy veteran, Bernal spent more than two decades leading the public campaign for a return of Blue Lake, tireless in his efforts on many fronts, almost frantic in his pleas for relief as he blocked out his words in heavily accented English, his second language.

The Taos Pueblo's campaign burns especially bright today because it was the first of its kind to succeed. Since the pueblo's success in 1970, tribes have made land recovery a major priority. Some acquisitions (including the dramatic developments in

Alaska recounted in this chapter) were done by congressional action or litigation and have tended to involve large expanses of land. Others, far more numerous, have been accomplished by purchase. Nearly every tribe has an active land acquisition program that buys former tribal land acre by acre, south forty by south forty.

Indian people not only stemmed the seemingly inexorable loss of land that had prevailed since the arrival of Europeans but reversed it. The landholdings of tribes hit their all-time low point—about 50.5 million acres—in the 1960s, after the termination statutes took effect. Since then, in addition to the vast Native holdings in Alaska, tribes have expanded the Indian land base in the contiguous states to a total of 58 million acres, an area larger than all but ten states. That is an increase of 15 percent, or 7.5 million acres—one and a half times the size of Massachusetts.

The breakthrough came with the Taos Pueblo's arduous and historic crusade to recover Blue Lake.

THE PUEBLO Indians of the Southwest—21 pueblos in the Rio Grande watershed with the Zuni and Hopi lying farther to the west—trace their ancestry in the region back at least 12,000 years. Initially hunting and gathering societies, they evolved into farming communities with the arrival of corn from Central America about 3,500 years ago and then began to live in villages, developing the adobe-style architecture still popular in the Southwest. The Taos Pueblo is the northernmost of the pueblos, its classic multistory adobe dwellings set against the sharp uplift of the Sangre de Cristo Mountains.

The Spanish began to settle the Rio Grande country in the late 1500s, long before Anglos moved into the trans-Mississippi West. If anything, the Spanish missionaries exceeded the Anglos to the north in their aggressive, often brutal treatment of the Natives. The pueblos, however, proved resilient in the face of cruel beatings, forced conversions to Christianity, and slavery. In modern times pueblo Indians typically ascribe to two religions, Catholicism and their own, but the traditional beliefs—steeped in

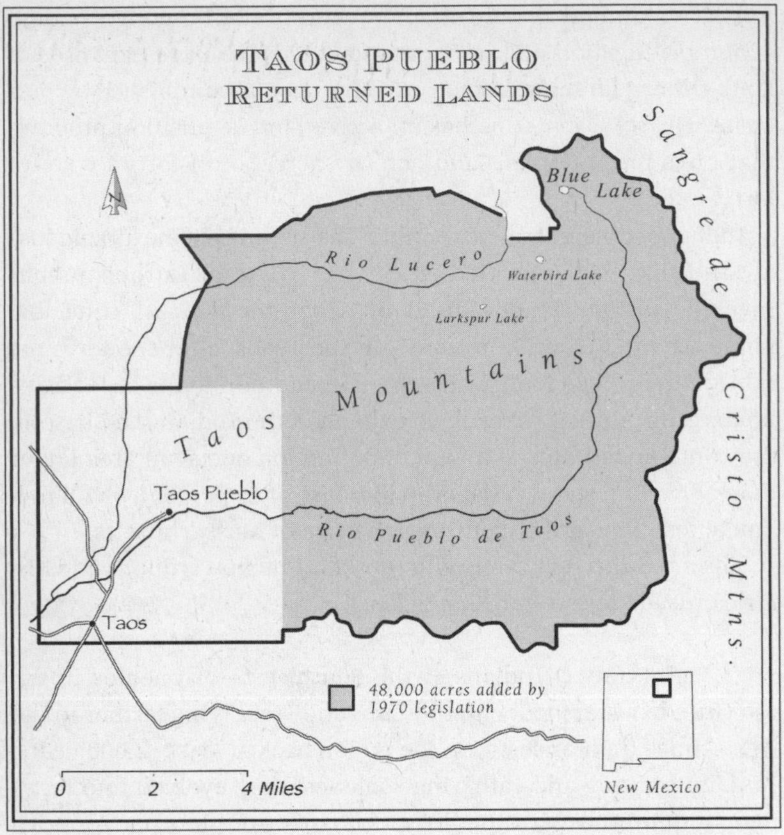
TAOS PUEBLO
RETURNED LANDS
Sangre de Cristo Mtns.
Blue Lake
Rio Lucero
Waterbird Lake
Larkspur Lake
Taos Mountains
Taos Pueblo
Rio Pueblo de Taos
Taos
48,000 acres added by 1970 legislation
0 2 4 Miles
New Mexico

secrecy, rooted in an intricate relationship with the natural world, and replete with elaborate songs, dances, and other rituals—run deeper.

The Rio Pueblo de Taos, which passes through the Taos Pueblo, begins as the outflow from Blue Lake, set in a forested bowl near the crest of the Sangre de Cristos not far from Wheeler Peak, the highest point in New Mexico. To reach Blue Lake in August for the pueblo's annual three-day ceremony, Taos people follow a rough, 25-mile-long trail that ascends from sagebrush terrain through aspen and ponderosa pine stands to the fir and spruce forest at the lake. Numerous shrines are found in the vicinity of the trail, home to stories and lessons from all the years. Among Blue Lake's many religious uses, all requiring strict privacy, the Taos Pueblo Indians instruct young people there during the six- to eighteen-month periods when children are removed from school for spiritual training. Further, as a federal commission found, "this area is used every day by at least a few Taos Pueblo Indians for private religious reflection." As Paul Bernal explained, the water in the river "is purified by nature and therefore is holy water coming from Blue Lake. . . . Blue Lake is our Indian church and we've been keeping this Indian church since the beginning of time. . . . We cannot practice our religion unless we own Blue Lake."

The pueblo's ownership came to an abrupt end under Gifford Pinchot, the patrician chief of the Forest Service during the Teddy Roosevelt years and one of the most influential figures in the history of the American West. In his illustrious career, he built the Forest Service into a respected and powerful administrative agency. Hand in hand with Roosevelt, Pinchot inspired perhaps the most notable conservation policy ever adopted, the set-aside of some 150 million acres of public land—7 percent of the entire nation—as national forests, withdrawn from homesteading and put under protective management.

But Pinchot had blind spots. He paid little attention to Indians in that era of the "Vanishing Indian" and on several occasions ran roughshod over their land rights. Always anxious to put land under his agency's protection, he recommended to Roosevelt that most of the Taos watershed, including Blue Lake, be designated a federal forest reserve under Forest Service control. Though never litigated, the action may well have been illegal. While the Taos Pueblo did not receive a written grant to Blue Lake (unlike the village, which the king of Spain had granted to the pueblo in 1551), American law has always recognized possessory rights to aboriginal land used by tribes, which surely included Blue Lake. Congress gave presidents broad authority to designate forest reserves, but those powers did not include extinguishing Indian land rights. But no matter. In 1906, Teddy Roosevelt proclaimed the Taos Forest Reserve, later named the Carson National Forest. From that point on, to all the world Blue Lake, for millennia the land of the Taos Pueblo, became land of the Forest Service.

The pueblo never stopped seeing Blue Lake as a sacred site, for use solely by its members. The Forest Service, conversely, operated under a mission calling for public use, including timber harvesting and recreation. The two were at loggerheads, but the federal agency had the leverage of possession. In 1904, during the government's study of forest reserve status, the tribe sought an exclusive use permit to assure privacy for its religious observances; after creation of the reserve, the agency brushed off the proposal. The pueblo then twice requested presidential declarations of exclusive pueblo use, but the Forest Service successfully opposed both. In 1916 the agency opened the area for public recreation, constructed trails, and stocked the lake with trout even though, as one anthropologist explained, outsiders created a "grave threat" to the religious ceremonies: "Their very presence, even if they observe nothing, is contaminating. It constitutes a serious invasion of religious privacy." A decade later forest rangers felled trees to build a cabin and horse corrals close to the lake. During the Franklin Roosevelt administration, BIA Commissioner John Collier advocated for the pueblo and succeeded in the passage of a 1933 statute directing the Forest Service to issue the pueblo a fifty-year permit, presumably for year-round exclusive use. For seven years the agency stalled and equivocated and finally issued a permit that allowed the pueblo exclusive use only during the three-day August ceremonies.

After World War II, now with Paul Bernal as the strategist, the pueblo's crusade continued. An unexpected opportunity presented itself. Congress had passed the Indian Claims Commission Act of 1946 as a way to square accounts with Indian tribes (and, with past wrongs resolved, pave the way for termination). The statute created the Indian Claims Commission and allowed tribes to sue for damages caused by federal actions, including the confiscation of tribal lands, no matter how long ago the land may have been taken. While the law can be viewed as an act of grace, Indian Claims Commission lawsuits had one very large catch: Tribes could recover only money, not land, and once a tribe received a cash payment, any legal claim to the land was forever barred.

The Taos Pueblo, which wanted Blue Lake, not cash, worked the machinery of the Indian Claims Commission to suit its pur-

poses. The pueblo decided to file, but not to obtain a money judgment. Instead, it sought a preliminary commission decision
declaring that the tribe had legally occupied the land when President Roosevelt put it into the forest reserve. With the help of Felix
Cohen, the pueblo found a law firm that would bring the case even
though it would not produce the generous fees that claims attorneys normally commanded. With the complaint filed in 1951, the
pueblo had reason to hope for a judicial finding that Blue Lake had
been wrongfully taken. While the commission had no authority to
return land, the strategy went, a strong statement from the commission would clarify the fundamental injustice for Congress,
which could then transfer Blue Lake back to the pueblo.

Several bills were introduced during the 1950s, but they went
nowhere. Despite their modest nature (rather than a land transfer
to the pueblo, the bills would have made permanent the existing
Forest Service use permit), Congress had in mind termination, not
expansion, of tribal rights. Further, the bills ran up against two
implacable foes that would fight the Taos Pueblo to the end.

One was the Forest Service, which assiduously cultivated the
western members of Congress who controlled public land matters. The agency remained firm in its insistence that it must make
decisions on the national forests. Beyond that, granting permanent use rights amounted to a transfer of the land itself, and it was
gospel within the service that no national forest acres should ever
pass out of the public land estate. This objection was accompanied
by two related arguments: A return of Blue Lake would open the
floodgates for similar claims by other tribes, and the Taos Pueblo,
whatever its present intentions, would eventually develop the
land commercially for its timber, minerals, or recreation potential. The Forest Service's position carried great weight. The
agency, though it would come under heavy criticism in the 1970s
for its excessive timber harvesting, rode a wave of public approval
during the 1950s.

The other obstacle was Clinton P. Anderson, the powerful New
Mexico senator who had to be on board for any legislation dealing
with public land in his home state. As secretary of agriculture during the Truman administration, Anderson had become imbued

with Pinchot's conservation legacy, the competence of the Forest Service (which is housed with the Department of Agriculture), and the "not one acre" rule against national forest land transfers. It helped the Taos Pueblo not at all that as a general matter the not one acre rule made good public policy. Our national forests are cherished public assets, and a flat prohibition against transfers served as protection against mining and timber companies that coveted national forest lands.

In 1960, with all progress on Blue Lake stalled, the pueblo decided to put off any further congressional initiatives until the Indian Claims Commission decided if the pueblo had held aboriginal ownership when the forest reserve was established. On the administrative front, the pueblo and the Forest Service continued to veer between heated disputes and sporadic but fruitless negotiations.

The Indian Claims Commission handed down its decision in 1965, and the ruling gave an enormous lift to the pueblo. The opinion (cosigned by none other than Arthur V. Watkins, who had been appointed to the commission after leaving the Senate) detailed, first, the Taos people's long and exclusive use of the area. It went on to recognize the need for privacy not just at the August ceremony but also during the individual prayers and religious reflection by Pueblo members that occurred daily at Blue Lake. The opinion concluded by ruling that when the United States obtained the area from Mexico in 1848, the Taos Pueblo had "held aboriginal or Indian title to [the Blue Lake watershed] and that it continued in the exclusive possession and use of said lands without interruption" until Roosevelt's 1906 proclamation.

Confronted with the commission's decision, Senator Anderson introduced legislation to return Blue Lake to the Taos Pueblo in 1966. In doing so, Anderson made it clear that he did not support the bill, that he had put it forward only as a courtesy to his constituents. Nonetheless, the pueblo now had the opportunity to press for what it had wanted all along, a full transfer of Blue Lake, not a permanent permit.

Many other factors enhanced the pueblo's cause. The tribal council, long at odds with the claims attorneys over their handling of the legislative matters, now turned to William Schaab, an Albu-querque attorney who dealt with members of Congress in a diplo-matic but firm way. Corinne Locker of the Association on American Indian Affairs helped coordinate the offers of support that poured in and proved to be a "master tactician." She also stood firm, working closely with Paul Bernal and the tribal council, against pressure from outsiders (including the claims attorneys and AAIA, her own organization) to settle short of a complete land transfer. Oliver La Farge, who had labored for the Taos cause dur-ing his years in the Collier administration and beyond, built up goodwill for the tribe. After La Farge died in 1963, his wife, Con-suela, chaired the national committee for return of Blue Lake. The pueblo also gained public understanding and support from Frank Waters's searing novel *The Man Who Killed the Deer*, about a young Pueblo Indian who goes hunting only to be arrested and ulti-mately entangled in the nightmare of the loss of Blue Lake and the Forest Service's obdurate determination to control the watershed in the name of conservation.

The Taos Pueblo campaign gathered good friends in Washing-ton, D.C., including Department of the Interior Secretary Stewart Udall, himself a southwesterner. A lover of history (Udall had just published the influential *The Quiet Crisis*, which included a lauda-tory chapter on Gifford Pinchot), he not only articulated the pueblo's religious needs but also explained to Congress why it never should have lost Blue Lake in the first place: "My own guess is that if Gifford Pinchot and Theodore Roosevelt would have known what they were doing—they were acting in great haste at the time and for the great good of the country—that they would not have taken these lands." Senator Robert Kennedy and his brother, Ted, came to the tribe's aid, as did Senator Barry Gold-water. Senator Fred Harris of Oklahoma, a Democrat and new to the Senate, bucked senior members of his party. His dashing and influential wife, LaDonna, a Comanche, was a dynamo, energeti-cally enlisting support in high places. The Wilderness Society gave eloquent backing.

Senator Anderson's 1966 bill did not pass, but Richard Nixon's victory in 1968, coupled with the steadily rising sympathy for

American Indian causes, finally tipped the balance in favor of the pueblo. The Indian advocates in the White House saw Blue Lake as an ideal opportunity to demonstrate support for Indian concerns. In particular, Bobbie Greene Kilberg, in the face of stiff opposition from some quarters, took the issue under her wing and, strategizing with LaDonna Harris, pressed it within the administration. As Nixon's comprehensive 1970 message to Congress on Indian affairs worked through the drafting stage, Blue Lake rose to the top to become first among his several priorities.

Nixon even timed his message to Congress to benefit the return of the lake. The House had already passed a Blue Lake land transfer bill. The problems lay with the Senate, especially with Anderson, Henry Jackson, and other Democrats. Nixon released the message at a highly publicized press conference on July 8, 1970, the day before the Senate subcommittee hearing on Blue Lake. The Taos Pueblo leaders attended the press conference and were greeted warmly by the president. The next day the *New York Times* carried a front-page photograph of the occasion. Bobbie Greene Kilberg remembered that at the White House staff meeting that morning "all those guys stood up and gave me a standing ovation and said, 'we don't believe it, he's on the front page of the *New York Times* doing something with a minority group that people like.' They could not believe it."

The Senate hearing on Blue Lake went well, but not smoothly. Realizing that passage was now close to inevitable, Senators Anderson and Lee Metcalf of Montana pressed and sometimes badgered tribal witnesses, trying to bolster the senators' arguments: that this land return would open the floodgates to other tribes and that the pueblo might want to make economic profit from the land. But the tribe had made an overwhelming case for the return of Blue Lake, showing circumstances that were, if not unique, rare; if other tribes could make equally compelling cases, then they too should be judged on their merits.

On the economic use issue, the exchange proved a fascinating study in disparate worldviews, harking back to Arthur Watkins's questioning of Klamath witnesses during the 1954 termination hearings. Repeatedly, Senator Quentin Burdick of North Dakota

After President Nixon's dramatic endorsement of the return of Blue Lake, he and Vice President Spiro Agnew met in the White House with Paul Bernal (left) and the cacique, Juan de Jesus Romero.

asked Bernal if the land should revert to the United States should the tribe decide to develop it. "There is no way," Bernal answered, "we are going to use this 48,000 acres for economic benefits." What, Burdick persisted, if gas or gold or uranium were found? Again, Bernal rejected the senator's premise: "[T]he Taos Indian is going to keep that in a natural state for only religious purposes, regardless of what he found." Suppose a livestock company wanted to lease it for grazing? "We don't want no stock. We don't want no cattle grazing. We do not want it for economic benefit, sir." If the land were used for mining or grazing, would you give it back to the United States? "We are going to use it only for religious purposes, sir." Suppose it ceased to be used for religious purposes? "It is not going to be ceased." The pueblo's attorney, William Schaab, intervened at that point, but one gains the firm impression that the questions and answers could have gone on forever, Senator Burdick sincerely believing that economic development would

always trump anything else if the price were right, Paul Bernal
sincerely believing that for his people development at Blue Lake
had no price, and never would.

Despite such often tense questioning, the hearing was most
characterized by its concluding testimony, the appearance of the
95-year-old cacique, Juan de Jesus Romero. Wearing his traditional shirt and wrap, his hair tied back in a knot, he helped himself along with his plain wooden cane. Romero had spent 65 years
praying and working for the return of Blue Lake. The cacique,
with Bernal interpreting, spoke briefly and deliberately not of
issues but of sacrifice, justice, the Great Spirit, love, and the commonality of all human beings. "He had extraordinary spiritual
power," Bobbie Greene Kilberg recalled. "He had a presence about
him, there was something about him that lit up a room."

When the cacique finished, the return of Blue Lake to his people had become a certainty. Beyond that, he and the others had
reversed a long-entrenched policy of the United States Congress.
Before Blue Lake, the watchword was "Not one acre for Indians."
After Blue Lake, the implicit understanding was that Congress
would return land to tribes when they could make deserving
cases.

Later, after President Nixon had signed the bill into law at a
teary-eyed ceremony, Paul Bernal looked back on the crusade that
had consumed a quarter century of his life. He had given so much.
Corinne Locker wrote that not "one of the non-Indians working on
the campaign, including myself, would have stuck it out without
his leadership and inspiration, and a willingness to do a large part
of the work year after year." Bernal reflected:

> After I finished this work . . . I guess you might say I have
> used the best part of my life. My prime time is what makes me
> able to handle and tackle these types of technical problems for
> the tribe. I felt like after we got this land and after we got this
> title back I'm still resting. I feel like I still need lots of rest. . . .
> Because part of my life God gave to me. I was overseas and fight-
> ing the Japanese out there and I said, "Maybe one day, God, if
> you let me go back, I'll go back. I'm going to do something for

Paul Bernal (1990s). Photograph courtesy of Richard Trudell.

my tribe; if my people want me to do something, I'll do it." So
really that particular request of God made the reality for me to
come back and do this. And I was glad. I really was glad to do
this.

DURING THE Blue Lake hearings, several witnesses for the
Taos Pueblo spoke to the argument that a return would open the
floodgates for other Indian land claims. Some testified that the
Taos claim was "singular" and that it would not serve as precedent.
That view carried weight in that the Taos claim had unique
aspects. At the same time, other witnesses acknowledged something else: that tribes across the country had long-standing grievances, all different from Blue Lake but all compelling in their own
right. John Belindo, for the National Congress of American Indians, defended the uniqueness of Taos ("There are no other claims
like that"), but he went on: "Even were the factual assumptions
correct that this would open the door to other claims for land,
since when does it make sense to argue that justice should be
denied in one instance, because granting what is obviously just

would lead others to seek justice in other instances?" Tandy Wilbur, also speaking for NCAI, was even more explicit: "You are quite concerned about doing something for the Indians and setting a small precedent. You shouldn't think that way because there are other Indians that deserve other lands that actually belonged to these Indian peoples. Right now, today, there are other lands that actually belonged to them. Let's set a precedent. Let's do something for the Indian people."

Out in central Oregon, on the east side of the Cascade Range, Delbert Frank and Olney Patt, Sr., knew that their tribe, the Warm Springs, deserved to have land returned. The two men never tired of making their point. "Let's pull over," Frank said to me one day as he was showing me around the reservation. "See that draw? Some of the McQuinn survey markers are up there. I'll show you." After a short hike, Frank was standing over a rock with a faint "U.S." chiseled on it. "See? There's one." Farther up the draw he identified another marker. "These continue up over the ridge up to the top of the Cascades. This is a lot of land, more than 77,000 acres."

Frank was pointing out the weathered original survey markers that identified the north edge of the McQuinn Strip. The tribe's 1855 treaty with the United States defined the northeast corner of the reservation as the midpoint of the Deschutes River opposite "the Mutton Mountains." A government surveyor, T. B. Handley, did the first survey sixteen years later—and did it wrong. Tribal members knew immediately that he had incorrectly set the northeast corner of the reservation; this error excluded from the reservation prime low-lying ponderosa pine stands and hunting grounds as well as spruce-fir forests, lakes, and huckleberry meadows in the high Cascades.

The Department of the Interior eventually agreed to a second survey, completed in 1887 by John A. McQuinn. McQuinn did his homework, interviewing many locals, including—unlike the Handley survey—Indian people. McQuinn also made sure that his survey lines comported with a rough map drawn during the treaty negotiations by Joel Palmer, one of the federal representatives. The McQuinn survey found that the true boundaries of the reservation should lie farther to the north and west by including the McQuinn Strip. The reason for the disparity between the two surveys? The name Mutton Mountains was applied to one ridge when the treaty was negotiated in 1855 and to another in 1871, causing the Handley survey to begin at the wrong point.

The tribe expected a prompt correction, but opposition from white settlers in the McQuinn Strip area blocked land return initiatives in 1890 and 1943. Warm Springs leaders, including Delbert Frank's grandfather and father and finally Delbert himself, kept the issue alive. Finally, in 1971, Senator Mark Hatfield and Representative Al Ullman, both of Oregon, reintroduced bills to return the McQuinn Strip. Much of the land now lay within national forests, and as with Blue Lake, the Forest Service objected. Nonetheless, the tribe had public opinion, as well as the clear surveying error, on its side. Compromises were made to accommodate various interests: Forest Service timber sales and state fish and game laws would continue for 20 years; several high lakes and the Pacific Crest Trail would remain open to the general public, and land within the Mount Jefferson Wilderness Area would not be returned to the tribe. In 1972, 101 years after the inaccurate Handley survey, President Nixon signed the remedial legislation.

Other tribes also convinced Congress to correct errors and injustices. In 1972 the Yakama Nation recovered 60,000 acres on the east and north slopes of Mount Adams that surveyors had mistakenly omitted from the reservation. The Quinault Indian Nation obtained the "North Boundary" area, 21,000 forested acres owed the tribe by treaty. The Siletz and Grand Ronde tribes of Oregon, made landless by termination, received reservation lands as part of their restoration legislation, as did other restored tribes. Congress passed numerous other land return statutes.

The return of former tribal lands just described generated controversy mostly at the local level, with opposition naturally coming from landowners and resource developers who had owned or used the areas. The national policy issues were important but abstract: whether to allow any tribal land returns at all and, if so, whether to keep national forest lands off limits. Two other sets of developments, however, attracted massive regional and national interest. Land claims in the eastern states and Alaska severely tested the nation's willingness to meet tribal demands that far exceeded the acreage in the Blue Lake return, the survey correction measures, or the grants to restored tribes.

IN 1957, Louise Sockabesin dug out some documents, which she had kept in a shoebox, and took them to John Stevens, governor of the Passamaquoddy Tribe in Maine. This is an Indian country tradition. Earnest tribal elders, who have suffered many injuries at the hands of the law, spend long hours scouring old documents and developing elaborate legal theories. More often than not, the process ends in frustration, turning up injustices beyond the legal system's ability to correct. But Stevens's meeting with Mrs. Sockabesin in far northeast Maine, near the New Brunswick line, set in motion sweeping legal events, for one of her documents was a copy of a treaty, signed in 1794, between the Passamaquoddy Tribe and the commonwealth of Massachusetts, which at the time included present-day Maine (in 1820, Maine separated from Massachusetts and became the twenty-third state).

Stevens had grown up hearing about wrongly confiscated tribal lands, but actually reading the treaty, which solemnly promised the tribe 23,000 acres and fifteen islands, galvanized him. The islands, plus 6,000 acres, all had slipped into private hands. Stevens's service in the Korean War had given him experience in dealing with the outside world, and the civil rights movement had shown him what minority groups could accomplish. The tribe's aboriginal domain covered much of Maine, with its sweeping stretches of pinewoods, rivers, coast, and all manner of wildlife. The 1794 treaty had taken almost all of it. Now the realization that still more had been lost angered and emboldened him. In Stevens's mind, seeing the treaty transformed the Passamaquoddy's loss of land from an abstract wrong into a legal violation deserving of a legal remedy.

In 1964, Stevens and other tribal members staged a sit-in when a white landowner started bulldozing a road and cutting timber for tourist cabins, all on land covered by the treaty. Stevens had been

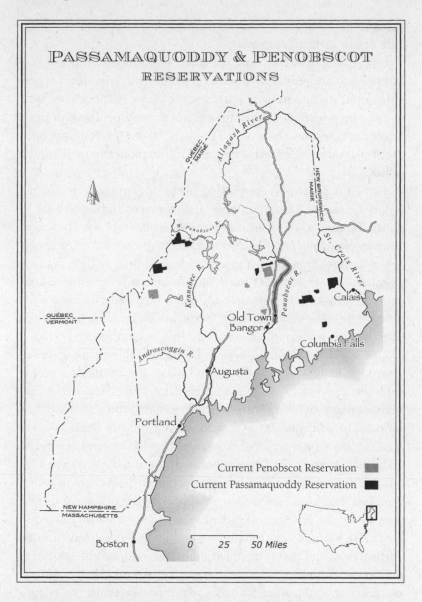

PASSAMAQUODDY & PENOBSCOT
RESERVATIONS

Current Penobscot Reservation
Current Passamaquoddy Reservation

0   25   50 Miles

looking for a lawyer to recover the lost land ever since his meeting with Mrs. Sockabesin, but no one would take the case. With criminal trespass charges pending against the demonstrators, a local attorney named Don Gellers came forward and, to calm the waters, reached a settlement that both the developer and the Passamaquoddy would stay off the disputed land until a judge could rule on the rightful ownership.

Gellers began researching the history of the land transactions but ran into troubles of his own (a conviction for "constructive possession" of marijuana) and parted ways with the tribe. The tribal council then turned to Tom Tureen, not a foregone decision since Tureen was just one year out of law school. But Tureen's appointment proved to be a fateful moment in the modern era of Indian policy.

Tureen had become committed to the Indian cause in college when he taught Sioux students at the Pierre Indian School in South Dakota. During summer break in law school at George Washington University, he had clerked with Gellers. After graduating, he took a staff position in Calais, Maine, with Pine Tree Legal Assistance, an OEO Indian legal service program, and continued to work on Passamaquoddy matters, mostly for individual tribal members. After taking on the tribe's treaty case, he plunged into the long and complex history of Indian land law.

One day, laboring at his desk in his second-story walk-up office above the Hathaway shirt outlet in Calais, Tureen made a breakthrough. Previously he had been concentrating on proving that Maine's roads and transfers of tribal lands amounted to treaty violations. In addition, he was puzzled about why the Passamaquoddy, poor (unemployment ran at 75 percent) and obviously Indians (several tribal members spoke only their native language), received no federal Indian services. In researching that question, he came upon BIA regulations saying that federal services would be provided only to Indians with trust or restricted lands. He learned that Indian law had been federalized from its earliest days and that it included many restrictions and restraints on the sale of Indian land. On that day he trained his attention on the foundational statute for Indian land transactions, the Nonintercourse Act of 1790, well ripened but still on the books, which required congressional approval of tribal land sales.

The discovery of this old statute changed everything. "You've been working," Tureen said to himself, "on the denial of federal services and the taking of the land described in the treaty. What about all the land they gave *up* in the 1794 treaty?" Was *that* land transfer legal?

This was 1970, the very eve of modern Indian law, and Tureen saw something no one else ever had. It was more than just a once-in-a-lifetime discovery, for few lawyers in their lifetimes ever make this kind of convention-shattering innovation. His basic proposition was disarmingly simple. Before the 1794 treaty, the Passamaquoddy Tribe held Indian title, a form of ownership that allowed the tribe exclusive occupation of the land within its aboriginal territory. Although the Nonintercourse Act, passed in 1790, had been used only sparingly during the twentieth century, it was still good law. It flatly prohibited any "purchase or grant" of Indian land unless approved by a "treaty or convention" *of the United States*. The 1794 treaty was a "purchase" of Indian land. The treaty was with a state, not the United States. Congress had never ratified it. Therefore, the treaty was void.

The Passamaquoddy Tribe, at least by the letter of the law, still owned all its aboriginal land and could sue to recover it.

The analysis, if valid, released the Passamaquoddy from the shackles that had always bound them. Under the Indian Claims Commission Act of 1946 and other statutes, tribes had long been pursuing only one choice—money damages—as a remedy for land wrongly taken. If Tureen was right, if the 1794 treaty was illegal, the tribe had two choices. It could concede that the land had been taken (after all, the title records showed it owned by others) and obtain congressional approval to sue the United States for a money award as recompense for the lost land or it could pursue this new legal theory by insisting that the treaty was a complete nullity and bring suit to confirm the tribe's continued ownership of the land.

Most tribes had lost the chance to recover land by going through the Indian Claims Commission process. Those money payments, once divided among the members (and usually amounting to a few thousand dollars or less per member), were final settlements that barred the tribes forever from reclaiming their lands. The Passamaquoddy had never gone to the Indian Claims Commission because the claims lawyers, scouring the western reservations for clients, overlooked the eastern "non-recognized" tribes. The Passamaquoddy still had the choice between money and land.

The neighboring Penobscot Tribe, Tureen realized, had a similar treaty and the same opportunity. Together, the two tribes had occupied 12 million acres in aboriginal times. According to the theory, the Passamaquoddy and Penobscot owned two-thirds of the state of Maine.

THE GREGARIOUS Tom Tureen, the quintessential hard charger, also had a sternly practical side and had no doubts about the political maelstrom these land claims would cause. To be sure, the tribes had equities on their side. The Nonintercourse Act of 1790 required congressional approval for Indian land sales for good reason—in order to regularize commercial relations with tribes and to protect them from unfair transactions. The policy was a principal foundation for the new nation in a time when it depended upon alliances with Indian tribes (both the Passamaquoddy and Penobscot proved valuable allies of the colonies in the Revolutionary War). The 23,000 acres allocated to the Passamaquoddy Tribe in the 1794 treaty with the state, and the Penobscot holdings of just 5,000 acres, were stingy amounts—near confiscations—compared with the much larger reservations in the federal treaties. The Passamaquoddy and Penobscot, their numbers decimated by disease and warfare, managed to continue on as traditional Indian communities in their remote forested homeland. In the 1970s they remained impoverished—and deserving of relief.

Yet there could be no doubting the force of the understandable outcry against the kind of bombshell Tureen was proposing. On these aboriginal lands lived 350,000 people, innocent of any wrongdoing. Timber companies, also blameless, had large forested holdings. Most Americans would find it outrageous, in a country that prides itself on the security of land title, to evict anyone on the basis of a technicality dredged up in some musty statute. George Washington had been president when the two treaties were signed!

Tureen proceeded carefully during 1971. In addition to book research, he cast a broad net for advice. Few lawyers knew much about Indian law at the time, and he tested his ideas with most of them. Tureen met with Bob Pelcyger, David Getches, and John Echohawk at the Native American Rights Fund. They not only agreed with Tureen but offered him a position as a staff attorney, and after he took on two more attorneys, Tureen's Calais operation became NARF's Maine office. Most lawyers who took time to wrestle seriously with the proposal for a Nonintercourse Act lawsuit saw many land mines but offered encouragement. Dissent came from private attorneys steeped in the Indian Claims Commission process, who dismissed any land return litigation out of hand.

By late 1971 the legal and political terrain was reasonably clear. As a legal matter, the state and landowners had many arguments, any one of which could defeat the tribes' claims. It was by no means clear that the Nonintercourse Act applied to the Passamaquoddy and Penobscot. Both had state reservations and received no federal services; did the federal statute cover nonfederally recognized tribes? The legislative history carried suggestions that Congress may have intended the Nonintercourse Act to apply only to the western tribes in unsettled areas, not to the original states.

Even if the tribes could come under the Nonintercourse Act, they had to overcome several defenses based on state property law and Maine's sovereignty. American law is fiercely protective of long-standing possession of land. Adverse possession grants full ownership to a person or company that openly possesses land for a fixed period of time, twenty-four years in Maine. Statutes of limitation require lawsuits to be filed within a certain time, four years for real estate disputes in Maine. Further, Maine, as a sovereign government, could claim sovereign immunity, which might bar any suit for land owned by the state, however valid the claim might otherwise be.

There was one other kicker. The only defect to non-Indian land title was the Nonintercourse Act's requirement of congressional approval. That meant that the claims could be voided by a one-

line federal statute approving the treaty of 1794. Such a move
would be pure politics, and the Passamaquoddy and Penobscot
hardly counted as a significant voting bloc.

Given the hard realities—legal hurdles, Congress's broad power
over Indian matters, and the logistical impossibility of evicting
350,000 citizens from their homes—Tureen knew that any ultimate solution had to be political and approved by Congress. Reac-
quiring most of the land in Maine was unrealistic, but obtaining a
lot of land was not. Other tribal objectives, federal recognition and
services, could be achieved in a comprehensive congressional settlement. But many imponderables lay between unleashing an
untested theory and the day of a congressional settlement, if it
ever were to arrive.

In December 1971 Tureen made a formal presentation to the
Passamaquoddy tribal council, recommending that the tribe drop
the lawsuit for the 6,000 acres taken from the 1794 treaty reservation. Instead, the tribe should declare the treaty, and its small
reservation, invalid and file the Nonintercourse Act land claim for
all the tribe's aboriginal territory. In fine detail, he set out his theory and the brutal political and legal battles that lay ahead. Unhesi-
tatingly, the tribal council decided to file. Speaking of his time in
Korea, John Stevens said, "I told myself if I ever got home there
was another war to be fought." The Penobscot soon joined in.

Like the tribal attorneys in the Northwest fishing cases, Tureen
desperately wanted the case argued in federal court, where judges
would be less swayed by state politics and more comfortable with
the idea of national laws overriding state prerogatives. Of all the
issues, Maine's sovereign immunity defense worried him most.
Tureen decided to address both concerns by having the Department of Justice sue in federal court as trustee for the tribes, since
Maine could not claim sovereign immunity against the United
States.

Early in 1972, Tureen began pressing interior and justice
department lawyers to file a federal suit on the Passamaquoddy's
and Penobscot's behalf. Time was short. In 1966, Congress had
passed a statute putting a six-year time limit on trespass claims
brought by the United States. The statute would not affect the land

claim itself, but it would bar a claim for trespass damages dating back to 1794. The claim would be lost unless the United States filed before midnight, July 18, 1972. Despite the tribe's many entreaties, interior and justice refused to act. The political stakes were too high, the legal theory was too much a stretch. One Department of the Interior lawyer cracked that "it was high time the Indians accepted the facts of life."

In June the tribe filed a lawsuit that heaped one seemingly preposterous theory upon another: Tureen asked the federal district court in Maine to order the United States to sue the state of Maine. Not only was the land claim theory untested, but so too was the idea that a court could order the United States to file a lawsuit: The doctrine of prosecutorial discretion gives the Department of Justice near-total discretion to decide whether to bring lawsuits. The issue was critical to the tribe, because a suit by the United States would overcome Maine's sovereign immunity defense, but federal lawyers hooted at the possibility of a judge's directing the United States to bring any suit, much less one based on Tureen's Nonintercourse Act theory. And by July 18?

The case was assigned to Judge Edward Gignoux, who set an expedited hearing for June 16, just two weeks after filing. At the end of the tense hearing he ordered government attorneys to decide within six days whether the United States would file the complaint against Maine—and if not, to explain why. Six days later the government lawyers based their response on one argument: Owing to the lack of a federal treaty or other continuous dealings with the Passamaquoddy and Penobscot, there was no trust relationship between the United States and the tribes; therefore, the government was not required to file suit against the state to protect tribal rights. Judge Gignoux, rejecting this argument, found that a trust duty did exist for the purposes of the Nonintercourse Act (which broadly referred to "any nation or tribe of Indians") and ordered the government to file *United States v. Maine,* which it did. So far, so good for the tribes.

Judge Gignoux's order, so sweeping, woke all the lawyers and federal and state officials involved to a certainty that the Passamaquoddy and Penobscot claim was serious. The court skirmish, however, had raised little public awareness. Further, however broad the ramifications might be, the 1972 ruling was a preliminary protective order that put *United States v. Maine* in abeyance until the court could fully consider the case and make a final ruling. That decision by Judge Gignoux, for the tribe on all counts, came in January 1975, and the court of appeals affirmed it in December (the United States did not take the case to the Supreme Court). Not even the appeals court ruling excited a public reaction. An Indian claim to two-thirds of Maine remained only vaguely unsettling.

The financial institutions caught on quickly, however. In the summer of 1976 the blue-ribbon Boston law firm advising New England municipal bond issuers concluded that it could not give unqualified approval to municipal bonds within the tribes' aboriginal territory. A shadow had suddenly fallen across municipal bonds, land sales, and mortgages, across landownership itself. Ordinary citizens, people who carried no grudge against Indians, exploded. John Peterson, a deputy state attorney general, called it "the worst crisis I've ever seen in state government. There were meetings going on in the cabinet room at 1:00 in the morning, trying to find solutions to it. It was extraordinary."

The scene shifted to Washington, D.C., where Congress had power to resolve the tribal claims. Tureen, Stevens, and other tribal leaders were always heard, and their proposals taken seriously and largely given respect. Nonetheless, the furious backlash from Maine, and from other eastern states where Indian land claims were germinating, made for an environment where Indian sympathizers were few and guarded.

The frenetic political activity continued for four years. For assistance, the tribe retained Archibald Cox, eminent Harvard law professor, solicitor general in the Kennedy administration, and special Watergate prosecutor; Maine called in Edward Bennett Williams, one of the nation's top trial lawyers. Maine introduced proposals to force an involuntary settlement on the tribes or to extinguish the claims altogether. President Jimmy Carter appointed Judge William Gunter of the Georgia Supreme Court to mediate, and when Gunter's report proved useful but not dispositive, Carter created a White House work group to continue the search for a solution that would bring fairness to both the tribes and non-Indian landowners. High officials in the Departments of Justice and the Interior walked a zigzag path of changing and contradictory positions. Related litigation moved through state and federal courts. All the while, state, tribal, and federal representatives engaged in often heated back-channel negotiations over land, money, jurisdiction, fairness, and politics. Finally, the many participants reached an accord.

President Carter signed into law the Maine Indian Claims Settlement Act in October 1980. The statute ratified the state treaties, thus eliminating all claims for Indian title under the Nonintercourse Act. In return, it provided $81.5 million, much of which would be used by the tribes to purchase 300,000 acres—more than 450 square miles of land—from willing sellers, including timber companies that had already been identified. The tribes received formal federal recognition and began receiving federal services for health, education, economic development, and other purposes. Detailed provisions dealt with state and tribal jurisdiction on tribal lands.

The compromise fell well short of the tribe's original claim as well as the state's initial position that the claims should be extinguished altogether. In the last analysis, two things are certain: The legislation both resolved a bitterly divisive public issue and allowed the tribes to take giant steps out of the bleak circumstances they had faced just a decade earlier, when John Stevens couldn't even find a lawyer to block further land grabs from what remained of the small reservation set aside in 1794.

Some two dozen tribes from New England down the eastern seaboard and west to Alabama, Louisiana, and Texas filed Nonintercourse Act claims based on invalid treaties with states. One tribe, the Mashpee of Massachusetts, lost its case outright. Otherwise, nearly all the tribal cases have gone to congressional resolutions structured similarly to the Maine settlement, providing land, funds, and federal recognition to small and previously overlooked tribes.

. . .

President Jimmy Carter, shown here signing the Maine Indian Claims Settlement Act of 1980, did not take sides in the dispute and tried to facilitate a negotiated agreement. In doing so, he probably spent more time on an Indian issue than any president in the twentieth century.

CLEARLY, land returns have mattered tremendously to many tribes, and tribal land acquisition programs continue apace. Even so, numerous efforts to return former homelands have been stymied. Although tribes did not realize it at the time, the final money-only judgments of the Indian Claims Commission, a legacy of termination-era thinking, interred any hopes of land claims under the Nonintercourse Act for most tribes. The Western Shoshone of Nevada have spent decades trying to establish ownership to the vast territory encompassed in the 1863 Treaty of Ruby Valley, only to be blocked by an Indian Claims Commission judgment: The Supreme Court found that the entry of the award by the court clerk eliminated the land claim, even though the tribe has refused the payment because it wants the land, not dollars. The tribes of the Great Sioux Nation have hit the same brick wall with respect to the government's taking of the Black Hills in the quest for gold. The Sioux want the Black Hills, not the money judgment now totaling over $700 million, which remains in the federal treasury, collecting interest.

Nor have land claims settlements always proved as satisfactory in later years as they appeared at the time of negotiation. The Passamaquoddy, for example, have made great strides in land acquisition and economic development. Maine, however, has aggressively used the unique provisions of the settlement act to extend state jurisdiction over tribal lands by, among other things, blocking a proposed tribal casino and regulating tribal fishing.

This theme, of historic land returns that sometimes carried dour consequences unseen by Native leaders, played out dramatically in the largest claims settlement of all: Alaska.

WHEN ALASKA came into the Union in 1959, the new state won the right to select 104 million acres from the federal public domain, by far the largest grant to any state. Surveyors and state officers soon appeared in the villages and hunting grounds of the vast, remote backcountry—"bush Alaska"—evaluating land for its value to the state for oil and gas production, mines, dams and reservoirs, recreation, and roads. Senator Ernest Gruening was laying plans for construction of the massive Rampart Dam, which would impound the mighty Yukon River and flood numerous Native villages and traditional hunting and fishing grounds. Word of the intrusions spread like wildfire among the Natives, already jumpy about the security of their land and subsistence hunting and fishing rights because of statehood.

Alaska Natives stood in a related but different situation from the Passamaquoddy. The Maine tribe originally possessed Indian title, seemingly transferred it to the state in 1794, and then sued to void the transaction and reestablish Indian title. Alaska, however, remained so distant and lightly populated, even as late as statehood, that there had been little pressure for settlement in Native territory and virtually no land dealings with Natives at all —not by Russia, which claimed it until 1867, or by the United States. The federal government had established just nine reservations, making up a small part of the state. Otherwise, Alaska

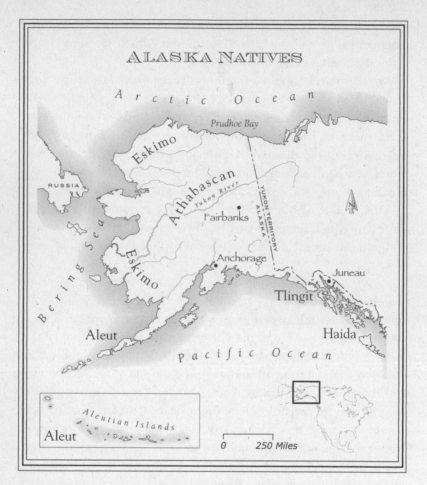

Natives lived on the land much as they always had. Willie Hensley, an Eskimo who became a leader in the land claims effort, grew up before statehood outside Kotzebue, in northwest Alaska on the Arctic Ocean. "I was raised out in the country. The land was open. Our people had lived there for ten thousand years. We had our dog teams, and we hunted and fished and lived at different places at different times of the year." To Hensley, to the Natives all across Alaska, most of the state remained theirs.

Alaska Natives fall into four separate geographic groupings: Tlingit, Haida, and Eyak of the southeastern panhandle; the Athabascan of central Alaska; the Inupiat and Yupik Eskimos of the northern and western Arctic; and the Aleut of the southwestern Alaska Peninsula and the Aleutian Islands. All moved rapidly to protect their rights as Alaska approached statehood. They had filed a few land claims with the Department of the Interior before 1959, but spurred on by a handful of lawyers and supportive BIA employees, the number of claims mushroomed when the threat of state land selections in bush Alaska became real. In 1966, Hensley, a young graduate student at the University of Alaska–Fairbanks, wrote a research paper arguing for the validity of Native land claims. The brief, well-documented, and readable paper made its way into Anchorage and bush newspapers and newsletters and attracted wide notice. The work of Hensley, mild-mannered and soft-spoken but passionately committed to Native rights, and others in Anchorage and Fairbanks fortified the determination out in the bush. Later, in 1966, the Alaska Federation of Natives came into being as a statewide activist organization with a mission of protecting Native land rights. By the end of the 1960s administrative claims filed by Natives blanketed most of the state.

This was a few years before the courts began handing down decisions in the eastern land claims cases, so an understanding of Indian title—the idea that Alaska Natives might have a right to occupy most of the state—depended upon judicial opinions handed down long ago and under different circumstances. Indian title claims in Alaska received a decidedly mixed reaction in governmental circles. The Alaska office of the Bureau of Land Management, with a strong mining constituency, denied the Native administrative claims, but the BIA appealed the BLM rulings to the Department of the Interior in Washington, D.C. The assistant secretary with authority over both agencies simply shelved the appeals, issuing no rulings and thereby defusing the controversy for the moment. Senator Gruening weighed in with his opinion that the claims to Indian title were based on "dubious grounds."

But not dubious to Secretary of the Interior Stewart Udall. He sided with the Natives on both legal and moral grounds. In 1963 one thousand Natives from twenty-four villages petitioned the interior secretary to impose a freeze on land transfers to protect Native land rights. The Tanana Chiefs Conference and other regional organizations followed suit. In October 1966, at the first statewide meeting of Alaska Natives in history (the gathering that led to the formation of the Alaska Federation of Natives), the assemblage requested Udall to impose a land freeze. Udall had visited Alaska several times and met regularly with Native leaders there and in Washington, D.C. Now he responded in dramatic fashion. In December 1966, citing a need to prevent conflicts over Native claims, he issued an informal freeze on state land selections and the issuance of federal oil and gas leases. Then, in early 1969, shortly before leaving office, Udall took it to a new level by issuing the Deep Freeze, a formal withdrawal order declaring Alaska's public domain lands, over 90 percent of the state, off limits to statehood selections, mineral leases, homesteading, and other forms of federal land transfer.

Udall's 1969 Deep Freeze, one of the most sweeping actions ever taken with respect to federal lands, took on even greater significance owing to a transcendent event the year before, the confirmation of fabulous oil reserves at Prudhoe Bay on Alaska's North Slope. To Alaska's boosters, this find, along with the proposed 700-mile Trans-Alaska Pipeline transecting the state from north to south, would at long last secure Alaska's future. Oil would far eclipse the 1898 gold rush. Except that Udall's Deep Freeze stood in the way.

This gigantic stalemate, sprawling across 365 million acres, 18 percent of the nation's land area, made major congressional land legislation inevitable. Proposals regularly stall in Congress because one powerful interest group or another wishes to preserve the status quo and therefore opposes any legislation. But by 1969 in Alaska, while their objectives differed, all the players wanted congressional relief. The state wanted to make its statehood land selections. The energy and construction companies wanted the oil and gas drilling and accompanying pipeline. The labor unions wanted jobs from all the construction and resource extraction. The Natives wanted a secure land base. Even the emerging environmental movement saw an opportunity for large conservation set-asides. Alaska—"the last pork chop," as one writer dubbed it— was about to be carved up.

The oil companies, labor unions, and state political leaders, marginally concerned at best with Native issues but avid for a drilling and construction boom, put pressure on Senator Henry Jackson and Congressman Wayne Aspinall, as ever vested with control over their committees and steadfastly deaf to Native rights. All of these Alaska interests wanted Washington to concoct a settlement that the Natives would support but that would involve as little land as possible. Both congressional leaders initially came in with settlement offers far below the 1969 proposal that the Alaska Federation of Natives put on the table: 40 million acres, $500 million, and a 2 percent royalty on all public land development, including oil and gas. Jackson's offer, in 1970, allowed seven million acres, Aspinall's initial bill much less, just 100,000 acres.

As lobbyists and negotiators worked Capitol Hill through 1970 and 1971, the center of gravity moved steadily toward the Natives' position. The Alaska Federation of Natives, led by Don Wright, John Borbridge, Emil Notti, Laura Bergt, Hensley, and others, held the whip hand and used it well. AFN delegates made an estimated 120 trips to Washington. Only the Arctic Slope Native Association, one of twelve regionally based groups within AFN, broke with the statewide organization, and that split came late in the process. Before then Arctic Slope representatives Joe Upicksoun and the fiery Charlie Edwardsen made valuable contributions in shaping and pushing the AFN position and strategy. A key moment came in April 1971, when President Nixon yielded to the Indian advocates in the White House. Nixon enjoyed the favorable public reaction to Blue Lake, and he was no less eager than the energy company executives to get oil flowing through the Alaska pipeline. So he picked a magic number, a 40-million-acre land base for the Natives. His position hardly sat well with Jackson or Aspinall, but it satisfied most of the Alaska interests. The president signed the final legislation, titled the Alaska Native Claims Settlement Act, into law on December 18, 1971.

ANCSA, which closely resembled the Alaska Federation of Natives' proposal, finally set aside 45 million acres and paid nearly one billion dollars to Alaska Natives. The statute extinguished

Before signing the Alaska Native Claims Settlement Act into law, President Nixon professed concern that the measure be acceptable to Alaska Natives. Although there never was a true Native plebiscite, the Alaska Federation of Natives called a special meeting of delegates to vote upon the measure, which they overwhelmingly approved. Later that day many of the delegates, above, clustered around speakerphones to hear a telephone call from the president telling them that he had just put his signature to the act. Photograph courtesy of the Ukpeagvik Inupiat Corporation and Tuzzy Consortium Library of Barrow, Alaska.

Indian title to the remaining 320 million acres of land. Udall's Deep Freeze was lifted, state selections resumed, and Prudhoe Bay drilling and the pipeline moved forward. ANCSA also called for an environmental study that led to more than 100 million acres being added to national parks and forests and to the wilderness and wild and scenic rivers system.

IT IS HARD to overstate the magnitude of the Alaska Natives' achievement. At the time of statehood in 1959, they were the invisible Alaskans, living off the land and widely separated from one another, mostly located in some two hundred bush villages spread across a terrain that, if superimposed on a map of the lower forty-eight states, would stretch from San Diego to Florida. They had no established interests on their side. Nothing in recent history supported their claim to possession of the land; Senator Gruening called their view of Indian title "tenuous." Legislation could easily have veered away from the land claim to the path—so familiar at that time—toward money payments that would soon evaporate. Instead, they found a way to organize themselves into AFN, the driving force that led to ANCSA's unprecedented grant—12 percent of Alaska and nearly as large as all the Native reservations in the lower forty-eight states combined.

Still and all, ANCSA's blockbuster land provisions came at a cost. Even though the United States recognized Alaska Native village governments as tribes, the land was transferred not to the tribes but to newly created village and regional corporations, all chartered under Alaska state corporate law. Each Alaska Native received shares of stock in the local village corporation and the associated regional corporation. This created an inequity identical to the termination acts: Children born after the passage of ANCSA—"after-borns"—received no shares under the statute, although they could become shareholders by inheritance. In addition, ANCSA put continuing Native control of the corporations in jeopardy: Shares could be inherited by non-Natives and, after a 20-year period, could be sold on the open market. This raised the specter that outside companies could take over the Native corporations—and the land.

In addition, ANCSA failed to honor Native sovereignty. Because ANSCA land was held by state-chartered private corporations, not tribal governments, Alaska state regulatory law applied on all of it. This led to one especially ominous consequence. ANCSA extinguished all aboriginal hunting and fishing rights, making subsistence living—the core of cultural and economic life in bush Alaska—subject to state law, the situation that treaty tribes in the lower forty-eight states fought so hard to prevent. So, the land provisions aside, ANCSA had much that pleased Senator Jackson and Congressman Aspinall.

ANCSA created a system strikingly similar to the discredited experiment that the federal government imposed on the Menominee. The question sounded: Is ANCSA termination in disguise?

Alaska Natives did head off some of the termination-style damage that ANCSA might have caused. In 1980 they persuaded Congress to adopt significant, though not complete, protections for subsistence hunting and fishing. In 1987, before the 20-year protective period ended, they convinced Congress to allow Native corporations to issue stock to children born after the passage of ANCSA in 1971. The 1987 law also gave Natives the equipment to block corporate takeovers by making the 20-year ban on stock transfers permanent, unless individual corporations chose to make the shares transferable, a step no corporation has yet taken. The land, however, remained under corporate ownership and subject to state jurisdiction over such matters as law and order, regulation of environmental and business affairs, and laws relating to culture and language.

Paradoxically, the idea of vesting Native land in state corporations traces to the proposal the Alaska Federation of Natives put forth in 1969. Strategically the Natives were pushed in that direction by Senator Henry Jackson's antipathy toward Indian reservations in general and Alaska reservations in particular. Even more fundamentally, between 1966 through 1971, when the die was being cast for ANCSA, the promise of Indian self-determination had not yet taken hold. "Reservation" was a pejorative term, signifying poverty and an overbearing federal paternalism. The Natives themselves wished for a better way, and so they turned to the corporate model.

Sovereignty played no part in the discussions at that time. Alaska Natives sought "land," to them a broad and evocative term enfolding their social, economic, and spiritual relationship with the natural world. They did not conceive that to the law, land meant land title only—a deed—not the right to govern it or take animals from it. Willie Hensley recalled: "Our focus was on land. Land was our future, our survival. In my region all we wanted was to get control of our space so we could live on it and hunt and fish on it and make our own way into the twentieth century at our own pace. Our focus was on land, not structure. The vehicle for administering the land was not our focus. We weren't lawyers. We were battling the state tooth and tong. We were always afraid the president might create a pipeline corridor. We were afraid of failure, of not getting a settlement and not protecting the land for our future generations. As a minority group we knew we could only press the country so far. But none of us ever envisioned a loss of tribal structure. We never thought that tribal control would not continue."

The contemporary recognition and respect for tribal sovereignty did not begin to emerge until a few years after the passage of ANCSA, when the Supreme Court, which had not previously used the word "sovereignty" in connection with tribal governments during the twentieth century, began handing down decisions that showed the potential for tribal governments. The powers of sovereigns far exceed those of corporations, for a sovereign can engage in the entrepreneurial pursuits of corporations and can exercise governmental authority as well. A sovereign can tax yet not be taxed. A sovereign can pass laws, establish police forces, try criminal and civil cases, and make basic societal choices. Sovereigns—and perhaps only sovereigns—can perpetuate the unique, communal cultures of land-based aboriginal peoples.

ANCSA's corporate framework had long raised questions about whether and how the governmental powers of Alaska tribes would apply on land held by regional and village corporations. When Alaska Natives reached the Supreme Court in the 1998 *Venetie* case, the Court ruled that under ANCSA the Native tribal governments have a sharply limited geographic reach of their governmental authority—"sovereignty without territoriality." All, or nearly all, of the land granted by ANCSA is subject to state jurisdiction.

WAS ANCSA termination in disguise? Yes, at bottom it was. But Alaska Natives never let it hit the bottom. Determined and resilient, they smoothed some of the 1971 law's sharpest edges. They amended it to enable children born after 1971 to become shareholders and to block takeovers of Native shares, corporations, and land. They overrode its extinguishment of hunting and fishing rights and established preferential rights to take the salmon, geese, caribou, moose, whales, and all the other animals they had depended upon since time immemorial. They worked within a constraining framework to keep in the village tribal governments some significant sovereign powers, such as over the adoption and guardianship of Native children. They continue to press at the state and federal levels for recognition of broader sovereignty over their land and members. And they have effectively used the capitalist side of ANCSA: The Alaska Native regional corporations have become key players in Alaska's economic and political life.

So the opponents of tribal rights who had so much influence over ANCSA obtained half of what they wanted. The dead hand of termination maintains its grasp on Alaska Native sovereignty. The other hand, though, missed its mark, and that is the surpassing achievement of Alaska Natives: They have held on to the grand expanses of ancestral land they obtained through ANCSA. For as long experience has shown, whether at Blue Lake to the south or Eskimo territory to the far north, land will always permeate what it means to be Native.

10.

Sovereignty in Congress and the Courts

Ultimately, the progress envisioned by the modern Indian movement could be manifested only by bettering the lives of Native people, primarily in Indian country, the homelands. As the first phase of reaching that goal, Indian leaders sought the modern recognition of traditional but long-dormant legal rights: tribal sovereignty; the government's trust obligations; hunting, fishing, and water rights; religious freedom; and the federal duty to protect Indian land possession. Firming up those rights had to be done in the courts and Congress. With that framework in place, governmental, social, and economic progress could be achieved at home.

The fishing rights decisions in the courts and the early congressional actions on self-determination, reversal of termination, and land returns were only the beginning. Starting in 1959 and continuing into the early twenty-first century, the Supreme Court became exceptionally active in Indian law, handing down 120 decisions, more than in fields such as international, securities, bankruptcy, and environmental law. Until the late 1980s the clear majority of the opinions ran in the tribes' favor. Then the Court turned, and Indian legal rights received a crabbed reading. While the tribes' legal position remains far more favorable than it was in the 1950s, the later decisions laid down several significant setbacks. Congress, on the other hand, despite an angry backlash against tribal rights and the small number of Indian votes in most elections, has been far more consistent. The national legislature, where tribal leaders maintain favorable ongoing relationships, has stood by its announced self-determination policy and the trust relationship.

The current legal structure, largely the result of tribal initiatives, does not afford Indian people all they would wish, but it sets a generally favorable context for an expansive tribal self-determination. Of course, tribal leaders must always keep a watchful eye on Washington, D.C. Congress has nearly unlimited power to adjust or eliminate Indian rights, and the Supreme Court has encompassing authority to interpret treaties and old and new statutes. That is why, although a major event over the past half century has been the resurrection and creation of laws favorable to American Indians, perhaps an even larger advance has been the underlying reason for the progress: the tribes' surprising ability to influence their own destiny in the courts and Congress—an ability the tribes are determined to preserve and enhance in the future.

BY THE EARLY 1970s tribes had at their disposal an emerging litigation capability, something they had never before possessed. OEO legal services programs served clients in much of Indian country and had good communications with one another. The nonprofit national Indian law firm, the Native American Rights Fund, opened its doors in 1969 and quickly grew to an operation of some fifteen lawyers with its main office in Boulder, Colorado, and field offices in Washington, D.C.; Calais, Maine; and Anchorage, Alaska. The Indian Law Resource Center, which works on international as well as domestic cases, established offices in Helena, Montana, and Washington, D.C. As Indian Claims Commission cases wound down, private firms broadened their work to include the breaking areas of tribal sovereignty and resource rights. Tribes soon developed in-house law firms, variously styled as tribal attorney general's or tribal attorney's offices, with staffs ranging from a handful of lawyers to the Navajo Nation's attorney general's office with more than twenty attorneys. For the first time Indian people began moving into the legal profession. A driving force was the Pre-Law Summer Institute for

John Echohawk, executive director of the Native American Rights Fund, and the author at NARF's Boulder offices in the 1980s. Photograph courtesy of Ray Ramirez, Native American Rights Fund.

American Indians and Alaska Natives at the University of New Mexico, which oriented prospective Indian law students to the law by giving them a rigorous two-month summer course before their first year of legal studies. After law school, most of the summer session lawyers practiced Indian law or took policy-oriented positions in Indian affairs.

This cadre of knowledgeable attorneys, modest in size at the beginning but steadily expanding ever since, included most of the country's experts in a still little-known field. In the early days of the sovereignty movement, the network of Indian lawyers held out the promise—when things broke right (as they did in the fishing cases and land claims)—of an effective, coordinated legal offensive.

AN EARLY OPPORTUNITY to set major legal precedent presented itself in prosaic fashion, a routine notice from the state of Arizona to the Phoenix-based Great Western Bank branch office in Window Rock, the capital of the Navajo Nation. The notice, mailed out in 1967, directed the bank to withhold state income taxes from the paychecks of all employees. Rosalind McClanahan, a Navajo tribal member and bank employee, knew that the Navajo tribal tax department wanted to challenge Arizona's ability to tax tribal members who lived and worked within the Navajo Reservation. She met with Bruce Bridegroom, an intake lawyer in the Window Rock office of DNA, the OEO legal services program serving Navajos (DNA is an abbreviation for *Dinebeiina Nahiilna Be Agaditahe*, meaning "lawyers who help with the revitalization of the Navajo people"). DNA, though new to the reservation, already had earned a reputation as a place to go for redress.

The DNA lawyers handled many small and medium-size disputes, often involving debts, but also had a law reform unit with an eye out for test cases. Bridegroom and his colleagues quickly saw the potential in the McClanahan situation, and the conviction grew as they discussed the case with other Indian lawyers around the country. Navajo and the other tribes wanted self-determination, the right to make their own laws and be free of state regulation. Even though the amount withheld from McClanahan's paycheck was just $16.20, here was a chance to establish essential principles of tribal sovereignty to guide a modern body of Indian law.

The cornerstone would be Chief Justice John Marshall's 1832 decision in *Worcester v. Georgia,* one of our greatest judge's greatest opinions. Even today, among all the Supreme Court decisions written in any field of law before the Civil War, *Worcester v. Georgia* is one of the most commonly cited.

The conflict in *Worcester v. Georgia* arose from Georgia's hostility toward the growing political and economic power of the Cherokee Nation and the federal treaties recognizing the tribe and its large territory. Georgia resolved to eliminate the Cherokee Nation. Passing a series of statutes in the late 1820s, it outlawed the Cherokee legislature and courts, divested the nation of its land, and regulated all traffic into the reservation. The Cherokee's challenge to the Georgia laws went to the Supreme Court. The national political environment was explosive as pressures were already building toward the state and federal schism that led to the Civil War, and Marshall's views on federal supremacy were anathema to Georgia and the other southern states. When the Supreme

Court decision came down in favor of the Cherokee, President Andrew Jackson, determined to remove the Cherokee and the other Five Civilized Tribes from the Southeast, vehemently supported Georgia and angrily dismissed the ruling. "John Marshall has made his decision," Jackson reportedly said of *Worcester v. Georgia*. "Now let him enforce it."

In deciding the case, Marshall explained Indian land rights and sovereignty—nationhood—during aboriginal times, at the times of treaties with Britain and America, and later. He acknowledged tribes as "separate nations . . . having institutions of their own, and governing themselves by their own laws." Cherokee sovereignty continued, separate and apart from Georgia's, after the federal treaties and after statehood. Concluding, Marshall laid down his, and the Supreme Court's, unflinching declaration that Georgia laws could not reach into the reservation of the sovereign Cherokee Nation and were utterly void: "The Cherokee nation, then, is a distinct community, occupying its own territory, with boundaries accurately described, in which the laws of Georgia can have no force. . . ."

But nearly a century and a half separated Georgia's laws and Arizona's attempt to withhold its taxes from Rosalind McClanahan's paycheck. While Felix Cohen helped keep Marshall's views alive in his monumental 1942 treatise on Indian law, the long oppression of Indian people prevented tribes from exercising their powers. Consequently, few cases on tribal authority had arisen during the twentieth century. This changed, beginning in the late 1950s. The Supreme Court in *Williams v. Lee* in 1959 issued a strong ruling in support of tribal governance, characterizing *Worcester* as "one of [Marshall's] most courageous and eloquent opinions" and finding that "the broad principles of that decision came to be accepted as law."

But then, just three years later, the Court lurched in the other direction in *Kake v. Egan*, emphasizing how circumstances had changed since Marshall's day and suggesting that state law can regularly intrude into Indian country.

The next opinion, and the most recent taxation case before Rosalind McClanahan received her tax notice, shifted ground once again as the justices felt their way through this old-yet-new field. In the 1965 *Warren Trading Post* case, also involving the Navajo reservation, the Court invalidated an Arizona gross proceeds tax on a non-Indian trading post. The opinion relied in part on *Worcester* but also looked to a federal statute that had no bearing on the McClanahan situation.

The DNA attorneys reasoned that the *McClanahan* case could be the vehicle for resolving the inconsistent precedents by setting a bright line test: that state law hardly ever applies to Indians within the reservations; that the only exception would be if Congress clearly and expressly provided for state jurisdiction (as it had, for example, in Public Law 280). Such a rule, faithful to Chief Justice Marshall's vision of a vigorous tribal sovereignty, would leave to tribal legislatures, courts, and administrative agencies a broad sweep of court, tax, and regulatory matters when Indians were involved. What better place than Navajo—the nation's largest reservation, so easily understood as a separate place—to litigate this bright line approach?

The DNA lawyers filed an administrative protest, then took *McClanahan* to the state courts, where the Arizona Court of Appeals upheld the tax and the state supreme court declined to review. The case then went to the United States Supreme Court.

By 1973, when the Court began deliberating on *McClanahan*, Indian law had gained considerably more visibility, and the ramifications for the majority society had grown more evident. In the eight years since *Warren Trading Post*, the Court had decided twelve Indian cases, including two major fishing rights cases, and had under consideration an eastern land claim case, another fishing rights case, and a difficult affirmative action issue. Justices read the newspapers and doubtless knew of Indian activism and the land cases still in the lower courts. The time had come to decide whether Marshall's opinion in *Worcester v. Georgia* was just a long-ago document, erased for the Cherokee in their forced Trail of Tears march to Oklahoma and eradicated for all other tribes in the rush of manifest destiny and terminationist policies, or whether the chief justice's words would still be heard over the chasm of time.

The *McClanahan* opinion proceeded gingerly on the issue of

tribal sovereignty and by no means offered the tribes total victory, but the comprehensive decision struck down the Arizona tax and gave Indians a major precedent that clarified and toughened modern Indian law. The Court, citing Marshall's concept of tribal sovereignty, found that "'the policy of leaving Indians free from state jurisdiction and control is deeply rooted in the Nation's history.'" Indian treaties "'are read with this tradition of sovereignty in mind' and 'doubtful expressions are to be resolved in favor of'" the Indians.

This rule of interpretation, requiring judges to read treaties in favor of Indians, stands on historical realities: the relative powerlessness of tribes and the fact that treaties were written by the United States in a language largely foreign to the tribes. The approach has been applied broadly in Indian cases, of which *McClanahan* is a leading example. The text of the Navajo Treaty of 1868, negotiated 44 years before Arizona statehood, gave little guidance on the question of whether a future state could tax Rosalind McClanahan's income, providing only that the reservation was set aside "for the use and occupation of the Navajo tribe of Indians." The treaty made no mention of jurisdiction or taxes. Nonetheless, under the Court's conception in *McClanahan* of Indian reservations as places where the tradition of tribal sovereignty controls and where state jurisdiction is limited, the state tax could not be "reconciled with tribal self-determination."

The Court had laid down the bright line test sought by the DNA lawyers: State laws cannot be applied to reservation Indians without explicit congressional approval.

The *McClanahan* litigation displays many of the reasons why tribes met with success in the Supreme Court during the 1960s, 1970s, and most of the 1980s. The issue was driven by the tribe— the Navajo tax department, DNA, and Rosalind McClanahan in this instance. The case was strategically selected. Legal representation was strong: Richard Collins, the litigation director at DNA and a former law clerk to Judge Charles Merrill on the Ninth Circuit Court of Appeals, brilliantly headed up the case before the Supreme Court.

In addition, the Solicitor General's Office, the branch of the

Department of Justice that handles all Supreme Court cases, has continually played a key role in Indian cases and did so in *McClanahan*. From the late 1960s, when Harry Sachse argued the *Puyallup* case, into the twenty-first century, Sachse, Louis Claiborne, and Edwin Kneedler, experts in Indian law all, made a point of steeping themselves in the details of each Indian case and presenting fairly the tribal side during deliberations within the department. The solicitor general's position, and the way it is expressed, carries great weight with the Court not only because of the office's prestige but also because the Court often requests friend of the court briefs from the solicitor general in cases where the federal government is not involved.

Further, *McClanahan* illuminates the course of Indian law because Justice Thurgood Marshall wrote the opinion. The first African-American on the Court and the civil rights attorney who argued *Brown v. Board of Education*, the school desegregation case, this second Marshall plainly saw himself as a guardian of Indian rights. During his tenure, which ended in 1991, he wrote more opinions in this field than any other justice, espousing a judicial philosophy based on strong tribal sovereignty and a limited state role in Indian country.

TRIBAL SOVEREIGNTY forms the bedrock of the modern court decisions and statutes. To most people, the word "sovereignty" carries an aura of dignity as well as complexity. Classical sovereignty, which traces to the sixteenth-century French philosopher Jean Bodin, was equal parts theology (the sovereign— the crown—derives power directly from God) and metaphysics (sovereignty is both supreme and absolute; it cannot be divided up). The notion never made sense in the United States, where religion and government are kept separate and where power is divided many different ways; Thomas Jefferson remarked that sovereignty in its absolutist sense was "an idea belonging to the other side of the Atlantic." The term, however, remains very much in use, although today it carries a different, simpler meaning: In modern America a sovereign is a government—that is, it has the power to make laws and enforce them.

Over the course of two generations American Indian tribes breathed life into a basic principle of American law and political science widely recognized in the early days of the Republic but dormant since the late 1800s. There are three branches of sovereignty within the American constitutional system: the United States, the states (cities and counties are subdivisions of state sovereignty), and the Indian tribes. To be sure, the actual extent of tribal power is less than that of the federal government and the states. Nevertheless, tribal sovereignty, which some tribes (and Supreme Court opinions) describe as nationhood, is real and often very substantial. Scores of tribes have actual, real-world legal, political, and economic power equal to or greater than that of large rural county governments.

Mark it down also that sovereignty in America is an emotional, contentious field of play, whether it be the states decrying federal intervention or tribes and states standing off against each other over the right to exercise jurisdiction. The stakes can be relatively small, such as Arizona's attempt to tax Rosalind McClanahan's paycheck earned within the boundaries of the Navajo Nation, or large—witness Washington state's crusade to impose its laws on tribal fishers. Either way, they reflect a primal need of all sovereigns, nations, governments—call them what you will—to assert their right to self-determination, their right to live well by their own rules.

IN THE 1980S a major boost to tribal sovereignty came out of the Jicarilla Apache reservation in the mountains of northern New Mexico. Jicarilla land—at 820,000 acres, a bit more than 1 percent of the state—overlay precious oil and gas deposits that the BIA had leased to oil and gas companies dating back to 1953. The leases made no mention of tribal taxation, and the tribal constitution in force at the time did not delegate tax authority to the tribal council. Frustrated by the companies' underpayment of royalties and anxious to increase revenues for tribal programs, in 1969 the tribe amended its constitution to authorize tribal taxation, and in 1976 it enacted a mineral severance tax ordinance.

The outraged oil and gas companies, raising serious issues of

Oren Lyons, chief of the Onondaga Nation and faithkeeper of
the Haudenosaunee (the Six Nations of the Iroquois Confederacy), speaking to the delegates of the United Nations General
Assembly. Lyons is one of many Native Americans who have
worked in international forums for the human rights of indigenous peoples, including the right of sovereignty. He gave this
opening address in 1992 in New York to begin the ceremonies
declaring 1993 "The Year of the Indigenous Peoples." Photograph courtesy of the United Nations Photo Library.

fairness, sued. The leases had been negotiated at a time when tribal taxation was impossible because the tribe's constitution had not provided for it. The tribe, the companies argued, was trying to change the rules—retroactively.

Merrion v. Jicarilla Apache went to the Supreme Court in 1982. The opinion approached the problem by directly comparing tribal sovereignty with the powers of other governments. The Court found that a tribe, like federal, state, and local governments, has "a role as a commercial partner" and a "role as a sovereign." Governments engaged in commercial transactions, the Court found, can adopt new taxes and increase existing rates without raising issues of retroactivity: "[S]overeign power, even when unexercised, is an enduring presence that governs all contracts subject to the sovereign's jurisdiction, and will remain intact. . . ." Tribes, like other sovereigns, must have such flexibility, in order to provide revenues for municipal services. One of the Court's comments in this regard—Justice Thurgood Marshall wrote the opinion—must be especially delicious to Indian people, who are all too familiar with generations of attempts to "civilize" Indians: "The petitioners [the energy companies] avail themselves of the 'substantial privilege of carrying on business' on the reservation. They benefit from the provision of police protection and other governmental services, as well as from 'the advantages of a civilized society' that are assured by the existence of tribal government. . . . Under these circumstances, there is nothing exceptional in requiring [the energy companies] to contribute through taxes to the general cost of tribal government."

During the 1970s and 1980s the tribal position lost out in some important cases. The Court, for example, upheld broad state court jurisdiction to hear Indian water rights cases; permitted some state taxation within Indian country; ruled that some reservation boundaries had been implicitly diminished during the allotment era, thereby reducing the geographic reach of tribal jurisdiction; and allowed national forest road building that infringed on tribal ceremonies at sacred sites.

From the late 1950s through the late 1980s, however, the tribes prevailed in the Supreme Court decisions numerically as well as in most of the highest-stakes cases. The Court upheld the Boldt decision on Pacific Northwest fishing rights in an opinion by Justice John Paul Stevens. The eastern land claim of the Oneida Nation succeeded in a 5–4 decision that applied broadly and allowed most of the remaining land claim cases to go ahead. The Cabazon and Morongo bands of Mission Indians established their right to operate gaming operations free of California law in another opinion that applied to most tribes. In 1974, when affirmative action had already become a deeply sensitive issue in the country and within the Court, *Morton v. Mancari* upheld a federal statute setting an Indian hiring preference for BIA employees: The unanimous opinion conceptualized the preference not as being race-based but rather as being an element of the government-to-government relationship between the United States and tribes. Among the many other cases resolved in favor of the tribes, Supreme Court decisions approved broad tribal court jurisdiction; held invalid state taxation of non-Indian business and recreational activities on the reservations, thus leaving room for tribal taxation; and restricted the reach of state jurisdiction under Public Law 280 by finding that states had no jurisdiction on the reservations over regulatory matters, including taxation and land use regulation.

HOWEVER MUCH American Indian cases may have increased in importance and populated the Court's docket, the justices themselves have displayed little affection for this legally intricate, often arcane field. Bob Woodward and Scott Armstrong made that point in *The Brethren*, and Professor David Getches has referred to "a fabled unpopularity of Indian cases among the Court's members." At the same time, a number of justices, acknowledging the Constitution's solicitude for minority groups, have seen themselves as protectors of Indian rights. Certainly that applies to Thurgood Marshall. Warren Court members Hugo Black, William O. Douglas, and William Brennan and, later, Harry Blackmun and Lewis Powell all wrote opinions consistently sensitive to tribal sovereignty and other Indian rights. On the current Court, John Paul Stevens, Sandra Day O'Connor, Stephen Breyer, David Souter, and Ruth Bader Ginsburg sometimes vote for the

Indian side, and sometimes not, but all of them give the tribes a fair shake by laboring through the often daunting maze of treaties, statutes, court opinions, and history that make up Indian law. So, over a period of years and to varying degrees, a sizable number of justices have paid considerable heed to the foundational principles of John Marshall.

The arrival of William Rehnquist in 1972 and his performance in Indian law, first as associate justice and then as chief justice, and his subsequent alliance with Antonin Scalia and Clarence Thomas when they joined the Court in 1986 and 1991, gradually changed the calculus. All three looked skeptically on assertions of minority rights and held strong states' rights agendas. The *Oliphant* case, handed down in 1978, when the Court was generally taking a protribal stance, set the new tone.

In August 1973 the Suquamish Tribe in northwest Washington held its traditional annual ceremony, Chief Seattle Days. The celebration took place at the tribal encampment grounds, where Indian people camped overnight. At four in the morning a fight broke out. Tribal police officers tried to restore order, but Mark Oliphant, a local non-Indian resident, would have none of it. Oliphant was charged in tribal court with assaulting a police officer and resisting arrest. He filed a habeas corpus petition in federal court to challenge the tribe's jurisdiction.

In October of the next year Oliphant was involved in another late-night incident, this time as a passenger in Daniel Belgrade's car. Carl Big Man, tribal chief of police, spotted Belgrade's pickup truck speeding through the town of Suquamish around midnight. Belgrade, like Oliphant a non-Indian, refused to pull over, and a high-speed chase ensued, with Big Man's blue lights flashing and siren screaming. When Belgrade was finally cornered, he rammed Big Man's police car with his vehicle. The tribe charged Belgrade with reckless driving and destruction of tribal property. Belgrade also filed a habeas corpus petition in federal court, and his case was joined with Oliphant's.

The situation presented a close and difficult issue with little direct precedent. By the mid-1970s tribal jurisdiction over non-Indians had become a white-hot emotional issue. Further, the setting differed radically from *McClanahan*, which arose on the remote, state-size Navajo Reservation. The small Suquamish reservation, on the Olympic Peninsula just across Puget Sound from Seattle, had been heavily allotted, so that 63 percent of the 7,200 acres had passed into non-Indian ownership. The demographics were even more extreme: 3,000 non-Indians resided on the reservation, but just 50 tribal members lived there.

The federal district court and court of appeals both upheld tribal criminal jurisdiction. With no direct case authority—given the BIA's strong hand, the tribes had not been asserting criminal jurisdiction over non-Indians since the mid-1800s—the courts worked from the general principles of *Worcester* and other cases, finding that tribes possess all sovereign powers except those granted away by them or extinguished by Congress. Since tribal criminal jurisdiction had not been so limited, the lower courts held, the Suquamish Tribe had authority over non-Indians within reservation boundaries even if non-Indian land was involved.

Justice Rehnquist wrote the opinion for the Supreme Court, which reversed the lower court decisions and ruled that Indian tribes lack criminal jurisdiction over non-Indians. Without doubt, many Americans would question the tribal position—at first blush, it seems wrong that U.S. citizens could be subjected to imprisonment by judges and juries of another race—and the justices likely reacted in that manner. Still, the tribal position had its merits. Non-Indian defendants had safeguards against unfair treatment since they could obtain habeas corpus review of the tribal action in federal court. The Court itself had recently ruled that federal and tribal relations must be thought of as government-to-government, not racial. And Indian people are routinely brought before white judges and juries in cases arising beyond reservation borders.

Whether or not the Court should have upheld tribal criminal jurisdiction over non-Indians, the manner in which the *Oliphant* decision was written has little to recommend it. Instead of a narrow ruling based on the civil liberties concerns, Rehnquist's opinion launched an attack on long-standing basic principles of Indian law. The Supreme Court normally demands clear congressional action to abridge tribal sovereignty. Rehnquist's opinion, however, relied heavily on a reference in the legislative history of the 1834 western territory bill, a most unorthodox and unreliable indicator of legislative intent since Congress never passed it. Even then the Rehnquist opinion acknowledged that the sketchy legislative statements over the years showed only the "unspoken assumption" of Congress that tribes lack criminal jurisdiction over non-Indians. But instead of conducting the rigorous examination for clear congressional intent to limit tribal rights that judges from John Marshall to George Boldt had insisted upon in order to protect these dispossessed peoples, the *Oliphant* opinion denied tribes those powers "inconsistent with their status," leaving the boundaries of tribal sovereignty to the vicissitudes of the value judgments of the courts.

Oliphant's potential impact did not hit home immediately. Just two weeks later the Court issued *United States v. Wheeler*, a ringing endorsement of tribal sovereignty. Other supportive decisions would follow. Yet seeds of destruction had been sown. By the late 1990s Rehnquist, Scalia, and Thomas were finding partners in some, though not all, cases in the enterprise of strapping still more shackles on tribal powers.

The decisions most adverse to tribes came in the area of civil jurisdiction over non-Indians. While no imprisonment is involved, civil jurisdiction includes significant matters, such as taxing authority, environmental regulation, and litigation over business transactions and personal injuries. This means reconciling the ability of tribes to govern their homelands with the rights of non-Indians, who cannot hold office or participate in tribal elections.

When the Supreme Court first addressed the issue, it adopted a promising approach. Its 1981 *Montana* opinion held that *Oliphant's* absolute bar against tribal criminal jurisdiction over non-Indians did not apply to tribal civil jurisdiction. Instead, tribes retained civil authority under the tribal interest test that allowed tribal regulatory jurisdiction when non-Indian conduct "threatens or has some direct effect on the political integrity, the economic security, or the health or welfare of the tribe." The test was fair and nuanced, putting limits on tribal authority over non-Indians and their land but leaving in place the tribe's sovereign right to make decisions on the matters that directly affect important tribal concerns. Yet, even though the tribal interest test was of such recent vintage, opinions in the 1980s and 1990s read it narrowly to restrict tribal zoning power and court jurisdiction.

Two cases in 2001 demonstrated beyond any doubt the Supreme Court's reluctance to uphold tribal civil jurisdiction over non-Indians. The *Atkinson Trading Company* case tested whether the Navajo Nation could exact a hotel occupancy tax on a hotel, originally an Indian trading post, located on non-Indian land within the reservation. The hotel plainly benefited from its site, since many customers were drawn to the establishment by Navajo culture. The tribe provided numerous services to the area, including police patrol, ambulance service, and fire protection. Given the hotel's many entanglements with the Navajo Nation, this must be a situation, it seemed, with a significant tribal interest to justify the tax. In spite of this commonsense notion and the Court's own language in *Merrion v. Jicarilla Apache* that municipal governments must be able to raise revenues through taxation, the *Atkinson Trading Company* opinion struck down the tribal tax. The opinion by Chief Justice Rehnquist left the tribal interest test in shreds.

Then came *Nevada v. Hicks*. Its facts weighed heavily against tribal jurisdiction. A tribal member sued a state police officer in tribal court for money damages under federal civil rights statutes, alleging an illegal search and seizure. The case could easily have been resolved on narrow grounds. State officials, including police officers, possess immunities from lawsuits that might well have decided the litigation.

Justice Scalia, however, wrote a very different kind of opinion in *Nevada v. Hicks*, essentially throwing in the kitchen sink in a far-ranging assault on tribal sovereignty. Typical of Scalia's style, the opinion included all manner of pointed asides and observations that went far beyond the legal points necessary to decide the case. Justice O'Connor sharply objected to Scalia's "sweeping opinion," finding that it was "unmoored from our precedents" and that it "without cause, undermines the authority of tribes to 'make their own laws and be ruled by them.' "

As one example of Scalia's crusade to denigrate tribal sovereignty and exalt state authority over the reservations, he asserted in *Nevada v. Hicks* that " 'ordinarily,' it is now clear, 'an Indian reservation is considered part of the territory of the state.' " In support of this proposition—the exact reverse of the whole course of modern Supreme Court Indian law—he cited two roundly discredited sources, a remark in the 1962 *Kake v. Egan* case and the 1958 interior department revision of *Felix Cohen's Handbook of Federal Indian Law*. The comment in *Kake v. Egan* had no basis at the time it was made, nor was it relevant to the case, and the leading 1973 *McClanahan* opinion expressly disavowed it. The 1958 rewriting of the original 1942 Cohen treatise was as sorry an episode as one will find in American law, a raw political move by the termination-bent Department of the Interior to debase Cohen's heralded scholarship in order to promote extreme assimilationist policies.

No one can yet say how the revisionary Scalia-Rehnquist-Thomas view of tribal sovereignty will fare in the years to come. Scalia did manage to put together a majority in *Nevada v. Hicks*. Yet most of the opinion was dictum—unnecessary to the opinion—and courts often give little deference to dictum, particularly when it is overdrawn. This new approach may fundamentally change Indian law, or it may be an isolated aberration. Time will tell.

RECENT Supreme Court opinions have clearly departed from the Court's own modern rulings. These decisions also are discordant because they clash with the approach of Congress, which holds primary authority over Indian affairs under the Constitution. The Indian voice has been heard, and regularly heeded, on Capitol Hill as Congress has held remarkably steady in support of self-determination over the course of thirty years. While President Nixon's message in 1970 owed much to the efforts of non-Indian White House staffers, the pattern soon emerged of tribally driven legislation in the tradition of early work by the Taos Pueblo,

258   BLOOD STRUGGLE

the Warm Springs and Menominee tribes, and Alaska Natives. A prime example involved the welfare of children.

In the fall of 1967, Louie and Janet Goodhouse of the Devil's Lake Sioux Tribe (now the Spirit Lake Tribe) contacted the Association on American Indian Affairs in New York about a child placement case. North Dakota county authorities wanted to remove Ivan Brown, a six-year-old boy, from his Indian home and place him with an adoptive white family. The boy was living with an elderly tribal member, Mrs. Alex Funey, a grandmother by tribal custom, though not by blood.

Bert Hirsch, a young lawyer with AAIA, went out to the reservation. After pinning down the facts, he brought suit to block the adoption proceedings. No one had alleged neglect. The county made only one argument for removing the boy from his Indian home: Mrs. Funey was 63 years old and therefore was unfit to care for the boy. The tribe saw nothing wrong in this—it was a tribal tradition. Eventually the county authorities backed off.

Hirsch and other staff members at AAIA, suspecting that the incident at Devil's Lake might be part of a larger problem, gathered statistics and learned that, astonishingly, no fewer than one-third of all Devil's Lake Sioux children had been removed from their families and placed in non-Indian homes. The data transformed Ivan Brown's individual circumstances into a cause. The Goodhouses traveled to New York for a summer 1968 press conference at the Overseas Press Club that received sympathetic coverage.

AAIA then began a national effort to assess the seriousness of the practice of removing children from Indian homes. Research showed that Devil's Lake was the norm, not the exception. The problem was nationwide, and its magnitude staggering: Of all Indian children across the country, 25 to 35 percent had been removed from their homes. Depending on the state, the ratio of adopted-out Indian children compared to non-Indian children was many times higher: 4–1 in several states, 10–1 in Wyoming, 15–1 or higher in Maine, Washington, Wisconsin, the Dakotas, and Utah.

AAIA, working closely with tribal leaders and other Indian

organizations, took the lead in bringing the issue to Congress. Hirsch and other lawyers drafted corrective legislation to clarify the primary authority of tribal courts, limit the jurisdiction of state courts, and rein in overly zealous state and local child welfare workers. Senator James Abourezk of South Dakota introduced it in 1972.

Indian people offered their experiences to Congress. Valencia Thacker from Southern California related: "I can remember [the child welfare worker] coming and taking some of my cousins and friends. I didn't know why and I didn't question it. It was just done and it had always been done." "One of the most serious failings of the current system," Chief Calvin Isaac of the Mississippi Band of Choctaw testified, "is that Indian children are removed from the custody of their natural parents by non-tribal governmental authorities who have no basis for intelligently evaluating the cultural and social premises underlying the Indian home life and childrearing. . . . [C]ulturally, the chances of Indian survival are significantly reduced if our children, the only real means for the transmission of tribal heritage, are raised in non Indian homes and denied exposure to the ways of their people." Louis La Rose, tribal chairman of the Winnebago Tribe of Nebraska, expressed his despair:

> I think the cruelest trick that the white man has ever done to Indian children is to take them into adoption courts, erase all of their records and send them off to some nebulous family that has a value system that is A-1 in the State of Nebraska and that child reaches 16 or 17, he is a little brown child residing in a white community and he goes back to the reservation and he has absolutely no idea who his relatives are, and they effectively make him a non-person and I think . . . they destroy him. And if you have ever talked to an individual like that when he comes to a reservation . . . I get depressed.

The Church of Jesus Christ of Latter-day Saints, the Mormon Church, played a major role in this. Always active in proselytizing and converting Native Americans, the church initiated its Indian Student Placement Program after World War II. Church members aggressively recruited Indian parents in remote areas (recruitment was especially widespread at Navajo and Hopi) to send their children to live in Mormon homes during the school year. However well-meaning it may have been, the Mormon program not only took children from their homes and tribes but also imposed intense pressure to convert. By the early 1970s some five thousand Indian children from various tribes lived in Mormon homes.

Racism played its part in the drain of children, but much of the loss can be attributed to an unfamiliarity with Native culture. Many Indian children came from broken homes, often caused by problem drinking. State caseworkers and judges instinctively leaned toward neighborhoods with lawns and white picket fences. No doubt they honestly believed that the child would be better off in the suburbs. They failed to appreciate the extended family tradition, as with Ivan Brown living with an Indian grandmother at Devil's Lake; the value of growing up in a tribal culture; or the disorientation facing a child in bridging the gulf between his or her homeland and the foreign white world. In some cases, Indian children would benefit from being adopted out, but tribal alternatives needed to be evaluated knowledgeably and thoroughly. The system had spun way out of kilter.

The proposed Indian child welfare legislation faced concerted opposition. The Mormon Church of course objected; some states joined in to oppose the unprecedented federal intervention into family law, an area traditionally left to the states and coveted by them. After Congress passed the bill, which had been amended only slightly from the version proposed by the Indian organizations, it hit still more storms. Several cabinet officers urged President Jimmy Carter to veto it. In response, AAIA placed ads in the *Washington Post* and *New York Times*, and tribes enlisted church groups to support the bill. In the end, the central figure may have been Congressman Morris Udall, who had been moved by the Indians' cause and had shepherded the bill through the Interior Committee he chaired. The powerful Arizonan made his case directly to the president and let it be known that he would block a civil service bill, a White House favorite, unless the child welfare act was signed.

Carter did sign the historic legislation in 1978. The Indian Child Welfare Act, perhaps the most far-ranging legislation ever enacted in favor of Indian rights, reaffirmed Supreme Court cases upholding exclusive tribal court jurisdiction over custody proceedings involving children who lived on the reservation. For off-reservation children, ICWA set liberal transfer rules mandating state court judges to shift many cases to tribal courts. For those cases that did remain in state court, ICWA required judges to give stringent presumptions in favor of Indian families before placing Indian children with non-Indian families. The statute allowed Public Law 280 tribes to petition the Interior Department so that their tribal courts could exercise ICWA jurisdiction, and most of those tribes have successfully done so.

State child welfare agencies initially resisted the implementation of ICWA, and state judges, accustomed to exclusive state jurisdiction over family matters, have narrowly interpreted some of the statute's provisions. Nonetheless, the Supreme Court has upheld the act, and the practice of adopting Indian children into white families has been greatly reduced. Tribal and state child welfare workers increasingly cooperate in the administration of Indian child placement. The Indian Child Welfare Act, which Indian people created and which fortifies the futures of tribes by giving them the tools to protect their children, stands as testament to how Indian leaders have mobilized in order to define and implement priorities.

TRIBAL LEADERS have pushed through an impressive array of federal legislation during the modern era. As noted, Congress dealt with the restoration of terminated tribes, the return of tribal lands, and the reform of the BIA through the self-determination policy. More than twenty water rights settlements have recognized tribal water rights and resolved complex, contentious western water disputes. Federal laws now address tribal forest management, agriculture, and fisheries management. The federal environmental laws, including the Clean Water Act and Clean Air Act, give tribes the option of being treated as states for regulatory programs on the reservations. To assist tribes in reducing the

One of the leading Indian attorneys, Susan Williams, of the Sisseton-Wahpeton Dakota Nation, graduated from Harvard Law School and practiced with the Fried, Frank firm in Washington, D.C., before moving her practice to Albuquerque. A dynamic advocate for tribes in courts and Congress, she specializes in tax, water, and environmental law and successfully defended the water rights of the Wind River Tribe in the Supreme Court.

impact of allotment, Congress passed legislation for reservation land restoration and consolidation.

A large body of law, based on proposals from Indian country, has addressed social and cultural issues. Congress has enacted several comprehensive health and education statutes. Tribal colleges draw an increasing amount of federal support. Appropriations statutes treat tribes as states for federal revenue sharing. The American Indian Religious Freedom Act of 1978 is a policy statement directing federal agencies to assure Indians access to, and privacy for ceremonies at, sacred sites on public lands; true, AIRFA was honored mostly in the breach at first, but the National Park Service, Forest Service, and Bureau of Land Management gradually began to respond to traditional Native people and move toward a fuller compliance with the spirit of the act. States may no longer prosecute Indian practitioners for using peyote in traditional religious ceremonies. The powerhouse Native American Graves Protection and Repatriation Act of 1990, presented to Congress by a coalition of religious practitioners with Walter Echo-Hawk of the Native American Rights Fund as the lead attorney, protects Indian graves on federal and tribal lands, prohibits the sale or transport of Native human remains, and requires "repatriation" by directing all government and federally funded museums to return to the tribes identifiable human remains and sacred objects. In an attempt to reverse the loss and dilution of Indian languages, Congress funds tribal-language programs.

Just as it is true that the spate of modern federal legislation—and there are hundreds of other laws, large and small—would have never happened if it were not for the tribes' assertiveness, so too none of this would have occurred without federal legislators who responded to the tribal proposals. Morris Udall of Arizona, George Miller of California, and Sid Yates of Illinois, in the House, and John McCain of Arizona, Ben Nighthorse Campbell of Colorado, and Mark Hatfield, in the Senate, all qualified as giants, people who stood tall out of conviction rather than political gain.

But no legislator in American history can equal the performance of Hawaii's Senator Daniel K. Inouye as a champion for American Indian rights. A Japanese-American born in Honolulu, Inouye enlisted in the army during World War II and fought in brutal battles in France and Italy, where he lost his right arm to a grenade. Recipient of the Medal of Honor and many other military decorations, Inouye used the GI Bill to earn his law degree from George Washington University and, upon Hawaiian statehood, won election as the state's first U.S. representative. In 1962 he became a U.S. senator. By the dawn of the twenty-first century he had represented Hawaii every year since statehood, served on the Senate Watergate Committee, and, fourth in seniority, had earned a position in the Senate "club." With the military so critical to the Islands, Inouye became chair (or vice-chair when the Democrats were in the minority) of the powerful Defense Appropriations Subcommittee.

Inouye had served on the temporary committee on Indian affairs since 1977 and had been mostly inactive until 1987, when he stepped forward to take the chairmanship out of a sense of duty. "No one else was very interested," he said, straight-faced. "This was before *Dances with Wolves* came out." He soon traveled out to the reservations, first to Northwest tribes, then to the pueblos. Inouye had grown up in poverty. Now he visited Indian people in their homes and was taken down into a kiva on Second Mesa for a ceremony. Both comfortable with and profoundly moved by the Indian people he met, Inouye felt, as one aide put it, that "a door in his soul opened up," and he pledged himself to respond because "people were relying on me to help them."

Senator Inouye put together a first-rate staff and held hearings at a breakneck pace. He also began the unprecedented practice of conducting informal listening sessions, often several each year, with tribal leaders in different regions. The format was simple. The senator delivered a short opening statement, saying that he had come to learn their needs, which he hoped to meet by helping turn them into law when it was feasible. He then listened all day, taking time off only for lunch, and at the end gave his sense of which concerns might have a chance in Congress and which would probably not. Routinely, he offered staff assistance in drafting the promising proposals and reformulating the doubtful ones.

Virtually all the Indian legislation from 1987 on has Inouye's mark on it. A meticulous legislator, he saw that no bill came forward until tribes had the language right and that no hearing was held until the testimony was in order. At the same time, he was bold, urging Indians to push for their priorities, and lifted their spirits, calling them "my brothers and sisters" in his formal yet

Senator Inouye meeting with Seminole Tribe of Florida members Joel and Marci Frank and their granddaughter Adelina. Photograph courtesy of Richard Trudell.

affectionate way. He also called in his chits as a senior senator. In 1990 the Supreme Court found that the *Oliphant* rule against tribal criminal jurisdiction over non-Indians extended to non-member Indians (meaning that the Navajo Nation was barred from trying a Sioux as well as an Anglo). Inouye acted promptly. Appreciating the tribes' universal indignation at the decision, he attached a legislative override of the offending Supreme Court decision to the defense appropriations bill that came out of his subcommittee and refused to budge. Asked how a tribal jurisdiction issue fell into the sphere of the defense appropriations subcommittee, Senator Inouye replied with a smile, "How can you have true national security if you don't have proper law and order in Indian country?" The measure passed.

THE TRIBAL SUCCESSES in Congress and the courts spurred a backlash, initially driven by the Northwest fishing decisions, that built up a head of steam by the mid-1970s and has yet to let up. The objections to Indian rights lie on several levels. Some are philosophical, coming from those opposed to "special rights" for any group, a belief sharpened when a race is involved. Assertions

Dr. Patricia Zell, a skilled and committed legislative aide, served as staff director and chief counsel of the Senate Indian Affairs Committee under Senator Inouye's leadership from 1987 through 2004. Photograph courtesty of Richard Trudell.

of tribal governmental powers almost always spur opposition from some state and local agencies and their constituencies, whether the subject is natural resources, taxation, gaming, child welfare, land use, law enforcement, or other areas of governmental and economic development activity.

Many private rights' holders, in addition, believe that recognizing ancient tribal rights—cases involving fishing, land claims, water, and jurisdiction over non-Indians come up most often— simply affect established interests too much. In one congressional report, for instance, Congressman Lloyd Meeds of Washington concluded that "doing justice by Indians does not mean doing injustice by non-Indians." Outright racism also plays a part. The Wisconsin Indian fishing rights controversy spawned verbal and bumper sticker epithets such as "How do you starve an Indian? Put his food stamps under his work boots"; "Save two walleyes, spear a pregnant squaw"; and "Red nigger."

All backlash reactions present one common problem to the tribes and their advocates: Public understanding of distinctive Indian issues comes slowly, and understandably so. Indian rights are indeed "special" in that they are uniquely complex and history-based, emerging from the distant past rather than arising from well-known modern circumstances. The same essential questions and their answers apply to walleye and muskellunge in Wisconsin, whitefish and lake trout in Michigan, salmon and steelhead in Washington and Oregon, eagles in Wyoming and Idaho, water in Colorado and Utah, tax collection in Minnesota and Nebraska, casinos in Connecticut and California, peyote in Nevada and New Mexico, custody of young Indian children in Montana and Illinois, land title in Maine and New York, economic development in Florida and Oklahoma, tribal taxation and court jurisdiction over non-Indians in Arizona and the Dakotas, and Native sovereignty in Alaska and Hawaii. The list could go on. In every instance, the Native position is fragile because it ultimately depends on the capacity and willingness of the majority society to explore unfamiliar intellectual terrain.

Given the nature of the Indian rights and a lack of Indian political weight, it seems likely that opponents to tribal rights would fare well in Congress. Various bills have been introduced to abrogate Indian fishing, hunting, and water rights; prohibit tribal taxation of non-Indians; overrule court decisions upholding tribal land claims; limit the powers of tribal courts; weaken the Indian Child Welfare Act; prohibit tribal gaming; and generally extend state authority over the reservations.

The modern tribes' ability to fend off such confiscatory measures has been as important as the ability to put through their own proposals. On the whole, tribal leaders have done well in defending their rights; the exceptions are few. The tribes did suffer budget cuts in important program areas, especially during the 1980s. After the Supreme Court upheld the right of tribes to engage in gaming free of state regulation, antigaming forces were able to gain federal legislation placing restrictions on casino and other large gaming operations in Indian country. Other than those (and the gaming law can be looked at as a victory for the tribes since it began as a bill to outlaw Indian gaming altogether), no statute of significance has been passed over Indian opposition since the end of the termination era in the early 1970s.

How could this be so? The sheer inertia of getting any bill

through Congress is surely a factor, but the core of it has to be the skillful and compelling defenses by tribal leaders. The proposals to abolish tribal rights, all supported by powerful interests, were defeated by Indian people able to articulate the historical, legal, and moral predicates for laws that are inconvenient to some but that are based on long-standing policies and promises and on modern circumstances that, once understood, provide justification for their continuation.

THE TRIBES have of course achieved no complete victory in their modern litigation and legislative initiatives. Virtually every pro-Indian court decision or statute involves some element, often a significant one, of compromise. Many legislative proposals went nowhere. In the 1990s the Supreme Court opinions took a turn for the worse.

Even so, from the early 1950s to the early 2000s, the situation turned from night to day. When Buck Chosa, Fred Dakota, and Bill Jondreau first decided to litigate their Chippewa fishing rights against the state of Michigan in the mid-1960s, they believed that overturning the old *Chosa* opinion might reinvigorate the tribe's sovereignty and give the tribe "room to move." Their work, and all the other efforts all across Indian country, did that and more. They put the essential legal structure in place.

Yet Supreme Court opinions and United States statutes can be just paper. This is especially true in Indian matters. Making the fishing cases bring fish to market and ceremony, enforcing the Indian Child Welfare Act to keep Indian children in Indian families, using the tribal rights installed in the federal environmental laws to heal the land and the rivers, making those and many other laws *real*, would require a great deal of effort. All those things and many, many more must be done in Indian country, not in Washington, D.C. That story fills the rest of this book.

Part Four

REVIVING the HOMELANDS

11.

Revitalizing Tribal Communities

However favorable the new legal and policy framework might be, every Indian tribe in the postwar years faced challenges befitting a third world nation—some have called aboriginal peoples the fourth world. The needs, numerous and diverse, included education at all levels: health, housing, jobs creation, economic development, protection of hunting, fishing, and water rights, natural resource and environmental management, alcoholism treatment, child care, elder care, cultural preservation, language preservation, archaeological protection, sewage disposal, roads, communications, police protection, jails, and civil and criminal courts. The Indians' societies had been blown nearly apart in the nineteenth century or earlier. Now after a long deadening time, they had to rebuild their communities to capture the best of their traditional ways and also meet the demands and opportunities of the modern industrial superpower within which they lived.

The underpinning for the revivals would be a working tribal sovereignty, true self-rule, not a false-front version where the BIA or the state had the final say. Experience in Indian economic development, for example, has shown that strong and effective tribal governments, anchored in tribal culture, are critical for economic progress. Professor Joseph Kalt, codirector of the Harvard Project on American Indian Economic Development at the Kennedy School of Government, reported: "We cannot find a single case of sustained economic development where the tribe is not in the driver's seat. . . . The only thing that is working is self-determination—that is, *de facto* sovereignty."

Outside control can never play out in quite the right key. Federal and state officials have their own agendas and must meet the budgetary and policy expectations of their superiors in state capitals or Washington, D.C. Indian people may resist federal and state programs, however well intentioned, out of deeply ingrained distrust. Tribal leaders, on the other hand, must face reelection. They know the reservation's people, their needs and expectations. Should the timber harvest be ramped up or scaled back to protect sacred areas and wildlife habitat? Is a gaming operation consistent with tribal values? If so, how large should the casino be, and where should it be located to minimize the disruption? Does juvenile justice, or expansion of the health clinic, trump housing for the people who want to move back home? How much money should be allocated to college scholarships? Are children and families ready for the rigors of a tribal-language immersion program in the elementary school?

Inevitably, while all tribes have made progress, success has been uneven across Indian country. The Confederated Tribes of the Warm Springs reservation of Oregon present one of many examples of how tribes have made dramatic improvements since the 1950s. The predicate for the Warm Springs experience has been a stable and culturally based tribal government.

WARM SPRINGS is called a confederated tribe because it includes three distinct groups. In 1855, when the hard-driving Isaac Stevens negotiated the treaties with the Nez Perce and other Northwest tribes during his determined crusade to open the region for settlement, he selected two tribes in the mid-Columbia area—the Warm Springs (living in the Deschutes River watershed) and the Wasco (whose territory was farther down the Columbia)—and included both in one treaty. In 1879 the government located a band of Paiute on the reservation. Despite their ethnological differences, the three became recognized as one tribe under federal law.

In the 1855 treaty the Wasco and Warm Springs were forced to cede away more than ten million acres of land on the mid-Columbia Plateau, but they retained a large and spectacular landscape as their reservation. The western border lies in the high spruce-fir forests of the Cascade Range and reaches 10,000 feet in elevation. The reservation slopes down toward the east through fine ponderosa pine country and open rangeland to the broad, fast-running Deschutes, the fabled salmon, steelhead, and trout river that marks the eastern boundary of the reservation, as low as 1,000 feet. Much of the land is arid with just ten inches of precipitation a year (western Oregon is wet, but the Pacific storms dissipate in the Cascades and throw little moisture east of there). In addition to the high volcanic peaks and full forests in the mountains, the lower reaches of the Warm Springs Reservation possess a bracing high-desert beauty of sheer cliff faces, massive rock outcrops, spring-fed streams, hot springs, and long vistas. The reservation includes 640,000 acres, slightly more than 1 percent of Oregon.

In the early 1950s Warm Springs people endured the kinds of troubles endemic to Indian country. The tribe had adopted a constitution back in 1938, but by 1945 it employed just one part-time employee, housed in the basement of the BIA office building. The first tribal timber sale had been made in 1942, affording tribal members small per capita payments, but transportation was tough; no paved road ran into the reservation and floating logs down the Deschutes was a treacherous endeavor. As Wasco Chief Nelson Wallulatum put it, the people of Warm Springs "were just floatin' around lookin' at the land."

In 1958, the tribe made a pivotal decision. The Army Corps of Engineers had flooded Celilo Falls on the Columbia, the traditional fishing grounds for Warm Springs tribal members, compensating the tribe in the amount of $4 million. For decades Congress, reflecting the low state of tribalism, had distributed such claims money by per capita payments to individuals even though the tribe, not its members, owned the lost land. Thus, when the Celilo Falls payment came out, past practice and the expectations of tribal members pointed toward per capita payments.

Tribal council members Charlie Jackson, Alvin Smith, Olney

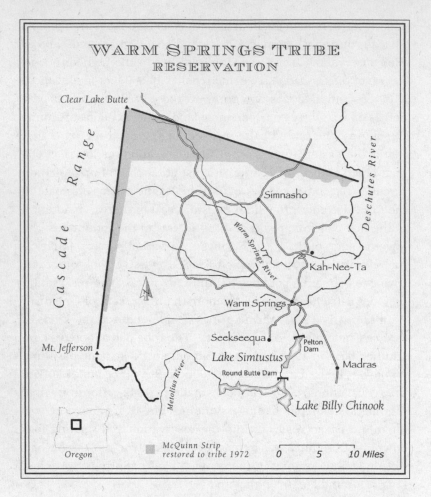

WARM SPRINGS TRIBE
RESERVATION

Clear Lake Butte

Cascade Range

Deschutes River

Simnasho

Warm Springs River

Kah-Nee-Ta

Warm Springs

Seekseequa

Mt. Jefferson

Pelton Dam

Lake Simtustus

Madras

Metolius River

Round Butte Dam

Lake Billy Chinook

Oregon

McQuinn Strip
restored to tribe 1972

0   5   10 Miles

Patt, Sr., Delbert Frank, and Secretary/Treasurer Vernon Jackson
had a different idea. They wanted to allocate most of the payment
to the tribe. The tribal government, still small, fewer than a dozen
employees, could use this money to get the tribe up on its feet.
The issue went to an emotional community meeting, where a consensus emerged. Tribal members, nearly all of them well below
the poverty line, would divide $1 million in the per capita pay-
ments but would commit $3 million to the tribal government.

This bold statement in the name of tribalism, made during the
depths of the termination era, brought near- and long-term gains

and set in place traditions of the highest order for Warm Springs governance.

The investments of the Celilo Falls compensation put Warm Springs on a new track. The tribe bought back a large parcel of land, encompassing a long stretch of the Warm Springs River and outstanding hot springs, which had passed out of Indian hands. This splendid locale became the site of Kah-Nee-Ta, the tribe's resort complex and a productive financial enterprise.

The purchase of the Kah-Nee-Ta parcel, coupled with the successful campaign to reacquire the McQuinn Strip by rectifying the nineteenth-century surveying error, initiated a tribal land acquisition program funded through the tribal budget. The reservation had been only lightly allotted, but nonetheless, thousands of acres made their way into non-Indian hands. By the beginning of the twenty-first century, other than a few small government inhold-

Lillie Heath, blending the old and new, cooks salmon in the traditional way on alder sticks over an open fire for guests at the Warm Springs Tribe's Kah-Nee-Ta lodge, shown in the background. Photograph by Cynthia D. Stowell, reprinted with permission from Faces of a Reservation: A Portrait of the Warm Springs Indian Reservation.

ings, there were virtually no non-Indian lands within reservation boundaries.

Reaching beyond the reservation, the tribe went on to reacquire land in the 10-million-acre area ceded in the 1855 treaty where the tribe had off-reservation hunting, fishing, gathering, and pasturing rights, a place of powerful emotional attachments. Soon the tribe owned the area surrounding Sherars Bridge on the Deschutes River, where tribal fishers still work their hoop nets from their traditional platforms, lifting salmon up out of the foam. It also acquired four properties in the John Day River basin, including a 35,000-acre parcel that carries with it grazing and water rights associated with 15,000 acres of public land. Between 1997 and 2002 alone, the tribe expended $18 million for land acquisition.

It also revamped its wood products program. The tribal council used Celilo Falls money to buy a private timber mill in the town of Warm Springs. This, along with the purchase in the 1960s of a plywood company in the off-reservation city of Madras, greatly expanded the tribe's capabilities. Instead of merely selling stumpage, the tribe now could mill the logs, then make and sell plywood and lumber. Naturally, tribal jobs steadily increased. One tribal member had worked in the reservation sawmill when it was in private hands. By 2003 more than 100 (of 140 employees) were Indians.

Warm Springs Forest Products and the Kah-Nee-Ta vacation resort became the first Warm Springs enterprises—tribal businesses chartered by the tribal council but operationally separate from it, thus keeping day-to-day commercial decisions apart from tribal politics. Today the tribe has six additional enterprises: an elegant cultural museum, a source of great pride to tribal members; a small plaza shopping center; a composite products venture; an energy enterprise on the Deschutes River that owns a reregulating dam and comanages with Portland General Electric Company the large dam-and-reservoir operation, the Pelton-Round Butte Project; Warm Springs Ventures, the tribe's investment arm; and the Indian Head Gaming Center, a small casino established in the 1990s and located at Kah-Nee-Ta, distant from tribal residential areas.

The Celilo Falls investment in tribal government spawned still another development in the early years. The tribal council engaged a group of faculty members at Oregon State University to study potential economic opportunities and prepare a resource development plan keyed to both job creation and cultural tradi- tions. This plan led to the initial tribal enterprises and to other comprehensive long-range plans, the kind that is actually used rather than shelved.

At Warm Springs, the forestlands play a central role in reserva- tion life. They have long been viewed as a pillar of the tribe's eco- nomic prospects. In addition, tribal members use the woodlands for huckleberry gathering, recreation, and religious ceremonies, and the forest habitat assures salmon, deer, and elk for abundant dinner tables. Suspicion grew that the BIA had overharvested the timber stands during the 1960s, 1970s, and early 1980s. In 1985 the tribe hired a team, again led by Oregon State faculty, which recommended that the timber harvest be reduced for cultural rea- sons even though a larger cut was sustainable in purely commer- cial forestry terms. At this point the tribal council, alarmed at the intensity of the timber harvest, initiated an integrated resource management plan.

The IRMP recommended a reduction in the timber harvest through 1992. By then the BIA was managing the forest according to the priorities of the tribal council, and the agency lowered the annual harvest. In 2001 the council brought down the timber cut still further. In all, the cut dropped from 105 million board feet in 1985 to 42 million by 2001. The tribe was willing to forgo the higher financial returns, and some job loss in the mill, in return for other benefits engrained in the culture. Reservation deer pop- ulations have increased fourfold, elk tenfold, and the salmon runs have been the best since the big dams went in. Bull trout, listed as a threatened species in many western rivers, are plentiful at Warm Springs.

The reduction in logging is just one of many testaments to the vibrant Warm Springs culture. Tribal members engage in ongoing feasts and celebrations in the longhouses and attend elaborate burial ceremonies. A reverence for the salmon, deer and elk, and huckleberries, for all the reservation land and the aboriginal expanse beyond, infuse the gatherings and day-to-day life. Visitors revel in the open, gracious, and welcoming atmosphere.

The Warm Springs Tribe now has 700 full-time employees on the government side of tribal operations. The tribal government provides the full array of services carried out by local governments: education, health, police, administration of justice, and so forth. Warm Springs' largest branch is natural resource management, about 120 strong.

The full-time tribal work force totals 1,100 when the enterprises' 400 employees are included. The figure swells to about 1,500 with summer seasonal hires, making the tribe in some years the largest employer in central Oregon. When only governmental functions are considered, Warm Springs is smaller than Deschutes County, where Bend is located, but considerably larger than other county and city governments in central Oregon. In little more than a generation the Warm Springs Tribe had gone from a subordinate and almost invisible adjunct of the BIA to an effective and respected governmental and economic force.

One effort deserves special mention. In 1965 the tribal council started a college scholarship program, and in 1986 tribal members approved a referendum creating a permanent fund of $6 million for scholarships. By the early twenty-first century the endowment had reached $12 million and guaranteed to every Warm Springs young person tuition at any institution of higher education, plus a portion of living expenses. Today about one hundred Warm Springs members are enrolled in higher education from junior colleges through graduate schools.

Warm Springs shines as an example of a stable, responsive, and capable tribal governance grown organically from the soil of its own culture and traditions. Several institutions that contributed to the revival may be traced to the tribe's 1938 constitution. This is unusual because many tribal constitutions of that era, developed under John Collier's Indian Reorganization Act, were boiler plate

documents prepared by the BIA. Indeed, the Warm Springs constitution has several provisions (including BIA approval of many
tribal actions) that seem to stem from Washington, not from the
east slope of the Cascades.

Still, many tribes, Warm Springs among them, insisted on culturally appropriate provisions in their governing documents.
Thus the Warm Springs constitution set up an eleven-person tribal
council. Eight members come from three districts: Simnasho
(mostly composed of Indians who are ethnologically from the
original Warm Springs bands), with three council members; Warm
Springs (mostly Wasco people), with three members; and the
smaller Seekseequa District (mostly Paiute), with two members.
The other three council members are hereditary chiefs, one from
each tribe. The chiefs, steeped in the culture and holding long
tenures, serve for life and lend stability to the council; as of 2002,
the Wasco chief, Nelson Wallulatum, had served since 1959, Delvis
Heath of the Warm Springs Tribe since 1985. Elected council
members have contributed to the continuity. During the second
half of the twentieth century, leaders such as Olney Patt, Sr., Delbert Frank, Bernice Mitchell, Zane Jackson, and Wilson Wewa, Sr.,
served in most, though not all, terms.

Stability also is enhanced by the office of the secretary/treas-
urer, another institution created by the 1938 constitution. The sec-
retary/treasurer, who is appointed by the council and carries out
duties similar to those of a chief executive officer, has provided a
steadying influence in part because of the stature of the people
holding the position. There is a powerful continuity among the
three men, all tribal members, who have occupied the office the
longest. Vernon Jackson, the tribe's first college graduate in 1958,
served continuously (except for the four years when he earned his
degree) from the early 1950s until his death in 1970. Jackson,
among other things, drove the dedication of the Celilo Falls funds
to the tribe. Ken Smith, the tribe's second college graduate, succeeded Jackson and served until his 1981 appointment as assistant
secretary of the interior for Indian affairs. He later was named to
the board of directors for the San Francisco District of the Federal
Reserve Board. Smith, at once amiable and tough-minded, was

known for his financial acumen and returned to the secretary/
treasurer post from 1989 until the mid-1990s. Charles Jackson
went to Columbia University, worked for the BIA and the tribe,
and then became secretary/treasurer in 1998. The three men,
able and respected, amount to a line: Vernon Jackson was mentor
to Ken Smith, and Charles Jackson was Smith's protégé as well as
Vernon's son.

There was continuity, too, in legal representation. In 1955 the
tribe hired the talented and folksy Owen Panner, a prominent public figure in central Oregon and later a federal judge. When Panner left private practice for the bench, his firm was kept on, with
Dennis Karnopp, James Noteboom, and Howard Arnett later
assuming primary duties.

Another constitutional provision promotes stability by installing democratic processes. Public hearings on the annual budgets
(invariably loud and well attended) are constitutionally mandated
and a public referendum is required to approve any nonbudgeted
expense above $25,000. A tradition has evolved of resolving large
expenditures and matters of great importance by referendum,
even if they could be included as regular budget items. This combination of public involvement and accountability requires
elected officials to do much walking the membership, as it is
called, and contributes to a buy-in by the membership of tribal
decisions.

Warm Springs, like all governments, tribal and otherwise, has
its share of internal dissension, erratic behavior, and other shortcomings. But the tribe's constitution, its leaders, and their decisions are accepted as legitimate by its citizenry. Businesses and
other governments know that Warm Springs can be trusted. Many
other tribes can claim the same, and all understand the need for
a stable and democratic working sovereignty. For an Indian reservation to become a true and permanent homeland, the tribe, as its
first job, must construct the sovereignty brick by brick.

SOVEREIGNTY BUILDING has proceeded on every reservation. The particulars differ from Warm Springs but everywhere,
even where progress has come more slowly, tribes have been cre-

ative and doggedly persistent in the gargantuan task of piecing societies back together. Two areas where this can be seen, both lying at the heart of any government's sovereignty, are tribal reform of Indian education and the rebuilding of tribal justice systems.

In the 1950s the landscape of Indian education displayed little but wreckage. The BIA ran a sprawling system of boarding schools and on-reservation day schools, which suffered from low funding, poorly trained and dispirited teachers, and programs that, despite some dedicated teachers who fought the system, usually ignored Indian culture and often actively sought to rub it out. Few Native people graduated from high school, almost none from college. The many arenas made reform all the more complex: preschool, elementary and secondary schools, higher education, congressional funding and policy direction, and the BIA. Within the tribes, educational reform had to overcome the cultural detritus of all the bad years: dysfunctional tribal families and discouraged, nonparticipatory communities. Still, Indian people knew that education held the key to everything from better tribal administration to reduction of poverty.

In the early 1960s, when it finally became possible to dream, some tribal leaders asked, "Why don't we control our own educational system?" Navajo moved first. After ferment brewed at the grass roots level, Raymond Nakai campaigned on the issue and was elected tribal chairman. The Rough Rock Demonstration School, the OEO-funded elementary school founded in the dawn of the self-determination era, opened its doors in 1966 as the first tribally controlled school in modern times. The Rough Rock breakthrough led to the creation of Navajo Community College (now Diné College), which began offering classes in 1969 with funding from the tribe, the OEO, and the Donner Foundation. By then steam was building in Indian country for tribal control of education at all levels.

The Rosebud Sioux Reservation in South Dakota was one of many places where the spirit of tribal control over education came alive. In the 1960s Stanley Redbird had a vision of a college at Rosebud, that despite the poverty and small rural population, there could be a place, as Redbird used to say, where teachers could help students find their dreams and make them come true. He yoked his vision to tireless organizing and brought together a critical mass of believers. Redbird, with tribal members Julia Lambert, Winnie Wood, Olive Pretty Bird, and Gerald Mohatt, a non-Indian community activist, hatched the idea of a tribal college at Rosebud.

Even with the election of the tribal chairman Webster Two Hawk, an early supporter of the tribal college concept, progress came slowly as the impoverished tribe (even today unemployment runs at 45 percent) struggled to develop housing, roads, and antipoverty programs. Nonetheless, fueled by a desire to introduce Lakota culture and language into schools, Redbird and a burgeoning number of supporters managed to craft a blueprint for a college and patch together funding. Undoubtedly, there was some of the hesitation that Avis Three Irons experienced during the founding of the Crow Tribe's Little Big Horn College: "It took several council meetings to get it chartered. People were unsure with chartering a college. People didn't feel like a sovereign yet." Finally, in 1971, the Rosebud Sioux tribal council unanimously approved a tribal charter for the new college and celebrated the event by a powwow, where traditional leaders blessed the new effort.

The Rosebud Sioux named their new college Sinte Gleska, after Spotted Tail, the tribe's *wicasa itancan*, or highest leader, during the Sioux Nation's cataclysmic events of treaty, reservation, Little Bighorn, loss of the Black Hills, and treaty renegotiation. Sinte Gleska professed that to survive, the tribe had to learn the methods of white society while retaining Lakota ways. In a defining episode, in 1880 he agreed to send his grandchildren to Carlisle, the BIA boarding school in Pennsylvania, only to learn that they had been baptized as Episcopalians, dressed as soldiers, and ordered to farm. He promptly brought them home, making his stand for bicultural, bilingual education.

Sinte Gleska University began as a two-year college. Today it enrolls more than one thousand students and offers a full four-year undergraduate program and a master's degree in education.

In addition to the customary liberal arts and business curricula, the university has a strong Lakota studies department and two research centers, the Sicangu Policy Institute and the Bison Project. The student body includes 10 to 15 percent non-Indians. Frank Pommersheim, a leading Indian law scholar at the University of South Dakota, who has taught at Sinte Gleska, has this to say:

> During the time I taught at Sinte Gleska University, I was repeatedly struck by the transformative nature of these exchanges, particularly as they affected non-Indians. Non-Indians reacted most favorably in three areas: (1) to the rigor and quality of education they were receiving; (2) to the fact that they were welcomed and not discriminated against; and (3) to the opportunity to meet Indians and their cultures in a non-threatening, nonstereotyped situation.
>
> The most striking attributes of these exchanges are legitimacy and humanity: legitimacy in the sense that most non-Indians begin to recognize and appreciate the legal and ethical thrust of Indian people to develop and to improve their institutions and government; and humanity in the sense that they begin to appreciate the human faces behind these exertions. Non-Indians gain a perception that, despite differences in culture and historical circumstances, a common thread of effort binds both sides to the task of improving the quality of opportunity and life in one's family and community. This alone, of course, does not solve difficult questions, but it is important in shaping discussions concerning such pressing issues as the alleviation of discrimination, the Black Hills controversy, and the recognition of authentic tribal government permanence in Indian country. The education process, which has often held so much promise for fulfillment in the dominant community, holds equal sway in tribal communities. Yet there is also the added potential for the emergence of a precious ethic of common understanding and respect.

Tribal colleges now number thirty-two. Most offer two-year degrees, but the trend is toward four-year and master's programs. Sinte Gleska and the rest operate under many handicaps. Their budgets average about 40 percent less per student than public community colleges. Although some—notably Diné College at Navajo and Salish Kootenai College at Flathead—have good facilities and new construction is under way on several campuses, many of the physical plants remain inadequate. Classes sometimes must be taught in double wides or renovated BIA offices. Teacher salaries are low, and turnover is high on some campuses.

Nonetheless, the progress is evident, and tribal colleges have become mainstays in their communities. Congress is voting more money, tribes have a greater capability to provide funding, and several foundations have responded enthusiastically. Graduates show high employment rates. Faculty members do important, reservation-specific research—work that would not otherwise be done—into tribal history, culture, language, law, and economic conditions. At every tribal college the culture is pervasive. It shows up in the Indian-focused courses and the special research programs and is integrated into otherwise standard courses found in Anglo curriculums. At Sinte Gleska the university makes the land omnipresent. The guiding maxim is "Never forget where you come from."

The tribal colleges bring higher education to remote areas and to people who otherwise could not attend school. It is said that the typical tribal college graduate is a thirty-year-old single mother. At Sitting Bull College on the Standing Rock Sioux reservation, I witnessed a graduation ceremony custom. After the red-robed graduates had marched in to the beat of a tribal drum and received their diplomas, blessed by burning sage and the wave of an eagle feather, each graduate handed out a dozen red roses to people who had helped him or her obtain their degrees. The president of the college whispered to me, "Most of those roses are going out to baby-sitters."

Tribal control of elementary and secondary education presented different problems. Before the 1960s higher education did not exist in Indian country. A tribal college could step in and fill a void. Primary education, conversely, had a long, stern history dominated by the BIA and the states.

In the 1870s, after decades of funding scattered reservation day

schools (most of them administered by churches), the federal government ambitiously expanded its role in Indian education with
the opening of the BIA boarding schools, noted for their strong
religious and military academy influences. By 1928, year of the
comprehensive Meriam Report on Indian affairs, 40 percent of all
Indian children in school were away at boarding schools. Others
attended on-reservation federal and church day schools or public
schools near reservations and in the cities. Tens of thousands of
school-age children had dropped out or never enrolled in the
first place.

The Meriam Report criticized nearly every aspect of the federal
schools: facilities, quality of teachers, the standardized national
curriculum, food, disciplinary practices, and funding levels. Congress responded in the 1930s by upping appropriations for Indian
education and authorizing the BIA to pay state schools to take
Indian children. Then, in the 1950s, as part of the termination-era
philosophy of assimilation and increased state authority over
Indian affairs, Indian children were directed to state schools in
ever-greater numbers as the BIA closed some schools and Congress offered states federal money for educating Indian children.

In 1969 came a major Senate report, "Indian Education: A
National Tragedy—A National Challenge," issued by a special subcommittee chaired first by Senator Robert Kennedy and then by
his brother, Senator Edward Kennedy. This gloomy document
concluded that little ground had been gained. In public schools,
Indian children faced widespread discrimination and saw little or
no evidence of their cultures in the classroom. Generally, they
experienced feelings of "alienation, hopelessness, [and] powerlessness." The BIA schools remained entrenched in their old ways.
The report excoriated the federal policy of "coercive assimilation"
as disastrous for the education of Indian children and recommended various measures: increased funding, the inclusion of
Indian culture and language in the curriculum, and more Indian
control over school administration.

Despite broad support generated by the Kennedy Report, tribal
reformers in the 1960s and 1970s faced an unyielding, many-
headed system. Indian children were being placed in five kinds of

schools: BIA day schools; BIA boarding schools; mission schools; on-reservation state schools, with mostly Indian students; and off-reservation state schools, with large Indian enrollments in some towns near reservations and small Indian enrollments in the cities. Each presented its own challenges, but all had one thing in common: a staunch resistance to Indian control, exemplified by the BIA employee who, when confronted with an all-Navajo school board at Rough Rock during the early self-determination days, snorted that the proposed school "won't last 6 months."

But Rough Rock did last, and it gave heart to Indian people elsewhere. In 1969, Indian educators founded the National Indian Education Association, which quickly became an active force for Indian education at all levels. The dynamic Coalition of Indian Controlled School Boards formed two years later, vowing to start tribal chartered schools wherever possible, mostly by converting BIA day schools. The coalition members also worked to install majority-Indian school boards for state schools within or near reservations. Unlike tribal schools, these would remain under state jurisdiction, but the strong Indian influence on the boards would assure an infusion of tribal culture—and a sensitivity to the special needs of Indian children.

The Rosebud Sioux Tribe, energized by the success of Sinte Gleska University, also acted inventively in elementary and secondary education. In the 1950s, South Dakota, in the drive toward assimilation, had taken over the five BIA schools at Rosebud. Although one remaining mission school was turned over to the tribe in the 1970s, the tribe lacked resources to administer the state schools directly. By the 1980s it had become clear that the system was not working. Concern among private and tribal leaders about the primary schools coalesced. As Sherry Red Owl put it, "truancy at both public and tribal schools had reached a crisis point."

The tribe, working with the Native American Rights Fund and educational consultants RJS & Associates, stepped back, took stock of education at all levels at Rosebud, and put in place a tribal education code and a tribal education department to administer it. The code identified four target areas: curriculum and education standards, staffing and teacher training, alcohol and substance abuse, and parental involvement. At bottom lay the pride and sense of self-worth deriving from tribal culture, spirituality, and language. As Albert White Hat, instructor of Lakota thought and philosophy at Sinte Gleska, explained matter-of-factly and not in anger, the white man "taught us English only so we could take orders, not so that we might dream."

The Rosebud Sioux Tribe's exercise of sovereignty over education (more than 80 other tribes also have education departments) has produced results. State schools on the reservation have embraced the tribe's curriculum. Tribal and Sinte Gleska educators have worked collaboratively with South Dakota administrators to implement it. Rosebud's dropout rate plummeted from 36 percent to 7 percent while its graduation rate grew from 24 percent to 69 percent. Like so many self-determination efforts, Rosebud's tribal education department took years to install and must operate at less than full funding, but it possesses a golden attribute, the legitimacy of emanating from within the tribe itself.

As the century has turned, tribes now run more than 100 tribal elementary and secondary schools. Another 1,200 schools—most of them, as at Rosebud, public and in or near Indian country—have Indian student enrollments of at least 25 percent. These public schools with high Indian populations enroll about 40 percent of America's Indian children. Native influence in nearly all of them is strong, whether through Indian representation on the school boards, tribal education codes, or parental involvement. The education community understands Indians much better. Non-Indians have a greater appreciation that Indian children should be educated in a culturally appropriate setting.

I remember visiting a Utah elementary school near the Navajo Reservation in the early 1970s. Most students were Navajo, but the building displayed no evidence—art, posters, books, photographs, or quotations—of any Indian heritage. A colleague said to me, "This school could be in a St. Louis suburb." Ten years later I returned to find the Navajo presence everywhere, from the books on the shelves to the walls in the entryway, adorned with murals of Navajo rugs and a landscape of Monument Valley.

Indian education remains no easy matter. Modern Indian leaders have accomplished reform, not revolution. Dropout and absentee rates remain high, and academic achievement is below average. Adults are active in some districts and distant in others. Indian parents and elders often view formal education with suspicion bred of a century of abuse, and the tradition of achieving higher education is still young. Nevertheless, we can take heart at the progress. High school graduation rates have steadily gone up. The number of Indian people in college has climbed from about 2,000 in the 1950s to 10,000 in 1970 to 147,000 in 2000.

Those are not just numbers. They are doctors, biologists, engineers, businesspeople, historians, lawyers, economists, poets, teachers, and generalists. Many of them will come home and lend a valued hand. Individually, their educations can bring them and their families a kind of security and personal satisfaction long denied Indian people.

IN ABORIGINAL TIMES Indian tribes had legal systems; they made laws, adjudicated disputes, and inflicted punishments. Some, the Iroquois Confederacy, for instance, were formal and elaborate; others much less so. Punishments—whippings and other forms of torture—could be cruel by today's standards, but Native law hewed to concepts of punishment that any system of justice could aspire to: Rather than revenge or retribution, tribes relied on banishment and restitution to victims and their families. Just as tribes had political heads, religious leaders, and warriors, so did they also have peacemakers who resolved disputes. In a celebrated, politically charged incident at Rosebud in 1881, Crow Dog killed Sinte Gleska, the highest civil leader and advocate of bilingual and bicultural education. After a tribal council meeting and mediation by tribal elders, the two families agreed to a plan of forward-looking restitution rather than imprisonment or capital punishment: Crow Dog's family would pay to Sinte Gleska's family eight horses, $600, and a blanket.

The federal government, aiming to supplant tribal ways, officially took over law enforcement in Indian country in 1883 by adopting in the Code of Federal Regulations a set of administrative laws and courts for Indian country. These CFR courts, with their BIA police and jails, clamped down on traditional practices, including healing by medicine men and ceremonies such as Sun Dance at Sioux. When extreme assimilation policies came under fire in the 1930s, tribes began installing true tribal courts to replace the federal CFR courts. Still, as late as 1970, there were only 85 operating tribal courts.

Much has changed in thirty-five years. Most of the 562 federally recognized tribes have created courts under their own constitutions or laws. This requires considerable infrastructure. Tribal justice systems need courtrooms and office spaces, judges for both trials and appeals, prosecutors, court clerks, tribal defenders in criminal cases, police, counselors, child welfare workers, and jail facilities. In addition to personnel, tribal justice systems must have civil and criminal laws, rules of court procedure, law libraries, and, typically, intergovernmental agreements with federal and state agencies for child welfare, environmental regulation, and criminal law. Cross-deputization agreements in such fields must be negotiated because overlaps of tribal, federal, and state law enforcement authority within reservations are so complex.

Tribal courts work in different ways, often depending on the size of the tribes. The number of law-trained tribal judges has steadily climbed, but there is still a place for lay judges; in addition to funding limitations, some tribes prefer judges without formal law school training but steeped in traditional community mores and tribal history. Judges may be full- or part-time; in some cases tribes retain active or retired state court judges to sit as tribal judges. Tribes may run their own jail facilities or contract with a nearby county or city. A tribal court may be casual or very formal with a modern courtroom, a judge in robes, and tribal, United States, and state flags behind the bench. For appeals, tribes variously have their own appeals courts, allow further appeals to intertribal courts of appeals, or have no appeals at all from trial judges' decisions. Most of the New Mexico pueblos have highly traditional and secretive courts in which "court procedures are unwritten, and the only laws applied are customary laws of the pueblo."

Funding for tribal justice, as with tribal education, is improving but only slowly. Tribal judges as a group are extraordinarily dedicated but sorely underpaid. Another difficulty is the independence of tribal judiciaries. Many tribes still operate under the BIA-drafted constitutions of the 1930s that vested tribal councils with executive power—line authority, with the power to hire and fire—over all reservation entities, including the courts. Although such instances are in decline, from time to time members of tribal councils have pressured judges for favorable treatment to family and friends. In response, some tribes have set up procedures for separation of executive, legislative, and judicial powers. In any event, on the matter of overall competence and fairness, tribal courts have fared well. Critics of tribal sovereignty and courts have spurred a number of hearings and investigations by congressional committees and the Civil Rights Commission. Those inquiries have consistently affirmed the work of the tribal courts and urged greater federal financial support.

Tribal justice systems must continually reconcile two different objectives. On the one hand, out of necessity they have a certain "Anglo" cast to them. As a matter of federal law, the Indian Civil Rights Act requires tribal courts to afford due process and other civil liberties. In addition, Indian courts try to provide a procedural setting familiar to lawyers; this is fair to the attorneys and helps blunt outside criticism that they are not "real" courts. Thus tribal courts commonly adopt rules of evidence, pleading, and other procedural requirements similar to those in federal and state courts.

Conversely, tribes want to integrate tribal traditions into their justice systems. Consider the Navajo Nation courts and the way they have addressed the melding of American law and tribal customary law.

In 1959, after thirty years under a CFR court, the Navajo Nation formed its own judiciary. Today, in the vast Navajo landscape, home to more than 220,000 people, the nation has seven district courts with 14 trial judges. Appeals can be taken to a three-judge supreme court. The Navajo courts have a distinguished history. Among other things, rules call for Navajo court advocates to represent parties that cannot afford lawyers; attorneys who wish to join the Navajo bar must pass a separate bar exam; the justices have authored many formal written opinions, some in Navajo; and the courts have stood firm for the principle of separation of powers in the face of various assaults on judicial independence. The Navajo judicial system hears about 100,000 cases a year, of which 28,000 involve criminal charges.

A foundation of Navajo justice is Navajo common law, similar in method but not result to English and American common law, in which the judges develop legal rules that reflect the society's history, traditions, economy, and natural resources. In one case, for instance, the Navajo Supreme Court interpreted a Navajo code provision allowing a case to be heard in any district where a defendant "resides." The suit was filed in the Shiprock District even though the defendant currently lived in the Window Rock District. The court found that Navajo common law allowed the suit to go ahead in the Shiprock District. The defendant "resided" in the Shiprock District because he had grown up in the village of Teec Nos Pos, within the Shiprock District, and his mother still lived there. "By custom," the justices explained, "Navajos consider themselves to be from the same area as their mothers are from. Thus, wherever they may be, they return home frequently for religious ceremonies and family functions, as well as to vote."

Robert Yazzie, chief justice of the Navajo Supreme Court from 1992 through 2003, has been the leading spokesman for the Navajo justice system and for the Indian tribal courts nationally as well. Chief Justice Yazzie, who grew up in a traditional household and ties his hair up in a *tsiyeeł*, the Navajo-style bun, graduated from Oberlin and obtained his law degree from the University of New Mexico. Yazzie, with a penetrating legal mind and a gentle, friendly demeanor, has made a point of educating the public about justice at Navajo. Like former Chief Justice Tom Tso and Justice Raymond Austin, he has written articles in the law journals about the Navajo Nation's courts and has spoken widely on the subject

Here Chief Justice Robert Yazzie talks with law students after the Navajo Supreme Court held court at the University of Oregon Law School. Photograph courtesy of Jack Liu, University of Oregon Law School.

to national, state, and local groups. The Navajo Supreme Court also has heard oral arguments—not moot courts but proceedings in actual cases with the justices, court personnel, and attorneys all being flown in—at the Arizona, Arizona State, New Mexico, Colorado, Harvard, UCLA, Oregon, and Stanford law schools. I have attended some of those hearings and rarely seen audiences so rapt, immersed in new meanings of "law" and "justice," engrossed in the stature of the judges, the dignity of the occasion, the formulation of Navajo common law, and the sprinkling of Navajo words by the judges and attorneys.

In 1982 the Navajo Judicial Branch broke new ground by initiating an innovative process called the Peacemaker Court, and peacemaking has steadily grown in use and stature at Navajo and other reservations as well. Traditionally, Navajo called in a *naat'áanii,* or peacemaker, to mediate disputes. Today the Navajo court system includes more than one hundred peacemakers— medicine men, elders, and other respected people chosen by chapters, the local units of government at Navajo. Peacemakers have the respect of the parties and the skill to get people talking out their problems with one another. Parties in court can, if they wish, leave the adversarial system behind and decide to resolve their disputes, civil or criminal, in the Peacemaker Court. This has prompted interest among leaders in the national alternative dispute resolution movement now gaining force in the state and federal courts.

I once heard Chief Justice Yazzie offer an explanation of the reasons behind peacemaking. He described the Anglo-American courts as representing what he called a vertical system of justice. "Judges," he said, "sit at the top over lawyers, jury members, parties, and all the other participants in court proceedings. Judges possess a tremendous amount of power, [and] the parties involved in the dispute do not have as much power."

Traditional Navajo justice, as Chief Justice Yazzie described it, is horizontal. He explained that "in the Navajo peacemaking system, all human beings are treated as equals. There are no rules to dictate how proceedings should be controlled. In the peacemaker process you can speak with the mediator. [The peacemaker] aims at one goal and one goal only: restoring true justice among individuals, families, and the larger community and society. This is done by allowing the wrongdoer and victims to 'talk things out.' No one is treated as the 'good guy' or the 'bad guy.' The peacemaker process is meant to restore the minds, physical being, spirits, and emotional well-being of all people involved." Peacemaking creates individualized solutions, often ratified through the healing powers of a traditional ceremony. Sometimes the solutions include restitution to the victim's family, community service, or a reuniting in a family or divorce case. There is, as Justice Yazzie put it, none of the "eye for an eye, tooth for a tooth" notion of retribution implicit in the Code of Hammurabi and in our vertical judicial system.

James Zion, solicitor to the courts of the Navajo Nation, has reported some of the cases heard in peacemaking. This is Zion's summary of what he calls "The Case of the Troubled War Veteran":

> A man told a Navajo Nation peacemaker that since he returned from Vietnam he had been troubled. He couldn't sleep, he drank too much, and he had problems dealing with his family.

The peacemaker knew of the special Navajo ceremony used for those who return from war to cleanse them of the evil they had experienced.

Navajos believe that war is evil and that what warriors see during the war can affect their spirit. Today, we call it post-traumatic stress disorder (PTSD). The ceremony exorcises the evil.

The peacemaker told the man he should have the ceremony done, and he replied, "I couldn't afford one when I got back from Vietnam, and besides, I don't really believe in that traditional stuff." But he had the ceremony done anyway.

The peacemaker followed up on the case, asking the man how he felt. He explained that he didn't know why, but the ceremony had worked. He could now sleep through the night without waking with bad dreams. He felt at peace.

Navajos have traditional wisdom about what to do with returning warriors. They know the evil effects of war, and PTSD is considered a "monster" in the Navajo way of thinking. To the Navajos, it isn't a disorder—it's an evil that must be slain or weakened in ceremonies.

The use of traditional concepts of justice has played an increasingly large role in the Navajo justice system. In 2000 the Navajo Nation legislature deemphasized the prison approach to crime by eliminating jail time and fines for 79 offenses. The legislature also required the use of peacemaking, which had previously been optional, in all criminal cases.

INDIAN TRIBES are at once the oldest and the youngest governments on the continent. In their current incarnations many tribal institutions are early in their evolution, just a few decades old. Nonetheless, we can count 70 or more tribes, whose members constitute the vast majority of American Indians, that have tribal institutions—working sovereignties—roughly as substantial as the Warm Springs Tribe in Oregon with, say, more than 300 tribal employees excluding gaming operations. As one gentleman from the Nez Perce Tribe of Idaho, looking back to the 1970s, has put it,

Wilma Mankiller, principal chief of the Cherokee Nation from 1985 to 1995, delivers the annual State of the Tribe address in 1992 at the tribal capital in Tahlequah, Oklahoma. Mankiller, who as the first female principal chief greatly improved tribal health care and created many jobs through community development, received the Medal of Freedom from President Clinton in 1998.

tribal government at Nez Perce has grown from "a mom-and-pop store to a supermarket."

It is astonishing, really. Two generations ago Indian tribes were prevented from providing any meaningful level of services to their people. Now scores of tribal governments compare favorably in size and operational capability with nearby county and municipal governments. Even smaller tribes nowadays commonly employ staffs of 50 or 100 or more.

If the accomplishments have been impressive, the challenges remain formidable. Serious discussions with Indian people about contemporary social and health difficulties on the reservations regularly turn to the corrosive effects of a century of aggressive assimilation. Such pressure especially impacted Indians born in the early twentieth century, when the efforts to erase Native culture were the most intense. Richard Trudell, a lawyer and executive director of the American Indian Resources Institute, agonizes over those lost generations: "In the 1940s and 1950s, when I was growing up, there just weren't any models. I hate so much to say it because it wasn't their fault, but entire generations were social casualties, no parenting skills, no sense of what a family was, just no self-esteem. Those boarding schools taught them their Indian side was no good and gave them nothing but a cold, institutional life. They were just submerged in that mechanized environment."

The reservations continue to face an array of problems associated with cultural dislocation and poverty. One major concern is violence among young people, often related to alcohol abuse. Youth homicides and suicides have gone down but still occur at twice and almost three times the national rates respectively. A Sioux woman reflected on the weight and legacy of history: "You have to realize how much cultural confusion there has been. For generations we were taught that all the answers were found in the majority society's way. Finally a lot of Indian people are saying that gangs and violence aren't the Indian way. In fact our cultures were exactly the opposite, built on respect. But we've had an alien way of looking at the world imposed on us. We have to look within, that's where the answers are, but it's hard, it's hard to find our place."

The theme of looking within, of Indian communities themselves taking responsibility for addressing the health problems and social ills, has taken hold. Impressive progress has been made—owing in significant part to an underfunded but dedicated Indian Health Service—with respect to infant mortality, life expectancy, and infectious diseases. Nonetheless, American Indians still face too many cases of heart disease, cirrhosis, and diabetes, all resulting from harmful lifestyle practices. Tribes have become fully engaged, taking over management of some Indian Health Service clinics and using medicine men and traditional healing practices—inside and outside the formal health system—to meet patients' needs.

Alcoholism, while progress has been made and while drinking practices vary significantly among tribes, remains a scourge. And alcoholism is itself infectious; witness fetal alcohol syndrome, automobile accidents, and violence in the family and community.

Indian leaders are responding. It is a rare tribe that lacks an alcoholism program, and family and community peer pressure is
increasing. This will be a long and painful crusade, but Indian people have acknowledged the causes and depths of the problem, and
the determination is palpable. As one Hopi man told me, "We
never had poverty before. We never had trouble with alcohol. We
had full, productive lives. And you know what we have learned?
The only way to restore the balance we once had is to use traditional means: the families, the medicine men, the ceremonies, the
dances. And we are finding ways to do that."

At the Tohono O'odham Nation in Arizona we can see both the
magnitude of the problems and some of the ways sovereign tribal
communities are addressing them.

THE TOHONO O'ODHAM have lived for millennia in the
Sonoran desert country of southwest Arizona and the Mexican
state of Sonora. They necessarily built their lives around the rain,
which many years leaves as little as five inches. The people gathered wild fruits when they bloomed and diverted the floodwaters
to fields planted in beans, corn, chilies, and squash. They moved
around to locate deer, rabbits, and javelinas and to gather salt and
seafood from the Gulf of California, fifty miles west of the modern
border town of Sonoyta.

The literature of the Tohono O'odham obsessively carries titles
like *Rainhouse Ocean, Ocean Power, Of Earth and Little Rain,* and
The Desert Smells Like Rain. This parched land and the rare, fickle
rains made them wait, and as always, they remain a calm, patient,
and low-key people. The Tohono O'odham poet Ofelia Zepeda,
professor of linguistics at the University of Arizona, a MacArthur
Fellow, and the city of Tucson's poet laureate, makes this obser-
vation: "The O'odham lack grand ritual paraphernalia that call for
attention. Instead they wear muted white clay paint on their faces
and bodies. The songs of the people are accompanied by hard
wood rasps that succeed only in making music that is swallowed
by the desert floor. The drumming is on overturned woven baskets,
sounds that also reverberate only short distances. The people have
no grand, colorful powwows and such social dancing. Instead,

TOHONO O'ODHAM NATION
RESERVATION

their dancing is quiet barefoot skipping and shuffling on dry dirt—
movements that cause dust to rise quietly toward the atmosphere,
dust that the people believe helps to form rain clouds."

Today the Tohono O'odham hold a 2.8-million-acre reservation,
the nation's second largest after the Navajo, with its southern border running 75 miles along the Mexican line. The population of
20,000, mostly poor and traditional (the O'odham language is
widely spoken), is centered in the town of Sells, but tribal members also live in widely scattered reservation villages and in Tucson and other nearby towns. Subsistence hunting and gathering
have declined but remain a food source for many families. The tie
to the land endures, with one ever-present reminder especially

prominent: The sacred peak, Baboquivari, rises to 11,000 feet and is visible from most places on the expansive reservation.

The Tohono O'odham may be calm and patient as a people, but they have tenaciously protected and exercised their sovereignty to create a society able to cope with the circumstances the tribe now faces. In 1986 the tribe took back its name (the earlier one, Papago, may be traced to a mispronunciation by the Spanish) and adopted a modern constitution with executive and judicial branches and a legislature composed of representatives from eleven districts with voting weighted according to population. For decades the tribe has attempted to resolve a problem that had festered ever since the straight-line international border was drawn by the Gadsden Purchase from Mexico in 1853: Many Tohono O'odham people—an estimated 1,400—live south of the line, and family members cannot freely cross back and forth to visit. Controversy of course swirls around border-crossing issues, but the tribe has put together enough support that its long campaign seems likely to result in administrative or congressional action to facilitate passage across the international line.

The Tohono O'odham Nation boasts a full-service government with an impressive new tribal center featuring a large auditorium-style tribal council chamber and a justice complex with five courtrooms and a 60-person police force. Tribal programs run the gamut from preschool to a community college to a natural resources department to a meals-on-wheels program for elders to a burial fund that helps support elaborate O'odham funerals often lasting up to two days.

In recent times the reservation has been infected by an upswing in juvenile delinquency and the emergence of gang activity—the Crips and Bloods, along with reservation-bred gangs as well. The tribal council has responded with a holistic approach, directed to youth, their families, and the broader community. The program includes awareness forums, student and parent workshops, one-on-one counseling, and substance abuse programs. The tribe has opened a group home for boys and another for girls.

The Tohono O'odham Nation, in addressing the needs of youth, has made an impressive commitment of budget dollars. In 1990 the Tohono O'odham had just eight people in the probation staff serving both children and adults. By 2002 the broad-based tribal program serving children and young people had grown to a staff of forty-four.

When I visited the reservation in 2002, the chief justice was Malcolm Escalante. He has given top priority to the young people's problems, and the justice system has moved in new directions. The judges, he explained, have tried to streamline what was once a cumbersome system for giving detained juveniles access to medicine men, or maka'i. "Parents say, 'This is an O'odham illness. We want him to be seen by a maka'i.' There's nothing on paper, but we do our best to move quickly. There's been a lot to overcome—stuff brought to us by the missionaries and the boarding schools. But being seen by a maka'i is an essential part of our existence. It's basic to the wellness of O'odham people." For adults, including young people caught up in the gang activity, the court system now offers peacemaking as an option in criminal cases. "More and more," Chief Justice Escalante passionately asserted, "we're moving back toward our traditions. We're tapping into that strength. We're heading in the right direction now. I don't know that we'll get there in my lifetime, but I'm encouraged."

And then there is, for the Tohono O'odham, a tragic tangle of water, health, and outside values and actions that have hammered away at individual well-being and life itself.

The Tohono O'odham had always farmed, using diversion canals and relying as well on flash floods that overflowed riverbanks. Families dug shallow wells for household use. But after World War II the city of Tucson boomed, and municipal water agencies, copper mining companies, and large farming operations sank deep, high-lift wells near reservation boundaries. The new pumping drew the aquifers down, below the reach of the Tohono O'odham family wells. The Santa Cruz River, the only major surface water in the region, received some of its flow from rains, but more from aquifers that fed into the river. As the pumping depleted the aquifers, the river floods became infrequent, then ceased altogether. Today the Santa Cruz is bone dry, a casualty of intensive modern development.

Farther inland on the reservation, where some water from small, ephemeral streams was still available, the BIA's assimilationist policies during the mid-twentieth century wounded the tie to subsistence farming. Anxious to move the Tohono O'odham into the cash economy, agency employees encouraged tribal members to abandon their own crops and take jobs as laborers in large, irrigated cotton fields off the reservation. The family of the poet Ofelia Zepeda was one of many to depart their communities for half the year or more, leaving their fields untended:

As far as the eye could see,
flat, green fields appearing to end at the foot of distant
    mountains.
Mountains, a reminder of what the fields once looked like.
Fields saturated with water pulled from its secret storage place
beneath the earth's surface.

We are called "the people of the cotton fields"
because of the labor our families did.
For us there was no reservation, no Housing & Urban Devel-
    opment, no tribal support.
We were a people segregated in row houses
all lined up along the roads of our labor.

For many, although not Zepeda herself, this uprooting led to physical illness on top of the sadness of separation. In the past generation the Tohono O'odham people have suffered a severe diabetes crisis that has taken limbs and lives from them. The curse of diabetes has swept across Indian country, and is rising nationally and globally as well, but adult-onset diabetes has hit the Tohono O'odham people especially hard, perhaps more harshly than any society in the world.

Nutritionists have learned why. Traditionally the Tohono O'odham depended, in addition to the desert's natural bounty, on the corn, squash, chilies, and, especially, tepary beans from their own fields. As tribal agriculture declined and many families, like the Zepedas, left their farms altogether, the Tohono O'odham adopted a more Western diet, including fast food. Studies confirmed that tepary beans and other traditional foods had regulated blood sugar and therefore held diabetes in check. Field research done at Tohono O'odham as early as the 1930s helps tell the story of how Anglo culture has afflicted Native people. One statistic stands out: In 1938 the average weight of Tohono O'odham men was 158 pounds; by 1978 it was 202 pounds.

The Tohono O'odham fought back. One task, to establish tribal water rights, took persistence. Charles Dickens, who wrote in *Bleak House* of the waste and expense of England's court proceedings, would be impressed by the tortoise-slow pace of western water litigation. Still, after decades of litigation and negotiation, and finally settlement, the tribe has a congressional promise of Central Arizona Project water, to go on line in the early 2000s.

In the meantime, the tribe has been able to obtain pumped water and is using some of it on traditional crops. Out in the villages a nonprofit group, Tohono O'odham Community Action, works with farmers to use floodwaters for raising tepary beans and other traditional foods. The tribe's focus on native plants has also benefited the larger society. A much-heralded nonprofit cooperative, Native Seeds/Search, inspired by the Tohono O'odham experience and voice, with both non-Indian and Indian board members, now distributes nutritious desert seeds to consumers throughout the Southwest and beyond.

FOR THE LAST interview of my three visits to the Tohono O'odham reservation, I talked with Daniel Preston. He served for years as vice-chairman of the Tohono O'odham Nation's San Xavier District, on the east side of the reservation close to the dry bed of the San Pedro River. Daniel's family has been hit hard by diabetes; he himself lost a leg below the knee.

A reformer, Daniel is part of a tribal effort that has restored some land to farming and aims to rehabilitate much more. "Genetically we are attuned to the desert, to making it on the edge of starvation. Now we have sugar and greasy stuff. Our bodies aren't built for that. We need to educate not only the O'odham but the whole United States about how valuable our traditional foods are to this country. Tepary beans, when you eat them, they're like medicine."

When I drove back to Tucson, I felt drained, choked up, in a way I seldom have. The Tohono O'odham had shown so much strength over thousands of years in adapting to such a severe environment, only to be crippled in just fifty years by an uncomprehending outside society. It's still too early, all the hard work notwithstanding, to know the outcomes for border crossing, gangs, water, and diabetes. We can be sure of one thing, though, whether at Tohono O'odham, Warm Springs, or other reservations: The best outcomes will be inspired by Indian people themselves and carried out by their own institutions.

12.

Stewards of the Land

Ronnie Lupe speaks Apache and uses it whenever he can. The language captivates him, and he lovingly explores its premises and the insights the language gives into the Apache culture and worldview. Lupe, longtime chairman of the White Mountain Apache Tribe, fixes on the word *ni'*, which despite its brevity is packed with meaning. A central aspect of *ni'* is that it encompasses both mind and land, evoking the stories, back through the ages, about the eastern Arizona homeland that rises from the desert floor to the White Mountains themselves, thick with fir, spruce, and ponderosa pine.

The White Mountain Apache take their land and stories seriously. Keith Basso's insightful book *Wisdom Sits in Places* speaks of the tribe and the land. In one passage, Basso recounts a visit he made to a wetland with two Apache cousins, Charles and Morley Cromwell. Basso, although he possessed a basic grasp of the Western Apache language, experienced great difficulty pronouncing the place's elaborate name. After four tries, he gave up.

> "I'm sorry Charles, I can't get it. I'll work on it later, it's in the machine. It doesn't matter."
>
> "It's matter," Charles says softly to me in English. And then, turning to speak to Morley, he addresses him in Western Apache:
>
> "What he's doing isn't right. It's not good. He seems to be in a

hurry. Why is he in a hurry? It's disrespectful. Our ancestors made this name. They made it just as it is. They made it for a reason. They spoke it first, a long time ago! He's repeating the speech of our ancestors. He doesn't know that. Tell him he's repeating the speech of our ancestors!"

To Basso's relief, Charles, out of politeness and friendship, relented and urged him to try again. Fully chastened, Basso finally got it right and Charles told him the story behind the place, *Goshtł'ish Tú Bił Sikáné*, meaning "Water Lies With Mud in an Open Container." Long ago the ancestors came to the land, but everything was new, and they wanted to find good places. They liked this place, a marshy swale filled with wild grasses and ringed by willows. Deer and turkey came to eat and drink. The plants might be useful for medicines. To be sure to remember the place, they gave it a name. "Now they had a picture they could carry in their minds," Charles told Basso. "You can see for yourself. It looks like its name."

Indian people elsewhere take the stories embedded in their places seriously. The land is alive with stories as well as with animals, vegetation, soil and rocks, and weather. Vine Deloria, Jr., has reflected that "Indians can be unhappy, but I do not think that Indians are ever lonely. They are never alone. The plains, the canyons all have so many stories."

Tribes now have reasserted control over the human actions on their lands, but for generations it was not so. Tribes lacked authority during the deadening years when the Bureau of Indian Affairs ruled the reservations. They lost even more control over the land, and the stories, after World War II, as the baby boom led to the national expansion and the beefed-up dam building, timber harvesting, and mining on the reservations.

The high-speed years of the postwar era spawned a dark episode at Hopi that told volumes about how outsiders made the decisions on Indian land.

THE HOPI RESERVATION in dry, remote north Arizona encompasses most of Black Mesa, a large formation shaped like a human hand as it gently slopes north toward its highest elevation at about 8,000 feet. The tribe's habitation, based on the skilled dry farming of corn, squash, chilies, and other vegetables, goes back thousands of years. Today the Hopi live in pueblo villages on First, Second, and Third Mesas, fingers that reach out from the lower, southern end of Black Mesa. Beneath the mesa lies one of the largest and finest coal deposits in the world, high in energy-producing BTUs and low in polluting sulfur.

Mining companies learned of Black Mesa's fabulous coal reserves a century ago, but the sleepy western cities—the Phoenix area, now with a population of more than 3 million, had just 250,000 residents in 1945—did not winch up their demand for such far-away energy until the 1960s. By then the Big Buildup of the Southwest from Denver to Los Angeles had moved into high gear. The western states and energy companies were close to ramming through Congress a Christmas tree bill of dams, power plants, highways, and transmission lines in the interior West. Because Arizonans held key positions in Congress, the legislation's centerpiece, without which the whole package would fail, was the Central Arizona Project, a mega-water aqueduct project designed to bring water 200 miles from the Colorado River east to Phoenix and Tucson.

The geography posed a problem since much of the aqueduct route ran uphill. A new power source would be needed to push millions of tons of water every year up to the distant, newly sprouting suburbs. Initially, the operating assumption was simple: Dam the Grand Canyon, and use the hydroelectricity for the Central Arizona Project. David Brower of the Sierra Club and Secretary of the Interior Stewart Udall finally put an end to that idea by the mid-1960s, but this was nothing if not an age of big thinking. Along came Plan B. As an alternate substitute energy source, the development forces would mine Black Mesa coal and construct a railroad to ship the coal 60 miles north to Page, Arizona, on the Colorado River, where water could be obtained for a coal-fired power plant big enough to generate the electricity to drive the Central Arizona Project. A second Black Mesa project crept into the planning as well; a coal slurry pipeline would transport coal, crushed and mixed with water from the aquifer underlying the mesa, to still another new coal-fired plant in Laughlin, Nevada.

This gigantic scenario would create one of the largest mining complexes in history, a complex rendered even grander because all the other water and energy projects in the proposed legislation depended on Black Mesa coal and groundwater. The Hopi (and the Navajo, who owned part of the Black Mesa coal deposit) had enormous leverage.

But the pages of the Indian coal leases, which the tribal councils approved in 1966, hardly evidenced leverage. Instead, they were financial travesties, unfair transactions that deprived the Hopi and Navajo of tens of millions of dollars. Among other provisions, the Hopi received inadequate payments for the coal and sold their water for the slurry pipeline at the egregiously low rate of $1.67 per acre foot.

In addition to lost revenue, the Hopi suffered severe environmental consequences. Dynamite and heavy earthmoving equipment gouged canyon-size strips on Black Mesa, destroying the landscape and all manner of shrines and archaeological sites, along with the age-old stories they held. Further, the springs used by the Hopi for farming, household use, and prayer began to dry up in the 1990s. The Peabody Coal Company's studies deny that its pumping has depleted the springs, but other analyses show a probable connection between the pumping and the aquifer where the springs originate. The Hopi way of life depends on the springs, for parched Black Mesa has no year-round streams.

It seems almost certain that if the Hopi had gotten their way, there would have been no coal mining or water pumping at all. The Hopi Kikmongwi, traditional village leaders, fought the project in every way they knew, but to no avail. Vernon Masayesva, who, like many, believes to his depths that Peabody's high-lift pumps are destroying the life-giving springs, laments, "All of our songs are about rain. Our poetry, our kachinas are about rain. The mining of our water violates our beliefs. When you sell something sacred, it doesn't sit right, it bothers you, it sits on your conscience."

If the Hopi did not choose to mine Black Mesa, who did? How did it happen?

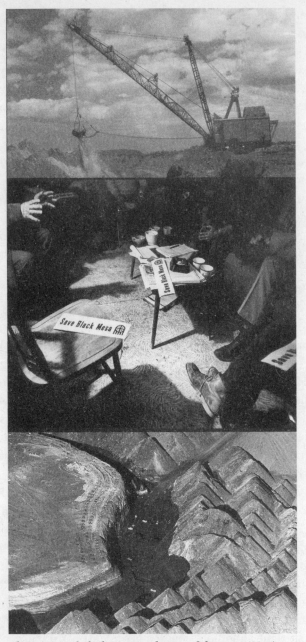

The mining of Black Mesa and some of the many Hopi people who opposed it. Photographs courtesy of Ray Ramirez, Native American Rights Fund.

For years Black Mesa buzzed with suspicions that John Boyden, the Hopi lawyer, had secretly represented Peabody Coal during the coal negotiations. The Kikmongwi commissioned an investigation by the Indian Law Resource Center. The center's investigation, which was thorough and covered all evidence known at the time, revealed that Boyden had represented Peabody on other transactions, but it could find no conclusive connection to the coal lease. In the 1990s, I discussed this with John Echohawk of the Native American Rights Fund, who represented the Kikmongwi in their attempts to overturn the lease. John confirmed my own instincts that Boyden, a respected Salt Lake City figure who twice narrowly lost races for governor, probably had not committed such a contemptible act and that even if he had, no one would likely ever know.

In 1994, without expecting to turn anything up, I asked my research assistant Cherche Prezeau to look through Boyden's papers (he had died in 1981) at the University of Utah Library. Shortly before, the library had completed its cataloging of a new batch of Boyden's papers and released them for public review. In them, misfiled under "Summer Vacations," Cherche discovered a sheath of correspondence and attorney billings showing conclusively that Boyden had secretly represented Peabody on Black Mesa coal and water rights during the decisive years of 1964 through 1971. His duplicity and violations of duty to his tribal client were even displayed in the salutations of his letters to Ed Phelps, Peabody's general counsel: When Boyden wrote in his capacity as the Hopi attorney, the letters began "Dear Mr. Phelps"; when he corresponded as Peabody's lawyer, it was "Dear Ed."

The outsiders had done their work carefully and in the shadows. First, Peabody and Boyden cut their deal. Next they enlisted the Bureau of Indian Affairs, arguing that the projects would be good for the Southwest and would bring needed money to the tribe. Then Boyden, the Hopi's trusted attorney, without any public hearings or other notice to the general tribal membership, brought the coal lease before the Hopi Tribal Council for rubber-stamping.

The scale of John Boyden's excesses and disloyalties was the exception rather than the rule. But his actions present a graphic image of decision making on Indian reservations during the deadening years. The ways that Indian people thought and felt about their sacred lands and waters and stories were inconsequential. Outsiders with agendas other than the best interests of Indian people viewed Native American natural resources not as domains of the tribes but as wide-open, low-cost opportunities.

AN INITIAL SPARK for reasserting tribal authority over land and natural resources came from Judge George Boldt's landmark 1974 decision upholding tribal treaty rights to harvest Pacific salmon. Judge Boldt, who ruled that the treaties guaranteed to the tribes the opportunity to harvest 50 percent of the salmon runs, also addressed tribal governmental authority. Opposition to such tribal powers was formidable. Washington, like other states, insisted upon an exclusive right to regulate the salmon harvest, but Boldt upheld a significant role for tribal regulation: "This court hereby finds and holds that any one of the plaintiff tribes is entitled to exercise its governmental powers by regulating the treaty right fishing of its members without any state regulation thereof."

Uplifted by this historic endorsement of their sovereignty, the tribes of northwest Washington expanded and formalized their regulatory systems to provide for fishing codes, licenses, procedures for tagging and monitoring salmon catches, and game wardens. The tribes soon moved beyond regulating fishing to improving the salmon runs by hiring staffs of fisheries scientists. The Bureau of Indian Affairs, now beginning to see itself as a trustee with a duty to support rather than rule tribal governments, provided supplemental funding.

The Puget Sound tribes together invented a new kind of institution, the professional intertribal natural resources organization. Within a year after Judge Boldt's 1974 opinion, the 23 tribes of the region founded the Northwest Indian Fisheries Commission to leverage and consolidate resources for scientific management and policy analysis. Today the commission's programs include ocean groundfish and shellfish as well as salmon; some fifty fisheries scientists work on staff and its state-of-the-art laboratory specializes in fish genetics and fish health.

Shortly after the creation of the commission, the four Columbia River tribes—Nez Perce, Umatilla, Warm Springs, and Yakama— joined together and started the Columbia River Intertribal Fish Commission, with offices in Portland, Oregon. CRITFC, staffed at about the level of the Northwest Commission, also has a strong scientific capability, an extensive enforcement division, and a laboratory conducting research on fish genetics and water quality. In addition to the intertribal organizations, all the Pacific Northwest tribes have their own fisheries agencies with on-reservation staffs of fisheries scientists.

The Northwest tribes are now accepted as comanagers of the salmon resource, along with the federal and state governments. This means that hundreds of tribal fisheries scientists—the total numbers are approximately equal to the numbers of state scientists—labor out in the watersheds, taking water-quality samples, tagging fish, measuring water flows and temperatures, identifying insect life, counting smolts and returning fish, analyzing ocean conditions, assessing fish health, planting native vegetation in riparian areas, and interviewing elders to obtain the traditional knowledge that enriches tribal resources management. Other tribal scientists carry out research in the laboratories and collaborate in meeting rooms or on conference calls to set, with their federal and state colleagues, the flow regimes from the dams in order to assist the migrating fish. If the far-flung effort to preserve the endangered wild Pacific salmon succeeds, the work of the tribes will have been a central reason.

Out along the Great Lakes, the Chippewa, fresh from several treaty rights victories and turning an eye toward the two Northwest intertribals, formed an intertribal organization of their own in the 1980s. The Great Lakes Indian Fish and Wildlife Commission has a budget of $4 million and a work force of more than 60 that swells to 150 during the springtime harvest. Like the Northwest intertribals, GLIFWC must deal with the complex and confrontational setting of off-reservation fishing, where Indian net

Billy Frank, Jr., was arrested many times for exercising his Nisqually tribal fishing rights during Washington's salmon wars of the 1960s and 1970s. Here, as long-time chair of the Northwest Indian Fisheries Commission, Frank testifies in 2003 on proposed salmon enhancement legislation in the U.S. Senate Indian Affairs Committee hearing room. In 1992, Frank received the prestigious Albert Schweitzer Prize for Humanitarianism from Johns Hopkins University. Photograph courtesy of Steve Robinson, Northwest Indian Fisheries Commission.

fishers and non-Indian commercial and sports fishers share the same waters. James Schlender, the executive administrator, emphasizes the key role of science: "Otherwise, you would have politics entering into business and natural resources management, and that's one of the things that we're here to not let happen."

In the Northwest, Great Lakes, and nationally, relationships between the states and the tribes over natural resources have often been thorny. States saw the tribes as infringing on their traditional primacy over fish and wildlife management. Tribes relentlessly pressed for recognition of their treaty rights and governmental status. Gradually a much more productive relationship developed as state and tribal professionals, both dedicated to the resource and both facing funding limitations, began to work together cooperatively. George Meyer, former secretary of the Wisconsin Department of Natural Resources, reflects on the rapprochement: "This didn't start out as a marriage made in heaven. [After a major court decision affirmed tribal fishing rights in the Great Lakes in 1983], it was a very tumultuous time for about ten years. I think it has evolved into a situation where the entire staff has strong respect for the biologists and law enforcement staff of the GLIFWC. It wasn't that way fifteen years ago, but sometimes people have to retire, new people have to come in, and—just over time—they can see the benefits. I mean, they have top-notch biologists. You know, there's always going to be disagreements among professionals, but that happens between the state of Minnesota and the state of Wisconsin. They are on a professional level and handled on a professional basis."

RONNIE LUPE, of the White Mountain Apache Tribe—who, as we have seen, is dedicated to his native language and the way the land, the Apache mind, and all the stories are captured in the word *ni'*—epitomizes the long path tribal leaders have walked to exercise self-determination over their reservation lands. When Lupe became tribal chairman in 1966 (he served into the 1990s), the chairman's office was right across the street from the BIA superintendent's. The superintendent regularly presented documents to the chairman for signature and sat near him at tribal council meetings, giving directions. "When I was first chairman, we couldn't even open our own mail. It all went into the BIA's hands."

Young and new at the job though he was, Lupe knew he had to make a change, however long it might take. He knew too the shape the change had to take: "I am an Apache. I look at the world differently than anybody else who doesn't live on this reservation, who wasn't born and raised here. People are always asking me how things change or how they can change for the better, and I tell them that if things are to change, they have to change from the Apache view. The way I do things, the things I believe, the choices I make are all because I am an Apache."

The problems at Hawley Lake especially stuck in Lupe's craw.

Before he took office, the tribe had built low dams to create several recreation lakes in the high pine country of the White Mountains. I have visited these lakes, gems each one, but Hawley stands
out. As Lupe says, "On a fall day the lake is calm, and the color of
the surrounding trees explodes off it." The other lakes were
opened to non-Indians for fishing and camping in the 1950s, but
the BIA convinced the tribal council to take a different tack at
Hawley. Starting in 1959, the tribe issued the first of 482 leases for
homesites. The grossly low lease payments in this glory country
ranged from $40 to $180 per year, with each lease to run for 25
years. The lessees then raised buildings ranging from small recreational cabins to elaborate year-round houses.

Resentment against the leases built up within the tribal council, because of both the token lease payments and the way that the
new settlement at Hawley Lake had changed for the worse the
character of an important place on the reservation. In 1977 the
council adopted a resolution prohibiting the issuance of any new
leases as against tribal interests "both culturally and financially."
A ban on future leases was one thing. What about the ones already
issued and the homes that had been erected? As 1984 and the end
of the 25-year period for the initial leases drew closer, the talk
among Lupe and other council members increasingly turned to
the issue of whether the tribe should renew the existing leases.

It decided not to renew. The homeowners' association hit the
roof, but the council held its ground. Lupe received a number of
threats and had FBI protection for some public appearances off
the reservation. The homeowners' administrative appeal to the
Interior Department was denied: No written assurance of renewal
existed, and vague oral promises, of dubious legal validity anyway,
were never proved. By 2001 all the leases had expired, and some
houses and cabins had been donated to the tribe, some moved to
other locations, and some damaged or destroyed by angry former
tenants. At least one homeowner took a different stance, express-
ing his gratitude to Lupe "for the privilege of living up here—the
garden spot of the world."

The situation at Hawley Lake in 1984 deserves reflection. Most
homeowners doubtless assumed in good faith that their leases

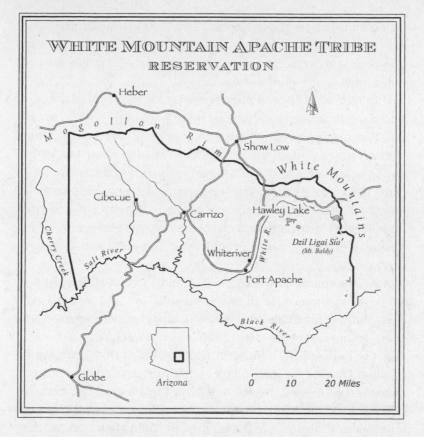

WHITE MOUNTAIN APACHE TRIBE
RESERVATION

Heber

Mogollon Rim

Show Low

White Mountains

Cibecue

Carrizo

Hawley Lake

Cherry Creek

Salt River

Whiteriver

White R.

Dzil Ligai Sía'
(Mt. Baldy)

Fort Apache

Black River

Globe

Arizona

0   10   20 Miles

would be renewed. The nonrenewal was, they said, "a raw deal."
Yet Lupe could act with a clear conscience on two counts: The law
was on his side, and he himself was rectifying a raw deal. Twenty-
five years earlier government officials had presented his predecessors on the tribal council with leases to sign. Now the tribe was
the government, and as government officials he and his fellow
council members could act solely on what was best for the White
Mountain Apache.

The White Mountain Apache Tribe also took on the vexing issue
of reservation logging. In the 1960s the BIA, which managed the
tribe's large forest holdings, sharply increased the annual timber
cut. Alarm spread among tribal members as logging crews clear-
cut forests, leveling whole stands of mature trees and leaving gap-

ing openings across the landscape. This increased the runoff, but
hillsides and streambanks eroded away. Great river bottom cot-
tonwoods, noncommercial trees that consumed large amounts of
water, were chainsawed down.

Outraged tribal council members were convinced that the BIA
jacked up the timber yield to send more water downstream to the
Salt River Project, which supplied water to the fast-growing
Phoenix metropolitan area. The Salt River Project, holder of
senior water rights to the Salt River, had diverted the entire flow
of the river from its banks into a network of large irrigation canals
just east of Phoenix. Certainly water users in Phoenix stood to gain
from logging that increased runoffs from the White Mountain
Apache forestlands, source of more than one-half the Salt River's
annual flow.

Any agreement between the BIA and the Salt River Project
would have been made by a wink and a nod and would have
been hard to prove. The tribal council, however, pointed to a BIA-
commissioned study by a Dr. Wilm to examine how water yield
might be enhanced by a higher timber cut and to Dr. Wilm's assertion at a Phoenix meeting that a higher timber cut would indeed
increase the flow and that the Salt River Project would be "greatly
benefited." If the BIA did act to further the Salt River Project's
interests at the expense of the tribe's, the White Mountain Apache
forests were caught up in the same mid-1960s dynamic that
afflicted the Hopi's Black Mesa coal, the Tuscarora's Allegheny
River, and many other tribal lands and waters: Heed the calls of
the growing cities, develop the reservations, and to hell with the
Indians.

The White Mountain Apache, under Ronnie Lupe's leadership,
moved on several fronts to gain control of their forestlands, among
the finest in the Southwest. By 1975 the tribe had expanded its
tribal timber mill, the Fort Apache Timber Company, into a good-
size, fully modern operation. That done, the tribe refused to
renew its contract with Southwest Forest Industries, which for
decades had a lock on reservation logging and milling. This move
created jobs for tribal members and increased tribal revenues,
since now the Apache were producing sawn timber rather than

receiving only stumpage fees from outside companies that did the milling. Then, in 1981, as the impact of the BIA's high-yield timber cut set in, the tribal council adopted the first in a series of resolutions strenuously opposing the bureau's logging program. The BIA was approving timber contracts for a 93-million board feet harvest annually, far above the sustainable yield of about 61 million board feet. Finally, in the early 1990s, the tribe used the self-determination legislation to contract with the BIA and take over timber management.

The White Mountain Apache reservation is now under tribal management, and the timber harvest held to a sustainable level. To be sure, the new regime is not without its difficulties. Federal funding for tribal forestry remains low. Downsizing the timber cutting has cost the tribe valuable jobs. The Rodeo-Chediski fire, in the West's terrible 2002 fire season, ravaged Apache forestlands. Yet a larger truth stands: The tribe itself now determines how tribal land, and the stories it holds, will be treated.

One decision at White Mountain is especially noteworthy. A number of tribes have put large land areas off limits from development as "wilderness." Under tribal law, these set-asides are not what we call wilderness (a foreign concept to Indian societies, which do not divide the natural world in that fashion) but rather places to be saved for cultural and spiritual reasons. To the White Mountain Apache, their sacred peak is Mount Baldy, known to tribal members as *Dzil Ligai Si'án*, the highest area on the reservation. The tribal council has closed all of the mountain's west slope to entry by nonmembers. Even tribal members are not permitted to enter without permission from the council. By taking this action, surely among the strictest land use classifications in the country, the council ensured that commercially valuable timber stands will be left pristine.

AMERICAN INDIAN TRIBES, as land-based peoples, have moved into natural resource stewardship with great gusto. You see it everywhere. Nearly every tribe has a formal institutional capability. Tribes that a generation ago had two- or three-person natural resource offices—or none at all—now operate mature agencies

*A hundred Apache tribal members form an annual procession toward their cere-
mony at the summit of the tribe's sacred mountain* Dzil Ligai Si'án. *Photograph
courtesy of Bill Hess and* National Geographic.

with staffs of 25, 50, 100, or more. The Navajo Nation's natural
resources department employs 460 people.

A prominent development has been the tribes' use of the self-
determination statutes to contract with the BIA and assume for
themselves management of tribal forests. This is crucial ground
both spiritually and economically; more than a third of all Indian
land is forested, with many sacred sites and stories, and at the
same time more than 70 tribes have commercial timber operations that generate nearly 50,000 jobs. For most of the twentieth
century, the BIA's high-harvest, low-dollar logging program that
hammered the Warm Springs and White Mountain Apache forests
protected neither the spirituality nor the sustainability of Indian
country.

Most tribes with timbered lands took control of reservation
forests. As discussed in Chapter 1, at the Quinault reservation in
Washington, BIA management tore into the thick big-tree forests
over the many complaints of tribal members who knew that the
logging trashed the land, made no provision for stocking young
trees, gave a return well below market value, and far exceeded sus-

tained yield forestry. Beginning in the late 1960s, the tribe seized the initiative. In a key move, Chairman Jim Jackson persuaded Joe DeLaCruz, just 30 at the time, to return to the reservation as business manager of the Quinault Nation. Blessed with charisma and a fine-tuned strategic sense, DeLaCruz became one of Indian country's foremost leaders, as both president of the National Congress of American Indians and, after Jackson's retirement, president of the Quinault Nation from 1970 through 1994.

Joe DeLaCruz knew how and when to be diplomatic, but he was also a man of action. In 1971, backed by a vote of the tribal general council, he barricaded the Chow Chow Bridge with his pickup truck, blocking timber company access across the Quinault River to a broad reach of timber stands. This shot across the bow captured the attention of the BIA and the logging companies, ITT Rayonier and Aloha, and led to settlements that addressed the tribe's grievances. A history of the Quinault Nation, commissioned by the tribe, explained how the incident at the Chow Chow Bridge changed the way the tribe conceived of its own possibilities:

> The barricade of Chow Chow was a telling confrontation, one that perhaps established the first glimmer of respect in the Bureau, and one that put the Tribe itself on its present course. The confrontation reveals more than any single incident since the Treaty of 1855 that, united, the Quinault Indian Nation can wield its power with wisdom and can absorb and exploit modern technology to enhance the present and future of its citizens. By their physical, yet symbolic actions at the entrance to and on the unique bridge, the new tribal activists put an end to an era and marked an aggressive new beginning. The Tribe was now permanently involved in the welfare of its timberlands and the advance toward fulfilling its goal of self-sufficiency.

Concurrently, the Quinault moved ahead with a very different kind of task, the building of permanent governmental institutions. DeLaCruz, Jim Jackson, and the tribal natural resources director Guy McMinds knew that agreements with the BIA and the timber companies were not the long-term solution; the Quinault Nation

Joe DeLaCruz blocks timber companies from entering Quinault forests on the far side of the Chow Chow Bridge. In later years, as president of the Quinault Nation, DeLaCruz strengthened tribal relations with state and county governments. He was a prime mover behind the 1989 Centennial Accord, signed by Governor Booth Gardner, in which Washington became one of the first of many states to formalize their government-to-government relationships with Indian tribes. Copyright 1971, Seattle Post-Intelligencer. *Reprinted with permission.*

could assure proper forest management only by becoming the primary decision maker. They brought in able resource specialists, including Gary Morishima, Larry Workman, and Larry Gilbertson, most of them Ph.D.'s, who remained on staff into the 2000s. While the early 1970s workspace was hardly commodious—a single-wide trailer—the excitement and momentum were as fresh and real as the nearby ocean winds.

Quinault studies had shown a direct correlation between heavy BIA logging and declines in the salmon runs. The tribe moved quickly after Congress passed the 1975 Self-Determination Act. Within a few years it negotiated contracts with the BIA and assumed management of its forestlands, bringing financial equity to the tribe and much greater environmental protection to the forests and rivers. As Joe DeLaCruz explained, "I think all we're saying, the Quinault people, is that what we have left is ours. Even though it's not in very good shape . . . let us alone, or maybe help us rebuild it."

Quinault coupled its expertise in forestry with a comprehensive fisheries program. Fisheries scientists operate two hatcheries and set seasons and catch limits for the several salmon runs, including the prized Quinault River blueback. Quinault management also encompasses two other treaty-protected resources: ocean groundfish including halibut, and the shellfish, notably the succulent razor clams, along the tribe's 26 miles of beach. On the diplomatic side, Quinault representatives have played significant roles in the far-flung Pacific salmon management effort that includes northwestern states up to Alaska and the governments of the United States, Canada, Russia, and Japan. DeLaCruz underscored the priority his tribe has placed on its fisheries program: "We don't need to be gigantic business successes, we don't need to be gigantic property developers. We should protect the basic things of our life, the fishing, the forest, the beach, the game, and the rivers."

Nationally, most of the other timber tribes are following the Quinault, Warm Springs, and White Mountain Apache in rebuilding their forests through more conservative harvesting regimes. Tribal forestry routinely experiments with progressive techniques to promote land health, including ecosystem management, streambank stabilization, and the use of fire to replicate natural processes. As Jody Calica of the Warm Springs Tribe observed, "Some reservations out there are managing in 250–300-year time frames, managing old-growth forests—that's visionary."

Tribal aspirations to care for the land run far beyond salmon and forest management. After the state of Idaho refused to participate, the Nez Perce Tribe contracted with the U.S. Fish and Wildlife Service and now administers the federal wolf reintroduction program statewide. Tribes in the Great Plains and beyond have reestablished bison herds. Most federal environmental laws treat tribes as states, affording them the opportunity to petition the Environmental Protection Agency for authority and funding to regulate pollution on the reservations. Under the Clean Water

Gail Small, attorney and member of the Northern Cheyenne Tribe of Montana, leads Native Action, an activist group that for years has fought the Colstrip power plant and five open-pit coal mines adjacent to the reservation. The operations continue, but the Northern Cheyenne have reduced the pollution levels. In 1977 the tribe became the first government in the country to declare its territory a Class I Airshed under the Clean Air Act. Photograph courtesy of Ken Kania.

Act, the Pueblo of Isleta adopted a water quality standard with a long reach. The Rio Grande, New Mexico's largest river, runs through the pueblo, whose standard required that the water be clean enough for tribal ceremonial purposes. Federal courts upheld, on the basis of the pueblo's sovereignty, the regulation as applied to the city of Albuquerque, which discharged excessive amounts of sewage effluents—even though the city was off the reservation, five miles upstream. Under the Clean Air Act, which demands highly technical scientific technology and assessment, more than a hundred tribes are in various stages of research and implementation in their efforts to protect human health and clear skies. The Oglala Sioux Tribe of South Dakota had a different kind of problem. During World War II the military used a large area of the reservation as a bombing range. This left a hazardous situa-

Mickey Pablo, a traditionalist also comfortable in dealing with state and federal governments, served as chairman of the Flathead Nation for ten years until his death in 1999. Pablo led the Montana tribe in a number of progressive efforts, including bison recovery, an aggressive land acquisition campaign, the negotiation of a cooperative hunting and fishing agreement with the state, and the attainment of "treatment as a state" status under the Clean Water Act that established sovereign tribal authority, over non-Indian as well as Indian water users, throughout the reservation. Photograph courtesy of the Confederated Salish and Kootenai Tribes of the Flathead Nation and Marcia Pablo.

tion—unexploded ordnance and toxic substances posed many dangers—but nothing was done. Finally, in the 1990s, the tribe persuaded the Department of Defense to fund a cleanup and put the tribe in charge of it, a decades-long but badly needed project.

In addition to initiating programs in established areas of land and water management, Indian country is exploring new ground in resource analysis, in the ways we think about the natural world. The Tulalip Tribe is one of a growing number to integrate noncommercial species, including traditional medicines, into land management programs. Tulalip elders are interviewed to identify culturally significant species and their habitat. The information is displayed by geographic information services (GIS) on a sophisticated computer map that superimposes the cultural data over commercial data, such as tree species, mineral deposits, and the like. Armed with this kind of analysis, the tribe can identify land where cultural and commercial values overlap. This gives the tribe the opportunity to limit development or, if the land is not owned by the tribe, acquire it in order to protect plants important to the Tulalip culture, species such as black lily, marsh tea, and Indian rice.

AN INTANGIBLE FACTOR runs through this broad discourse. Wrangling over biology, economics, state and tribal sovereignty, and administrative programs can be clinical and dull, even insensitive. Interjecting the Indian voice, reflecting the centrality of land in the Indian worldview, lends beauty, humanity, and spirituality to what can be gray, technocratic processes. The Indian voice, at once evocative and precise, can take the public discussion to a higher plane and lead to wiser decisions. We are speaking here, after all, about more than the "environment" or "natural resources."

Among the many times I have been struck by this, the tribal effort to achieve reform of the Endangered Species Act is one that stands out. By the late 1990s Indian country held strong views on the ESA. First, tribes received many benefits from federal species protection. Often ESA requirements thwarted irresponsible development near reservations. Indians wanted those provisions enforced, especially against projects affecting tribal hunting, fishing, and cultural rights.

The tribes' other set of interests concerning the ESA was different. For all the commitment to protecting the land, tribes also engage in economic development, and that has sometimes put them crosswise with environmental organizations, which are normally allies, and with federal agencies that administer environmental laws, including the ESA. These tensions are inevitable, for tribal councils are torn: They feel responsible for land health and, at the same time, face unemployment rates of 20 percent, 30 percent, higher in some places. Consequently, questions of environmental compliance have sometimes arisen from such tribal development activities as timber sales, water projects, and casino and housing construction.

Basically, the tribes wanted more flexibility when it came to technical aspects of protecting species. Their projects invariably made up only a tiny percentage of the environmental impacts on a particular place, but the tribal projects came on the scene last—because tribal activities had been suppressed for so long—and took the brunt of ESA regulation. Further, the tribes passionately believed they were doing the right thing as a matter of good land stewardship. During the 1980s and 1990s most of the larger tribes adopted comprehensive ecosystem management plans that evaluated land health across entire watersheds—in contrast with the narrower single-species approach of the ESA, which has been roundly criticized on this ground by environmentalists. The tribes believed that ESA compliance would work smoothly if federal officials would just make the effort to consider the specific circumstances in Indian country.

It took time, but eventually federal administrators made sensible accommodations in administering the ESA. After lengthy negotiations between high-level departmental representatives and tribal leaders, in 1997 Secretary of the Interior Bruce Babbitt and Secretary of Commerce William Daley signed a joint secretarial order laying out elaborate procedures for cooperative federal and tribal administration of the ESA.

I am left with many memories of the events leading up to the joint secretarial order. My strongest impressions involve not the details of the negotiations (in which I participated) but the tribal leaders' informed, heartfelt viewpoints that, once understood by the federal side, made the secretarial order possible. Consider the first organizational meeting, for tribal members and invited guests only, held in Seattle in February 1995.

The language was notably different from that at Anglo-dominated meetings. Instead of generic allusions to "forests," "rivers," and "species," the discourse rang with specific references to eagles, hawks, ducks, geese, salmon and steelhead, suckers, sea lions, wolves, bison, ferns, wocus, berries, meadows, mountains, hillsides, rocks, soil, and other aspects of the natural world. Most of these references were not made with respect to some issue or conflict. Instead, they were made to illustrate how humans are connected to all nature or were offered in an almost offhanded way, not to make any specific point but simply as an organic part of a statement by a person who knew the natural world and felt a part of it. Ted Strong, a member of the Yakama Nation and director of the Columbia River Intertribal Fish Commission, alluded to this mutual gene, saying, "That is something the elders speak about continuously—the idea of knowing something about where we come from, why we are here, and the appropriate names for species, suggesting a reverence for the reasons these species exist."

Elwood Miller, of the Klamath Tribe in Oregon, followed an Indian custom of prefacing his remarks by explaining what his homeland is like. "In our neck of the woods, that's where the waters begin. It jumps out of the ground right there in the Klamath country and begins its trek toward the ocean and ends up down in Yurok territory on the coast." Billy Frank, Jr., who has lived his life along the Nisqually River, told the gathering of his homeland near Mount Rainier, not far from the meeting site: "As you see, our mountain is sticking up today. . . . Our salmon here travel a long way. They travel up to the Aleutian Islands when they leave these rivers along this mountain and they travel clean out as far as the Japanese waters to Russia and they come home, right back to these waters here." Later Frank alluded to the habits of one of the Northwest's protected species: "The marbled murrelet stays in the old growth trees, in this canopy, along our coast, along our Puget Sound, along our range of mountains. We can't see them but they're living there. Early in the day, they go out into the ocean, and they float around like ducks, out in the Sound, out in the Strait of Juan de Fuca."

One enduring message from the Seattle meeting, then, emerged from the texture of the language—low-key, subtle, and instinctive— a reminder of how much knowledge exists in Indian country and how Native people have always lived the science of ecology's central premise that our species is tied to all nature. As Chairman Ronnie Lupe observed, "White Mountain Apaches never saw themselves as separate from Mother Earth. We are one with the land. Hunting was not for sport but to provide food and clothing. We have always been taught to respect the land and living things

Ronnie Lupe, former tribal chairman of the White Mountain Apache Tribe, with Secretary of the Interior Babbitt (right) and Secretary of Commerce Daley (left), at the signing of the joint secretarial order on the Endangered Species Act in 1997.

because we have a sacred responsibility for the stewardship of the lands that the Creator has provided us."

The federal representatives entered formal ESA negotiations with the tribes motivated by a pragmatic desire to resolve a nettlesome dispute by agreement rather than litigation. Along the way, in addition to learning about the size and expertise of tribal natural resource management agencies, they were swayed by the sincerity and gentle eloquence of the tribal leaders. This led to a valuable secretarial order anchored not in romanticism or guilt but in a land ethic, authentic and ecological, articulated in the distinctive Indian voice.

THE WORDS AND EMOTION of the Indian voice for the land are the same they always have been. For centuries the voice was put aside, kept apart, unheard even in Indian country. But modern tribes have gained the power to steward their lands, an area larger than Minnesota, according to their own stories and the values they reflect. They also participate beyond the reservations in forums that set regional, national, and even international policy on the environment. How unlikely it was, just a few generations ago, that a growing number of decisions about America's land, water, animals, and air would be made by expert tribal staffs—and by stepping back and listening to stories first told more generations ago than can be counted.

13.

Casino Lights and the Quandary of Indian Economic Progress

By the turn of this century Indian tribes had put in place much of the ambitious agenda that tribal leaders advanced in the 1950s and 1960s. They stopped termination and replaced it with self-determination. They ousted the BIA as the reservation government and installed their own sovereign legislatures, courts, and administrative agencies. They enforced the treaties of old and, with them, the fishing, hunting, and water rights. They earned the right to follow their own traditions and cultures and see them reflected in schools, health care, and land management. Nowhere have these changes been absolute or pure. In most cases the advances represent works in progress, but they have been deep and real.

If we may call the tribal victories over governmental and cultural suppression transforming, we must see economic progress as falling well short of that. To be sure, the stark, oppressive poverty of the 1950s has lifted from most reservations. Unemployment is down and personal income up. A few tribes have made dramatic strides. But there it stops; the improvement has been spotty, greatly variable from reservation to reservation. Why? Certainly, Indians started from an abysmally low point. Often their lands were not economically productive and, to boot, were located far from the markets. At the core, however, Native Americans have held true to their own cultures and have not fully bought into an alarm-clock, balance-sheet ethic. Tribal peoples

have not thrown off their traditional slower pace and their nur-
tured relationships with family, friends, and the natural world,
nor does it seem likely that they intend to do that. It may be that
American Indians have implicitly decided to give our hustling
national economic system a half embrace: to acknowledge that
some will wish to pursue economic prosperity and, as well, to
maintain Indian country as a welcoming place for those who wish
to forgo success as measured in material terms.

But, increasingly, in order to address poverty, Native Americans will be dealing with reservation economic development in
some form. Most particularly, they will have to confront the glo-
ries and hexes of tribal gaming. It must be emphatically stated
that tribes have engaged in many other kinds of ventures—the
emerging reality of economic development in Indian country is
the kind of diversified jobs and enterprise program found on the
Warm Springs reservation. More than half of all tribes either have
no casinos or have gambling operations that barely pay for themselves. Nonetheless, we must start with gaming because it has
produced the single largest infusion of income into Indian country in history. As such, it is a leading example of the many benefits of the painstaking sovereignty building done by modern
tribes.

IN THE LATE 1960s and 1970s, as tribes began to take the initiative, they searched for ways to use their sovereignty to enhance
revenue-producing ventures. This modest, early economic activity included resorts, recreational hunting and fishing programs,
and sales of arts and crafts. These enterprises could be marginally
more competitive because state tax and licensing laws normally
do not reach into Indian reservations. Better, when the Navajo,
Jicarilla Apache, and other tribes with mineral resources added to
their royalties by imposing taxes on the extraction of coal, oil, and
gas, those taxes were generally upheld in court. Not many reservations, however, held such treasure underground.

A number of tribes, struggling to scratch out some income,
lured customers to smoke shops that sold tax-free cigarettes and
sometimes liquor and fireworks. The courts soon eliminated

much of this competitive advantage by ruling that tribal members did not owe state taxes, but that non-Indian customers (who made the bulk of the purchases) did. The rationale for denying these exemptions from state tobacco and liquor taxes was that the tribes did not manufacture the products or produce the raw material. Thus there was, in the Supreme Court's words, no "value generated on the reservation." This was a new notion in Indian law; existing cases supported the tribes' position, but the justices fretted that tribes were "marketing their tax exemption" to draw customers away from nearby off-reservation communities. Of course, cities and states routinely employ tax breaks to lure business.

A few tribes came at it from another direction. In most states, gambling in one form or another is quite legal. Why not on the reservations and why not with prizes above the maximums set by state laws? And there the troubles began. The governors, attorney generals, and sheriffs erupted, unleashing invective about the evils of gaming and the potential for infiltration by organized crime. Lawsuits and congressional bills flew around, all aimed at removing the blight of Indian gaming. But as Senator Daniel Inouye made clear, the real issue was the competitive advantage tribes might secure over church bingo rooms, the proliferating private casinos authorized under liberalized state laws, and the lotteries and other games of chance so dear to the states themselves: "We should be candid about the interests surrounding [Indian gaming]. The issue has never really been one of crime control, morality, or economic fairness. . . . At issue is economics. . . . Ironically, the strongest opponents of tribal authority over gaming on Indian lands are from States whose liberal gaming policies would allow them to compete on an equal basis with the tribes. . . . We must not impose greater moral restraints on Indians than we do on the rest of our citizenry."

Beginning in the late 1970s, the outcome hung in the balance for a decade. The legality of tribal operations, valid under tribal law but contrary to state law, proved to be a razor-close question in the Supreme Court. Defending tribal gaming against attacks in Congress proved at least as difficult. All the while, as the tribes argued for their sovereign right to govern their reservations, the

debate bristled with harsh characterizations of the tribal position—so easy to portray as "illegal gambling," so susceptible to
honest concerns about compulsive gambling and organized crime.

The Seminole Tribe of Florida took the lead. Under the aggressive leadership of tribal chairman Howard Tommie, the Seminole
built a high-stakes bingo hall on reservation ground about seven
miles from Fort Lauderdale. As planned, the facility would be
open six days a week (Florida law held bingo halls to twice
weekly), and the tribal jackpots exceeded the state limit of $100.
Early on, Robert Butterworth, sheriff of Broward County, made his
position clear. He would begin making arrests the moment the
Seminole hall opened its doors.

The tribe sued, seeking a federal court injunction against Butterworth from enforcing the state laws. The case went before District Judge Norman Roettger, sitting in Fort Lauderdale, who had
sent dozens of mobsters to prison and received death threats in
the process. In 1980, Judge Roettger came down decisively in
favor of tribal sovereignty. Citing Chief Justice Marshall's opinion
in *Worcester v. Georgia*, he upheld the Seminole's position, finding
that "Indian nations have always been dealt with exclusively by
the federal government. . . . The Federal Government has long
permitted Indian Nations largely to govern themselves, free from
state interference." The Court of Appeals for the Fifth Circuit
affirmed, and the Supreme Court declined to review the case.

A victory, to be sure, but only the beginning of the legal war.
Out on the West Coast, California Indians were dirt-poor and short
of land. Many of the tribes had negotiated treaties in the early
1850s only to have them blocked by senators from the new state
of California; most of the tribes had come away with nothing. In
the late 1970s the tiny southern California reservation of the
Cabazon Band of Mission Indians near Indio "was completely
impoverished. . . . It was like everything stopped at the borders of
the reservation. Everything just stopped there." At the nearby
Morongo Reservation, "there were some HUD buildings and a few
trailers, but that was about it. There was really nothing there. The
people simply didn't have a lot." Both tribes turned to gaming.

The Cabazon Band opened its bingo and poker club in 1980.

Two days later the Indio police department shut the operation down, arresting more than a hundred employees and customers. The tribe promptly sued and won in the federal court of appeals, on a narrow ruling that applied only to the city of Indio. When the Cabazon reopened, the sheriff of Riverside County stepped in, asserting that the appeals court ruling against Indio did not bar county enforcement. He raided the club, issued citations, and impounded records and cash on hand. The Cabazon Band then brought suit against Riverside County.

Lawsuits may be slow, but the idea of gaming was spreading fast. Two months later the Morongo Tribe, also in Riverside County, had a bingo hall ready to go. Knowing that the county was preparing to raid it too, the Morongo filed suit. The federal judge consolidated the two cases, which would decide whether Indian gaming could legally proceed outside state law.

The Cabazon Band and Morongo Tribe prevailed in the lower courts. But the matter would not be settled there, for the U.S. Supreme Court accepted the case in 1986. The states weighed in against the tribes with twenty-one of them supporting California's position in the widely watched litigation. In addition to the stiff opposition from most of the states with Indian reservations, the timing was not auspicious for the tribes: As the cigarette tax cases and others showed, the Court had already exhibited signs of moving away from its traditionally protective stance toward tribal sovereignty.

Nonetheless, the tribes achieved a resounding triumph. In a 6–3 opinion handed down in 1987, the Supreme Court found that the Cabazon and Morongo bingo halls could operate under tribal laws. If the tribes' gaming is to be regulated from the outside, it must be done by Congress, not California. "Tribal sovereignty," Justice Byron White wrote for the majority, "is dependent on, and subordinate to, only the Federal Government, not the States." The Court emphasized the compelling need for economic development on these reservations: "The Cabazon and Morongo Reservations contain no natural resources which can be exploited. The tribal games at present provide the sole source of revenues for the operation of the tribal governments and the provision of tribal services. They are also the major sources of employment on the reservations. Self-determination and economic development are not within reach if the Tribes cannot raise revenues and provide employment for their members."

A main issue in the *Cabazon* case was whether the tribes were "marketing their tax exemptions," as in the on-reservation sale of cigarettes, where the Court allowed state taxation of sales to non-Indians. Instead, the Court found that the gaming tribes were "generating value on the reservation." The situation was comparable, not to smoke shops, but to tribal wildlife management programs, where an earlier Supreme Court opinion had struck down state jurisdiction:

> [T]he Tribes are not merely importing a product onto the reservations for immediate resale to non-Indians. They have built modern facilities which provide recreational opportunities and ancillary services to their patrons, who do not simply drive onto the reservations, make purchases and depart, but spend extended periods of times there enjoying the services the Tribes provide. The Tribes have a strong incentive to provide comfortable, clean, and attractive facilities and well-run games in order to increase attendance at the games. The tribal bingo enterprises are similar to the resort complex, featuring hunting and fishing, that the Mescalero Apache Tribe operates on its reservation through the "concerted and sustained" management of reservation land and wildlife resources.

While the *Cabazon Band* case worked its way through the courts during the mid-1980s, Indian gaming, and the boom in legalized gambling generally, had attracted considerable attention. Congress had been deliberating for several years on bills to regulate Indian gaming. And make no mistake about it: While the states could not outlaw or regulate Indian gaming, Congress could.

Senators Daniel Inouye and John McCain and Congressman Morris Udall took the lead in supporting the tribes, but in the teeth of strong states' rights advocacy. Senator Chic Hecht of Nevada was one of many arguing for full state authority: "Legal gaming on Indian lands should be subject to the same rules and regulations which non-Indian games must abide. Indian gaming should also be taxed the same way." Congressman Norman Shumway of California asserted that "Indian communities have taken unfair advantage of the unique jurisdictional status of their reservations by establishing large-scale gambling operations. . . . The Indian nations' unique position in the federal system . . . have made the Indians a separate, unaccountable segment of society who claim many rights but deny accountability for commensurate responsibilities." In addition to defending state sovereignty, opponents of Indian gaming, such as Congressman James Bilbray of Nevada, regularly raised the specter, never proved, of crooked dealings and organized crime: "The States have a constitutional responsibility to protect their citizens from harm, here in the form of fraudulent manipulation by the operators of the games and of victimization by criminal elements that may infiltrate the legal games operated on Indian lands."

By early 1987, just before *Cabazon* came down, Congress was close to settling on a bill that would have sharply curtailed tribal gaming. A key issue was Class III gaming—basically, casinos, jai alai, and racetracks. The most prominent bill would have allowed Class III gaming in Indian country only if legal in the state and if approved by the state in a tribal-state compact. Given the states' resistance, Indian gaming would have withered.

Cabazon changed the calculus. The law as handed down by the courts, previously uncertain, had now been clarified: States had no jurisdiction over bingo halls, which were classified as Class II, and presumably lacked authority over most Class III gaming as well. Congress could alter the judge-made law, but now the tribes had the status quo in their favor.

Congress finally passed the monumental Indian Gaming Regulatory Act in 1988. While shot through with compromise— inevitably so, given gambling's complexities—IGRA preserved tribal power to develop casino-style operations that could improve, even transform governmental services and economic conditions in Indian country.

Amid the many provisions of IGRA, some stand out. The starting point is that tribes have "exclusive right" to regulate gaming in

Indian country except when gambling is contrary to federal law or when a state completely prohibits a form of gaming. Class I— traditional tribal gambling, such as stick and bone games—is under sole tribal jurisdiction. Class II gaming—bingo, pull tabs, and other listed games—is regulated by the tribes with oversight by the National Indian Gaming Commission, an independent federal agency created by the 1988 statute. Class III—the large-scale gambling operations—may be conducted in a state that allows such gaming, even if it permits only low-level operations. But Class III operations are subject to agreed regulatory procedures in tribal-state compacts, which states are required to negotiate in "good faith." The National Indian Gaming Commission has broad investigative and regulatory authority, principally to ensure against influence by organized crime.

The provision in IGRA for tribal-state compacts, without which no tribal casino can go forward, has been especially objectionable to the tribes. True, the requirement of good faith negotiating is binding on the states. The Supreme Court, however, citing state sovereign immunity under the Eleventh Amendment, held that tribes cannot sue the states to enforce the requirement. The tribes are left with a right without a remedy. Numerous other disputes have arisen, with the tribes and states accusing the other of over-reaching. A sort of standoff exists. IGRA grants states authority not recognized by *Cabazon*. At the same time, the tribes held on to the ultimate prize: The 1988 statute preserved both an expansive role for tribal regulatory authority and a chance for American Indian tribes to produce needed revenue streams for tribal purposes.

BOTH *Cabazon* and the passage of the Indian Gaming Regulation Act made national news, but no one could have predicted the magnitude of the events that would unfold over the ensuing years. Approximately 200 tribes (of 562 federally recognized tribes) set up casinos or high-stakes bingo operations. In 1988, when President Reagan signed IGRA, total Indian gaming revenues, mostly from bingo halls, stood at $100 million. By 2003 the total take had shot up to $16.7 billion—more than a hundredfold increase. About twenty megacasinos generate 50 to 60 percent of all revenue; each of these make over $400 million annually, and the largest, the Mashantucket Pequot Nation and Mohegan Tribe casinos in Connecticut, bring in about $1 billion apiece annually. That is a lot of money, but it does not put Indians in a commanding position in the gaming business. Nearly half the states allow casinos (only Utah and Hawaii outlaw all forms of gambling), and 80 percent of the yield nationally flows to non-Indian gaming establishments.

The numbers just given represent gross receipts. Most tribes do not release net revenue figures, but after accounting for salaries, payments to states and local communities, equipment, advertising, debt service, and other management expenses, the tribes probably net about 30 percent of the $16.7 billion gross tribal revenues. Leaving aside the 20 highest-revenue tribes for a moment and recognizing that we cannot apply the term "average" in any meaningful way, we can conclude that most of the remaining 180 tribes net, say, in the neighborhood of $5 to $15 million a year. Without doubt, this is a significant infusion of money for any tribe but still not enough to put in place all the education, health, economic, and social programs needed to lift reservations out of poverty. Let us remember too that more than half of the tribes have no gaming operations, either because they oppose the concept or because their reservations are so isolated that gaming could not be economically viable.

Most gaming tribes have used their revenues well. Common expenditures include health insurance, new clinics and hospitals, college scholarships, tribal elementary and secondary schools, tribal colleges, land acquisition, and new housing. Nationwide, the casinos have generated some 75,000 new jobs for tribal members. Investments have been funneled into many nongaming tribal ventures: museums, banks, hydroelectric dams, farms, hotels, restaurants, and grocery stores.

The tribes and the National Indian Gaming Commission have taken care to foster relationships with nearby communities and to ease the off-site costs that may result from reservation gaming.

Significant moneys go to local charities and communities for maintenance of roads and water and sewage systems, schools, hospitals, law enforcement, and other public services. The spin-off effects of Indian casinos are not trivial. Local construction firms, gas stations, hotels, restaurants, and other businesses benefit directly from the reservation gaming activity. Three-fourths of the 300,000 casino jobs are filled by non-Indians, and those paychecks have a multiplier effect as they work their way through the communities. Also, and blessedly for all, a much-feared byproduct of Indian gaming—the influence of organized crime—has never come to pass.

Still and all, Indian gaming gives pause to many Americans. A good percentage of the public objects to any gaming at all, Indian or otherwise. Yet Indian gambling generates the highest heat, perhaps traceable to racism, perhaps to a reflexive, often unspoken notion that the system tilts toward Indians. It is somehow seen as illegitimate to some when Indians obtain wealth. Never mind that wealthy Indians are few and that the great majority of Indians, even now, remain a good distance away from the middle class.

Another, more justifiable concern involves basic perceptions of democracy. Americans understandably assume that they should have a say about something as controversial as gambling, especially when a casino may rise up within a few miles of their neighborhoods. It is true that state laws also can permit a close-to-home casino and true too that non-Indians do have a say on Indian casinos through the state-tribal compacting process. Still, the fact remains that non-Indians feel a sense of powerlessness. In most cases, the tribes make the basic decisions on reservation gaming, just as they do for other activities on their homelands. Much depends on good will being displayed on both sides.

There is no single story about tribal gaming. It is especially a subject where "for instances" and "for examples" are treacherous. There are as many stories as there are tribes, including the nongaming tribes. But if we put aside the megacasinos and the failed and marginal operations, the experience of the Poarch Band of Creeks has many of the elements found in the stories of the other tribes and can bring some depth to the subject.

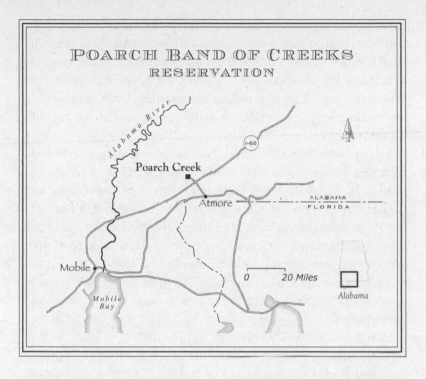

POARCH BAND OF CREEKS
RESERVATION

Alabama River

Poarch Creek

I-65

Atmore

ALABAMA
FLORIDA

Mobile

0   20 Miles

Mobile
Bay

Alabama

.   .   .

WHEN the Creek War broke out in 1813, the Poarch Band
lived in southwestern Alabama, near the edge of the vast Creek
territory. The Creek Nation split over the war, some Creek towns
choosing to fight the incoming settlers and the United States,
while other towns wanted peace. The Poarch, like "friendly
Creeks" in several other towns, sided with the United States and
General Andrew Jackson. After the United States emerged victo-
rious, the Poarch's loyalty came mostly to naught. In the 1814
Treaty of Fort Jackson, they and other bands were forced to sign
away some 21 million acres. The treaty did provide that any
"friendly" Creeks would be entitled to land grants of 640 acres.

The Poarch were spared the Trail of Tears of the 1830s, when,
with Andrew Jackson now president, federal troops marched
most Creeks and the other Five Civilized Tribes west to Oklahoma.
Probably the Poarch were allowed to remain in Alabama because
of their wartime loyalty (several families proudly displayed land

grant certificates and letters of gratitude for their military service), but at that point the United States lost interest, and the
Poarch received none of the federal benefits thereafter available
to Indians. Poor and notably "Indian-looking," they stayed where
they were, a distinct and isolated community, marrying largely
among themselves. Historians have labeled them the "lost" or "forgotten" Creeks.

By the early years of the twentieth century Poarch people were
enduring a relentless discrimination that they bitterly remember
to this day. Local schools were segregated—white, black, and
Indian. So were the churches. The Indians believed that they had
been defrauded out of their land through transactions lost in the
mist of history. In a hardscrabble economy dominated by timber
and cotton, the Poarch Creeks labored in the forests, farmed the
few family parcels still left, or worked as sharecroppers. They held
on to a strong sense of society but had no land base or organized
government.

Poarch history took a new turn in 1947 under the leadership of
Calvin McGhee, a direct descendant of Lynn McGhee, a prominent Creek who had managed to avoid the Trail of Tears. Calvin's
life is celebrated in annual ceremonies at Poarch, and with reason.
Early on, he outlined a plan with three objectives: end school segregation, prosecute a Poarch claims case for the lost land, and
revive tribal government. McGhee was an imposing fellow, tall,
erect, and handsome in his Plains Indian regalia, complete with
war bonnet, which he wore on many public occasions because it
was so recognizably Indian, though in no way Creek. He seemed
to be everywhere—calling tribal meetings, pressing school officials, visiting governors, and taking some hundred trips to Washington, D.C.

The effort paid off. First came the matter of education discrimination. In the early 1950s Escambia County provided Poarch
Band children an Indian-only elementary school and nothing
more; Indian students could not attend the high school in Atmore,
seven miles away. School buses bound for Atmore drove straight
through the Creek settlements, never stopping for Indian children. McGhee filed a lawsuit but got no relief. Finally, in an inci-

dent that the Poarch still recount in fond detail, McGhee organized the men of the band; one morning they spread out across the
main road, hands joined. The bus stopped, the Indian children got
on, and from that point onward Indian children were accepted in
the Atmore high school.

The land claim took more than twenty years to resolve and produced a paltry award, barely $113 for each Poarch Creek member.
Even so, the people took it as an acknowledgment of past wrongs.
One Poarch member said, "I'll always say it was that Indian money
which freed us from bondage . . . because so many who had been
so down on the Indians had to face up to us over that money." In
the area of tribal government, the Poarch, though not recognized
by the United States, adopted a constitution in 1950 and elected
McGhee chairman (he was known, in and out of Poarch society,
as the Chief), a post he held until his death in 1971. Sadly, Calvin
McGhee never saw the third part of his dream come true. In 1984
the federal government formally recognized the Poarch Band of
Creeks as a sovereign nation.

The second stage of modern Poarch history began with that federal recognition. By then the tribal chairman was Eddie Tullis,
who has served even longer than Calvin McGhee, giving the tribe
remarkably stable leadership over more than half a century.

Tullis and the tribal council, with federal recognition finally in
hand, knew of the Florida Seminole's early success with bingo—
and since Alabama and Florida were both in the Fifth Circuit
Court of Appeals, the Poarch Band could rely on the Seminole's
favorable decision in the early 1980s in a way California tribes
could not. A tribe may, however, run casinos only on tribal trust
land, and by the spring of 1985 the BIA still had not taken the
tribe's 229 acres in trust. As for the bingo hall, it was up and ready
to open. Tullis, soft-spoken and deliberate, every bit the southern
gentleman, is nonetheless a master at applying pressure. He
finally ran out of patience on April 13, 1985. "We told those guys
stalling up in Washington, that we're goin' to play bingo tonight at
six, whether you sign the papers or not." The bureaucrats did sign
the papers, and the Poarch Creek Bingo Palace opened its doors—
legally and on Tullis's schedule.

The new bingo palace, the largest gaming operation in Alabama and just 56 miles from Mobile, took off. Within days, busloads of players were pouring into the 1,700-seat facility. In the years to follow the band opened two other bingo halls, one in Montgomery, the state capital. All are Class II operations (which do not require tribal-state compacts) because the Poarch Creek and the state could not agree on a compact; the tribe's court case based on the state's failure to negotiate in good faith under IGRA was thrown out because of Alabama's immunity from suit, thus blocking hopes for a blockbuster Class III casino. Today the three bingo enterprises employ 400 people.

The Poarch gaming halls have helped bring steady, constructive change to the tribe. Jobs in the gambling operations and other tribal enterprises have reduced unemployment, although the rate remains above 25 percent. Some proceeds have been invested in tribal enterprises, starting with a Best Western motel and restaurant on Interstate 65. The tribe also purchased a large machine shop, Muskogee Metal Works, and bought up farmlands; Perdido Farm now has 265 head of brood cows and the largest pecan orchard in the county. The Poarch Band has obtained federal economic development grants over the years, but Tullis much prefers Poarch enterprises to the government contracts. "Anything we ever got was more strings than resources."

Housing has been a top priority, and HUD grants and bingo palace profits built 80 single-family homes and rental units. By the turn of the century the reservation, sporting paved roads and tidy green lawns, was welcoming ten new houses every year: The tribal members must supply the land and the tribe provides no-interest thirty-year loans. The tribal land base has grown to 2,000 acres with more purchases in the pipeline. In addition to housing projects and enterprise facilities, there are several new tribal buildings: a spacious tribal office and community center, a fire station, a senior citizens' center, and a health clinic. The Poarch Band has money for college scholarships in its education trust fund, though not yet enough for the full rides it would like to offer to its students.

Unfortunately, prejudice against the Poarch Creeks may have

abated, but it still runs strong. Buford Rolin, the buttoned-down tribal vice-chair, obviously a man of substance, gave this lament: "It'll take generations to change, if it ever does. The challenge now is that prejudice against Indians is growing with each success. People think we're trying to set up a kingdom down here. . . . But we have accomplished so much in such a short time since recognition.

"This is what just burns me up now. People in town take no pride in what we are doing. They still say, 'those people *out there.*' But it is us, the tribe, that is giving jobs, creating enterprise. And none of them have ever been here. Everything we are doing is positive, and that town is drying up, and still, we're the ones who are 'out there.' "

THE POARCH CREEK experience tells a lot about how gaming works in Indian country. Like the Poarch, most tribes nationally also have done a good job in putting their revenues into beneficent tribal programs. A key step for the Poarch was phasing out its management firm. Tribes, like most counties and cities wanting to build large recreation or convention facilities, have hired outside firms to construct the facilities and establish management practices. The band accelerated its payments to the management firm and became full owner of the Creek Bingo Palace within five years. Too many tribes in the early years of gaming were burned by management firms (now limited by IGRA to a ceiling of 40 percent of net revenues over a maximum of seven years). Today tribes negotiate those contracts with experience and from a position of strength. As for the frustrations tribes feel over the state role under IGRA, the Poarch Creeks' failure to attain Class III status is emblematic: Alabama's reliance on its sovereign immunity completely shut down the tribe's efforts to open a casino. We'll never know if Alabama negotiated with the Poarch in good faith, as IGRA directs.

About one-quarter of the gaming tribes, although not the Poarch, distribute some revenues as per capita payments to tribal members. These kinds of payments are an anomaly since the casinos are governmental, not individual, ventures. But they have a history, tracing back to Congress's practice, during the deadening years of the early twentieth century, of passing proceeds from land claims directly to individuals despite the fact that the lost lands had belonged to the tribe. With tribalism suppressed, Congress then thought of tribes as collections of individuals, not as governments. Tribal members, however, became used to the per capita payments, although they never did more than offer a fleeting break from poverty. Now, with gaming proceeds available, tribal members often pressure their councils for the distributions.

Most of the per capita distributions from gaming range from minimal payments in the nature of a Christmas bonus to amounts large enough to pay the rent. The widely publicized distributions—as high as hundreds of thousands a year per tribal member—have been made by no more than a dozen tribes, all of them with small enrollments. Tribal councils normally take the long view, knowing that they need to build a solid permanent structure to provide for education, health, land management, law and order, and other basic governmental responsibilities. Eddie Tullis is clear on this: "There is some pressure to start per capita payments to members, so the leadership needs to demonstrate that it can do more for the community by providing services. I believe in self-help, not handouts."

In addition to the attention on the few examples of fabulous per capita payments, publicity has been trained on small tribes that are "not Indian" and exist only for the casino money. The Poarch Band, "forgotten" for so many decades, faced this during the recognition process before satisfying the BIA that it was a distinct Indian band with a tradition of governance and a specific geographic location. Far more concerted attacks were leveled at other southern and eastern tribes and at tiny California rancherias, who may have memberships as small as several dozen or even just one family.

Leave no doubt that the premise is correct: These tribes, all of whom lived in deep poverty before gaming, *are* small of population and land. These are the Native peoples who caught the sharpest edges of European settlement. Take the Mashantucket Pequot of Connecticut, who developed one of the largest casinos in the world and have had the harshest "not Indian" charges leveled against them. This tribe was devastated first by epidemics and then by the brutal Pequot Wars of the 1630s. In California, after the smallpox and the onslaught of the gold rush—one of the largest migrations in human history—the tribes, weak and greatly reduced in numbers, signed treaties to preserve some land, but the Senate of the United States reneged on the solemnly negotiated documents.

So yes, by the 1970s the Mashantucket Pequot population had dwindled. And yes, tribal chair Richard "Skip" Hayward, berated for being a "low-blood," was just that, a "low-blood." But if you spend time with Skip Hayward, it is hard to doubt his sincerity and burning determination to save what is left of his people and their blood. And yes, the Viejas Band of Kumeyaay Indians in San Diego County can count only a few hundred members, but you cannot doubt the Indianness or the sincerity of its chairman, Anthony Pico.

Are some Indian people in Connecticut and California interested mainly in working the system for the money? Undoubtedly. Is there a greater truth, found at Poarch Creek and scores of other reservations, a truth woven of staying power, minority rights, avenues out of poverty, and blood commitment to culture, to what peoples irrevocably *are*? Undoubtedly. In the end, it may be entirely consistent for a person to oppose gambling and at the same time, out of an understanding of history and justice, to support Indian gambling.

MANY of the gaming tribes have, like the Poarch Band of Creeks, used casino revenues to start up other business ventures. Others have diversified without any gaming or with casino income playing a minor role. Of the latter, the Southern Ute Indian Tribe is one of the most economically successful.

When Leonard Burch took over as chairman of the Southern Ute in 1966, the tribal budget consisted of a few thousand dollars. A personable, outgoing navy veteran, Burch went on to serve as chairman of the Colorado tribe almost continuously for 36 years. Early on, he called for a comprehensive long-term plan. Sam Maynes, of Durango, who acted as tribal attorney into the twenty-first century and became one of western Colorado's finest lawyers, agreed to help out.

One unexpected consequence of history leaped out at the planners. To be sure, the Southern Utes' reservation in the Four Corners area of southwestern Colorado was the residue of treachery. Governor Frederick Pitkin, determined to open the state's western slope for settlement by non-Indians, inflamed the citizenry in the 1870s with anti-Ute rhetoric and succeeded in blasting apart the magnificent 1868 treaty reservation and relocating tribal members on three much smaller plots. The treachery, though, had its irony, for the modern Southern Ute reservation overlay part of the San Juan Basin. This storied geological region contained major natural gas, coal, and coalbed methane resources. The tribe, however, received few benefits from the old-style mineral management. Burch fumed that between the energy companies' connections and BIA incompetence, "We were at the mercy of development."

The tribal council and Burch moved forward to take control of the energy resources. Most of the revenues, such as they were, went out to tribal members in the form of per capita payments. Burch put a stop to these and saw to it that the lease revenues went to the tribal government. He and tribal leaders from other reservations founded the Council of Energy Resource Tribes, one of the first intertribal organizations, dedicated to pooling mineral and legal expertise. In 1974, buying time for building the tribe's management capability, the tribal council declared a moratorium on new mineral leases. In the 1980s the tribe enacted a severance tax on reservation mineral production.

By the early 1990s Burch had been in office for a quarter century and had assembled a solid staff and good research. The Southern Ute were ready to break the mold. The most profitable opportunities in the energy industry are found on the production side. Passively receiving royalties, as all tribes traditionally did, has no risks, but the potential yields pale in comparison. The Southern Ute formed Red Willow Production Company and began buying back drilling rights and hiring its own oilmen to operate the wells. Today Red Willow owns interests in nearly 1,000 wells and works about half of those, making it one of the top natural gas producers in Colorado. The tribe also entered the natural gas transportation business. The Red Cedar Gathering Company now owns more than 700 miles of pipelines, moving about 1 percent of the nation's daily natural gas supply.

Despite the success of this vertical integration, Burch worried about dry wells and rainy days. "One day, we might wake up and there's no income from oil and gas." By the turn of the century, with net revenues from Red Willow and Red Cedar totaling about $100 million annually (the Sky Ute Casino, by comparison, returns about $8 million), the Southern Ute looked to the future. First, it established the Permanent Fund, a conservatively invested endowment to satisfy tribal government and core service needs in perpetuity, which now stands at about $650 million. A Growth Fund, housed in a modern building in the tribal capital of Ignacio, manages existing tribal businesses and develops new ventures. Between the two funds, the Southern Ute Tribe, among other things, has made many successful business investments. Its bonds hold the ultimate AAA Fitch rating (better, tribal leaders lightheartedly point out, than Japan or Canada). The tribe provides elders with annual pensions of $54,000, administers excellent health and housing programs, operates a tribal elementary school and a generous college scholarship fund, and runs KSUT, Four Corners public radio, with six different FM frequencies on your dial.

While only a few tribes can claim the Southern Utes' kind of financial result, every reservation has experienced an upswing in economic activity. There can be three kinds of businesses in Indian country: those run by the tribe, by individual Indians, or by outside, non-Indian interests. A generation ago the outsiders accounted for what little economic activity there was. Since then, as we have seen at Southern Ute, Poarch Creek, White Mountain Apache, Tohono O'odham, and Warm Springs, tribes have launched a wide variety of business enterprises, even including the chartering of banks. Moreover, individual Indian entrepreneurship has

Peterson Zah served two terms, 1983–1987 and 1991–1995, as chairman and (when the position was renamed) president of the Navajo Nation. Recognizing that mining will eventually dry up, Zah initiated the Permanent Trust Fund, where mineral revenues are invested, with proceeds used to meet education, health, and other needs. By 2003 the fund held more than $500 million. The nation honored him by naming its handsome new building in Window Rock the Peterson Zah–Navajo Nation Museum and Library. Photograph courtesy of Richard Trudell.

taken off. Indian-owned businesses, on the reservations and in the cities, have mushroomed from 3,000 in 1969 to around 200,000 at the turn of the century.

As always, we must remember the beginning point. Until recently Indian country lacked any semblance of an economic infrastructure. There was no place to buy gas, a bag of groceries, a pair of jeans, or a meal. This lack of small businesses caused "leakage": Instead of dollars being spent on the reservation and turned over several times, tribal members made their purchases in off-reservation communities, which received the direct and indirect economic benefits. Gradually, reservation economies are maturing. In addition to tribal and individual Indian businesses, outside companies—which now come into Indian country on the tribes' terms—increasingly see opportunities on the reservations. The result is not always pretty, consisting as it sometimes does of

Burger Kings, ragtag Indian jewelry stores, an occasional ATM, scruffy auto repair shops, tribal timber mills, 7-Elevens, and the like, but it represents the emergence of a diverse base of at-home goods, services, and jobs.

While the trends are promising, poverty still stalks Indian country. On-reservation unemployment has dropped from 50 percent in 1960 to 26 percent in 1990 to 22 percent in 2000 (these figures somewhat understate real unemployment because the census excludes from the work force those people so discouraged that they have stopped looking for work). Median family income on reservations is $24,000, a major jump from the 1950s, when families lived on $870 a year (only $6,500 in 2002 dollars). Still, family income in Indian country remains just one-half of the national average. In some areas, especially the upper Great Plains, circumstances are especially dire. On the Pine Ridge reservation, where the Lakota have taken back their governance from the BIA and fought off the cultural and religious suppression, unemployment still stands at 80 percent in the winter and 60 percent in the summer.

Several ameliorating features take an edge off these poverty figures. Income for urban Indians is much higher and approaches the national average. Bartering and trading are staples of daily reservation life—a side of venison for a 1985 Chevy engine—and the sentiment of Elsa Stands in Timber from Northern Cheyenne in Montana holds for all tribes: "Our old people fought and gave their lives so we would have this land. We have a lot of poverty and unemployment here but you can always find somebody on the reservation who will take you in and that's the way we are supposed to be." The formal structures matter a great deal also, for tribes now offer an array of programs ranging from child care to housing to health to scholarships to elder care. Day by day, tribal councils labor to build the effective governments that come from strong, stable legislatures, courts, and agencies. This is heartening, for Professors Joseph Kalt and Stephen Cornell of the Harvard Project on American Indian Economic Development rightly identify nation building as the foundation: "Economic development on

Indian reservations is first and foremost a political problem. At the heart of it lie sovereignty and the governing institutions through which sovereignty can be effectively exercised."

A person can wonder whether statistics, such as the census numbers, will ever match up with the nation as a whole. Pueblo dancers may take two or three weeks preparing for a ceremony, and some of the Texas Kickapoo set aside January through March for religious purposes. Those kinds of schedules are hard for employers to accommodate. A Sioux friend tells of a man who spotted an elk when driving to work. By the time he stalked, shot, and dressed the animal it was midafternoon. Another dissatisfied boss. A related phenomenon is that an Indian person may lose respect in the community by "starring around" or "going white" through getting an education or a good-paying job. Anthropologist Kathleen Pickering explains that an Indian person, by amassing financial capital, may risk losing "social capital"—the high respect (and when needed, the material gifts from strong social relationships) that comes with being a traditionalist. The tug, and the worth, of the Indian way keeps some Indian people poor in money but rich in spirit and community support.

One thing is for sure: No matter how many casinos, tribal enterprises, federal programs, and other investments there may be, it will take a long time, if ever, before poverty as measured by dollars will fade from Indian country. When the Europeans stripped away the wealth that Indian people created from their caribou, buffalo, salmon, and cornfield economies, the newcomers never replaced it. Native Americans received only the many generations of the deadening years. Economists see the task of breaking from BIA control to tribal democracy as comparable to rebuilding the government-controlled economies of Eastern Europe. Johnson Holy Rock, the Oglala Lakota elder statesman, made the point in his own way:

> As our land mass was diminished, the Oglalas were assigned to the Pine Ridge reservation. When they finally realized that they no longer had freedom of movement they had already become slaves. They had to live under the concepts of this other

civilization and they found it very hard. They could see then that this was a vast prison where they were concentrated and that's when they knew that they were enslaved to a system that was not theirs. But it was too late then to do anything. . . .

Addressing what might be called our social and economic crisis on this reservation could be real difficult because this is something that has developed over almost a century and a half. These things cannot be changed with the flick of a wand. . . .

14.

Preserving the Old Ways

"My grandmother died in 1969." This was Rick Williams speaking, Oglala Sioux from Pine Ridge, executive director of the American Indian College Fund, one of the three largest Indian nonprofits along with the Native American Rights Fund and First Nations Development Institute. "She knew she was dying, and several times she told me what to do at her funeral. She said, 'Do this for me because I'm the last one to be buried this way.'

"So she went to her grave believing that Indian people had lost their culture. Had she lived another five years, she would have changed her mind. Because that was right at the beginning of so many things happening. We went from being victims of racism to being an important part of America.

"My grandmother didn't know about Alcatraz or AIM or self-determination; all that would follow. She would have been absolutely shocked to see that Sun Dance has returned, that there are sweat lodges all over the reservation, that the Lakota still do burials the old way. She'd be shocked that I have my long braids. She'd be shocked that her great-grandchildren speak Lakota."

IN THE EARLY 1970s, as tribal governments began to assume more powers and responsibilities, the authority of the BIA and the churches receded. This released a surge of cultural pride; at last it became safe to be Indian. The main litigation and legislative initiatives bore directly on culture. Rights to land and hunting and

fishing are bathed in ceremony and spirituality. The right to be
heard in tribal, rather than state, court means that a controversy
will probably come before a judge sensitive to cultural concerns.
The sovereign rights to charter and regulate schools and colleges
means that tribes can assure culturally appropriate classrooms.

It is the great irony of nineteenth-century Indian policy that the
sharply reduced tribal landholdings, which Native people bitterly
protested, later became cherished homelands and the foundation
for the modern sovereignty movement. The great irony of the twentieth century is that contemporaneously with the rise of Indian
entrepreneurship in general and gaming in particular, Indian people experienced a resurgence in traditionalism. Everywhere there
are more dances, songs, and ceremonies, more pottery, jewelry,
and rugs, more longhouses and tribal museums, more native language classes. Indian painting and sculpture are thriving, with
scores of artists now following in the tracks of post–World War II
giants Oscar Howe (whose painting *The Singer* graced the jacket of
this book's hardcover edition), Allan Houser, Fritz Scholder, Dick
West, Woody Crumbo, and R. C. Gorman. The explosion of Indian
writers includes N. Scott Momaday, Louise Erdrich, James Welch,
Sherman Alexie, Linda Hogan, Leslie Marmon Silko, Gerald
Vizenor, Suzan Shown Harjo, Vine Deloria, Jr., and Joy Harjo. Compare this with the late 1920s through the late 1950s, when D'Arcy
McNickle and the Osage novelist and historian John Joseph Math-
ews were the only Indian public intellectuals visible to the outside
world, the sole Native voices for Indian nationalism.

This is not to say that Indian culture of today is exactly that of
yesteryear. Shadings of old and new are common: Some of the
drummers at the powwow may be wearing running shoes, light
skins may be dancing among the dark skins, and after the dancing, Jell-O with marshmallows may sit next to the venison and
roots on the potluck table. In the earlier time, virtually all the people held the Indian worldview. (More than 500 tribal groups live
in the United States, each a separate people and each endowed
with unique traditions. Yet I am satisfied that most, if not all, the
tribal peoples share ideas and overarching values. It is that common body of thought I mean by "Indian worldview.") Of course the

Allan Houser, Chiricahua Apache, born in 1914, studied art at the Santa Fe Indian School and Utah State University. For years he created his sculptures and paintings by night and worked in construction by day. After receiving a Guggenheim Fellowship in 1949, he was able to practice his art full-time and became one of the world's finest sculptors. Shown in the photograph is the mold for Sacred Rain Arrow, *which, when bronzed, he donated to the U.S. Senate Committee on Indian Affairs hearing room, dedicated in 1991. Houser passed away in 1994. Photograph by David Hoptman, reprinted with permission.*

Indian worldview is attenuated today. The battles of more than two centuries have been waged over Indians' minds as well as land and sovereignty, and the battalions of assimilation have marched on every tribe.

The tenacity behind the worldview has made its mark too. Even in the cities most Native people maintain ties with their homeland and value their culture, and a good many are culturally Indian by any definition. Out in Indian country, some traditional Indians hold the worldview essentially intact. Nearly every Native person on the reservations holds some of the orientation and direction of the old ways; most of them, and this is quite a large number of people, hew to the Indian way as their main compass. Wherever they may be in the spectrum of the Indian worldview, these are people, targeted for termination not long ago, who have found their places and intend to hold their ground.

THE INDIAN worldview is elaborate and demanding—Vine Deloria, Jr., writes that "tribal religions are actually complexes of attitudes, beliefs, and practices fine-tuned to harmonize with the lands on which the people live"—but the broad philosophy is often manifested in simple acts of respect toward other people and the natural world. It is a pervasive custom, for example, not to interrupt others when they are speaking. Similarly, since Native people know they are part of nature, Indians have ways of showing respect for the skies, land forms, rocks, plants, and animals. Consider deer and ceremony.

The Texas, or Mexican, Band of Kickapoo is one of the most culturally conservative group of Indians in the United States. Originally a woodland tribe of the Great Lakes, many Kickapoo refused to negotiate treaties with the United States under any circumstances and were pushed south. By the 1850s the band had moved all the way down to Mexico, to the state of Coahuila.

There they became a favorite of the Mexican government because of their admirable warrior mentality and because they had liberated hundreds of thousands head of cattle from the Texans. (One thing the Kickapoo and the Mexicans held in common was contempt for Texans.) In gratitude, Benito Juárez granted them an *ejido*, a large, commonly held parcel of land.

After I had gone into teaching, I worked for the Kickapoo Band on a consulting arrangement with the Native American Rights Fund. Many of the Kickapoo men seasonally went to and from the United States for work. The band wanted to put a bill through Congress (they subsequently did), clarifying their border crossing rights and creating a small reservation near Eagle Pass, Texas, their crossing point.

I visited the Kickapoo at their home in Mexico in the spring of 1982. Their splendid *ejido* lay in open-range country on the eastern slope of the Sierra Madre. A clear stream ran down through Naciamento, as their settlement was called. The Kickapoo were mostly full-blood and monolingual in Kickapoo.

On this trip, I went for supper to the home of a middle-aged gentleman named Ketchima and was served a meal of deer meat. Ketchima had told me once, through an interpreter, that the force of the Great Spirit, Manitou, was found in all nature, and he used deer as an example. "Where did you get this deer? Are the deer good here?" I asked at the dinner table. I had heard that they were.

Ketchima answered in his own language, and a younger Kickapoo man translated for me, saying the word "he" with a particular fullness.

"He came right up to me. He often does. He knows that I need him. I shot him, then I honored him and prayed for him. I know that he will come back."

A deer also played a role in a story I heard far to the north in Montana. Pat Smith, an Assiniboine from Fort Peck, worked for ten years in the six-lawyer tribal attorney's office at the Confederated Salish and Kootenai Tribes of the Flathead Reservation. Now he has his own firm in Missoula and represents tribes around the West.

A few years ago, when we were out on a hike, Pat told me a story. He told it slowly and softly, in wonderment.

Not long before, Pat had been in the middle of making a major life decision. He could think about little else and felt he needed a sign.

After a meeting in Great Falls and before going to bed, he sensed that a deer might be waiting for him, signaling that what he was planning to do was right. "It was a premonition, one of the strongest I'd ever had."

He got up at 4:00 A.M. and headed west toward home. Along the way Pat, who doesn't smoke, stopped to buy some tobacco. Then he went on, rising toward the Jocko Divide at daybreak. Near the top he saw the deer, a three-point buck, in a clearing by the side of the road. He shot him immediately.

The son of the Cheyenne artist Dick West, W. Richard West represented Indian tribes in private practice for 19 years. In 1990 he was named the founding director of the National Museum of the American Indian. West shaped the philosophy of the museum—to present, in collaboration with Indian people, the long Indian experience "that has eluded American history from the beginning"—and spearheaded the design and construction of the magnificent facility that opened in 2004 on the last available space on the National Mall. Here Gordon Yellowman presents West with an eagle-feathered war bonnet at the ceremony making West a Cheyenne peace chief. Photograph courtesy of Richard West and the Museum of the American Indian.

"I knew that was going to happen," Pat told me. "He was there, and that made me know my decision was right. I took some time to reflect on it all. Then I honored that deer. I blew some smoke up his nostrils and scattered some tobacco on the ground."

"Why," I asked, "did you use that ceremony?"

"I don't know exactly. I knew I had to stop for the tobacco. Indian people have a protocol. If you kill anything, you ought to leave something. You ought to pay honor."

INDIAN PEOPLE, like Ketchima and Pat Smith, have their private ways, but there is also a more formal governmental aspect to the cultural revival, tasks that go with the obligations of sovereignty. The tribes of the Great Plains and the Intertribal Bison

Cooperative are working hard to bring back the buffalo, central to Sioux life and religion. Said Harry Charger of the Cheyenne River Sioux: "The buffalo are coming back, and with them our strength as a people." Many of the lands ceded away at treaty time are now managed by federal public land agencies; since the 1980s tribes have advocated for religious practitioners who wish to use sacred sites on those lands for ceremonies and to gather medicines. Dealing government to government, tribal agencies and federal land offices have negotiated cooperative agreements to ensure access to those sites. Powwows (cultural and social events usually open to the public but invariably closed to alcohol) are put on annually by most tribes.

I have witnessed few events as satisfying as the powwow hosted in November 1977 by the Siletz Tribe of Oregon. It was timed to celebrate President Carter's signing of the Siletz Restoration Act, which reversed termination and recognized Siletz sovereignty. In the grand entry, the opening processional, a hundred or more colorfully garbed marchers from the Siletz and other Northwest tribes strode in to the beat of many drums. Those ancient, sharp sounds, pounded out on tautly drawn rawhide, had not resounded on the Oregon coast in more than thirty years. The setting was humble, just the the worn-out building at the county fairgrounds, for the penniless Siletz tribe still had no facilities of its own—and the heating had gone out on the dank, near-freezing evening. But the spectators in the packed gym looked on in respect and wonder, savoring the pageantry, the rhythms, and the revival of a tribe that termination nearly hounded into extinction.

ANOTHER major reconstruction effort in Indian country, which displays in full colors the perseverance and valor of modern Indian people, is the campaign to preserve and resurrect native languages.

Linguists emphasize how much a culture depends upon its language, for language expresses the way a society sees itself and the world. Each language thus becomes the repository for the values, philosophies, and individuality of a people. How do we show respect, value family, perceive nature, define property, allocate

A singer-drummer at a Red Lake Chippewa powwow cups his hand to amplify his voice and to isolate his voice from the sound of the drums. Photograph courtesy of the Charles Brill family, reprinted with permission from Red Lake Nation— Portraits of Ojibway Life.

authority, settle disputes, and treat sicknesses? Listen to our language. Anthropologist Russell Bernard, making the comparison commonly made between species loss and language loss, warns of the subtle but profound effects of losing the world's languages: "[A]ny reduction of language diversity diminishes the adaptational strength of our species because it lowers the pool of knowledge from which we can draw. We know that the reduction of biodiversity today threatens all of us. I think we are conducting an experiment to see what will happen to humanity if we eliminate 'cultural species' in the world. This is a reckless experiment. If we don't like the way it turns out, there's no going back."

An estimated one-half of all the world's languages have already been lost. Of the 6,000 or so still spoken, roughly one-half are at risk because they are used by the children sporadically or not at all. Only a few hundred can be considered "safe" from extinction.

Language loss in the United States is steady and pronounced. At the beginning of the twentieth century most American Indian people spoke their native tongues as a first or second language. By the end of the century, of some 300 original North American languages, just one-half were still spoken. The languages tended to be strongest in the Southwest and Alaska. Of the 36 tribes with more than 1,000 speakers, Navajo has by far the most, with 150,000; next are the Choctaw, Apache, Cherokee, O'odham, and Yupik. The pueblos of New Mexico and Arizona, which have smaller tribal populations, also have high percentages of speakers. In most tribes, however, native languages are spoken only by the middle-aged and elderly or, more precarious yet, by a handful of elders.

The pressures have long been intense. In 1888, at the outset of allotment and assimilation, President Grover Cleveland declared that Indians should not be permitted "to indulge in their barbarous language." For generations during the deadening years, the BIA and the churches discouraged Native talk—and in some cases sanctioned violators by beating them or washing out their mouths with yellow lye soap. Before the Indian Child Welfare Act of 1978, state courts and placement agencies adopted out children in droves to non-Indian families. Those young people lost the opportunity to learn their native languages. Oren Lyons, chief and faithkeeper of the Onondaga Nation of New York, has his history right when he says: "Indigenous languages were never 'lost.' That term implies that somehow Indian nations are responsible for our own demise. Our languages were taken, in some cases destroyed, as a deliberate federal policy." Given all that, linguist Michael Krauss calls it "remarkable" that so many languages remain alive, even if barely, and describes the survival as "powerful testimony to the cultural and spiritual strength of Native America."

The obliteration and damage have been grievous. Professor Krauss has written: "There are no 'primitive' languages. Every human language is an exquisitely complex intellectual master-piece, created and polished by untold generations, as the ever per-fect expression of their culture and experience, of intimate knowledge of their specific environment, and of their own special interpretation of universal human experience." Many Indian peo-ple believe that they can pray to their ancestors only in their own language. Lakota reminds us of one of the mysteries of human existence: The word *tehi* is the root for both "love" and "difficult." Louise Erdrich, the Turtle Mountain Chippewa writer who learned her native tongue as an adult, explains how its concepts expanded her perception of the world. "The word for stone, *asin*, is animate. Stones are called grandfathers and grandmothers and are extremely important in Ojibwe philosophy. Once I began to think of stones as animate, I started to wonder whether I was pick-ing up a stone or it was putting itself into my hand. Stones are not the same as they were to me in English. I can't write about a stone without considering it in Ojibwe and acknowledging that the Anishinabe universe began with a conversation between stones."

Still, however grievous the loss of a language might be, how could people dare assume the job of reversing such patently inevitable forces? How would you even begin to go about it?

The Blackfeet Tribe of Montana was one of the first to take the initiative in Native language revival. Darrell Robes Kipp, raised on the reservation, an army veteran, and the holder of a master's in education from Harvard, realized when he came back home that the tribe had few speakers left, almost none under the age of fifty. In 1987 he and two other tribal members founded the Piegan Insti-tute, dedicated to researching and preserving the Blackfeet and other native languages. Knowing that more had to be done, Kipp and his colleagues traveled to Hawaii in 1994 to visit Pūnana Leo, America's first native language immersion school. Within two years, mightily inspired by the accomplishments of the Native Hawaiians, the Piegan Institute had opened Moccasin Flat School,

Darrell Robes Kipp with Blackfeet language school children. Photograph courtesy of Lynn Donaldson.

kindergarten through eighth grade. Two others, Cuts Wood and Lost Child schools, soon followed.

The three Blackfeet schools are immersion programs, the most demanding and effective method for children to learn a new language. Throughout the school day, students do their learning in Blackfeet; it is the medium of instruction and social communication, not a course. With the language, tribal history takes on a deeper meaning and context. Teachers regularly schedule field trips to traditional places, where elders can tell the old stories in their true tongue. The commitment among the Blackfeet to their tribe's schools runs strong; the waiting list (necessary because of financial limitations) holds 100 names. Darrell Kipp explained why tribal members are so supportive. "Same reason you don't burn down your libraries is why we keep our language. Our language is our library. And Blackfeet is totally unlike English, so it gives the child another thinking blueprint. For example, in Blackfeet, there is no gender, so the world can be suddenly seen in a different fashion." One of the students explained the attachment to the language in her own way: "People look up to us because we can speak Indian."

Nationally, in addition to the classes and research and Blackfeet Community College and the other tribal colleges, the tribal language movement now has in place about one hundred programs. Some are small, offering after-school or evening classes for children and adults, and some operate in tribal schools as bilingual-bicultural programs. A few public schools on or near reservations have established courses in a tribal language to meet the curriculum requirement of a second foreign language. The most ambitious approach, the full-blown immersion program for young people found at Blackfeet and Pūnana Leo, has been undertaken at Mohawk, Cherokee, Lac Courte Oreilles, Navajo, and several other tribes. Native educators are fortified by the knowledge that learning a tribal language brings the same intellectual benefits as learning a foreign language. Students of course learn English also, in society outside the immersion schools and in high school, since the immersion programs are preschool or K–8. Leanne Hinton, chair of the department of linguistics at the University of California at Berkeley, has observed that Native-speaking children have good foundations for college: "We know through their intense hard work and leadership that these systems work successfully to educate students to be literate and fluent in their ancestral language and accustomed to using it in daily communications and also literate and fluent in English, and fully prepared to go on to higher education in English-speaking institutions."

Even some of the most dispossessed tribes have taken on the task of language restoration. The Washoe Tribe of Nevada, for example, would seem a most unlikely candidate for such an effort. The center of the Washoe's existence was Lake Tahoe, one of the world's glory spots, but nineteenth-century settlers and commer-

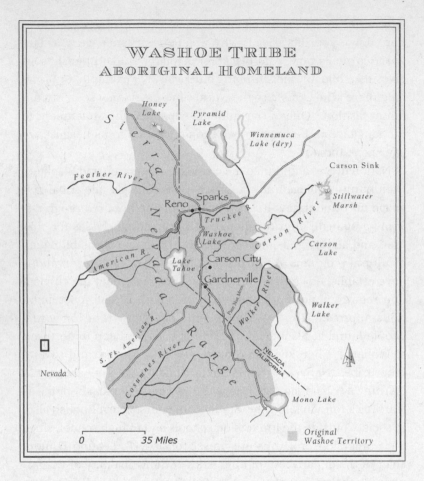

cial fishers quickly took it for its beauty and fishery. The gold rush in California and the silver strikes in Nevada overwhelmed Washoe territory to the west and east of Tahoe. In a flash the land was gone. That, and disease and poverty, led to predictions that the Washoe would soon be extinct.

The Washoe Tribe began to make breakthroughs. It gradually reacquired some land and adopted a constitution. It established hunting rights, and the ability to manage the deer herd, on the tribal land in the Pinenut Range through a court decision in 1980. Government grants provided funds for housing, a senior citizens' center, a new tribal building, and other tribal facilities. Then, when it had become ever clearer that their language, Washiw, was in free fall, the Washoe determined to take action. In 1997, in a small, unprepossessing tribal building in Gardnerville, Nevada, a group of Washoe elders and native language activists opened the doors of Washiw Wagayay Mangal, meaning "The House Where Washiw Is Spoken."

The Washoe tribal chairman, Brian Wallace, an intellectual who himself has taken community language classes, has been an unremitting advocate for the Washoe school, providing tribal financial support and pressing for congressional appropriations. He explains that for Native people their languages are "the baskets that cradle our culture" and that learning an indigenous language promotes the same kind of growth as instruction in Spanish or Japanese. The local language may not be as useful in the larger world, but—Wallace often cites the Catalan language of Spain as an example—it binds the community together and gives it pride. He likes to quote Benny Fillmore, a board member of Washiw Wagayay Mangal, who says that the Washoe school makes the children "twice as smart."

Quite so, but to make their languages healthy once again, the Washoe, the Blackfeet, and the growing number of other tribes with formal language programs face a monumental undertaking. Their schools all encounter difficulties meeting state accreditation standards. Certified teachers who speak the languages are rare, requiring extensive use of elders short of formal academic training. Adult as well as youth programs are needed. Course materials must be produced at all levels. Certainly not least is the matter of documentation: Elders need to be recorded, dictionaries and primers written, literature created, and works from other languages translated into Indian languages.

Almost all the schools struggle to find financial and human resources. Federal and foundation funding has helped but does not begin to meet all the needs. While language has become a priority, tribal budgets are strained and councils beset by many priorities; the list of pressing economic, social, and natural resource projects seems without end. Lack of funding, for instance, forced the Washoe Tribe to suspend its immersion school in 2003, although Washiw Wagayay Mangal continues an active program of language classes for children and elders. Rebuilding societies from the ground up is no enterprise for the half committed.

Still, the drive to preserve native languages continues to build. The gravity of the threat, and the sense of empowerment in Indian country to address it, are new; most of the formal programs started in the 1990s or later. The tribal colleges have emerged as crucial support bodies. Tribal radio stations broadcast programs in their own languages, and videos and CDs have been produced. The states are pitching in; some have adjusted their certification requirements, and Hawaii's constitution makes both English and Hawaiian the official state languages. Importantly, the academic community nationally has placed vastly greater emphasis on language loss during the past generation; one linguist observed, "[T]here has never, in my recollection, been such a universal upsurge of professional linguistic concern." With expanded research and course offerings in the universities, the number of formally trained specialists in Native American languages now exceeds 700.

Is there hope for native languages in the United States? Many experts would say no, or probably not. One of them is William Jacobsen, retired professor of linguistics at the University of Nevada, whose work helped The House Where Washiw Is Spoken through his book on Washoe grammar. Asked about the future of Washiw, he replied, "It's hopeless. Languages are dying like flies all over the place." We can understand his point. Basically, Indian-language revival faces the same forces that Indian culture faces across the board: the allure of television, the Internet, shopping malls, and Eminem.

Yet there is another course. Most experts agree that the future of Indian languages depends on the tribes themselves, on the will of Indian country. That gives cause for optimism. To those who see the tribal efforts as a passing fancy, Janine Pease, of the Crow Tribe, sighed: "Saying language programs are a fad is like saying tribal colleges were a fad thirty years ago. The work is much too difficult to be a fad." Brian Wallace, the tribal chairman from Washoe, explains his tribes' transformation to a dogged ethic of language preservation: "Whatever the future of Washiw Wagayay Mangal may be, it started a movement across the whole tribe. It showed us the cliff we were about to go over. Language repatriation has become a kind of natural thing. Now we know that we can think the way our ancestors thought only if we have the language. Now we know that the land is a caregiver, but we must be caretakers of the land and we can do that only if we can speak the language of the land, Washiw.

"Now the language effort has dispersed beyond the school to the communities, Dresslerville, Gardnerville, Woodfords, Stewart, Reno-Sparks. Now they have their own gatherings, which we call language circles. They have elders and others fluent in Washiw tutor the children after they get home from the public schools. They use the curricular materials from Washiw Wagayay Mangal, but now it's gone way beyond any institution."

We won't know the outcomes for a good while. But given the dignity of the destination, it is likely that few will regret the quest.

KAHO'OLAWE, one of the places where the modern Hawaiian movement first welled up, is the island the tourists don't know about. Eleven miles long and seven miles wide, it is graced with expanses of sand beaches and some thirty bays. The giving ocean waters teem with colorful Hawaiian sea life. After voyagers from Polynesia settled Kaho'olawe more than 1,000 years ago, the island drew relatively few residents, probably never more than a few hundred, because of its aridity; its high point of 1,477 feet, low compared with the volcanoes on other islands, does not catch many rain-bearing storms.

Although always small in permanent population, Kaho'olawe has a powerful religious significance. The island is the body form of Kanaloa, one of the Hawaiian Natives' four principal gods. Hawaiians have always considered it a *wahi pana*, or sacred place, and worshipers of Kanaloa traveled from other islands to hold ceremonies. Historian Edward Kahalele has explained the meaning of *wahi pana*: "The sacred places of Hawaii or wahi pana of Hawaii, were treated with great reverence and respect. These are places believed to have mana or spiritual power. . . . Our ancestors

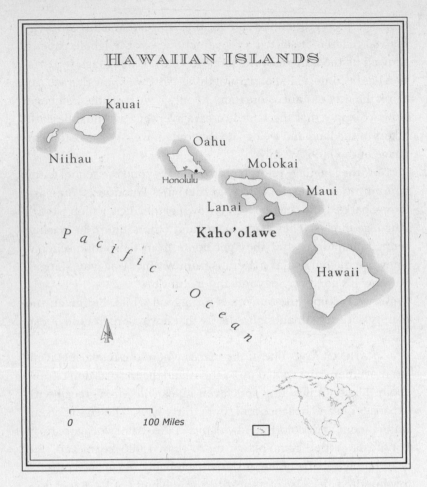

honored the earth and life as divine gifts of the gods. In fishing and farming wahi pana were respected. Their activities never encouraged or allowed overuse of the resources of the land or the sea. To do so would dishonor the gods. 'The earth must not be desecrated,' is a native Hawaiian value."

Desecration has nonetheless strafed across Kaho'olawe. Diseases carried by British and American settlers struck all of Hawaii's peoples, including those on Kaho'olawe. Wars waged by Hawaiian chiefs took still more lives. In the 1820s, when hard-driving missionaries had won over King Kamehameha II, the crackdown on

This lele *is found on Moa'ulaiki, the second highest point on Kaho'olawe. Here, annual offerings are made to Lono, Hawaiian god of agriculture, to seek his help in bringing back the island's native vegetation. Maui lies in the distance. Photograph by Franco Salmoiraghi.*

Native religion had driven practitioners from the sister islands to find refuge for their ceremonies on the more isolated Kaho'olawe.

The land suffered a cancerous insult in 1858. As part of the Great Mahele, a land distribution policy forced upon King Kamehameha III by Westerners to separate Hawaiians from their land, rancher Robert Wyllie obtained a lease to all of Kaho'olawe for a pittance. Eventually Wyllie and his sublessees let loose 9,000 sheep and 12,000 goats, which ripped out the grasses from most of the island and sent two million tons of soil to the low-lying areas, reefs, and coastal waters. Even today, the broad red swaths of bare soil are visible from Maui. Up close, the reddened landscape is hardpan, cut through with eroded-out gullies and ravines. It is as ruined as grazing land can get.

The bombing of Kaho'olawe by the United States military began in earnest in 1941, just seven months before Pearl Harbor. The bombardment started under a lease with the ranchers, but on December 8, 1941, one day after the Japanese attack, the army invoked martial law, ordered all persons off the island, and declared the whole of Kaho'olawe subject to military use. Stepped-up shelling came from the air and from navy destroyers and other ships practicing support for marine shore-landing maneuvers.

At war's end, Kaho'olawe enjoyed a lull in the bombing, but worse military injuries were still to come. In 1953 President Eisenhower issued an executive order setting the island aside for navy military purposes. Bombing activity intensified during the Korean and Vietnam wars. Uncounted tens of thousands of bombs fell over more than three decades, blasting huge craters, killing off vegetation, and tearing up the soils. Rusted, twisted skeletons of target vehicles—trucks and planes—dotted Kaho'olawe's landscape. The most dangerous legacy, however, was the unexploded ordnance, rocket-propelled grenades, Tiny Tim rockets, 100- and 250-pound bombs, and many others. All lay in wait on the surface, underneath it, and in the bays and coastal waters off the island.

NATIVE SOVEREIGNTY in Hawaii developed differently from Indian self-government on the mainland. During the nineteenth century the United States and other nations recognized the Kingdom of Hawaii through treaties and other international accords. Outside Western interests grew in influence, but as of the late nineteenth century, the kingdom was still acknowledged as an international sovereign. If there had been a United Nations, Hawaii would have been a member.

This came to a perfidious end in 1893, when U.S. officials in Hawaii conspired with sugar plantation owners and other commercial interests to overthrow the Hawaiian kingdom. The insurrectionists placed Queen Lili'uokalani—elegant, gentle composer of many songs, including the lilting Hawaiian love song, "Aloha Oe"—under house arrest in her palace. Interestingly, in this time of manifest destiny, President Grover Cleveland argued forcefully against the overthrow. In a message to Congress that described the overthrow as an "armed invasion," he called for the restoration of the Kingdom of Hawaii, asserting that the United States "[c]an not allow itself to refuse to redress an injury inflicted through an abuse of power by officers clothed with its authority and wearing its uniform; . . . the United States can not fail to vindicate its

honor and its sense of justice by an earnest effort to make all possible reparation."

It was to no avail. In 1898, with Cleveland out of office, Congress annexed the Hawaiian Islands by joint resolution. And to
this day Native Hawaiians still lack any sovereign government
recognized by the United States.

The modern Hawaiian movement, which began in the early
1970s, was propelled by powerful currents of culture and sovereignty, often blending together. When you spend time with
Hawaiians, you are swept away by the authenticity of their cul
ture and their devotion to it. The fire of Native identity and sovereignty burns as hot in Hawaii as anywhere in America.

On the cultural side, Hawaiians reacted to the rampaging development that swept over the Islands during the 1960s and 1970s.
New oceanfront hotels and luxury houses, which blocked access
to beaches and fishing grounds, disrupted traditional communities that revolve around fishing and taro farming. Inspired by the
national civil rights activity and the American Indian Movement,
Hawaiians mounted scores of protests on every island. These
activists aroused their share of critics, including some Natives, but
the cause received support across all color lines. Native Hawaiians
constitute close to 20 percent of the population. Their ancient culture is held in high respect by much of the state's citizenry. In
modern times the state legislature and courts of Hawaii, to a
degree not found in any other state, have recognized and supported an array of traditional rights relating to beach access, fishing, water, access to sacred sites, and language.

As for sovereignty, the overthrow of their government back in
1893 remained an open wound to Native Hawaiians in the 1970s.
They had to restore the honor of their Queen Lili'u, as Hawaiian
leader Mililani Trask sometimes refers to her. It was as though she
were still here, right in the next room, at the piano, playing and
composing her songs in the smooth, flowing island rhythms,
patiently awaiting the day when she would be called back to serve
the common people she loved so.

Kaho'olawe embodied all the injuries to the land, the culture,
and the sovereignty. On January 3, 1976, seven young men and

two women pushed off from Maui's Maʻalaea Beach and rowed their fishing boat toward Kahoʻolawe. They well knew that with the island under military rule, their landing violated federal law. Their leader was George Helm, a guitarist and singer of traditional Hawaiian music. His songs, sung with a soaring falsetto, can still be found in music stores.

Another was a young doctor named Noa Emmett Aluli. The years since have proved him a remarkable man. He has devoted himself to his medical practice, never remunerative, among the rural Hawaiian people of Molokaʻi. He has also given his adult life to the bombed-out, sheep-ravaged *wahi pana* of Kahoʻolawe, making visits by sea, bringing lawsuits, fighting then negotiating with military officials, testifying before Congress, and serving as the driving force behind the commissions that would chart the future course for the island.

But in January 1976 all of that lay ahead for the short, lithe Aluli, half bedside manner, half steel. On that first voyage he was still searching, wanting to learn more. He knew that Helm, raised in the traditional way on Molokaʻi, was the right teacher, by far the most grounded of all the voyagers in the many meanings of Kahoʻolawe. "Only George," Aluli said, "really understood why we were there." Helm made certain that the group respected all the customs. When Hawaiians approach an island in the traditional way, it is proper to ask permission to land. This is the chant composed for Kahoʻolawe:

Mele Komo	Request to Enter
He haki nu ʻanuʻa nei kai	Indeed a rough and crashing sea
ʻo ʻawa ana i uka.	Echoing into the uplands
Pehea e hiki aku ai?	How is it that the one lands?
ʻO ka leo	It is the voice
Mai paʻa I ka leo	Please don't hold back the voice.

The government kept tight security on the island. Upon landing, seven of the group were promptly arrested and taken back to Maui. Aluli and Walter Ritter, somehow avoiding capture, hiked Kahoʻolawe for two days before turning themselves in. Aluli remembered vividly both the profane and the sacred: "The ordnance was everywhere. Everywhere. But we could see the beauty and the culture also. We were so fortunate to be there."

The group called itself the Protect Kaho'olawe 'Ohana (*'ohana* means "family" in Hawaiian). Steadily growing, the 'Ohana made another landing two weeks later, and many others to follow, always to pray and give honor to Kanaloa. Lawsuits landed in federal court: one from the 'Ohana (Aluli was the plaintiff) against the navy to halt the bombing and to allow the religious exercises, one from the United States for criminal trespass. The litigation affirmed the right of 'Ohana members to exercise their religion. In a seminal victory for Hawaiians, Judge William Schwarzer approved a consent decree allowing access by Hawaiian practitioners four days each month and requiring a stop to the bombing during those times. Otherwise the bombing continued.

In 1987 and 1988 I met on Oahu with Hawaiian leaders from the different islands. By then, having established a good measure of support in the state, they had begun to set an agenda for the Hawaiian movement. Priorities included the recognition of Native Hawaiian sovereignty, the protection of traditional beach access rights, and the environmental restoration of Kaho'olawe and transfer of the island to a new Native government. The issue of sovereignty had a divisive edge to it, which continues. Some Hawaiians argue that the Natives should accept only full-blown international sovereignty; the Kingdom of Hawaii possessed those powers and was wrongfully overthrown, and modern Hawaiians should accept nothing less. Others see the rectitude of that position yet pragmatically support a "nation within a nation" model similar to the status of mainland tribes.

I had expected the spirit and sense of momentum on those issues. What took me aback was the primacy the Hawaiians placed on receiving an apology from the United States for the overthrow of Queen Lili'uokalani and her kingdom in 1893. Hawaiians took that as a slight to the queen and all Hawaiians, then and now. They passionately insisted that the apology be listed as the first priority. Acknowledgment of that wrong was required as a matter of morality and propriety; in addition, an understanding of the overthrow would lay a foundation for the rights to land, sovereignty, and culture they also cherished.

Hawaiians have made progress few would have predicted when the protests began in the 1970s. In a unique gesture, Congress indeed issued in 1993 an unconditional apology to the Hawaiian people for the overthrow of the kingdom, along with a lengthy and historically accurate explanation of the sordid incident. As of 2004, Hawaiian leaders, working closely with Senator Daniel Inouye and other members of the Hawaiian delegation, are apparently close to achieving enactment of legislation that would lead to a sovereign Hawaiian government, with powers analogous to the mainland tribes. The measure passed the House of Representatives in 2002 only to be stalled in the Senate by one senator who put a "hold" on the bill. A similar bill, which is expected to pass in time, has since been introduced by Senator Daniel Akaka of Hawaii.

In some ways most remarkable of all, Kahoʻolawe is being put right—as a physical landscape and as a *wahi pana*, the spiritual place of Kanaloa. In 1990 the first President Bush answered the calls of Native Hawaiians, and many other residents activated by the Protect Kahoʻolawe ʻOhana, by ordering a halt to the bombing. Congress then chartered the Kahoʻolawe Island Conveyance Commission to study the feasibility of restoring the island and conveying it to the state of Hawaii. The 1993 commission report, rich in its treatment of Hawaiian culture (Aluli served as commission vice-chair), recommended full-scale environmental restoration and transfer to the state. The commission also took the bold step of recommending that the state set the land and surrounding ocean aside "exclusively for the study and practice of traditional and contemporary Native Hawaiian culture" with strict environmental protections.

This was not a report to be filed away and forgotten. Congress authorized $400 million for the cleanup. The United States has transferred Kahoʻolawe to the state. The state in turn has passed a law mandating that the island be used exclusively for traditional Hawaiian culture. The Hawaiian legislature, at the urging of

Natives, went even farther than Congress or the commission by directing that the state shall transfer Kahoʻolawe to a sovereign Native government once it is established. One sadness persists. George Helm, whose voice in song and activism inspired the revival of an island and the chants and ceremonies organic with it, died in 1977 in choppy seas returning from Kahoʻolawe with Kimo Mitchell, a colleague in the Protect Kahoʻolawe ʻOhana.

I had long wanted to visit Kahoʻolawe. Finally, in 2002, I went there along with two of my sons, David and Ben, courtesy of the Kahoʻolawe Island Reserve Commission. KIRC, the state agency in charge of managing the island, is staffed mostly by Hawaiians. Collette Machado, an ʻOhana member, is now the commission chair, having succeeded Aluli. After crossing from Maui on a 40-passenger military helicopter, we toured the island by Jeep and on foot. I have so many impressions. One is the sheer magnitude of the cleanup effort, which is heavy industry all the way: stacks of unexploded ordnance waiting to be trucked down to the docking facility to be taken out by barge; junk heaps of blasted-apart target vehicles; all manner of trucks far too heavy, noisy, and dusty for a sacred place. Cleaning up a bombing range is dangerous, nasty business.

Another kind of effort proceeds at the same time. KIRC staffers, along with religious practitioners and other volunteers, have been carrying out the laborious process of reestablishing native vegetation destroyed by the sheep, goats, and bombs. They are making some headway. Pili and other grasses have spread out over some slopes and plantings of shrubs, kawelu, and aweoweo have taken hold. Every year the hardpan gives way by a few acres. The bombing did not get all the ceremonial sites. I saw two shrines that remain intact, mountaintop circles of rocks where Hawaiians say chants to greet the sunrise.

It was a long day, dusty and hot, tiring. Of course the real work has been done by thousands of people putting in their long days, journeying to the island in violation of federal law, traveling to Washington, D.C., sitting through tedious meetings, gingerly searching for ordnance, sprinkling seeds and planting shrubs, learning and speaking the chants. This is going to take a very long time—Dr. Noa Emmett Aluli has told me quietly, "I realize that this will not be finished during my lifetime"—but because of a kind of dedication that cannot fully be understood by the Western mind, the outcome now is assured. The day will come when Kahoʻolawe will once again be Kahoʻolawe.

SO MANY tribes, so many stories. The state of Indian culture and sovereignty, the state of the future, can be understood only through many stories from many places. One from Quinault, the Olympic Peninsula ocean and river people, is among the most telling I know.

In the 1980s, with pride in Quinault culture surging, Phillip Martin had a conversation with Emmett Oliver. Both were tribal members, Phillip in his fifties at the time, Emmett a generation older. Emmett raised the idea of building an ocean canoe. He said that other tribes in the Pacific Northwest were thinking about bringing back the canoes and that the Quinault ought to join in.

Emmett's suggestion inflamed Phillip. All the Quinault knew about these canoes of legend, hallmarks of coast Indian culture along with the totem poles. Historically, the Quinault had two classes of canoe: large, durable ocean canoes and lighter, lower, more maneuverable river craft. The ocean canoes, in particular, lay at the heart of tribal existence. Quinault people depended on the ocean's bounty of seafood. The coast tribes engaged in a thriving trade economy that, without the canoes, would have been thwarted by the thick forests, with their big trees and dense brush, and the mountains, steep valleys, and deep rivers. Nor would land travel have allowed the extensive socializing among the tribes of the region.

Specialized canoe carvers, trained by their ancestors, built the ocean canoes. They used giant cedar logs, known for their strength, buoyancy, and resistance to decay. The craft, as large as fifty feet long and eight feet wide, could transport up to 10,000 pounds of cargo, such as fish, seal, and whale. Able to withstand the powerful ocean swells, they made it possible to travel up and down the coast, especially north to British Columbia to trade and visit with sister tribes.

In addition to their utility, the ocean canoes were works of art. What a sight they made, gliding into a harbor, manned by eight or more pullers with their paddles synchronized: colorful, finely crafted vessels with sweeping, graceful lines rising up to the decorative sterns and bows.

Yet events took their toll. Whaling declined. Overland routes were constructed to transport freight. The Bureau of Indian Affairs exerted pressure to jettison cultural ways. When Phillip Martin and Emmett Oliver had their discussion in the 1980s, a few Quinault river canoes could still be seen, but not the ocean canoes. Employed continuously for thousands of years, they had gone out of use by the 1940s.

Phillip remembered the ocean vessels well. His uncle had taken him, just seven or eight then, out on the waters up and down the Olympic Peninsula in the family sealing canoe. He had seen many others, and the images stuck in his mind.

But he had no idea how to make one, nor did anyone else at Quinault, for none of the carvers was still alive. Along with fellow tribesmen Guy Capoeman and Shakey Jackson, Phillip started going to museums to examine ocean canoes on exhibit, even to Ivar's Restaurant in Seattle, which has a fine specimen hung from the ceiling. Then he came across Steve Brown, a curator at the University of Washington's Burke Museum of Natural History and Culture. Brown, a non-Indian, had not only studied the ocean canoes of the Northwest tribes as an academic but actually learned how to carve them. And Brown gave generously of his time, traveling down to Taholah to pass on his knowledge about the intricate process of constructing ocean canoes in the traditional way.

Phillip, Guy, Shakey, and other tribal members, calling themselves the Quinault Canoe Club, went to work. They found a downed 700-year-old cedar, split it, cut it into lengths, and let it dry. Intending to build two vessels, with much elbow grease they hollowed out two long sections, for each canoe was essentially one piece. They attached the stern and bow and seats for the pullers. Employing no nails, they instead pounded in 50 to 60 dowels per canoe. Finally, they carved designs into the canoes and painted them, with red the dominant color. Phillip had not been counting, but when I asked him, he estimated that in total the labor required about 2,000 man-hours.

By this time the Quinault had a clear objective: the Canoe Journey of 1994. Emmett Oliver, who first presented the ocean canoe idea to Phillip Martin, had been busy with other tribes as well. As newly carved canoes were launched, Emmett and others decided to revive an ancient traditional practice, of having an annual gathering of all canoe tribes. This included the tribes of British Columbia because for millennia—long before any United States–Canada border line—the tribes of the two nations had had extensive commercial, social, and family relationships. During the deadening years, though, the contacts had waned, and they did not rekindle until recent times, with tribal nationalism rising on both sides of the border. One part of that renewal took place in 1989: the reinitiation of the annual summer gathering, now called the Canoe Journey, of American and commonwealth canoes. Seattle hosted the event, and it was a wild success.

By 1994 the Quinault had made two canoes ocean-ready, the *May-ee* (meaning "the new beginning") and *Tso-Kapoo* ("wolf coat"). That year the Canoe Journey would be held in Victoria, on Vancouver Island. They decided to paddle up on the *Tso-Kapoo*, 39 feet long with ten pullers and a captain, and a skiff that served as a supply boat.

"It was a bright, clear summer morning. Guy Capoeman was the captain, and I was handling the supply boat," remembers David Martin, Phillip's son and former vice-president of the Quinault Indian Nation. "When we got past Queets, the weather kicked up on us. By the time we got to the mouth of the Hoh River, we were facing swells of probably four to six feet. We had to wait off the mouth of the Hoh to see if conditions would get better.

"They never did, so we decided to spend the night on the shore of the Hoh River. But the mouth of the Hoh is rocky, different than down here, different currents. We made one run but couldn't make it in. On the second try we got in trouble, got caught in a sleeper, got sideways.

QUINAULT CANOE JOURNEY
ROUTE

Vancouver Island
BRITISH COLUMBIA

Sooke
Victoria

Strait of Juan de Fuca

Neah
Bay

Pacific
Ocean

Olympic
Mountains

Soleduck River

Elwah River

Hoh River

Queets R.

Queets

Quinault R.

Quinault

Taholah

0   20 Miles

Washington

"We had to abandon the canoe. We all had life jackets, and we all made it in except one, who got caught in a rip current and got knocked unconscious. When we got to him in the skiff, he had no energy to get in, but we pulled him up.

"When we got back to the shore, the canoe came back to the beach in pieces."

The people were distraught, some crying, some walking around retrieving paddles and pieces of the canoe, some just staring out at sea. Capoeman, the captain, was "devastated," carrying responsibility for the voyage, blaming himself, although the events were beyond his or anyone else's control. Finally, exhausted, they lay down on the beach, some people resting their heads on neighbors' backsides. Everyone went quiet, half asleep or contemplating the wreckage.

Then one of the pullers split the silence wide open. An athletic young woman named Phoebe Bryan, "one hundred pounds soaking wet," according to Phillip Martin, jumped to her feet and shouted, "*Well!* Are we going to go back and get that other canoe or *what?*"

Two days later the oceangoers headed out on another beautiful summer morning, this time aboard the slightly smaller *May-ee*, fitted out with eight pullers. They paddled up the western side of the Olympic Peninsula and turned east at Makah to the mouth of the Elwah. From there, they rode the "Canoe Trail," a current in the Strait of Juan de Fuca, well known to Indian people, that carries vessels over to the harbor at Sooke, near Victoria. On the way across they hit even worse weather, swells of six to eight feet.

But the *May-ee* made it. When the Quinault paddled into Victoria Harbor, an assemblage was there to welcome them. "What a scene!" exclaimed an excited Phillip Martin, by then in his sixties, as he witnessed a dream he had helped make come true. "There might have been three thousand people out on the docks, screaming and cheering, applauding, taking pictures as we came in. I mean it. What a scene!"

In 2002 the Quinault Indian Nation enthusiastically hosted the Canoe Journey, a three-day celebration with a potlatch, games, and dancing. By then the *Tso-Kapoo* had been put back together with dowels and made seaworthy, and a third ocean canoe was in the water. Carvers would soon be working on a fourth, named in honor of Phillip Martin. An estimated 5,000 people from the United States and Canada came to Taholah that year to celebrate the canoes, the ocean, the salmon people. Natalie Charlie observed, "To see the canoes together asking for permission to come ashore in Taholah, it was like for the day time turned back. You were back to when our ancestors were inviting visitors to come eat and celebrate with us. It's really hard to describe that feeling."

And so yet another piece of the old fabric had been woven back together, different now but also the same.

*The captain and pullers of the Quinault Indian Nation, at sea in the May-ee,
approach the landing area in the Quileute village of LaPush on their way to the
intertribal Canoe Journey held in August 2002 in Taholah, the home of the Quinault Indian Nation. The Quinault crew had paddled up the coast to meet other
canoes so that they could come into Taholah with colleagues from other tribes.
Photograph courtesy of Debbie Preston, Northwest Indian Fisheries Commission.*

CODA
The Outlook

Indian people still have many miles to walk before their reservations are the secure and prosperous homelands, places of both modernity and tradition, that they want them to be. Many tribes have yet to turn the corner economically. Difficult health and social problems remain. The highest court too often abdicates its traditional role as the final protector of minority rights.

Nor can we turn away from the most fundamental question of all: Can the Indian voice endure?

For more than 500 years, white society on this continent has discussed how long it would be before Indian people finally disappeared into the general society. Not if, but when. In a generation? Three? Five?

But now we have data: five centuries of survival under the most excruciating pressure of killing diseases, wars, land expropriation, and official government policy—forced assimilation, then outright termination. Yet the tribes are now the strongest they have been in a century and a half. Never has this land seen such staying power.

I don't know what "forever" means. But I believe that tribal people will be planting their corn seeds in the red southwestern soil; taking the big chinook from the Northwest's rivers; knocking wild rice from the stalks in the shallow lakes of the upper Midwest; singing the old songs and dancing the old dances; providing for the economic, social, and spiritual well-being of their members; and gently urging a deeper land ethic upon all the people—I believe they will be doing those things across the enduring landscape of Indian country *forever.*

NOTES

CHAPTER 1: Indian Country, August 1953

3 *Roger Jourdain.* Roger Jourdain, interviews with author, Bemidji, Minnesota, March 23–24, 2001. Some of Jourdain's early construction work included working on Alaska's highway systems as well as projects in and around Red Lake. The union politics and connections he made through this work helped him become a tribal leader. Jim Parsons, "Critics Don't Quell Jourdain's Quest to Keep Red Lake Post," *Minneapolis–St. Paul Star-Tribune*, p. 1A (May 22, 1990); Chuck Haga, "Roger Jourdain 1912–2002," *Minneapolis–St. Paul Star-Tribune*, p. 1A (March 23, 2002).

4 *Unemployment generally.* Unemployment at Red Lake ran well above 50 percent. A congressional subcommittee study done in 1950 found just 151 jobs, probably including part-time employment, leaving 60 percent of the work force unemployed. House Committee on Public Lands, Subcommittee on Indian Affairs, "Compilation of Material Relating to the Indians of the United States and the Territory of Alaska, Including Certain Laws and Treaties Affecting Such Indians," 81st Congress, 2d Session, p. 729 (Washington, DC: U.S. Government Printing Office, 1950) [hereinafter "Compilation"]. On social conditions for Minnesota Indians in the 1950s generally, see State of Minnesota, Governor's Human Rights Commission, "Minnesota Indian Workers: A Survey Analysis" (St. Paul: State of Minnesota, Governor's Human Rights Commission, 1957); State of Minnesota, Governor's Human Rights Commission, "Minnesota Indians: Yesterday and Today" (St. Paul: State of Minnesota, Governor's Human Rights Commission, 1959); State of Minnesota, Interim Commission of Indian Affairs, "Report of the 1958 Interim Commission on Indian Affairs to the Hon. Orville L. Freeman, Governor of Minnesota, and the Members of the Minnesota Legislature" (St. Paul: State of Minnesota, Interim Commission of Indian Affairs, 1959).

4 *Fewer than 100 people.* League of Women Voters of Minnesota, *Indians in Minnesota*, p. 40 (Minneapolis: League of Women Voters of Minnesota, 1962).

4   *$1,250.* "Compilation," p. 730.

4   *$3,200.* U.S. Department of Commerce, Bureau of the Census, "Historical Statistics of the United States: Colonial Times to 1970," Bicentennial Edition, pt. 2, p. 297 (Washington, DC: U.S. Government Printing Office, 1975) [hereinafter "Historical Statistics"].

4   *Living conditions at Red Lake.* Jourdain, interview; Kathryn Beaulieu, interview with author, Red Lake Reservation, Minnesota, March 23, 2001; Cellestine Maas, interview with author, Bemidji, Minnesota, March 24, 2001.

4   *"we had running water."* Jourdain, interview.

5   *the freedom it brings them.* On the land and daily living, see three most useful books, Project Preserve, *To Walk the Red Road: Memories of the Red Lake Ojibwe People* (Red Lake, MN: Red Lake Board of Education, 1989); Project Preserve, *We Choose to Remember: More Memories of the Red Lake Ojibwe People* (Red Lake, MN: Red Lake Board of Education, 1991); Charles Brill, *Red Lake Nation: Portraits of Ojibway Life* (Minneapolis: University of Minnesota Press, 1992). During my interviews in 2001, Roger Jourdain, Kathryn Beaulieu, and Larry Stillday also offered insights into the relationship between the people of Red Lake and the lands around them.

5   *Most families kept home gardens. See, e.g.*, Project Preserve, *To Walk*, pp. 45, 59, 76, 81, 82, 84; Project Preserve, *We Choose*, pp. 2, 91.

6   *Nonetheless, in the 1950s.* Beaulieu, interview; Maas, interview.

6   *"The BIA and the missions."* Jourdain, interview.

6   *"They were a bunch of bums."* Ibid.

7   *"no sense of entitlement."* Larry Stillday, interview with author, Red Lake reservation, Minnesota, March 23, 2001.

7   *"You talk about losing land."* Ibid.

7   *"It was a confusing time."* Ibid.

7   *Pine Ridge.* On the Pine Ridge Reservation in the years after World War II, see generally Murray L. Wax et al., *Formal Education in an American Indian Community*, pp. 15–19 (Kalamazoo, MI: Society for the Study of Social Problems, Monograph, 1964); Will H. Spindler, *Tragedy Strikes at Wounded Knee: And Other Essays on Indian Life in South Dakota and Nebraska*, pp. 77–81 (Vermillion, SD: Dakota Press, 1985); Thomas Biolsi, *Organizing the Lakota: The Political Economy of the New Deal on the Pine Ridge and Rosebud Reservations* (Tucson: University of Arizona Press, 1992); Raymond J. De Mallie, "Pine Ridge Economy: Cultural and Historical Perspectives," *in* Sam Stanley, ed., *American Indian Economic Development*, pp. 260–93 (The Hague: Mouton Publishers, 1978). Also helpful were interviews conducted at Pine Ridge. Mario Gonzales, interview with Matt O'Malley, research assistant, Rapid City, South Dakota, Aug. 3, 2001; Thomas Short Bull, interview with Matt O'Malley, research assistant, Pine Ridge, South Dakota, June 26, 2001.

7   *"Mother's heart."* The source of this quote, as well as a good narrative on the Black Hills, is Frank Pommersheim, "Black Hills," *in* Mary B. Davis, ed.,

Native America in the Twentieth Century: An Encyclopedia, p. 73 (New York: Garland Publishing, 1994).

8   *Sioux treaties and the Black Hills. See generally* Roxanne Dunbar Ortiz, *The Great Sioux Nation: Sitting in Judgment on America* (New York: American Indian Treaty Council Information Center; Berkeley, CA: Moon Books, 1977); Edward Lazarus, *Black Hills, White Justice* (New York: HarperCollins Publishers, 1991); Frank Pommersheim, "Making All the Difference: Native American Testimony and the Black Hills," vol. 69, no. 2 *North Dakota Law Review,* p. 337 (1993).

9   *" 'The Company.' "* Wax et al., "Formal Education," p. 18.

9   *rates well below market value.* Janet A. McDonnell, *The Dispossession of the American Indian, 1887–1934,* pp. 60–61, 66–67 (Bloomington: Indiana University Press, 1991).

9   *"you'd need permission."* Gonzales, interview; *see also* Biolsi, *Organizing,* pp. 16, 117–18, 168–69; McDonnell, *The Dispossession,* pp. 60–70.

9   *"Back then."* Personal communication from Marla Powers received by Matt O'Malley, research assistant (date unknown); *see also* Biolsi, *Organizing,* pp. 16–17.

9   *"when we heard drums."* Fergus M. Bordewich, *Killing the White Man's Indian: Reinventing Native Americans at the End of the Twentieth Century,* p. 224 (New York: Doubleday, 1996).

10 *Every Monday.* Joe Starita, *The Dull Knifes of Pine Ridge: A Lakota Odyssey,* p. 257 (New York: G. P. Putnam's Sons, 1995).

10 *Sun Dance.* For general information on Sun Dance, see William K. Powers, *Oglala Religion* (Lincoln: University of Nebraska Press, 1977).

10 *One experienced Sun Dancer.* Personal communication received by Michelle Roche, research assistant (complete date unknown, 2000).

10 *Sun Dance ceremony.* Powers, *Oglala Religion,* pp. 95–100. For photographs of Sun Dance, see Thomas E. Mails, *Sundancing: The Great Sioux Piercing Ritual* (Tulsa, OK: Council Oak Books, 1998).

11 *"Every time a break."* Sarah Olden, "The People of Tipi Sapa," *in* Vine Deloria, Jr., *Singing for a Spirit: A Portrait of the Dakota Sioux,* p. 197 (Santa Fe, NM: Clear Light Publishers, 1999). For other methods of piercing, see David Little Elk, *Wicoh'an Otehike (The Difficult Path): An Itazipco Version of Lakota Existence,* p. 101 (Dupree, SD: Hehaka7 Productions, 1987).

11 *outlawed Sun Dance.* On the ban and the eventual lifting of Sun Dance, see Clyde Holler, *Black Elk's Religion: The Sun Dance and Lakota Catholicism,* pp. 110–38 (Syracuse, NY: Syracuse University Press, 1995); Mails, *Sundancing,* pp. 2–9, and the authorities cited there; Powers, *Oglala Religion,* p. 139.

11 *Wounded Knee.* On the massacre at Wounded Knee, see Angie Debo, *A History of the Indians of the United States,* pp. 292–94 (Norman: University of Oklahoma Press, 1970); James H. McGregor, *The Wounded Knee Massacre: From the Viewpoint of the Sioux* (Rapid City, SD: Fenske Printing, 1987); Dee

388 Notes

Brown, *Bury My Heart at Wounded Knee: An Indian History of the American West*, pp. 415–46 (New York: Holt, Rinehart and Winston, 1975); Robert M. Utley, *The Last Days of the Sioux Nation*, pp. 200–30 (New Haven, CT: Yale University Press, 1974).

11   *the Sioux kept it alive. See, e.g.*, Mails, *Sundancing*, pp. 3–9; Rick Williams, interview with author, Denver, Colorado, July 30, 2003.

12   *"I went to St. Louis."* Personal communication from Sadie Janis received by Matt O'Malley, research assistant, Pine Ridge, South Dakota, Aug. 4, 2001.

13   *Rations.* On rations, see Biolsi, *Organizing*, p. 113.

13   *Quinault Nation.* On the Quinault generally, see Pauline K. Capoeman, ed., *Land of the Quinault*, 2d ed. (Taholah, WA: Quinault Indian Nation, 1991); Gary Morishima and Larry Workman, *Portrait of Our Land: A Quinault Tribal Forestry Perspective* (Taholah, WA: Quinault Indian Nation, Department of Natural Resources, 1978); Hal Neumann et al., *The Forests of the Quinault: Forest Management on the Quinault Indian Reservation, 1855–1996* (Missoula, MT: Heritage Research Center, 1997); Frank C. Fickeisen, *The Quinaults, Their Land, Their Waters* (Portland, OR: American Friends Service Committee, 1971).

13   *"I remember it vividly."* Phillip Martin, interview with author, Taholah, Washington, Dec. 28, 2001.

13   *family income amounted. Compare* House Committee on Interior and Insular Affairs, Subcommittee on Indian Affairs, "Statistical Charts Regarding the Indians of the United States," 82d Congress, 2d Session, p. 4 (Washington, DC: U.S. Government Printing Office, 1952) [hereinafter "1952 Statistical Charts"] (Quinault family income of $2,160 in 1950) *with* "Historical Statistics," p. 297 (State of Washington family income of $3,523 in 1949).

13   *"We knew, of course."* Pearl Capoeman-Baller, interview with author, Taholah, Washington, Dec. 18, 2001.

14   *some 200 jobs.* "Compilation," pp. 790, 792.

15   *Taholah had two churches.* Capoeman-Baller, interview; Phillip Martin, interview; Francis McCrory, interview with author, Taholah, Washington, Dec. 19, 2001.

16   *Quinault allotments.* On allotment and forest management at Quinault, see Neumann et al., *The Forests.* On allotment generally, see also the discussion of allotment at the Nez Perce Reservation, *infra* ch. 2, pp. **47–51**.

17   *"When I came back."* David Martin, interview with author, Taholah, Washington, Dec. 18, 2001.

18   *The U.S. Bureau of Sports Fisheries and Wildlife.* Neumann et al., *The Forests*, pp. 232–33.

18   *The Army Corps. Ibid.*, p. 234.

18   *"the Bureau of Indian Affairs." Ibid.*, p. 217 (quoting E. Wayne Chapman, Area Road Engineer, Sacramento Area Office, memorandum to Commissioner of Indian Affairs, Bureau of Indian Affairs, "Re: Logging Roads—Quinault Reservation" [March 24, 1972]).

18   *"it is a known fact."* Joint Hearings Before the Senate Committee on Interior and Insular Affairs, Special Subcommittee on the Legislative Oversight Function, and the House Government Operations Committee, Subcommittee on Public Works and Resources, "Federal Timber Sale Policies," 84th Congress, 1st Session, pt. 2, p. 1635 (Nov. 28, 1955) (Washington, DC: U.S. Government Printing Office, 1956) (cited in *Mitchell v. United States*, 10 Cl. Ct. 63, 68 [1986]).

18   *"I think it is a very sorry situation."* Senate Committee on Interior and Insular Affairs, Subcommittee on Indian Affairs, "Timber Sales—Quinaielt [sic] Indian Reservation," 85th Congress, 1st Session, p. 170 (Apr. 15, 1957) (Washington, DC: U.S. Government Printing Office, 1957); *see also* House Report No. 2960, "Federal Timber Sales Policies· Thirty-first Intermediate Report of the Committee on Government Operations," 84th Congress, 2d Session, pp. 15–16 (Washington, DC: U.S. Government Printing Office, 1956) (suggesting that continuing the timber practices of the time "could constitute a serious breach of trust by the Federal Government").

19   *Public Law 280.* On Public Law 280, see generally Carole E. Goldberg, "Public Law 280: The Limits of State Jurisdiction over Reservation Indians," vol. 22 *U.C.L.A. Law Review*, p. 535 (Feb. 1975); *Bryan v. Itasca County*, 426 U.S. 373 (1976). Much later, decisions held that tribal courts could continue to exercise concurrent jurisdiction with state courts in Public Law 280 states. *See, e.g., Walker v. Rushing*, 898 F.2d 672 (8th Cir. 1990). In practice, however, once Public Law 280 went into effect and state police and judges had jurisdiction, tribal courts became inactive. In the case of Washington, Public Law 280 allowed the state to assume jurisdiction over reservations unilaterally.

19   *Washington law.* On the procedures for assumption of state jurisdiction under Public Law 280, see Goldberg, "Public Law 280," pp. 563–75.

19   *"it was a pretty hectic time."* Francis Rosander, interview with author, Taholah, Washington, Dec. 19, 2001.

19   *"Our sovereignty is sacred to us."* Phillip Martin, interview.

19   *Three separate times. State v. Bertrand*, No. 50,082, mem. dec. 167, 174 (Super. Ct. Wash. Grays Harbor County filed Dec. 15, 1959); *see also* Minutes of Special Meeting of Quinault General Council, p. 5 (Feb. 1, 1958) (on file with author).

20   *"I have strong reason to believe."* *Bertrand*, p. 168. For later decisions on the matter of Public Law 280 at Quinault, see *Quinault Tribe v. Gallagher*, 368 F.2d 648 (9th Cir. 1966); *State v. Bertrand*, 378 P.2d 427 (Wash. 1963); *Comenout v. Burdman*, 525 P.2d 217 (Wash. 1974).

20   *State game officials.* An important and thorough work on the confrontations between tribes and the state of Washington over fishing rights is American Friends Service Committee, *Uncommon Controversy: Fishing Rights of the Muckleshoot, Puyallup, and Nisqually Indians* (Seattle: University of Washington Press, 1970).

20   *ugly confrontations at off-reservation sites.* Phillip Martin, interview; McCrory, interview; Rosander, interview.

20   *At least one Quinault fisherman was shot at.* Rosander, interview.

20   *a main reason.* Phillip Martin, interview; McCrory, interview; Rosander, interview.

21   *The Bureau.* On the BIA during this era, see generally Kenneth R. Philp, *Termination Revisited: American Indians on the Trail to Self-Determination, 1933–1953* (Lincoln: University of Nebraska Press, 1999); Alvin M. Josephy, Jr., *Now That the Buffalo's Gone: A Study of Today's American Indians*, pp. 217–58 (New York: Alfred A. Knopf, 1982); Edgar S. Cahn, ed., *Our Brother's Keeper: The Indian in White America*, pp. 141–73 (Washington, DC: New Community Press, 1969).

21   *"When I got on the council."* Earl Old Person, telephone interview with Heather Corson, research assistant, Sept. 27, 2001.

22   *"Agents of the Bureau of Indian Affairs."* Josephy, *Buffalo's Gone*, p. 87.

22   *"During this time."* Old Person, interview.

22   *Life expectancy.* Hearing Before the House Committee on Interior and Insular Affairs, Subcommittee on Indian Affairs, "A Review of the Indian Health Program," 88th Congress, 1st Session, p. 21 (May, 23, 1963) (Washington, DC: U.S. Government Printing Office, 1963).

22   *Infant mortality.* David H. Getches et al., *Cases and Materials on Federal Indian Law*, 4th ed., p. 17 (St. Paul, MN: West Group, 1998).

22   *Children stayed away.* "Compilation," p. 691. According to figures from the 1950 Census, only about 67 percent of all Indian children between the ages of five and thirteen were enrolled in school. This percentage is well below the national average of school enrollment for the same age-group at that time of 82 percent. U.S. Department of Commerce, Bureau of the Census, vol. 4, pt. 5 "U.S. Census of Population: 1950," Special Reports, Chapter B, Education, p. 5B-26 (Washington, DC: U.S. Government Printing Office, 1953).

22   *Less than 5 percent of Indian people held high school degrees.* According to estimates compiled by the BIA in 1950, there were fewer than 15,000 Indian high school graduates out of an estimated total Indian population of 360,000. "Compilation," pp. 641–875.

22   *Of course, still far fewer entered higher education.* The BIA in 1950 estimated fewer than fifteen hundred Indian college graduates in 1950. "Compilation," pp. 641–875. The statistics are cloudy, however, because of the lack of studies during this era. One scholarly work noted that "in 1957, some crude figures support an estimate that there were about two thousand Indian students in colleges and other post-secondary school institutions." Estelle Fuchs and Robert J. Havighurst, *To Live on This Earth: American Indian Education*, p. 261 (Garden City, NY: Doubleday and Co., 1972). Margaret Connell Szasz notes that in 1961, the first year that such information was mentioned in the annual reports of the BIA, sixty-six Indians graduated from four-year college institutions. *Education and the American Indian: The Road to Self-Determination Since 1928*, p. 134 (Albuquerque: University of New Mexico

Press, 1999). Whatever the exact numbers, it is clear that there were very few Indian people studying and graduating from postsecondary institutions in the early 1950s.

22   *The number of Indian lawyers.* Nearly a generation later there were only a dozen lawyers. *See* Rennard Strickland, "Redeeming Centuries of Dishonor: Legal Education and the American Indian," vol. 1970, no. 3 *University of Toledo Law Review*, pp. 861–66 (1970). In a study published in 1980, Dean Chavers, then of Bacone College, noted that a Ford Foundation report from 1971 found only eighteen Indians holding Ph.D.'s in the United States at that time. "Isolation and Drainoff: The Case of the American Indian Educational Researcher," vol. 9 *Educational Researcher*, p. 12 (Oct. 1980). Like the data for Indians in postsecondary institutions, the information regarding Indians in postgraduate institutions is incomplete.

22   *Median income.* Alan L. Sorkin, "Trends in Employment and Earnings of American Indians," *in* Joint Congressional Economic Committee, Subcommittee on Economy in Government, "Toward Economic Development for Native American Communities: A Compendium of Papers," 91st Congress, 1st Session, p. 115 (Washington, DC: U.S. Government Printing Office, 1969) (citing U.S. Department of Commerce, Bureau of the Census, "U.S. Census of Population: 1950," Special Reports, "Characteristics of the Nonwhite Population by Race," p. 32, tbl. 10, p. 72, tbl. 21 (Washington, DC: U.S. Government Printing Office, 1953) (the cited figures are for 1949).

22   *The unemployment rate.* Alan L. Sorkin, *American Indians and Federal Aid*, p. 12 (Washington, DC: Brookings Institution, 1971) (citing House Committee on Interior and Insular Affairs, "Indian Unemployment Survey: A Memorandum and Accompanying Information from the Chairman of the Committee on Interior and Insular Affairs, House of Representatives, to the Members of the Committee," 88th Congress, 1st Session, Questionnaire Returns, pt. 1 [Washington, DC: U.S. Government Printing Office, 1963]).

22   *never rose above 25 percent.* Frederick E. Hosen, *The Great Depression and the New Deal*, p. 257 (Jefferson, NC: McFarland and Co., 1992); Sorkin, *American Indians*, p. 13.

23   *"There were some tough times."* Marlon Sherman, telephone interview with Cynthia Carter, faculty assistant, Sept. 20, 2001.

23   *In the early 1950s.* Alan L. Sorkin, *The Urban American Indian*, p. 10 (Lexington, MA: Lexington Books, 1978).

23   *Incomes for off-reservation Indians. See generally* Sorkin, "Trends," pp. 114–17.

23   *"Adjusting to urban life."* Donald L. Fixico, *The Urban Indian Experience in America*, p. 4 (Albuquerque: University of New Mexico Press, 2000).

23   *Hill 57.* On conditions at Hill 57 generally, see Senate Committee on Interior and Insular Affairs, Executive Session, "Various Bills," 84th Congress, 1st Session (July 26, 1955) (Washington, DC: Alderson Reporting Co., 1955); Hearings Before the Senate Committee on Interior and Insular Affairs, Subcommittee on Indian Affairs, "Federal Indian Policy: On S. 809, S. Con. Res.

3, and S. 331 (Bills Pertaining to Federal Indian Policy)," 85th Congress, 1st Session, pp. 47–100 (May 16, 1957) (Washington, DC: U.S. Government Printing Office, 1957).

24   *income levels.* For average family income by tribe, see "Compilation," pp. 641–875; for average family income by state, see U.S. Department of Commerce, Bureau of the Census, vol. 2, pt. 1 "Census of Population: 1950," Characteristics of the Population, United States Summary, pp. 1-136–1-137 (Washington, DC: U.S. Government Printing Office, 1953) [hereinafter "1950 Census"].

24   *Quinault.* "Compilation," p. 793; "1950 Census," p. 1–137.

24   *The Klamath Tribe. See infra* ch. 3, p. **77** (citing Theodore Stern, *The Klamath Tribe: A People and Their Reservation*, p. 190 [Seattle: University of Washington Press, 1966]).

24   *The Blackfeet of Montana.* Estimated family incomes by tribe are found in "1952 Statistical Charts," pp. 1–5.

24   *Oklahoma Indians.* On Oklahoma Indians, see generally Angie Debo, *And Still the Waters Run: The Betrayal of the Five Civilized Tribes* (Princeton, NJ: Princeton University Press, 1972); Angie Debo, *The Rise and Fall of the Choctaw Republic* (Norman: University of Oklahoma Press, 1961); Francis Paul Prucha, *American Indian Policy in Crisis: Christian Reformers and the Indian, 1865–1900*, pp. 373–401 (Norman: University of Oklahoma Press, 1976).

24   *The remaining lands.* For information regarding social and economic conditions of the Five Civilized Tribes, see "Compilation," pp. 767–74.

25   *Thus, by 1950.* "Compilation," pp. 768, 773.

25   *poverty-stricken conditions. See Ibid.*, pp. 768–69, 773.

25   *When oil was discovered. See generally* Donald L. Fixico, *The Invasion of Indian Country in the Twentieth Century: American Capitalism and Tribal Natural Resources*, pp. 27–49 (Niwot: University Press of Colorado, 1998).

25   *The boom had faded.* "1952 Statistical Charts," p. 3.

25   *"every oil-rich Osage."* Joane Nagel et al., "The Politics of American Indian Economic Development: The Reservation/Urban Nexus," *in* C. Matthew Snipp, ed., *Public Policy Impacts on American Indian Economic Development*, p. 42 (Albuquerque: University of New Mexico Press, Native American Studies, 1988) (quoting U.S. Department of Commerce, "Federal and State Indian Reservations and Indian Trust Areas," p. 463 [Washington, DC: U.S. Government Printing Office, 1974]).

CHAPTER 2: The Deadening Years

27   *Nez Perce and their land.* On Nez Perce tribal history, see generally Alvin M. Josephy, Jr., *The Nez Perce Indians and the Opening of the Northwest*, abridged ed., pp. 6–7 (New Haven, CT: Yale University Press, 1971); Dan Landeen and

Jeremy Crow, eds., *A Nez Perce Nature Guide: I Am of This Land: Wetes pe m'e wes*, p. 19 (Clarkston, WA: Western Printing, 1997); *see also* Merrill D. Beal, *"I Will Fight No More Forever": Chief Joseph and the Nez Perce War* (Seattle: University of Washington Press, 1963).

29 *Early Anglo travelers.* Charles F. Wilkinson, *Crossing the Next Meridian: Land, Water, and the Future of the West*, p. 184 (Washington, DC: Island Press, 1992).

29 *"In the springtime."* Dan Landeen and Allen Pinkham, *Salmon and His People: Fish and Fishing in Nez Perce Culture*, p. 54 (Lewiston, ID: Confluence Press, 1999).

29 *Nez Perce using their land.* See Deward E. Walker, Jr., *Indians of Idaho*, p. 71 (Moscow: University Press of Idaho, 1982); Josephy, *The Nez Perce*, p. 17.

29 *Nez Perce and horses.* See Walker, *Indians of Idaho*, pp. 71–72; Josephy, *The Nez Perce*, p. 19; Beal, *"I Will Fight,"* pp. 9–11.

29 *Natural geography of defense.* Josephy elaborates on this throughout the first five chapters of his book, but Chapter 1 seems to be the most comprehensive discussion. *See generally* Josephy, *The Nez Perce*, pp. 3–35; *see also* David Lavender, *Let Me Be Free: The Nez Perce Tragedy*, pp. 1–20 (Norman: University of Oklahoma Press, 1992).

29 *"brought an abrupt end."* Elizabeth A. Fenn, *Pox Americana: The Great Smallpox Epidemic of 1775–82*, pp. 22–23 (New York: Hill and Wang, 2002). On smallpox and the other epidemics that devastated Native Americans, see generally Jared Diamond, *Guns, Germs, and Steel: The Fates of Human Societies* (New York: W. W. Norton and Co., 1997).

30 *Disease and Nez Perce population.* On the early Nez Perce epidemics, see Lavender, *Let Me Be Free*, pp. 26–27. For population estimates, see David Agee Horr, ed., "Historical and Population Information," in *Nez Perce Indians*, pp. 21–22 (New York: Garland Publishing, 1974).

30 *In addition to actual deaths.* Russell Thornton, *American Indian Holocaust and Survival: A Population History Since 1492*, p. 54 (Norman: University of Oklahoma Press, 1987).

30 *The use of sweat baths.* Lavender, *Let Me Be Free*, pp. 26–27; Henry F. Dobyns, *Their Number Become Thinned: Native American Population Dynamics in Eastern North America*, p. 16 (Knoxville: University of Tennessee Press, 1983).

30 *No tribe escaped.* See generally Dobyns, *Their Number*; Thornton, *Indian Holocaust*.

30 *"Seeing themselves disfigured."* Ronald Wright, *Stolen Continents: The Americas through Indian Eyes Since 1492*, p. 103 (New York: Houghton Mifflin Co., 1992).

31 *"The Kiowa remember."* James Mooney, *Calendar History of the Kiowa Indians*, pp. 173, 289 (Washington, DC: Smithsonian Institution Press, 1979).

31 *"The first symptom."* Thornton, *Indian Holocaust*, p. 98.

31 *The commonly accepted range. Ibid.*, pp. 25–32.

31   *In 1900.* U.S. Department of Commerce, Bureau of the Census, "Indian Population in the United States and Alaska: 1910," pp. 10–11 (Washington, DC: U.S. Government Printing Office, 1915).

31   *From early colonial days. See, e.g.,* Francis Paul Prucha, *The Great Father: The United States Government and the American Indians,* abridged ed., pp. 8–9 (Lincoln: University of Nebraska Press, 1986).

32   *In 1802. Ibid.,* pp. 40–41.

32   *They learned the best trails.* David Lavender, *The Rockies,* p. 90 (New York: Harper and Row Publishers, 1968).

32   *While they used liquor.* Allan M. Winkler, "Drinking on the American Frontier," vol. 29 *Quarterly Journal of Studies on Alcohol,* pp. 421–22 (June 1968); American Indian Policy Review Commission, "Report on Alcohol and Drug Abuse: Task Force Eleven: Alcohol and Drug Abuse: Final Report," p. 31 (Washington, DC: U.S. Government Printing Office, 1976) ("Most of the respectable traders discouraged the use of alcohol as regular payment for furs. . . .").

32   *"liquor became a desperate problem."* Josephy, *The Nez Perce,* p. 398.

32   *"This first taste."* Angie Debo, *A History of the Indians of the United States,* p. 43 (Norman: University of Oklahoma Press, 1970).

33   *European debates over Indian rights. See generally* Robert A. Williams, Jr., *The American Indian in Western Legal Thought: The Discourses of Conquest* (New York: Oxford University Press, 1990); Felix S. Cohen, "The Spanish Origin of Indian Rights in the Law of the United States," vol. 31 *Georgetown Law Journal,* p. 1 (Nov. 1942).

33   *"You have to understand."* Personal communication received by author (circa 1990).

33   *Missionaries converted significant numbers. See generally* Hilary E. Wyss, *Writing Indians: Literacy, Christianity, and Native Community in Early America* (Amherst: University of Massachusetts Press, 2000).

33   *On the whole. See, e.g.,* Prucha, *Great Father,* pp. 3–8; *see generally* R. Pierce Beaver, *Church, State, and the American Indians: Two and a Half Centuries of Partnership in Missions Between Protestant Churches and Government* (St. Louis: Concordia Publishing House, 1966).

33   *Washington.* Prucha, *Great Father,* pp. 48–53.

34   *"we have the power."* *Ibid.,* p. 54.

34   *Treaties of the era.* Francis Paul Prucha, *American Indian Policy in the Formative Years: The Indian Trade and Intercourse Acts, 1790–1834,* pp. 219–24 (Cambridge, MA: Harvard University Press, 1962).

34   *Nez Perce and Christianity.* The standard authority on Nez Perce political and religious acculturation is Deward E. Walker, Jr., *Conflict and Schism in Nez Perce Acculturation: A Study of Religion and Politics* (Pullman: Washington State University Press, 1968). On Spaulding's arrival, see Lavender, *Let Me Be Free,* pp. 90–106.

34   *"The missionaries at first."* Allen P. Slickpoo, Sr., vol. 1 *Noon Nee-Me-Poo (We,
      The Nez Perces): Culture and History of the Nez Perces*, p. 72 (Lapwai: Nez Perce
      Tribe of Idaho, 1973).

34   *Spaulding and his methods.* See Francis Haines, *The Nez Perces: Tribesmen of
      the Columbia Plateau*, pp. 76–79 (Norman: University of Oklahoma Press,
      1955); Slickpoo, *Noon*, pp. 72–75; Walker, *Conflict and Schism*, pp. 40–41.

35   *"The external stress."* Walker, *Conflict and Schism*, p. 5.

35   *"Later we realized."* Slickpoo, *Noon*, p. 72.

35   *Nez Perce population.* Various estimates were made of the Nez Perce popula-
      tion at different times during the nineteenth century. The figure of three
      thousand seems to be the best estimate for the mid-nineteenth century. *See*
      Stuart A. Chalfant, "Aboriginal Territory of the Nez Perce Indians," *in* Horr,
      Nez Perce Indians, pp. 45–47.

35   *Isaac Stevens.* On Isaac Stevens, see generally Kent D. Richards, *Isaac I.
      Stevens: Young Man in a Hurry* (Provo, UT: Brigham Young University Press,
      1979).

35   *The December 1854 treaty.* Treaty with the Nisquallys and Other Tribes, Dec.
      26, 1854, 10 Stat. 1132 (1855).

36   *Chief Leschi and the Nisqually.* On the Nisqually, Chief Leschi, and the strug-
      gles both faced, see generally Cecelia Svinth Carpenter, *Fort Nisqually: A
      Documented History of Indian and British Interaction* (Tacoma, WA: Tahoma
      Research Service, 1986); Cecelia Svinth Carpenter, *Leschi: Last Chief of the
      Nisquallies* (Orting, WA: Heritage Quest, 1986); Charles Wilkinson, *Messages
      from Frank's Landing: A Story of Salmon, Treaties, and the Indian Way*, pp.
      10–19 (Seattle: University of Washington Press, 2000).

36   *An estimated 5,000 Indian people.* Josephy, *The Nez Perce*, p. 309.

36   *"a thousand warriors."* Ibid., p. 308.

36   *Isaac Stevens used strong-arm tactics.* See Darrell Scott, ed., "A True Copy of
      the Record of the Official Proceedings at the Council in the Walla Walla Val-
      ley, June 9th and 11th, 1855" (Fairfield, WA: Ye Galleon Press, 1985) [here-
      inafter "Official Proceedings"].

36   *the creation of three reservations. Ibid.; see also* Treaty Between the United
      States of America and the Nez Percé Indians, arts. 1–2, June 11, 1855, 12 Stat.
      957, 957–58 (1863) [hereinafter 1855 Treaty]. With respect to Nez Perce
      treaty rights, I have drawn material from Charles F. Wilkinson, "Indian
      Tribal Rights and the National Forests: The Case of Aboriginal Rights of the
      Nez Perce Tribe," vol. 34, no. 3 *Idaho Law Review*, p. 435 (1998).

36   *Alvin Josephy.* For publication information, see *supra* ch. 2, p. **394**.

36   *the stereotype of the Indian leaders. See, e.g.,* "Official Proceedings,"
      pp. 52–63.

37   *They strung the proceedings out. See Ibid.*

37   *They made their arguments. See, e.g., Ibid.*, pp. 64–65.

37   *"by calm reasoning."* Herbert Joseph Spinden, "The Nez Percé Indians," vol.
     2, pt. 3 *Memoirs of the American Anthropological Association*, p. 243 (1964).

37   *"made our bodies from the earth."* "Official Proceedings," p. 58; *see also* Jose-
     phy, *The Nez Perce*, p. 317.

37   *"I wonder if this ground."* "Official Proceedings," p. 55; *see also* Josephy, *The
     Nez Perce*, pp. 316–17.

38   Johnson v. McIntosh. 21 U.S. (8 Wheat.) 543 (1823).

38   *"rightful occupants of the soil." Ibid.*, p. 574.

38   *tribes had a legal right. See Felix S. Cohen's Handbook of Federal Indian Law*,
     1982 ed., pp. 486–93 (Charlottesville, VA: Michie Bobbs-Merrill, 1982) [here-
     inafter *1982 Cohen Handbook*].

38   *trespassers upon the tribal title. See, e.g., Oneida Indian Nation v. County of
     Oneida*, 414 U.S. 661, 667–74 (1974). The inability of states or settlers to extin-
     guish the tribal right to occupancy was first announced by the Court in *John-
     son*, 21 U.S. at 587–88. According to *Tee-Hit-Ton Indians v. United States*, 348
     U.S. 272, 279–85 (1955), compensation is not required under the Fifth
     Amendment to the Constitution if the right of occupancy is extinguished;
     rather, compensation depends upon voluntary "congressional contributions."
     Ibid. at 290. Tribal title held by treaty, however, is vested in the tribe and pro-
     tected under the Fifth Amendment. *See, e.g., United States v. Shoshone Tribe*,
     304 U.S. 111 (1938); *1982 Cohen Handbook*, pp. 473–77.

38   *"My people."* Josephy, *The Nez Perce*, p. 319.

38   *Looking Glass . . . went to Stevens's map. Ibid.*, p. 321. There is a question
     whether the "Official Proceedings" support Josephy's version of this event.
     A later exchange during the negotiations among Stevens, Looking Glass, and
     Palmer went as follows:

>   GOV. STEVENS: Looking Glass is satisfied with the Nez Perce
>   line. . . .
>
>   LOOKING GLASS: I said yes to the line I marked myself, not to your line.
>
>   GOV. STEVENS: I will say to the Looking Glass, we cannot agree.
>
>   GEN. PALMER: I would say to the Looking Glass, what use is it to pur-
>   chase his country and give it all back again. "Official Proceedings,"
>   p. 77.

39   *The Nez Perce chiefs. Ibid.*, p. 79.

39   *The Nez Perce retained. Nez Perce Tribe v. United States*, 18 Indian Cl. Comm'n
     1, 131 (1967); *see also* Josephy, *The Nez Perce*, pp. 324–25, 329–30.

39   *Stevens and Palmer assured them.* "Official Proceedings," pp. 25, 46–50, 67, 76.

39   *"the right of taking fish."* 1855 Treaty, art. III.

40   *Miners turned up traces of gold.* Josephy, *The Nez Perce*, pp. 382–89.

40   *major strikes in the Clearwater watershed. Ibid.*

40   *"reservation was overrun."* H. H. [Helen Hunt Jackson], *A Century of Dishonor:*

A Sketch of the United States Government's Dealings with Some of the Indian Tribes, p. 118 (New York: Harper and Brothers, 1881).

40   *the Nez Perce were no exception.* See *Ibid.*; see also Debo, *A History*.

40   *The inevitable land reduction treaty.* Treaty Between the United States of America and the Nez Percé Tribe of Indians, June 9, 1863, 14 Stat. 647 (1868) [hereinafter 1863 Treaty].

40   *leaders of several Nez Perce bands refused to show up.* See, e.g., Dennis Baird et al., eds., "The Nez Perce Nation Divided: Firsthand Accounts of Events Leading to the 1863 Treaty," pp. 346–47, 257, 264, 266, 368–69, 375 (Moscow: University of Idaho Press, 2002) (reprinting General Services Administration, National Archives and Records Administration, "Documents Relating to the Negotiations of Ratified and Unratified Treaties with Various Tribes of Indians, 1801–1869," Records of the Bureau of Indian Affairs, Record Group 75, Roll 6 [Washington, DC: U.S. Government Printing Office, 1960]).

40   *"In the end."* Josephy, *The Nez Perce*, p. 421.

40   *The 1863 treaty ceded away.* Landeen and Crow, *Nature Guide*, p. 21.

40   *treaty expressly left in place.* 1863 Treaty, art. III.

41   *"fraudulent."* Josephy, *The Nez Perce*, p. 420; Debo, *A History*, p. 261.

41   Lone Wolf v. Hitchcock. 187 U.S. 553 (1903).

41   *One chief who refused.* Josephy, *The Nez Perce*, p. 421.

41   *"I buried him."* Debo, *A History*, p. 261.

41   *"They will teach us."* Slickpoo, *Noon*, p. 164.

41   *Young Nez Perce warriors.* Beal, *I Will Fight*, pp. 45–51.

42   *Chief Joseph's march.* See generally *Ibid.*

42   *Chief Joseph's final battle. Ibid.*, pp. 233, 258.

42   *"Hear me, my chiefs." Ibid.*, p. 229.

42   *Some went to Lapwai.* See Josephy, *The Nez Perce*, p. 624.

43   *Congress launched a policy.* General Allotment Act, ch. 119, Feb. 8, 1887, 24 Stat. 388 (1887) (codified as amended at 25 U.S.C. §§ 331–34, 339, 341–42, 348–49, 354, 381 [2000]). The standard work on the allotment policy is Frederick E. Hoxie, *A Final Promise: The Campaign to Assimilate the Indians, 1880–1920* (Lincoln: University of Nebraska Press, 2001).

43   *Not so incidentally.* See generally Vine Deloria, Jr., and Clifford M. Lytle, *American Indians, American Justice*, pp. 8–12 (Austin: University of Texas Press, 1983); see also Frank Pommersheim, *Braid of Feathers: American Indian Law and Contemporary Tribal Life*, p. 20 (Berkeley: University of California Press, 1995).

43   *a loss of nearly 90 million acres.* Alvin M. Josephy, Jr., *Now that the Buffalo's Gone: A Study of Today's American Indians*, p. 132 (New York: Alfred A. Knopf, 1982); see Pommersheim, *Braid of Feathers*, p. 20.

43   *"a mighty pulverizing engine."* Brian W. Dippie, *The Vanishing American: White*

Attitudes and U.S. Indian Policy, p. 244 (Middletown, CT: Wesleyan University Press, 1982).

43 *"irresistible as that of Sherman's to the sea."* Statement by Representative Springer of Dec. 18, 1879, vol. 10, pt. 1 *Congressional Record*, 46th Congress, 2d Session, p. 178 (Washington, DC: U.S. Government Printing Office, 1880).

43 *A House subcommittee minority report.* D. S. Otis, *The Dawes Act and the Allotment of Indian Lands*, p. 19 (Norman: University of Oklahoma Press, 1973) (quoting House Report No. 1576, "Lands in Severalty to Indians," 46th Congress, 2d Session, p. 10 (Washington, DC: U.S. Government Printing Office, 1880)). On the passage of the General Allotment Act, see generally Otis, *The Dawes Act*, pp. 3–56; Francis Paul Prucha, *American Indian Policy in Crisis: Christian Reformers and the Indian, 1865–1900*, pp. 248–57 (Norman: University of Oklahoma Press, 1976); Hoxie, *A Final Promise*, pp. 70–78.

46 *"The time has now come."* Robert Winston Mardock, *The Reformers and the American Indian*, p. 32 (Columbia: University of Missouri Press, 1971) (quoting Lydia Maria Child, *An Appeal for the Indians* [New York: William P. Tomlinson, 1868]). On the Friends of the Indian, see generally William T. Hagan, *The Indian Rights Association: The Herbert Welsh Years, 1882–1904* (Tucson: University of Arizona Press, 1985); Mardock, *The Reformers*; Prucha, *Policy in Crisis*, pp. 143–68.

46 *Allotment, individualism, and evangelical Christians.* On the emphasis on individualism generally and by Christian evangelicals in particular, see Prucha, *Policy in Crisis*, pp. 151–53.

46 *Henry L. Dawes.* On Dawes, see Leonard Schlup, "Henry Laurens Dawes," *in* John A. Garraty and Mark C. Carnes, eds., vol. 6, *American National Biography*, pp. 250–52 (New York: Oxford University Press, 1999). On Dawes's Indian views, see Henry L. Dawes, "The Indian Territory," vol. 52 *Independent*, p. 2561 (Oct. 1900), *at* http://emedia.netlibrary.com/reader/reader.asp?product_id=2010700 (Charlottesville: University of Virginia Library; Boulder, CO: NetLibrary, 1995) (last visited Aug. 18, 2003) (on file with author).

46 *"If I stand alone in the Senate."* Statement by Senator Teller of Jan. 20, 1881, vol. 11, pt. 1 *Congressional Record*, 46th Congress, 2d Session, p. 783 (Washington, DC: U.S. Government Printing Office, 1881).

47 *Alice C. Fletcher.* On Fletcher, see Thurman Wilkins, "Fletcher, Alice Cunningham," *in* Edward T. James, ed., vol. 1, *Notable American Women 1607–1950: A Biographical Dictionary*, pp. 630–33 (Cambridge, MA: Belknap Press, 1971); Fredrick E. Hoxie and Joan T. Mark, eds., and "Introduction," *in* E. Jane Gay, *With the Nez Perces: Alice Fletcher in the Field, 1889–1892*, pp. xxvii–ix (Lincoln: University of Nebraska Press, 1981).

47 *"There is tangible silence within."* Gay, *With the Nez Perces*, pp. 22–24.

49 *Findings of competency.* Debo, *A History*, pp. 276–77; Hoxie, *A Final Promise*, pp. 181–83.

49 *"I don't know what happened."* Walker, *Conflict and Schism*, p. 78; *see also* Slickpoo, *Noon*, pp. 220–27.

49   *Smoholla. See* Josephy, *The Nez Perce,* pp. 424–26.

49   *"You ask me to plow the ground." Ibid.,* p. 426.

49   *10 percent of the land was being cultivated.* Otis, *The Dawes Act,* p. 133.

49   *98 percent of the 136,000 acres.* Hoxie and Mark, "Introduction," p. xxv (citing U.S. Department of the Interior, Office of Indian Affairs, "Annual Report of the Commissioner of Indian Affairs," p. 152 [Washington, DC: U.S. Government Printing Office, 1911] [hereinafter "Annual Report"]).

50   *The General Allotment Act required.* Prucha, *Policy in Crisis,* p. 253.

50   *Federal Indian agents dictated the terms. See, e.g.,* Bruce Hampton, *Children of Grace: The Nez Perce War of 1877,* pp. 372–73, n. 49 (New York: Henry Holt and Co., 1994); Wilcomb E. Washburn, *The Assault on Indian Tribalism: The General Allotment Law (Dawes Act) of 1887,* p. 8 (Philadelphia: J. B. Lippincott Co., 1975).

50   *Christian "progressives."* Slickpoo, *Noon,* pp. 223–24.

50   *The tribe received three dollars an acre. Ibid.,* p. 224.

50   *the rush for Nez Perce land. Ibid.,* p. 226.

50   *"It gives the Indian a chance."* Otis, *The Dawes Act,* p. 133 (citing U.S. Department of the Interior, Office of Indian Affairs, "Report of the Board of Indian Commissioners," pp. 22–23 [Washington, DC: U.S. Government Printing Office, 1898]).

51   *"perhaps the single most important change."* Walker, *Conflict and Schism,* p. 77.

51   *Of the 750,000 acres.* L. Scott Gould, "The Consent Paradigm: Tribal Sovereignty at the Millennium," vol. 96 *Columbia Law Review,* p. 831, n. 139 (May 1996) (citing U.S. Department of Commerce, Bureau of the Census, "1990 Census of Population and Housing: Summary Population and Housing Characteristics: United States," p. 422 tbl. 10 [Washington, DC: U.S. Government Printing Office, 1992]; U.S. Department of Interior, Bureau of Indian Affairs, Office of Trust Responsibilities, "Annual Report of Indian Lands," p. 26 [Washington, DC: U.S. Government Printing Office, 1985]).

51   *The rest.* Slickpoo, *Noon,* pp. 221–25; *see also* Lavender, *Let Me Be Free,* p. 334.

52   *"idea of a weaker race."* J. Walker McSpadden, *Famous Sculptors of America,* p. 281 (Freeport, NY: Books for Libraries Press, 1968); *see generally* Dean Krakel, *End of the Trail: The Odyssey of a Statue* (Norman: University of Oklahoma Press, 1973).

52   *the "Vanishing Indian."* For a full treatment, see generally Dippie, *The Vanishing Indian.*

53   *a "Presbyterian reservation."* Slickpoo, *Noon,* p. 156.

53   *"[A]ll the Indian there is."* Scott Riney, *The Rapid City Indian School, 1898–1933,* p. 8 (Norman: University of Oklahoma Press, 1999).

53   *"to fight them is cruel."* Alice Littlefield, "Learning to Labor: Native American Education in the United States, 1880–1930," *in* John H. Moore, ed., *The Polit-*

ical Economy of North American Indians, p. 49 (Norman: University of Oklahoma Press, 1993).

53   *by 1900.* Riney, *Rapid City*, p. 20.

53   *BIA officials and school administrators.* See, e.g., Clyde Ellis, *To Change Them Forever: Indian Education at the Rainy Mountain Boarding School, 1893–1920*, p. 93 (Norman: University of Oklahoma Press, 1996).

53   *The teachers meted out.* Margaret Connell Szasz, *Education and the American Indian: The Road to Self-Determination Since 1928*, pp. 2, 28 (Albuquerque: University of New Mexico Press, 1999).

53   *"The boarding schools were highly regimented."* See, e.g., Slickpoo, *Noon*, pp. 227–37.

54   *Many in the subjugated citizenry.* On indigenous peoples resisting assimilation, including specific examples, *see generally* Michael E. Brown and Sumit Ganguly, eds., *Government Policies and Ethnic Relations in Asia and the Pacific*, pp. 539–41 (Cambridge, MA: MIT Press, 1997).

54   *"Enforced social change.."* Ruth Hill Useem and Carl K. Eicher, "Rosebud Reservation Economy," in Ethel Nurge, ed., *The Modern Sioux: Social Systems and Reservation Culture*, p. 8 (Lincoln: University of Nebraska Press, 1970).

54   *"When a relative needed help."* Michael Joseph Francisconi, *Kinship, Capitalism, Change: The Informal Economy of the Navajo, 1868–1995*, p. 65 (New York: Garland Publishing, 1998).

54   *BIA officials in the early twentieth century.* Leonard A. Carlson, *Indians, Bureaucrats, and Land: The Dawes Act and the Decline of Indian Farming*, pp. 105–06 (Westport, CT: Greenwood Press, 1981).

54   *"the Indians' hospitality."* *Ibid.*, p. 105.

55   *fault lines within the tribes.* See, e.g., Brian C. Hosmer, *American Indians in the Marketplace: Persistence and Innovation among the Menominees and Metlakatlans, 1870–1920*, p. 80 (Lawrence: University of Kansas Press, 1999) (noting the power shift to entrepreneurs in the Menominee tribe); Ralph Linton, ed., *Acculturation in Seven American Indian Tribes*, pp. 187–88 (Gloucester, MA: Peter Smith, 1963) (identifying a generational conflict among the Southern Ute "precipitated by the economic independence of the younger generation").

55   *"The money economy has caused."* Caroline James, *Nez Perce Women in Transition, 1877–1990*, p. 217 (Moscow: University of Idaho Press, 1996).

55   *"It will be."* Hoxie and Mark, "Introduction," p. xxv (citing "Annual Report," p. 152).

55   *the five-year plan.* On the Nez Perce revival during the 1920s through the 1940s, see generally Slickpoo, *Noon*, pp. 242–77; Walker, *Conflict and Schism*, pp. 124–26.

55   *Some elements of a constitution.* A master's thesis on the history of Nez Perce governance describes the 1923 document as a constitution; *see* Robert James

Riley, "The Nez Perce Struggle for Self Government: A History of the Nez Perce Governing Bodies, 1842–1960," pp. 58–61, M.A. thesis, University of Idaho (1961) (on file with author). Slickpoo's authorized history of the tribe, however, does not, and its minimal provisions on governance do not seem to rise to the level of constitutionalism as we normally think of it, as evidenced, for example, in the Nez Perce constitution of 1948. See Slickpoo, *Noon,* pp. 242–51, which reprints the five-year plan.

55   *actions had to be approved.* Walker, *Conflict and Schism,* p. 124.

56   *1948 constitution.* For the text of the 1948 constitution, *see Ibid.,* pp. 163–66.

CHAPTER 3: Termination

57   *House Concurrent Resolution 108.* 83rd Congress, 1st Session, Aug. 1, 1953, 67 Stat. B132 (1953). The phrase "termination" was chosen over the equally ominous "liquidation." *See* Charles F. Wilkinson and Eric R. Biggs, "The Evolution of the Termination Policy," vol. 5, no. 1 *American Indian Law Review,* p. 166, n. 3 (1977) (citing Hearings Before the Senate Committee on Public Lands, Subcommittee on Indian Affairs, "Klamath Indians, Oregon: On S. 1222 [A Bill to Remove Restrictions on the Property and Moneys Belonging to the Individual Enrolled Members of the Klamath Indian Reservation in Oregon, to Provide for the Liquidation of Tribal Property and Distribution of the Proceeds thereof, to Confer Complete Citizenship upon Such Indians, and for Other Purposes]," 80th Congress, 1st Session [Washington, DC: U.S. Government Printing Office, 1947]).

57   *Two weeks after.* On Public Law 280, see *supra* ch. 1, pp. **18–19.**

58   *Although sometimes ascribed.* On the buildup to termination during the 1940s and early 1950s, see Kenneth R. Philp, *Termination Revisited: American Indians on the Trail to Self-Determination, 1933–1953* (Lincoln: University of Nebraska Press, 1999).

58   *John Collier.* On Collier, see S. Lyman Tyler, "Indian Affairs: A Study of the Changes in Policy of the United States Toward Indians," pp. 62–82 (Provo, UT: Brigham Young University, Institute of American Indian Studies, 1964).

58   *Meriam Commission.* Lewis Meriam et al., Institute for Government Research, "The Problem of Indian Administration" (Baltimore: Johns Hopkins Press, 1928).

58   *"an overwhelming majority." Ibid.,* p. 3.

58   *Its recommendations. Ibid.,* pp. 21, 50–51.

59   *"The national government." Ibid.,* p. 22.

59   *John Collier's high-visibility.* For Collier's son reflecting on his father's appointment, see John Collier, Jr., "Foreword" *in* Lawrence Kelly, *The Assault on Assimilation: John Collier and the Origins of Indian Policy Reform,* pp. xvii–iii (Albuquerque: University of New Mexico Press, 1983).

59   *"They had what the world has lost."* John Collier, *The Indians of the Americas,* p. 15 (New York: W. W. Norton and Co., 1947).

59   *Radical though his views.* On the passage of Collier's agenda, see Elmer R.
     Rusco, *A Fateful Time: The Background and Legislative History of the Indian
     Reorganization Act* (Reno: University of Nevada Press, 2000); *see also* Kelly,
     The Assault; Kenneth R. Philp, *John Collier's Crusade for Indian Reform* (Tuc-
     son: University of Arizona Press, 1977).

60   *Indian Reorganization Act.* Pub. L. No. 383, ch. 576, June 18, 1934, 48 Stat. 984
     (1934) (codified as amended at 25 U.S.C. §§ 461–79 [2000]).

60   *"no interference with."* Francis Paul Prucha, vol. 2, *The Great Father: The United
     States Government and the American Indians*, p. 951 (Lincoln: University of
     Nebraska Press, 1984).

60   *wreckage of allotment.* The study is D. S. Otis, *The Dawes Act and the Allotment
     of Indian Lands* (Norman: University of Oklahoma Press, 1973).

60   *The FDR administration.* Cohen's seminal treatise is Felix S. Cohen, *Hand-
     book of Federal Indian Law* (Washington, DC: U.S. Government Printing
     Office, 1942). The 1982 revision of the Cohen treatise contains a discussion
     of the preparation of the original edition, its importance in American law,
     and a complete listing of Cohen's many scholarly publications. *See Felix S.
     Cohen's Handbook of Federal Indian Law*, pp. vii–xi (Charlottesville, VA:
     Michie Bobbs-Merrill, 1982).

61   Worcester v. Georgia. 31 U.S. (6 Pet.) 515 (1832).

61   *"Considered as distinct, independent political communities."* Ibid. at 559.

61   *"Perhaps the most basic principle."* 1982 Cohen Handbook, p. 122.

61   *"It is a pity."* Felix S. Cohen, "The Erosion of Indian Rights, 1950–1953: A Case
     Study in Bureaucracy," vol. 62 *Yale Law Journal*, p. 390 (Feb. 1953).

62   *Especially at Hopi and in Sioux country.* On Hopi, see, for example, Charles
     Wilkinson, *Fire on the Plateau: Conflict and Endurance in the American South-
     west*, pp. 281–84 (Washington, DC: Island Press, 1999). On Sioux, see, for
     example, Murray L. Wax et al., "Formal Education in an American Indian
     Community," *in Social Problems*, SSSP Monograph, p. 18 (Kalamazoo, MI:
     1964) ("Culturally a non-Indian form [the Tribal Council] is honored by no
     one. It has been the target of conservative Indian suspicion since its initia-
     tion in the 1930s.").

62   *Whatever shortcomings Collier had. See, e.g.*, Vine Deloria, Jr., and Clifford M.
     Lytle, *The Nations Within: The Past and Future of American Indian Sovereignty*,
     pp. 111–12, 116–18, 132 (New York: Pantheon Books, 1984); Prucha, *Great
     Father*, p. 999.

63   *The document attacked. Ibid.* On Collier's battles with congressional leaders,
     see generally *Ibid.*, pp. 997–1005.

63   *Senate Report 310. Ibid.*, pp. 1000–01, n. 14 (citing Senate Report No. 310, "Sur-
     vey of Conditions Among the Indians of the United States: Analysis of the
     Statement of the Commissioner of Indian Affairs in Justification of Appro-
     priations for 1944, and the Liquidation of the Indian Bureau," 78th Congress,

1st Session [Washington, DC: U.S. Government Printing Office, 1943]).

63   *The House Committee.* Hearings Before the House Committee on Indian Affairs, "Investigate Indian Affairs: On H. Res. 166 (A Bill to Authorize and Direct and Conduct an Investigation to Determine Whether the Changed Status of the Indian Requires a Revision of the Laws and Regulations Affecting the American Indian)," 78th Congress, 1st and 2d Sessions, pts. 1–2 (Washington, DC: U.S. Government Printing Office, 1943) [hereinafter H. Res. 166 Hearings].

63   *"In other words." Ibid.*, pt. 2, p. 78 (Feb. 9, 1944).

63   *committee members made no secret. See, e.g., Ibid.*, pt. 1, p. 5 (March 23, 1943).

63   *"the purpose of the Indian Bureau." Ibid.*, p. 6.

63   *"give us concrete suggestions." Ibid.*, pt. 2, p. 59 (Feb. 2, 1944).

64   *The committee ordered him to supply.* Harold E. Fey and D'Arcy McNickle, *Indians and Other Americans: Two Ways of Life Meet*, p. 133 (New York: Harper and Brothers Publishers, 1959); Philp, *Termination*, p. 70; *see also* Hearings Before the Senate Committee on Civil Service, "Officers and Employees of the Federal Government: On S. Res. 41 (A Resolution to Investigate Certain Matters Relating to Officers and Employees of the Federal Government)," 80th Congress, 1st Session, pt. 3, pp. 526, 541–42 (Feb. 6, 1947) (Washington, DC: U.S. Government Printing Office, 1947) [hereinafter Civil Service Hearings].

64   *Zimmerman hastily prepared a list.* Fey and McNickle, *Indians*, p. 134.

64   *breaking tribes down into three groups.* Prucha, *Great Father*, p. 1026; *see also* Zimmerman's list and his initial explanation to the committee in Civil Service Hearings, pt. 3, pp. 544–47 (Feb. 8, 1947).

64   *While this list resembled. See* H. Res. 166 Hearings, 2d Session, pp. 59–63 (Collier's list). To compare Zimmerman's and Collier's lists, see Philp, *Termination*, pp. 71–76, which reprints both.

64   *Dozens of Indian land sale. See, e.g.*, Wilcomb E. Washburn, *Red Man's Land/White Man's Law: The Past and Present Status of the American Indian*, 2d ed., pp. 82-83 (Norman: University of Oklahoma Press, 1995).

64   *"The basis for historic Indian culture."* Commission on Organization of the Executive Branch of the Government, "Social Security and Education— Indian Affairs: A Report to Congress," Special Task Force Report, pp. 54–55 (Washington, DC: U.S. Government Printing Office, 1948) (quoted in Prucha, *Great Father*, p. 1029).

64   *President Truman found. See generally* Richard Drinnon, *Keeper of Concentration Camps: Dillon S. Myer and American Racism*, pp. 78–116 (Berkeley: University of California Press, 1987).

64   *"A man of unimpeachable integrity."* Cohen, "The Erosion," p. 389, n. 158.

65   *"blundering and dictatorial tin-Hitler."* Drinnon, *Keeper*, p. 194.

65   *Myer left no doubt.* On Myer, see generally Fey and McNickle, *Indians*,

pp. 183–85; Wilkinson and Biggs, "Evolution," pp. 147–49 and accompanying notes.

65   *Myer's activist administration.* The Myer administration has been widely analyzed. *See, e.g.,* Prucha, *Great Father,* pp. 1030–36; Donald L. Fixico, *Termination and Relocation: Federal Indian Policy, 1945–1960,* pp. 63–77 (Albuquerque: University of New Mexico Press, 1986); Philp, *Termination,* pp. 87–139; Wilkinson and Biggs, "Evolution," pp. 147–48 and accompanying notes.

65   *Myer implemented his extreme views. Ibid.*

65   *To Myer's credit.* William Zimmerman, Jr., "The Role of the Bureau of Indian Affairs Since 1933," vol. 311 *Annals of the American Academy of Political and Social Science,* p. 35 (May 1957).

65   *But his reappointment was not to be. See* Philp, *Termination,* p. 168.

67   *"So I went to Washington."* Arthur V. Watkins, *Enough Rope,* p. 9 (Englewood Cliffs, NJ: Prentice Hall, 1969). On Watkins, see also Kenneth T. Jackson et al., eds., *Dictionary of American Biography,* Supp. 9, 1971–1975, pp. 841–43 (New York: Charles Scribner's Sons, 1994).

67   *"acquitted himself with firmness and dignity."* "Arthur V. Watkins Dies at 86; Led McCarthy Censure Inquiry," vol. 4 *New York Times Biographical Edition,* p. 566 (Sept. 1973); *see also* Watkins, *Enough Rope,* pp. 37–42, 125–29 (recounting illustrative exchanges between Watkins and McCarthy).

67   *the withholding of tribal funds.* For example, after a bill providing for per capita payment of a judgment of $8 million for a 50-year-old Menominee claim against the Forest Service routinely passed the House of Representatives in 1953, Senator Watkins held the bill in committee. He explained to the Menominee at a tribal hearing that they could not obtain their funds unless they agreed to termination. Gary Orfield, "A Study of the Termination Policy," *in* Senate Committee on Labor and Public Welfare, Subcommittee on Indian Education, "The Education of American Indians: The Organization Question," 91st Congress, 1st Session, vol. 4, pp. 695–96 (Washington, DC: U.S. Government Printing Office, 1970).

67   *Perhaps because he believed. Ibid.,* p. 691. *See also* Gary Orfield, *A Study of the Termination Policy,* p. 14 (Washington, DC: National Congress of American Indians, 1966); Theodore Stern, *The Development of the Klamath Termination Policy,* p. 36 (unpublished manuscript, on file with the author); Oliver La Farge, "Termination of Federal Supervision: Disintegration and the American Indians," vol. 311 *Annals of the American Academy of Political and Social Science,* p. 44 (May 1957) (suggesting that the strength of "Indian opposition" explained the rough tactics of "disintegrationists" like Watkins).

67   *doubted the validity of Indian treaties. See* Joint Hearings Before the Committees on Interior and Insular Affairs, Subcommittees, "Termination of Federal Supervision over Certain Tribes of Indians: On S. 2749 and H. R. 7322," 83rd Congress, 2d Session, pt. 5, p. 457 (Mar. 5, 1954) (Washington, DC: U.S. Government Printing Office, 1954) [hereinafter Joint Hearings on Termination]

("Senator Watkins. You have raised a question on which I would like to comment, and that is with respect to the so-called treaties. A treaty is ordinarily an agreement between two sovereign nations. Under the practice, and as time has gone on, we have arrived at the point where we do not recognize now within the confines of the United States any foreign nations. You have now become citizens of the one nation. Ordinarily the United States does not enter into treaties, as they are understood, in an international sense, between any of its citizens and the Federal Government. They enter into contracts, not treaties. So it is doubtful now that from here on treaties are going to be recognized where the Indians themselves have gone to the point where they have accepted citizenship in the United States and have taken advantage of its opportunities. So that that question of treaties, I think, is going to largely disappear.").

67   *misleading assurances. See, e.g.*, Joint Hearings on Termination, pt. 4, pp. 261, 274–75 (Feb. 23, 1954); *see also* Wilkinson and Biggs, "Evolution," p. 178, n. 74 and accompanying text.

67   *erroneous information. See, e.g.*, Joint Hearings on Termination, pt. 4, pp. 655–56 (Feb. 23, 1954). When one witness found the sudden emphasis on termination "just a bit peculiar," Watkins stated that "the State itself suggested the idea that it ought to terminate, and we assumed that the State had been working on it." *Ibid.*, pt. 6, p. 655 (March 10, 1954). One commentator remarked that "this assertion was false, but it was not challenged." Orfield, "A Study," p. 699.

68   *He asked leading questions.* The following exchange is an example.

> SENATOR WATKINS. The fact of the matter is that most of the whites [in the area of the Klamath Reservation] would have a business experience far above the average white man in the United States. Is that not true?
>
> MR. PRYSE. I expect so.
>
> SENATOR WATKINS. And they would be reputable people, who could give [the Indians] good sound advice?
>
> MR. PRYSE. Yes, sir.

Joint Hearings on Termination, pt. 4, p. 219 (Feb. 23, 1954). In fact, the opposite of what Watkins had suggested occurred at termination; the Klamath lost most of their per capita payments, largely through the highly questionable business practices of non-Indians in the area. *See* American Indian Policy Review Commission, "Task Force Ten: Report on Terminated and Nonfederally Recognized Indians," 94th Congress, 2d Session, pp. 58–59 (Washington, DC: U.S. Government Printing Office, 1976) [hereinafter "Task Force Ten"]. These unfair business practices by the local non-Indian community at the time of the Klamath termination were documented by the Federal Trade Commission during hearings in Klamath Falls in 1972. U.S. Department of Commerce, Federal Trade Commission, Seattle Regional Office, "A Report of the Consumer Problems of the Klamath Indians: A Case for Action," (Washington, DC: U.S. Government Printing Office, 1973).

68   *critical and incredulous.* Orfield, "A Study," pp. 690–91.

68   *devoutly religious.* Watkins, *Enough Rope*, p. 10.

68   *"They want all the benefits."* Orfield, "A Study," p. 690.

69   *"They would have learned."* Statement by Senator Watkins of May 10, 1954, vol. 100, pt. 5 *Congressional Record*, 83rd Congress, 2d Session, p. 6253 (Washington, DC: U.S. Government Printing Office, 1954).

69   *"Following in the footsteps."* Arthur V. Watkins, "Termination of Federal Supervision: The Removal of Restrictions over Indian Property and Person," vol. 311 *Annals of the American Academy of Political and Social Science*, p. 55 (May 1957).

69   *E. Y. Berry.* On Berry's background, see Orfield, "A Study," p. 677.

69   *joint Senate-House subcommittee hearings.* The sessions were transcribed; *see* Joint Hearings on Termination, pts. 1–12.

70   *At the outset.* Martha C. Knack, *Boundaries Between: The Southern Paiutes, 1775–1995*, p. 254 (Lincoln: University of Nebraska Press, 2001); Ronald L. Holt, *Beneath These Red Cliffs: An Ethnohistory of the Utah Paiutes*, p. 77 (Albuquerque: University of New Mexico Press, 1992).

70   *"For discussion purposes."* Joint Hearing on Termination, pt. 1, p. 46.

70   *education and income levels.* See *Ibid.*, pp. 12–16, 27–29.

70   *The committee received a letter. Ibid.*, p. 61.

70   *"He represents some oil company." Ibid.*, p. 60.

70   *When Joe Garry. See Ibid.*, pp. 77–79.

70   *"Is this an act that enfranchises." Ibid.*, p. 86.

70   *"Not in my judgment." Ibid.*

71   *Although Watkins repeatedly said. See, e.g., Ibid.*, pt. 6, p. 743 (March 12, 1954).

71   *"absolute terror spread through Indian country."* Vine Deloria, Jr., *Custer Died for Your Sins: An Indian Manifesto*, p. 70 (New York: Avon Books, 1970).

71   *The Menominee forest.* Nicholas C. Peroff, *Menominee Drums: Tribal Termination and Restoration, 1954–1974*, p. 43 (Norman: University of Oklahoma Press, 1982); Thomas Davis, *Sustaining the Forest, the People, and the Spirit*, pp. 12, 14–15, 21, 23, 145–46 (Albany: State University of New York Press, 2000).

71   *Loggers recognized its commercial value.* Patricia K. Ourada, *The Menominee Indians: A History*, pp. 170–71 (Norman: University of Oklahoma Press, 1979).

71   *He also got funding. Ibid.*, p. 172.

71   *the mill served the tribe well.* Peroff, *Menominee Drums*, pp. 43–44.

71   *$2,300 annual family income.* Joint Hearings on Termination, pt. 6, p. 590 (March 10, 1954).

72   *$1,200 family income.* Compare House Committee on Interior and Insular

Affairs, Subcommittee on Indian Affairs, "Statistical Charts Regarding the Indians of the United States," 82d Congress, 2d Session, p. 2 (Washington, DC: U.S. Government Printing Office, 1952).

72 *$3,300 statewide family income.* U.S. Department of Commerce, Bureau of the Census, "Historical Statistics of the United States: Colonial Times to 1970," Bicentennial Edition, pt. 2, p. 297 (Washington, DC: U.S. Government Printing Office, 1975) [hereinafter Historical Statistics].

72 *five college graduates.* Stephen J. Herzberg, "The Menominee Indians: From Treaty to Termination," vol. 60, no. 4 *Wisconsin Magazine of History*, p. 297 (1977).

72 *settlement of $8.5 million. Menominee Tribe of Indians v. United States*, 119 Ct. Cl. 832, 832 (1951).

72 *holding the claims award hostage.* Wilkinson and Biggs, "Evolution," p. 178, n. 174; Peroff, *Menominee Drums*, pp. 53–55.

72 *Before the hearings. See generally* Hertzberg, "The Menominee Indians," pp. 311–16.

72 *"told the tribal members."* Verne F. Ray, *The Menominee Tribe of Indians, 1940–1970*, p. 14 (Escanaba, MI: Photo Offset Printing Co., 1972) (originally in Plaintiff's Exhibit no. R-1, *Menominee Tribe of Indians v. United States*, 607 F.2d 1335 [Ct. Cl. 1979] [No. 134-67]).

72 *[D]o you feel that." Ibid.*, p. 16.

72 *"Yes, I do." Ibid.*

72 *After a short discussion. See, e.g.*, Herzberg, "The Menominee Indians," p. 314.

72 *less than a month later. See, e.g., Ibid.*, p. 316; *see also* Deborah Shames, ed., *Freedom with Reservation: The Menominee Struggle to Save Their Land and People*, p. 8 (Madison, WI: National Committee to Save the Menominee People and Forests, 1972).

73 *"But here we have a group."* Joint Hearings on Termination, pt. 6, p. 678.

73 *As for coordination with the state.* Acting Commissioner Zimmerman had identified state willingness as one of four criteria. Philp, *Termination*, p. 71. The Interior Department asserted that it used this approach. *See, e.g.*, Joint Hearings on Termination, pt. 1, p. 17.

73 *"Now it is my feeling."* Joint Hearings on Termination, pt. 6, p. 651.

73 *"If you are basing that." Ibid.*

73 *"So the State of Wisconsin." Ibid.*, pp. 650–62.

73 *Harder and Wisconsin Congressman Laird. Ibid.*, pp. 594–605.

73 *Another unusual aspect.* Orfield, "A Study," p. 688.

73 *"We became convinced."* Shames, *Freedom with Reservation*, p. 8.

73 *Several tribal witnesses requested.* Joint Hearings on Termination, pt. 6, p. 741 (March 12, 1954).

74   *"MR. WAUPOCHICK. Thank you very much." Ibid.*, pp. 743–44 (emphasis added).

75   *The Klamath Tribe of Oregon.* On the Klamath Tribe, see generally Stern, *The Klamath*. Land loss to the surveying error, national park designation, and allotment is summarized in *Oregon Department of Fish and Wildlife v. Klamath Indian Tribe*, 473 U.S. 753, 755–61 (1985). On the wagon road grant, see generally Jerry A. O'Callaghan, "Klamath Indians and the Oregon Wagon Road Grant, 1864–1938," vol. 53 *Oregon Historical Quarterly*, p. 23 (March 1952).

77   *Hunting was a major activity.* Theodore Stern, *The Klamath Tribe: A People and Their Reservation*, p. 192 (Seattle: University of Washington Press, 1966).

77   *$4,000 family income.* Joint Hearings on Termination, pt. 4, p. 208 (Feb. 23, 1954); *see* Historical Statistics, p. 297.

77   *$800 per capita payments. Ibid.*; Stern, *The Klamath*, p. 190.

77   *tribal members had little incentive. Ibid.* A study by a statutorily required group of "management" specialists concluded that unemployment probably was about two-thirds. "Task Force Ten," p. 49.

77   *Low education levels. See* Orfield, "A Study," pp. 686.

77   *"a very special economic niche."* Stern, *The Klamath*, p. 195.

77   *As early as the 1920s.* Rusco, *Fateful Time*, pp. 128–30.

77   *Crawford's followers. See, e.g.*, Philp, *Termination*, pp. 158–59.

77   *In the years leading up to termination. See, e.g.*, Joint Hearings on Termination, pt. 4, pp. 220–22, 269–74, 276–82 (Feb. 23, 1954).

77   *confused the Klamath.* Stanford Research Institute, "Preliminary Planning for Termination of Federal Control over the Klamath Indian Tribe," Project I-1440, pp. 25, 28–29 (1956) (cited in Doug Foster, "Landless Tribes: Termination of the Klamath Reservation," vol. 1, no. 2 *Oregon Heritage*, p. 6 [1994]).

77   *American Indian Policy Review Commission.* "Task Force Ten," pp. 54–55.

78   *"new policy to give the Indians."* Joint Hearings on Termination, pt. 4, p. 290 (Feb. 24, 1954).

78   *"REPRESENTATIVE BERRY. I would just like to ask this question." Ibid.*, p. 217 (Feb. 23, 1954).

79   *"MR. JACKSON. It seems to me that the present move." Ibid.*, pp. 258–59, 263.

81   *Six termination acts.* For a listing of all terminated tribes, see Wilkinson and Biggs, "Evolution," p. 151.

81   *Termination affected at least. Ibid.*

81   *The Menominee plan.* U.S. Department of the Interior, Bureau of Indian Affairs, "Plan for the Future Control of Menominee Indian Tribal Property and Future Service Functions," vol. 26, no. 82 *Federal Register*, p. 3727 (April 29, 1961).

81   *Every terminated tribe floundered.* On terminated Western Oregon tribes, *see*, for example, "Task Force Ten," pp. 61–65; Hearing Before the Senate Select Committee on Indian Affairs, "Establishment of a Siletz Indian Reservation:

On S. 2055 (To Establish a Reservation for the Confederated Tribes of Siletz Indians of Oregon), 96th Congress, 1st Session (Washington, DC: U.S. Government Printing Office, 1980).

82   *"What it did to the tribe."* Foster, "Landless Tribes," p. 7.

82   *The Menominee managed to avoid. See generally* Stephen J. Herzberg, "The Menominee Indians: Termination to Restoration," vol. 6, no. 1 *American Indian Law Review*, p. 143 (1978).

82   *The tribe had expended.* Personal communication from Joseph Preloznik, Menominee tribal attorney, received by author (date unknown).

82   *After Congress terminated federal services.* On Menominee health care, see Shames, *Freedom with Reservation,* pp. 41–45

82   *widespread discrimination.* Kenneth A. Mines, Regional Civil Rights Director, Office for Civil Rights, Department of Health, Education, and Welfare, letter to Arnold A. Gruber, Superintendent, Shawano Board of Education (Oct. 4, 1972) (on file with author).

83   *fraud and exploitation.* The Federal Trade Commission documented consumer abuse at the time of termination in U.S. Department of Commerce, Federal Trade Commission, Seattle Regional Office, "A Report of Consumer Problems of the Klamath Indians: A Case for Action" (Washington, DC: U.S. Government Printing Office, 1973).

83   *A small minority of remaining members.* "Task Force Ten," pp. 57–58.

83   *"few lasting benefits from termination."* W. T. Trulove and David Bunting, "The Economic Impact of Federal Indian Policy: Incentives and Response of the Klamath Indians," in David H. Getches et al., *Cases and Materials on Federal Indian Law*, 1st ed. p. 95 (St. Paul, MN: West Publishing Co., 1979).

83   *A comprehensive survey.* Klamath Tribes Comprehensive Needs Assessment Staff, "The Klamath Tribes' Comprehensive Needs Assessment: Report and Analysis—Summary," pp. 156–57 (Chiloquin, OR: Klamath Tribes, 1989).

84   *non-Indians . . . took most of the animals.* In *Kimball v. Callahan*, 590 F.2d 768, 773, 775–77 (9th Cir. 1979), after a decade of tribal members' being denied any treaty rights, the tribe did establish that termination did not abrogate these treaty rights—that is, the ability of the tribe rather than the state, to set seasons, bag limits, and other regulations for tribal members. The tribe, however, did not seek exclusive rights, so that tribal members must compete with non-Indians licensed under Oregon law for fish and game on the former reservation.

84   *Forest Service clear-cutting.* Rick Ward, telephone interview with Jonathan Fero, research assistant, Nov. 6, 2003; *see also* Harold James Salwasser, "Ecology and Management of the Devil's Garden Interstate Deer Herd and Range," p. 79, Ph.D. dissertation, University of California, Berkeley (1979) (on file with author).

84   *Public Law 280. See generally* Carole E. Goldberg, "Public Law 280: The Limits of State Jurisdiction over Reservation Indians," vol. 22 *U.C.L.A. Law Review*, p. 535 (Feb. 1975).

84   *In 1968, Congress curtailed.* 25 U.S.C. §§ 1321(a), 1322(a), 1326 (2000).

85   *numerous tribes.* Vine Deloria, Jr., and Clifford M. Lytle, *American Indians,
      American Justice,* p. 176 (Austin: University of Texas Press, 1983); Christine
      Zuni, "Strengthening What Remains," vol. 7, no. 1 *Kansas Journal of Law and
      Public Policy,* p. 21 (1997); Orville N. Olney and David H. Getches, *Indian
      Courts and the Future: Report of the NAICJA Long Range Planning Project,* pp.
      11–12 (Washington, DC: U.S. Government Printing Office, 1978).

85   *"there was a lot of pressure."* Joseph H. Cash and Herbert T. Hoover, eds., *To
      Be an Indian: An Oral History,* p. 138 (New York: Holt, Rinehart and Winston,
      1971).

85   *100,000 Indians.* Donald L. Fixico, *The Urban Indian Experience in America,*
      p. 25 (Albuquerque: University of New Mexico Press, 2000).

85   *a similar number left.* On relocation, see generally Fixico, *Termination,* pp.
      134–57; Prucha, *Great Father,* pp. 1079–84; Fixico, *Urban Indian,* pp. 8–25.

85   *Urban life. See generally* Fixico, *Urban Indian,* pp. 13–16.

85   *Many returned home. Ibid.,* p. 20.

85   *"I think next week I'll go."* Personal communication received by author (com-
      plete date unknown, 1971).

85   *Although relocation provided few benefits. See, e.g.,* Fixico, *Urban Indian,* p. 25.

86   *"an acknowledged guide for the Supreme Court."* Philip B. Kurland, ed., *Of Law
      and Life and Other Things that Matter: Papers and Addresses of Felix Frank-
      furter, 1956–1963,* p. 143 (Cambridge, MA: Belknap Press, 1965).

86   *"Much of the earlier Federal law."* U.S. Department of the Interior, Office of the
      Solicitor, *Federal Indian Law,* p. 1 (Washington, DC: U.S. Government Print-
      ing Office, 1958).

86   *later cases in fact supported them. See Menominee Tribe of Indians v. United States,*
      391 U.S. 404, 410–13 (1968) (holding that the tribe's treaty hunting and fishing
      rights survived the Menominee Termination Act); *Washington v. Washington
      State Commercial Passenger Fishing Vessel Ass'n,* 443 U.S. 658, 674–79 (1979)
      (upholding the Pacific Northwest tribes' treaty right to take up to 50 percent
      of the harvestable fish passing through the tribes' usual and accustomed fish-
      ing places).

CHAPTER 4: The Making of a Movement

90   *"sustaining Indian figures."* Hank Adams, letter to author (April 15, 2001).

91   *Charles Eastman.* On Eastman, see generally his autobiography, Charles A.
      Eastman, *From the Deep Woods to Civilization: Chapters in the Autobiography
      of an Indian* (Lincoln: University of Nebraska Press, 1977).

92   *"as it was before."* Charles Alexander Eastman, *The Soul of the Indian: An Inter-
      pretation,* pp. ix–x (Lincoln: University of Nebraska Press, 1980).

92   *"The worship of the 'Great Mystery.' "* Ibid., pp. 4–5.

93   *"We believed that the spirit." Ibid.*, pp. 14–15, 47.

93   *"The native American." Ibid.*, pp. 9–10.

94   *"As a child." Ibid.*, p. 88.

94   *Black Elk embarked.* John G. Neihardt, *Black Elk Speaks: Being the Life Story of a Holy Man of the Oglala Sioux*, p. xi (Lincoln: University of Nebraska Press, 1961).

94   *conversations with fish. Ibid.*, p. 65.

95   *Black Elk's scalping. Ibid.*, p. 113.

95   *the naming of every month. Ibid.*, pp. 92, 95.

95   *the sweat lodge. Ibid.*, p. 187.

95   *the Lakota's love of the land. Ibid.*, p. 153.

95   *"You have noticed." Ibid.*, pp. 194, 195–96.

95   *"I know now what this meant." Ibid.*, p. 39.

96   *"After the heyoka ceremony." Ibid.*, pp. 194, 196.

96   *"As I made these shirts." Ibid.*, p. 243.

96   *"I did not know then." Ibid.*, p. 270.

96   *In later editions. Ibid.*, front matter.

96   *Joseph Epps Brown.* The book is Joseph Eppes Brown, ed., *The Sacred Pipe: Black Elk's Account of the Seven Rites of the Oglala Sioux* (Norman: University of Oklahoma Press, 1988).

97   *The medicine man. See generally* Michael F. Steltenkamp, *Black Elk: Holy Man of the Oglala* (Norman: University of Oklahoma Press, 1993).

97   *Christian-Indian relationships. See* Mary Young, "Pagans, Converts, and Backsliders, All: A Secular View," *in* Calvin Martin, ed., *The American Indian and the Problem of History*, pp. 78–79 (New York: Oxford University Press, 1987); Robert A. Brightman, "Toward a History of Indian Religion: Religious Changes in Native Societies," *in* Colin G. Calloway, ed., *New Directions in American Indian History*, pp. 239–40 (Norman: University of Oklahoma Press, 1988).

97   *In Black Elk's case. See generally* Clyde Holler, *Black Elk's Religion: The Sun Dance and Lakota Catholicism*, pp. 204–23 (Syracuse, NY: Syracuse University Press, 1995); *see also* Thomas E. Mails, *Fools Crow: Wisdom and Power*, pp. 19–20 (Tulsa, OK: Council Oak Books, 1991).

97   *Important too was the social work. See generally* Steltenkamp, *Black Elk.*

97   *Black Elk's granddaughter. Writings of Black Elk*, C-SPAN American Writers, VHS (Washington, DC: National Cable Satellite Corp., 2001).

97   *"The most important aspect."* Vine Deloria, Jr., "Introduction," *in* Neihardt, *Black Elk Speaks*, pp. xii–xiii.

98   *The third animating Indian voice.* Lawrence W. Towner, "Afterword," *in* D'Arcy McNickle, *The Surrounded*, p. 303 (Albuquerque: University of New Mexico Press, 1936); James Ruppert, *D'Arcy McNickle*, p. 6 (Boise, ID: Boise State

University Printing and Graphics Services, 1988); Birgit Hans, "Wards of the Government: Federal Indian Policy in 'How Anger Died,' " in John Lloyd Purdy, ed., *The Legacy of D'Arcy McNickle: Writer, Historian, Activist*, pp. 169–70 (Norman: University of Oklahoma Press, 1996).

98 *D'Arcy McNickle.* On McNickle's life, see generally Dorothy R. Parker, *Singing an Indian Song: A Biography of D'Arcy McNickle* (Lincoln: University of Nebraska Press, 1992); Purdy, *Legacy*; Ruppert, *D'Arcy McNickle*.

98 *McNickle's first published work.* Oliver La Farge, "Review of *The Surrounded*," *Saturday Review of Literature*, p. 10 (March 14, 1936); Ruppert, *D'Arcy McNickle*, p. 10.

98 *"magnificent barricade."* McNickle, *Surrounded*, p. 44.

98 *"a mirror to the sky."* Ibid., p. 43.

98 *Collier's inner circle. See, e.g.,* Parker, *Singing*, pp. 93–94.

99 *he explained federal tribal history. Indians and Other Americans* was coauthored with Harold Fey, but McNickle took the lead on the book. *See, e.g.,* Ruppert, *D'Arcy McNickle*, p. 36.

99 *In 1959.* Harold E. Fey and D'Arcy McNickle, *Indians and Other Americans: Two Ways of Life Meet*, pp. 47, 55–56 (New York: Harper and Brothers, 1959).

99 *"Trouble had come."* D'Arcy McNickle, *They Came Here First: The Epic of the American Indian*, pp. vii–ix (New York: Harper and Row, 1975).

101 *McNickle's last book.* On McNickle's process of writing *Wind from an Enemy Sky*, see, for example, Hans, "Wards."

101 *"The problem is communication."* D'Arcy McNickle, *Wind from an Enemy Sky*, p. 125 (San Francisco: Harper and Row, 1978).

102 *Association on American Indian Affairs.* On AAIA, see Thomas W. Cowger, *The National Congress of American Indians: The Founding Years*, pp. 35–36 (Lincoln: University of Nebraska Press, 1999); *Reference Encyclopedia of the American Indian*, 6th ed., p. 74 (West Nyack, NY: Todd Publications, 1993); Duane Champagne, ed., *The Native North American Almanac*, p. 222 (Detroit: Gale Research, 1994).

102 *Society of the American Indian.* On the SAI and the Teepee Order, see, for example, Hazel W. Hertzberg, *The Search for an American Indian Identity: Modern Pan-Indian Movements*, pp. 31–38, 199–200, 213–21 (Syracuse, NY: Syracuse University Press, 1971).

102 *McNickle and fellow BIA employees.* On these early organizational efforts, see Parker, *Singing*, pp. 105–06; Cowger, *National*, pp. 25, 30–33; Alison R. Bernstein, *American Indians and World War II: Toward a New Era in Indian Affairs*, pp. 112–13 (Norman: University of Oklahoma Press, 1991); Kenneth R. Philp, *Termination Revisited: American Indians on the Trail to Self-Determination, 1933–1953*, pp. 13–14 (Lincoln: University of Nebraska Press, 1999).

102 *The inaugural convention.* Parker, *Singing*, p. 106; "Indian Tribal Parley Closes

with Election: National Congress May Return to Denver for 1945 Meeting," *Denver Post*, p. 12 (Nov. 19, 1944).

102 *"Basil Two Bears was asked."* Parker, *Singing*, p. 107.

103 *Turning to less exciting matters.* Cowger, *National*, p.44.

103 *The concept was right.* Wilcomb E. Washington, ed., vol. 4 *History of Indian-White Relations, in* William C. Sturtevant, ed., *Handbook of North American Indians*, p. 312 (Washington, DC: Smithsonian Institution, 1988); Cowger, *National*, p. 109. On McNickle's influence, *see Ibid.*, p. 33. The original NCAI constitution allowed off-reservation Indian groups and voluntary organizations membership, but that was amended in the 1955 to limit voting to "bonafide Indian tribes." Washington, *Indian-White Relations*, p. 315; Cowger, *National*, p. 109.

103 *Twenty-five thousand. See* Bernstein, *American Indians*, p. 40; U.S. Department of Commerce, Bureau of the Census, "Historical Statistics of the United States: Colonial Times to 1957," p. 8 (Washington, DC: U.S. Government Printing Office, 1960).

103 *They gained a reputation.* Bernstein, *American Indians*, pp. 54–61.

103 *On coming home. See Ibid.*, pp. 149–50.

103 *"Some spent a few days."* Vine Deloria, Jr., "This Country Was a Lot Better Off when the Indians Were Running It," sec. 6 *New York Times Magazine*, p. 50 (March 8, 1970); *see also* Frederick E. Hoxie, ed., *Encyclopedia of North American Indians*, p. 653 (New York: Houghton Mifflin Co., 1996) (suggesting that World War II played a direct role in moving American Indians to cities).

104 *"World War Two."* Bernstein, *American Indians*, p. 158.

104 *Arizona Supreme Court case. Harrison v. Laveen*, 196 P.2d 456, 459, 462–63 (Ariz. 1948).

104 *In the New Mexico case.* Bernstein, *American Indians*, pp. 139–40 (quoting *Trujillo v. Garley*, No. 1353 [D.N.M. Aug. 11, 1948] [three-judge court]). In 1956, Utah became the last state to lift the restrictions on Indian suffrage. Vine Deloria, Jr., ed., *American Indian Policy in the Twentieth Century*, p. 108 (Norman: University of Oklahoma Press, 1985).

104 *Joe Garry.* On Garry, see John Fahey, *Saving the Reservation: Joe Garry and the Battle to Be Indian* (Seattle: University of Washington Press, 2001).

105 *Lacking money.* Robert L. Bennett et al., "Relocation," *in* Kenneth R. Philp, ed., *Indian Self-Rule: First-Hand Accounts of Indian-White Relations from Roosevelt to Reagan*, p. 170 (Salt Lake City: Howe Brothers, 1986).

105 *"Hang on to your lands."* Fahey, *Saving*, p. 53.

105 *Garry appeared.* Joint Hearings Before the Committees on Interior and Insular Affairs, Subcommittees, "Termination of Federal Supervision over Certain Tribes of Indians: On S. 2749 and H. R. 7322," 83rd Congress, 2d Session, pt. 1, pp. 77–79 (Feb. 15, 1954) (Washington, DC: U.S. Government Printing Office, 1954) [hereinafter Joint Hearings on Termination].

105 *"We had little understanding."* Philp, *Indian Self-Rule*, pp. 169–70.

105 *They called an emergency conference.* Fahey, *Saving*, p. 5.

105 *Held just two weeks. Ibid.*, p. 6; Cowger, *National*, pp. 114.

105 *"one-sided approach."* Bernstein, *American Indians*, p. 174; Cowger, *National*, p. 116.

106 *more than 100 participants. Ibid.*

106 *Their presence. See generally* Joint Hearings on Termination, pt. 7 (Feb. 25–27, 1954); Larry W. Burt, *Tribalism in Crisis: Federal Indian Policy, 1953–1961*, pp. 36–38 (Albuquerque, University of New Mexico Press, 1982).

106 *Deloria . . . grew up.* Vine Deloria, Jr., interviews with author, Golden, Colorado, June 8, 2000, and Boulder, Colorado, Aug. 4, 2000.

107 Williams v. Lee. 358 U.S 217 (1959).

107 *"What you could see."* Deloria, interview, Aug. 4, 2000.

107 *His three years. See, e.g.*, Cowger, *National*, pp. 148–49.

107 *"This is when I started writing."* Deloria, interview, Aug. 4, 2000.

108 Custer Died for Your Sins. Vine Deloria, Jr., *Custer Died for Your Sins: An Indian Manifesto* (New York: Avon Books, 1969).

109 *"We will survive." Ibid.*, p. 221.

110 *"This is all I have to offer."* Paul Chaat Smith and Robert Allen Warrior, *Like a Hurricane: The Indian Movement from Alcatraz to Wounded Knee*, p. 42 (New York: New Press, 1996). On Warrior, see generally *Ibid.*, pp. 36–59; Stan Steiner, *The New Indians*, pp. 66–72 (New York: Dell Publishing Co., 1968); Hoxie, *Encyclopedia*, pp. 665–66; Deloria, interview, June 8, 2000.

110 *Hank Adams.* Hank Adams, interviews with author, Olympia, Washington, Nov. 5, 1997, and June 23, 2001; *see also* Smith and Warrior, *Like a Hurricane*, 44–46; Champagne, *Native North American*, pp. 996–97.

111 *"We had decided."* Steiner, *New Indians*, p. 40. On Thom, see, for example, Smith and Warrior, *Like a Hurricane*, pp. 43, 53, 99.

111 *Declaration of Indian Purpose. See generally* Alvin M. Josephy, Jr., *Red Power: The American Indians' Fight for Freedom*, pp. 49–52 (New York: American Heritage Press, 1971).

111 *"We, the Indian people." Ibid.*, p. 49.

111 *National Indian Youth Council. See, e.g.*, Steiner, *New Indians*, pp. 40–41, 66–72; Cowger, *National*, pp. 140–41; Champagne, *Native North American*, pp. 566–67.

111 *The four fed off one another.* Deloria, interview, June 8, 2000.

111 *Hundreds of people attended.* On Warrior's funeral, see Hoxie, *Encyclopedia*, p. 666.

CHAPTER 5: Leadership on the Reservations

114 *he traveled to Philadelphia.* Joy A. Bilharz, *The Allegany Senecas and Kinzua Dam: Forced Relocation Through Two Generations*, pp. 9–10 (Lincoln: University of Nebraska Press, 1998).

114 *Four years later.* A Treaty Between the United States of America, and the
     Tribes of Indians Called the Six Nations, Nov. 11, 1794, 7 Stat. 44, 45 (1846);
     see generally Bilharz, *Allegany Senecas*, pp. 9–11; Anthony F. C. Wallace, *The
     Death and Rebirth of the Seneca*, pp. 168–79 (New York: Alfred A. Knopf, 1969).

114 *"particularly essential that our word."* Laurence M. Hauptman, *The Iroquois
     Struggle for Survival: World War II to Red Power*, p. 109 (Syracuse, NY: Syra-
     cuse University Press, 1986).

114 *"Flooding the Conewango Valley."* *Ibid.*, p. 114.

115 *Justice and interior promptly reversed.* Bilharz, *Allegany Senecas*, pp. 48–54;
     Hauptman, *Iroquois Struggle*, pp. 105–14.

115 *The corps designed.* Alvin M. Josephy, Jr., *Now that the Buffalo's Gone: A Study
     of Today's American Indians*, pp. 127–28, 140 (New York: Alfred A. Knopf,
     1982); Hauptman, *Iroquois Struggle*, pp. 85–92.

115 *Habitat, uprooting, and the longhouse.* Bilharz, *Allegany Senecas*, pp. 1, 62, 75.

115 *Thousands of Seneca graves.* Josephy, *Buffalo's Gone*, p. 141.

115 *Working without any staff.* Bilharz, *Allegany Senecas*, pp. 50–52. Hauptman,
     Iroquois Struggle, p. 114.

116 *Moved deeply by the Indian cause.* Josephy has written extensively on Indi-
     ans. *See, e.g.*, Alvin M. Josephy, Jr., *The Nez Perce Indians and the Opening of
     the Northwest*, abr. ed. (New Haven, CT: Yale University Press, 1971); Jose-
     phy, *Buffalo's Gone*; Alvin M. Josephy, Jr., "The Murder of the Southwest,"
     vol. 73 *Audubon* (July 1971).

116 *For the wrongs at Seneca. See* Alvin M. Josephy, Jr., "Cornplanter, Can You
     Swim?," vol. 20 *American Heritage*, p. 4 (Dec. 1968).

116 *The memorial purports.* Josephy, *Buffalo's Gone*, pp. 146, 150.

117 *The tribe's court challenges.* The two cases are *Seneca Nation of Indians v.
     United States*, 338 F.2d 55 (2d Cir. 1964); *Seneca Nation of Indians v. Brucker*,
     162 F. Supp. 580 (D.D.C. 1958). The Seneca Nation's basic position was that
     although Congress had granted the Army Corps of Engineers general author-
     ity to build water projects throughout the Ohio River basin, the statutes
     never suggested any intention to break Indian treaties. *Seneca*, 162 F. Supp.
     at 581. The Seneca's claims came just a few years too early; by the late 1960s
     modern Indian law had begun to mature, and the judicial decisions, looking
     to early opinions by Chief Justice John Marshall requiring high respect for
     Indian treaties, ruled that administrative agencies could not violate Indian
     treaties without clear congressional direction. *See, e.g.*, *United States v. Win-
     nebago Tribe of Nebraska*, 542 F.2d 1002, 1004–05 (8th Cir. 1976); *Confederated
     Tribes of the Umatilla Indian Reservation v. Alexander*, 440 F. Supp. 553, 555–56
     (D. Or. 1977). *See generally Menominee Tribe of Indians v. United States*, 391
     U.S. 404, 410–13 (1968); *Felix S. Cohen's Handbook of Federal Indian Law*, 1982
     ed., pp. 282–86 (Charlottesville, VA: Michie Bobbs-Merrill, 1982).

117 *In the West.* On the Army Corps of Engineers, Bureau of Reclamation, and
     the postwar era in the West, see generally Marc Reisner, *Cadillac Desert: The
     American West and Its Disappearing Water* (New York: Viking, 1986); Peter

Wiley and Robert Gottlieb, *Empires in the Sun: The Rise of the New American West* (Tucson: University of Arizona Press, 1985); Charles Wilkinson, *Fire on the Plateau: Conflict and Endurance in the American Southwest* (Washington, DC: Island Press, 1999); Charles F. Wilkinson, *Crossing the Next Meridian: Land, Water, and the Future of the West* (Washington, DC: Island Press, 1992).

118   *five Sioux reservations.* Michael L. Lawson, *Dammed Indians: The Pick-Sloan Plan and the Missouri River Sioux, 1944–1980*, p. 29 (Norman: University of Oklahoma Press, 1982); John E. Thorson, *River of Promise, River of Peril: The Politics of Managing the Missouri River*, pp. 80–83 (Lawrence: University Press of Kansas, 1994).

118   *Among the upriver tribes.* Marjane Ambler, *Breaking the Iron Bonds: Indian Control of Energy Development*, p. 204 (Lawrence: University Press of Kansas, 1990) (The flooded land comprised "nearly all the reservation's commercial timber, most of the wildlife habitat, and many of the accessible coal seams."); Thorson, *River of Promise*, pp. 80–83.

118   *The dams flooded. See, e.g.*, Mark D. O'Keefe et al., *Boundaries Carved in Water: An Analysis of River and Water Management in the Upper Missouri Basin*, p. 19 (Missoula, MT: Northern Lights Research and Education Institute, 1986) (discussing the flooding caused by Garrison Dam in North Dakota).

118   *The agencies stonewalled. See, e.g.*, the most extensive study, Lawson, *Dammed Indians*, p. 29, 80–134.

118   *Federal negotiators. See, e.g., Ibid.*, pp. 60–61, 84–86.

118   *Payments averaged. See Ibid.*, pp. 60–62.

119   *"the tribe just couldn't." Ibid.*, p. 86. On the tribes' dealings with the Corps regarding the Pick-Sloan Agreement, see generally *Ibid.*, pp. 69–87.

119   *Tribal chairmen Martin Cross.* On Cross and the Garrison Dam, *see* Paul Van-Develder, *Coyote Warrior: One Man, Three Tribes, and the Trial That Forged a Nation* (New York: Little, Brown and Company, 2004).

120   *"You know that famous photograph."* Susan Johnson, interview with author, Verde Valley, Arizona, March 19, 2002.

121   *"In little more than one generation."* Vera Springer, "Power and the Pacific Northwest: A History of the Bonneville Power Administration," p. 101 (Washington, DC: U.S. Government Printing Office, 1976).

122   *salmon runs were in free fall.* Wilkinson, *Crossing*, p. 201.

122   *The salmon tribes. See, e.g.*, Richard White, *The Organic Machine*, pp. 91, 93 (New York: Hill and Wang, 1995); *see also* Wilkinson, *Crossing*, p. 198 ("feeling powerless . . . the Indians' main reaction was to express wonderment at why the white man would do such things").

122   *"in the history of the United States."* National Water Commission, Final Report, pp. 474–75; *see also* Wiley and Gottlieb, *Empires*, pp. 234–38; Wilkinson, *Fire*, pp. 165–68, 197–203.

122 *Coal, oil, and gas.* See generally Ambler, *Breaking*, pp. 31–61.

123 *"You pass all kinds of laws."* Wilkinson, *Fire*, p. 293. On the Hopi, Black Mesa, and Boyden, *see generally Ibid.*, pp. 280–94.

123 *"The ultimate answer."* Thomas Biolsi, *"Deadliest Enemies": Law and the Making of Race Relations on and off Rosebud Reservation*, p. 104 (Berkeley: University of California Press, 2001).

123 *A perfect mechanism.* See supra ch. 1, pp. 17–18.

123 *Although South Dakota officials.* Richmond L. Clow, "State Jurisdiction on Sioux Reservations: Indian and Non-Indian Responses, 1952–1964," vol. 11, no. 3 *South Dakota History*, p. 173 (1981).

124 *"the Wounded Knee of 1963." Ibid.*, p. 178.

124 *Within two weeks. Ibid.*, p. 179.

124 *Sioux leaders. Ibid.*, pp. 173–84.

124 *90 percent of Sioux people voted.* Stan Steiner, *The New Indians*, p. 248 (New York: Harper and Row, 1968).

125 *The referendum passed.* Biolsi, *"Deadliest Enemies,"* p. 115.

125 *The tribal newspaper headline.* Steiner, *New Indians*, p. 249.

125 *"You are not giving." Ibid.*, p. 196.

125 *In the early 1960s.* Cellestine Maus, interview with author, Bemidji, Minnesota, March 24, 2001.

125 *"We can build them better."* Roger Jourdain, interview with author, Bemidji, Minnesota, March 24, 2001.

125 *He began paving the way.* On the health facility, see "Jourdain/Perpich Nursing Home Is Dedicated," *in* Red Lake Nation, *30 Years of Leadership* (Red Lake, MN: Red Lake Nation, 1990); Red Lake Band of Chippewa Indians, Tribal Council, "Red Lake Hospital and Health Care Facility and Staff Housing Project" (Red Lake, MN: Red Lake Band of Chippewa Indians, date unknown) (both on file with the author).

125 *the Minnesota Supreme Court later ruled. Red Lake Band of Chippewa Indians v. State*, 248 N.W.2d 722, 727–29 (Minn. 1976).

126 *"Indian people should make."* Edward Helmore, "Obituary: Wendell Chino," *Independent-London*, p. 6 (Nov. 30, 1998).

126 *He wrested control. Ibid.*

126 *"Navajos . . . make rugs." Ibid.*

126 *Cato Valandra.* Joseph H. Cash, "Dakota Images: Cato W. Valandra," vol. 19, no. 3 *South Dakota History*, p. 453 (1989).

127 *Robert Jim and Eagle Seelatsee.* See *infra* ch. 7.

127 *Other influential tribal leaders.* Vine Deloria, Jr., interview with author, Boulder, Colorado, Aug. 4, 2000.

127 *"Look, in many ways."* Vine Deloria, Jr., interview with author, Golden, Colorado, June 8, 2000.

127 *Capital Conference.* Alvin M. Josephy, Jr., *Red Power: The American Indians' Fight for Freedom*, pp. 65–66 (New York: American Heritage Press, 1971); *see also* James E. Officer, "The Bureau of Indian Affairs Since 1945: An Assessment," vol. 436 *Annals of the American Academy of Political and Social Science*, p. 65 (March 1978); S. Lyman Tyler, *A History of Indian Policy*, p. 211 (Washington, DC: U.S. Government Printing Office, 1973).

128 *When the OEO legislation passed.* Although they were not authorized explicitly by the statute as originally passed, Economic Opportunity Act of 1964, Pub. L. No. 88-452, Aug. 20, 1964, 78 Stat. 508 (1965) (codified as amended at 42 U.S.C. §§ 2701–2996 [2000]), there was a widespread understanding that tribal community action projects could receive direct funding, and tribal CAPs in fact received OEO grants from the beginning. Sar A. Levitan, *The Great Society's Poor Law: A New Approach to Poverty*, pp. 263–68 (Baltimore: Johns Hopkins University Press, 1969); *1982 Cohen Handbook*, p. 713 (citing American Indian Law Center, "Study of Statutory Barriers to Tribal Participation in Federal Domestic Assistance Programs," pp. 1, 31–32 [Albuquerque, NM: American Indian Law Center, 1975]); *see also* House Report No. 1458, "Economic Opportunity Act of 1964," 88th Congress, 2d Session, p. 10 (Washington, DC: U.S. Government Printing Office, 1964). Three years later Congress amended the statute to provide expressly for direct OEO funding to tribal governments. Economic Opportunity Amendments of 1967, Pub. L. No. 90-222, sec. 104, Dec. 23, 1967, 81 Stat. 672, 692 (1968) (codified at 42 U.S.C. §§ 2790[a], [f] [Supp. V 1964], repealed by Omnibus Budget Reconciliation Act of 1981, Pub. L. No. 97-35, sec. 683, Aug. 13, 1981, 95 Stat. 357, 519 [1982]).

128 *"The 1960s was above all else."* Philip S. Deloria, "The Era of Indian Self-Determination: An Overview," *in* Kenneth R. Philp, ed., *Indian Self-Rule: First-Hand Accounts of Indian-White Relations from Roosevelt to Reagan*, p. 196 (Logan: Utah State University Press, 1995).

CHAPTER 6: Red Power

129 *"In the minds of most people."* Vine Deloria, Jr., *Custer Died for Your Sins: An Indian Manifesto*, pp. 179–80 (Norman: University of Oklahoma Press, 1988). Deloria does a fine job on these issues in his chapter "The Red and the Black," *in Ibid.*, pp. 169–96.

129 *Indians, then, stayed away.* Vine Deloria, Jr., interview with author, Aug. 4, 2000.

129 *Some Indians did march.* Deloria, *Custer*, p. 183.

130 *The Lumbee Tribe.* On the Lumbee, see generally Karen I. Blu, *The Lumbee Problem: The Making of an American Indian People* (New York: Cambridge University Press, 1980); Adolph L. Dial, *The Lumbee* (New York: Chelsea

House Publishers, 1993); Adolph L. Dial and David K. Eliades, *The Only Land I Know: A History of the Lumbee Indians* (Syracuse, NY: Syracuse University Press, 1996); Gerald M. Sider, *Lumbee Indian Histories: Race, Ethnicity, and Indian Identity in the Southern United States* (New York: Cambridge University Press, 1993).

131 *The local Ku Klux Klan.* A detailed firsthand account of these events is Charles Craven, "The Robeson County Indian Uprising Against the KKK," vol. 57, no. 4 *South Atlantic Quarterly*, p. 433 (1958). The episode is also given major treatment in each of the histories cited in the prior note. The evening was sufficiently chaotic that the various sources differ on such details as the exact location of the event, the number of people in attendance, whether the light was shot out or knocked out with a shotgun barrel, and so forth. I have done my best to resolve such inconsistencies.

131 *"I can't control this crowd." Ibid.*, p. 439.

132 *A shot from an Indian rifle. See Ibid.*, pp. 439–40.

132 *A Robeson County judge.* On sentencing, see *Ibid.*, p. 441. For the *Life* magazine article, see "Bad Medicine for the Klan: North Carolina Indians Break Up Ku Klux Meeting," vol. 44, no. 4 *Life*, p. 26 (1958).

132 *One scholar tells.* Blu, *Lumbee Problem*, p. 89.

132 *Kelvin Sampson.* Dave Krieger, "Sooners' Grit Reflection of Sampson's Dad," *Rocky Mountain News*, p. 1D (March 30, 2002).

132 *Mohawk boycotted public schools.* Stephen Cornell, *The Return of the Native: American Indian Political Resurgence*, p. 189 (New York: Oxford University Press, 1988).

132 *Cherokee protested. Ibid.*

132 *Indians in the Northwest. Ibid.*; see *infra* ch. 7, pp. **168–70**.

132 *Navajo and Hopi demonstrated. See Ibid.*, pp. 197, 201; Alvin M. Josephy, Jr., "The Murder of the Southwest," vol. 73 *Audubon*, pp. 54, 64 (July 1971).

132 *Alaska Natives picketed. See, e.g.*, Robert D. Arnold, *Alaska Native Land Claims*, p. 131 (Anchorage: Alaska Native Foundation, 1978).

132 *Native Hawaiians sat in.* Michael Reese and Martin Kasindorf, "The Comeback for Hawaii," *Newsweek*, p. 43 (Sept. 13, 1982); *see also* Viveca Novak, "Hawaii's Dirty Secret," *Common Cause*, pp. 16–17 (Nov./Dec. 1989) (discussing Native Hawaiians' organized opposition against a large geothermal energy project).

133 *"Native people often came."* Wilma Mankiller and Michael Wallis, *Mankiller: A Chief and Her People*, pp. 192–93 (New York: St. Martin's Press, 2000).

133 *Alcatraz.* The landing is described in the most detailed source on the Alcatraz occupation, Troy R. Johnson, *The Occupation of Alcatraz Island: Indian Self-Determination and the Rise of Indian Activism*, pp. 46–75 (Urbana: University of Illinois Press, 1996); *see also* Adam Fortunate Eagle, *Alcatraz! Alcatraz!: The Indian Occupation of 1969–1971*, pp. 71–74 (Berkeley, CA: Heyday

Books, 1992); Paul Chaat Smith and Robert Allen Warrior, *Like a Hurricane: The Indian Movement from Alcatraz to Wounded Knee*, pp. 18–24 (New York: New Press, 1996).

134 *Alcatraz Proclamation.* Fortunate Eagle, *Alcatraz!*, pp. 44–48; Smith and Warrior, *Like a Hurricane*, pp. 28–30.

134 *"Alcatraz was symbolic."* Richard Oakes, "Alcatraz Is Not an Island," vol. 11 *Ramparts*, p. 40 (Dec. 1972).

134 *The media response. See, e.g.*, Johnson, *The Occupation*, pp. 55, 63, 93; Smith and Warrior, *Like a Hurricane*, pp. 11–16.

135 *the Coast Guard.* Fortunate Eagle, *Alcatraz!*, pp. 74–77.

135 *There were celebrities. See, e.g., Ibid.*, p. 120; Mankiller and Wallis, *Mankiller*, p. 191.

136 *Richard Oakes's little daughter.* Adam Fortunate Eagle, *Heart of the Rock: The Indian Invasion of Alcatraz*, pp. 165–66 (Norman: University of Oklahoma Press, 2002).

136 *Accentuating the social ills.* Smith and Warrior, *Like a Hurricane*, p. 61.

136 *federal negotiators made a serious offer.* Johnson, *The Occupation*, p. 190–91.

137 *the last fifteen occupiers. Ibid.*, pp. 212–13; Smith and Warrior, *Like a Hurricane*, pp. 108–10.

137 *"There was one old man."* Oakes, "Not an Island," p. 40.

137 *"It affected how I think of myself."* Troy Johnson et al., "American Indian Activism and Transformation: Lessons from Alcatraz," *in* Johnson et al., *American Indian Activism: Alcatraz to the Longest Walk*, p. 31 (Urbana: University of Illinois Press, 1997).

137 *"Although Alcatraz ultimately would not remain."* Mankiller and Wallis, *Mankiller*, pp. 192–93.

138 *Minnesota's jails.* Peter Matthiessen, *In the Spirit of Crazy Horse*, p. 34 (New York: Viking Penguin, 1991); Vine Deloria, Jr., *Behind the Trail of Broken Treaties: An Indian Declaration of Independence*, pp. 35–36 (New York: Delacorte Press, 1974); *see also* Judith Rosenblatt, ed., *Indians in Minnesota*, 4th ed., pp. 241–42 (Minneapolis: University of Minnesota Press, 1985) (citing significant statistical differences for arrests and court treatments among the Indian and white populations).

138 *To head off trouble.* On the early days of AIM, see, for example, Deloria, *Behind the Trail*, pp. 34–37; Matthiessen, *In the Spirit*, pp. 34–37; Rex Weyler, *Blood of the Land: The Government and Corporate War Against the American Indian Movement*, pp. 35–37 (New York: Everest House, 1982).

138 *an estimated 100,000 listeners.* Johnson, *Occupation*, p. 85.

138 *Russell Means.* On Means, see generally his autobiography, Russell Means, *Where White Men Fear to Tread* (New York: St. Martin's Press, 1995).

138 *Yet Means never lost touch. Ibid.*, pp. 11–15.

139 *AIM instigated.* Weyler, *Blood*, p. 46 (Fort Snelling and Milwaukee Coast Guard base); Smith and Warrior, *Like a Hurricane*, p. 144 (Fort Sill Indian School).

139 *"kitchen justice."* Weyler, *Blood*, p. 48.

139 *In Gordon, Nebraska.* On the Yellow Thunder incident, see generally Smith and Warrior, *Like a Hurricane*, pp. 112–26.

139 *The pattern was all too familiar.* Deloria, *Behind the Trail*, pp. 48–53; Smith and Warrior, *Like a Hurricane*, p. 140; Weyler, *Blood*, pp. 48–49.

140 *"The Caravan must be."* Smith and Warrior, *Like a Hurricane*, p. 143. On the organization of the Trail of Broken Treaties, see generally *Ibid.*, pp. 141–43.

141 TRAIL OF BROKEN TREATIES, UNITED STATES. Means, *White Men*, p. 225.

141 *The Minneapolis meeting.* On Adams's drafting of the Twenty Points, see *Ibid.*, pp. 227–28; Smith and Warrior, *Like a Hurricane*, p. 144.

141 *Adams's central premise.* On the Twenty Points, see generally Deloria, *Behind the Trail*, pp. 48-53; Vine Deloria, Jr., and Clifford M. Lytle, *The Nations Within: The Past and Future of American Indian Sovereignty*, pp. 237-39 (New York: Pantheon Books, 1984).

141 *To be sure, AIM dominated.* See Robert Burnette and John Koster, *The Road to Wounded Knee*, p. 203 (New York: Bantam Books, 1974); Means, *White Men*, p. 226; Smith and Warrior, *Like a Hurricane*, p. 147.

142 *press coverage of the colorful entourage.* See, *e.g.*, William M. Blair, "Indians to Begin Capital Protests," *New York Times*, p. 31 (Oct. 31, 1972).

142 *BIA officials refused.* See, *e.g.*, Weyler, *Blood*, pp. 49–50.

142 *the occupiers . . . tore the place apart.* On the occupation, see generally Smith and Warrior, *Like a Hurricane*, pp. 149–68; Weyler, *Blood*, pp. 49–57.

143 *Now the occupiers chose.* Smith and Warrior, *Like a Hurricane*, pp. 162–63.

143 *A white man had knifed.* See Rolland Dewing, "South Dakota Newspaper Coverage of the 1973 Occupation of Wounded Knee," vol. 12, no. 1 *South Dakota History*, pp. 61–62 (1982).

143 *charges of racism rang out.* Smith and Warrior, *Like a Hurricane*, pp. 182–85; Weyler, *Blood*, pp. 67–69.

144 *The tension soon built.* The 1973 Wounded Knee takeover has generated much controversy and treatment in the literature. *See, e.g.*, Matthiessen, *In the Spirit*, pp. 58–82; Smith and Warrior, *Like a Hurricane*, pp. 218–44; Weyler, *Blood*, pp. 58–96. Stanley David Lyman, *Wounded Knee 1973: A Personal Account* (Lincoln: University of Nebraska Press, 1991) is a useful account by the BIA superintendent at Pine Ridge. John William Sayer, *Ghost Dancing the Law: The Wounded Knee Trials* (Cambridge, MA: Harvard University Press, 1997) examines the prosecutions that followed the occupations. For additional information, see also Rolland Dewing, *Wounded Knee II* (Chadron, NE: Great Plains Network, 2000); Bill Zimmerman, *Airlift to Wounded Knee* (Chicago: Swallow Press, 1977); *Voices from Wounded Knee, 1973: In the Words*

of the Participants (Rooseveltown, NY: Akwesasne Notes, Mohawk Nation, 1979).

144   *The stocky, burr-cut Wilson.* Means, *White Men*, pp. 218.

144   *Wilson doled out jobs.* Matthiessen, *In the Spirit*, p. 60.

144   *Now the government wanted.* Weyler, *Blood*, pp. 71–72.

144   *a tribal civil rights group.* Smith and Warrior, *Like a Hurricane*, pp. 191–93; Weyler, *Blood*, pp. 73–74.

144   *the reservation was aswarm.* On law enforcement, see, for example, Smith and Warrior, *Hurrricane*, pp. 196–97; Weyler, *Blood*, pp. 72–74.

145   *Wilson's "goons."* See, e.g., Deloria, *Behind the Trail*, pp. 71–72; Matthiessen, *In the Spirit*, p. 61; Weyler, *Blood*, pp. 32, 60–61.

145   *"We decided that we did need."* Sayer, *Ghost Dancing*, p. 32.

145   *"Go ahead and do it."* Smith and Warrior, *Like a Hurricane*, p. 200.

146   *"The Sioux issued a series of demands." Ibid.*, p. 204.

146   *South Dakota senators.* Means, *White Men*, p. 266.

146   *President Richard Nixon.* Smith and Warrior, *Like a Hurricane*, p. 208.

146   *Across the country. See, e.g., Ibid.*, p. 207.

147   *the government forces fired. See, e.g.*, Weyler, *Blood*, pp. 91–93.

147   *Buddy Lamont and Frank Clearwater.* Smith and Warrior, *Like a Hurricane*, p. 259.

147   *Lloyd Grimm. Ibid.*, p. 234.

147   *"As Wounded Knee unfolds."* Dewing, "South Dakota," p. 54. For an assessment of AIM's "coup d'etat" of media coverage, see Desmond Smith, "Wounded Knee: The Media Coup d'Etat," vol. 216, no. 26 *Nation*, p. 806 (1973).

147   *While Indians sometimes broke. See* Zimmerman, *Airlift*, pp. 268–70.

147   *The federal government controlled. See, e.g.*, Deloria, *Behind the Trail*, p. 79; Smith and Warrior, *Like a Hurricane*, pp. 261–68.

148   *The Department of Justice then proceeded.* Smith and Warrior, *Like a Hurricane*, p. 270 (562 total arrests); Sayer, *Ghost Dancing*, pp. 44.

148   *William Kunstler. Ibid.*, p. 45; Smith and Warrior, *Like a Hurricane*, p. 271. On Kunstler, see generally his autobiography, William M. Kunstler, *My Life as a Radical Lawyer* (New York: Birch Lane Press, 1994).

148   *The defendants regularly charged government misconduct. See, e.g.*, Sayer, *Ghost Dancing*, pp. 58, 79, 167–70; Weyler, *Blood*, pp. 105–31.

148   *Judges threw out some charges.* Sayer, *Ghost Dancing*, p. 4.

148   *"I think to some extent." Ibid.*, p. 228 (quoting David Gienapp, assistant U.S. attorney, who with R. D. Hurd prosecuted the Means-Banks St. Paul trial).

149   *"virtually every AIM leader."* Weyler, *Blood*, p. 96.

149   *In a movement directed toward.* Means also came close to election as tribal chairman at Pine Ridge in 2002. Robert E. Pierre, "Oglala Sioux Choose

Steele over Means; Victor Favors Incremental Change," *Washington Post*, p. A3 (Nov. 21, 2002).

149 *"We had to obtain."* Vine Deloria, Jr., interview with author, Aug. 4, 2000.

CHAPTER 7: The Salmon People

150 *"We are salmon people."* Sue Masten, interview with author, Boulder, Colorado, June 15, 1990.

150 *The Supreme Court has knocked down.* On the repudiation of state ownership of wildlife, see *Hughes v. Oklahoma*, 441 U.S. 322, 335–36 (1979), overruling *Geer v. Connecticut*, 161 U.S. 519 (1896) (abandoning the "19th century legal fiction of state ownership" of wildlife within its borders). On federal supremacy over state wildlife laws, see *Washington v. Washington State Commercial Passenger Fishing Vessel Ass'n*, 443 U.S. 658, 685 (1979) (upholding, regardless of contrary state laws, the Pacific Northwest tribes' treaty right to take up to 50 percent of the harvestable fish passing through the tribes' usual and accustomed fishing places); *Minnesota v. Mille Lacs Band of Chippewa Indians*, 526 U.S. 172, 204–05 (1999) (upholding the Chippewa's right to hunt, fish, and gather on ceded lands free from unreasonable, unnecessary, and discriminatory state regulations); *see generally* George Cameron Coggins, "Wildlife and the Constitution: The Walls Come Tumbling Down," vol. 55 *Washington Law Review*, p. 295 (April 1980).

151 *The most serious argument.* On the evolution of state wildlife agencies, see Ruth S. Musgrave and Mary Anne Stein, *State Wildlife Laws Handbook*, pp. 6–20 (Rockville, MD: Government Institutes, 1993); Laurence R. Jahn, "Highlights in a Century of Wildlife Conservation," paper presented to Wildlife Society, Virginia Chapter, meeting, Richmond, Virginia (March 2, 2000), *at* http://fwie.fw.vt.edu/vatws/HistoryJahn.htm (last visited Jan. 24, 2004) (on file with author).

151 *Invariably, large-scale harvests.* See *infra* ch. 7, pp. **159–60** and accompanying notes.

152 *Nez Perce 1855 Treaty.* See *supra* ch. 2, p. **39**.

152 *off-reservation treaty rights battles. See, e.g., Crow Tribe of Indians v. Repsis*, 73 F.3d 982 (10th Cir. 1995); *Cheyenne-Arapaho Tribes of Oklahoma v. Oklahoma*, 618 F.2d 665 (10th Cir. 1980); *State v. Keesee*, 521 S.E.2d 743 (S.C. 1999); *State v. Cutler*, 708 P.2d 853 (Idaho 1985); *State v. Coffee*, 556 P.2d 1185 (Idaho 1976); *State v. Stasso*, 563 P.2d 562 (Mont. 1977).

152 *The Chippewa. See generally* Helen Hornbeck Tanner, *The Ojibwa* (New York: Chelsea House Publishers, 1992); Basil Johnston, *Ojibway Heritage* (Lincoln: University of Nebraska Press, 1976). For oral histories, see also Gerald Vizenor, *The People Named the Chippewa: Narrative Histories* (Minneapolis: University of Minnesota Press, 1984).

153 *With the end of the War of 1812.* On the Michigan treaties, see generally, Charles E. Cleland, *Rites of Conquest: The History and Culture of Michigan's*

Native Americans, pp. 205–62 (Ann Arbor: University of Michigan Press, 1992). On what Native Americans thought regarding their rights under these treaties, see, for example, *Ibid.*, p. 228; Robert Doherty, *Disputed Waters: Native Americans and the Great Lakes Fishery,* pp. 86–100 (Lexington: University Press of Kentucky, 1990); *United States v. Michigan,* 471 F.Supp. 192, 215–16, 219–49 (W.D. Mich. 1979).

153 *nineteenth-century technology.* On pound nets, see Margaret Beattie Bogue, *Fishing the Great Lakes: An Environmental History,* pp. 38–39 (Madison: University of Wisconsin Press, 2000); on gill nets, see *Ibid.*, pp. 39, 49–50.

154 *The introduction of steam-driven boats. Ibid.*, p. 49.

154 *2,121 miles of nets. Ibid.*, pp. 49–50.

154 *So too was hook-and-line.* On hook gangs, see *Ibid.*, p. 258.

155 *100 million pounds. Ibid.*, pp. 256–57.

155 *huge losses because of waste.* Frederick W. True, "The Fisheries of the Great Lakes," in George Brown Goode, *The Fisheries and Fishery Industries of the United States,* Senate Miscellaneous Document No. 124, 47th Congress, 1st Session, pt. 3, p. 645 (Washington, DC: U.S. Government Printing Office, 1887) (cited in Bogue, *Fishing,* p. 100); Hugh M. Smith and Merwin-Marie Snell, "Review of the Fisheries of the Great Lakes in 1885," in House Miscellaneous Document No. 113, U.S. Commission of Fish and Fisheries, *Report: 1887,* Appendix, 50th Congress, 2d Session, p. 281 (Washington, DC: U.S. Government Printing Office, 1891) (cited in Bogue, *Fishing,* p. 100).

155 *"What of the great lakes?"* Bogue, *Fishing,* p. 239 (quoting Howell, "Food Supply of Fresh Waters," *Chicago Times,* p. 10 [Aug. 20, 1881]).

155 *Then came the sea lampreys.* For a map depicting the sea lamprey invasion route, see *Ibid.*, p. 328. Similar sea lampreys had been found in Lake Ontario for many decades; whether they migrated there or became landlocked after the glaciers retreated is inconclusive. Either way, the Welland Canal was completed in 1919, and fishermen began finding sea lampreys in Lake Erie as early as 1921. *Ibid.*, p. 330.

155 *"collapsed catastrophically."* Michael J. Hansen and James W. Peck, "Lake Trout in the Great Lakes," at http://biology.usgs.gov/s+t/noframe /m2130.htm (last visited Apr. 29, 2002) (on file with author); see generally Thomas C. Kuchenberg, *Reflections in a Tarnished Mirror: The Use and Abuse of the Great Lakes* (Sturgeon Bay, WI: Golden Glow Publishing, 1978). For an illustration of the sea lamprey's feeding technique, see Bogue, *Fishing,* p. 329.

155 *They had sold fish.* Doherty, *Disputed Waters,* pp. 24–32.

155 *A. Booth and Company.* See generally Bogue, *Fishing,* pp. 264–72.

155 *By the 1930s.* Doherty, *Disputed Waters,* p. 66.

156 *Confrontational non-Indians.* See generally Ronald N. Satz, "Chippewa Treaty Rights," vol. 79, no. 1 *Transactions* (1991).

156 *The state supreme courts.* In Michigan, see, for example, *People v. Chosa*, 233 N.W. 205 (Mich. 1930). In Wisconsin, see, for example, *State v. Morrin*, 117 N.W. 1006 (Wis. 1908); *State v. Johnson*, 249 N.W. 284 (Wis. 1933); *see also* Satz, *Chippewa*, pp. 85–88; Charles F. Wilkinson, "To Feel the Summer in the Spring: The Treaty Fishing Rights of the Wisconsin Chippewa," vol. 1991, no. 3 *Wisconsin Law Review*, pp. 393–95 (1991).

156 *the Chippewa never stopped fishing.* The most extensive accounts of this were developed at trial, and found as fact by the court, in *Michigan*, 471 F.Supp. at 225 ("Indian fisherman still live in the same areas and fish on the same fishing grounds as did their ancestors for centuries past. Indian fishing of today is remarkably like Indian fishing in 1836, and not much different from Indian fishing two millennia before that"); *see also* Doherty, *Disputed Waters*, p. 67; James M. McClurken, *Gah-Baeh-Jhagwah-Buk*, pp. 50, 54 (East Lansing: Michigan State University Museum, 1991).

156 *"give the tribe room to move."* John McCarthy, tribal attorney, telephone interview with author, May 15, 2002.

157 *"when one becomes a citizen."* Chosa, 233 N.W. at 207.

157 *"foreign to our system." Ibid.*

157 *state officials arrested Jondreau.* The facts of Bill Jondreau's arrest are set out in *People v. Jondreau*, 185 N.W. 2d 375, 376–77 (Mich. 1971).

157 *The court of appeals. People v. Jondreau*, 166 N.W. 2d 293, 294–95 (Mich. Ct. App. 1969).

158 *The very definition.* Timothy Egan, *The Good Rain: Across Time and Terrain in the Pacific Northwest,* p. 22 (New York: Vintage Departures, 1990).

158 *"When I look at a salmon."* Jim Lichatowich, *Salmon Without Rivers: A History of the Pacific Salmon Crisis,* p. 23 (Washington, DC: Island Press, 1999).

159 *42 million pounds.* Northwest Power Planning Council, "Compilation of Information on Salmon and Steelhead Losses in the Columbia River Basin," pp. 66–76 (Portland, OR: Northwest Power Planning Council, 1986).

159 *Development of the Columbia River. See generally* Charles F. Wilkinson, *Crossing the Next Meridian: Land, Water, and the Future of the American West,* pp. 175–218 (Washington, DC: Island Press, 1992); Richard White, *The Organic Machine,* pp. 15–24, 89–92 (New York: Hill and Wang, 1996); Roberta Ulrich, *Empty Nets: Indians, Dams, and the Columbia River,* pp. 4–12, 147–58 (Corvallis: Oregon State University Press, 1999).

159 *While the tribes . . . learned to limit their take. See, e.g.,* Lichatowich, *Salmon,* p. 19; White, *Organic Machine,* p. 20. On the signals to other fishermen to cease fishing, see Chuck Williams, *Bridge of the Gods, Mountains of Fire: A Return to the Columbia Gorge,* p. 73 (San Francisco: Friends of the Earth, 1980); *see generally* Deward E. Walker, *Mutual Cross-Utilization of Economic Resources in the Plateau: An Example from Aboriginal Nez Perce Fishing Practices,* pp. 14–15 (Pullman: Washington State University, Laboratory of Anthropology, 1967).

159 *The Columbia's first cannery.* On early canneries, see Anthony Netboy, *The*

Columbia River Salmon and Steelhead Trout: Their Fight for Survival, pp. 20–21 (Seattle: University of Washington Press, 1980); Arthur F. McEvoy, *The Fisherman's Problem: Ecology and Law in the California Fisheries, 1850–1980*, pp. 69–72 (Cambridge, UK: Cambridge University Press, 1986); Courtland L. Smith, *Salmon Fishers of the Columbia*, p. 16 (Corvallis: Oregon State University Press, 1979).

159 *"the salmon fisheries."* President Theodore Roosevelt, "Special Message to Congress" (Dec. 8, 1908), *in* James D. Richardson, vol. 10 *Messages and Papers of the Presidents*, p. 7610 (New York: Bureau of National Literature and Art, 1913).

159 *"[T]he helpless salmon's life."* See Anthony Netboy, *Salmon: The World's Most Harassed Fish*, p. 213 (London: André Deutsch, 1980) (reprinting the full text of Dr. Stone's address).

159 *That was before the dams.* Wilkinson, *Crossing*, pp. 180, 196–98.

159 *Bonneville and Grand Coulee. Ibid.*, pp. 198–203, 295.

160 *Today's runs.* Lichatowich, *Salmon*, p. 198; Northwest Power and Conservation Council, "Return to the River," Council Doc. 2000-12, pp. 101–24, 304–05 (Portland, OR: Northwest Power Planning Council, 2000) *at* http://www.nwcouncil.org/library/return/2000-12.htm (last visited Nov. 12, 2003) (on file with author) (discussing current run status, catch, and artificial production); Fen Montaigne, "A River Dammed," vol. 199 *National Geographic*, pp. 10, 31 (Apr. 2001).

160 *2,000 fishers.* White, *Organic Machine*, p. 100.

160 *The tribal councils objected. See, e.g., Ibid.*, pp. 91–93, 100; Ulrich, *Empty Nets*, pp. 81–82, 84–85.

161 *a "direct and outstanding contribution."* White, *Organic Machine*, p. 101; *see also* Ulrich, *Empty Nets*, pp. 80–81 ("The prevailing belief seems to have been: get rid of the Indian fishing and there will be plenty of fish for the rest of us").

161 *"There goes my life."* Wilkinson, *Crossing*, p. 199.

161 *After the flooding.* Tim Weaver, Yakama tribal attorney, telephone interviews with author, May 6 and 13, 2002.

161 *Indian fishing. Ibid.*; Ulrich, *Empty Nets*, p. 117.

162 *The fishers returned. Ibid.*

163 *The agencies adopted. Ibid.*, p. 116.

163 *State wardens.* Judge Owen Panner, former Warm Springs tribal attorney, interview with author, Portland, Oregon, May 8, 2002; Ulrich, *Empty Nets*, pp. 118–20.

164 *state officials "thought." Ibid.*, p. 119.

164 *Between them, Dysart and Hovis.* Weaver, interview, May 6, 2002.

164 *Most of the juries. Ibid.*; *see* Ulrich, *Empty Nets*, p. 129.

165 *The Yakama Nation.* On tribal regulations during the 1960s, see, for example,

Ibid., pp. 129–32. For a federal court case in which the Yakama enforced its codes, see *Settler v. Lameer*, 507 F.2d 231 (9th Cir. 1974).

165 *"a miracle."* Panner, interview.

165 *Judge Belloni's decision. Sohappy v. Smith*, 302 F.Supp. 899 (D. Or. 1969).

165 *"fair share." Ibid.*, at 911.

165 *"fishermen of all kinds."* Laura Berg, "Let Them Do as They Have Promised: A History of *U.S. v. Oregon* and Four Tribes' Fight for Columbia River Salmon," vol. 3, no. 1 *Hastings West-Northwest Journal of Environmental Law and Policy*, p. 15 (1995).

165 *"the case took a toll."* Panner, interview.

165 *He crafted his fair share test.* On the events following Judge Belloni's decision, see generally Ulrich, *Empty Nets*, pp. 147–58.

167 *6 percent of the overall harvest.* Bruce Brown, *Mountain in the Clouds: A Search for the Wild Salmon*, p. 155 (New York: Simon and Schuster, 1982); *see also* American Friends Service Committee, *Uncommon Controversy: Fishing Rights of the Muckleshoot, Puyallup, and Nisqually Indians*, pp. 123–24, 126–27 (Seattle: University of Washington Press, 1970).

167 *State officers mounted.* On the salmon wars, see generally *Ibid.*, pp. 107–40; Fay G. Cohen, *Treaties on Trial: The Continuing Controversy over Northwest Indian Fishing Rights*, pp. 67–76 (Seattle: University of Washington Press, 1986); Brown, *Mountain*, pp. 152–57; Charles Wilkinson, *Messages from Frank's Landing: A Story of Salmon, Treaties, and the Indian Way*, pp. 32–46 (Seattle: University of Washington Press, 2000). *Messages from Frank's Landing* covers many of those events, and I have drawn upon that book here.

167 *The Muckleshoot Tribe.* Dennis Anderson, Gerald Moses, and Vernon Star, all Muckleshoot tribal members, interviews with author, Muckleshoot reservation, May 23, 2002.

168 *"just take, take, take."* Moses, interview.

168 *The fishing at Muckleshoot.* Anderson, Moses, and Star interviews.

169 *"These guys had a budget."* Wilkinson, *Messages*, p. 33.

170 *"No thanks." Ibid.*, p. 40.

170 *"This was . . . an injustice."* Ralph W. Johnson, interview with author, Seattle, Washington, November 5, 1997.

170 *The litigation aspect. See* Wilkinson, *Messages*, pp. 44–46.

170 *a dozen or so Indian lawyers. See* Rennard Strickland, "Redeeming Centuries of Dishonor: Legal Education and the American Indian," vol. 1970, no. 3 *University of Toledo Law Review*, pp. 861–66 (1970).

170 *"Here. Take this book."* Guy McMinds, interview with author, Spokane, Washington, November 28, 2001.

170 *"not much less necessary." United States v. Winans*, 198 U.S. 371, 381 (1905).

171 *The cases since.* For federal cases, see, for example, *Tulee v. State of Washing-*

ton, 315 U.S. 681 (1942); *Maison v. Confederated Tribes of Umatilla Indian Reservation*, 314 F.2d 169 (9th Cir. 1963); *Makah Indian Tribe v. Schoettler*, 192 F.2d 224 (9th Cir. 1951). For state cases, see, for example, *State v. Moses*, 422 P.2d 775 (Wash. 1967); *State v. McCoy*, 387 P.2d 942 (Wash. 1963); *State v. Towessnute*, 154 P. 805 (Wash. 1916).

171 *NARF involvement*. Wilkinson, *Messages*, pp. 50–51; David Getches, interview with author, St. George, Utah, May 2, 2002; Alan Stay, telephone interview with author, May 6, 2002.

172 *"to keep his powder dry."* Getches, interview.

172 *In the trial of Vietnam protesters*. United Press International, "Seattle 7's Bail Held Up by Judge: He refuses to Act Despite Order of Appeals Court," *New York Times*, p. 34 (Dec. 29, 1970); United Press International, "Bail for Seattle 7 Is Stayed by Court," *New York Times*, p. 23 (Dec. 30, 1970). For more information about the Seattle Seven, see generally "Radicals: 'The Seattle Seven,'" *Newsweek*, p. 54 (Dec. 14, 1970); Roger Lippman, "Looking Back on the Seattle Seven Conspiracy Trial" (Dec. 1990), *at* http://terrasol.hom .igc.org/trial.htm (last visited April 5, 2004) (on file with author) (a firsthand account by one of the accused protesters).

173 *"We had a whole lot of bad experiences."* Billy Frank, Jr., interview with author, Olympia, Washington, May 22, 2002.

CHAPTER 8: Turning Points

178 *Termination gradually waned*. Watkins was then defeated for reelection in 1958. James Reston, "Democrats Gain 13 Senate Seats: Add 46 in House in Taking Republican Strongholds Throughout Nation," *New York Times*, pp. 1, 16 (Nov. 6, 1958).

178 *Acknowledging the contentiousness*. Charles F. Wilkinson and Eric R. Biggs, "The Evolution of the Termination Policy," vol. 5, no. 1 *American Indian Law Review*, p. 163 (1977).

178 *Termination proposals continued*. Vine Deloria, Jr., interview with author, June 8, 2000; Frank Ducheneaux, interview with author, Washington, D.C., June 6, 2002; *see, e.g.*, Nebraska Ponca Act, Pub. L. No. 87-629, Sept. 5, 1962, 76 Stat. 429 (1963) (codified as amended at 25 U.S.C. §§ 971–80 [2000]); S. 1413, 89th Congress, 1st Session (1965) (Colville termination bill proposed by Senator Jackson).

178 *several senators expressed*. Hearing Before the Senate Committee on Interior and Insular Affairs, "Interior Nomination: On the Nomination of Robert La Follette Bennett, of Alaska, to be Commissioner of Indian Affairs," 89th Congress, 2d Session, pp. 13–14 (April 1, 1966) (Washington, DC: U.S. Government Printing Office, 1966).

178 *terminate the Seneca Nation*. Joy A. Bilharz, *The Allegany Senecas and Kinzua Dam: Forced Relocation Through Two Generations*, p. 100 (Lincoln: University of Nebraska Press, 1998).

178   *Senator Henry "Scoop" Jackson.* On Jackson, see Peter J. Ognibene, *Scoop: The Life and Politics of Henry M. Jackson* (Briarcliff Manor, NY: Stein and Day, 1975); William W. Prochnau and Richard W. Larsen, *A Certain Democrat: Senator Henry M. Jackson: A Political Biography* (Englewood Cliffs, NJ: Prentice-Hall, 1972).

178   *A hawk on military issues.* Prochnav and Larson, *A Certain Democrat*, pp. 233–43; H. R. Haldeman, "The Nixon White House and Presidency," in Kenneth W. Thompson, ed., *The Nixon Presidency*, p. 79 (Lanham, MD: University Press of America, 1987).

179   *Public Law 772.* Colville Restoration Act, Pub. L. No. 772, ch. 684, July 24, 1956, 70 Stat. 626 (1957) (not codified); *see also* Hearings Before the House Committee on Appropriations, Subcommittee on Department of the Interior and Related Agencies, "Department of the Interior and Related Agencies Appropriations for 1958," 85th Congress, 1st Session, p. 380 (Jan. 17, 1957) (Washington, DC: U.S. Government Printing Office, 1957). Jackson cosponsored the Senate bill, S. #2120. Introduction of S. 2120 by Mr. Magnuson (for himself and Mr. Jackson), vol. 101, pt. 6 *Congressional Record*, 84th Congress, 1st Session, p. 7310 (Washington, DC: U.S. Government Printing Office, 1955). See generally Larry W. Burt, *Tribalism in Crisis: Federal Indian Policy, 1953–1961*, p. 80 (Albuquerque: University of New Mexico Press, 1982).

179   *termination seemed a possible solution.* On attitudes toward termination, see Kathleen A. Dahl, "The Battle over Termination on the Colville Indian Reservation," vol. 18, no. 1 *American Indian Culture and Research Journal*, p. 29 (1994); Donald L. Fixico, *Termination and Relocation: Federal Indian Policy, 1945–1960*, p. 194 (Albuquerque: University of New Mexico Press, 1992); John Alan Ross, "Factionalism on the Colville Reservation," pp. 82–97, M.A. thesis, Washington State University (1967) (on file with author); Susanna Adella Hayes, "The Resistance to Education for Assimilation by the Colville Indians, 1872 to 1972," pp. 183–90, Ph.D. dissertation, University of Michigan (1973) (on file with author); *see also* Ruth Scofield, "Behind the Buckskin Curtain," unpublished manuscript, Seattle Pacific College (1977) (on file with author) (containing numerous interviews).

180   *"To keep the Indians."* Dahl, "Battle," p. 40.

180   *"I do not want termination."* Ibid., p. 43.

180   *As for the financial issues.* Ibid., pp. 33–34, 47.

180   *protermination candidates took over the council.* On the protermination tribal council, see Ross, "Factionalism," pp. 87–94; Dahl, "Battle," pp 35–36.

180   *"We all rode."* The American Character: Lucy Covington: Native American Indian, Odyssey Productions, 16mm (Chicago: Encyclopaedia Britannica Educational Corp., 1978).

181   *she made whirlwind trips.* Julie Titone, "Law of the Land: Indian Tribes Embrace Role of Self-Governing as a Way to Preserve Their Language, Values and Heritage," *Spokesmen-Review* (Dec. 25, 2000), *at* http://www.spokesman

review.com/news/newslibrary.asp (last visited May 30, 2003) (on file with author).

182 *"Termination . . . is like."* Dahl, "Battle," p. 29.

182 *To expose the damage.* Deloria, interview; Jim White and Elnathan Davis, personal communications with author, Chiloquin, Oregon, complete date unknown, 1974; *see also* Hayes, "Resistance," pp. 185–88.

182 *With their reservations liquidated. See, e.g.*, American Indian Policy Review Commission, "Task Force Ten: Report on Terminated and Nonfederally Recognized Indians," 94th Congress, 2d Session, pp. 62–65 (Washington, DC: U.S. Government Printing Office, 1976); William A. Brophy and Sophie D. Aberle, *The Indian: America's Unfinished Business,* pp. 193–96 (Norman: University of Oklahoma Press, 1966) (Southern Paiute of Utah); Parker M. Nielson, *The Dispossessed: Cultural Genocide of the Mixed-Blood Utes* (Norman: University of Oklahoma Press, 1998) (Mixed-Blood Ute of Utah). On the effects of Menominee termination, see Stephen J. Herzberg, "The Menominee Indians: Termination to Restoration," vol. 6, no. 1 *American Indian Law Review,* p. 143 (1978); Deborah Shames, ed , *Freedom with Reservation: The Menominee Struggle to Save Their Land and People* (Madison, WI: National Committee to Save the Menominee People and Forests, 1972); Nicholas C. Peroff, *Menominee Drums: Tribal Termination and Restoration, 1954–1974* (Norman: University of Oklahoma Press, 1982); Hearings Before the Senate Committee on Interior and Insular Affairs, Subcommittee on Indian Affairs, "Menominee Restoration Act: On S. 1687 (A Bill to Repeal the Act Terminating Federal Supervision over the Property and Members of the Mcnominee Indian Tribe of Wisconsin, etc.)," 93rd Congress, 1st Session (Washington, DC: U.S. Government Printing Office, 1973) [hereinafter Senate Restoration Hearings]; Hearings Before the House Committee on Interior and Insular Affairs, Subcommittee on Indian Affairs, "Menominee Restoration Act: On H.R. 7421 (To Repeal the Act Terminating Federal Supervision over the Property and Members of the Menominee Indian Tribe of Wisconsin, etc.)," 93rd Congress, 1st Session (Washington, DC: U.S. Government Printing Office, 1973) [hereinafter House Restoration Hearings].

183 *Menominee Enterprises, Inc.* On the structure of MEI, see Shames, *Freedom,* pp. 18–23; David H. Getches et al., *Cases and Materials on Federal Indian Law,* 4th ed., pp. 221–24 (St. Paul, MN: West Group, 1998); Senate Restoration Hearings, pp. 44–58 (Sept. 17, 1973); House Restoration Hearings, pp. 85–89 (May 25, 1973).

183 *The corporation's dearth of cash reserves.* Herzberg, "Menominee," p. 171.

183 *Indian children.* Kenneth A. Mines, Regional Civil Rights Director, Office for Civil Rights, Department of Health, Education, and Welfare, letter to Arnold A. Gruber, Superintendent, Shawano Board of Education (Oct. 4, 1972) (on file with author).

184 *With tribal jobs eliminated.* House Restoration Hearings, p. 203 (May 26,

1973). On Menominee socioeconomic difficulties, see Herzberg, "Menominee," pp. 170–86; Shames, *Freedom*, pp. 36–66.

184   *Legend Lake.* Shames, *Freedom*, pp. 29–35.

184   *In the mid-1970s the Menominee.* For example, in 1975, young members of the Menominee Warrior Society took over the Alexian Brothers' Novitiate as a protest against implementation of the restoration legislation. Patricia K. Ourada, *The Menominee Indians: A History*, p. 221 (Norman: University of Oklahoma Press, 1979); *Alexian Brothers Novitiate: Gresham, Wisconsin*, Congregation of Alexian Brothers, History, *at* http://www.alexian brothers.org/English/history/America/hist-nov-wis.html (last visited Jan. 29, 2004) (on file with author).

185   *To disrupt the Legend Lake.* Peroff, *Menominee Drums*, p. 185.

185   *More than 200 protesters. Ibid.* On DRUMS activism, see generally *Ibid.*, pp. 163–90; Shames, *Freedom*, pp. 83–96.

185   *"We read it."* Peroff, *Menominee Drums*, p. 163 (quoting William Greider, "The Menominee: Victims of Experiment," *Washington Post*, pp. A1, A12 [Oct. 3, 1971]).

186   *"We felt we had to go."* Shames, *Freedom*, p. 91.

187   *Senator Jackson listened.* Jackson began to move away from support of termination in the early 1970s. In 1971 he supported the repeal of House Concurrent Resolution 108, the 1953 congressional announcement of the termination policy. *See, e.g.,* Statement by Senator Jackson of Dec. 11, 1971, vol. 117, pt. 35 *Congressional Record*, 92d Congress, 1st Session, p. 46382 (Washington, DC: U.S. Government Printing Office, 1971); Senate Report No. 92-561, "National American Indian Policy," 92d Congress, 1st Session (Washington, DC: U.S. Government Printing Office, 1971); *see also* Ognibene, *Scoop*, pp. 133–35.

187   *The House presented.* On Aspinall, see generally Steven C. Schulte, *Wayne Aspinall and the Shaping of the American West* (Boulder: University Press of Colorado, 2002); Stephen C. Sturgeon, *The Politics of Western Water: The Congressional Career of Wayne Aspinall* (Tucson: University of Arizona Press, 2002).

187   *Lewis Sigler and Dillon Myer.* Kenneth R. Philp, *Termination Revisited: American Indians on the Trail to Self-Determination, 1933–1953*, p. 91 (Lincoln: University of Nebraska Press, 1999).

187   *Sigler explained.* Personal recollection of author (complete date unknown, Jan. 1972).

187   *"I have spent."* Kenneth R. Philp, ed., *Indian Self-Rule: First-Hand Accounts of Indian-White Relations from Roosevelt to Reagan*, p. 138 (Salt Lake City: Howe Brothers, 1986).

188   *In 1972 Henry Jackson.* Peroff, *Menominee Drums*, p. 229; Ognibene, *Scoop*, pp. 133–35.

188   *A few months after.* Schulte, *Wayne Aspinall*, p. 277.

189 *President Nixon signed.* Menominee Restoration Act of 1973, 25 U.S.C. §§ 903–903f.

189 *That done, in April 1975.* The final transfer documents are in possession of the author, who attended the 1975 signing ceremony.

189 *Charles Eastman had argued.* Charles A. Eastman (Ohiyesa), "The Indian's Plea for Freedom," vol. 6, no. 4 *American Indian Magazine,* p. 164 (1919).

189 *"Mr. Chairman, it is peculiar."* Frederick E. Hoxie, ed., *Talking Back to Civilization: Indian Voices from the Progressive Era,* pp. 136–37 (Boston: Bedford/St. Martin's, 2001) (quoting Senate Report No. 219, "Crow Tribe of Indians in Montana," 66th Congress, 1st Session, pp. 8–9 [Washington, DC: U.S. Government Printing Office, 1919]).

190 *After World War II.* Harold E. Fey and D'Arcy McNickle, *Indians and Other Americans: Two Ways of Life Meet,* p. 56 (New York: Harper and Brothers, 1959).

190 *And though his prose.* Roger Jourdain, interview with author, Bemidji, Minnesota, March 23–24, 2001; see *supra* ch. 1, p. **6**.

191 *Further, the direct-funding provision.* On the Capital Conference and direct funding, see *supra* ch. 5, pp. **127–28**. On OEO Indian programs, see Sar A. Levitan, *The Great Society's Poor Law: A New Approach to Poverty,* pp. 263–70 (Baltimore: Johns Hopkins University Press, 1969).

191 *"raw cash."* Ibid., p. 264.

191 *"a program which mobilizes."* 42 U.S.C. § 2782 (1964) (repealed by Pub. L. No. 90-222, sec. 104, Dec. 23, 1967, 81 Stat. 672, 691 [1968]).

191 *Tribal councils authorized.* Hearings Before the House Committee on Appropriations, "Departments of Labor and Health, Education, and Welfare Appropriations for 1969," 90th Congress, 2d Session, pt. 6, p. 305 (Washington, DC: U.S. Government Printing Office, 1968) (cited in Levitan, *Great Society's,* p. 266).

191 *Tribal CAPs dedicated.* Levitan, *Great Society's,* pp. 267–68.

191 *The eight northern pueblos.* Alfonso Ortiz et al., "The War on Poverty," in Philp, *Indian Self-Rule,* p. 222.

191 *"secured money for a training program."* Philip S. Deloria, "The Era of Self-Determination: An Overview," in Philp, *Indian Self-Rule,* p. 198.

192 *Rough Rock Demonstration School.* On the founding of Rough Rock, see Teresa L. McCarty, *A Place to Be Navajo: Rough Rock and the Struggle for Self-Determination in Indigenous Schooling,* pp. 71–81 (Mahwah, NJ: Lawrence Erlbaum Associates, 2002); Robert A Roessel, Jr., *Navajo Education, 1948–1978: Its Progress and Its Problems,* pp. 49–58 (Rough Rock, AZ: Navajo Curriculum Center, 1979).

192 *"Whatever OEO did."* McCarty, *A Place,* p. 81.

192 *Skeptics in the BIA.* Ibid., p. 83.

192 *They were wrong.* For the most comprehensive study of Rough Rock, see gen-

erally *Ibid.*; *see also* Robert A. Roessel, Jr., *Navajo Education in Action: The Rough Rock Demonstration School* (Chinle, AZ: Navajo Curriculum Center, 1977); Robert A. Roessel, Jr., "An Overview of the Rough Rock Demonstration School," vol. 7 *Journal of American Indian Education* (May 1968).

193 *Other tribes soon set up. See generally* Daniel M. Rosenfelt, "Indian Schools and Community Control," vol. 25 *Stanford Law Review*, p. 489 (1973).

193 *Rough Rock and Navajo Community College.* Roessel, *Navajo Education*, p. 59.

193 *Tribal colleges nationally. See generally* Norman T. Oppelt, *TheTribally Controlled Indian Colleges: The Beginnings of Self-Determination in American Indian Education* (Tsaile, AZ: Navajo Community College Press, 1990); *American Indian Higher Education Consortium*, American Indian Higher Education Consortium, Main Page, *at* http://www.aihec.org/ (last visited Nov. 3, 2003) (on file with author).

193 *The school . . . has attracted.* For articles on Rough Rock, see, for example, McCarty, *A Place*, pp. 201–13; Roessel, *Navajo Education*, p. 149; Cathie Jordan, "Creating Cultures of Schooling: Historical and Conceptual Background of the Keep/Rough Rock Collaboration," vol. 19 *Bilingual Research Journal*, p. 83 (Winter 1995); Yumiko Mizuno, "Dine bi Olta or School of the Navajos: Educational Experiments at Rough Rock Demonstration School, 1966–1970," no. 9 *Japanese Journal of American Studies*, p. 143 (1998).

193 *It became almost a mantra.* For an article on this notion, see Robert A. Roessel, Jr., "The Right to Be Wrong and the Right to Be Right," vol. 7 *Journal of American Indian Education*, p. 1 (Jan. 1968).

194 *"We had never been given."* Ducheneaux, interview.

194 *The president's staff. See generally* Richard Nixon, *In the Arena: A Memoir of Victory, Defeat, and Renewal*, pp. 272–74 (New York: Simon and Schuster, 1990); John Ehrlichman, *Witness to Power: The Nixon Years*, pp. 82–83 (New York: Simon and Schuster, 1982); Haldeman, "Nixon," pp. 79–82.

194 *The three pushed hard.* On the organizations and personalities in Indian issues in the Nixon White House, see George Pierre Castile, *To Show Heart: Native American Self-Determination and Federal Indian Policy, 1960–1975*, pp. 80–87 (Tucson: University of Arizona Press, 1998).

195 *A new way of doing business.* Ducheneaux, interview; Forrest Gerard, interview with author, Albuquerque, New Mexico, Oct. 17, 2002.

195 *Bill King and Stewart Udall.* On King and the emergence of the self-determination policy during the Johnson-Udall years, see Castile, "To Show," pp. 42–72.

195 *In 1968, Johnson delivered.* Special Message to the Congress on the Problem of the American Indian: "The Forgotten American" by President Johnson of March 6, 1968, *in* General Services Administration, National Archives and Records Administration, Office of the Federal Register, vol. 1, "Public Papers of the Presidents of the United States: Lyndon B. Johnson, 1968–1969," p. 336 (Washington, DC: U.S. Government Printing Office, 1970).

196   *Many well-intentioned people.* On development of Nixon's message, see Alvin
      M. Josephy, Jr., *Red Power: The American Indians' Fight for Freedom*, pp.
      223–42 (New York: American Heritage Press, 1971) (reprinting Nixon's mes-
      sage with a brief introduction); Castile, "To Show," pp. 48–49, 78–79; Vine
      Deloria, Jr., *Custer Died for Your Sins: An Indian Manifesto*, p. 142 (New York:
      Avon Books, 1970); Deloria and Lytle, *The Nations Within*, p. 216; Duche-
      neaux, interview; Alvin M. Josephy, Jr., *A Walk Toward Oregon: A Memoir*,
      pp. 298–99 (New York: Alfred A. Knopf, 2000); Gerard, interview.

196   *Nixon's 1970 message.* Special Message to the Congress on Indian Affairs by
      President Nixon of July 8, 1970, *in* General Services Administration,
      National Archives and Records Administration, Office of the Federal Regis-
      ter, "Public Papers of the Presidents of the United States: Richard Nixon,
      1970," pp. 564–76 (Washington, DC: U.S. Government Printing Office, 1971).

196   *Congress would in time.* See generally Daniel H. Israel, "The Reemergence of
      Tribal Nationalism and Its Impact on Reservation Resource Development,"
      vol. 47 *University of Colorado Law Review*, pp. 624–29 (1976).

197   *The centerpiece of the Nixon message.* Indian Self-Determination and Educa-
      tion Assistance Act, Pub. L. No. 93-638, Jan. 4, 1975, 88 Stat. 2203, 2206–07
      (1976) (codified as amended at 25 U.S.C. § 450 (2000)). On the self-determi-
      nation legislation, see Francis Paul Prucha, vol. 2, *The Great Father: The
      United States Government and the American Indians*, pp. 1157–62 (Lincoln:
      University of Nebraska Press, 1984); Vine Deloria, Jr., and Clifford M. Lytle,
      American Indians, American Justice, pp. 103–04 (Austin: University of Texas
      Press, 1983).

197   *Funding often proved inadequate.* For criticisms of the self-determination leg-
      islation, see, for example, Earl Old Person et al., "Contracting Under the Self-
      Determination Act," *in* Philp, *Indian Self-Rule*, pp. 251–59; *see also* Michael P.
      Gross, "Indian Self-Determination and Tribal Sovereignty: An Analysis of
      Recent Federal Indian Policy," vol. 56 *Texas Law Review*, pp. 1199–1218 (Aug.
      1978).

197   *Statutes expanded tribal rights.* On improvement of self-determination and
      related laws, see, for example, Deloria and Lytle, *American Indians*, pp.
      104–05; Cornell, *Return of the Native*, pp. 204–05; Getches et al., *Cases and
      Materials*, p. 231.

197   *"In the 1960s, self-determination."* Cornell, *Return of the Native*, p. 205.

197   *Courts, in ruling on the nature. See, e.g., Bryan v. Itasca County*, 426 U.S. 373,
      388 n. 14 (1976) (relying in part on the contemporary self-determination pol-
      icy in striking down the imposition of a state tax that that statute sought to
      justify under the termination-era Public Law 280).

198   *"Rigged" proceeding.* See *supra* ch. 7, pp. **172–73**.

198   *Back in Michigan. People v. Jondreau*, 185 N.W. 2d 375, 379–81 (Mich. 1971).

198   *In Idaho, Indian fishermen. State v. Tinno*, 497 P.2d 1386, 1390 (Ida. 1972).

199   *The U.S. Supreme Court. Department of Game v. Puyallup Tribe*, 414 U.S. 44,

398 (1973) (*Puyallup II*) (striking down, as discriminatory against Indians, a state regulation that completely banned net fishing for steelhead trout); *Mattz v. Arnett*, 412 U.S. 481, 497 (1971) (Yurok treaty hunting and fishing rights upheld because "allotment . . . is completely consistent with continued reservation status"); *Menominee Tribe of Indians v. United States*, 391 U.S. 404 (1968) ("We decline to consider the Termination Act as a backhanded way of abrogating the hunting and fishing rights of these Indians"). In *Puyallup II*, the Court greatly diminished the states' conservation argument, finding that the real intent of Washington state's efforts to regulate Indian fishing was not to achieve true conservation but rather to allocate more fish to non-Indian sports and commercial fishers. The Court adopted the distinction between conservation and allocation first put forth by Professor Ralph W. Johnson in his article "The States Versus Indian Off-Reservation Fishing: A United States Supreme Court Error," vol. 47 *Washington Law Review,* pp. 232–36 (1972).

199 *"The Solicitor General's office."* Harry R. Sachse, letter to author (Apr. 13, 2001). The case that Sachse argued was *Puyallup II.*

200 *"the right of taking fish." See, e.g.*, Treaty with Nisquallys & c., art. III, Dec. 26, 1854, 10 Stat. 1132 (1855).

200 *The Supreme Court said long ago. See, e.g., United States v. Winans*, 198 U.S. 371, 380–81 (1905); *Winters v. United States*, 207 U.S. 564, 576 (1908). For modern cases, see *United States v. Dion*, 476 U.S. 734, 738–40 (1986); *Minnesota v. Mille Lacs Band of Chippewa Indians*, 526 U.S. 172, 195–96, 202–03, 206 (1999).

200 *The law has always. See generally* Charles F. Wilkinson and John M. Volkman, " Judicial Review of Indian Treaty Abrogation: 'As Long as Water Flows, or Grass Grows Upon the Earth'—How Long a Time Is That?," vol. 63 *California Law Review*, p. 601 (May 1975).

200 *The rule of reading Indian treaties. Felix S. Cohen, Handbook of Federal Indian Law*, pp. 220–25 (Charlottesville, VA: Michie Bobbs-Merrill, 1982.)

200 *calling her findings. United States v. Washington*, 384 F. Supp. 312, 350 (D. Wash. 1974).

200 *"in summary, the court finds." Ibid.*

201 *"Historically, the Indians would never."* "Fishing Decision Was 'Just and Right,' Says Judge," *Seattle Times*, p. E6 (Feb. 8, 1979).

201 *Some lawyers in the case.* David Getches, interview with author, St. George, Utah, May 2, 2002; Mason Morisset, interview with author, June 7, 2002.

201 *"once when my grandfather."* Transcript of Proceedings at 2696, Sept. 10, 1973, *Washington* (Civ. No. 9213).

201 *"We gave up our land." Ibid.*, at 3020–21, Sept. 12, 1973.

201 *"Q: Mr. Kinley, you just said." Ibid.*, at 3023.

201 *he intentionally chose Lincoln's birthday.* "Fishing," p. E6.

202 *He had immersed himself in the case, Ibid.*

202   *Judge Boldt boldly moved.* For analysis of the Boldt decision, see, for example, Fay G. Cohen, *Treaties on Trial: The Continuing Controversy over Northwest Indian Fishing Rights,* pp. 3–17 (Seattle: University of Washington Press, 1986); Charles Wilkinson, *Messages from Frank's Landing: A Story of Salmon, Treaties, and the Indian Way,* pp. 49–65 (Seattle: University of Washington Press, 2000).

202   *"With a single possible exception."* Washington, 384 F. Supp. at 338–39, n. 26.

202   *A state and federal "buy-back" program.* 42 U.S.C. § 2782 (2000); *see also* House Report No. 96-1243, "Salmon and Steelhead Management and Enhancement," 96th Congress, 2d Session, pp. 33–35 (Washington, DC: U.S. Government Printing Office, 1980) (discussing the overcapacity problem).

203   *"Massive illegal fishing."* Cohen, *Treaties,* p. 93.

203   *183,000 salmon. Ibid.,* p. 100.

203   *Eventually the Boldt decision.* A notable example of this is a piece written by sportswriter John de Yonge in a special issue of the *Seattle Post-Intelligencer* in 1984 to commemorate the tenth anniversary of the Boldt decision:

> Judge George Boldt is dead. In his case the good he did will not be interred with his bones.
>
> Boldt did a lot of good over a tremendously long career as a U.S. District Court judge sitting in Tacoma and elsewhere. . . .
>
> It happens that the [Indian treaty] decision hurt and angered a lot of people, non-Indian commercial fishermen and sports anglers whose catches up until then were coming out of the Indian's share.
>
> To speak personally, in the short run and perhaps for the rest of my life, Judge Boldt's interpretation of the treaty words has knocked the hell out of my annual catch of salmon and steelhead on my favorite streams, the Skagit River and its tributaries. . . .
>
> But in rational moments I have praised Judge Boldt for accomplishing two things with his decision.
>
> First, he was fair. To the Indians he restored a right under the law which for a hundred years had been nibbled away by the conscious and unconscious greed of people like me and by the state government's conscious and unconscious mismanagement of its fisheries wealth.
>
> Second, and this is the good that ultimately should profit society in general, Judge Boldt's decision is forcing all of us to take a close look at how we must take care of our fisheries.
>
> We have been poor stewards. Overfishing, dam building, rapacious logging, the sucking up of river flows for irrigation, the dumping of chemical poisons into our waters, the institution of poorly understood hatchery systems—these at the state, national and international levels have so hurt the fish runs that in some cases Indians and others each have a right to take 50 percent of next to nothing. . . .
>
> There is an irony that at the end of a distinguished career as a judge and as a citizen, Boldt found himself being hung in effigy and reviled for his decision on Indian treaty rights to fish.

He refused to be swayed by public opinion. "It is not an essential or even necessarily desirable factor that a conscientious judge should even consider," he said.

True. But if we're brave enough to deal rationally with the effects of his decision, I predict that someday the "Boldt Decision" will be remembered as when this state and its people (Indians included) began, however unwillingly and haltingly, to save the salmon and steelhead runs from oblivion.

John de Yonge, "Boldt's Good Deeds Will Live After Him,"
Seattle Post-Intelligencer, p. A11 (March 21, 1984)

203   *The federal court of appeals affirmed. United States v. Washington*, 520 F.2d 676 (9th Cir. 1975)

203   *the Supreme Court declined to hear. Washington v. United States*, 423 U.S. 1086 (1976).

203   *Taking a circuitous procedural route. Washington v. Washington State Commercial Passenger Fishing Vessel Ass'n*, 443 U.S. 658 (1979).

203   *"The State's extraordinary machinations." Ibid.*, at 696, n. 36.

CHAPTER 9: Reclaiming Heartlands

206   *Juan de Jesus Romero.* R. C. Gordon-McCutchan, *The Taos Indians and the Battle for Blue Lake*, pp. 182–83 (Santa Fe, NM: Red Crane Books, 1995).

206   *"If our land is not returned." Ibid.*, p. 185.

206   *The cacique rarely spoke in public.* The most thorough account of the Taos Pueblo's campaign to return Blue Lake is *Ibid.* For a more concise summary, see also William F. Deverell, "The Return of Blue Lake to the Taos Pueblo," vol. 49, no. 1 *Princeton University Library Chronicle*, p. 57 (1987); *The Sacred Lake of Taos*, Beta SP (ABC News, date unknown).

207   *seemingly inexorable loss of land.* The one exception to the steady drain of Indian land took place during the Franklin Roosevelt administration, when the Interior Department transferred federal lands to some tribes under section 3 of the Indian Reorganization Act. See *supra*, ch. 3, p. **60**.

207   *7.5 million acres.* In 1963, Indian lands held in trust by the federal government totaled 50,483,517 acres. U.S. Department of the Interior, Bureau of Indian Affairs, "U.S. Indian Population (1962) and Land (1963)," p. 6 (Washington, DC: U.S. Government Printing Office, 1963). By 1997 total trust acreage had grown to 55,737,452 acres. U.S. Department of the Interior, Bureau of Indian Affairs, "Annual Report of Indian Lands" (Washington, DC: U.S. Government Printing Office, 1997). Communications by my research assistant, Kristi Denney, with three BIA regional offices (Billings, Navajo, and Sacramento) and five tribes (Colville, Navajo, Oneida, Rosebud Sioux, and Salish-Kootenai) in April 2004 revealed that at least an additional 2,250,000 acres have been placed in trust or are held in fee since the 1997 report. Thus current land holdings are approximately 58 million acres. This

is a conservative estimate because only a sample of tribes were contacted and BIA figures are commonly low.

207   *The pueblo Indians . . . trace their ancestry.* In aboriginal times the pueblo people were more mobile than is commonly realized. Many sites were constructed, abandoned, resettled, then abandoned again. One of the largest outmigrations involved the Ancestral Puebloans (or Anasazi), who populated the Four Corners area until about eight hundred years ago. Then tens of thousands of people dispersed—perhaps because of drought, outside raiding, or their own inclinations—to Hopi, Zuni, and the pueblos of the Rio Grande. *See generally* Robert H. Lister and Florence C. Lister, *Those Who Came Before*, pp. 40–42 (Tucson: University of Arizona Press, 1983); Linda S. Cordell and George J. Gumerman, eds., *Dynamics of Southwest Prehistory*, pp. 163–69 (Washington, DC: Smithsonian Institution Press, 1989); Linda S. Cordell, *Ancient Pueblo Peoples*, pp. 131–33 (Washington, DC: Smithsonian Books, 1994); Charles Wilkinson, *Fire on the Plateau: Conflict and Endurance in the American Southwest*, pp. 251–66 (Washington, DC: Island Press, 1999).

207   *The pueblos—Spanish missionaries and modern circumstances.* On the pueblos generally, *see* Joe S. Sando, *Pueblo Nations: Eight Centuries of Pueblo Indian History* (Santa Fe, NM: Clear Light Publishers, 1992); Stephen Trimble, *The People: Indians of the American Southwest*, pp. 38–120 (Santa Fe, NM: SAR Press, 1993). My thanks to Joe Sando for a background interview on the pueblos in Albuquerque, New Mexico, on October 16, 2002.

207   *Spanish missionaries exceeded the Anglos. See generally* Ramón Gutiérrez, *When Jesus Came, the Corn Mothers Went Away: Marriage, Sexuality, and Power in New Mexico, 1500–1846*, pp. 40–55 (Stanford, CA: Stanford University Press, 1991).

207   *The pueblos . . . proved resilient. See, e.g.*, John J. Bodine, *Taos Pueblo: A Walk Through Time*, p. 43 (Santa Fe, NM: Lightning Tree, 1977); *Sacred Lake*, Beta SP.

208   *To reach Blue Lake.* Gordon-McCutchan, *Taos Indians*, pp. 10–17.

209   *"this area is used every day." Pueblo of Taos v. United States*, 15 Ind. Cl. Comm. 666, 675 (1965).

209   *"purified by nature." Sacred Lake*, Beta SP.

209   *Gifford Pinchot.* On Pinchot, see generally his biography, Char Miller, *Gifford Pinchot and the Making of Modern Environmentalism* (Washington, DC: Island Press, 2001); *see also* Charles F. Wilkinson, *Crossing the Next Meridian: Land, Water, and the Future of the West*, pp. 120, 124–31 (Washington, DC: Island Press, 1992). His autobiography is Gifford Pinchot, *Breaking New Ground* (Washington, DC: Island Press, 1998). In Charles F. Wilkinson, *The American West: A Narrative Bibliography and a Study in Regionalism*, pp. 36–37 (Niwot: University Press of Colorado, 1989), I listed him as one of the seven most influential persons in the history of the American West.

209   *Pinchot . . . paid little attention. See, e.g.*, Wilkinson, *Fire*, p. 154 (inclusion of Ute reservation land in the Uinta Forest Reserve); Gordon-McCutchan, *Taos*

Indians, p. 14 (in New Mexico Pinchot included Indian lands, in addition to Blue Lake, in national forests and charged Indians Forest Service grazing fees).

209 *Spanish grant.* Frank Waters, "Foreword," *in* Gordon-McCutchan, *Taos Indians*, p. vii.

209 *Congress gave presidents.* Presidential authority to create forest reserves is based upon a rider to the 1891 General Appropriations Act, and there was no mention of delegating to the president the power to extinguish Indian land rights. Charles F. Wilkinson and H. Michael Anderson, *Land and Resource Planning in the National Forests*, pp. 17–18 (Washington, DC: Island Press, 1987). Under similar circumstance, courts have struck down executive action; see, for example, *Cramer v. United States*, 261 U.S. 219 (1923); *United States v. Winnebago Tribe of Nebraska*, 542 F.2d 1002 (8th Cir. 1976); *Felix S. Cohen's Handbook of Federal Indian Law*, 1982 ed., pp. 225–28 (Charlottesville, VA: Michie Bobbs-Merrill, 1982).

209 *Taos Forest Reserve.* Proclamation by President Roosevelt of Nov. 7, 1906, 34 Stat. 3262 (1907); Gordon-McCutchan, *Taos Indians*, pp. 11–12.

210 *The agency opened the area.* Gordon-McCutchan, *Taos Indians*, p. 15; *see also* Hearings Before the Senate Committee on Interior and Insular Affairs, Subcommittee on Indian Affairs, "Taos Indians—Blue Lake Amendments: On S. 750 and H.R. 471 (Bills to Amend Section 4 of the Act of May 31, 1933 [48 Stat. 108], to Add Certain Lands to the Wheeler Park Wilderness, Carson National Forest, New Mexico, and for Other Purposes)," 91st Congress, 2d Session, pp. 113, 115–17, 125–27, 163, 292, 296 (July 9–10, 1970) [hereinafter 1970 Hearings].

210 *a "grave threat."* John J. Bodine, associate professor, American University, letter to Hon. Lee Metcalf, senator, U.S. Senate (July 10, 1970), *in* 1970 Hearings, p. 298.

210 *"Their very presence." Ibid.,* p. 299.

210 *The agency stalled. Ibid.,* pp. 12–32. *See also* Gordon-McCutchan, *Taos Indians*, pp. 11–22.

210 *Indian Claims Commission. See generally 1982 Cohen Handbook*, pp. 160–62, 205.

211 *The pueblo decided to file.* Gordon-McCutchan, *Taos Indians*, pp. 43–45.

211 *wave of public approval.* Wilkinson, *Crossing*, pp. 131–35.

212 *pueblo and the Forest Service.* Hearings Before the House Committee on Interior and Insular Affairs, Subcommittee on Indian Affairs, "On H.R. 471 (To Amend Section 4 of the Act of May 31, 1933)," 91st Congress, 1st Session, pp. 21–23 (May 15–16, 1969) [hereinafter 1969 Hearings].

212 *The Indian Claims Commission handed down. Pueblo of Taos*, 15 Ind. Cl. Comm., at 666.

212 *need for privacy. Ibid.,* at 675.

212   *The opinion concluded.* Ibid., at 682.

212   *Senator Anderson introduced.* "Bills Introduced," March 15, 1966, vol. 112, pt.
       5 *Congressional Record*, 89th Congress, 2d Session, p. S5889 (Washington, DC:
       U.S. Government Printing Office, 1966); see generally Gordon-McCutchan,
       Taos Indians, pp. 85–106.

212   *Many other factors.* Gordon-McCutchan, *Taos Indians*, pp. 111–15.

212   *The tribal council.* For Schaab's performance under aggressive questioning by
       Senators Metcalf and Burdick, see, for example, 1970 Hearings, pp. 125–34
       (July 9, 1970).

213   *Corinne Locker.* Gordon-McCutchan, *Taos Indians*, p. 126.

213   *She also stood firm.* Ibid., pp. 125–26 (focusing on conflicts with Senator
       Anderson and AAIA).

213   *After La Farge died.* 1969 Hearings, p. 74.

213   *The pueblo also gained.* The publication information is Frank Waters, *The
       Man Who Killed the Deer* (New York: Farrar and Rinehart, 1942).

213   *"My own guess."* 1970 Hearings, p. 59 (July 9, 1970)

213   *Senator Robert Kennedy.* Stewart Udall, telephone interview with author, Oct.
       21, 2002.

213   *The Wilderness Society gave.* 1970 Hearings, pp. 149–50 (July 9, 1970).

214   *The Indian advocates.* See, e.g., Deverell, "Return," pp. 67–69.

214   *Nixon's 1970 message.* See Richard Nixon, "Message from the President: Pro-
       posed Recommendations Relating to the American Indians," vol. 116, pt. 17
       Congressional Record, 91st Congress, 2d Session, pp. 23259–60 (Washington,
       DC: U.S. Government Printing Office, 1970).

214   *Press conference day before hearings.* Gordon-McCutchan, *Taos Indians*, pp.
       185–87.

214   *"all those guys stood up."* Ibid., p. 187.

214   *Repeatedly, Senator Quentin Burdick . . . asked.* On the exchange between Bur-
       dick and Bernal, see 1970 Hearings, p. 131–132 (July 9, 1970).

216   *The cacique's appearance.* 1970 Hearings, p. 257 (July 9, 1970).

216   *"He had extraordinary spiritual power."* Gordon-McCutchan, *Taos Indians*, p.
       189.

216   *Later, after President Nixon had signed.* For a summary of the law and the Taos
       Pueblo's long struggle to regain Blue Lake, see generally John J. Bodine,
       "Blue Lake: A Struggle for Indian Rights," vol. 1, no. 1 *American Indian Law
       Review*, p. 23 (1973). As finally passed, the statute contained a provision that
       except for firewood gathering and other low-level personal uses, the land
       would be kept wild in accordance with the provisions of the Wilderness Act
       of 1964. Blue Lake Restoration Act, Pub. L. No. 91-550, Dec.15, 1970, 84 Stat.
       1437 (1971) (not codified).

216   *not "one of the non-Indians working."* Deverell, "Return," p. 64.

216 *"After I finished this work."* Paul Bernal, video interview (date unknown).

217 *Some testified. See, e.g.,* 1970 Hearings, p. 59 (Stewart Udall), p. 66 (Thomas O'Leary, representative of the Indian Rights Association) (July 9, 1970).

217 *"There are no other claims . . . Even were the factual assumptions correct."* 1969 Hearings, p. 88.

218 *"You are quite concerned."* 1970 Hearings, p. 242 (July 9, 1970).

218 *"Let's pull over."* Delbert Frank, interview with author, June 30, 1988.

218 *The tribe's 1855 treaty.* Treaty Between the United States and the Warm Springs and Wasco Tribes of Middle Oregon, June 25, 1855, 12 Stat. 963 (1863). On the surveys, see *A History of the McQuinn Strip,* pp. 7–8 (Warm Springs, OR: Tribal Council of the Confederated Tribes of the Warm Springs Indian Reservation, 1972).

218 *The Department of the Interior eventually agreed.* Harrison Loesch, Assistant Secretary, U.S. Department of the Interior, letter to Hon. Henry M. Jackson, Senator, U.S. Senate (June 14, 1972), *in* Senate Report No. 92-999, 92d Congress, 2d Session, pp. 5–6 (Washington, DC: U.S. Government Printing Office, 1972); *see McQuinn Strip,* pp. 7–8.

219 *remedial legislation.* Pub. L. No. 92-427, September 21, 1972, 86 Stat. 719 (1973) (not codified).

219 *In 1972 the Yakama Nation.* Executive Order No. 11670, "Providing for the Return of Certain lands to the Yakima Indian Reservation," vol. 37, no. 100 *Federal Register,* p. 10431 (May 23, 1972).

219 *The Quinault Indian Nation obtained.* An Act to declare that certain lands be held in trust for the Quinault Indian Nation, and for other purposes, Pub. L. No. 100-638, Nov. 8, 1988, 102 Stat. 3327 (1990) (not codified); *see also* Hal Neumann et al., *The Forests of the Quinault: Forest Management on the Quinault Indian Reservation, 1855–1996,* pp. 315–17 (Missoula, MT: Heritage Research Center, 1997).

219 *The Siletz and Grand Ronde tribes.* Siletz Restoration Act, Pub. L. No. 96-340, Sept. 4, 1980, 94 Stat. 1072 (1981) (not codified but set out at 25 U.S.C. § 711[e] [2000]) (3,630 acres); Grand Ronde Restoration Act, Pub. L. No. 98-165, Nov. 22, 1983, 97 Stat. 1064 (1985) (codified at 25 U.S.C. § 713[f] [2000]).

219 *Congress passed.* On tribal land claims and other restored tribes, see *1982 Cohen Handbook,* pp. 477–81, 562–67.

220 *Maine's separation from Massachusetts.* On the separation, see generally James S. Leamon et al., "Separation and Statehood, 1783–1820," *in* Richard W. Judd et al., eds., *Maine: The Pine Tree State from Prehistory to Present,* p. 169 (Orono: University of Maine Press, 1995); Henry E. Dunnack, *The Maine Book,* pp. 58–61 (Augusta, ME: publisher unknown, 1920); Massachusetts Act of Separation, 1819 Mass. Acts, ch. 161, § 1. Maine agreed to "assume and perform all the duties and obligations" of Massachusetts toward the Indians. *Joint Tribal Council of Passamaquoddy Tribe v. Morton,* 388 F. Supp. 649, 652, n. 2 (D. Me. 1975).

220 *Stevens had grown up.* Tom Tureen, telephone interview with author, July 31, 2002.

220 *deserving of a legal remedy.* The most complete and reliable account of the Passamaquoddy and Penobscot land claim cases is Paul Brodeur, *Restitution: The Land Claims of the Mashpee, Passamaquoddy, and Penobscot Indians of New England* (Boston: Northeastern University Press, 1985); *see also* Robert McLaughlin, "Giving It Back to the Indians," vol. 239 *Atlantic Monthly*, p. 70 (Feb. 1977); Kim Isaac Eisler, *Revenge of the Pequots: How a Small Native American Tribe Created the World's Most Profitable Casino*, pp. 63–81 (New York: Simon and Schuster, 2001).

222 *Gellers began researching.* Brodeur, *Restitution*, p. 83; Robert H. White, *Tribal Assets: The Rebirth of Native America*, pp. 29–30 (New York: Henry Holt and Co., 1990).

222 *"You've been working."* Tureen, interview.

223 *His basic proposition.* The Nonintercourse Act claims brought by the Passamaquoddy and other tribes work on a simple premise but also have bred a large and intricate body of law. For a brief summary, see William C. Canby, Jr., *American Indian Law in a Nutshell*, pp. 41–42 (St. Paul, MN: West Group, 1998). Early in his work, Tureen wrote a short law review article of interest, Francis J. O'Toole and Thomas N. Tureen, "State Power and the Passamaquoddy Tribe: 'A Gross National Hypocrisy?,'" vol. 23, no. 1 *Maine Law Review*, p. 1 (1971). *1982 Cohen Handbook*, pp. 510–16, also sets out the basics; *see also* Tim Vollmann, "A Survey of Eastern Indian Land Claims: 1970–1979," vol. 31, no. 1 *Maine Law Review*, p. 5 (1979); Robert N. Clinton and Margaret Tobey Hotopp, "Judicial Enforcement of the Federal Restraint on Alienation of Indian Land: The Origins of the Eastern Land Claims," vol. 31, no. 1 *Maine Law Review*, p. 17 (1979).

225 *Tureen met with.* Tureen, interview.

225 *Most lawyers. See* Brodeur, *Restitution*, pp. 83–84.

225 *Adverse possession.* 14 Me. Rev. Stat. § 6651 (2003).

225 *Statutes of limitation.* 14 Me. Rev. Stat. § 801 (2003).

226 *"I told myself."* Roberta Scruggs, "The Fight of a Lifetime: An 'Aggressive Strategy' that Questioned the Validity of Maine's Claims to Indian Land Led to the Landmark 1980 Settlement," *Portland Press Herald*, p. A11 (Aug. 20, 2000).

227 *"it was high time."* Brodeur, *Restitution*, p. 89.

227 *prosecutorial discretion. See, e.g., Dunlop v. Bachowski*, 421 U.S. 560 (1975); Richard J. Pierce, Jr., vol. 3, *Administrative Law Treatise*, 4th ed., pp. 1227–28, 1322 (New York: Aspen Law and Business, 2002).

227 *Judge Gignoux, rejecting this argument, found. Passamaquoddy Tribe*, 388 F. Supp. at 655–63.

228 *court of appeals. Joint Tribal Council of Passamaquoddy Tribe v. Morton*, 528 F.2d 370 (1st Cir. 1975).

228 *In the summer of 1976.* Brodeur, *Restitution*, p. 97.

228 *"the worst crisis."* Scruggs, "Fight."

228 *The frenetic political activity. See generally* Brodeur, *Restitution*, pp. 127–31.

229 *President Carter signed.* The statute included the Houlton Band of Maliseets as well as the Passamaquoddy and Penobscot. On the act, see generally David H. Getches et al., *Cases and Materials on Federal Indian Law*, 4th ed., p. 297 (St. Paul, MN: West Group, 1998).

229 *One tribe, the Mashpee. Mashpee Tribe v. New Seabury Corp.*, 592 F.2d 575 (1st Cir. 1979).

229 *Otherwise, nearly all the tribal cases. See, for example*, the congressional settlements for the Seminole, Pub. L. No. 100-228, Dec. 31, 1987, 101 Stat. 1556 (1989) (codified at 25 U.S.C. § 1772 [2000]), Puyallup, Pub. L. No. 101-41, June 21, 1989, 103 Stat. 83 (1991) (codified at 25 U.S.C. §1773 [2000]), and Seneca, Pub. L. No. 101-503, Nov. 3, 1990, 104 Stat. 1292 (1991) (codified at 25 U.S.C. § 1774 [2000]), tribes. But see a summary of the Cayuga judgment, Margaret Cronin Fisk, "200-Year-Old Land Dispute Nets $247.9M: Suit Centered on Land of Cayuga Indian Nation," *National Law Journal*, p. A6 (Oct. 22, 2001), in which Congress rejected a state settlement of $8 million and the tribe ultimately won $36.9 million for land value and rent and fair use plus $211 million in interest, though no land was received.

230 *The Western Shoshone of Nevada. See generally* Steven J. Crum, *The Road on Which We Came: A History of the Western Shoshone*, pp. 175–83 (Salt Lake City: University of Utah Press, 1994).

231 *The Sioux want.* Tim Giago, "Black Hills Claims Settlement Revisited," *Lakota Journal* (Aug. 2–9, 2002), *at* http://www.dlncoalition.org/dln_issues/black_hills_articles.htm (last visited Nov. 9, 2003) (on file with author).

231 *The Passamaquoddy, for example.* On land acquisition and economic development, see, for example, White, *Tribal Assets*, pp. 11–20, 41–53, 115–32; Roberta Scruggs, "The Fight of a Lifetime: An 'Aggressive Strategy' that Questioned the Validity of Maine's Claims to Indian Land Led to the Landmark 1980 Settlement," *Portland Press Herald*, p. 11A (Aug. 20, 2000); "Do Not Shift Indians Outside of State Law: Key Laws Govern Them that Govern All in Maine," *Portland Press Herald*, p. 8A (March 6, 1997).

231 *Maine, however, has aggressively used. See* Roberta Scruggs, "An Unsettled Settlement: Twenty Years After the Signing of the Historic Maine Land Claims Settlement, Many Tribal Leaders Regret the Compromise, Judging It Not by What Was Gained, But by All that Was Lost," *Portland Press Herald*, p. 1A (Aug. 20, 2000); Brian MacQuarrie, "Casino Plan for Maine Rejected by Wide Margin," *Boston Globe*, p. A1 (Nov. 5, 2003).

231 *Senator Ernest Gruening and Rampart Dam. See, e.g.*, "Alaska Hopeful on Yukon Power," *New York Times*, p. 57 (June 18, 1961); Lawrence E. Davies, "Alaskans Press for a Hydroelectric Dam on Yukon," *New York Times*, p. 174

(Dec. 1, 1963); Ernest Gruening, "Gruening Backs Alaska Dam: State's Senator Challenges Agency Forecast of Wildlife Loss," *New York Times*, letter to ed., p. 18 (Sept. 5, 1964); Ernest Gruening, "Gruening Backs Hydro Power for Rampart," *New York Times*, letter to ed., p. 44 (March 17, 1965); Mary Clay Berry, *The Alaska Pipeline: The Politics of Oil and Native Land Claims*, pp. 42–43 (Bloomington: Indiana University Press, 1975).

231 *Word of the intrusions.* Donald Craig Mitchell, *Sold American: The Story of Alaska Natives and Their Land, 1867–1959: The Army to Statehood* (Hanover, NH: University Press of New England, 1997). On Alaska statehood, see generally Joseph Rudd, "Who Owns Alaska?—Mineral Rights Acquisition amid Rapidly Changing Land Ownership," vol. 20 *Rocky Mountain Mineral Law Institute*, p. 109 (1975). On state land selections and Native rights, see Berry, *Alaska Pipeline*, pp. 34–52; Kornelia Grabinska, "History of Events Leading to the Passage of the Alaska Native Claims Settlement Act," paper presented at the Tanana Chiefs Conference (Jan. 1983), *at* http://www.alaskool.org/projects/ancsa/tcc2/TananaChiefs.html#top (last visited June 10, 2003) (on file with author).

232 *'I was raised.'* Willie Hensley, telephone interview with author, Sept. 17, 2002.

232 *To Hensley, to the Natives.* The Alaska Natives' belief in their aboriginal ownership is reflected in the law. On aboriginal title in Alaska, see David Case and David A. Voluck, *Alaska Natives and American Laws*, 2d ed., pp. 35–63 (Fairbanks: University of Alaska Press, 2002); *1982 Cohen Handbook*, pp. 743–46; Robert D. Arnold, *Alaska Native Land Claims*, pp. 61–92 (Anchorage: Alaska Native Foundation, 1978).

233 *They had filed a few.* Mitchell, *Sold American*, p. 379; *see* Arnold, *Alaska Native*, p. 112.

233 *Willie Hensley research paper. Ibid.*, pp. 112–17; John McPhee, *Coming into the Country*, pp. 141–44 (New York: Bantam Books, 1979); John Strohmeyer, *Extreme Conditions: Big Oil and the Transformation of Alaska*, pp. 13–21, 63–69 (Anchorage, AK: Cascade Press, 1997).

233 *By the end of the 1960s.* Arnold, *Alaska Native*, pp. 118–19; Berry, *Alaska Pipeline*, p. 44.

233 *Alaska Native claims and the Alaska Native Claims Settlement Act.* The most detailed account of the events leading up to ANCSA is Donald Craig Mitchell, *Take My Land, Take My Life: The Story of Congress's Historic Settlement of Alaska Native Land Claims, 1960–1971* (Fairbanks: University of Alaska Press, 2001). Thomas Berger, a Canadian judge working under the authority of the Inupiat Circumpolar Council, held hearings in the 1980s and filed a colorful and influential report on ANCSA and its aftermath, Thomas R. Berger, *Village Journey: The Report of the Alaska Native Review Commission* (New York: Hill and Wang, 1985). Mary Berry, a journalist, has written a fine shorter account, *Alaska Pipeline; see also* Arnold, *Alaska Native*; Strohmeyer, *Extreme Conditions*; Ramona Ellen Skinner, *Alaska Native Policy in the Twentieth Cen-*

tury (New York: Garland Publishing, 1997); Kirk Dombrowski, *Against Culture: Development, Politics, and Religion in Indian Alaska* (Lincoln: University of Nebraska Press, 2001); Norman A. Chance, *The Iñupiat and Arctic Alaska: An Ethnography of Development* (Fort Worth, TX: Holt, Rinehart and Winston, 1990).

233 *The Alaska office of the Bureau.* Mitchell, *Sold American*, p. 379.

233 *The assistant secretary . . . shelved the appeals. Ibid.*

233 *Senator Gruening weighed in.* Berry, *Alaska Pipeline*, p. 41.

233 *But not dubious to . . . Stewart Udall.* The more Udall looked into the matter, the more he became convinced of the Natives' side on the land claims. Stewart Udall, interview with author, Santa Fe, New Mexico, Oct. 17, 2002. On the conflicts within the Department of the Interior, especially between Solicitor Frank Barry, who favored the Natives' position, and Assistant Secretary John Carver, who did not, see Mitchell, *Take My Land*, pp. 74–75, 91–92, 147–48.

233 *one thousand Natives.* Arnold, *Alaska Native*, p. 102; *see also* Mitchell, *Take My Land*, pp. 83–195 (examining the land freezes in detail).

233 *The Tanana Chiefs Conference. See, e.g.*, Grabinska, "History," p. 10.

234 *In October 1966.* Mitchell, *Sold American*, p. 380; Grabinska, "History," pp. 11–13.

234 *Udall had visited.* Hensley, interview.

234 *In December 1966. See, e.g.*, Berry, *Alaska Pipeline*, p. 49; Arnold, *Alaska Native*, pp. 117–19.

234 *Udall's formal withdrawal.* Public Land Order No. 4582, "Alaska: Withdrawal of Unreserved Lands," Jan. 23, 1969, vol. 34, no. 15 *Federal Register*, p. 1025 (Washington, DC: U.S. Government Printing Office, 1969).

234 *North Slope oil.* Mary Berry captures the near hysteria over the Prudhoe Bay find in Berry, *Alaska Pipeline*, pp. 89–97. On the Alaska pipeline, see generally Peter A. Coates, *The Trans-Alaska Pipeline Controversy: Technology, Conservation, and the Frontier* (Bethlehem, PA: Lehigh University Press, 1991).

234 *"the last pork chop."* Edward Abbey, "The Last Pork Chop," *in The Best of Outside: The First Twenty Years*, p. 13 (New York: Villard Books, 1997).

235 *Both congressional leaders initially came in. See, e.g.*, Grabinska, "History," p. 16; Arnold, *Alaska Native*, p. 130.

235 *Jackson's offer.* Berry, *Alaska Pipeline*, p. 124; *see also* Mitchell, *Take My Land*, pp. 269–79.

235 *Aspinall's initial bill.* Arnold, *Alaska Native*, p. 137; Grabinska, "History," p. 20. Aspinall's revised bill allowed a land grant of just 500,000 acres. Mitchell, *Take My Land*, pp. 390, 403. The Aspinall bills would have allowed for additional lands for subsistence hunting and fishing under federal permits. *Ibid.*

235 *The Alaska Federation of Natives.* On AFN's effectiveness, see Berry, *Alaska Pipeline*, p. 214; Arnold, *Alaska Native*, pp. 137–41.

235 *AFN delegates made.* Strohmeyer, *Extreme Conditions*, p. 72.

235 *Charlie Edwardsen.* For a biography of Edwardsen, see H. G. Gallagher, *Etok: A Story of Eskimo Power* (New York: G. P. Putnam's Sons, 1974).

235 *A key moment.* Mitchell, *Take My Land*, pp. 368–75, 396–401; Gallagher, *Etok*, p. 216.

235 *ANCSA. See generally* Case and Voluck, *Alaska Natives*, pp. 155–185; *see also* George Cameron Coggins et al., *Federal Public Land and Resources Law*, 5th ed., pp. 144–47 (New York: Foundation Press, 2002). On the environmental study, see *Ibid.*; 43 U.S.C. § 1616(d)(2) (2000); *see generally* Robert Cahn, *The Fight to Save Wild Alaska* (New York: National Audubon Society, 1982); Glenn E. Cravez, "The Alaska National Interest Lands Conservation Act: Directing the Great Land's Future," vol. 10, no. 1 *UCLA-Alaska Law Review*, p. 33 (1980).

237 *Still and all, ANCSA's blockbuster.* Case and Voluck, *Alaska Natives*, pp. 159–60; *1982 Cohen Handbook*, pp. 746–56; Monroe E. Price, "A Moment in History: The Alaska Native Claims Settlement Act," vol. 8, no. 2 *UCLA-Alaska Law Review*, p. 89 (1979).

237 *In 1980 they persuaded.* Case and Voluck, *Alaska Natives*, pp. 283–93; Getches et al., *Cases and Materials*, pp. 924–28.

237 *In 1987, before the 20-year.* J. Tate London, "The '1991 Amendments' to the Alaska Native Claims Settlement Act: Protection for Native Lands?," vol. 8 *Stanford Environmental Law Journal*, p. 200 (1989); Case and Voluck, *Alaska Natives*, pp. 173–74.

238 *Paradoxically, the idea of vesting.* Donald Mitchell traces the idea of land title being held by state-chartered corporations to Barry Jackson, an Anglo lawyer assisting the Alaska Federation of Natives. Jackson, who was well respected among Natives, had little background in Indian law. Mitchell, *Take My Land*, pp. 155–61.

238 *Strategically the Natives were pushed. See, e.g.*, Mitchell, *Sold American*, pp. 294, 303, 343, 375.

238 *"Our focus was on land."* Hensley, interview.

239 *Contemporary Supreme Court opinions at the time ANCSA passed.* The Supreme Court did not hand down the leading *McClanahan* opinion on tribal sovereignty until 1973, two years after passage of ANCSA. See *infra* ch. 10, pp. **243–49**.

239 *When Alaska Natives reached. Alaska v. Native Village of Venetie Tribal Government*, 522 U.S. 520 (1998).

239 *All, or nearly all, of the land granted.* Apparently, Native allotments remain subject to tribal government jurisdiction, and Native tribes have jurisdiction under the Indian Child Welfare Act, 25 U.S.C. §§1901–63 (2000). See *infra* ch. 10, pp. **258–61.** On Native jurisdiction after *Venetie*, see Erin Goff Chrisbens, "Indian Country After ANSCA: Divesting Tribal Sovereignty by Interpretation in *Alaska v. Native Village of Venetie Tribal Government*," vol. 76, no. 1

Denver University Law Review, pp. 326–29 (1998).

240 *They continue to press.* On negotiations between Alaska Native tribes and the
federal and state governments, *see, e.g.,* Case and Voluck, *Alaska Natives,* p.
431–32; "Alaska Natives Press Unity on Sovereignty," *at* http://www.indanz
.com/News/show.asp?=2002/10/25/afn (last visited May 12, 2004 (on file
with author).

CHAPTER 10: Sovereignty in Congress and the Courts

241 *Until the late 1980s the clear majority.* The scholarship on Indian law has been
voluminous. For comprehensive analyses, see, for example, William C.
Canby, Jr., *American Indian Law: In a Nutshell,* 3d ed. (St. Paul, MN: West
Group, 1998); Vine Deloria, Jr., and Clifford M. Lytle, *The Nations Within:
The Past and Future of American Indian Sovereignty* (New York: Pantheon
Books, 1984); Vine Deloria, Jr., and Clifford M. Lytle, *American Indians,
American Justice* (Austin: University of Texas Press, 1983); Charles F. Wilkin-
son, *American Indians, Time, and the Law* (New Haven, CT: Yale University
Press, 1987); David H. Getches, "Conquering the Cultural Frontier: The New
Subjectivism of the Supreme Court in Indian Law," vol. 84 *California Law
Review,* p. 1573 (1996); David H. Getches, "Beyond Indian Law: The Rehn-
quist Court's Pursuit of States' Rights, Color-Blind Justice and Mainstream
Values," vol. 86 *Minnesota Law Review,* p. 267 (2001); Philip P. Frickey, "Com-
mentary: Adjudication and Its Discontents: Coherence and Conciliation in
Federal Indian Law," vol. 110 *Harvard Law Review,* p. 1754 (1997); S. James
Anaya, "The United States Supreme Court and Indigenous Peoples: Still a
Long Way to Go Toward a Therapeutic Role," vol. 24, *Seattle U. Law Review,* p.
229 (2000); Robert N. Clinton, "Isolated in Their Own Country: A Defense of
Federal Protection of Indian Autonomy and Self-Government," vol. 33 *Stan-
ford Law Review,* p. 979 (1981); Nell Jessup Newton, "Federal Power over Indi-
ans: Its Sources, Scope, and Limitations," vol. 132 *University of Pennsylvania
Law Review,* p. 195 (1984). The origins of the field are explored in Robert A.
Williams, *The American Indian in Western Legal Thought: The Discourses of
Conquest* (New York: Oxford University Press, 1990) and Robert A. Williams,
*Linking Arms Together: American Indian Treaty Visions of Law and Peace,
1600–1800* (New York: Oxford University Press, 1997). Frank Pommersheim
offers a superb study of tribal justice systems in *Braid of Feathers: American
Indian Law and Contemporary Tribal Life* (Berkeley: University of California
Press, 1995). The literature is enriched by the articles and books of many
additional scholars, some of which are referenced in the notes that follow.

242 *By the early 1970s tribes had.* On Indian legal service programs during this
time, see generally David H. Getches, "Difficult Beginnings for Indian Legal
Services," vol. 30 *NLADA Briefcase,* p. 181 (May 1972).

242 *Native American Rights Fund.* The founding of NARF is discussed in *Ibid.* and
Ralph W. Johnson, "Indian Tribes and the Legal System," vol. 72 *Washington
Law Review,* pp. 1035–36 (Oct. 1997); *see also* Native American Rights Fund,
NARF: Our First Twenty Years (Boulder, CO: Native American Rights Fund,

1990); Marlise James, *The People's Lawyers*, pp. 350–60 (New York: Holt, Rinehart and Winston, 1973). NARF maintains a Web site, accessible *at* http://www.narf.org.

242   *Tribes soon developed.* On the emergence of in-house tribal attorneys, see Johnson, "Indian Tribes," p. 1039.

242   *A driving force. See generally* Heidi Estes and Robert Laurence, "Preparing American Indians for Law School: The American Indian Law Center's Pre-Law Summer Institute," vol. 12, no. 2 *Northern Illinois University Law Review*, p. 278 (1992); *see also* Johnson, "Indian Tribes," pp. 1037–38. The institute's Web site may be accessed *at* http://lawschool.unm.edu/ AILC/plsi/index.htm.

244   *Rosalind McClanahan and DNA.* Richard Collins, who refreshed his memory by talking with Bruce Bridegroom, provided this background on the *McClanahan* case. Richard Collins, telephone interview with author, Aug. 13 and 15, 2002.

244   *The conflict in* Worcester v. Georgia. On the background of the Cherokee cases, see generally Francis Paul Prucha, vol. 1, *The Great Father: The United States Government and the American Indians*, pp. 190, 224–48 (Lincoln: University of Nebraska Press, 1984); Allen Guttman, *States' Rights and Indian Removal: The Cherokee Nation v. the State of Georgia* (Boston: D.C. Health, 1965); Wilson Lumpkin, *The Removal of the Cherokee Indians from Georgia* (New York: Arno Press, 1969); Joseph C. Burke, "The Cherokee Cases: A Study in Law, Politics, and Morality," vol. 21 *Stanford Law Review*, p. 500 (Feb. 1969).

245   *He acknowledged tribes as "separate nations."* Worcester v. Georgia, 31 U.S. (6 Pet.) 515, 542–43 (1832).

245   *"The Cherokee nation, then." Ibid.* at 561.

245   *The Supreme Court. Williams v. Lee*, 358 U.S. 217, 219 (1959).

245   *But then, just three years later.* "The general notion drawn from Chief Justice Marshall's opinion in Worcester v. Georgia . . . that an Indian reservation is a distinct nation within whose boundaries state law cannot penetrate, has yielded to closer analysis when confronted, in the course of subsequent developments, with diverse concrete situations. By 1880 the Court no longer viewed reservations as distinct nations. On the contrary, it was said that a reservation was in many cases a part of the surrounding State or Territory, and subject to its jurisdiction except as forbidden by federal law." *Organized Village of Kake v. Egan*, 369 U.S. 60, 72 (1962).

246   *In the 1965* Warren Trading Post *case. Warren Trading Post v. Arizona State Tax Commission*, 380 U.S. 685, 688–92 (1965).

246   *Public Law 280.* See *supra* ch. 1, pp. **18–20** (state jurisdiction at the Quinault Reservation), ch. 5, pp. **123–25** (state jurisdiction in South Dakota).

246   *The DNA lawyers filed. McClanahan v. State Tax Commission*, 484 P.2d 221 (Ariz. Ct. App. 1971).

246   *In the eight years since.* For cases decided, *see, e.g., Menominee Tribe of Indi-
      ans v. United States,* 391 U.S. 404 (1968) (upholding the tribe's retention of its
      treaty hunting and fishing rights, despite the Termination Act of 1954);
      Puyallup Tribe v. Department of Game (Puyallup I), 391 U.S. 392 (1968)
      (upholding the state's authority to regulate the manner in which a tribe exer-
      cises its off-reservation treaty fishing rights where such regulations are rea-
      sonable and necessary to conserve fish and wildlife resources and are
      nondiscriminatory). For cases under consideration, *see, e.g., Oneida Indian
      Nation v. County of Oneida,* 414 U.S. 661 (1974) (land claim); *Morton v. Man-
      cari,* 417 U.S. 535 (1974) (affirmative action).

247   *The* McClanahan *opinion.* The result in *McClanahan* strongly supported
      tribal sovereignty, and so did much of the Court's language, but the opinion
      also found that the doctrine had undergone "considerable evolution" since
      Worcester:

> The trend has been away from the idea of inherent Indian sover-
> eignty as a bar to state jurisdiction and toward reliance on federal pre-
> emption. The modern cases thus tend to avoid reliance on platonic
> notions of Indian sovereignty and to look instead to the applicable
> treaties and statutes which define the limits of state power.
>   The Indian sovereignty doctrine is relevant, then, not because it pro-
> vides a definitive resolution of the issues in this suit, but because it pro-
> vides a backdrop against which the applicable treaties and federal
> statutes must be read. It must always be remembered that the various
> Indian tribes were once independent and sovereign nations, and that
> their claim to sovereignty long predates that of our own Government.
> Indians today are American citizens. They have the right to vote, to use
> state courts, and they receive some state services. But it is nonetheless
> still true, as it was in the last century, that "[t]he relation of the Indian
> tribes living within the borders of the United States . . . [is] an anom-
> alous one and of a complex character. . . . They were, and always have
> been, regarded as having a semi-independent position when they pre-
> served their tribal relations; not as States, not as nations, not as pos-
> sessed of the full attributes of sovereignty, but as a separate people,
> with the power of regulating their internal and social relations, and
> thus far not brought under the laws of the Union or of the State within
> whose limits they resided. *McClanahan v. State Tax Commission of Ari-
> zona,* 411 U.S. 164, 172–73 (1973) (citations omitted) (quoting *United
> States v. Kagama,* 118 U.S. 375, 381–82 [1886]).

247   " 'the policy of leaving Indians.' " *Ibid.* at 168 (quoting *Rice v. Olson,* 324 U.S.
      786, 789 [1945]).

247   *Indian treaties* " 'are read.' " *Ibid.* at 173–74 (quoting *Carpenter v. Shaw,* 280 U.S.
      363, 367 [1930]).

247   *The text of the Navajo Treaty.* Treaty Between the United States of America
      and the Navajo Tribe of Indians, June 1, 1868, 15 Stat. 667, 668 (1869).

247   *Nonetheless, under the Court's conception. McClanahan,* 411 U.S. at 179.

247 *In addition, the Solicitor General's office.* For a firsthand reflection of the
     Court's treatment of Indian law cases, see Louis Claiborne, "The Trend of
     Supreme Court Decisions in Indian Cases," vol. 22, no. 1 *American Indian
     Law Review*, p. 585 (1998).

248 *During his tenure.* On Thurgood Marshall's central role in the Court's Indian
     law opinions, see Getches, "Conquering," pp. 1589–620.

248 *Tribal sovereignty forms. See generally* Wilkinson, *American Indians,* pp.
     54–63.

249 *Jicarilla land . . . overlay precious oil.* Robert J. Nordhaus et al., "Revisiting *Mer-
     rion v. Jicarilla Apache Tribe*: Robert Nordhaus and Sovereign Indian Control
     over Natural Resources on Reservations," vol. 43, no. 1 *Natural Resources
     Journal,* pp. 234–36 (2003). The Jicarilla Apache were not alone in battling
     oil and gas companies over leases. *See, e.g.,* Robert William Alexander, "The
     Collision of Tribal Natural Resource Development and State Taxation: An
     Economic Analysis," vol. 27, no. 2 *New Mexico Law Review*, p. 394 (1997).

249 *The leases made no mention. See Merrion v. Jicarilla Apache Tribe*, 455 U.S. 130,
     134–36, 147 (1982).

249 *the tribe amended its constitution.* Some tribes, especially under constitutions
     prepared by the BIA in the 1930s and 1940s, required bureau approval of
     tribal ordinances and/or constitutional amendments. The Jicarilla Apache
     Tribe had such a requirement, and the BIA approved the constitutional
     amendment and tax ordinance at issue in the case. *Ibid.* at 134–36.

251 *The opinion approached the problem. Ibid.* at 145.

251 *"[S]overeign power, even when unexercised." Ibid.* at 148.

251 *"The petitioners [the energy companies]." Ibid.* at 137–38 (citations omitted).

251 *broad state court jurisdiction to hear Indian water rights cases. Colorado River
     Water Conservation District v. United States*, 424 U.S. 800 (1976); *Arizona v. San
     Carlos Apache Tribe of Arizona*, 463 U.S. 545 (1983).

251 *permitted some state taxation. Washington v. Confederated Tribes of the Colville
     Indian Reservation*, 447 U.S. 134 (1980) (upholding the imposition of state cig-
     arette and sales taxes on on-reservation sales by a tribe to nonmembers of
     the tribe); *Cotton Petroleum Corp. v. New Mexico*, 490 U.S. 163 (1989) (state
     severance tax on a non-Indian oil and gas company operating on reservation
     land was not precluded by imposition of a tribal tax or federal law).

251 *ruled that some reservation boundaries. See, e.g., DeCoteau v. District County Court
     for Tenth Judicial District*, 420 U.S. 425 (1975); *Rosebud Sioux Tribe v. Kneip*, 430
     U.S. 584 (1977). Other decisions, however, held that boundaries had not been
     diminished. *See, e.g., Mattz*, 412 U.S. 481; *Solem v. Bartlett*, 465 U.S. 463 (1984).

251 *allowed national forest road building. Lyng v. Northwest Indian Cemetery Pro-
     tective Ass'n*, 485 U.S. 439 (1988); *see also Employment Division, Department
     of Human Resources of Oregon v. Smith*, 494 U.S. 872 (1990) (upholding state
     denial of unemployment benefits where job termination resulted from cer-
     emonial peyote use, which violated state drug laws).

252 The Court upheld the Boldt decision. *Washington v. Washington State Commercial Passenger Fishing Vessel Ass'n*, 443 U.S. 658 (1979); *see supra* ch. 8, pp. **198–204**.

252 The eastern land claim. *Oneida County, New York v. Oneida Indian Nation of New York State*, 470 U.S. 226 (1985).

252 The Cabazon and Morongo bands. *California v. Cabazon Band of Mission Indians*, 480 U.S. 202 (1987).

252 affirmative action. *Mancari*, 417 U.S. 535.

252 broad tribal court jurisdiction. See, e.g., *Fisher v. District Court*, 424 U.S. 382 (1976); *Santa Clara Pueblo v. Martinez*, 436 U.S. 49 (1978); *National Farmers Union Insurance Cos. v. Crow Tribe of Indians*, 471 U.S. 845 (1985); *Iowa Mutual Insurance Co. v. LaPlante*, 480 U.S. 9 (1987).

252 held invalid state taxation. See, e.g., *White Mountain Apache Tribe v. Bracker*, 448 U.S. 136 (1980); *Ramah Navajo School Board, Inc. v. Bureau of Revenue of New Mexico*, 458 U.S. 832 (1982).

252 and restricted the reach of state jurisdiction. *Bryan v. Itasca County, Minnesota*, 426 U.S. 373 (1976).

252 The Brethren. Bob Woodward and Scott Armstrong, *The Brethren: Inside the Supreme Court*, pp. 57–58, 359, 412–13 (New York: Simon and Schuster, 1979).

252 "a fabled unpopularity." Getches, "Conquering," p. 1632; *see also* Claiborne, "The Trend."

253 Supreme Court justices. For analysis of the approaches of different judges, see generally Getches, "Conquering;" Claiborne, "The Trend."

253 Facts of Oliphant and Belgrade cases. Respondents' Brief to the District Court, "Return of Suquamish Respondents on Petition for Writ of Habeas Corpus," Jan. 31, 1975, in Appendix at 94–95, *Oliphant v. Suquamish Indian Tribe*, 435 U.S. 191 (1978) (No. 76-5729).

253 white-hot emotional issue. See, e.g., American Indian Policy Review Commission, vol. 1, "Final Report," pp. 583–90 (May 17, 1977) (Washington, DC: U.S. Government Printing Office, 1977) (separate dissenting views of Representative Lloyd Meeds) [hereinafter Final Report].

254 The small Suquamish reservation. *Oliphant*, 435 U.S. at 193, n. 1.

254 Lower court rulings. *Oliphant v. Schlie*, 544 F.2d 1007 (9th Cir. 1976); *Oliphant v. Schlie*, "District Court—Memorandum Opinion of U.S. District Judge Morill E. Sharp," (W.D. Wash. Filed April 5, 1974), in Appendix at 48, *Oliphant*, 435 U.S. 191.

254 Justice Rehnquist wrote the opinion. *Oliphant*, 435 U.S. 191.

254 The Court itself had recently ruled. *Mancari*, 417 U.S. at 551–54.

254 Instead of a narrow ruling. *Oliphant*, 435 U.S. at 197, 203, 206, 208.

254 The Supreme Court normally demands. *Ibid.* at 201–03; Robert A. Williams, Jr., "The Algebra of Federal Indian Law: The Hard Trail of Decolonizing and Americanizing the White Man's Indian Jurisprudence," vol. 1986 *Wisconsin Law Review*, pp. 267–74 (1986); Ball, "Constitution," p. 125.

255 *Even then the Rehnquist opinion. Oliphant*, 435 U.S. at 203.

255 *instead of conducting the rigorous examination. Ibid.* at 208.

255 United States v. Wheeler. 435 U.S. 313 (1978).

255 *Tribal civil jurisdiction over non-Indians.* Non-Indians under tribal jurisdiction
     are also affected by Supreme Court decisions ruling that most cases in tribal
     court cannot be reviewed by the federal courts. This anomaly in our legal
     system, based on the independent sovereignty of tribes, contrasts with the
     practice for the rulings of state and lower federal courts, which can be
     reviewed by the U.S. Supreme Court to assure compliance with due process
     guarantees and other requirements of federal law. *Santa Clara*, 436 U.S. 49;
     National Farmers, 471 U.S. 845; *Iowa Mutual*, 480 U.S. 9; *see generally* Canby,
     American Indian Law, pp. 204–09; Wilkinson, *American Indians*, pp. 113–16.
     The rule applies only in civil cases. Criminal defendants in tribal courts can
     obtain habeas corpus relief in federal courts to contest their convictions. 25
     U.S.C. § 1303 (2000). Justice Souter has discussed the ways in which tribal
     courts differ from other American courts in his concurring opinion in
     Nevada v. Hicks, 533 U.S. 353, 383–86 (2001).

255 *The 1981* Montana *opinion. Montana v. United States*, 450 U.S. 544, 565–67
     (1981).

256 *Yet, even though the tribal interest. Brendale v. Confederated Tribes and Bands
     of the Yakima Indian Nation*, 492 U.S. 408 (1989); *Strate v. A-1 Contractors*, 520
     U.S. 438 (1997).

256 *In spite of this commonsense notion. Atkinson Trading Co., Inc. v. Shirley*, 532
     U.S. 645 (2001).

256 Nevada v. Hicks. 533 U.S. 353 (2001).

256 *Immunity. See, e.g., Westfall v. Erwin*, 484 U.S. 292 (1988) (official immunity);
     Harlow v. Fitzgerald, 457 U.S. 800, 815–19 (1982) (qualified immunity). Jus-
     tice O'Connor would have looked first to the immunity issues before
     addressing Indian law questions. *Nevada*, 533 U.S. at 387–401.

256 *Typical of Scalia's style.* See the concurring opinion of Justice O'Connor, *Ibid.*;
     Getches, "Beyond," pp. 331–35.

256 *Justice O'Connor sharply objected. Nevada*, 533 U.S. at 397. Justice Stevens
     called Scalia's analysis "exactly backwards." *Ibid.* at 402.

257 *As one example of Scalia's crusade. Ibid.* at 361–62.

257 *The comment in Kake v. Egan had no basis.* The *McClanahan* opinion took the
     trouble to limit the *Kake v. Egan* language three separate times. *McClanahan*,
     411 U.S. at 172, n. 8, 176, n. 15, 180, n. 20.

257 *The 1958 rewriting.* Professor Robert Clinton described the 1958 treatise as "a
     total bastardization" of Felix Cohen's 1942 work, in his article, "There Is No
     Federal Supremacy Clause for Indian Tribes," vol. 34, no. 1 *Arizona State Law
     Journal*, p. 232 (2002), and cited other such judgments; *see also* the assess-
     ment of the editors of the 1982 revision, *Felix S. Cohen's Handbook of Federal
     Indian Law*, 1982 ed., p. ix (Charlottesville, VA: Michie Bobbs-Merrill, 1982).

257 *Primary congressional authority over Indian affairs.* The Constitution grants power over Indian matters by means of the commerce clause, which includes the Indian commerce clause. Congress is authorized to "regulate Commerce with foreign Nations, and among the several States, and with Indian tribes." U.S. Const. art. I, § 8, cl. 3; *see generally 1982 Cohen Handbook*, pp. 207–28.

258 *In the fall of 1967, Louie and Janet Goodhouse.* Bert Hirsch, telephone interview with Anna Ulrich, research assistant, Oct. 12, 2000.

258 *Bert Hirsch, a young lawyer. Ibid.*

258 *The Goodhouses traveled to New York. See, e.g.,* "Welfare Workers Assailed on Treatment of Indians," *New York Times*, p. 86 (July 17, 1968).

258 *The problem was nationwide.* American Indian Policy Review Commission, "Report on Federal, State, and Tribal Jurisdiction: Task Force Four," *in* Senate Report No. 95-597, "The Indian Child Welfare Act of 1977," 95th Congress, 1st Session, p. 44 (Washington, DC: U.S. Government Printing Office, 1977) [hereinafter "Task Force Four"].

258 *Depending on the state. Ibid.,* pp. 46–50.

259 *"I can remember." Ibid.,* p. 43.

259 *"One of the most serious failings."* Hearings Before the Senate Select Committee on Indian Affairs, "Indian Child Welfare Act of 1977: On S. 1214," 95th Congress, 1st Session, p. 152 (Aug. 4, 1977) (Washington, DC: U.S. Government Printing Office, 1977).

260 *"I think the cruelest trick."* "Task Force Four," p. 43.

260 *five thousand children . . . in Mormon homes.* Daniel H. Ludlow, ed., vol. 2, *Encyclopedia of Mormonism: The History, Scripture, Doctrine, and Procedure of the Church of Jesus Christ of Latter-day Saints*, p. 679 (New York: Macmillan Publishing Co., 1992); *see also* Molly Ivins, "Mormons' Aid to Indian Children Preserved by New Law," *New York Times,* p. A16 (Dec. 26, 1978); Rex Weyler, *Blood of the Land: The Government and Corporate War Against the American Indian Movement,* p. 149 (New York: Everest House Publishers, 1982).

260 *The Mormon Church of course objected.* Hearing Before the Senate Select Committee on Indian Affairs, "Indian Child Welfare Act of 1977: On S. 1214 (To Establish Standards for the Placement of Indian Children in Foster or Adoptive Homes, to Prevent the Breakup of Indian Families, and for Other Purposes)," 95th Congress, 1st Session, pp. 204–08 (Aug. 4, 1977) (Washington, DC: U.S. Government Printing Office, 1977) (Mormon testimony concerning the church's placement program, asking that it be protected from federal interference); Weyler, *Blood,* p. 150 (identifying the Mormon lobbying pressure).

260 *Several cabinet officers.* Molly Ivins, "Indians' Tribal Courts Prepare to Take over Child Custody Cases," *New York Times,* p. 14 (Dec. 25, 1978) (explaining that Udall championed the bill and Carter signed it in the face of opposition from within the executive branch); Bert Hirsch, interview with Anna Ulrich, research assistant, Oct. 12, 2000.

261 *The Indian Child Welfare Act.* On ICWA, see the act itself, Indian Child Wel-
     fare Act of 1978, Pub. L. No. 95-608, Nov. 8, 1978, 92 Stat. 3069 (1980) (codi-
     fied as amended at 25 U.S.C. §§ 1901–63 [2000]), and the following articles:
     Manuel P. Guerrero, "Indian Child Welfare Act of 1978: A Response to the
     Threat to Indian Culture Caused by Foster and Adoptive Placements of
     Indian Children," vol. 7, no. 1 *American Indian Law Review*, p. 51 (1979);
     Michael C. Snyder, "An Overview of the Indian Child Welfare Act," vol. 7, no.
     3 *St. Thomas Law Review*, p. 815 (1995); Brian D. Gallagher, "Indian Child
     Welfare Act of 1978: The Congressional Foray into the Adoption Process,"
     vol. 15, no. 1 *Northern Illinois University Law Review*, p. 81 (1994).

261 *State child welfare agencies initially resisted.* One such narrow interpretation
     is the "existing Indian family exception." *See generally In re Bridget R. v. Cindy
     R.*, 49 Cal. Rptr. 2d 507 (Cal. Ct. App. 1996); Samuel Prim, "The Indian Child
     Welfare Act and the Existing Indian Family Exception: Rerouting the Trail of
     Tears?," vol. 24 *Law and Psychology Review*, p. 115 (Spring 2000); David H.
     Getches et al., *Cases and Materials on Federal Indian Law*, 4th ed., pp. 678–82
     (St. Paul, MN: West Group, 1998).

261 *Nonetheless, the Supreme Court has upheld. Mississippi Band of Choctaw Indi-
     ans v. Holyfield*, 490 U.S. 30 (1989).

261 *Reduced adoption. See, e.g.,* Ann E. MacEachron et al., "The Effectiveness of
     the Indian Child Welfare Act of 1978," vol. 70 *Social Service Review*, pp. 456–58
     (Sept. 1996); Margaret C. Plantz et al., "Indian Child Welfare: A Status
     Report," *in* Hearing Before the Senate Select Committee on Indian Affairs,
     "Indian Child Welfare Act: On S. 1976 (To Amend the Indian Child Welfare
     Act)," 100th Congress, 2d Session, pp. 224–25, 229–31 (May 11, 1988) (Wash-
     ington, DC: U.S. Government Printing Office, 1988); *see also* Mi'iko T'cha,
     "Indian Child Welfare Act Now 25 Years Old," *Sho-Ban News* (Sept. 24, 2003)
     (on file with author) (placement in an outside culture reduced from 80 to 85
     percent to about 25 percent of cases). These studies examine adoptions of
     Indian children in state courts; placement of Indian children living on reser-
     vations must be heard in tribal courts under ICWA, and the rate of place-
     ment in non-Indian homes is doubtless much lower.

261 *More than twenty water rights settlements. See generally* Getches et al., *Cases
     and Materials*, pp. 844–52 (containing a tribal water settlements summary
     table); Lloyd Burton, *American Indian Water Rights and the Limits of the Law*,
     pp. 63–86 (Lawrence: University Press of Kansas, 1991); *see, e.g.,* Daniel
     McCool, *Command of the Waters: Iron Triangles, Federal Water Development,
     and Indian Water*, pp. 234–36 (Berkeley: University of California Press, 1987)
     (Tohono O'odham Nation settlement).

261 *Federal laws now address.* Forests: National Indian Forest Resources Manage-
     ment Act, Pub. L. No. 101-630, title III, Nov. 28, 1990, 104 Stat. 4531, 4532
     (1991) (codified as amended at 25 U.S.C. §§ 3101–20 (2000)); *see also* the entire
     issue of "Forestry on Tribal Lands," *Journal of Forestry* (Nov. 1997), especially
     the article by Gary S. Morishima, "From Paternalism to Self-Determination,"
     p. 4. Agriculture: American Indian Agricultural Resource Management Act,

Pub. L. No. 103-177, Dec. 3, 1993, 107 Stat. 2011 (1994) (codified as amended at 25 U.S.C. §§ 3701–46 [2000]). Fisheries: 16 U.S.C. §§ 3632–34 (2000); 16 U.S.C. §§ 3311–12 (2000); 16 U.S.C. §§ 1852(f), 1855(i) (2000).

261   *The federal environmental laws. See, e.g.*, 42 U.S.C. § 7410(o) (2000) (Clean Air Act).

261   *To assist tribes.* Indian Lands Consolidation Act, Pub. L. No. 97-459, title II, Jan. 12, 1983, 96 Stat. 2515, 2517 (1984) (amended by Indian Lands Consolidation Act Amendments of 2000, Pub. L. No. 106-462, Nov. 7, 2000, 114 Stat. 1991 [2001] [codified at 25 U.S.C. §§ 2201–19 (2000)]).

262   *several comprehensive health and education statutes. See, e.g.*, Indian Health Care Improvement Act, Pub. L. No. 94-437, Sept. 30, 1976, 90 Stat. 1400 (1978) (codified as amended at 25 U.S.C. §§ 1601–83 (2000)) (health); Tribally Controlled Schools Act of 1988, Pub. L. No. 100-297, title V, pt. B, April 28, 1988, 102 Stat. 130, 385 (1990) (codified as amended at 25 U.S.C. §§ 2501–11 [2000]) (education).

262   *Tribal colleges draw. See, e.g.*, Higher Education Tribal Grant Authorization Act, Pub. L. No. 102-325, title XIII, pt. B, July 23, 1992, 106 Stat. 448, 798 (1993) (codified at 25 U.S.C. §§ 3301–07 [2000]).

263   *Appropriations statutes treat tribes. See, e.g.*, Pub. L. No. 103-322, title III, Sept. 13, 1994, 108 Stat. 1867 (1994) (codified at 31 U.S.C. § 6705 [2000]).

263   *The American Indian Religious Freedom Act. Lyng*, 485 U.S. at 454–55 (describing AIRFA as a policy statement). On recent actions, see generally Charlton H. Bonham, "Devils Tower, Rainbow Bridge, and the Uphill Battle Facing Native American Religion on Public Lands," vol. 20, no.2 *Law and Inequality: A Journal of Theory and Practice*, p. 157 (2002).

263   *Traditional peyote use.* 42 U.S.C. 1996a(b)(1) (2000); Rebecca Tsosie, "Reclaiming Native Stories: An Essay on Cultural Appropriation and Cultural Rights," vol. 34, no. 1 *Arizona State Law Journal*, pp. 339–40 (2002).

263   *The Native American Graves Protection and Repatriation Act.* Pub. L. No. 101-601, Nov. 16, 1990, 104 Stat. 3048 (1991) (codified as amended at 25 U.S.C. §§ 3001–13 [2000]); Roger C. Echo-Hawk and Walter A. Echo-Hawk, *Battlefields and Burial Grounds: The Indian Struggle to Protect Ancestral Graves in the United States* (Minneapolis: Lerner Publications Co., 1994).

263   *In an attempt to reverse. See* Native American Languages Act of 1992, Pub. L. No. 102-524, Oct. 26, 1992, 106 Stat. 3434 (1992) (codified at 42 U.S.C. § 2991b–3 [2000]); Native American Languages Act, Pub. L. No. 101-447, title I, Oct. 30, 1990, 104 Stat. 1152, 1153 (1991) (codified as amended at 25 U.S.C. §§ 2901–06 [2000]). As authorized by the 1992 Act, the Administration for Native Americans funded twenty-three language programs in fiscal year 2003 with a total of $2.6 million, *at* http://www2.acf.hhs.gov/programs/ana/news/2003_Language_application_status.html (last visited May 20, 2004).

263   *Other federal laws. See, e.g.*, Bruce Elliot Johansen, ed., *The Encyclopedia of*

Native American Legal Tradition (Westport, CT: Greenwood Press, 1998) (providing brief summaries of numerous statutes relating to Indians).

263   *Daniel K. Inouye.* Daniel K. Inouye, interview with author, San Francisco, California, July 1, 2003. *See generally Biography of Senator Daniel K. Inouye,* U.S. Sentate (*at* http://www.senate/gov/~/inouye/bio.htm) (last visited April 18, 2004) (on file with author); *see also* the senator's autobiography, Daniel K. Inouye, *Journey to Washington* (Englewood Cliffs, NJ: Prentice-Hall, 1967).

264   *"No one else was very interested."* Personal communication received by author (complete date unknown, 1995).

264   *Both comfortable with and profoundly moved.* Patricia Zell, interview with author, Louisville, Colorado, June 26, 2003.

264   *He also began the unprecedented practice.* I attended several of these hearings and each time witnessed Inouye's receptiveness to the tribal leaders and the prompt follow-through on the assurances he made.

265   *Tribal jurisdiction over non-member Indians and legislative override.* The Supreme Court case is *Duro v. Reina,* 495 U.S. 676 (1990). The 1991 congressional override of the case is codified as an amendment to the Indian Civil Rights Act, 25 U.S.C. §§ 1301(2), 1301(4). The override has been upheld. *See United States v. Lara,* 124 S. Ct. 1628 (2004).

265   *The tribal successes . . . spurred a backlash. See generally* Jill Nogren and Petra T. Shattuck, "Still Fighting the Indians: America's Old-Fashioned Response to Native Legal Victories," *Juris Doctor,* p. 30 (Oct./Nov. 1978). Regarding treaties, see, for example, Ross Anderson, "Look Who's Clamming in My Yard—Rulings Pit Tribes Against Landowners," *Seattle Times,* p. B1 (Feb. 15, 1998); C. Herb Williams and Walt Nebrech, *American Nightmare: Indian Treaties* (Seattle: Outdoor Empire Publishing, 1976). On the gaming backlash, see, for example, Iver Peterson, "Despite Promise of Easy Money, Indian Casinos Meet Resistance," *New York Times,* p. 29 (Feb. 1, 2004). Tribal tax exemptions have also been criticized. *See, e.g.,* Deborah Barfield, "Indians Map Tax Fight: NY Sales-Levy Plan Called Sovereignty Assault," *Newsday,* p. A4 (April 16, 1996). Of course, the backlash has extended over tribal natural resource management as well. *See, e.g.,* Tania Branigan, "Groups Lock Horns over Bison Range; Conservationists Criticize Administration Plan that Would Let Tribes Run Montana Refuge," *Washington Post,* p. A19 (Sept. 2, 2003).

266   *"doing justice by Indians."* American Indian Policy Review Commission, "Final Report," p. 612 (separate dissenting views of Representative Lloyd Meeds).

266   *Racism.* Charles F. Wilkinson, "To Feel the Summer in the Spring: The Treaty Fishing Rights of the Wisconsin Chippewa," vol. 1991 *Wisconsin Law Review,* p. 376 (1991). *See generally* Rick Whaley and Walter Bresette, *Walleye Warriors: An Effective Alliance Against Racism and for the Earth* (Philadelphia: New Society Publishers, 1994), especially pp. 23–46, 50–51.

267 *Various bills have been introduced. See, e.g.*, Robert S. Johnson, "Backlash Politics—Solons Trying 'Backdoor' Approach to Defeat Indians," vol. 6 *Indian
Voice*, p. 7 (Oct. 1978) (discussing a congressional strategy to nullify tribal
legal victories); Bill Keller, "Capital Stew: Anti-Indian Bill Draws Precious Little Laughter," *Sunday Oregonian*, p. E3 (Oct. 16, 1977) (mentioning various
introduced backlash bills); *see also* Getches et al., *Cases and Materials*, pp.
251–52. On attempts to prohibit Indian gaming, see *infra* ch. 13, pp. **334–35**.

267 *antigaming forces. Ibid.* The case upholding the right of tribes to engage in
gaming is *Cabazon*, 480 U.S. 202, and the subsequent legislation is the Indian
Gaming Regulatory Act, Pub. L. No. 100-497, Oct. 17, 1988, 102 Stat. 2467
(1989) (codified at 25 U.S.C. §§ 2701–21 [2000]). Both are discussed *infra* ch.
13, pp. **330–36**.

CHAPTER 11: Revitalizing Tribal Communities

271 *the fourth world. See, e.g.*, Thomas R. Berger, *Village Journey: The Report of the
Alaska Native Review Commission*, pp. 176–81 (New York: Hill and Wang,
1985).

271 *"We cannot find."* Hearing Before the Senate Committee on Indian Affairs,
"Economic Development on Indian Reservations," 104th Congress, 2d Ses-
sion, pp. 6–7 (Sept. 17, 1996) (Washington, DC: U.S. Government Printing
Office, 1996). The work of the Kennedy School—Kalt's codirectors are
Stephen Cornell and Manuel Begay—has been extensive and enlightening.
See, e.g., Stephen Cornell and Joseph P. Kalt, eds., *What Can Tribes Do? Strate-
gies and Institutions in American Indian Economic Development* (Los Angeles:
American Indian Studies Center, date unknown); Stephen Cornell and
Joseph P. Kalt, *Sovereignty and Nation-Building: The Development Challenge in
Indian Country Today* (Cambridge, MA: Harvard Project on American Indian
Economic Development, 1998); Joseph P. Kalt, *Policy Foundations for the
Future of Nation Building in Indian Country* (Cambridge, MA: Harvard Uni-
versity Native American Program, 2001).

272 *Warm Springs Reservation and history. See generally* Cynthia D. Stowell, *Faces
of a Reservation: A Portrait of the Warm Springs Indian Reservation* (Portland:
Oregon Historical Society Press, 1987); Mary B. Davis, ed., *Native America in
the Twentieth Century: An Encyclopedia*, pp. 140–42 (New York: Garland Publishing, 1996); *A Short History of the Confederated Tribes of the Warm Springs
Reservation*, pamphlet (Warm Springs, OR: Tribal Council of the Confederated Tribes of the Warm Springs Indian Reservation, 1976) (on file with
author); Nat Shaw, *Historical Perspective of the Confederated Tribes of the Warm
Springs Indian Reservation of Oregon*, Oregon State University, Warm Springs
Extension, Warm Springs Public Information Department, *at* http://
osu.orst.edu/extension/warmsprings/pid.htm (last visited Dec. 4, 2002) (on
file with author); *Warm Springs Indian Reservation*, Oregon State University,
Warm Springs Extension, Warm Springs Community Profiles, *at*
http://osu.orst.edu/extension/warmsprings/comprof.htm (last visited

Dec. 4, 2002) (on file with author) [hereinafter *Community Profile*]. The tribe also maintains its own Web site accessible *at* http://www.warmsprings.com.

273 *just one part-time employee.* Charles Jackson, telephone interview with author, Dec. 3, 2002.

273 *The first tribal timber sale.* Nelson Wallulatum, interview with Monte Mills, research assistant, Warm Springs, Oregon, Oct. 31, 2002.

273 *"were just floatin' around." Ibid.*

273 *Celilo Falls distribution and ensuing events. A Short History*, p. 5; Jackson, interview; Judge Owen Panner, interview with author, Portland, Oregon, May 8, 2002; Olney Patt, Jr., interview with Monte Mills, research assistant, Warm Springs, Oregon, Oct. 31, 2002.

276 *Acquisition generally.* Jackson, interview.

276 *$18 million expended for land acquisition.* Terri Luther, interview with Monte Mills, research assistant, Warm Springs, Oregon, Oct. 30, 2002.

276 *The wood products program.* Stowell, *Faces of a Reservation*, pp. 139–41; Jackson, interview; Larry Potts, interview with Monte Mills, research assistant, Warm Springs, Oregon, Oct. 31, 2002.

276 *Tribal enterprises. A Summary of Reservation Economic Enterprises*, Oregon State University, Warm Springs Extension, Warm Springs Tribal Enterprises, *at* http://www.orst.edu/extension/warmsprings/enterp.htm (last visited Dec. 4, 2002) (on file with author).

278 *Tribal members engage.* Stowell, *Faces of a Reservation*, pp. 137–41; Jackson, interview; Luther, interview.

278 *Tribal government today.* Jackson, interview.

278 *The full-time tribal work force.* Jackson, interview.

278 *The figure swells. Confederated Tribes of Warm Springs*, Northwest Portland Area Indian Health Board, Tribal Profiles, *at* http://www.npaihb.org/profiles/tribal_profiles/interface.htm (last visited May 21, 2003) (on file with author); Jackson, interview; *People of the Warm Springs*, Oregon State University, Warm Springs Extension, Warm Springs People, *at* http://osu.orst.edu/extension/warmsprings/people.htm (last visited May 21, 2003) (on file with author) [hereinafter *Warm Springs People*].

278 *When only governmental functions are considered. Ibid.*

278 *Tribal scholarships.* Stowell, *Faces of a Reservation*, pp. 175–77; Jackson, interview.

279 *Warm Springs constitution. See, e.g., Constitution and By-Laws of the Confederated Tribes of Warm Springs Reservation of Oregon as Amended*, pmbl., art. I, The Confederated Tribes of Warm Springs, *at* http://www.warmsprings.com/history/treaty/const.htm (last visited May 21, 2003) (on file with author).

280 *Public hearings. Ibid.*, arts. V, § 1(t) (referendum), VI (public hearing).

281 *In the 1950s the landscape of Indian education.* On Indian education generally, see Margaret Szasz, *Education and the American Indian: The Road to Self-Determination, 1928–1973* (Albuquerque: University of New Mexico Press, 1974); Allison M. Dussias, "Let No Native American Child Be Left Behind: Re-Envisioning Native American Education for the Twenty-First Century," vol. 43 *Arizona Law Review*, p. 819 (Winter 2001). *See also supra* ch. 1, p. **22**.

281 *"Why don't we control."* Wayne J. Stein, "A History of the Tribally Controlled Community Colleges: 1968–1978," pp. 31–38, Ed.D. dissertation, Washington State University (1988) [hereinafter "Community Colleges"]. On Indian-controlled schools generally, see Szasz, *Education*, pp. 169–80.

281 *The Rough Rock Demonstration School.* See *supra* ch. 8, pp. **192–93**.

281 *The Rough Rock breakthrough led.* Stein, "Community Colleges," p. 43.

281 *Stanley Redbird.* Letter from Frank Pommersheim to author, Nov. 17, 2003.

282 *45 percent unemployment. See Community Profile.*

282 *"It took several council meetings."* Avis Three Irons, telephone interview with Heather Corson, research assistant, Nov. 3, 2000.

282 *The Rosebud Sioux named.* On Sinte Gleska (Spotted Tail) and the naming of the college, see *History of Sinte Gleska (Spotted Tail) 1823–1881*, Sinte Gleska University, General Catalog, pp. 5–6, *at* http://www.sinte.edu/catalog/SGUctlg005.html (last visited May 21, 2003) (on file with author); Stein, "Community Colleges," p. 114; George E. Hyde, *Spotted Tail's Folk: A History of the Brulé Sioux*, pp. 277–78, 289–93 (Norman: University of Oklahoma Press, 1961).

282 *Today [Sinte Gleska University] enrolls. Degrees Offered*, Sinte Gleska University, General Catalog, p 16, *at* http://www/sinte.edu/catalog/SGUctlg010 .html (last visited May 21, 2003) (on file with author).

283 *"During the time I taught."* Frank Pommersheim, *Braid of Feathers: American Indian Law and Contemporary Tribal Life*, pp. 32–33 (Berkeley: University of California Press, 1995).

283 *Tribal colleges.* On tribal colleges generally, see *Tribal College Journal of American Indian Higher Education* and the Web sites of American Indian Higher Education Consortium (http://www.aihec.org) and the American Indian College Fund (http://www.collegefund.org), which link to the Web sites of individual colleges; *see also* Paul Boyer, *Native American Colleges: Progress and Prospects* (San Francisco: Jossey-Bass Publishers, 1997); C. Patrick Morris, "Indian Self-Determination and the Tribal College Movement: A Good Idea that Not Even the Government Can Kill," *in* Lyman H. Legters and Fremont J. Lyden, eds., *American Indian Policy: Self-Governance and Economic Development*, p. 71 (Westport, CT: Greenwood Press, 1994).

284 *Their budgets average.* "Tribal Colleges to Lead in Creating 1,000 Indian Teachers," *Tribal Colleges Today* (Feb. 2000).

284 *Congress is voting more money. Ibid.*

284   *several foundations have responded. See, e.g., Ibid.*; Paul Boyer, "Rewriting the
      Way Foundations Do Business in Indian Country," vol. 12 *Tribal College Jour-
      nal*, p. 15 (Fall 2000).

284   *Graduates show high employment.* Boyer, *Native American Colleges*, pp. 68–69.

284   *The guiding maxim.* Marjane Ambler, "Never Forget Where You Come From,"
      vol. 12 *Tribal College Journal*, p. 9 (Winter 2000).

284   *Elementary and secondary education.* On Indian primary education, see gen-
      erally Szasz, *Education*; Michael C. Coleman, *American Indian Children at
      School, 1850–1930*, pp. 36–54 (Jackson: University Press of Mississippi, 1993);
      Estelle Fuchs and Robert J. Havighurst, *To Live on This Earth: American
      Indian Education* (Garden City, NY: Doubleday and Co., 1972); Dussias, "Let
      No Native"; Raymond Cross, "American Indian Education: The Terror of His-
      tory and the Nation's Debt to the Indian Peoples," vol. 21, no. 4 *University of
      Arkansas at Little Rock Law Review*, p. 941 (1999); Melissa Campobasso, "The
      State of Indian Education and New Schools of Thought," *Washington State Bar
      News*, p. 47 (Nov. 2000).

285   *Meriam Report.* Lewis Meriam et al., Institute for Government Research,
      "The Problem of Indian Administration" (Baltimore: Johns Hopkins Press,
      1928), discussed *supra* ch. 3, pp. **58–59**.

285   *40 percent. See, e.g.*, Dussias, "Let No Native," pp. 848–49.

285   *Congress responded. Ibid.*, pp. 841–42.

285   *1969 Senate report.* Senate Report No. 91-501, "Indian Education: A National
      Tragedy—A National Challenge," 91st Congress, 1st Session (Washington,
      DC: U.S. Government Printing Office, 1969) [hereinafter "Kennedy Report"].

285   *In public schools. See generally Ibid.*, pp. 24–34; *see also* NAACP Legal Defense
      and Educational Fund, *An Even Chance*, pp. 41–57 (New York: NAACP Legal
      Defense and Educational Fund, 1971) (with several firsthand accounts from
      Indian country); Edgar S. Cahn, ed., *Our Brother's Keeper: The Indian in White
      America*, pp. 25–54 (Washington, DC: New Community Press, 1969).

285   *The BIA schools remained. See generally* "Kennedy Report," pp. 55–104.

285   *the federal policy of "coercive assimilation." See generally Ibid.*, pp. 105–38.

286   *"won't last 6 months."* See *supra* ch. 8, p. **192**.

286   *"truancy at both public and tribal schools."* On Rosebud Sioux Primary Educa-
      tion, see "Rosebud Sioux Education Department Reduces Truancy Among
      Tribal Secondary Students," vol. 24, no. 2 *NARF Legal Review* (1999), *at*
      http://www.narf.org/pubs/nlr/nlr24-2.html (last visited Dec. 19, 2002) (on
      file with author); Dussias, "Let No Native," pp. 899–903. For a brief discus-
      sion of the role of parental and community involvement in education, focus-
      ing on Alaska, see McDowell Group, "Alaska Native Education Study: A
      Statewide Study of Alaska Native Values and Opinions Regarding Education
      in Alaska, Literature Review: Community Involvement," *at* http://www
      .ankn.uaf.edu/summit/McDowell/reviewcommunity.html (last visited
      May 22, 2003) (on file with author).

287 *the white man "taught us."* Pommersheim, *Braid of Feathers*, p. 21.

287 *more than 80 other tribes.* Campobesso, "Indian Education," p. 50; "Rosebud Sioux," p. 2.

287 *Dropout rates.* National Center for Education Statistics, U.S. Department of Education, "Characteristics of American Indian and Alaska Native Education: Results from thc 1990–91 and 1993–94 Schools and Staffing Surveys," pp. B-49–B-50, B-83 (Washington, DC: U.S. Government Printing Office, 1997) [hereinafter "NCES Report"].

287 *more than 100 tribal elementary and secondary schools.* Carmen Taylor, Director, National Indian School Board Association, telephone interview with author, Feb. 6, 2004; Dussias, *"Let No Native,"* p. 866.

287 *Another 1,200 schools.* "NCES Report," p. iii.

287 *"This school could be."* Personal communication received by author (Sept. 1974).

288 *Dropout and absentee rates.* "NCES Report," pp. B-49–B-50, B-83.

288 *High school graduation rates.* D. Michael Pavel, "Schools, Principals, and Teachers Serving American Indian and Alaska Native Students," *ERIC Digest*, EDO-RC-98-9 (Jan. 1999), *at* http://www.ael.org/eric/page.cfm?&scope = ai&id = 217&pub = x (last visited May 22, 2003) (on file with author).

288 *2,000 in the 1950s.* Fuchs and Havighurst, *To Live*, p. 260.

288 *10,000 in 1970. Ibid.*

288 *147,000 in 2000.* Laura G. Knapp et al., "Enrollment in Postsecondary Institutions, Fall 2000 and Financial Statistics, Fiscal Year 2000," p. 13, tbl. 1, National Center for Educational Statistics, Report 2002212 (Sept. 2002), *at* http://nces.ed.gov/pubsearch/pubsinfo.asp?pubid = 2002212 (last visited May 22, 2003) (on file with author).

288 *Traditional Indian legal systems.* Two acclaimed tribal justice systems have been examined in classic jurisprudential studies: Karl Llewellan and E. Adamson Hoebel, *The Cheyenne Way* (Norman: University of Oklahoma Press, 1941) and Rennard Strickland, *Fire and the Spirits: Cherokee Law from Clan to Court* (Norman: University of Oklahoma Press, 1975). Perhaps the richest source of material on traditional tribal governments is a forty-eight-volume series of government-commissioned annual studies, U.S. Bureau of American Ethnology Annotated Reports (1879–80 to 1930–31). While all volumes are out of print, publication information for each may be found in Smithsonian Institution, Bureau of American Ethnology, "List of Publications of the Bureau of American Ethnology with Index to Authors and Titles," electronic ed., Bulletin 200 (Washington, DC: Smithsonian Institution, 1997), *at* http://www.siris-libraries.si.edu/#focus.htm (last visited April 18, 2004); *see also* Harold E. Driver, *Indians of North America*, 2d ed., pp. 287–308 (Chicago: University of Chicago Press, 1969).

288 *Crow Dog.* Sidney L. Harring, "Crow Dog's Case: A Chapter in the Legal History of Tribal Sovereignty," vol. 14, no. 2 *American Indian Law Review*, pp. 197–99 (1989).

289   *History of CFR and tribal courts. See generally* William T. Hagan, *Indian Police and Judges: Experiments in Acculturation and Control* (Lincoln: University of Nebraska Press, 1980); David H. Getches, ed., *Indian Courts and the Future* (National American Indian Court Judges Association, 1978).

289   *85 operating tribal courts.* David H. Getches et al., *Cases and Materials on Federal Indian Law*, 1st ed., p. 322 (St. Paul, MN: West Publishing Co., 1979).

289   *Modern tribal courts. See generally* David H. Getches et al., *Cases and Materials on Federal Indian Law*, 4th ed., pp. 388–418 (St. Paul, MN: West Group, 1998); Getches, *Indian Courts*; Pommersheim, *Braid of Feathers*; Nell Jessup Newton, "Tribal Court Praxis: One Year in the Life of Twenty Tribal Courts," vol. 22, no. 2 *American Indian Law Review*, p. 285 (1998).

290   *"court procedures are unwritten."* U.S. Department of the Interior, Bureau of Indian Affairs, Branch of Judicial Services, "Native American Tribal Court Profiles," pp. 77, 91 (Washington, DC: U.S. Government Printing Office, 1985) (cited in United States Commission on Civil Rights, "The Indian Civil Rights Act," p. 33 [Washington, DC: U.S. Government Printing Office, 1991] [hereinafter "ICRA Report"]).

290   *Critics of tribal sovereignty.* On the strengths and weaknesses of tribal courts, see generally Getches, *Indian Courts*, pp. 88–102; "ICRA Report," pp. 29–70.

290   *hearings and investigations. See generally* Newton, "Tribal Court Praxis," pp. 285–89. For a listing of congressional and commission inquiries, see *Ibid.*, pp. 287–89, nn. 13–16.

290   *Navajo judiciary. See, e.g.,* James W. Zion, "Court Lawyering in the Navajo Nation" (Cambridge, MA: Harvard Law School, Navajo Supreme Court Clinical Program, 2001); Tom Tso, "The Process of Decision Making in Tribal Courts," vol. 31, no. 2 *Arizona Law Review*, p. 225 (1989); Getches et al., *Cases and Materials*, pp. 393–418.

290   *"By custom."* Halona v. MacDonald, 1 Navajo Rptr. 189, 5 Indian L. Rep. 119 (Navajo 1978).

291   *Articles by Navajo Justices. See, e.g.,* Tom Tso, "Indian Nations and the Human Right to an Independent Judiciary," vol. 3 *New York City Law Review*, p. 105 (May 1998); Tso, "The Process," p. 225; Raymond D. Austin, "Freedom, Responsibility, and Duty: ADR and the Navajo Peacemaker Court," vol. 32, no. 3 *Judges' Journal*, p. 8 (1993); Robert Yazzie, " 'Watch Your Six': An Indian Nation Judge's View of 25 Years of Indian Law, Where We Are and Where We Are Going," vol. 23, no. 2 *American Indian Law Review*, p. 497 (1998–99); Robert Yazzie, "Navajo Peacemaking: Technology and Traditional Indian Law," vol. 10 *St. Thomas Law Review*, p. 95 (Fall 1997); Robert Yazzie, " 'Hozho Nahasdlii'—We Are Now in Good Relations: Navajo Restorative Justice," vol. 9 *St. Thomas Law Review*, p. 117 (Fall 1996).

292   *Court sessions at law schools.* Nancy Waring, "The Law of Their Land: Navajo Nation Makes a Case at HLS," *Harvard Law Bulletin* (Summer 1999), *at* http://www.law.harvard.edu/alumni/bulletin/backissues/summer99/article5.html (last visited May 22, 2003) (on file with author).

293   *I once heard.* Chief Justice Robert Yazzie, interview with author, Window
      Rock, Arizona, March 23, 1993.

293   *He described the Anglo-American.* On Navajo peacemaking, see generally
      Yazzie, "Navajo Peacemaking," p. 95; Tom Tso "The Process of Decision Mak-
      ing in Tribal Courts," vol. 31, no. 2 *Arizona Law Review*, p. 225 (1989); Matt
      Arbaugh, "Making Peace the Old Fashioned Way: Infusing Traditional Tribal
      Practices into Modern ADR," vol. 2, no. 2 *Pepperdine Dispute Resolution Law
      Journal*, p. 303 (2002).

293   *Navajo horizontal justice.* See Robert Yazzie, "Life Comes from It: Navajo Jus-
      tice Concepts," vol. 24 *New Mexico Law Review*, pp. 181–87 (Spring 1994).

293   *"A man told a Navajo Nation."* Jim Zion, "Stories from the Peacemaker Court,"
      no. 38 *In Context*, p. 31 (Spring 1994), *at* http://www.context.org/
      ICLIB/IC38/Yazzie.htm#zion (last visited May 22, 2003) (on file with
      author).

294   *The legislature also required.* Robert Yazzie, "Navajo Justice," no. 15 *Yes!*, p. 36
      (Fall 2000), *at* http://www.futurenet.org/15prisons/yazzie.htm (last visited
      May 22, 2003) (on file with author).

294   *70 or more tribes.* The figure of 70 tribes roughly as substantial as Warm
      Springs—with at least 300 employees, not counting gaming operations—
      seems to be conservative. I've done no formal inventory on this but have
      relied on my own knowledge of tribal governments and interviewed several
      people familiar with tribal operations around the country. My interviews
      included: Rennard Strickland (Nov. 5, 2003); John Echohawk (Nov. 11, 2003);
      Billy Frank, Jr. (Dec. 2, 2003); Jim Anderson (Dec. 2, 2003); Kathy Gorospe
      (Apr. 1, 2004); Dick Trudell (Apr. 3, 2004); Marlon Sherman (May 11, 2004);
      Jim Enote (May 14, 2004); and Jim Schlender (May 20, 2004). The tribes are
      as follows: *Arizona:* Colorado River Indian Tribes, Fort McDowell Yavapai
      Nation, Fort Mojave Indian Tribe, Gila River Indian Community, Hopi Tribe,
      Navajo Nation, Pasqua-Yaqui Indian Community, Salt River Indian Com-
      munity, San Carlos Apache Tribe, Tohono O'odham Nation, White Mountain
      Apache Tribe; *California:* Agua Caliente Band of Cahuilla Indians, Hoopa Val-
      ley Tribe; *Colorado:* Southern Ute Indian Tribe, Ute Mountain Tribe; *Con-
      necticut:* Mashantucket Pequot Tribe, Mohegan Indian Tribe; *Florida*:
      Miccosukee Tribe, Seminole Tribe; *Idaho:* Nez Perce Tribe, Shoshone-
      Bannock Tribes; *Maine*: Passamaquoddy Tribe, Penobscot Tribe; *Michigan*:
      Saginaw Chippewa Tribe, Sault St. Marie Tribe; *Minnesota*: Mille Lacs Band
      of Ojibwa, Red Lake Band of Chippewa, Shakopee Mdewakanton Sioux,
      White Earth Band of Chippewa; *Mississippi:* Mississippi Band of Choctaw
      Indians; *Montana:* Assiniboine and Sioux Tribe of Fort Peck reservation,
      Blackfeet Tribe, Confederated Salish & Kootenai Tribes, Crow Tribe, Fort
      Belknap Indian Community; *New Mexico*; Jicarilla Apache Nation, Laguna
      Pueblo, Mescalero Apache Tribe, Zuni Pueblo; *New York:* Oneida Nation, St.
      Regis Band of Mohawk Indians, Seneca Nation; *North Carolina:* Eastern Band
      of Cherokee Indians; *Oklahoma:* Cherokee Nation, Cheyenne-Arapaho
      Tribes, Chickasaw Nation, Choctaw Nation, Comanche Nation, Kiowa Indian

Tribe; Muscogee (Creek) Nation, Osage Tribe, Seminole Nation, Shawnee Tribe; *Oregon:* Confederated Tribes of the Grand Ronde Community, Confederated Tribes of the Siletz reservation, Confederated Tribes of the Umatilla reservation, Confederated Tribes of the Warm Springs reservation; *South Dakota:* Cheyenne River Sioux Tribe, Oglala Sioux Tribe, Rosebud Sioux Tribe, Standing Rock Sioux Tribe; *Utah:* Ute Indian Tribe of the Uintah and Ouray reservation; *Washington:* Confederated Tribes of the Colville reservation, Confederated Tribes and Bands of the Yakama Nation, Lummi Tribe, Muckleshoot Indian Tribe, Puyallup Tribe, Quinault Indian Nation, Tulalip Tribes; *Wisconsin:* Ho-Chunk Nation, Menominee Indian Tribe, Oneida Tribe.

295 *"a mom-and-pop store."* Del White, telephone interview with Andrew Huff, research assistant, Apr. 27, 1998.

296 *"In the 1940s and 1950s."* Richard T. Trudell, telephone interview with author, Aug. 13, 2003.

296 *One major concern is violence.* George R. Brenneman, "Maternal, Child, and Youth Health," *in* Everett R. Rhoades, ed., *American Indian Health: Innovations in Health Care, Promotion, and Policy,* p. 147 (Baltimore: Johns Hopkins University Press, 2000). The editor, Dr. Everett, himself an Indian, served a distinguished term as director of the Indian Health Service.

296 *Youth homicides and suicides. Ibid.,* pp. 146–47.

296 *"You have to realize how much."* Personal communication received by author (Sept. 10, 2003).

296 *Impressive progress has been made. See generally* George R. Brenneman et al., "Health Status and Clinical Indicators," *in* Rhoades, *American Indian Health,* p. 103. "During the past 30 to 40 years, the health status of American Indians has in many respects generally improved, sometimes profoundly. However, current data shows that Indians still experience an excess burden of illness. Responding to effective prevention and treatment, infectious diseases (e.g., tuberculosis, pneumonia, and influenza) have significantly diminished in importance." *Ibid.* For gains in infant mortality and life expectancy, see, for example, Abraham B. Bergman et al., "A Political History of the Indian Health Service," vol. 77, no. 4 *Milbank Quarterly,* p. 573 (1999).

296 *Nonetheless, American Indians still face.* Brenneman et al., "Health Status," p. 103.

296 *Tribes have become fully engaged. See generally* Everett R. Rhoades and Dorothy A. Rhoades, "Traditional Indian and Modern Western Medicine," *in* Rhoades, *American Indian Health,* p. 401; Susan L. Johnston, "Native American Traditional and Alternative Medicine," vol. 583 *Annals of the American Academy Political and Social Science,* p. 195 (Sept. 2002); *see, e.g.,* Wade Davies, *Healing Ways: Navajo Health Care in the Twentieth Century,* pp. 153–92 (Albuquerque: University of New Mexico Press, 2001); Brooke Olson, "Meeting the Challenges of American Indian Diabetes: Anthropological Perspectives on

Prevention and Treatment," *in* Clifford E. Trafzer and Diane Weiner, eds., *Medicine Ways: Disease, Health, and Survival Among Native Americans*, pp. 173–76 (Walnut Creek, CA: AltaMira Press, 2001).

296 *Alcoholism, while progress.* Marlita A. Reddy, ed., *Statistical Record of Native North Americans*, 2d ed., p. 576, tbl. 442 (Detroit: Gale Research, 1995) (reduction of Indian alcoholism death rate from 58 deaths per 100,000 population in late 1970s to 37 deaths per 100,000 in late 1980s, a 35 percent decrease).

296 *while drinking practices vary. See, e.g.*, Fred Beauvais, "American Indians and Alcohol," vol. 22, no. 4 *Alcohol Health and Research World*, pp. 253–54 (1998).

297 *It is a rare tribe that lacks an alcoholism program. See Ibid.*, p. 258; *see also* Fred Beauvais and S. LaBoueff, "Drug and Alcohol Abuse Intervention in American Indian Communities," vol. 20, no. 1 *International Journal of the Addictions*, pp. 139–71 (1985); Eugene R. Oetting et al., "Assessing Community Readiness for Prevention," vol. 30, no. 6 *International Journal of the Addictions*, pp. 659–83 (1995).

297 *"We never had poverty."* Personal communication received by author (July 30, 1994).

297 *Tohono O'odham Reservation and history.* On the Tohono O'odham, see generally Winston P. Erickson, *Sharing the Desert: The Tohono O'odham in History* (Tucson: University of Arizona Press, 1994); Ofelia Zepeda, *Ocean Power: Poems from the Desert* (Tucson: University of Arizona Press, 1995); Ruth M. Underhill et al., *Rainhouse and Ocean: Speeches for the Papago Year* (Flagstaff: Museum of Northern Arizona Press, 1979); Gary Paul Nabhan, *The Desert Smells like Rain: A Naturalist in Papago Indian Country* (San Francisco: North Point Press, 1982); Bernard L. Fontana, *Of Earth and Little Rain· The Papago Indians* (Tucson: University of Arizona Press, 1989).

297 *"The O'odham lack grand ritual."* Zepeda, *Ocean Power*, p. 89.

299 *Border crossing. See generally* Tohono O'odham Nation, Office of the Chairman and Vice Chairman, *Briefing Book: The Case for Amending Present Nationality Law to Make All Members of the Tohono O'odham Nation United States Citizens, Now and Forever* (Sells, AZ: Tohono O'odham Nation, date unknown) (reprinting Stephanie Innes, "Aliens in Their Own Land," *Arizona Daily Star* [May 16, 2000]); Ken Ellingwood, "Tribes Are Caught on the Border," *Los Angeles Times* (May 8, 2000).

299 *burial fund.* Ofelia Zepeda, interview with author, Tucson, Arizona, March 5, 2002.

299 *Juvenile delinquency and gangs.* Carmen Duarte, "Gangs Find New Land, Membership Up," *Arizona Daily Star* (Nov. 24, 2002), *at* wysiwyg://4/http://www.azstarnet.com/star/sun/21124RESERVATIONGANSOK-O.html (last visited Nov. 25, 2002) (on file with author).

299 *The tribal council has responded.* Tohono O'odham Nation, Judiciary Branch, *Children's Program* (Sells, AZ: Tohono O'odham Nation, 1998).

300   *Staff growth.* Chief Justice Malcolm Escalante, Solicitor Russell Dillon, and staff of the Tohono O'odham Nation's children's program, interviews with author, Sells, Arizona, March 7, 2002.

300   *"Parents say."* Escalante, interview.

300   *Water conflicts.* Ruth Underhill, *The Papago Indians of Arizona and their Relatives the Pima,* pp. 12–14, 63 (Washington, DC: U.S. Office of Indian Affairs, Education Division, 1940) (describing traditional Tohono O'odham farming methods and water usage); William H. Kelly, *The Papago Indians of Arizona: A Population and Economic Study,* pp. 30–32 (Tucson: University of Arizona, Department of Anthropology, Bureau of Ethnic Research, 1963) (summarizing pre– and post–World War II water development on the reservation); House Report No. 97-422, "Papago Indian Claims," 97th Congress, 2d Session, pp. 7–8, 11 (Washington, DC: U.S. Government Printing Office, 1982) (identifying the tribe's water competitors and resulting supply problems); Arizona Commission of Indian Affairs, "The Papago Reservation," p. 9 (Phoenix: Arizona Commission of Indian Affairs, 1962) (noting that "in most instances . . . it was necessary to go from 500 to 700 feet [deep] for very small quantities of water").

301   *"As far as the eye could see."* Zepeda, *Ocean Power,* p. 30.

301   *Diabetes crisis.* On the crisis generally and elevated rates among Indians, particularly the Tohono O'odham, see Dorothy M. Gohdes and Kelly Acton, "Diabetes Mellitus and Its Complications," in Rhoades, *American Indian Health,* p. 221; Daniel Lopez et al., "The Impact of Food Assistance Programs on the Tohono O'odham Food System: An Analysis and Recommendations," pp. 13, 17–18 (Sells, AZ: Tohono O'odham Community College, and Tohono O'odham Community Action, 2001) (citing Indian Health Service, "Special Diabetes Program for Indians: Interim Report to Congress" [Albuquerque, NM: IHS National Diabetes Program, 2000]); Pauline Arillaga, "Illness Ravages Tribes: Program Seeks to Stem Diabetes," *Denver Post,* p. 29A (Nov. 9, 2001); Gary Paul Nabhan, *Coming Home to Eat: The Pleasures and Politics of Local Foods,* p. 247 (New York: W. W. Norton and Co., 2002); *see also* Lorelei De Cora, "The Diabetes Plague in Indian Country: Legacy of Displacement," vol. 16, no. 1 *Wicazo Sa Review,* p. 9 (2001) (with an emphasis on the Winnebago Indians).

301   *Traditionally the Tohono O'odham depended.* Lopez et al., "Impact of Food," pp. 16–19.

302   *the average weight of Tohono O'odham men.* Nabhan, *Coming Home,* p. 247.

302   *Charles Dickens, who wrote. Bleak House,* pp. v, 433–44 (London: Chapman and Hall, 1881).

302   *Still, after decades of litigation.* Southern Arizona Water Rights Settlement Act of 1982, Pub. L. No. 97-293, sec. 301, Oct. 12, 1982, 96 Stat. 1261, 1274 (1983) (not codified); Southern Arizona Water Rights Settlement Technical Amendments Act of 1992, Pub. L. No. 102-497, sec. 8, Oct. 24, 1992, 106 Stat. 3255, 3256–57 (1993) (not codified). On the settlement, see Daniel McCool, *Com-*

mand of the Waters: Iron Triangles, Federal Water Development, and Indian Water, pp. 234–36 (Tempe: University of Arizona Press, 1994); Erickson, *Sharing the Desert*, pp. 164–65; Lloyd Burton, *American Indian Water Rights and the Limits of Law*, pp. 71–73 (Lawrence: University Press of Kansas, 1991).

302 *Out in the villages.* Cristián A. Sierra, "Room to Grow," *Tucson Weekly* (April 18–24, 2002), *at* http://www.tucsonweekly.com/tw/2002-04-18/curr.html (last visited May 22, 2003) (on file with author); Tohono O'odham Community Action, "Program Overview," pamphlet (Sells, AZ: Tohono O'odham Community Action, date unknown) (on file with author). On current Tohono O'odham agricultural initiatives, I also benefited from interviews with Daniel Preston, San Xavier, Arizona, March 7, 2002, and Terrell Johnson and Tristan Reader, Sells, Arizona, March 7, 2002.

302 *A much-heralded nonprofit.* The cooperative maintains a Web site accessible *at* http://www.nativeseeds.org. On Native Seeds/Search and its activities on the reservation, see Bijal P. Trivedi, "Planting Tradition: Seeds Native to Tribal Areas Are Healthier, Hardier," *Columbus Dispatch*, p. 4A (Aug. 6, 2002); Paul L. Allen, "Growing Native," *Tucson Citizen*, p. 1E (July 26, 2002).

302 *"Genetically we are attuned."* Preston interview.

CHAPTER 12: Stewards of the Land

304 *Ronnie Lupe speaks Apache.* Over the years I have had several conversations with Ronnie Lupe about language, land, culture, and his years as chairman. For a published explanation of *ni'*, see John R. Welch and Ramon Riley, "Reclaiming Land and Spirit in the Western Apache Homeland," vol. 25, no. 1 *American Indian Quarterly*, p. 5 (2001). I also benefited from conversations with Bob Brauchli and Charlie O'Hara and from several interviews conducted on the White Mountain Apache Reservation by my research assistant, Monte Mills, Oct. 10–11, 2002.

304 *"I'm sorry Charles."* Keith H. Basso, *Wisdom Sits in Places: Landscape and Language Among the Western Apache*, p. 10 (Albuquerque: University of New Mexico Press, 1996).

304 *To Basso's relief. Ibid.*, pp. 11–13.

305 *"Now they had a picture." Ibid.*, p. 12.

305 *"Indians can be unhappy."* Vine Deloria, Jr., interview with author, Boulder, Colorado, Feb. 7, 1996.

305 *The high-speed years.* I have explored these events at some length in Charles Wilkinson, *Fire on the Plateau: Conflict and Endurance in the American Southwest*, pp. 276–313 (Washington, DC: Island Press, 1999).

306 *Beneath the mesa.* BHP–Utah Minerals International, *Navajo Mine*, p. 10 (BHP–Utah Minerals International, 1990); Senate Committee on Interior and Insular Affairs, "Problems of Electrical Power Production in the Southwest," 92d Congress, 1st Session, p. 5 (Washington, DC: U.S. Government Printing Office, 1972).

306   *The geography posed a problem.* For a map, see Wilkinson, *Fire*, p. 183.

307   *But the pages of the Indian coal leases.* Reid Peyton Chambers, telephone interview with author, July 15, 1994; s*ee generally* Wilkinson, *Fire*, pp. 301–07.

307   *Further, the springs used.* Joanne Ditmer, "Running on Empty," *Denver Post*, p. 1A (March 20, 1994); Sil Perla and Fern Vest, interview with author, Black Mesa, Arizona, March 24, 1993; Marguerite Michaels, "Indians v. Miners: The Hopi and the Navajo Take on the Country's Largest Coal Miner over Scarce and Sacred Water," *Time*, p. Y13 (Nov. 5, 2001); *see generally* David Beckman et al., "Drawdown: Groundwater Mining on Black Mesa" (New York: Natural Resources Defense Council, 2000), *at* http://www.nrdc.org/water/conservation/draw/drawinx.asp (last visited Jan. 29, 2004).

307   *The Hopi Kikmongwi. See generally* Wilkinson, *Fire*, pp. 304–05, and the authorities cited there.

307   *"All of our songs."* Vernon Masayesva, interview with author, Boulder, Colorado, June 23, 1994.

309   *John confirmed my own instincts.* John Echohawk, interview with author, Boulder, Colorado, 1993 (complete date unknown).

309   *In 1994, without expecting to turn anything up.* Wilkinson, *Fire*, pp. 300–01; *see also* Richard P. Conerly, vice-president and general counsel, Peabody Coal Company, letter to John S. Boyden (Aug. 2, 1967) (on file with author); John S. Boyden, letter to Richard P. Conerly, vice-president and general counsel, Peabody Coal Company (Aug. 10, 1967) (on file with author).

309   *The scale of John Boyden's excesses.* Two other documented instances of attorney infidelity involve the Klamath and Osage. *See, e.g.,* the discussion of attorney misconduct toward Klamath Indians during termination in American Indian Policy Review Commission, "Task Force Ten: Report on Terminated and Nonfederally Recognized Indians," 94th Congress, 2d Session, pp. 58–59 (Washington, DC: U.S. Government Printing Office, 1976) (citing U.S. Department of Commerce, Federal Trade Commission, Seattle Regional Office, "A Report of the Consumer Problems of the Klamath Indians: A Case for Action," pp. 18, 20–22 [Washington, DC: U.S. Government Printing Office, 1973]). Legal historian Rennard Strickland has said this of the widespread fraud and violence during the Osage oil boom of the early decades of the twentieth century: "There is no more tragic nor bitter example of the failure of law and of lawyers than the experiences of the Osage people following the great oil boom." *See* Rennard Strickland, "Osage Oil: Mineral Law, Murder, Mayhem, and Manipulation," vol. 10, no. 1, *Natural Resources and Environment*, p. 43 (1995).

310   *"This court hereby finds." United States v. Washington*, 384 F. Supp. 312, 340 (D. Wash. 1974). The opinion set a process for tribes to qualify for self-regulation. *Ibid.* at 340–42.

310   *Within a year after Judge Boldt's 1974 opinion. An Overview of NWIFC*, Northwest Indian Fisheries Commission, About Us, *at* http://nwifc.wa.gov/about us/overview.asp (last visited April 2, 2004) (on file with author); *see also* Fay

G. Cohen, "Treaty Indian Tribes and Washington State: The Evolution of Tribal Involvement in Fisheries Management in the U.S. Pacific Northwest," in Evelyn Pinkerton, ed., *Co-Operative Management of Local Fisheries: New Directions for Improved Management and Community Development*, p. 39 (Vancouver: University of British Columbia, 1989).

310 *Today the commission's programs.* Charles Wilkinson, *Messages from Frank's Landing: A Story of Salmon, Treaties, and the Indian Way*, pp. 92–94 (Seattle: University of Washington Press, 2000).

311 *Shortly after the creation.* On CRITFC, see generally its Web site, http://www.critfc.org, and Charles Hudson, "Columbia River Inter-Tribal Fish Commission Celebrates Its 25th Anniversary," vol. 27 *Fisheries*, p. 32 (May 2002).

311 *This means that hundreds.* Wilkinson, *Messages*, pp. 93–94.

312 *"Otherwise, you would have politics entering."* James Schlender, telephone interview with Jonathan Fero, research assistant, Oct. 28, 2002.

313 *"This didn't start out as a marriage made in heaven."* George Meyer, telephone interview with Jonathan Fero, research assistant, Nov. 26, 2002. On the several intertribal organizations specializing in fisheries, see *Tribal Fisheries Co-Management Symposium*, proceedings of conference, Portland, Oregon (Jan. 30–31, 2003) (on file with author).

313 *Ronnie Lupe.* Ronnie Lupe, interview with Monte Mills, research assistant, Oct. 11, 2002; Robert Brauchli, White Mountain Apache tribal attorney, interview with author, Tucson, Arizona, Feb. 25, 2002.

313 *"When I was first chairman."* Lupe, interview, Oct. 11, 2002.

313 *"I am an Apache." Ibid.*

314 *"On a fall day the lake." Ibid.*

314 *Starting in 1959, the tribe.* On the dispute, see *Hawley Lake Homeowners' Ass'n v. Deputy Assistant Secretary*, 13 I.B.I.A. 276, 277–78 (1985); Associated Press "Apaches End Leases and a Resort Is Fading," *New York Times*, p. A15, June 12, 1984.

314 *In 1977 the council adopted.* Resolution No. 77-248 (Dec. 13, 1977); *Hawley Lake*, 13 I.B.I.A. at 279.

314 *It decided not to renew.* Lupe, interview, Oct. 11, 2002.

314 *The homeowners' administrative appeal. Hawley Lake*, 13 I.B.I.A. at 280–81, 286 (dismissing the appeal on the basis that the Interior Board of Indian Appeals lacked jurisdiction and that the homeowners' association had no standing).

314 *By 2001 all the leases. Community Development Corporation*, White Mountain Apache Tribe, *at* http://wmat.us/aboutcdc.html (last visited June 16, 2003) (on file with author).

314 *"for the privilege of living up here."* Associated Press, "Apaches End," p. A15.

315 *Increased logging and runoff.* These developments are set out in a series of

tribal council resolutions beginning in 1981. Resolution No. 81-41 (Feb. 10, 1981); Resolution No. 81-223 (Sept. 21, 1981); Resolution No. 85-01 (Jan. 10, 1985); Resolution No. 85-298 (Dec. 4, 1985); Resolution No. 86-73 (March 11, 1986); Resolution No. 86-150 (May 27, 1986); Resolution No. 86-381 (Dec. 4, 1986); Resolution No. 05-87-173 (May 15, 1987); Resolution No. 12-87-346 (Dec. 21, 1987); Resolution No. 11-90-262 (Nov. 21, 1990); Resolution No. 11-90-266 (Nov. 29, 1990); Resolution No. 01-91-25 (Jan. 24, 1991); Resolution No. 03-91-77 (March 14, 1991); Resolution No. 02-94-060 (Feb. 24, 1994).

316 *The tribal council, Dr. Wilm, and the Salt River Project.* Resolution No. 11-90-266 (Nov. 29, 1990).

316 *By 1975 the tribe had expanded its tribal timber mill.* Ronnie Lupe, telephone interview with author, Nov. 20, 2003; Brauchli, interview.

317 *series of resolutions strenuously opposing the bureau's logging.* See *supra* under "Increased logging and runoff."

317 *The White Mountain Apache reservation.* Brauchli, interview; Lupe, interview, Oct. 11, 2001.

317 *Rodeo-Chediski fire.* On the fire's effects on the reservation, see Joseph Reaves, "Hell Comes to White Mountains," *Arizona Republic* (June 30, 2002), *at* http://www.azcentral.com/news/specials/wildfires/0630hellcomes.html (last visited Feb. 6, 2002) (on file with author); Judy Nichols, "Apaches Cope with Multiple Blows," *Arizona Republic* (June 15, 2003), *at* http://www.azcentral.com/news/specials/wildfires/fire-apache.html (last visited Feb. 6, 2004) (on file with author).

317 *A number of tribes. See, e.g.,* Diane L. Krahe, "A Sovereign Prescription for Preservation: The Mission Mountains Tribal Wilderness," *in* Richmond L. Clow and Imre Sutton, eds., *Trusteeship in Change: Toward Tribal Autonomy in Resource Management,* p. 195 (Boulder: University Press of Colorado, 2001); Charles Wilkinson, "Land Use, Science, and Spirituality: The Search for a True and Lasting Relationship with the Land," vol. 21 *Public Land and Resources Law Review,* p. 13, n. 57 (2000).

317 *The tribal council has closed.* Alex Puglisi and Roland Ethelbaugh, interview with Monte Mills, research assistant, Oct. 10, 2002. For the geography of the closed area, see *White Mountain Apache Reservation Map,* White Mountain Apache Tribe, *at* http://162.42.237.6/wmatod/wmatmap.shtml (last visited Dec. 17, 2003).

318 *460 Navajo employees.* Arvin Trujillo, director, Navajo Nation Department of Natural Resources, interviews with author, Boulder, Colorado, Dec. 7, 2001, and Window Rock, Arizona, March 26, 2003.

318 *A prominent development.* On tribal forestry, see generally the entire issue of "Forestry on Tribal Lands," *Journal of Forestry* (Nov. 1997), especially the article by Gary S. Morishima, "From Paternalism to Self-Determination," p. 4, and the entire issue of "Forestry in Indian Country: Progress and Promise," *Evergreen* (June 1998); *see also* Darla J. Mondou, "Our Land Is What Makes

Us Who We Are: Timber Harvesting on Tribal Reservations After the NIFRMA," vol. 21, no. 2 *American Indian Law Review*, p. 259 (1997); Indian Forest Management Team, *An Assessment of Indian Forests and Forest Management in the United States* (Intertribal Timber Council, 1993).

318 *50,000 timber jobs.* Morishima, "From Paternalism," p. 5.

319 *Joe DeLaCruz.* "Tribes Mourn Loss of DeLaCruz," vol. 5 *Sin-Wit-Ki (All Life on Earth)*, p. 1 (April 2000); Cate Montana, "Timing Was Everything for Late Quinault Leader," *Indian Country Today* (May 3, 2000), at http://indiancountry.com/?858 (last visited Jan. 27, 2004) (on file with author). For a dated but excellent discussion on DeLaCruz, see also Desmond Wilcox, *Americans*, pp. 145–71 (New York: Delacorte Press, 1978).

310 *"The barricade of Chow Chow."* Pauline K. Capoeman, ed., *Land of the Quinault*, 2d ed., pp. 206–08 (Taholah, WA: Quinault Indian Nation, 1991). On the Chow Chow Bridge incident and the rise of modern tribal land management at Quinault, *see Ibid.*, pp. 205–07, 211–18.

320 *Quinault Nation natural resource staffing. Ibid.*, pp. 211–36; Gary Morishima, Larry Workman, Guy McMinds, Ed Johnstone, and others, interviews with author, Dec. 17–19, 2001.

320 *Quinault studies. See, e.g.*, Quinault Tribal Business Committee, *Quinault Comprehensive Plan: Existing Conditions*, p. 67 (Taholah, WA: Quinault Tribal Business Committee, 1974).

320 *Within a few years.* Hal Neumann et al., *The Forests of the Quinault: Forest Management on the Quinault Indian Reservation, 1855–1996*, pp. 267–69 (Missoula, MT: Heritage Research Center, 1997); *see generally* Capoeman, *Land of the Quinault*, pp. 214–36.

320 *"I think all we're saying." Frontline: Indian Country*, transcript (Public Broadcasting System, 1998).

321 *On the diplomatic side. See* Quinault General Council, *Report*, March 30–31, 2001, p. 69 (Taholah, WA: Quinault General Council, 2001).

321 *far-flung Pacific salmon management effort. See generally* Charles F. Wilkinson and Daniel Keith Conner, "The Law of the Pacific Salmon Fishery: Conservation and Allocation of a Transboundary Common Property Resource," vol. 32, no. 1 *Kansas Law Review*, pp. 94–99 (1983).

321 *"We don't need to be gigantic."* Wilcox, *Americans*, p. 171 (DeLaCruz explaining advice he received, and took, from Henry Mason, a Quinault elder).

321 *Nationally, most of the other timber tribes.* Morishima, "From Paternalism," p. 9; Mandou, "Our Land," p. 259.

321 *"Some reservations out there."* Charles Wilkinson, "The Role of Bilateralism in Fulfilling the Federal-Tribal Relationship: The Tribal Rights-Endangered Species Secretarial Order," vol. 72 *Washington Law Review*, p. 1071 (Oct. 1997) (citing *Tribal Workshop on the Endangered Species Act*, proceedings of conference, Seattle, Washington [February 1–2, 1996] [on file with author] [hereinafter *Tribal Workshop*]).

321   *Nez Perce wolf recovery.* U.S. Department of the Interior, Fish and Wildlife Ser-
      vice, "Nez Perce Tribal Wolf Recovery and Management Plan for Idaho," No.
      14-48-0001-95-538 (Aug. 8, 1995); Cate Montana, "Nez Perce and Grey Wolf:
      Both Banished, They Recover Together," *Indian Country Today*, pp. B1–B2 (Feb.
      15–22, 1999); Sandi B. Zellmer, "Conserving Ecosystems Through the Secre-
      tarial Order on Tribal Rights," vol. 14, no. 3 *Natural Resources and Environment*,
      p. 212 (2000); Jaime Pinkham, telephone interview with author, Sept. 3, 1997.

321   *Tribes in the Great Plains.* Carol Goodstein, "Buffalo Comeback: Native Amer-
      icans Try Restoring a Spiritual Economy Based on Bison," vol. 17, no. 1 *Ami-
      cus Journal*, p. 34 (1995); "Everyday Heroes: Bring Back the Buffalo,"
      Newsweek, p. 32 (May 29, 1995); *see* Lloyd Burton, "Wild Sacred Icon or
      Woolly Cow? Culture and the Legal Reconstruction of the American Bison,"
      vol. 23 *Political and Legal Anthropology Review*, p. 21 (Nov. 2000).

321   *Most federal environmental laws. See generally* David H. Getches et al., *Cases
      and Materials on Federal Indian Law*, 4th ed., pp. 620–35 (St. Paul, MN: West
      Group, 1998); Judith V. Royster and Michael C. Blumm, *Native American Nat-
      ural Resources Law: Cases and Materials*, pp. 217–53 (Durham, NC: Carolina
      Academic Press, 2002); Steffani A. Cochran, "Treating Tribes as States Under
      the Federal Clean Air Act: Congressional Grant of Authority—Federal Pre-
      emption—Inherent Tribal Authority," vol. 26, no. 2 *New Mexico Law Review*,
      p. 323 (1996); James M. Grijalva, "Tribal Governmental Regulation of Non-
      Indian Polluters of Reservation Waters," vol. 71, no. 2 *North Dakota Law
      Review*, p. 433 (1995).

321   *Under the Clean Water Act. City of Albuquerque v. Browner*, 97 F.3d 415 (9th
      Cir. 1996).

322   *Under the Clean Air Act.* My thanks to Jana Milford, a former student at the
      University of Colorado School of Law, for her thoughtful and exhaustive
      research paper "Tribal Authority Under the Clean Air Act: How Is It Work-
      ing?" (2003) (on file with author).

322   *bombing range. See generally* Oglala Sioux Tribe, *Badlands Bombing Range Pro-
      ject* (Pine Ridge, SD: Oglala Sioux Tribe, 1996); U.S. Department of the Inte-
      rior, Bureau of Indian Affairs, "Investigation of Pine Ridge Aerial Gunnery
      Range Taking for the Committee on Interior and Insular Affairs, United
      States House of Representatives," (Washington, DC: U.S. Department of the
      Interior, 1952).

323   *The Tulalip Tribe.* Terry Williams, interview with author, Tulalip Reservation,
      May 10, 2002; *see generally Tulalip Natural Resources: Cultural Stories*, CD-
      ROM (Tulalip Tribes, date unknown).

325   *Single-species criticism. See, e.g.*, James Drozdowski, "Saving an Endangered
      Act: The Case for a Biodiversity Approach to ESA Conservation Efforts," vol.
      45, no. 2 *Case Western Reserve Law Review*, p. 553 (1995); Dianne K. Conway
      and Daniel S. Evans, "Salmon on the Brink: The Imperative of Integrating
      Environmental Standards and Review on an Ecosystem Scale," vol. 23, no. 4
      Seattle University Law Review, p. 977 (2000).

325 *After lengthy negotiations.* On the development of the secretarial order, see generally Wilkinson, "The Role of Bilateralism," pp. 1063–81.

326 *"That is something the elders."* Ibid., p. 1067 (quoting *Tribal Workshop*).

326 *"In our neck of the woods."* Ibid. (quoting *Tribal Workshop*).

326 *"As you see, our mountain."* Ibid., pp. 1067–68 (quoting *Tribal Workshop*).

326 *"The marbled murrelet stays."* Ibid., p. 1068 (quoting *Tribal Workshop*).

326 *"White Mountain Apaches never."* Ibid., p. 1069 (citing *Tribal Workshop*).

CHAPTER 13: Casino Lights and the Quandary of Indian Economic Progress

330 *Economic development difficulties in the 1960s and 1970s. See, e.g.,* Stephen Cornell, *The Return of the Native: American Indian Political Resurgence,* pp. 199–201, 210–11 (New York and Oxford: Oxford University Press, 1988).

330 *Tribal mineral extraction tax programs.* See *Merrion v. Jicarilla Apache Tribe,* 455 U.S. 130 (1982) and *Kerr-McGee Corp. v. Navajo Tribe of Indians,* 471 U.S. 195 (1985), in which the Court upheld tribal taxes; *see also Cotton Petroleum Corp. v. New Mexico,* 490 U.S. 163 (1989) (upholding tribal tax but also allowing state tax, thus establishing a dual taxation regime that created a disincentive to develop tribal mineral resources); David H. Getches et al., *Cases and Materials on Federal Indian Law,* 4th ed., pp. 602–03 (St. Paul, MN: West Group, 1998) (discussing the *Crow Tribe of Indians v. Montana* cases).

330 *The courts soon eliminated. Washington v. Confederated Tribes of the Colville Reservation,* 447 U.S. 134, 156–57 (1980) (cigarettes); *Rice v. Rehner,* 463 U.S. 713 (1983) (liquor).

331 *Local government tax breaks. See, e.g.,* "New England Revival," *Wall Street Journal,* p. 24 (Sept. 22, 1980); Paul B. Brown and Laura Rohmann, "Taxing Matters: It Pays to Shop Around," *Forbes,* pp. 68–70 (Oct. 25, 1982); Sam Allis, "States Pay Dearly, Gain Little in Competition to Lure Industry," *Wall Street Journal,* p. 25 (July 1, 1980).

331 *"We should be candid."* W. Dale Mason, *Indian Gaming: Tribal Sovereignty and American Politics,* p. 62 (Norman: University of Oklahoma Press, 2000).

332 *District Judge Norman Roettger.* Larry Lebowitz and Meg Laughlin, "Norman Roettger, Judge, Dies at 72," *Miami Herald,* p. 1B (July 29, 2003).

332 *"Indian nations have always." Seminole Tribe of Florida v. Butterworth,* 491 F. Supp. 1015, 1018 (S.D. Fla. 1980).

332 *The Court of Appeals. Seminole Tribe of Florida v. Butterworth,* 658 F.2d 310 (5th Cir. 1981). Florida is a Public Law 280 state, see *supra* ch. 1, pp. **18–19**, but the judges in the *Seminole* litigation, relying on *Bryan v. Itasca County,* 426 U.S. 373 (1976), found that Public Law 280 allows only state "prohibitory" laws, not "regulatory" laws, to apply on Indian reservations. Since the Florida law did allow some bingo operations, and did not completely prohibit such gaming, the Florida law was considered regulatory and inapplicable to the

Seminole bingo hall. *See Seminole*, 658 F.2d at 314–15; *Seminole*, 491 F. Supp. at 1020.

332 *California treaties. See, e.g., Felix S. Cohen's Handbook of Federal Indian Law*, 1982 ed., p. 97 (Charlottesville, VA: Michie Bobbs-Merrill, 1982).

332 *"completely impoverished."* Glenn Feldman, Cabazon Band attorney, telephone interview with Jeremy Lakin, research assistant, Nov. 17, 2000.

332 *"there were some HUD buildings."* Barbara Karchmer, Morongo tribal attorney, interview with Jeremy Lakin, research assistant, Berkeley, California, Oct. 18, 2001.

332 *The Cabazon Band opened.* Mason, *Indian Gaming*, p. 48.

333 *the timing was not auspicious.* See *supra* ch. 10, pp. **252–57**.

333 *In a 6–3 opinion. California v. Cabazon Band of Mission Indians*, 480 U.S. 202 (1987). California, like Florida, is a Public Law 280 state, and among other things, the Supreme Court found, like the opinions in *Seminole*, that the California law was "regulatory, not prohibitory," so that the state could not claim jurisdiction under Public Law 280. *Ibid.* at 210–12. Since Public Law 280 could only benefit the state, the *Cabazon* ruling definitely applied in non-Public Law 280 states, in which most reservations are located.

333 *"Tribal sovereignty," Justice Byron White wrote. Ibid.* at 207 (quoting *Colville*, 447 U.S. at 154).

333 *"The Cabazon and Morongo Reservations." Ibid.* at 218–19.

334 *"[T]he Tribes are not merely importing." Ibid.* at 219–20.

334 *Senators Daniel Inouye and John McCain.* On the various court decisions and the congressional process, see generally Mason, *Indian Gaming*, pp. 46–69; Roland J. Santoni, "The Indian Gaming Regulatory Act: How Did We Get Here? Where Are We Going?," vol. 26, no. 2 *Creighton Law Review* pp. 395–403 (1993).

334 *"Legal gaming on Indian lands."* Hearing Before the Senate Select Committee on Indian Affairs, "Gaming Activities on Indian Reservations and Lands: On S. 555 (To Regulate Gaming on Indian Lands) and S. 1303 (To Establish Federal Standards and Regulations for the Conduct of Gaming Activities on Indian Reservations and Lands, and for Other Purposes)," 100th Congress, 1st Session, p. 80 (June 18, 1987) (Washington, DC: U.S. Government Printing Office, 1988) [hereinafter Senate Gaming Hearing].

335 *"Indian communities have taken."* Hearing Before the House Committee on Interior and Insular Affairs, "Indian Gambling Control Act: On H.R. 4566 (To Establish Federal Standards and Regulations for the Conduct of Gambling Activities within Indian Country, and for Other Purposes)," 98th Congress, 2d Session, pp. 322–23 (June 19, 1984) (Washington, DC: U.S. Government Printing Office, 1984).

334 *"The States have a constitutional responsibility."* Senate Gaming Hearing, p. 201 (June 18, 1987).

335 *By early 1987.* Mason, *Indian Gaming,* pp. 61–62; Santoni, "Indian Gaming,"
      pp. 400–01.

335 *Amid the many provisions of IGRA.* On IGRA, 25 U.S.C. §§ 2701–21, see gen-
      erally Getches et al., *Cases and Materials,* pp. 749–53; Mason, *Indian Gam-
      ing,* pp. 64–69; *see also* Kathryn R. L. Rand and Steven A. Light, "Virtue or
      Vice? How IGRA Shapes the Politics of Native American Gaming, Sover-
      eignty, and Identity," vol. 4, no. 2 *Virginia Journal of Social Policy and the Law,*
      pp. 398–401 (1997); Kelly B. Kramer, "Current Issues in Indian Gaming:
      Casino Lands and Gaming Compacts," vol. 7 *Gaming Law Review,* p. 329 (Oct.
      2003).

336 *Class III gaming and low-level operations.* Initially, courts had given the tribes
      broad leeway on the form of Class III gaming under IGRA. For example, a
      state law permitting churches or fraternal organizations to hold "Las Vegas
      nights" as fundraisers would be sufficient to allow full-scale tribal casinos.
      Later a major opinion tightened the requirement to the detriment of the
      tribes: "IGRA does not require a state to negotiate over one form of a gam-
      ing activity simply because it has legalized another, albeit similar form of
      gaming." *Rumsey Indian Rancheria of Wintun Indians v. Wilson,* 41 F.3d 421,
      427 (9th Cir. 1994), *cert. denied by Sycan Band of Mission Indians v. Wilson,*
      521 U.S. 1118 (1997) (state law allowing keno and other games in a nonelec-
      tronic format does not require the state to negotiate over the tribe's proposal
      to allow the games in an electronic format).

336 *state sovereign immunity. Seminole Tribe of Florida v. Florida,* 517 U.S. 44
      (1996).

336 *In 1988, when President Reagan signed.* Mason, *Indian Gaming,* p. 44.

336 *By 2003 the total take. Tribal Gaming Revenues,* National Indian Gaming Com-
      mission, Tribal Data, *at* http://www.nigc.gov/nigc/nigcControl?
      option = TRIBAL_REVENUE (last visited Sept. 6, 2004) (on file with author)
      [hereinafter *Gaming Revenues*].

337 *About twenty megacasinos generate.* National Gambling Impact Study Com-
      mission, *Report,* p. 6-2 (Washington, DC: U.S. Government Printing Office,
      1999) [hereinafter *Gambling Report*]; Katherine Spilde, telephone interviews
      with Jonathan Fero, research assistant, July 14 and July 25, 2003; *see also*
      Mason, *Indian Gaming,* p. 44 ("Eight tribal gaming operations account for 40
      percent of total Indian gaming revenues").

337 *Gaming nationally. See generally* Anthony N. Cabot, *Casino Gaming: Policy,
      Economics, and Regulation* (Las Vegas, NV: Trace Publications, 1996); Robert
      Goodman, *The Luck Business: The Devastating Consequences and Broken
      Promises of America's Gambling Explosion* (New York: Free Press, 1995); *Gam-
      bling Report; see also* Patricia A. McQueen, "North American Gaming at a
      Glance," *International Gaming and Wagering Business,* p. 36 (Sept. 1998)
      (twenty-two states allowed casinos in 1995).

337 *80 percent of the yield. Industry Information Fact Sheet,* American Gaming
      Association, *at* http://www.americangaming.org/industry/factsheets/statis

tics_detail.cfv?id = 7 (last visited Sept. 6, 2004) (on file with author).

337 *Net and gross revenue. Gaming Revenues, supra;* Richard Trudell, interview with author, Portland, Oregon, July 23, 2003; Spilde, interview, July 14, 2003.

337 *Let us remember too. Gambling Report,* p. 6-2; see Mason, *Indian Gaming,* pp. 44–45; *Indian Gaming Facts,* National Indian Gaming Association, NIGA Resource Library, *at* http://www.indiangaming.org/library/index.html #facts (last visited July 7, 2003) (on file with author) [hereinafter *Gaming Facts*].

337 *Most gaming tribes have used. See, e.g., Gambling Report,* pp. 6-14–6-16; Associated Press, "Casino Boom Helps Tribes Reduce Poverty and Unemployment," *New York Times,* p. 16 (Sept. 3, 2000); Dirk Johnson, "Manna in the Form of Jobs Comes to the Reservation," *New York Times,* pp. 4–6 (Feb. 21, 1999); Kit Miniclier, "Reservations Look Beyond Casinos," *Denver Post,* p. 29A (Dec. 16, 2001); Kit Miniclier, "Indians Buy Back Ancestral Lands: Casinos' Revenue Fuels Acquisition," *Denver Post,* p. 1B (Dec. 17, 2000); Cheryl Simrell King and Casey Kanzler, *Background to Dreams: Impacts of Tribal Gaming in Washington State* (Olympia, WA: First American Education Project, 2002).

337 *75,000 new jobs. Gaming Facts; Gambling Report,* pp. 6-15 (identifying as much as 100,000 jobs).

337 *The tribes and the National Indian Gaming Commission.* King, *Background; Gambling Report,* pp. 6-12–6-14.

338 *The spin-off effects. See generally* Katherine Spilde, "Creating a Political Space for American Indian Economic Development," *in* Maggie Fishman and Melissa Checker, eds., *Local Actions: Cultural Activism, Power, and Public Life in America* (New York: Columbia University Press, forthcoming 2004); Katherine Spilde, "The Work of Indian Nations: Tribal Governmental Gaming and Nation Building," unpublished article (on file with author).

338 *Lack of organized crime influence.* Everyone I and my assistants have interviewed about Indian gaming has confirmed this. Nonetheless, contrary suggestions continue to be made in the press. *See, e.g.,* Michael Rezendes, "Tribal Gamble: The Lure and Peril of Indian Gaming: Big-Money Draw Spurs Corruption," *Boston Globe,* p. A1 (Dec. 13, 2000); Barlett, "Wheel," p. 48.

338 *Indian gambling generates the highest heat.* For an illuminating study of the "rich Indian," see Spilde "Creating."

339 *When the Creek War.* On Poarch Creek history, see generally J. Anthony Paredes, "Federal Recognition and the Poarch Creek Indians," *in* J. Anthony Paredes, ed., *Indians of the Southeastern United States in the Late 20th Century,* p. 120 (Tuscaloosa: University of Alabama Press, 1992); J. Anthony Paredes, "The Emergence of Contemporary Eastern Creek Indian Identity," *in* Thomas K. Fitzgerald, ed., *Social and Cultural Identity: Problems of Persistence and Change,* p. 63 (Athens: University of Georgia Press, 1974); Catherine Sells, ed., *Creek Nation East of the Mississippi: Yesterday, Today, and Tomorrow* (Creek Nation East of the Mississippi, 1975).

340 *Poarch history took a new turn. Ibid.; see also The Chief: Calvin McGhee and the*

Notes

477

Forgotten Creeks, VHS (University of Alabama, Center for Public Television, 1995); Eddie Tullis, interview with Michelle Roche, research assistant, Poarch, Alabama, Oct. 10, 2002; Buford Rolin, interview with Michelle Roche, research assistant, Poarch, Alabama, Oct. 11, 2002.

341 *'I'll always say it was."* Sells, *Creek Nation*, p. 28.

341 *Poarch recognition. Ibid.*, p. 35. *See also* U.S. Department of the Interior, Bureau of Indian Affairs, "Final Determination for Federal Acknowledgment of the Poarch Band of Creeks," June 11, 1984, vol. 49, no. 113 *Federal Register*, p. 24083 (Washington, DC: U.S. Government Printing Office, 1984).

341 *"We told those guys stalling."* Tullis, interview.

342 *The new bingo palace.* J. Anthony Paredes, *Indians of the Southeastern United States in the Late 20th Century*, p. 135 (Tuscaloosa: University of Alabama Press, 1992).

342 *Unemployment rate.* U.S. Department of Commerce, Bureau of the Census, "Profile of Selected Economic Characteristics, 2000 (Poarch Creek Reservation and Off-Reservation Trust Land, AL-FL)," Quick Table DP3, Summary File 3, *at* American FactFinder, http://factfinder.census.gov/main/www/cen2000.htm (last visited July 29, 2003) (on file with author). Census figures, it should be noted, often understate actual unemployment. See *infra* ch. 13, p. **496**.

342 *tribal enterprises.* Tullis, interview; *Economic Development*, Poarch Band of Creek Indians, *at* http://www/poarchcreekindians-nsn.gov/economic _development.htm (last visited Jan. 16, 2004) (on file with author).

342 *"Anything we ever got."* Tullis, interview.

342 *Housing has been a top priority.* Paredes, *Indians*, p. 136.

342 *new houses every year.* Rolin, interview.

342 *The tribal land base.* Tullis, interview.

342 *"It'll take generations to change."* Rolin, interview.

343 *IGRA limitations on management firms.* 25 U.S.C. § 2711(b)(5) (2000) (seven-year maximum); 25 U.S.C. § 2711(c) (40 percent of net revenues).

344 *History of per capita payments. See* Felix S. Cohen's *Handbook of Federal Indian Law,* 1982 ed., pp. 572–74 (Charlottesville, VA: Michie Bobbs-Merrill, 1982).

344 *The widely publicized distributions. Gaming Facts, supra*; Spilde interview.

344 *"There is some pressure."* Tullis, interview.

344 *Criticism of Mashantucket Pequot. See, e.g.*, Kim Isaac Eisler, *Revenge of the Pequots: How a Small Native American Tribe Created the World's Most Profitable Casino*, pp. 63–81 (New York: Simon and Schuster, 2001).

345 *Pequot Wars. See generally* Alden T. Vaughan, *Roots of American Racism: Essays on the Colonial Experience*, pp. 177–99 (New York: Oxford University Press, 1995).

345 *California gold rush.* J. S. Holliday, *The World Rushed In: The California Gold*

Rush Experience, pp. 26, 452–53 (New York: Simon and Schuster, 1981); Rodman W. Paul, *California Gold: The Beginning of Mining in the Far West*, pp. 23–25 (Lincoln: University of Nebraska Press, 1965).

345 *When Leonard Burch took over.* Sam Maynes and Tom Shipps, tribal attorneys, interviews with Monte Mills, research assistant, Durango, Colorado, July 1, 2002; Leonard Burch, interview with Monte Mills, research assistant, Ignacio, Colorado, July 2, 2002; Karen Abbott, "Burch Helped Lead Utes to Prosperity," *Rocky Mountain News*, p. 16C (Aug. 2, 2003); Electa Draper, " 'We've Lost Our Giant:' Pioneer Leonard Burch Blazed a Trail for Indian Leaders," *Denver Post*, p. A23 (Aug. 3, 2003).

346 *the Southern Utes' reservation. See generally* Robert Emmitt, *The Last War Trail: The Utes and the Settlement of Colorado* (Norman: University of Oklahoma Press, 1954); Charles Wilkinson, *Fire on the Plateau: Conflict and Endurance in the American Southwest*, pp. 124–47 (Washington, DC: Island Press, 1999).

346 *"We were at the mercy."* Burch, interview.

346 *The tribal council and Burch.* Shipps, interview.

346 *The Southern Ute formed Red Willow.* Shipps, interview; *see generally* Fitch IBCA, Duff and Phelps, "Tribal Finance Credit Analysis: Southern Ute Indian Tribe, Colorado," pp. 4–6 (Aug. 21, 2001) (on file with author) [hereinafter "Fitch Report"]; Ianthe Jeanne Dugan, "New Tribal Tradition: Counting Its Millions," *Rocky Mountain News*, p. 8A (June 14, 2003); Electa Draper, "Southern Utes Get Rare AAA Bond Rating," *Denver Post*, p. 3B (June 8, 2001).

347 *Despite the success.* Burch, interview.

347 *"One day, we might wake up."* Dugan, "New Tribal," p. 8A.

347 *net revenues.* "Fitch Report," p. A-15.

347 *the Permanent Fund. Ibid.*, p. A-12.

347 *Between the two funds.* Burch, interview; Shipps, interview; *see also* "Fitch Report," pp. 3, 7; Dugan, "New Tribal," p. 8A; Draper, "Southern Utes," p. 3B.

347 *businesses in Indian country. See, e.g.*, Richard J. Ansson, Jr., and Ladine Oravetz, "Tribal Economic Development: What Challenges Lie Ahead for Tribal Nations as They Continue to Strive for Economic Diversity?," vol. 11, no. 2 *Kansas Journal of Law and Public Policy*, pp. 463–65 (2001–2002); Aldo Svaldi, "Hope Deposited in Native American Bank," *Denver Post*, p. 1C (April 8, 2002).

347 *Moreover, individual Indian entrepreneurship.* U.S. Department of Commerce, Bureau of the Census, "American Indians and Alaska Natives: 1997 Economic Census Survey of Minority-Owned Business Enterprises," p. 9 (Washington, DC: U.S. Government Printing Office, 2001), *at* http://www.census .gov/prod/ec97/e97cs-6.pdf (last visited Dec. 18, 2003); Paula Moore, "Indians See Biz Success on the Rise," *Denver Business Journal*, p. 22A (May 25–31, 2001).

347 *This lack of small businesses.* Robert J. Miller, "Economic Development in Indian Country: Will Capitalism or Socialism Succeed?," vol. 80, no. 3 *Oregon Law Review*, p. 829 (2001).

347 *unemployment.* Alan L. Sorkin, *American Indians and Federal Aid*, p. 12
     (Washington, DC: Brookings Institution, 1971) (50 percent in 1960); U.S.
     Department of Commerce, Bureau of the Census, sec. 2, "1990 Census of
     Population: Social and Economic Characteristics: American Indian and
     Alaskan Native Areas," p. 720, tbl. 9 (Washington, DC: U.S. Government
     Printing Office, 1993) (26 percent in 1990); U.S. Department of Commerce,
     Bureau of the Census, "Sex by Employment Status for the Population 16
     Years and Older (American Indian and Alaskan Native Alone)," Detailed
     Table P150C, Summary File 3, *at* American FactFinder, http://factfinder
     .census.gov/main/www/ccn2000.htm (last visited July 29, 2003) (on file
     with author) (22 percent in 2000). For the Census Bureau's definitions of
     "employed," "unemployed," and "labor force," see *Glossary*, U.S. Department
     of Commerce, Bureau of the Census, *at* http://www.census.gov (last visited
     July 29, 2003) (on file with author).

349 *Median family income.* See *supra* ch. 1, p. **22** (family income of $870 in 1950s).
     The 2002 dollars amount was calculated with an inflation rate conversion
     factor from Robert C. Sahr, "Consumer Price Index (CPI) Conversion Factors
     1800 to Estimated 2013 to Convert to Dollars of 2002," *at* http://oregon
     state.edu/Dept/pol_sci/fac/sahr/cv2002.pdf (last visited Dec. 18, 2003) (on
     file with author).

349 *Still, family income.* U.S. Department of Commerce, Bureau of the Census,
     "Profile of Selected Economic Characteristics, 2000," Quick Table DP3, Sum-
     mary File 3, *at* American FactFinder, http://factfinder.census.gov/
     main/www/cen2000.htm (last visited July 29, 2003) (on file with author)
     ($50,046 median family income in the United States, all races); U.S. Depart-
     ment of Commerce, Bureau of the Census, "Median Family Income in 1999
     (Dollars) (American Indian and Alaska Native Alone Householder),"
     Detailed Table P155C, Summary File 3, *at* American FactFinder, http://
     factfinder.census.gov/main/www/cen2000.htm (last visited July 29, 2003)
     (on file with author) [hereinafter "Median Family Income"] ($23,966 median
     family income in Indian country, American Indians and Alaska Natives).

349 *On the Pine Ridge Reservation.* President John Yellow Bird Steele of Oglala
     Sioux Tribe, interview with author, Pine Ridge, South Dakota, July 8, 2003.

349 *Income for urban Indians.* U.S. Department of Commerce, Bureau of the Cen-
     sus, "Families with a Householder Who Is American Indian and Alaskan
     Native Alone: Median Family Income in 1999," Custom Table, Data Element
     P155C001, Summary File 3, *at* American FactFinder, http://factfinder.cen
     sus.gov/main/www/cen2000.htm (last visited June 24, 2003) (on file with
     author) ($35,590 median family income in urban areas, American Indians and
     Alaska Natives).

349 *"Our old people fought."* Serle L. Chapman, ed., vol. 2, *We, The People: Of
     Earth and Elders*, p. 99 (Missoula, MT: Mountain Press Publishing Co.,
     2001).

349 *"Economic development on Indian reservations."* Stephen Cornell and Joseph P.
     Kalt, "Sovereignty and Nation Building: The Development Challenge in

Indian Country Today," vol. 22, no. 3 *American Indian Culture and Research Journal*, p. 212 (1998).

350 *"social capital."* See generally Kathleen Pickering, "Decolonizing Time Regimes: Lakota Conceptions of Work, Economy, and Society," vol. 106, no. 1 *American Anthropologist*, pp. 85–97 (2004).

350 *Economists see the task.* Eric Henson et al., *Native America at the New Millennium*, p. 106 (Cambridge, MA: Harvard Project on American Indian Economic Development, date unknown), *at* http://www.ksg.harvard.edu /hpaied/res_main.htm (last visited Nov. 21, 2003) (on file with author).

350 *"As our land mass was diminished."* Chapman, *We, the People*, pp. 45, 51.

CHAPTER 14: Preserving the Old Ways

352 *"My grandmother died."* Rick Williams, interview with author, Denver, Colorado, July 30, 2003.

353 *Indian painting and sculpture.* See generally Margaret Archuleta and Rennard Strickland, *Shared Visions: Native American Painters and Sculptors in the Twentieth Century* (New York: New Press, 1991); Edwin L. Wade and Rennard Strickland, *Magic Images: Contemporary Native American Art* (Norman: University of Oklahoma Press, 1981).

353 *Compare this. See, e.g.,* Louis Owens, *Other Destinies: Understanding the American Indian Novel* (Norman: University of Oklahoma Press, 1992); A. LaVonne Brown Ruoff, *American Indian Literatures* (New York: Modern Language Association of America, 1990); Paula Gunn Allen, *The Sacred Hoop: Recovering the Feminine in American Indian Traditions* (Boston: Beacon Press, 1986).

355 *"tribal religions are actually complexes."* Vine Deloria, Jr., *God Is Red: A Native View of Religion,* p. 70 (Golden, CO: Fulcrum Publishing, 1994).

355 *The Texas, or Mexican, Band of Kickapoo. See generally* A. M. Gibson, *The Kickapoos: Lords of the Middle Border* (Norman: University of Oklahoma Press, 1975).

355 *"I don't know exactly."* I first presented this material on deer, Ketchima, and Pat Smith as part of the Wallace Stegner Memorial Lecture at Montana State University in April 1996. The university published a monograph of the lecture titled "The Deer by the Road, Judge Wells, and Home Dance: A Quarter Century's Impressions of Tribal Sovereignty and the Indian Worldview," which may be accessed *at* http://www.montana.edu/wwwsf/chair/deer wellsdance.html.

357 *The tribes of the Great Plains.* John D. Berry, "Buffalo Rebound" (Nov. 19, 2002), South Dakota State University, News, *at* http:///www3.sdstate.edu (last visited Aug. 8, 2003) (on file with author); Pete Letheby, "Grasslands, Bison Indeed May Again Dominate the Plains," *Denver Post*, p. 4E (Aug. 10, 2003). The Intertribal Bison Cooperative maintains a Web site, *at* http://www.intertribalbison.org. On the IBC and bison restoration gener-

ally, see also Moneil Patel, "Restoration of Bison onto the American Prairie," B.S., senior seminar, University of California, Irvine (1997), *at* http://darwin .bio.uci.edu/~sustain/global/sensem/patel97.htm (last visited Jan. 29, 2004) (on file with author).

358 *"The buffalo are coming back."* Berry, "Buffalo Rebound."

358 *Intergovernmental agreements.* For example, in the Pacific Southwest region of the U.S. Forest Service, there are "dozens" of such agreements. Sonia Tamez, tribal relations program manager for Pacific Southwest Region, telephone interview with Jonathan Fero, research assistant, April 19, 2004. I have had many conversations with Patricia Parker, chief of the American Indian Liaison Office for the National Park Service, to the same effect. *See also Report of the Native American Sacred Lands Forum*, pp. 43–44, proceedings of conference, Boulder and Denver, Colorado (Oct. 9–10, 2001). For a survey of intergovernmental agreements in other contexts, such as hunting, fishing, and water rights, see David H. Getches, "Negotiated Sovereignty: Intergovernmental Agreements with American Indian Tribes as Models for Expanding Self-Government," vol. 1, no. 1 *Review of Constitutional Studies*, pp. 143–63 (1993).

359 *"[A]ny reduction of language."* Russell H. Bernard, "Preserving Language Diversity," vol. 51, no. 1 *Human Organization*, p. 82 (1992) (cited in Jon Reyhner, "Rational and Needs for Stabilizing Indigenous Languages," *in* Gina Cantoni, ed., *Stabilizing Indigenous Languages* [Flagstaff: Northern Arizona University, 1996], *at* http://www.ncela.gwu.edu/miscpubs/stabilize/ index.htm [last visited Jan. 28, 2004]) (on file with author).

360 *An estimated one-half of all the world's languages.* David Nettle and Suzanne Romaine, *Vanishing Voices: The Extinction of the World's Languages*, p. 2 (New York: Oxford University Press, 2000).

360 *Of the 6,000 or so. See, e.g.*, David Crystal, *Language Death*, pp. 18–19 (New York: Cambridge University Press, 2000).

360 *Only a few hundred. Ibid.* On world language loss, see also Robert H. Robins and Eugenius M. Uhlenbeck, eds., *Endangered Languages* (New York: St. Martin's Press, 1991).

360 *At the beginning of the twentieth century.* Mary B. Davis, ed., *Native America in the Twentieth Century: An Encyclopedia*, p. 310 (New York: Garland Publishing, 1996).

360 *By the end of the century.* James Estes, "How Many Indigenous Languages Are Spoken in the United States? By How Many Speakers?," no. 20 *AskNCELA* (Feb. 2002), *at* http://www.ncela.gwu.edu/askncela/20natlang.htm (last visited Oct. 27, 2002) (on file with author) (citing Barbara F. Grimes, ed., *Enthnologue: Languages of the World*, 13th ed. [Dallas, TX: Summer Institute of Linguistics, 1996]). In his article, Estes lists the Native American languages still spoken, along with the estimated number of speakers.

360 *spoken only by middle-aged and elderly.* Michael Krauss, "State of Native American Language Endangerment," *in* G. Cantoni, ed., *Stabilizing Indigenous Lan-*

guages (Flagstaff: Center for Excellence in Education, Northern Arizona University, 1996), *at* http://www.ncela.gwu.edu/miscpubs/stabilize/i-needs/status.htm (last visited Oct. 27, 2002) (on file with author). For a survey of the history, law, and policy of native languages in the United States, see Allison M. Dussias, "Waging War with Words: Native Americans' Continuing Struggle Against the Suppression of Their Languages," vol. 60, no. 3 *Ohio State Law Journal*, p. 901 (1999).

360 *"barbarous language."* "The Education of Indians: President Cleveland Expresses His Views," *New York Times*, p. 8 (April 4, 1888).

360 *"Indigenous languages."* Oren R. Lyons, "Tradition as a Foundation for Today's Tribal Successes," welcoming address at honoring ceremony for Honoring Nations 2002, Bismarck, North Dakota (June 18, 2002), *at* http://www.ksg.harvard.edu/hpaied/docs/Oren%20Lyons%20speech%20excerpted.pdf (last visited Oct. 11, 2003) (on file with author).

360 *"remarkable."* Hearing Before the Senate Committee on Indian Affairs, "Native American Languages Act Amendments: On S. 2688 (To Amend the Native American Languages Act to Provide for the Support of Native American Language Survival Schools)," 106th Congress, 2d Session, p. 105 (July 20, 2000) (Washington, DC: U.S. Government Printing Office, 2000).

361 *"There are no 'primitive' languages."* *Ibid.*, p. 104.

361 *Many Indian people believe.* James Brooke, "Indians Striving to Save Their Languages," *New York Times*, p. A22 (April 9, 1998) (cited in Dussias, "Waging War," p. 981).

361 *the word tehi.* David Little Elk, Lakota language and culture teacher, telephone interview with Autumn Bernhardt, research assistant, Nov. 12, 2003.

361 *"The word for stone."* Louise Erdrich, "Two Languages in Mind, but Just One in the Heart," *in Writers on Writing: Collected Essays from The New York Times*, p. 58 (New York: Times Books, 2001).

361 *Piegan Institute schools. See, e.g.,* Michelle Nijhuis, "Tribal Immersion Schools Rescue Language and Culture," *Christian Science Monitor*, p. 11 (June 11, 2002); Ron Selden, "Immersion Programs Ensure Cultural Survival," *Indian Country Today* (June 28, 2000) *at* http://www.indiancountry.com/?2530 (last visited June 1, 2004) [hereinafter Immersion Programs]; Ron Selden, "The Last Word," *Missoula Independent* (Nov. 11, 2000) *at* http://www.missoulanews.com/Archives/News.asp?no=1319 (last visited June 1, 2004). The Web site for the institute is http://www.pieganinstitute.org.

362 *Language immersion programs.* On Native programs, see, e.g., Janine Pease, "New Voices, Ancient Words: Language Immersion Produces Fluent Speakers, Stronger Personal and Cultural Identities," vol. 15, no. 3 *Tribal College Journal*, p. 14 (2004); Nettle and Romaine, *Vanishing Voices*, pp. 180–83 (discussing language immersion at Pūnana Leo). On language immersion generally, see Terry Piper, *Language and Learning: The Home and School Years*, 2d ed., pp. 97–100 (Upper Saddle River, NJ: Prentice Hall, 1998). My thanks

to Lisa Grayshield, of the Washoe Tribe, for helping me understand immersion programs.

363 *"Same reason."* Pete Fromm, "Raising Minipokaiax," *Big Sky Journal* (Fall 2003) *at* http://www.pieganinstitute.org/102703_raising.html (last visited June 1, 2004).

363 *"People look up to us."* Selden, "Immersion Programs."

363 *A few public schools. See, e.g.,* Peter Johnson, "Students Learn Blackfeet," *Great Falls Tribune* (Feb. 9, 2004) *at* http://www.pieganinstitute .org/020904_students_learn.html (last visited June 1, 2004); "Washiw Wagayay Mangal," *Washoe Tribe of Nevada California Newsletter*, p. 10 (March/Apr. 2004) (on file with author).

363 *"We know through their intense."* Christopher Steiner, "Blackfeet Push to Preserve Language," *Great Falls Tribune* (May 18, 2003) *at* http://www.piegan institute.org/blackfeet_language_051803.html (last visited June 1, 2004).

363 *The Washoe Tribe.* James F. Downs, *The Two Worlds of the Washo: An Indian Tribe of California and Nevada*, pp. 74–89 (New York: Holt, Rinehart and Winston, 1966).

364 *predictions that the Washoe.* Patrick McCartney, "Washoe Will Ask President to Return Land," *Tahoe Daily Tribune* (June 19, 1997), *at* http:// ceres .ca.gov/tcsf/PresidentialEvent/tribune_washoe_land.html (last visited Jan. 29, 2004 (on file with author); Jon Christensen, "At Tahoe Forum, a Tribe Wins a Deal," vol. 29, no. 15 *High Country News* (1997), *at* http://www .hcn.org/servlets/hcn.Article?article_id = 3568 (last visited Jan. 29, 2004) (on file with author); *see also* Jennifer Ragland, "Wa Shi Shiw: The People from Here," *Tahoe Daily Tribune* (July 27, 1997), *at* http://ceres.ca.gov/tcsf/ PresidentialEvent/tribune_wa_shi_shiw.html (last visited Jan. 29, 2004) (on file with author) (tribal population had decreased 80 percent by the late 1860s).

364 *Tribal land and constitution.* Jo Ann Nevers and Inter-Tribal Council of Nevada, *Wa She Shu: A Washoe Tribal History*, pp. 62–65, 89 (Salt Lake City: University of Utah Printing Service, 1976); Davis, *Native America*, p. 687; "The Washoe People in the Twentieth Century," paper presented to *Wa-She-Shu-Edeh* Festival of Native American Arts and Culture, Lake Tahoe, California (July, 30 1993) (on file with author).

364 *It established hunting rights. Ibid.*, pp. 688–90.

364 *grants provided funds.* Washoe Tribe of Nevada and California, *Washoe*, pamphlet (Gardnerville, NV: Washoe Tribe of Nevada and California, date unknown) (on file with author).

365 *In 1997, in a small, unprepossessing tribal building.* On the Washoe School, see generally *Washiw Wagayay Mangal*, pamplet (Gardnerville, NV: Washoe Tribe of Nevada and California, 1999) (on file with author); Jon Christensen, "Speaking the Language of the Land," *at* http://www.greatbasinweb.com/

millenium/washoe.html (last visited Dec. 20, 2002) (on file with author); Washoe Tribe of Nevada and California, "A. Brian Wallace, Chairman: Testimony in Support of S. 2688: Native American Languages Act Amendments of 2000," (July 20, 2000) (Gardnerville, NV: Washoe Tribe of Nevada and California, date unknown) [hereinafter "Wallace Testimony"].

365 *The Washoe tribal chairman. See, e.g.*, Washoe Tribe, "Wallace Testimony."

365 *"the baskets that cradle."* A. Brian Wallace, "A Reply to 'Holding a Mirror to "Eyes Wide Shut": The Role Native Cultures and Languages in the Education of American Indian Students,' " *at* http://www.indianeduresearch.net/A Wallace.htm (last visited Dec. 26, 2002) (on file with author).

365 *The local language may not.* Brian Wallace, interview with author, Reno, Nevada, Apr. 12, 2001.

365 *He likes to quote.* Wallace, "A Reply."

365 *formal language programs face a monumental undertaking. See generally* Nettle and Romaine, *Vanishing Voices*, pp. 176–204; Dussias, "Waging War," pp. 982–90; James Crawford, "Endangered Native American Languages: What Is to Be Done, and Why?," vol. 19, no. 1 *Bilingual Research Journal*, pp. 29–32 (1995).

365 *Lack of funding. See, e.g.*, Washoe Tribe of Nevada California Newsletter, p. 10.

366 *Tribal radio stations broadcast. See, e.g.*, Dussias, "Waging War," pp. 988–89.

366 *The states are pitching in.* Nettle and Romaine, *Vanishing Voices*, p. 182 (Hawaii efforts). On other state efforts generally, see Brooke, "Indians Striving," p. A22.

366 *"[T]here has never."* Crystal, *Language Death*, p. viii.

366 *With expanded research and course offerings in the universities.* Davis, *Native America*, p. 311.

366 *William Jacobsen.* Don Cox, "Reno Linguist Foremost Expert on Washoe Language," no. 52 *Canku Ota (Many Paths)* (Dec. 29, 2001), *at* http://www.turtle track.org/Issues01/Co12292001/CO_12292001_Washoe_Language.htm (on file with author). Jacobsen's text is William H. Jacobsen, Jr., *Beginning Washo* (Carson City: Nevada State Museum, 1996).

366 *"It's hopeless."* Cox, "Reno Linguist."

366 *"Saying language programs are a fad."* Marjane Ambler "Native Languages: A Question of Life or Death," vol. 15 *Tribal College Journal*, p. 9 (Spring 2004) (Quoting Janine Pease).

367 *"Whatever the future."* Brian Wallace, telephone interview with author, Aug. 26, 2003.

367 *Kahoʻolawe and Hawaiians.* On Kahoʻolawe and its history and significance to Native Hawaiians, see the excellent treatment in Final Report of the Kahoʻolawe Island Conveyance Commission to the Congress of the United States, *Kahoʻolawe Island: Restoring a Cultural Treasure*, pp. 16–29 (Washington, DC: U.S. Government Printing Office, 1993) [hereinafter "Final Report"]; Peter MacDonald, "Fixed in Time: A Brief History of Kahoʻolawe," vol. 6

Hawaiian Journal of History, p. 69 (1972). *See also* Inez Macphee Ashdown, *Recollections of Kaho'olawe* (Honolulu: Topgallant Publishing Co., 1979).

367 *"The sacred places of Hawaii."* Edward L. H. Kanahele, "Foreword," in Van James, *Ancient Sites of O'ahu: A Guide to Hawaiian Archeological Places of Interest,* p. ix (Honolulu: Bishop Museum Press, 1991).

368 *Diseases carried by British and American settlers.* For a graphic description of disease in Hawaiians, see O. A. Bushnell, *Ka'a'awa: A Novel About Hawaii in the 1850s,* pp. 407–17 (Honolulu: University of Hawaii Press, 1980).

370 *At war's end.* On the impacts of bombing, see "Final Report," pp. 42–48; Paul Higashino, interview with author, Kaho'olawe, Hawaii, June 24, 2002.

370 *During the nineteenth century.* On the rise of Western influence, see generally Ralph S. Kuykendall, vol. 1 *The Hawaiian Kingdom, 1778–1854: Foundation and Transformation* (Honolulu: University of Hawaii, 1938). The sovereignty of the Hawaiian Nation is discussed in Melody Kapilialoha MacKenzie, ed., *Native Hawaiian Rights Handbook,* pp. 95–98 (Honolulu: Native Hawaiian Legal Corporation, 1991), and in Mililani B. Trask, "Historical and Contemporary Hawaiian Self-Determination: A Native Hawaiian Perspective," vol. 8, no. 2 *Arizona Journal of Comparative Law,* p. 77 (1991). The United States enacted several treaties and conventions with the kingdom. *See, e.g.,* Charles F. Wilkinson, "Land Tenure in the Pacific: The Context for Native Hawaiian Land Rights," vol. 64 *Washington Law Review,* pp. 228–29, n. 11 (1989). Also, in its formal apology to Native Hawaiians, Congress acknowledged the kingdom's independence. Pub. L. No. 103-150, Nov. 23, 1993, 107 Stat. 1510 (1994) (not codified).

370 *the United States "[c]an not allow."* House Executive Doc. No. 47, "President's Message Relating to the Hawaiian Islands," 53d Congress, 2d Session, p. xv (Dec. 18, 1893) (Washington, DC: U.S. Government Printing Office, 1893). Cleveland left office in 1897.

371 *Hawaiians reacted to the rampaging development.* On Hawaiian activism, see Michael Kioni Dudley and Keoni Kealoha Agard, *A Call for Hawaiian Sovereignty,* pp. 107–16 (Honolulu: Nā Kāne O Ka Malo Press, 1993); Sally Engle Merry, "Legal Vernacularization and Ka Ho'okolokolonui Kanaka Maoli, the People's International Tribunal, Hawai'i 1993," vol. 19, no. 1 *Political and Legal Anthropology Review,* p. 67 (1996). On Hawaiian state law, see generally MacKenzie, *Native Hawaiian.*

372 *His songs, sung with a soaring falsetto.* Harry B. Soria, Jr., historical liner notes in "The Music of George Helm—A True Hawaiian," CD (Hana Ola Records, date unknown).

372 *"Only George . . . really understood."* Dr. Emmett Aluli, interview with author, Kahului, Hawaii, June 27, 2002.

372 Mele Komo—*Request to Enter.* Smithsonian Institution, *Kaho'olawe: Rebirth of a Sacred Hawaiian Island,* pamphlet (Washington, DC: Smithsonian Institution, 2002) (on file with author).

373 *"The ordnance was everywhere."* Aluli, interview.

373 *Lawsuits landed in federal court.* For a listing of the court decisions, see "Final Report," p. 127.

373 *Some Hawaiians argue. See, e.g.,* Haunani-Kay Trask, "Coalition-Building Between Natives and Non-Natives," vol. 43 *Stanford Law Review*, p. 1197 (1991); Haunani-Kay Trask, *From a Native Daughter: Colonialism and Sovereignty in Hawai'i*, pp. 25–132 (Honolulu: University of Hawaii Press, 1999); *see also* Ronna Bolante, "What Happened to Sovereignty?," vol. 38 *Honolulu*, p. 94 (Nov. 2003) (describing recent developments in the Native Hawaiian sovereignty movement).

374 *Congressional apology.* Pub. L. No. 103-150, 107 Stat. at 1510–14.

374 *A similar bill.* S. 344, 108th Congress, 1st Session (2003).

374 *Commission recommendation.* "Final Report," pp. 41–48.

374 *The commission also took. Ibid.,* p. 50.

374 *The United States has transferred Kaho'olawe.* Quitclaim Deed from the United States of America to the State of Hawaii for the island of Kaho'olawe, Hawaii (May 7, 1994).

374 *The state in turn has passed a law.* Haw. Rev. Stat. §§ 6K-3, 6K-9 (1993).

375 *One sadness persists.* Aluli, interview; Soria, "The Music," gives an account of the incident.

376 *"I realize that this will not be finished."* Aluli, interview.

376 *Quinault canoes.* Phillip Martin and David Martin, interviews with author, Taholah, Washington, Dec. 18, 2001; Phillip Martin, telephone interviews with author, Dec. 28, 2001, and Jan. 5, 2004; *see generally* David Neel, *The Great Canoes: Reviving a North Coast Tradition* (Seattle: University of Washington Press, 1995); George Durham, "Notes on the History of Indian Canoes in the Northwest," vol. 46, no. 2 *Pacific Northwest Quarterly*, pp. 33–39 (1955); Emmett Oliver, "Reminiscences of a Canoe Puller," *in* Robin K. Wright, ed., *A Time of Gathering: Native Heritage in Washington State*, pp. 248–53 (Seattle: Burke Museum, and University of Washington Press, 1991).

378 *1994 Canoe Journey.* Several people at Quinault mentioned this story, but Phillip and David Martin took the time to tell it to me in great detail. Phillip and David Martin, 2001 and 2004 interviews. For background on the experience of Phillip Martin and Emmett Oliver with ocean canoes, see Elaine Silzer, "Honors Paid to Tribal Elder," *Nugguam* (Quinault tribal newsletter), p. 5 (Sept. 2003).

380 *2002 Canoe Journey. See generally* D. Preston, "Tribal Canoe Journey Celebrates Ancestors," vol. 28, no. 2 *Northwest Indian Fisheries Commission News*, p. 4 (2002).

APPENDIX A

State and Federally Recognized Tribes

The following state-by-state list includes those Indian tribes or groups who are federally recognized and eligible for funding and services from the Bureau of Indian Affairs (BIA). The list also includes Indian tribes or groups that are recognized by the states. This acknowledges their status within the state but does not guarantee funding from the state or the federal government. State-recognized Indian tribes are not federally recognized; however, federally recognized tribes may also be state-recognized.

This list was accessed from the National Conference of State Legislatures, available at http://www.ncsl.org/programs/statetribe/tribes.htm (accessed January 26, 2004). The sources for compiling the list:

Federally Recognized Tribes: Federal Register, Friday, July 12, 2002.
State-Recognized tribes: National Indian Law Library; various state commissions on Indian affairs.

ALABAMA

Federally Recognized
Poarch Band of Creeks

State-Recognized
Mowa Band of Choctaws
Echota Cherokees
Cherokees of Southeast Alabama
MaChis Lower Alabama Creek Tribe
Star Clan-Muscogee Creek Tribe
Cherokees of Northeast Alabama

ALASKA

Federally Recognized
Village of Afognak
Native Village of Akhiok
Akiachak Native Community
Akiak Native Community
Native Village of Akutan
Village of Alakanuk
Alatna Village
Native Village of Aleknagik

Algaaciq Native Village (St. Mary's)
Allakaket Village
Native Village of Ambler
Village of Anaktuvuk Pass
Yupiit of Andreafski
Angoon Community Association
Village of Aniak
Anvik Village
Arctic Village (see Native Village of
Venetie Tribal Government)
Native Village of Atka
Asa'carsarmiut Tribe (formerly
Native Village of Mountain Village)
Atqasuk Village (Atkasook)
Village of Atmautluak
Native Village of Barrow Inupiat Tra-
ditional Government (formerly
Native Village of Barrow)
Beaver Village
Native Village of Belkofski
Village of Bill Moore's Slough
Birch Creek Village
Native Village of Brevig Mission
Native Village of Buckland
Native Village of Cantwell
Native Village of Chanega
(Chenega)
Chalkyitsik Village
Village of Chefornak
Chevak Native Village
Chickaloon Native Village
Native Village of Chignik
Native Village of Chignik Lagoon
Chignik Lake Village
Chilkat Indian Village (Kluckwan)
Chilkoot Indian Association (Haines)
Chinik Eskimo Community
(Golovin)
Native Village of Chistochina
Native Village of Chitina
Native Village of Chuathbaluk (Russ-
ian Mission, Kuskokwim)
Chuloonawick Native Village
Circle Native Community
Village of Clark's Point
Native Village of Council
Craig Community Association
Village of Crooked Creek

Curyung Tribal Council (formerly
Native Village of Dillingham)
Native Village of Deering
Native Village of Diomede (Inalik)
Village of Dot Lake
Douglas Indian Association
Native Village of Eagle
Native Village of Eek
Egegik Village
Eklutna Native Village
Native Village of Ekuk
Ekwok Village
Native Village of Elim
Emmonak Village
Evansville Village (Bettles Field)
Native Village of Eyak (Cordova)
Native Village of False Pass
Native Village of Fort Yukon
Native Village of Gakona
Galena Village (Louden Village)
Native Village of Gambell
Native Village of Georgetown
Native Village of Goodnews Bay
Organized Village of Grayling
(Holikachuk)
Gulkana Village
Native Village of Hamilton
Healy Lake Village
Holy Cross Village
Hoonah Indian Association
Native Village of Hooper Bay
Hughes Village
Huslia Village
Hydaburg Cooperative Association
Igiugig Village
Village of Iliamna
Inupiat Community of the Arctic
Slope
Iqurmuit Traditional Council (for-
merly Native Village of Russian
Mission)
Ivanoff Bay Village
Kaguyak Village
Organized Village of Kake
Kaktovik Village (Barter Island)
Village of Kalskag
Village of Kaltag
Native Village of Kanatak

Native Village of Karluk
Organized Village of Kasaan
Native Village of Kasigluk
Kenaitze Indian Tribe
Ketchikan Indian Corporation
Native Village of Kiana
Agdaagux Tribe of King Cove
King Island Native Community
King Salmon Tribe
Native Village of Kipnuk
Native Village of Kivalina
Klawock Cooperative Association
Native Village of Kluti Kaah (Copper
   Center)
Knik Tribe
Native Village of Kobuk
Kokhanok Village
New Koliganek Village Council (for-
   merly Koliganek Village)
Native Village of Kongiganak
Village of Kotlik
Native Village of Kotzebue
Native Village of Koyuk
Koyukuk Native Village
Organized Village of Kwethluk
Native Village of Kwigillingok
Native Village of Kwinhagak
   (Quinhagak)
Native Village of Larsen Bay
Levelock Village
Lesnoi Village (Woody Island)
Lime Village
Village of Lower Kalskag
Manley Hot Springs Village
Manokotak Village
Native Village of Marshall (Fortuna
   Ledge)
Native Village of Mary's Igloo
McGrath Native Village
Native Village of Mekoryuk
Mentasta Traditional Council (for-
   merly Mentasta Lake Village)
Metlakatla Indian Community,
   Annette Island Reserve
Native Village of Minto
Naknek Native Village
Native Village of Nanwalek (English
   Bay)

Native Village of Napaimute
Native Village of Napakiak
Native Village of Napaskiak
Native Village of Nelson Lagoon
Nenana Native Association
New Stuyahok Village
Newhalen Village
Newtok Village
Native Village of Nightmute
Nikolai Village
Native Village of Nikolski
Ninilchik Village
Native Village of Noatak
Nome Eskimo Community
Nondalton Village
Noorvik Native Community
Northway Village
Native Village of Nuiqsut (Nooiksut)
Nulato Village
Native Village of Nunapitchuk
Village of Ohogamiut
Village of Old Harbor
Orutsararmuit Native Village
   (Bethel)
Oscarville Traditional Village
Native Village of Ouzinkie
Native Village of Paimiut
Pauloff Harbor Village
Pedro Bay Village
Native Village of Perryville
Petersburg Indian Association
Native Village of Pilot Point
Pilot Station Traditional Village
Native Village of Pitka's Point
Platinum Traditional Village
Native Village of Point Hope
Native Village of Point Lay
Native Village of Port Graham
Native Village of Port Heiden
Native Village of Port Lions
Portage Creek Village (Ohgsenakale)
Pribilof Islands Aleut Communities
   of St. Paul and St. George Islands
Qagan Toyagungin Tribe of Sand
   Point Village
Rampart Village
Village of Red Devil
Native Village of Ruby

Village of Salamatoff
Organized Village of Saxman
Native Village of Savoonga
Saint George (see Pribilof Islands
    Aleut Communities of St. Paul and
    St. George Islands)
Native Village of Saint Michael
Saint Paul (see Pribilof Islands Aleut
    Communities of St. Paul and St.
    George Islands)
Native Village of Scammon Bay
Native Village of Selawik
Seldovia Village Tribe
Shageluk Native Village
Native Village of Shaktoolik
Native Village of Sheldon's Point
Native Village of Shishmaref
Shoonaq' Tribe of Kodiak
Native Village of Shungnak
Sitka Tribe of Alaska
Skagway Village
Village of Sleetmute
Village of Solomon
South Naknek Village
Stebbins Community Association
Native Village of Stevens
Village of Stony River
Takotna Village
Native Village of Tanacross
Native Village of Tanana
Native Village of Tatitlek
Native Village of Tazlina
Telida Village
Native Village of Teller
Native Village of Tetlin
Central Council of the Tlingit and
    Haida Indian Tribes
Traditional Village of Togiak
Native Village of Toksook Bay
Tuluksak Native Community
Native Village of Tuntutuliak
Native Village of Tununak
Twin Hills Village
Native Village of Tyonek
Ugashik Village
Umkumiute Native Village
Native Village of Unalakleet

Qawalangin Tribe of Unalaska
Native Village of Unga
Village of Venetie (see Native Village
    of Venetie Tribal Government)
Native Village of Venetie Tribal
    Government (Arctic Village and
    Village of Venetie)
Village of Wainwright
Native Village of Wales
Native Village of White Mountain
Wrangell Cooperative Association
Yakutat Tlingit Tribe

ARIZONA
Federally Recognized
Ak Chin Indian Community
Cocopah Tribe
Colorado River Indian Tribes
    (Arizona and California)
Fort McDowell Yavapai Nation
Fort Mojave Indian Tribe (Arizona,
    California, and Nevada)
Gila River Indian Community
Havasupai Tribe
Hopi Tribe
Hualapai Indian Tribe
Kaibab Band of Paiute Indians
Navajo Nation (Arizona, New Mexico,
    and Utah)
Pascua Yaqui Tribe
Quechan Tribe (Arizona and
    California)
Salt River Pima-Maricopa Indian
    Community
San Carlos Apache Tribe
San Juan Southern Paiute Tribe
Tohono O'odham Nation
Tonto Apache Tribe
White Mountain Apache Tribe
Yavapai-Apache Nation
Yavapai-Prescott Tribe

CALIFORNIA
Federally Recognized
Agua Caliente Band of Cahuilla
    Indians

Alturas Indian Rancheria
Augustine Band of Cahuilla Mission
  Indians
Bear River Band of the Rohnerville
  Rancheria
Berry Creek Rancheria of Maidu
  Indians of California
Big Lagoon Rancheria
Big Pine Band of Owens Valley
  Paiute Shoshone Indians
Big Sandy Rancheria of Mono Indians
Big Valley Band of Pomo Indians
Blue Lake Rancheria
Bridgeport Paiute Indian Colony
Buena Vista Rancheria of Me-Wuk
  Indians
Cabazon Band of Cahuilla Mission
  Indians
Cachil DeHe Band of Wintun Indians
  of the Colusa Indian Community
Cahuilla Band of Mission Indians
Cahto Indian Tribe
Campo Band of Diegueño Mission
  Indians
Capitan Grande Band of Diegueño
  Mission Indians
Barona Group of Capitan Grande
  Band of Mission Indians
Viejas (Baron Long) Group of Capi-
  tan Grande Band of Mission
  Indians
Cedarville Rancheria
Chemehuevi Indian Tribe
Cher-Ae Heights Indian Community
Chicken Ranch Rancheria of Me-Wuk
  Indians
Cloverdale Rancheria of Pomo
  Indians
Cold Springs Rancheria of Mono
  Indians
Colorado River Indian Tribes
  (Arizona and California)
Cortina Indian Rancheria of Wintun
  Indians
Coyote Valley Band of Pomo Indians
Cuyapaipe Community of Diegueño
  Mission Indians

Death Valley Timbi-Sha Shoshone
  Band
Dry Creek Rancheria of Pomo
  Indians
Elem Indian Colony of Pomo Indians
  of the Sulphur Bank Rancheria
Elk Valley Rancheria
Enterprise Rancheria of Maidu
  Indians
Fort Bidwell Indian Community
Fort Independence Indian Commu-
  nity of Paiute Indians
Fort Mojave Indian Tribe (Arizona,
  California, and Nevada)
Graton Rancheria
Greenville Rancheria of Maidu
  Indians
Grindstone Indian Rancheria of
  Wintun-Wailaki Indians
Guidiville Rancheria
Hoopa Valley Tribe
Hopland Band of Pomo Indians
Inaja Band of Diegueño Mission
  Indians
Ione Band of Miwok Indians
Jackson Rancheria of Me-Wuk
  Indians
Jamul Indian Village
Karuk Tribe
Kashia Band of Pomo Indians of the
  Stewart's Point Rancheria
La Jolla Band of Luiseño Mission
  Indians
La Posta Band of Diegueño Mission
  Indians
Los Coyotes Band of Cahuilla Mis-
  sion Indians
Lower Lake Rancheria
Lytton Rancheria
Manchester Band of Pomo Indians
Manzanita Band of Diegueño Mission
  Indians
Mechoopda Indian Tribe
Mesa Grande Band of Diegueño Mis-
  sion Indians
Middletown Rancheria of Pomo
  Indians

Mooretown Rancheria of Maidu
Indians
Morongo Band of Cahuilla Mission
Indians
Northfork Rancheria of Mono
Indians
Paiute-Shoshone Indians of the
Bishop Community
Paiute-Shoshone Indians of the Lone
Pine Community
Pala Band of Luiseño Mission Indians
Paskenta Band of Nomlaki Indians
Pauma Band of Luiseño Mission
Indians
Pechanga Band of Luiseño Mission
Indians
Picayune Rancheria of Chukchansi
Indians
Pinoleville Rancheria of Pomo
Indians
Pit River Tribe (includes Big Bend,
Lookout, Montgomery Creek, and
Roaring Creek Rancherias, and XL
Ranch)
Potter Valley Rancheria of Pomo
Indians
Quartz Valley Indian Community
Quechan Tribe (Arizona and
California)
Ramona Band or Village of Cahuilla
Mission Indians
Redding Rancheria
Redwood Valley Rancheria of Pomo
Indians
Resighini Rancheria (formerly
known as the Coast Indian Com-
munity of Yurok Indians of the
Resighini Rancheria)
Rincon Band of Luiseño Mission
Indians
Robinson Rancheria of Pomo Indians
Round Valley Indian Tribes (formerly
known as the Covelo Indian
Community)
Rumsey Indian Rancheria of Wintun
Indians
San Manual Band of Serrano Mission
Indians

San Pasqual Band of Diegueño Mis-
sion Indians
Santa Rosa Indian Community
Santa Rosa Band of Cahuilla Mission
Indians
Santa Ynez Band of Chumash Mis-
sion Indians
Santa Ysabel Band of Diegueño Mis-
sion Indians
Scotts Valley Band of Pomo Indians
Sheep Ranch Rancheria of Me-Wuk
Indians
Sherwood Valley Rancheria of Pomo
Indians
Shingle Springs Band of Miwok
Indians
Smith River Rancheria
Soboba Band of Luiseño Mission
Indians
Susanville Indian Rancheria
Sycuan Band of Diegueño Mission
Indians
Table Bluff Reservation-Wiyot Tribe
Table Mountain Rancheria
Torres-Martinez Band of Cahuilla
Mission Indians
Tule River Indian Tribe
Tuolumne Band of Me-Wuk Indians
Twenty-Nine Palms Band of Mission
Indians
United Auburn Indian Community
Upper Lake Band of Pomo Indians
Utu Utu Gwaitu Paiute Tribe
Washoe Tribe (Carson Colony,
Dresslerville Colony, Woodfords
Community, Stewart Community,
and Washoe ranches) (California
and Nevada)
Yurok Tribe

COLORADO

Federally Recognized

Southern Ute Indian Tribe
Ute Mountain Tribe (Colorado, New
Mexico, and Utah)

CONNECTICUT
Federally Recognized
Mashantucket Pequot Tribe
Mohegan Indian Tribe

State-Recognized
Golden Hill Paugussett Tribe
Paucatuck Eastern Pequot Tribe
Schaghticoke Bands

DELAWARE
State-Recognized
Nanticoke Indians

FLORIDA
Federally Recognized
Miccosukee Tribe of Indians
Seminole Tribe (Dania, Big Cypress,
    Brighton, Hollywood, and Tampa
    reservations)

GEORGIA
State-Recognized
Georgia Tribe of Eastern Cherokee
Lower Muscogee Creek Tribe
Cherokee of Georgia Tribal Council

IDAHO
Federally Recognized
Coeur d'Alene Tribe
Kootenai Tribe
Nez Perce Tribe
Shoshone-Bannock Tribes

IOWA
Federally Recognized
Sac & Fox Tribe of the Mississippi

KANSAS
Federally Recognized
Iowa Tribe (Kansas and Nebraska)
Kickapoo Tribe of Indians
Prairie Band of Potawatomi Nation
Sac & Fox Nation of Missouri (Kansas
    and Nebraska)

LOUISIANA
Federally Recognized
Chitimacha Tribe
Coushatta Tribe
Jena Band of Choctaw Indians
Tunica-Biloxi Indian Tribe

State-Recognized
Caddo Indian Tribe
Choctaw-Apache of Ebarb
Clifton Choctaw
Louisiana Choctaw
United Houma Nation

MAINE
Federally Recognized
Aroostook Band of Micmac Indians
Houlton Band of Maliseet Indians
Passamaquoddy Tribe
Penobscot Tribe

State-Recognized
Passamaquoddy Tribe
Penobscot Nation

MASSACHUSETTS
Federally Recognized
Wampanoag Tribe of Gay Head
    (Aquinnah)

State-Recognized
Hassanamisco

MICHIGAN
Federally Recognized
Bay Mills Indian Community
Grand Traverse Band of Ottawa and
    Chippewa Indians
Hannahville Indian Community
Huron Potawatomi, Inc.
Keweenaw Bay Indian Community
    of L'Anse and Ontonagon Bands of
    Chippewa Indians
Lac Vieux Desert Band of Lake Supe-
    rior Chippewa Indians
Little River Band of Ottawa Indians
Little Traverse Bay Bands of Odawa
    Indians

Match-e-be-nash-she-wish Band of
Pottawatomi Indians
Pokagon Band of Potawatomi Indians
Saginaw Chippewa Indian Tribe
Sault Ste. Marie Tribe of Chippewa
Indians

State-Recognized

Burt Lake Band of Ottawa and
Chippewa Indians
Gun Lake Band of Grand River
Ottawa Indians
Swan Creek Black River Confeder-
ated Ojibwa Tribes
Grand River Band of Ottawa Indians

MINNESOTA

Federally Recognized

Lower Sioux Indian Community of
Minnesota Mdewakanton Sioux
Indians
Minnesota Chippewa Tribe (six com-
ponent reservations: Bois Forte
Band [Nett Lake], Fond du Lac
Band, Grand Portage Band, Leech
Lake Band, Mille Lacs Band, and
White Earth Band)
Prairie Island Indian Community of
Minnesota Mdewakanton Sioux
Indians
Red Lake Band of Chippewa Indians
Shakopee Mdewakanton Sioux Com-
munity
Upper Sioux Community

MISSISSIPPI

Federally Recognized

Mississippi Band of Choctaw Indians

MISSOURI

State-Recognized

Northern Cherokee
Chickamauga Cherokee

MONTANA

Federally Recognized

Assiniboine and Sioux Tribes
Blackfeet Tribe

Chippewa-Cree Indians
Confederated Salish and Kootenai
Tribes
Crow Tribe
Fort Belknap Indian Community
Northern Cheyenne Tribe

NEBRASKA

Federally Recognized

Iowa Tribe (Kansas and Nebraska)
Omaha Tribe
Ponca Tribe
Sac & Fox Nation of Missouri (Kansas
and Nebraska)
Santee Sioux Tribe
Winnebago Tribe

NEVADA

Federally Recognized

Confederated Tribes of the Goshute
Reservation (Nevada and Utah)
Duckwater Shoshone Tribe
Ely Shoshone Tribe
Fort McDermitt Paiute and Shoshone
Tribes (Nevada and Oregon)
Fort Mojave Indian Tribe (Arizona,
California, and Nevada)
Las Vegas Tribe of Paiute Indians of
the Las Vegas Indian Colony
Lovelock Paiute Tribe of the Love-
lock Indian Colony
Moapa Band of Paiute Indians
Paiute-Shoshone Tribe
Pyramid Lake Paiute Tribe
Reno-Sparks Indian Colony
Shoshone-Paiute Tribes
Summit Lake Paiute Tribe
Te-Moak Tribes of Western Shoshone
Indians (four constituent bands:
Battle Mountain, Elko, South Fork,
and Wells)
Walker River Paiute Tribe
Washoe Tribe (Nevada and Califor-
nia) (Carson Colony, Dresslerville
Colony, Woodfords Community,
Stewart Community, and Washoe
ranches)

Winnemucca Indian Colony
Yerington Paiute Tribe
Yomba Shoshone Tribe

NEW JERSEY
State-Recognized
Rankokus

NEW MEXICO
Federally Recognized
Jicarilla Apache Nation
Mescalero Apache Tribe
Navajo Nation (Arizona,
   New Mexico, and Utah)
Pueblo of Acoma
Pueblo of Cochiti
Pueblo of Jemez
Pueblo of Isleta
Pueblo of Laguna
Pueblo of Nambe
Pueblo of Picuris
Pueblo of Pojoaque
Pueblo of San Felipe
Pueblo of San Juan
Pueblo of San Ildefonso
Pueblo of Sandia
Pueblo of Santa Ana
Pueblo of Santa Clara
Pueblo of Santo Domingo
Pueblo of Taos
Pueblo of Tesuque
Pueblo of Zia
Ute Mountain Tribe (Colorado,
   New Mexico, and Utah)
Zuni Tribe

NEW YORK
Federally Recognized
Cayuga Nation
Oneida Nation
Onondaga Nation
Seneca Nation
St. Regis Band of Mohawk Indians
Tonawanda Band of Seneca Indians
Tuscarora Nation

State-Recognized
Poospatuck
Shinnecock

NORTH CAROLINA
Federally Recognized
Eastern Band of Cherokee Indians

State-Recognized
Coharie
Haliwa-Saponi
Lumbee
Mcherrin
Waccamaw-Siouan

NORTH DAKOTA
Federally Recognized
Spirit Lake Tribe (formerly known as
   the Devil's Lake Sioux Tribe)
Standing Rock Sioux Tribe (North and
   South Dakota)
Three Affiliated Tribes of the Fort
   Berthold Reservation
Turtle Mountain Band of Chippewa
   Indians

OKLAHOMA
Federally Recognized
Absentee-Shawnee Tribe of Indians
Alabama-Quassarte Tribal Town
Apache Tribe
Caddo Indian Tribe
Cherokee Nation
Cheyenne-Arapaho Tribes
Chickasaw Nation
Choctaw Nation
Citizen Potawatomi Nation
Comanche Nation
Delaware Tribe of Indians
Delaware Nation
Eastern Shawnee Tribe
Fort Sill Apache Tribe
Iowa Tribe
Kaw Nation
Kialegee Tribal Town
Kickapoo Tribe
Kiowa Indian Tribe

Miami Tribe
Modoc Tribe
Muscogee (Creek) Nation
Osage Tribe
Ottawa Tribe
Otoe-Missouria Tribe
Pawnee Nation
Peoria Tribe
Ponca Tribe
Quapaw Tribe
Sac & Fox Nation
Seminole Nation
Seneca-Cayuga Tribe
Shawnee Tribe
Thlopthlocco Tribal Town
Tonkawa Tribe
United Keetoowah Band of
   Cherokee Indians
Wichita and Affiliated Tribes
   (Wichita, Keechi, Waco, and
   Tawakonie)
Wyandotte Tribe

OREGON
Federally Recognized
Burns Paiute Tribe
Confederated Tribes of the Coos,
   Lower Umpqua, and Siuslaw
   Indians
Confederated Tribes of the Grand
   Ronde Community
Confederated Tribes of the Siletz
   Reservation
Confederated Tribes of the Umatilla
   Reservation
Confederated Tribes of the Warm
   Springs Reservation
Coquille Tribe
Cow Creek Band of Umpqua Indians
Fort McDermitt Paiute and Shoshone
   Tribes (Nevada and Oregon)
Klamath Indian Tribe

RHODE ISLAND
Federally Recognized
Narragansett Indian Tribe

SOUTH CAROLINA
Federally Recognized
Catawba Indian Nation (Catawba
   Tribe)

SOUTH DAKOTA
Federally Recognized
Cheyenne River Sioux Tribe
Crow Creek Sioux Tribe
Flandreau Santee Sioux Tribe
Lower Brule Sioux Tribe
Oglala Sioux Tribe
Rosebud Sioux Tribe
Sisseton-Wahpeton Sioux Tribe
Standing Rock Sioux Tribe (North
   Dakota and South Dakota)
Yankton Sioux Tribe

TEXAS
Federally Recognized
Alabama-Coushatta Tribes
Kickapoo Traditional Tribe
Ysleta del Sur Pueblo

UTAH
Federally Recognized
Confederated Tribes of the Goshute
   Reservation (Nevada and Utah)
Navajo Nation (Arizona, New Mexico,
   and Utah)
Northwestern Band of Shoshoni
   Nation (Washakie)
Paiute Indian Tribe
Skull Valley Band of Goshute Indians
Ute Indian Tribe of the Uintah and
   Ouray Reservation
Ute Mountain Tribe (Colorado, New
   Mexico, and Utah)

VIRGINIA
State-Recognized
Eastern Chickahominy
Chickahominy
Mattaponi
Monacan
Nansemond

Pamunkey
Rappahannock
Upper Mattaponi

WASHINGTON

Federally Recognized

Confederated Tribes of the Chehalis
  Reservation
Confederated Tribes of the Colville
  Reservation
Confederated Tribes and Bands of
  the Yakama Nation
Cowlitz Indian Tribe
Hoh Indian Tribe
Jamestown S'Klallam Tribe
Kalispel Indian Community
Lower Elwha Tribal Community
Lummi Tribe
Makah Indian Tribe
Muckleshoot Indian Tribe
Nisqually Indian Tribe
Nooksack Indian Tribe
Port Gamble Indian Community
Puyallup Tribe
Quileute Tribe
Quinault Tribe
Samish Indian Tribe
Sauk-Suiattle Indian Tribe
Shoalwater Bay Tribe
Skokomish Indian Tribe
Snoqualmie Tribe
Spokane Tribe

Squaxin Island Tribe
Stillaguamish Tribe
Suquamish Indian Tribe
Swinomish Indians
Tulalip Tribes
Upper Skagit Indian Tribe

WISCONSIN

Federally Recognized

Bad River Band of the Lake Superior
  Tribe of Chippewa Indians
Forest County Potawotomi
  Community
Ho-Chunk Nation
Lac Courte Oreilles Band of Lake
  Superior Chippewa Indians
Lac du Flambeau Band of Lake
  Superior Chippewa Indians
Menominee Indian Tribe
Oneida Tribe
Red Cliff Band of Lake Superior
  Chippewa Indians
Sokaogon Chippewa Community
St. Croix Chippewa Indians
Stockbridge-Munsee Community
  of Mohican Indians

WYOMING

Federally Recognized

Arapahoe Tribe
Shoshone Tribe

APPENDIX B

Largest Landholding Tribes

Tribe	State	Tribal Trust Land	Individual Trust Allotments	Total Indian Land
Navajo	AZ, NM, UT	14,715,093	717,077	15,432,170
Tohono O'odham	AZ	2,773,850	320	2,774,170
Pine Ridge	SD	749,883	1,314,624	2,064,507
Cheyenne River	SD	1,150,546	872,843	2,023,389
San Carlos	AZ	1,826,541	0	1,826,541
Wind River	WY	1,710,169	101,196	1,811,365
White Mountain Apache	AZ	1,664,972	0	1,664,972
Hopi	AZ	1,560,993	220	1,561,213
Crow	MT	408,444	1,107,561	1,516,005
Standing Rock	ND, SD	422,512	825,822	1,248,334
Fort Berthold	ND	596,257	604,409	1,200,666
Rosebud	SD	1,135,230	641,009	1,776,239
Yakima	WA	904,411	225,851	1,130,262
Colville	WA	1,023,641	39,395	1,063,036
Uintah & Ouray	UT	1,007,238	14,318	1,021,556
Hualapai	AZ	992,463	0	992,463
Blackfeet	MT	302,072	635,630	937,702
Fort Peck	MT	391,769	512,914	904,683
Jicarilla	NM	823,580	0	823,580
Warm Springs	OR	592,143	51,348	643,491
Flathead	MT	581,907	45,164	627,071
Fort Belknap	MT	235,595	385,376	620,971
Ute Mountain	CO	588,825	8,483	597,308
Red Lake	MN	564,452	0	564,452
Fort Hall	ID	260,837	229,041	489,878

Sources: Annual Report of Indian Lands, BIA office of Trust Responsibilities, September 30, 1985; BIA area offices in Aberdeen, South Dakota; Billings, Montana; and Phoenix, Arizona

APPENDIX C
Most Populous Tribes

The following information is derived from the U.S. Census Bureau publication "The American Indian and Alaska Native Population: 2000" (published February 2002, available at www.census.gov/prof/2002pubs/c2kbr01-15.pdf), based on 2000 Census data. The following list is based upon those persons reporting to be "American and Alaska Native alone" (rather than in combination with one or more races) and reporting to belong to one tribe (as opposed to more than one tribe).

Tribe	Population	Tribe	Population
1. Cherokee	281,069	16. Potawatomi	15,817
2. Navajo	269,202	17. Yaqui	15,224
3. Native Hawaiians*	140,652	18. Tlingit-Haida	14,825
4. Sioux	108,272	19. Alaska Athabascan	14,520
5. Chippewa	105,907	20. Seminole	12,431
6. Choctaw	87,349	21. Aleut	11,941
7. Pueblo	59,533	22. Cheyenne	11,191
8. Apache	57,060	23. Puget Sound Salish	11,034
9. Lumbee	51,913	24. Comanche	10,120
10. Eskimo	45,919	25. Paiute	9,705
11. Iroquois	45,212	26. Crow	9,117
12. Creek	40,223	27. Kiowa	8,559
13. Blackfeet	27,104	28. Pima	8,519
14. Chickasaw	20,887	29. Yakama	8,481
15. Tohono O'odham	17,466	30. Delaware	8,304

* The population number for Native Hawaiians comes from the U.S. Census Bureau publication "Native Hawaiian and Other Pacific Islander Populations: 2000," (published December 2001, available at http://www.census.gov/prod/2001pubs/c2kbr01-14.pdf). As described above for the other tribal population numbers, this number represents persons reporting to be Native Hawaiian only (not in combination with any other Pacific Islander group and not in combination with any other race).

ACKNOWLEDGMENTS

I owe waves of thanks, some to those who helped me during my four years of work spent directly on writing this book, many others to the uncountable numbers of people who contributed to my understanding during the thirty-four years I have been working with Indian people.

From the time I first raised this book with John Echohawk, Dick Trudell, Rennard Strickland, Terry Tempest Williams, Patricia Limerick, and Rhea Suh, they understood my objectives and gave me advice and encouragement. Their support fueled me throughout this project. Early on, I had two long interviews with Vine Deloria, Jr. I had already, from my own experience and observations, formed my opinion on his enormous contributions to the modern tribal sovereignty movement. Yet as much as I have long known and admired him, I was taken aback by his skill as an historian: He put the modern era in perspective and identified all manner of events and personalities that were new to me and that became central to this book. Ed Barber, my demanding but gracious editor at W. W. Norton, believed in this book and gave generously the gifts of his expertise and time. Carl Brandt has been my adviser as well as agent for a decade and a half; his insights about literature and the world ride on my shoulder always.

The love, encouragement, and suggestions of my family (for they themselves have spent much time in Indian country) gave me sustenance all the way. I send out my most special gratitude to my life's partners—Ann and my four boys, Seth, Philip, Dave, and Ben. A particular joy for me was when Dave agreed to supply his sharp editing eye during the proofreading of galleys.

I spend a great amount of time with my research assistants and depend on both their detail work and their good judgment. Matt O'Malley, Monte Mills, Jon Fero, and Gregg deBie, in addition to working during the school year, worked full-time in various summers. Heather Corson, Michelle Roche, Jeremy Lakin, Kristi Denney, Autumn Bernhardt, and Christy McCann also made major contributions. To all of you: Thank you ever for all you have done for this book, from the tedium of endnotes, to your careful edits, to interviews, to the creativity of sending me off in directions I would not have explored on my own.

Cynthia Carter, a faculty assistant at the law school, has made contributions to every part of this book. She prepared the manuscript and did all manner of organizational work with my travels and research assistants. She also took full responsibility for locating the photographs and obtaining permissions—a demanding task that required hundreds of hours. Cynthia is also a skilled editor who knows this book inside out and made numerous suggestions that have improved it.

Several colleagues gave me the benefit of their suggestions. Rennard Strickland, Richard Collins, Vine Deloria, Jr., and Gary Morishima reviewed the entire manuscript in detail. A number of people read portions of the manuscript and made useful comments: Joe Sando, Patricia Zell, Marlon Sherman, David Case, Bob Brauchli, Charlie O'Hara, Ada Deer, Charles Jackson, Howard Arnett, Ken Smith, Brian Wallace, Lisa Grayshield, John McCarthy, Tom Shipps, Patricia Parker, Jody Beaulieu, Noa Emmett Aluli, Davianna McGregor, Bob Hershey, Phillip Martin, Kate Spilde, Frank Pommersheim, Robert Yazzie, James Zion, and Kathleen Pickering.

The interviews provided indispensable information and in many cases lent the Indian voice to these pages. My thanks to Roger Jourdain, Jody Beaulieu, and Larry Stillday (Red Lake Band of Chippewa); John Yellowbird Steele, Thomas Short Bull, Mario Gonzalez, Rick Williams, and Marlon Sherman (Oglala Sioux);

Pearl Capoeman-Baller, David Martin, Phillip Martin, Rose Martin, Guy McMinds, Francis Rosander, Francis McCrory, Ed Johnstone, Myrna Figg, and James Delacruz (Quinault); Jaime Pinkham, Allen Pinkham, and Del White (Nez Perce); Ofelia Zepeda, Austin Nuñez, Daniel Preston, Henry Ramon, and Malcolm Escalante (Tohono O'odham); Dennis Anderson, Gerald Moses, and Vernon Star (Muckleshoot); Nelson Wallulutum, Delvis Heath, Charles Jackson, Delbert Frank, Olney Patt, Olney Patt, Jr., and Zane Jackson (Warms Springs); Ronnie Lupe (White Mountain Apache); Earl Old Person and Forrest Gerard (Blackfeet); Frank Ducheneaux (Cheyenne River Sioux); Dick Trudell (Santee Sioux); Leonard Burch (Southern Ute); Eddie Tullis and Buford Rolin (Poarch Band of Creeks); Hank Adams (Assiniboine and Sioux); Billy Frank, Jr. (Nisqually); Vine Deloria, Jr. (Standing Rock Sioux); Susan Johnson (Three Affiliated Tribes of the Fort Berthold reservation); Sue Masten (Yurok); Delores Pigsley (Siletz); Joe Sando (Jemez Pueblo); Willie Hensley (Inuit); Avis Three Irons (Crow); Carmen Taylor (Flathead); Wilma Mankiller (Cherokee); Chief Justice Robert Yazzie, Justice Raymond Austin, and Arvin Trujillo (Navajo); Tom Fredericks (Mandan); John Echohawk (Pawnee); Vernon Masayesva (Hopi); Jim Schlender (Lac Courte Oreilles); Terry Williams (Tulalip); Brian Wallace and Lisa Grayshield (Washoe); Noa Emmett Aluli, Colette Machado, Mahealani Kamauu, and Kioni Fairbanks (Native Hawaiian).

I also thank, for their interviews, Cellestine Maas, Mariana Roca Shulstad, Larry Workman, Gary Morishima, Larry Gilbertson, Dawn Fuller, John McCarthy, Rick Ward, Tim Weaver, Judge Owen Panner, David Getches, Alan Stay, Mason Morisset, Tom Tureen, David Case, Richard Collins, Bruce Bridegroom, Bert Hirsch, Patricia Zell, Senator Daniel Inouye, Terri Luther, Larry Potts, Howard Arnett, Jim Noteboom, Dennis Karnopp, Doyce Waldrip, Jim Zion, Jim Anderson, Robert Pelcyger, Bruce Greene, Patricia Parker, Sonia Tamez, David Doe, Neil Eldredge, Bruce Jones, Charlie O'Hara, Bob Hershey, Tristan Reader, Terrell Johnson, Russell Dillow, Sam Maynes, Tom Shipps, Gary Nabhan, George Meyer, Barbara Karchmer, Glenn Feldman, Kate Spilde, and Paul Higashino.

Jim Robb, the cartographer at the Geography Department here at the University of Colorado, was invaluable in preparing the maps. I am proud to have Oscar Howe's artistry gracing the cover and send out my deep appreciation to the Howe family and Lisa Scholten, curator of the University of South Dakota Museum. Jan Dysart was very helpful in directing me to the papers of her husband, George. At W. W. Norton, Ed Barber's assistants Sarah Moriarty and Evan Carver, and copy editor Pearl Hanig made valuable contributions.

For their cooperative spirit in the acquisition of photographs, I and my faculty assistant, Cynthia Carter, would like to extend gratitude to Ray Ramirez, Dick Trudell, Larry Workman, Amy Drapeau, Shoshannah Flach, Carolyn McMahon, Tony Marinella, Maridee Quanbeck, Tim Riggs, Clara Gouy, the Image Collection Staff at National Geographic, the University of Oregon Law School, the Northwest Indian Fisheries Commission, the Charles Brill family, Wilma Mankiller, Ronnie Lupe, Jon Fero, Cynthia D. Stowell, Ken Kania, David Hoptman, Tony Meyer, Lois Allen, D. Fred Matt, and David Ongley.

This book could not have been possible without the financial support that gave me time to write and that allowed me, and in some cases my research assistants, to undertake extensive travels. The University of Colorado awarded me a sabbatical and Faculty Fellowship that gave me a full year and a half to dedicate to this book. My thanks to Chancellor Dick Byyny, Provost Phil DiStefano, and Dean of the Graduate School Carol Lynch. The William and Flora Hewlett Foundation provided a generous grant that supported my travel and summer salaries for research assistants. The Native American Rights Fund was kind enough to sponsor and administer the Hewlett grant, and I thank John Echohawk and Rose Brave. My two deans during this period, Hal Bruff and David Getches, gave me all manner of personal encouragement as well as support for travel and research assistants.

The large amount of historical and contemporary research material caused me to make heavy demands on libraries. Many thanks to the university's Norlin Library for allowing me to keep substantial numbers of books for long periods of time. At the law school, the library staff was—as they always are—diligent and cooperative in every possible way. My special appreciation to Barbara Bintliff, Jane Thompson, and Manuel Santos. Thanks also to the National Indian Law Library for access to its fine collection and to Ray Ramirez of the Native American Rights Fund for his hard work in taking and tracking down photographs.

While I have mentioned a number of people who contributed to this project, there is a much larger group, whose contributions are every bit as real. Since 1971 a great many Indian people, directly and indirectly, have taught me about the Indian experience in America. I could never understand it in the way they do, but I have been deeply moved by their challenges and successes, by their values and spirit, and by the way they see the world. My fondest hope is that these pages honor their work and reflect what they have seen and done.

INDEX

About the Author

CHARLES WILKINSON is the Moses Lasky Professor of Law at the University of Colorado and has been named Distinguished University Professor, one of twenty on the Boulder campus. A graduate of Denison University and Stanford Law School, Wilkinson practiced law with firms in Phoenix and San Francisco and then between 1971 and 1975 served as a staff attorney with the Native American Rights Fund, where he represented tribes in several successful court cases and legislative campaigns. He then entered academia with the University of Oregon School of Law and has continued to work closely with tribes, having visited nearly a hundred Indian reservations. The recipient of numerous awards, his twelve books include *American Indians, Time, and the Law* (1987), *The Eagle Bird* (1992), *Fire on the Plateau* (1999), and *Messages from Frank's Landing* (2000). Over the years Wilkinson has taken on many special assignments for the Departments of the Interior, Agriculture, and Justice. He was a member of the tribal team that negotiated the 1997 Joint Secretarial Order of the Interior and Commerce Departments concerning tribal rights under the Endangered Species Act. Wilkinson acted as facilitator in negotiations between the National Park Service and the Timbisha Shoshone Tribe concerning a tribal land base in Death Valley National Park; in 2000 Congress enacted legislation ratifying the resulting agreement. He is currently serving as mediator in two sets of negotiations, between the City of Seattle and the Muckleshoot Indian Tribe and between the Oglala Sioux Tribe and the National Park Service. Wilkinson is married to Ann Amundson and has four sons, Seth, Philip, David, and Ben. They make their home in Boulder, Colorado.